Fashion from Victoria to the New Millennium

Daniel Delis Hill

PEARSON

Boston Columbus Indianapolis New York San Francisco Upper Saddle River
Amsterdam Cape Town Dubai London Madrid Milan Munich Paris Montreal
Toronto Delhi Mexico City São Paulo Sydney Hong Kong Seoul Singapore Taipei Tokyo

Editorial Director: Vernon R. Anthony
Acquisitions Editor: Sara Eilert
Editorial Assistant: Doug Greive
Director of Marketing: David Gesell
Senior Marketing Manager: Harper Christopher
Marketing Assistant: Les Roberts
Senior Managing Editor: JoEllen Gohr
Associate Managing Editor: Alexandrina Benedicto Wolf
AV Project Manager: Janet Portisch
Senior Operations Supervisor: Pat Tonneman

Operations Specialist: Deidra Skahill
Art Director: Diane Ernsberger
Cover Designer: Kristina Holmes
Full-Service Project Management: Michael B. Kopf,
    S4Carlisle Publishing Services
Composition: S4Carlisle Publishing Services
Printer/Binder: Courier-Kendallville
Cover Printer: Lehigh-Phoenix Color/Hagerstown
Text Font: 45 Helvetica Light

Credits and acknowledgments borrowed from other sources and reproduced, with permission, in this textbook appear on page 555.

Library of Congress Cataloging-in-Publication Data

Hill, Daniel Delis.
    Fashion: from Victoria to the new millennium / Daniel Delis Hill.
        p. cm.
    ISBN-13: 978-0-13-227518-7
    ISBN-10: 0-13-227518-X
    1. Fashion—History—19th century.   2. Fashion—History—20th century.   3. Fashion
design—History—19th century.   4. Fashion design—History—20th century.   5. Fashion
designers—History—19th century.   6. Fashion designers—History—20th century.   I. Title.
    TT504.H55 2012
    746.9'2—dc23   2012022971

10 9 8 7 6 5 4 3 2 1

ISBN 10:   0-13-227518-X
ISBN 13: 978-0-13-227518-7

brief contents

3
Edwardianism
1900–1909

8
The Jet Age
1950–1959

9
The Space Age
1960–1969

contents

5 The Jazz and Gin Age 1920–1929 | 147

6 The Great Depression 1930–1939 | 189

7 The Second World War and a New Look 1940–1949 | 229

preface

The business of fashion in the twenty-first century developed from two primary economies that first emerged in the nineteenth century: the establishment of couture centered in Paris and the rapid expansion of mass production technologies during the Second Industrial Revolution.

Where once fashion was determined by society's elite and executed by skilled tailors and dressmakers, by the mid-1800s, fashion had become a more broadly commercial enterprise, driven by imaginative designers whose innovative creations set the trends of style for everyone. For more than a century from the 1850s into the 1960s, the dictates of Paris governed fashion around the world. Through mass production and mass marketing by ready-to-wear makers, fashions that originated in the ateliers of the couturiers were disseminated to all socioeconomic classes. This was the democratization of fashion. And although the radiant influence—some would say tyranny—of the couturier greatly diminished in the last decades of the twentieth century, modern fashion is, more than ever, a commercial commodity, conceived by creative minds and mass produced for a global consumer market.

It is largely from this commercial Euro-American perspective that this survey of modern era fashions has been compiled. The majority of images used as illustrations are of ready-to-wear adaptations of the prevailing fashions. The text provides corresponding descriptions and analysis of the key trends and style changes as they evolved decade by decade.

Each chapter has been formatted with introductory historical and geographical references. Chronological graphs at the start of each chapter feature highlights of historical events and cultural achievements relevant to the era. Selected maps show the shifting geopolitical boundaries of European nations since the nineteenth century. For those readers who have limited knowledge of world history, or wish a brief refresher of the topic, each chapter opens with a short overview of the significant historical, social, and cultural developments of the time.

The core text of each chapter is organized into sections for the dress of women, men, and children. The full range of dress is presented, including principal forms of daytime apparel, evening wear, outerwear, undergarments, sleepwear, swimwear, shoes, hats, jewelry and other accessories, and hairstyles and grooming trends. Key terms of clothing or accessory styles are emphasized with bold type. Varieties of garment silhouettes, constructions, fabrications, and decorative treatments are described in detail. To reinforce the accuracy of the descriptions, many primary sources of each era are cited, such as the fashion editorials of *Godey's, Harper's Bazaar, Vogue, Esquire,* and *GQ,* to name a few, as well as quotes from the designers themselves and other fashion cognoscenti. Other primary sources include images and copy from period retail or manufacturing catalogs and similar fashion marketing materials.

Each chapter concludes with a review that recaps the key types and characteristics of the fashions of each era. In addition, chapter questions aid readers in reviewing the broad themes and important details about dress. Recommended research and portfolio projects provide students with ideas for developing a more thorough understanding of the trends in a given period. A glossary at the end of each chapter catalogs the terms of fashion with brief definitions for easy reference.

A selected bibliography is provided at the end of the book with the focus on material written about historic dress since 1800. The index is extensive and provides numerous cross references to more easily locate content.

The Development of Dress

Evidence from the early Paleolithic period more than 30,000 years ago confirms that, since the dawn of the human race, people have transformed the appearance of their bodies in a wide assortment of ways. Prehistoric carvings and cave paintings have provided intriguing records that document forms of dress, ranging from simple ring ornaments to a variety of draped and wrapped clothing. Paleolithic gravesites have yielded artifacts such as stone scrapers for preparing hides, bone needles for sewing, and antler awls for punching holes for easier stitching. In addition, an abundance of stone beads, pierced shells, drilled animal teeth, and fish vertebrae suggests ring ornaments such as necklaces, bracelets, anklets, and girdles or, perhaps, beadwork stitched to clothing. Some early graves even revealed that prehistoric humans painted their bodies in striking hues of yellow or red ochre.

why people wear what they wear

But why? What motivated these early peoples to alter the appearance of their bodies? And were their impulses for dress so different from ours today?

Anthropologists, ethnologists, sociologists, and other scholars and researchers have attempted to delve into the question of why people wear what they wear. The four fundamental reasons for the development of human dress suggested most are for:

- protection
- decoration
- denoting status
- modesty

Clothing for Protection

Clothing worn for protection may be indexed into three categories. First is protection from the elements—cold, rain, snow, sun—which is often cited as the most basic reason for the origins of dress. As noted previously, artifacts have proven that Paleolithic peoples developed methods of preparing animal hides and stitching them together into warm, protective clothing. Yet there is no evidence that the need for warmth was the first, let alone the dominant, reason for the development of dress. Indeed, early humans first emerged in the warm, equatorial climates of Africa millennia before migrating into colder regions.

the most basic reason

A second form of protective dress was against physical injury. Some anthropologists suggest that, since early societies were under constant threat of extinction, they developed forms of dress principally to protect the genitals when running through underbrush, climbing trees, or other such dangerous activities. Hence, with injury averted, fertility would be better preserved. Similarly, injury caused by parasitic insects could be prevented by covering sensitive areas of the body or by wearing dangling or fringed items, which, by their swinging motion, could help fend off attacks. And following the examples from wildlife whose mud-wallows provided relief from stinging and biting insects, humans may have developed body painting from this need for protection.

The third form of protective dress was supernatural. Around the world today, people still wear mystical images and ornaments to ward off evil. In Africa, the batakari is a type of men's tunic embellished with appliques of handstamped magic squares and amulets to protect the wearer from a variety of calamities. Likewise, all along the eastern Mediterranean, various ethnic groups wear clothing and charms that bear stylized motifs representing eyes to shield against the evil eye of those believed to have the power to cast spells.

Clothing for Decoration

Decoration is, by and large, thought by most scholars to be the primary reason for the development of human dress. Even into the twenty-first century there are cultures in which clothing is not worn, but there are no cultures in which some form of body decoration does not exist. This awareness of self and the interest in body decoration is believed by many behavioral and social scientists to be a basic human trait that developed in our earliest stages of social evolution.

a basic human trait

The history of dress is populated with an endless array of clothing that served no practical function other than decorative. The garnishments worn by the Rococo society lady included towering hair arrangements and fifty-inch-wide wedding cake gowns made with fifty pounds of fabric, supports, swags, rosettes, bows, and other trimmings. Likewise, the Japanese counterpart of the French noblewoman decorated herself in twelve layers of kimonos with enormous sleeves and trains that, as a total look, symbolized types of flowers or seasonal foliage.

Clothing Symbolizing Status

Dress as a symbol of status, arguably, developed as a later phase of dress. Conveying status through dress can be so complex and subtle that to recognize its meaning usually requires special training from the earliest age within a society. Among the solitary or combinations of status that dress may communicate include gender, age, religion, nationality, ethnic group, profession or trade skill, military rank, social station, economic status, marital condition, family connection, and political or sports affiliation.

conveying status through dress

The occupational uniform is one of the most distinctive global forms of status dress in modern society. The accoutrement of the police officer, firefighter, and soldier are distinctive enough for us to recognize instantly. Yet, it is often only within each of the groups that the subtleties of rank and achievement are discernible. The four stars on the epaulets of a U.S. army general's tunic might be widely understood throughout American society, but the display of his ribbons and medals is more esoteric.

One of the most ancient forms of status dress is clothing reserved exclusively for those of social rank, hieratic privilege, or economic significance. At various times in history, certain types of apparel, accessories, fabrics, trimmings, dyes, and luxury goods were reserved for the exclusive use of the elite. These restrictions were often codified into sumptuary laws, which, by design, were enacted to keep society visibly stratified. In 1789, one of the catalysts for the French Revolution was the reinstating of sumptuary laws by the Estates-General; not only were the nobility required to wear certain types of opulent court clothing, but all other classes were excluded from wearing those styles even if they could afford them. Even within the ranking classes, sumptuary restrictions were established to denote status; for instance, in ancient Rome, the rare and precious murex purple was lavishly used as a dye for the clothing of the imperial family, but the color was limited to only border edging for the togas of senators.

Clothing for Modesty

In assessing modesty as a purpose for the development of any form of historic dress, researchers must guard against imposing their own ideas of modesty (or shame) into the analysis. The part of the body that may be freely and openly exposed in one society may be viewed as immodest in another. The notion of modesty and the emotion of shame at exposing a particular part of the body vary from culture to culture and from era to era. Ancient Athenian women disparaged their Spartan sisters as "hip displayers" for wearing a type of peplos that was open up the side, and the phrase to "dress in the Spartan manner" was a euphemism for indecent exposure. Yet the full nudity of the young Greek male in public was regarded as "a holy offering to the divine," according to Herodotus.

Dress in a Social Context

For the most part, humans prefer to live together in social groups. Over the millennia, various levels of communications developed within these groups, including dress as one of the more direct forms of visual communication. In some instances, dress as social communication also included sound, such as the jingle of the East Indian ghungrus (bell anklets), or smell, such as the distinctive scent of Chanel #5, or touch, such as the ikharo (raised scars) of certain African peoples for whom the feel is sensual.

dress as social communication

One of the key functions of these forms of dress as social communication is the differentiation of the sexes. Gender-role socialization is fundamental to all societies. Customs, roles, and standards of behavior that are particular to one sex often evolved over many generations, and their origins have been lost to time. In more recent eras, some customs and activities, such as sports in the nineteenth century like baseball and basketball, were specifically developed solely for one sex. Traditions of dress, likewise, reflected culturally determined views of each sex. In Western societies, men wore their hair cut short, with a few notable exceptions, from the time of Napoleon into the 1960s. Trousers, too, were exclusive to men from the earliest forms in the sixteenth century until the late 1800s when women began wearing versions for bicycling and other outdoor activities.

Another function of dress as a social communication is to designate age. In the early twentieth century, preteen boys wore knee-length pants called knickers; as they grew older, they looked forward to the rite of passage when they got their first pair of long pants. Similarly, the designation of age might also include body modification, such as the circumcision of prepubescent boys during manhood rites of some African peoples.

Dress also serves as an identification of a group within a society. A standardized uniform such as that of the Boy Scouts or a prep school might be both functional and a form of social communication. The look of an informal group might be based on certain similar components that allow variation and an expression of individuality within the group such as the dress of the hippies in the 1960s or the punks in the 1970s.

Possibly one of the most universal purposes of dress throughout history has been sexual attraction. In the study of historic dress, though, this can be subject to the pitfalls of interpretation based on modern precepts. In examining the artwork of the Minoans, some scholars have suggested that the brief contours of the men's genital pouch, which resembles men's bikini swimwear of today, and the corseted, bare-breasted bodices of women's dresses were designed for sexual attraction. But there is no evidence to support that assertion.

In some instances, though, some revealing cuts of garments and shaped exaggerations were clearly designed for sexual attraction. The padded codpiece of men's hose in the sixteenth century developed into pronounced proportions embellished with ribbons, embroidery, pinking, and other types of eye-catching decoration. Similarly, over the centuries, bodices of women's gowns either have been cut with revealing necklines to display the breasts or padded and contoured to emphasize the shape and dimensions of the bosom.

Dress as sexual communication within a society also includes forms other than clothing. The application of perfume and cosmetics or the modification of the body, such as surgical implants and injections, are prevalent forms of dress specific to sexual attractiveness and communication within many of our modern societies.

Cross-Cultural Influences

In the twenty-first century, there are few societies around the world that still live in isolation. From the most remote forests of the Amazon basin to the most desolate regions of the Sahara Desert and Arctic tundra, people have become globally connected in ways undreamt of even a generation ago. Satellite telecommunications instantaneously and continually link all five habitable continents of the planet. Languages can be translated automatically over the Internet by sophisticated software, and digitized images can be transmitted to wireless cell phones and laptops worldwide.

the global exchange of ideas

From these international connections, cross-cultural influences occur at an ever more rapid pace. Along with the global exchange of ideas in business, the sciences, technology, languages, art, and culture, also is the exchange of concepts, traditions, and designs of dress.

Since the emergence of the earliest settled communities, people have sought out and encountered other people in distant lands. The motives may have been for war or trade or, perhaps, simple curiosity about their neighbors. Then, as now, ideas of dress were exchanged. But it was rare that new concepts of dress introduced from one culture into another were not changed. When the ancient Egyptians were conquered by the Hyksos, the Egyptians adopted new forms of layered clothing from their new rulers but rejected the wool fabrics and textile patterns of the Hyksos; instead, the Egyptians transformed those new types of clothing with goffered white linen, a look that was compatible with two thousand years of Egyptian dress tradition. Similarly, concepts of dress are sometimes adopted from one culture with the same look but the meaning is transformed. The twenty-first century punks of Tokyo look like their British and American counterparts of the 1970s—replete with slashed black clothing, crested and spiked hairstyles, multiple body piercings, and heavy black makeup—but instead of exhibiting the antisocial behavior reputed of many Western punks, notably drug use and verbally assaulting people in public, the Japanese punks are polite and orderly.

Costume and Fashion

Much has been written and discussed in scholarly circles about the significance of using the term "dress" rather than the assortment of other words like "appearance," "costume," or "fashion." As researchers Joanne B. Eicher and Mary Ellen Roach-Higgins note, "The dressed person is a gestalt that includes the body, all direct modifications of the body itself, and all three-dimensional supplements added to it." In other words, the comprehensive catalog of forms of dress includes not just draped and tailored body enclosures but also attached and hand-held objects, body modifications ranging from clipped fingernails and haircuts to tattoos and piercings, and transformations of the muscular or skeletal system. Perfume and even breath mints are likewise components of dress.

changing trends in dress

Consequently, the differentiation between the terms costume and fashion is significant. In essence, costume is the traditional dress of a people that confirms a stable meaning in the culture even if customs change. For instance, despite foreign invasions and dramatic cross-cultural exchanges over the centuries, China's costume traditions remained fairly constant for thousands of years. The concept of fashion, though, emerged in the late Middle Ages. The affluent middle classes sought to elevate their social status by copying the appearance, lifestyle, and behavior of their social superiors. This included adopting the dress of the aristocracy. When sumptuary laws did not prevent the bourgeoisie from infringing on the special status of the elite classes, the nobility opted for new forms of dress to reestablish their social distinction. The cycle then began to repeat itself with an increasing frequency until changing trends in dress, or fashion, were of an ever shorter duration.

Sources for the Study of Dress

To more comprehensively study historic dress, the student of costume and fashion must assemble evidence from a wide variety of sources. The more source material that is available, the more complete the picture of dress from any given period. For some eras, evidence is abundant and may include extant examples of clothing and accessories, written records, and assorted visual references such as paintings and sculptures. In our modern times, consumer and marketing materials such as magazines, catalogs, TV commercials, and other forms of advertising are important sources. Period photos and diaries are valuable as well.

Movies are always a favorite source, having been a direct influence on mainstream fashion at times.

Certainly, the earlier the period of research, the scarcer and less clear the evidence. In these instances, the researcher must rely on secondary sources, particularly the insights and conclusions of scholars and writers with in-depth, specialized knowledge of historic dress. Even then, there is often dispute and contradiction—everything from descriptive interpretation of source material to the spelling of terms.

As the evidence is collected, each of the sources must be cross-checked against the others to ensure as accurate a picture of historic dress as possible. In examining paintings and sculptures, we must take into account the artistic conventions of the period. Sculptures of ancient Egyptian women appear to depict formfitting sheaths, but extant examples found in tombs reveal that the garments were made to fall from the shoulders loosely, somewhat like a modern chemise. Nor can extant examples of clothing always be credible; often garments from one fashion era were altered to the new

assembling evidence

styles of a subsequent period. This is one reason that none of the hundreds of opulent gowns owned by Elizabeth I have survived. Even with vintage photos some images may be suspect since negatives were often touched up, and hand-colored photographic prints were commonly painted from the imagination of the photographer rather than the actual model of the costume. Moreover, as in most portrait paintings, portrait photos usually depicted the sitters' "Sunday best" clothing instead of their everyday attire. And although movies provide animated, 360-degree views of contemporary clothing in motion, the styles often do not reflect the actual fashions of the time but, rather, were designed for creative effect, or sometimes even to enhance an actor's particular look. In her movies, Joan Crawford continued to wear garments made with broad, padded shoulders long after the look ceased to be popular in the early forties.

With all the aforementioned tenets in mind—the purposes and origins of dress, the impact of cross-cultural influences, and the importance of assembling evidence from a wide variety of sources—students of historic dress will be well armed in their journey through this history of modern fashion.

1 Prelude: The Empire and Romantic Eras 1800–1850

1800				1825
Napoleon crowned emperor 1804	War between U.S. and England 1812–1814	Napoleon defeated at Waterloo; exiled 1815	Reign of George IV of England 1820–1830	Reign of Charles X of France 1824–1830
U.S. purchased Louisiana from France 1803	Wars of independence in Latin America 1806–1828	Restoration of French monarchy; reign of Louis XVIII 1815–1824	U.S. Monroe Doctrine 1823	
	Goya's *Third of May, 1808* 1814	Spain ceded Florida to U.S. 1819	First steamship crossed the Atlantic 1819	Lord Byron's *Don Juan* 1824

1825				1850
U.S. Erie Canal opened 1825	Reign of William IV of England 1830–1837	Victoria ascended the English throne 1837	Victoria and Prince Albert wedded 1840	Elias Howe invented sewing machine 1846
Independence of Greece 1829	Louis Philippe ruled France 1830–1848	Samuel Morse developed the telegraph 1837	Turner's *Rain, Steam and Speed* 1844	U.S. war with Mexico 1846–1848
Victor Hugo's *Notre-Dame de Paris* 1831	Darwin's voyage of the *Beagle* 1831	Daguerreotype photography invented 1839		Charles Dickens' *David Copperfield* 1850

The New World Order 1800–1850

Perhaps more than in any other period in history, Europe and the Americas in the nineteenth century were dramatically altered by rapid and profound changes—political, social, and economic. In the 1800s, the borders of European and New World nations were gradually defined and carved into the framework of today's countries. Industrialization undermined the lingering vestiges of economic and social feudalism, and replaced it with an egalitarianism based on the manipulation of capital and labor rather than ownership of land. Science triumphed with

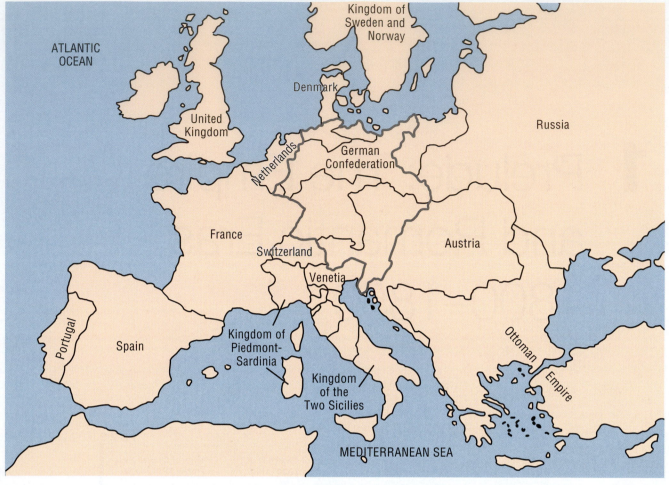

Map of Europe redrawn by the Congress of Vienna following the defeat of Napoleon in 1815.

advances in medicine and technology. In the arts, Neoclassicism was supplanted by the sublime emotionalism of Romanticism.

Initially, however, the political turmoil of the French Revolution extended into the following century, affecting the stability of all of Europe. In the closing months of the eighteenth century, the Directory of France had been dissolved and a consulate government formed with Napoleon Bonaparte as First Consul. In 1804, he crowned himself emperor and reestablished a royal court in Paris. Over the following ten years, Napoleon waged wars of conquest and defense across Europe until his defeat and exile in 1815. A provisional government established a constitutional monarchy and brought from exile the brother of Louis XVI as the new Bourbon king, Louis XVIII. For ten years he reigned with only a nominal part in the affairs of state. When his brother succeeded him as Charles X in 1824, though, the royal court attempted to restore the pre-revolutionary order of the ancien regime. The people of Paris revolted in 1830 and overthrew the Bourbons. The crown was then offered to Louis Philippe of the House of Orleans. Under the bourgeois Orleanists, France experienced a period of calm, economic expansion and prosperity for the following eighteen years. In 1848, the disenfranchised lower classes united into a socialist workers' revolution that ousted the monarchy and formed a second republic.

England in the first half of the 1800s was a strange contrast of the old and the new. Socially and politically, it remained essentially the same England of the eighteenth century with the landed aristocracy controlling the destiny of the nation. On the other hand, the Industrial Revolution was changing the basis of economic wealth from land holdings to industry and finance. Another contrast of the old and the new was the monarchy. The insanity of George III and the scandalous behavior of his son, who became George IV in 1820, weakened the monarchy, particularly in light of the powerful leaders in Parliament at the time. In 1830, the unpopular George IV was succeeded by the amenable but ineffectual William IV, who reigned only seven years. His niece, eighteen-year-old Victoria, became queen in 1837. Her reign spanned the remainder of the century, giving the era its name. The young queen immediately set about raising the status of the monarchy from the ignominy of previous reigns. She represented a moderating influence on politics by presenting the views of the people to the government. In 1840, she married her handsome cousin, Prince Albert of Saxe-Coburg-Gotha, who added his intelligence and moral purpose to the English monarchy.

Over the decades following the end of the Napoleonic wars, the nations of modern Europe took shape. In 1815, the thirty-nine German states that comprised the remnant of the Holy Roman Empire were organized into a German Confederation. Switzerland became an independent confederation of cantons. After a lengthy and bloody revolution, Serbia, Romania, and Greece won independence from the Ottoman Empire in 1829. The following year, with support from England and France, Catholic Belgium declared its independence from Protestant Netherlands.

Similarly, between 1811 and 1824, the nations of modern South America gained their independence. To the north, the United Provinces of Central America was formed as an independent nation in 1823, and a year later Mexico adopted its constitution.

In 1803, the United States more than doubled its territory with the Louisiana Purchase. A westward migration led to the addition of fourteen new states stretching coast to coast by 1850. The United States gained additional territory through Spain's ceding of Florida in 1819, the annexation of Texas in 1845, and the acquisition of Oregon from Britain in 1846.

Economics and Society 1800–1850

The new political order that evolved in Europe and the Americas during the first half of the nineteenth century occurred in part by changes in Western economics and society. The Industrial Revolution that had begun in England in the mid-eighteenth century grew at an increasingly rapid pace in the early decades of the 1800s. Mechanization in the spinning and weaving of textiles spread to France, Holland, and the United States, followed by techniques for the manufacture of iron and steel, and, finally, the actual means of generating power. Industrialization was slow to expand into Germany and Switzerland until mid-century, and into Italy and Spain only late in the 1800s. As industrialization rapidly increased, so, too, did the development of fast and efficient forms of transportation and communication. Nations entered into a frenzy of building turnpikes, canals, and railroads.

Advances in manufacturing technology broadened the accessibility and affordability of textiles and clothing that previously were available mostly for the privileged classes. In 1801, Joseph-Marie Jacquard perfected a loom for weaving textiles of intricate designs by raising

Invention of the Sewing Machine

The most important technological development in the fashion industry of the nineteenth century is the sewing machine. In 1830, Barthelemy Thimonnier of Lyon invented a crude machine that could sew about 200 stitches a minute, over five times faster than the swiftest hand-sewer. When he set up a factory to produce men's coats for the French military, an angry mob of tailors attacked and destroyed the operation. Thimonnier barely escaped with his life and abandoned the refinement of his invention to others.

In 1845, American watchmaker Elias Howe developed an improved sewing machine that incorporated a curved eye-point needle that moved horizontally with an underthread shuttle. Howe's sewing machine operated with a hand crank that could run 250 stitches a minute.

At about the same time, Isaac Singer developed a sewing machine with a straight needle that moved up and down and had an adjustable lever that held the fabric in place for easily stitching a long straight or curved seam. Equally important, Singer's machine was operated by a foot treadle, freeing the hands for the manipulation of the fabric.

In addition to sewing machines produced for commercial use, including versions for sewing leather, inexpensive models were widely available for home use by the 1850s. In 1860, *Godey's Lady's Book* declared the sewing machine "the queen of inventions." A table of comparisons produced by the magazine showed that a man's shirt sewn by hand took more than fourteen hours of sewing, but the same garment stitched on a machine took only one hour and sixteen minutes.

Home treadle sewing machine, 1894.

or lowering the warp. The type of textile with raised patterns still bears the inventor's name: **jacquard**. In 1808, John Heathcote developed a bobbinet lacemaking device, and during the next two decades established factories in England and France to mass produce machine-made lace. In 1816, Marc Brunel invented the circular knitting machine, which produced a tubular form of fabric with no seams. In 1839, U.S. inventor Charles Goodyear discovered the vulcanization process for rubber, which was added to threads for making **elasticized fabrics**.

In addition to new developments in manufacturing technology, new methods of work-flow production led to mass production. Standardized goods with uniform components could be produced rapidly and with a regulated quality—a precursor to the assembly line. In the clothing industry, certain types of garments such as cloaks, overcoats, and accessories like gloves, scarves, and caps were mass produced even in the late eighteenth century. In 1825, the first ready-to-wear factory was built in the United States to produce men's military attire—a significant portent of things to come.

These revolutions of industrialization, communication, and transportation sped the rise in power and wealth of the middle classes. The new, broader middle class of the nineteenth century encompassed social gradations that almost blended imperceptibly at the extremities.

At the top, banking families, manufacturing barons, and merchant princes were comparable in wealth to the landed aristocracy. At the opposite end of the middle class spectrum were the clerks and civil servants who retained a social superiority over the working classes, though they were not paid much better.

From this expanding middle class developed a pervasive bourgeois attitude in life and society that rejected the dazzling display of the revived European aristocracy and, instead, sought convenience and a familial intimacy. Fashion trends now largely emerged from the great ladies of the upper middle classes of Paris and London whose passion for elegance and refinement centered on their homes and intimate social circles. The uninspired and unimaginative royal courts of Louis XVIII, Charles X, and Louis-Philippe provided little fashion leadership during this period of social transition. The wave of Anglomania that had swept Paris at the end of the eighteenth century continued well into the first quarter of the 1800s, due in part to the salons of English ladies living there at the time. English dandyism, inspired by Beau Brummell and others of the circle of the Prince Regent, spread a refined romanticism of masculine fashion and manners to the Continent.

In literature, music, theatre, and the visual arts, the Neoclassicism of the late eighteenth century and of the Empire period dissolved into the Romantic Age. The arts offered escapism from the banalities of the new capitalistic social order. Writers, composers, and artists expressed in their works the sublime beauty of nature, the melodrama of romanticized history, and the picturesqueness of distant lands. The onion-top domes of the Brighton Pavilion of George IV conjured images from the *Tales from the Arabian Nights*. Lord Byron's lyrical poetry recounted sagas of Greek pirates and Muslim slaves. Eugene Delacroix's vivacious canvases depicted exotic narratives of Africa and the Near East. Beethoven's symphonies stirred the soul with exhilarating new sounds.

From these influences of the Romantic movement, fashion abandoned the prescriptions of Neoclassical costume to pursue variety. By the 1830s, fashions had adapted a wide assortment of elements from the costumes of earlier periods and distant cultures. A return of Elizabethan leg-of-mutton sleeves and corseted, cinched waists was inspired, in part, by performances of Shakespeare's plays, both in London and Paris. The revival of decorative treatments such as medieval dagging—the crenelated or scalloped cut of fabric edges—was an influence of the historical fiction of Victor Hugo and Sir Walter Scott. These and numerous other influences and inspirations of the Romantic Age fostered a confusing array of looks in which stylistic novelty rather than innovation prevailed. By mid-century, the Romantic movement had largely crystallized into an effete formula of eclectic borrowings. The time was right for something totally new. In the early 1850s, a new force of style and fashion took the lead—once again centered in Paris and once again emanating from a revitalized royal court.

Beginning in the early nineteenth century, the rapidity of change in the styles of women's fashions outpaced that of men's. Whereas the design of feminine apparel became increasingly more complex and varied, men's clothing was standardized into garments that articulated and encased the body with a uniformity that men strove to conform to. Women's fashion in the nineteenth century demanded novelty and rapid cycles of change, but men's clothing retreated from Rococo splendor into a codified bourgeois formula of sober plainness, largely eschewing color, decorative treatment, and especially abrupt change.

FIGURE 1.1. In the early years of the Empire period, Neoclassical gowns featured more complex designs than the earlier styles. The skirt and bodice were separate sections sewn together. Bodices were constructed of multiple pieces that usually included a center back closure and crossed sections in the front that lifted the bust. "Modes Asiatiques" from *Les Elegances de la Toilette*, 1802.

FIGURE 1.2. The Empire gown began to show influences of Romanticism. Sleeves displayed adaptations of medieval and Renaissance models. Necklines featured variations of the sixteenth-century Medici collar. Vivid colors and textile patterns were reintroduced. *Portrait of a Woman* by Henri-Francois Mulard, c. 1810.

Women's Empire Gowns 1800–1820

At the court of Napoleon, Neoclassicism was the inspiration for women's fashions. Although assorted interpretations of the Greek chiton had originated during the last decade of the eighteenth century, the look continued to prevail in both Paris and London. (Figure 1.1.) Today, the silhouette of a dress or coat with a high waistline just under the bosom is commonly called an **Empire waist**, named for the era in which Napoleon reigned as emperor. Initially, the columnar gowns were cut in one piece from the shoulders to the hem to drape about the figure and reveal the feminine form. The deep decollete necklines were shaped by drawstrings in the facings or by front edges that crossed on diagonal lines. A sash or ribbon sometimes secured the gown just beneath the bosom forming a high-waisted silhouette that emphasized the breasts. Some gowns were sleeveless but most had either T-cut or set-in short sleeves that bared much of the arms.

By 1802, though, some of the first influences of Romanticism began to alter the silhouette of the Neoclassical gown. Changes were subtle but significant over the remainder of the decade. The high-waisted bodice and skirt were constructed as separate pieces stitched together. The seam was usually concealed by a sash or ribbon. Bodices became complex designs sometimes made with multiple pieces like that shown in Figure 1.1. The **fall front bodice** featured a center panel in the narrow back section and two side panels into which were sewn two pieces of lining material that fastened across the inside front to lift the bust. The center back closure was ordinarily fastened with a row of buttons, tapes, pins, or tasseled cords. The fullness of the skirt in the back became extended into a train. Hemlines went to the floor.

Sleeves displayed the first distinct signs of the Romantic era's penchant for adapting styles of the past. Set-in long sleeves with flared cuffs covering the hands to the knuckles were modeled on styles of the Middle Ages. One of the most popular sleeve revivals was reminiscent of the Renaissance with its two-piece construction of a puffed upper section at the shoulders and a long, close-fitting cylinder to the wrist. (Figure 1.2.) Similarly, some sleeves were made slightly full in order to be bound with silk cords or ribbons to simulate the puffed styles of the late 1500s. Necklines also were transformed by Romantic revivals such as a variant of the Medici collar—a stand-up ruff high in the back and tapering to the front. The 1804 coronation gown of Josephine and those of her ladies-in-waiting were constructed with a combination of Romantic historical influences including adaptations of the Medici collar, the Renaissance puffed upper sleeve, and the knuckle-length cuff of the Middle Ages. Other types of soft, ruffled collar treatments like that shown in the Mulard portrait recalled the chemises of the late-seventeenth century.

Throughout the 1810s, the high waistline of the Empire gown remained the mode. However, the draping of the skirt l'antique was superceded by a more structured, conical cut. (Figure 1.3.) The front of the skirt fell straight and smooth while gathers or pleats at the back

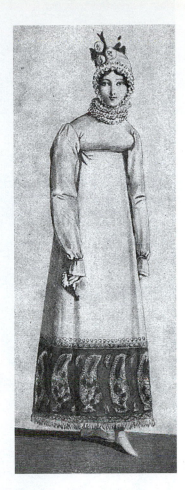

FIGURE 1.3. Through the 1810s, the draping of the Empire gown evolved from the chiton-inspired model to a structured conical shape. The silhouette retained the high waistline, though. Romantic Age treatments included borders of medieval dagging or East Indian paisleys. "Costumes de Promenade" from *Costume Parisien,* left, 1813; right, 1815.

FIGURE 1.4. By the second decade of the nineteenth century, Empire gowns were embellished with various historical elements inspired by Romantic art, literature, and theater. Medieval dagging, Renaissance slashing, and Elizabethan ruffs were often anachronistically combined. *Marie Marcoz, Vicomtesse de Senonnes* by Jean Dominique Ingres, 1814.

FIGURE 1.5. Another influence of Romanticism in women's fashion was the adaptation of exotic textile patterns. One of the most popular and enduring was the paisley motif, which was usually applied as a border treatment rather than an allover print. Left, *Marie-Francoise Beauregard, Madame Riviere* by Jean Dominique Ingres, 1806; right, detail of a cashmere shawl, c. 1815.

shaped the flared contours. Trains disappeared and hemlines rose to the ankles. Fabrics were opaque and less fluid, which, when coupled with the conical shape, made for an elegant sweeping motion when a woman walked or danced. Decorative treatments drew inspiration from Romanticism. Skirts were edged with crenulated tiers adapted from medieval dagging or with wide borders of richly patterned prints. A profusion of ruffles was added to collars, necklines, cuffs, sleeve caps, and skirts. Variations of the Elizabethan ruff were ubiquitous into the early 1820s. Even slashing reappeared. (Figure 1.4.)

Women's Outerwear, Undergarments, and Accessories 1800–1820

The primary types of outerwear for women of the early Empire period were wraps of assorted styles and sizes. Large shawls, long scarves, and stoles not only simulated the Greek himation but also served the same basic purpose as their ancient predecessors—to cover bare arms and shoulders in chilly, damp weather. As Romanticism began to influence fashions of the decade, exotic Eastern motifs replaced the Classical palmettes and Greek key designs as decorations on wrap garments. East Indian patterns, especially the gourd-shaped **paisley**, became immensely popular. (Figure 1.5.) Similarly the stylized buta floral shape was translated

FIGURE 1.6. During the Empire era, the fuller pelisse was usually fur lined and included large fur cuffs that served as a muff. The carrick was made with tiered layers of three to five capelets cropped to the line of the empire waist. Left, pelisse, 1816; right, carrick, 1815. Plates from *Costume Parisien.*

into the pinecone motif by English textile manufacturers. In fact, French and English textile designers assiduously reproduced and reinvented the "modes asiatiques," thus spreading the trend.

Fabrics of wrap garments ranged from airy silk **organdy** to thick wool. Selective breeding of sheep in England and Spain during the eighteenth century led to the development of the soft, supple **Merino wool** that was especially preferred for wraps. From India came downy-soft **cashmere**, a textile made from the silken hair of the goats from the Kashmir region.

In addition to the light wraps, heavy wool capes and cloaks, many with hoods, also continued to be common forms of outerwear for women of all classes.

The high-waisted silhouette of Empire gowns was applied to new coat forms by constructing a separate bodice with set-in sleeves and a long, conical skirt. The **pelisse** featured a fur lining or trim and wide cylindrical sleeves with long fur cuffs that served as a muff when the hands were clasped. In the mid-1810s, a feminine adaptation of the English coachman's coat called a **carrick** became widespread on the Continent. The carrick included layers of three to five capelets that covered the shoulders to the line of the Empire waist. (Figure 1.6.)

Another type of women's outerwear was an adaptation of a men's short jacket called the **spencer**. Because of the high-waisted silhouette of women's gowns, the hemline of the feminine spencer extended to just under the bosom. Variations of the spencer—some sleeveless—also were designed of lightweight wool or silk for indoor wear.

The assortment of undergarments for women became more complex and varied in the nineteenth century. The cotton or linen chemise remained the most prevalent type of underclothing. It was cut to conform to the short-sleeved or sleeveless gowns with their deep decolletage necklines. Women's knee-length drawers were more widely worn beginning in the Empire period. Most types of drawers were made of woven cotton or linen, but examples of knitted silk are known to have been worn by aristocratic women. The legs of drawers were left as loose tubes of fabric or were gathered into kneebands. The long version of drawers based on men's pantaloons was called **pantalettes**, which extended to mid-calf or even the ankles.

FIGURE 1.7. In the early years of the Empire period, women's hats reflected the influences of Neoclassicism with their elongated shape. By the 1810s, hats became tall and narrow, often excessively decorated with ornaments that emphasized the height. Hat plates from *Elegances of Fashion,* left, 1804; center, 1806; right 1816.

Hats of the Empire period were seemingly limitless in their variety. Key changes in silhouette were particularly notable with bonnets. (Figure 1.7.) In the first decade of the century the elongated shape followed the Neoclassical hairstyles arranged at the back of the head. Sometimes designs reversed the profile by extending the visor in the front to an exaggerated length. In the 1810s, bonnets became tall and narrow, often bristling with an abundance of ribbon loops, feathers, bows, and silk flowers. Brimless forms of these tall, tapering hats were called **toques**. The **capote** was a bonnet style made with a soft fabric crown and a stiff brim, often of straw. Silk and satin turbans became all the rage for evening wear following Napoleon's occupation of Ottoman Egypt in 1799.

Shoe styles in the early years of the 1800s remained complementary to the Neoclassical look although sandals were discarded entirely. Flat slippers without heels were the prevalent footwear into the late teens. Some featured long ribbons that laced across the instep and about the ankles. Upper-class women had satin shoes dyed to match perfectly the velvet and silk textiles of their gowns. For a promenade stroll, lace-up ankle boots, also heelless, were functional and fashionable.

Women's purses, called "pockets" at the time, had previously been attached to the underside of panniered skirts. But the close draping of the Empire gown required the bulky purse to be hand carried. Although numerous fashion plates depict these small purses carried as accessories, some contemporary literature suggested that carrying a purse—an article not so long ago concealed beneath the skirts—was in a similar category of immodesty with that of exposed arms and shoulders in daytime. Possibly this social criticism led to the origin of the other name for the purse—**reticule** or redicule. The small purses were of fabric, some richly embroidered, attached to a metal clasp frame or stitched with a draw-string closure.

Other feminine accessories included fans, parasols, lace trimmed handkerchiefs, long gloves, decorative combs, and muffs made of fur or down-filled fabric. Jewelry remained inconspicuous although bracelets à la grecque encircled the bare upper arms for evening wear.

FIGURE 1.8. In the early Romantic Age, the most innovative change to women's dresses was the immense expanse of the sleeves. Armscyes were dropped off the shoulder, shifting the fullness of the sleeves down the arm. By the end of the 1820s, the width of the sleeve was supported by padding, usually made from down-filled pillows. Brown silk gown, c. 1825–1830.

Women's Romantic Era Dresses 1820–1850

By 1820, women's fashions had moved completely away from the influences of Neoclassicism. Even the waistline that had remained in the Empire mode for two decades had dropped from just under the bosom to slightly above the natural waistline. Sleeves began to widen, increasing the breadth across the shoulders. To balance this horizontal profile, skirts also widened, taking a bell shape. Waists were rigidly corseted as small as physiologically possible to emphasize the new hourglass silhouette. Color became more vivid and ornamentation more fanciful. The Romantic Age was reaching a crescendo, and the anachronistic combinations of historical elements were unbridled. Textile patterns such as plaids and floral prints were bolder and more vividly hued.

The most innovative change to the silhouette of the late 1820s was the immense width of the sleeves. (Figure 1.8.) An adaptation of Elizabethan leg-of-mutton styles called a **gigot** may have been inspired by a renewed interest in Shakespeare, whose plays were avidly attended by the Romanticists in both London and Paris. Unlike the sixteenth-century sleeve, though, the armscyes of the 1820s were dropped off the shoulder, pushing the fullness of the sleeve down the arm.

Throughout the 1820s, skirts continued to widen, at first with the addition of gores and then later by a gathered or pleated fullness at the waist. Hemlines remained at the ankles. V-shaped necklines were formed either by a surplice front or by the pointed cut of the bodice front. Deep square or low, rounded necklines were usually reserved for evening gowns.

Decorative trim along the hemline of the skirts reinforced the widened silhouette. The gown in Figure 1.8 features two rows of three-dimensional scallops, which would have fluttered kinetically in the sweeping motion of the skirt. A similar trim called **vandyking** (named for the sharply pointed beard of the seventeenth-century painter Anthony Van Dyke) was a variant of the zigzag dagging of the Middle Ages. Flounces of sheer fabric, lace ruffles, banded tucks, ruching, appliques, and numerous other fussy treatments along the lower edge of the skirt functioned in the same manner.

Between 1828 and 1837, these exaggerated, flamboyant trends reached their apogee. (Figure 1.9.) Because of the excessive mix of decorative treatments, both in fashion and in interior design, this period is sometimes referred to as the Second Rococo.

Bodices were fitted and the waistline dropped to its natural position. Off-the-shoulder armscyes gave a long, sloping line to the profile of the neck and shoulders. Designs of the gigot sleeve were exceptionally diverse and fanciful. Tucks, pleats, and gathers ensured the maximum width. Ruffles and tiers of lace or other trimmings reinforced the breadth.

The expansiveness of the shoulder area was also enhanced by the cut and treatments of the neckline. For high necklines, wide cape-like collars extended over the shoulders like

FIGURE 1.9. The exaggerated, flamboyant trends of women's fashions in the Romantic Age reached their height between 1828 and 1837. Sleeves were enormous. Waistlines were cinched by rigid corsets. Skirts were widened to balance the top-heavy look of the shoulderline. All manner of decorative treatments ornamented surfaces and seams. Plates from *Le Follet Courrier des Salons,* 1830.

those shown in Figure 1.9. Open necklines daringly exposed the shoulders in a deep oval or V-cut. Additional lateral emphasis of the upper bodice was achieved with the attachment of a **bertha**—a wide, deep collar pinned to the edge or revers of the low, open neckline all around.

At the end of the 1830s, a distinct change in the silhouette of dresses was apparent. The gigantic sleeves had begun to diminish. By 1840, the transition to narrow sleeves had decisively occurred. (Figure 1.10.) The armscye continued to be placed off the shoulder until the end of the decade when the seam became more vertical. Around 1848, sleeves were shortened and widened at the wrists to display the sleeve of various underbodice garments.

Bodices were made tightly form-fitting with curved or slanted darts in the front and back. Most waistlines were cut straight although the deep V-front became increasingly popular throughout the 1840s. Queen Victoria's white satin wedding gown from 1840 featured a V-front waistline. The shape of necklines shifted from a horizontal expanse to a V-cut. A type

FIGURE 1.10. After 1840, the emphasis of women's dress designs shifted from the lateral expanse of the sleeves to a widening of the skirt. Bustles were more pronounced and hemlines dropped to the floor. Fitted bodices were constructed with curved or slanted darts in the front and back. Sleeves were narrow although the armscye remained off the shoulder until the end of the decade. Plates from *Godey's Lady's Book:* top, 1841; bottom two, 1849.

of underbodice or **camisole** called a **chemisette** filled the opening with assorted forms of contrasting decorative fronts including lace or ladders of tucks. Other V-fronts were inset with panels of the same material as the rest of the dress for a more unified look.

Whereas the expanse of sleeves was the most striking component of the silhouette in the 1830s, the spread of the skirt marked the 1840s and heralded the crinoline age. The shape of skirts was full and round. Numerous starched petticoats were needed to support the circular fullness of the widened skirt. Hemlines dropped to the floor.

Women's Outerwear, Undergarments, and Accessories 1820–1850

During the 1830s, when the massive sleeves of dresses made great-coats impossible, wrap garments—or "envelopes" as they were called at the time—such as shawls, capes, and cloaks, were the principal forms of outerwear. The variety of styles was similar to that of preceding decades except for the fuller, more circular cuts that were required to encase the padded sleeves and wide skirts. With the reduction of sleeves in the 1840s, coats reappeared although the various types of wraps had become so popular that they remained ubiquitous. Among the new styles of wraps was the **paletot**, a three-quarter length cape with two or more tiered layers and slits for the arms. (Figure 1.11.)

Once dress sleeves were reduced in size in the 1840s, fitted coats re-emerged. (Figure 1.12.) As with the silhouette of dresses, shoulders of coats were rounded with dropped armscyes. Waists were close fitting and skirts flared wide into a bell shape. Hemlines usually extended to a three-quarter length since the mud on a skirt hemline could be washed but a coat had to be laboriously brushed.

As skirts increasingly widened in the 1830s and 1840s, the petticoat evolved into new forms of support. Initially layers of starched petticoats provided the fullness necessary but the excess fabric about the legs was cumbersome. An innovative solution came in the form of the **crinoline petticoat**—not to be confused with the "cage" crinoline of the 1850s. **Crinoline** was a dense fabric woven of horsehair and linen. Thick bands of stiff crinoline were applied to the hems of petticoats up to about the knees, which effectively supported the spreading dome shape of skirts.

Drawers had become an indispensable undergarment by this time. Most styles extended only to the knees, contrary to Hollywood's preference in showing ankle-length pantalettes at the hemlines of women's costumes for this period.

Corsets grew in size to cover the bosom and flare over the hips. Day corsets even featured shoulder straps and cup shapes for support of the breasts. Whalebone corsets of the 1830s became so rigid and constricting that there was little give or bend. Women frequently fainted from lack of adequate respiration. By the 1840s, though, an important advance in the design of corsets was made possible with the perfecting of **rubberized thread**. The elasticized

FIGURE 1.11. Wrap garments had become the outerwear of choice during the 1830s when padded sleeves were so wide. Although a variety of coats was once again feasible in the 1840s, wraps continued to be a favored form of outerwear. A new type of wrap, called a paletot, featured tiered layers and slits for the arms. Detail of plate from *Godey's Lady's Book,* 1842.

FIGURE 1.12. New silhouettes of overcoats were introduced in the 1840s. Bodices were fitted and bell-shaped skirts were wide enough to fit over the dress. Detail of plate from *Godey's Lady's Book,* 1849.

bodice was commercially called the **corset amazone** because of the freedom of movement it afforded women.

With the raising of hemlines in the 1830s, greater attention was focused on stockings. White ribbed silk stockings were worn with all formal dresses. *Lady's Magazine* noted in 1833 that "most ladies, under their silk stockings, wear stockings of flesh-colored cashmere." Younger women were seen with embroidered sprays of flowers at the ankle of their stockings. On excursions to the country, women might wear gray or brown knit woolen varieties; black silk became the favorite for daytime dress.

Through much of the 1820s, women's hats were unobtrusive accents to the fashionable ensemble. Small toques, turbans, and bonnets fitted closely to the head and were trimmed more simply than in the previous decade. Beginning about 1828 through the end of the 1830s, though, hats became enormous to balance the lateral expansion of sleeves and skirts. (Figure 1.13.) Turbans were great, billowing puffs of fabric, and the brims of bonnets expanded into platter-sized arcs and disks. Adding to the oversized scale of these hats

FIGURE 1.13. At the height of the Romantic Age, women's hats became enormous to balance the wide sleeves and skirts of dresses. The top-heavy scale of hats was further emphasized by excessive ornamentation. Detail of plate from *Le Follet Courrier des Salons,* 1830.

were huge ribbon loops, clusters of feathers, lace ruffles, and cutwork rosettes. For evening wear, extravagant hairstyles imitated the excessive decorations of hats with elaborate arrangements of loops, plaits, and twists—some over wire supports—combined with plumes, strands of beads, jeweled combs, and all sorts of similar hair ornaments. As sleeves diminished in size in the 1840s, hats likewise reverted to smaller shapes with less decoration. (Figure 1.14.) The wide brimmed bonnet with a flat crown was the most prevalent hat style of the decade. A **bavolet bonnet** featured a ruffle at the back of the neck to protect against the sun. Decorative interest was primarily provided by vivid colors and the richness of fabric. For everyday domestic wear indoors, women continued to cover their hair with assorted types of white linen or muslin caps.

The most popular type of footwear in the 1820s and 1830s remained the flat, heelless slipper with ribbon lacings. When skirts were shortened during the 1830s, color and material were especially important for shoes. By the 1840s, when skirt hems once again dropped to the floor, lace-up ankle boots with low heels replaced slippers as the favored ladies' shoe, especially once it became publicized that Queen Victoria preferred the style. Bootmakers took advantage of the new, durable types of rubberized materials to add inserts of elasticized fabric at the sides of shoes for a more comfortable fit.

FIGURE 1.14. Women's hats of the 1840s were reduced in scale, and styles once again fitted more compactly to the head. Towering decorative trim was eliminated, replaced instead by drooping feathers and veils. Detail of plate from *Godey's Lady's Book,* 1841.

Men's Suits of the Empire Era 1800–1820

As a result of the turmoil of the French Revolution, many of Paris' best tailors fled to England where they set up shop. There, expatriate French clothing makers were influenced by the superlative cut and the subdued color palette of English menswear. During the Empire period, these sartorial influences filtered back across the Channel where they were eagerly adopted by Parisians during their Anglomania phase, despite the best efforts of Napoleon to make his court a scintillating center of fashion and style.

In London, the Prince Regent and his circle set the standards for a gentleman's dress and comportment. These dandies regarded clothing and etiquette worthy of a man's whole attention and study. Foremost among London's fashionably elite was George Bryan Brummell, known more familiarly as Beau Brummell. His claim to fame was a mastery of the art of being well dressed, a role he played until debt forced him to flee the country in 1816. He was not an innovator of fashion but, rather, built his reputation by proper grooming, the perfect fit of his clothing, and the correct details of fashion accoutrement. His fastidiously knotted cravats, for instance, were legendary.

The masculine suit of the Empire-Regency period evolved by degrees of refinement rather than by dramatic change in silhouette. (Figure 1.15.) The jacket retained the cut-in or stepped-back front cropped at the waist first seen in the 1790s. Square-front closures were both single- and double-breasted. Tails were cut separately and sewn to the jacket body. The swallowtail variety was attached at the front of the hips and swept in a diagonal line to the back. Spade-shaped tails were attached farther back at the sides and dropped vertically in a straight or slightly curved line. Collars were constructed with a wider band to sit high on the neck. The **notched collar** was formed by the intersection of the folded back lapels and the high turned-down collar.

The sleeveless vest was one of the two remaining men's garments—along with neckwear—that retained some degree of Rococo fancifulness in the nineteenth century. Many men indulged in vivid colors, prints, and patterns. In the 1810s, men even layered two or three vests of contrasting hues for added richness of color and dimension. To allow for the frill fronts of shirts and for the end lengths of the cravat to hang free, vests were either worn partially unbuttoned at the neckline or were cut with a deep U-front. Most vests were still cropped straight at the waist, usually a couple of inches longer than the bottom edge of the jacket front. High, stiff collars extended upright to the ears.

Men's shirts became more differentiated in style and purpose during the nineteenth century. Day shirts were made with a front panel of horizontal tucks or vertical ruching. Both evening and day shirts remained pullovers with keyhole front openings at the neckline. All were of crisp white linen or brilliantly bleached white muslin.

The **cravat** encircled the collar two to three times before being tied in various knots at the throat. The lengths of the ends varied from short bow-like tendrils—the precursor of the bow tie—to long, scarf-like lengths filling the shirt fronts and sometimes fixed with an ornamental stud.

Breeches and pantaloons were trim and formfitting. Buttons at the outside knees ensured a snug fit. Small side slash pockets, usually covered with button flaps, were inserted high on the hips.

Trousers gradually gained in popularity but did not begin to eclipse breeches until the 1820s. The fit of trousers in the Empire period was narrow and smooth like that of breeches. To reinforce the slender look, instep straps, or **stirrups**, were attached to the cuffs to prevent the legs from riding up and the knees bagging. The drop-front flap of breeches was also applied to trousers.

FIGURE 1.15. Men's suits of the Empire era changed little from the styles of the late eighteenth century. Neoclassicism prevailed still in the fitted tail coats with cut-in fronts and vests cropped at the waist. Fashion plate by Horace Vernet, 1814.

Men's Outerwear, Undergarments, and Accessories 1800–1820

Men's overcoats were greatly varied in the nineteenth century. The voluminous carrick with its layers of three to five capelets and high collar was similar to the women's version shown in Figure 1.6. In the 1810s, the French military greatcoat worn by Napoleon was widely adopted by civilians. It was a simple design with an ankle-length hemline, a double-breasted closure, and a high turned-down collar. Cloaks were more commonly worn for riding and travel.

Undergarments for men included a sort of pullover undershirt for winter, which was a simpler version of the day shirt with a short banded collar and plain front panel. Knee-length drawers were made of cotton, linen, silk, or for winter, thick worsted.

Top hats became the most prevalent type of headwear in the nineteenth century. Both tall and short crowns were combined with brims of varying widths. Prior to 1820, though, the most common shape was a tall, straight crown with a shallow, rolled brim that dipped in the front and back. (Figure 1.16.) The two-sided bicorne introduced in the late eighteenth century continued to be worn into the 1820s, though mostly by military men, even when not in uniform. General Andrew Jackson wore the bicorne pointed front to back, but Napoleon wore the style pointed laterally.

Slipper-style shoes with low, rounded heels and rounded toes were the most common form of men's indoor footwear in the Empire period. However, assorted types of boots were the most popular. The **Wellington boot**—named for the British general who defeated Napoleon in 1815—featured a high, curving top that extended to just under the knee but dipped lower in the back. The **jockey boot**, shown in Figure 1.16, was made with a tall, snug top that was worn turned down to display a contrast lining. The **Hessian boot** was named for the German mercenaries who spread the style of their military footwear as they fought in wars on both sides of the Atlantic. The top of the Hessian boot was cut in heart-shaped curve at the front, usually with a tassel at the dip in the center. Beau Brummell listed the Hessian as his favorite.

Other accessories of the gentleman included straight-handled walking sticks, pocket watches with a cluster of ornamental fobs, and made-to-measure kid gloves. Jewelry was limited to rings and the occasional stick pin for the spread cravat.

Powdered wigs had disappeared in the aftermath of the French Revolution although the temple curls and long queues at the nape of the neck had remained. Neoclassicism inspired the shearing of long hair to imitate the short, cropped styles of Greco-Roman busts. Wisps of hair were swept forward all around the clean-shaven face. In the 1810s, side whiskers were neatly shaped into crescents along the jawline.

FIGURE 1.16. Top hats remained the most popular headgear for most men except the lowest classes. Crowns of varying heights were combined with brims of assorted widths to provide a broad variety of choices. Fashion plate from *La Mesangere,* 1808.

Men's Suits of the Romantic Age 1820–1850

Although women's clothing had completely abandoned Neoclassicism by the second quarter of the nineteenth century, men's suits continued to evolve new interpretations of displaying the idealized silhouette of the antique hero: fitted coats were padded to shape sloping shoulders and pigeon-breasted chests, waists were cinched by a corset, and pantaloons and trousers were smooth and slim.

The Anglomania that had swept France in the Empire period left a lasting impression of the importance of well-tailored clothing on almost all men except those of the laboring classes. A wider audience of men became keenly conscientious of the cut, fit, and simplicity of line in men's apparel. From Paris and London, this masculine self-awareness was disseminated throughout Europe, its colonies, and the Americas during the Romantic Age. Even as ready-to-wear became increasingly available for the middle classes later in the century, men ordinarily had their manufactured suits altered for a more tailored fit, a practice still common today.

FIGURE 1.17. During the late 1820s, the men's full-skirted frock coat was revived. The new Romantic Age styling featured a tightly fitted, pigeon-breasted bodice, raised collar, and flared skirt extending below the knees.

FIGURE 1.18. Vests and neckwear were the two remaining garments worn in public with which men could still indulge in colorful self-expression. Bold checks, plaids, and prints in vibrant colors were popular throughout the period. Plate from *Modern Zeitung*, 1843.

In the 1820s, the full skirted frock coat was revived for daytime wear after a thirty-year absence. (Figure 1.17.) Coat skirts of the 1830s were full and flared; hemlines usually extended to the knees or below although some were cropped at mid-thigh. By the 1840s, skirts narrowed and were shortened above the knees. The bodice of the Romantic era frock coat featured most of the same design details as the tail coat including the fitted waist, pigeon-breasted front, high collar, and double- or single-breasted closure. In the late 1840s, the waistline of frock coats dropped to the hips in a long-line silhouette and padding was reduced. At about this time the frock coat surpassed the popularity of the tail coat for both day wear and formal occasions.

Vests continued to provide men of the Romantic Age with the opportunity for colorful self-expression in their wardrobes. Bold checks or prints and flashy hues endured into the 1840s.

Men still sometimes layered two vests for an extra dash of color and as an additional form of padding support for the pigeon-breasted contours of the coat. By the end of the 1830s, the length of the vest dropped to the hips where it has largely remained to this day. (Figure 1.18.)

Men's pullover suit shirts changed little in the second quarter of the century. The high, stiff collar that extended up to the jawline only receded in the late 1820s. Although some versions of the cuff link band appeared as early as the end of the 1790s, the link-hole cuff did not become widespread for formal dress until the 1840s. During the 1830s, detachable collars and cuffs were introduced. By midcentury, most ready-to-wear shirts were made with button bands for attaching a variety of collars and cuffs.

The double-wrapped volume of the Empire era cravat was reduced in the 1820s although, for another decade, dandies continued to favor the fuller styles with ends spread across the chest. Instead of a loose, rounded knot with tendril ends, a squared, flat bow was introduced about 1825. In the 1830s, black cravats became most prevalent for day wear, and white was worn only in the evening. By the 1840s, the cravat had been replaced by the narrow bow tie. Although black was the most common color for neckwear, by the late 1840s, some men jauntily sported bow ties of polka dots, stripes, or checks of varying color combinations.

Beginning in the 1820s, trousers became increasing preferred to breeches and pantaloons. Suspenders attached at the waistband by buttons, and instep stirrups at the cuff ensured a smooth fit of the legs without the discomfort of tightness. Through the 1830s, breeches and trousers were constructed with a **fall front closure**. (Figure 1.19.) In the 1840s, the drop front construction was gradually replaced by the revival of the concealed button **fly front**, which had been forgotten since the end of the seventeenth century. Also during this decade, the instep straps disappeared and cuffs were left to drape freely about the ankles. The proper cuff hemline covered the heel of the shoe and broke in front over the instep—the same length of suit trousers today.

FIGURE 1.19. Until the 1830s, breeches and trousers were constructed with a fall front closure. In the 1840s, the concealed button fly front gradually replaced the fall front.

Men's Outerwear, Undergarments, and Accessories 1820–1850

One of the new developments in the design of men's overcoats in the 1820s was the separate bodice and skirt construction. Previously the long military-style coat of the Empire period had been made in a single piece from the shoulder to the hem. The pelisse-styled greatcoats of the Romantic Age, though, became more fitted. Collar treatments followed the trends of the suit coats, including high rolled styles cut with and without lapels. Pockets were placed high on the hips sometimes at the waist seam with deep flaps. For the dandy, a pelisse-styled overcoat of the 1830s and 1840s featured a wide collar, often of velvet, a cinched waist, and a full bell-shaped skirt such as those shown in Figure 1.20. Greatcoats retained their comfortable boxy capaciousness through the entire period.

During the second quarter of the nineteenth century the great expansion of the Industrial Revolution spurred a rapid rise in business travel for many middle-class men. As a result, cloaks once again became a prevalent form of outerwear. The huge circular cloak of the Empire era was gradually narrowed and shortened to just below the knees after 1825. Some riding cloaks were made with a slit partially up the back that was secured by buttoned tabs that could be

FIGURE 1.20. Men's pelisse-styled overcoats of the 1820s and 1830s replicated the hourglass silhouette of women's versions. Collars were wide and bodices were fitted to a cinched waist. Skirts were full and bell shaped all around. Fashion plate of a Russian Pelisse from *Costume Parisien,* 1830.

FIGURE 1.21. During the second quarter of the nineteenth century, men's cloaks became shorter and more narrow than those of the Empire era. Cloaks were a more comfortable alternative to the snugly fitted overcoat for horseback riding and commuter train travel. Fashion plate from *Modern Zeitung,* 1844.

unfastened to more easily drape over the saddle. Most were constructed with wide collars that replicated the designs of fitted coats. (Figure 1.21.)

Manufactured rainwear first emerged during this period. In 1823, the Scottish chemist, Charles MacIntosh patented a waterproof fabric made by cementing thin sheets of India rubber between woven textiles. The resulting raincoat, called a **mackintosh**—a variation of the inventor's name—was not a commercial success because the coal-tar naphtha glue reeked an intolerable odor. Within a decade of the first mackintoshes, though, Thomas Burberry developed a closely-woven twill fabric, later patented as **gabardine**, that caused water droplets to run off the surface. The new weather-resistant textile was made into a variety of outerwear, which was later sold in his own retail shop. Today, the **Burberry** line of ready-made outerwear and rainwear is still a quality branded apparel line.

Men's drawers and undershirts remained basically the same as those developed in the 1810s. As trousers became more prevalent than breeches during the 1830s, a new form of ankle-length **trouser drawers** was introduced. After 1840, drawers were more commonly made of knit fabrics—cotton for summer and wool for winter. Also, at that time, the drop front flap was replaced with a button fly adapted from the new styles of trousers.

The cylindrical top hat remained the predominant headwear for both day and evening. (Figure 1.21.) The combinations of crown heights and brim widths continued to be as varied as those of the Empire period. After 1830, though, the dip in the front and back of the brim was less pronounced and the rolled lateral edges were more subtle. Sleek and shiny beaverskin or black silk was used for dress hats; straw suited a more casual street suit in summer.

Men's shoes of the 1820s were similar to the shallow slipper styles of the Empire period. In the late 1820s, lace-up shoes became more prevalent for day wear and the slipper styles were worn primarily in the evening. At this time, the heel became somewhat higher and toes were squared. Assorted types of boots were still the favored footwear for travel and outdoor activities.

In the 1820s, side whiskers began to lengthen and expand. By the 1840s, bushy **mutton chops**, resembling a fleecy leg of lamb, extended down the temples to the jawline. Beards and mustaches also returned after an absence of almost 150 years. The outer strands of each side of the mustache were waxed into upturned curled points. Hair remained cropped above the collar. By the 1840s, men's hair was closely cut and tamed with oils. To protect furniture upholstery against the oily heads of their menfolks, Victorian women began to cover the armrests and backs of chairs and sofas with crocheted and lace doilies called antimacassers named for the popular Macasser's hair oil.

Children's Clothing 1800–1850

Few changes occurred in the design of infants' clothing in the first half of the nineteenth century. The practice of swaddling—binding the baby's arms and legs—mostly had been abandoned by the end of the 1700s except for some isolated areas where superstitions and entrenched customs persisted. Instead, everyday clothing for infants became more loose and longer than ever before. The presentation and christening gowns were made of fine fabrics and laces and cut exceedingly long to display the family's affluence. One change was the disapproval of caps for babies by childcare authorities of the time. Caps and hats could harm "the delicate tissues of the head," warned one publication.

Even though infants' wear changed little from that of the eighteenth century during the first quarter of the nineteenth century, significant changes were made to children's clothing, which became increasingly regressive in the 1820s. Initially, though, girls continued to enjoy the ease and comfort of chemise-styled dresses made of cotton or linen although the silhouettes became more columnar like the Neoclassical gowns of their mothers. (Figure 1.22.) Further liberation was accorded small girls with hemlines shortened to mid-calf. As a girl got older, the hemline fell incrementally with age until her skirt reached the appropriate length of a young woman's dress—a practice that remained in effect through the First World War.

As hemlines rose on girls' dresses, the legs—or "limbs" in polite society—had to be covered. The solution was an appropriation of trousers similar in shape to the styles worn by their little brothers. These pantalettes were usually made of cotton and trimmed with lace, embroidery, or ruffles such as shown here in the *Portrait of Little Mary* by William Beechey.

During the 1830s and 1840s, the class-consciousness of the affluent middle classes influenced major changes in girl's apparel. The simple white chemise dress presented no cachet

FIGURE 1.22. The full, loose chemise-style dresses worn by girls in the last decades of the 1700s were replaced by short, columnar styles of the Empire period. For modesty, a form of trousers called pantalettes was adapted from menswear to fully cover the girl's "limbs." *Portrait of Little Mary* by William Beechey, c. 1810.

FIGURE 1.23. To reflect their success and affluence, the burgeoning middle classes of the Industrial Revolution dressed their girls in miniature versions of women's fashions, including constricting corsets. Preschool-age boys donned the new tunic suits, which included adaptations of women's dress silhouettes worn over trousers. Detail of plate from *Godey's Lady's Book,* 1841.

FIGURE 1.24. By the 1840s, suits for school-age boys featured various forms of a short coat and trousers. Plate from *Godey's Lady's Book,* 1849.

of social and financial status. Consequently, parents began to dress their girls in miniature versions of women's fashions. (Figure 1.23.) Like the fine furniture in their parlors, their children were upholstered in heavy fabrics trimmed with ruffles, fringe, and other decorative treatments. Girls as young as age three were forced into tight bodices made smooth by corsets. Bell-shaped skirts required petticoats made of stiff, heavy crinoline. Bonnets and oversized hats additionally restricted a girl's movements.

Boys, too, suffered a fate similar to that of their sisters. The eighteenth-century skeleton suit that had been so ideal for the freedom of active small boys was gradually replaced by a revival of dresses beginning in the late 1820s. In Charles Dickens' *Sketches from Boz* of 1838, the skeleton suit is referred to as an "ingenious contrivance" that had gone out of style. The adaptation of dresses for young boys was called the **tunic suit**. The five-year-old boy shown in Figure 1.23 wears a fancy version of this new tunic top from 1841. The tunic bodices were fitted and made with a full, knee-length skirt attached. Usually the waist was articulated by a belt, sash, or waistband. Beneath the tunic, boys wore trousers or, sometimes, even pantaloons trimmed with lace and ruffles.

Around the age of six or seven, depending on the child's height, boys graduated to the suit styles of their fathers. In the first quarter of the century, the components of the suit included breeches, vest, and tail coat. In the 1840s, the boy's basic suit changed to long trousers and a short jacket. (Figure 1.24.) Long-sleeved jackets were cropped at the waist with front openings cut straight or rounded to the hips. Various types of lapels and collars were applied to the new form of short jacket. In England, the short jacket, trousers, and white shirt with a turned-down collar came to be known as an **Eton suit**, named for the London boys' school where the ensemble was a mandated uniform. This style of suit would remain the predominant basic clothing for boys throughout the rest of the century.

Review

In the first two decades of the nineteenth century, the imperial dominance of Napoleonic France perpetuated influences of Neoclassicism throughout Western culture and society. Art, architecture, interior design, and fashions of the Empire period reflected the modes l'antique that had first emerged in the late 1700s. Women's gowns with the high waistline just under the bosom is still known today as the Empire waist. Skirts fluidly draped over the body, and bare arms and necklines simulated the look of the ancient Greek chiton.

However, within the first years of the nineteenth century, women's fashions began to show elements of change inspired by the countercultural movement that would become the Romantic Age. Sleeve styles from assorted past eras were adapted to the Empire silhouette. Versions of the ruff were revived. Textile prints incorporated exotic motifs and colors of Africa, the Islamic Empire, and the Far East.

By the end of the 1820s, Neoclassicism had been completely superceded by Romanticism. The waistline of women's dresses gradually dropped to its natural position becoming once again cinched by constricting corsets. Skirts, at first, became conical and then wide bell shapes in the 1830s. Sleeves presented the most innovative change with their immense lateral fullness supported with padding.

As Romanticism faded into Victorianism in the 1840s, the emphasis of dress designs shifted from sleeves to the ever-widening skirt. Petticoats made of a stiff horsehair and linen fabric called crinoline provided support for the great expanse of the circular skirts.

Men's suits of the Empire period also remained influenced by Neoclassicism. The fitted tail coat with its cut-in front cropped at the waist and the tight, short vest evolved in points of refinement rather than innovative change in silhouette. Breeches and pantaloons were tight and form fitting.

In the second quarter of the nineteenth century, the form of men's suits was dramatically altered with the revival of the closed-front frock coat and the transition from breeches to trousers. Colors became muted and ornament was minimized. Ostentatious neckwear receded to the simple bow tie. A middle class conformity developed that would dominate menswear well into the following century.

Children's clothing became regressive. Girls once again were dressed in miniature versions of women's styles including corsets and layers of crinoline petticoats. For young boys, the practical skeleton suit was replaced by tunic suits, which featured adaptations of feminine dresses worn over trousers. School-age boys wore versions of their father's somber suits.

review questions

1. What was the most significant technological development in the first half of the nineteenth century that revolutionized the production of clothing? Who were the three principal contributors and what were their achievements? What has been the impact of this technology?

2. How were advances in the refinement of rubber applied to textiles and clothing?

3. Which elements of the Empire gown featured influences of Neoclassicism? How was the Empire gown altered by influences of Romanticism?

4. What was the transition of the Empire gown from a Neoclassical profile to the Romantic silhouette in the 1810s and 1820s?

5. Identify the primary elements of dress design at the height of the Romantic Age in the 1830s.

6. What was the shift in emphasis on the design of dresses in the 1840s? What was a key development in textiles that made possible the new silhouette of the 1840s? To what purpose and how was this new fabric applied to women's garments?

7. How did men's suits of the Empire period reflect influences of Neoclassicism? What were the subtle changes of the Empire coat, vest, and collar from the styles of the late 1700s?

8. As men's clothing became more drab in color, what two garments afforded men some degree of personal expression with color and textile pattern?

9. What dramatic changes to men's suits occurred in the 1820s? What was significant about these changes? How did these new types of garments evolve in the 1840s?

10. Identify and describe the men's garment that emerged from the lower classes to become a widespread fashion in the 1840s.

11. How did children's clothing of the early nineteenth century become regressive?

research and portfolio projects

Research

1. Write a research paper on the Anglomania phases of French fashion in the first half of the nineteenth century. Explore the social and economic causes of the importation of English culture and how these forces impacted French style. Identify the specifics of French fashion design that were affected by Anglomania.

Portfolio

1. Compile a reference guide of women's accessories of the early nineteenth century designed with motifs "à la grecque." Research artwork of the period as well as modern auction catalogs and antiques magazines for:

   - 10 examples of jewelry
   - 10 examples of textiles used for accessories
   - 10 examples of any other items (fans, parasols, combs, reticules, handkerchiefs, belts)

   Next to each photocopy or digital scan include a written description of the item including details of the featured Greco-Roman motif.

dress terms

bavolet bonnet: a close fitting hat style with a ruffle at the back of the neck

bertha: a wide, deep collar usually attached to the edge of the low, open neckline of the Romantic dress

Burberry: any of a type of men's or women's outerwear or rainwear made of a weather resistant gabardine

camisole: a form of short sleeved or sleeveless underbodice

capote: a bonnet style made with a soft fabric crown and rigid brim

carrick: a men's or women's overcoat with layers of three to five capes sewn to the collar

cashmere: a soft textile made from the silken hair of goats from the Kashmir region of Central Asia

chemisette: a type of underbodice made with a decorative front panel to fill open necklines

corset amazone: a corset style made from elasticized fabric

cravat: men's neckwear variously tied or knotted at the front of the throat

crinoline: a dense fabric woven of horsehair and linen

crinoline petticoat: a petticoat made with wide, thick bands of crinoline applied around the hem

elasticized fabrics: textiles produced in the early nineteenth century from yarns made with rubber

Empire waist: a high waistline positioned just under the bosom

Eton suit: boy's short jacket, trousers, and white shirt with a turned-down collar named for the London boys' school where the ensemble was a required uniform

fall front bodice: two pieces of lining material that fastened across the inside front of an Empire waist bodice to lift the bust

fall front closure: the drop-front flap of men's trousers through the 1830s

fly front: the vertical slit in the front of men's trousers or drawers

gabardine: a closely woven twill fabric

gigot: a form of leg-of-mutton sleeve padded with feather pillows in the Romantic Age

Hessian boot: a men's high boot with a heart-shaped top and a tassel at the dip in the center

jacquard: a fabric with an intricately woven design of raised patterns

jockey boot: a men's tall boot worn with the snug top turned down

mackintosh: a raincoat made from layers of sheet rubber cemented to fabric; named for the inventor of the material, Charles MacIntosh

Merino wool: soft, supple wool from specially bred sheep in England and Spain

mutton chops: men's long, bushy side whiskers

notched collar: the V-cut gap formed at the intersection of the lapel and collar piece

organdy: a stiff, transparent fabric of silk or cotton

paisley: gourd or pod-shaped motifs richly decorated with intricate patterns

paletot: a women's three-quarter length cape with two or more layers and slits for the arms

pantalettes: women's long drawers of mid-calf or ankle length

pelisse: a long, capacious overcoat, usually lined with fur

reticule (also rediclue): a women's small purse of assorted types

rubberized thread: spun yarns reinforced with an application of vulcanized rubber used to create elasticized fabrics

spencer: a women's Empire jacket cropped to fit just below the bosom

stirrups: strips of fabric sewn to the cuff of men's trousers that fit under the instep of a shoe

toque: a woman's tall, brimless hat usually tapering to the top

trouser drawers: men's ankle length underwear commonly made of knit fabrics

tunic suit: a boy's skirted top worn over pantaloons or trousers

vandyking: a form of trim cut in points resembling the sharply pointed beard of the artist Anthony Van Dyck

Wellington boot: a men's high boot with a curving top in the front and a dipped curve in the back; named for the British general who defeated Napoleon at Waterloo

2 The Victorian Age 1850–1900

1850					1875
French Second Empire ruled by Napoleon III 1852–1870	Transatlantic Cable laid 1858	U.S. Civil War 1861–1865	U.S. purchased Alaska from Russia 1867	First electric motor 1869	Italy united 1870
Crimean War 1853–1855	Japan opened to the West by U.S. Commodore Perry 1854	Butterick paper patterns developed 1863	U.S. transcontinental railroad completed 1869		Germany united under the Second Reich 1871
Great Exhibition, London 1851	Walt Whitman's *Leaves of Grass* 1855	Darwin's *Origin of Species* 1859	*Harper's Bazaar* first published 1867	Suez Canal opened 1869	First exhibit of the Impressionists 1874

1875					1900
British buy Suez Canal 1875	Edison's electric light bulb 1879	First motorcar prototypes made in Germany 1885	George Eastman's first amateur cameras 1888	Marconi invented wireless telegraph 1895	Spanish-American War 1898
Mark Twain's *Tom Sawyer* 1875	Bell invented the telephone 1876	American Red Cross founded 1881	Safety bicycle introduced 1889	Roentgen discovered X-rays 1895	U.S. annexed Hawaii 1898
U.S. Centennial Exposition in Philadelphia 1876		Robert Louis Stevenson's *Treasure Island* 1882	Van Gogh's *Starry Night* 1889	First Olympics since ancient times 1896	Queen Victoria died 1901

Nationalism, Industrialism, and Victorianism 1850–1900

Where the first half of the nineteenth century was defined by dramatic and profound changes in technologies, economics, politics, and societies, the second half was marked by an ever-increasing rapidity of change across all these fronts. The former was deep and intimate—a redefining of the order of things in the post-revolutionary era; the latter was wide—an evangelizing of change through Western nationalism and socioeconomic imperialism around the world.

Map of Europe 1899.

This new, widely flung imperialism of technology, economics, and politics was showcased on the world stage in 1851 with the Great Exhibition in London. Gathered beneath the lofty iron-and-glass casing of the Crystal Palace were the technological wonders of the EuroAmerican Industrial Revolution and the astounding array of machine-made products it could produce. Equally significant, among the cultural displays from around the globe was a clear statement of the preeminence of Britain as the world's greatest colonial power. Queen Victoria had been on the throne for fourteen years when she opened the Great Exhibition, and she would reign another fifty years, giving her name to the era.

In France, a coup d'etat in 1852 by Louis Bonaparte, the nephew of Napoleon, led to the reestablishment of an imperial government. Louis became Napoleon III, and the period is known as the Second Empire. The following year the emperor married the beautiful Spanish countess, Eugenie, and established a glittering court in the Tuileries Palace. In their efforts to make Paris once again the cultural center of the world and reestablish the dominance of the French fashion industry, the emperor and empress surrounded themselves with fashionably dressed aristocrats. They held dazzling formal balls to which guests flocked wearing the newest finery from the fashion houses. Although the emperor succeeded in these cultural and economic endeavors, his foreign policy acumen was dismal, leading to a war with Germany in 1870. The Prussian army captured both Paris and the emperor, forcing him to abdicate and flee into exile with his family. The Third Republic that was formed after the departure of the emperor focused on the nation's industrialization and imperial expansion, especially colonies in Africa.

Prussia continued to be the most powerful and modernized state in the German Confederation. Under the leadership of its chancellor, Otto Von Bismarck, the thirty-seven German statelets were unified in 1870 under a constitutional monarchy headed by Prussian Kaiser Wilhelm. From this point of power, the new Germany embarked upon its own imperialistic ventures, acquiring large sections of Africa and establishing a colonial presence in China and Japan.

The last feudal stronghold in Europe was Italy. A peasant insurrection in 1860 was whipped into a nationalist rebellion led by Giuseppe Garibaldi. The varied Italian states and principalities were finally united into one nation in 1870 governed from Rome.

The rapid changes that occurred in the United States during the second half of the nineteenth century began with a "Manifest Destiny," a nationalist purpose in which Americans viewed the coast-to-coast expansion of the nation as a divinely ordained mission. The price, though, was a threat to the balance of power between slave states and free states—a dichotomy of cultures, societies, economies, and politics. The inevitable result was a prolonged, devastating civil war (1861–65). The costly national crisis preserved the union and strengthened the central government over that of individual states. In 1869, a symbol of this new unity was the completion of the transcontinental railroad. With the expansion of the western frontier and the rapid industrialization of the North during the Civil War, the United States was second only to Britain in manufacturing might by the time Americans celebrated their centennial with a grand exposition in 1876. By the end of the century, the United States had even become a global imperial power in 1898 with the annexation of Hawaii and the acquisition of Puerto Rico, Guam, and the Philippines following the Spanish-American War.

Revolutions in Science and the Arts

The astonishing force and speed with which the Industrial Revolution progressed throughout the nineteenth century were fueled by the rapid and continual advances in technology and science. Unlike the intellectual quests of enlightenment in the 1700s, the scientific and technological discoveries of the 1800s were made principally for the advancement of the Euro-American industrialized economic systems. Electric power replaced steam; electric lighting expanded the hours of a workweek; electric tools and machinery increased productivity. The telephone provided direct, instantaneous communication for businesses and the home in a way the telegraph could not. The internal combustion engine was adapted to automobiles and farm equipment.

Many of the singular discoveries of the era ultimately had broad applications that still impact our daily lives today. In attempting to solve spoilage problems for dairies and wineries, Louis Pasteur developed the process of "pasteurization"—the process of heating liquids to destroy bacteria. Joseph Lister developed antibiotics and antiseptics to fight disease and reduce postoperative fatalities. Wilhelm Roentgen discovered X-rays. Pierre and Marie Curie isolated radium, the first known radioactive element—the first step toward harnessing atomic energy.

Women's Trousers

The first audacious steps in introducing trousers for women had occurred in the late 1840s with the advent of the American women's movement. In 1848, a group of progressive women participated in a conference in rural western New York state to discuss a broad range of issues that laid the foundation for the American feminist movement in the nineteenth century. Among the demands outlined in their manifesto, the Seneca Falls Declaration of Sentiments, was dress reform. Besides proposing the abandonment of the corset, some women also advocated the adoption of trousers for women. The recommended form that preserved modesty as well as provided functionality and comfort was the **Turkish trouser**, which had full, baggy legs tied at the ankles and was worn under a knee- or calf-length skirt. (Figure 2.1.) Because the feminist lecturer, Amelia Bloomer, wore the ensemble on tour in the 1850s, the style came to be popularly called a **Bloomer dress**. When *Peterson's Magazine* presented the illustration shown here in 1851, the editors noted, "We must say that too few of the Bloomer costumes are graceful: they are either altogether uncouth or they are too theatrical."

The concept of trousers as street wear for women was soon abandoned, but the garment survived in forms of bathing suits. In the 1890s, shorter, less voluminous forms of bloomers were gradually accepted as a safe and comfortable alternative to long skirts for school athletics. Related to bloomers were **knickerbockers**—more commonly called knickers—which were a type of knee breeches that had been adopted by men in the 1860s for hunting and other country activities. By the mid-1890s, various forms of bloomers, knickers, and leggings for women's sports had become almost commonplace.

FIGURE 2.1. Although trousers for women were introduced in the late 1840s, it was the bicycling craze of the 1890s that provided a catalyst for a broader, though limited, acceptance of feminine versions. The popularity of the bicycle advanced women's clothing reform more rapidly than had forty years of feminist advocacy. Women discarded corsets and adopted practical clothing such as forms of breeches and shortened or split skirts. Left, Bloomer dresses from *Peterson's,* 1851; center, flannel bathing suit from *Godey's,* 1865; right, knickerbocker suits from *Vogue,* 1895.

Just as science and technology continually crossed new thresholds in the late nineteenth century, startling new social and cultural perspectives challenged established ideas and traditions. Charles Darwin's *Origin of Species* (1859) horrified the devoutly religious and further contributed to a secularization of Western society. Sigmund Freud and Havelock Ellis popularized psychology and opened a public dialog on the taboo subject of sexual motivation in human behavior.

The women's movement gained momentum with the widely publicized Declaration of Sentiments drafted at the 1848 conference of women in Seneca Falls, New York. Women's demands for equal citizenship, political rights, opportunities in education and employment, dress reform, and voluntary motherhood were thrust into the nation's public dialog. However, it was an advance in technology that provided the most significant boost in helping women achieve greater independence. In 1889, the chain-driven safety bicycle was introduced, launching a cycling craze that opened new gates for cloistered Victorian women. In droves, women escaped the confines of the kitchen and the nursery to explore horizons far and wide. Women gained confidence in their new-found independence and in their self-assuring operation of these mechanical conveyances. In addition, bicycling impelled clothing reform such as less constricting types of corsets and a broader acceptance of feminine forms of trousers. (Figure 2.1.)

In the visual arts of midcentury, Romanticism began to evolve in new directions. In France, America, and Russia, schools of naturalism produced highly realistic studies of nature populated with raw representations of common people. From the foundations of the naturalists developed the Impressionist movement in the 1870s and 1880s. Led by Monet, Degas, Renoir, and Pissarro, the Impressionists focused on the spontaneous recording of light and color. By the mid-1880s, a group of artists, later categorized as Post-Impressionists, reacted against Impressionism by developing expressive painting styles that forecast the modernist art of the next century. Cezanne, Van Gogh, and Gauguin reconstructed the natural world with imagination rather than fidelity to the actual appearance of things. For absolute realism, there was photography. Although photographic techniques had been developed in the 1830s, a reproducible negative was not invented until 1851. In 1888, George Eastman introduced the first amateur box camera, popularizing photography with the masses.

Although Neoclassicism and Romanticism had had significant influence on the design of clothing for both men and women, the principal art movements of the second half of the century had little effect on fashions. The exception was the Art Nouveau style of the 1890s. Art historian H. W. Janson describes Art Nouveau as "primarily a decorative style, inspired by Rococo forms and based on sinuous curves that often suggest organic shapes." The look had wide appeal and was applied to architecture, furniture, home decorative items, mass media design, and fashion and accessories through the 1910s. (Figure 2.2.)

Worth and Couture

Prior to the mid-nineteenth century, the arbiters of fashion were the great ladies of the various eras such as Isabella d'Este in the sixteenth century, Catherine de Medici in the seventeenth century, and Madame de Pompadour in the eighteenth century. Very few dressmakers and tailors achieved the status of fashion designer to whom their patrons yielded style direction.

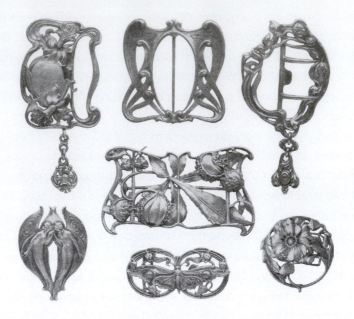

FIGURE 2.2. From the 1890s through the First World War, the decoration of women's fashions and accessories featured elements of the Art Nouveau movement. Surfaces and contours were dissolved into sinuous, undulating lines and soft, organic shapes. Left, dress with inset panels of an Art Nouveau pattern, 1896; right, Gorham silver jewelry, 1901.

Notable exceptions were Rose Bertin who designed for Marie Antoinette and was nicknamed the "Minister of Fashion" in the 1780s, and Louis Leroy who designed Neoclassical styles for both Empresses Josephine and Marie Louise.

In the 1850s, though, a young Englishman forever altered the course of fashion production with inventive new marketing methods. Charles Frederick Worth had worked at various jobs in Paris dress shops for several years when he began to design dresses for his wife to wear at her job as a sales assistant in the upscale Maison Gagelin. When customers began to request similar gowns, Worth was permitted to establish his own dressmaking operation in the shop. By 1858, he had become so successful that he partnered with a wealthy Swede cloth merchant to open his own salon. The following year, Worth's wife presented her husband's design portfolio to the newly arrived Princess Pauline de Metternich, wife of the ambassador from the court of the Austro-Hungarian Empire. When the princess wore one of Worth's gowns to a court ball, the ensemble caught the eye of the Empress Eugenie who asked about its creator. Worth's fortune was made. (Figure 2.3.) For the next thirty-five years, he set the fashion trends not only for Paris but for all the style centers of the world. His designs were worn by the Empress of Austria, the Queen of Italy, the Czarina of Russia, and through her own dressmakers, Queen Victoria. After the collapse of the Second Empire during the Franco-Prussian War of 1870, the House of Worth continued to prosper despite a brief setback from the loss of his aristocratic patrons. With equal flair he designed for the wealthy bourgeoisie of the Third Republic as well as for innumerable Americans on the Grand Tour.

FIGURE 2.3. In the 1850s and 1860s, the elegance and fashion leadership of Empress Eugenie and the court of the Second Empire advanced France's preeminence in fashion and style throughout the world. *The Empress Eugenie and her ladies-in-waiting* by Franz Xaver Winterhalter in 1855.

As a designer Worth is often credited with the revival of the hooped petticoat, or cage crinoline, as it came to be known. Whether or not this is true, he popularized the look in the 1850s and 1860s. His authority as fashion master was particularly evident in his radical alteration of the gown silhouette in 1866. He eliminated the crinoline and narrowed the skirt with a draping to the back, a look which launched the bustle era. One of Worth's most quoted statements is his claim that he "dethroned the crinoline."

Worth's marketing acumen paved the path for all couturiers from the late nineteenth century to today. Among the innovative practices he established was the use of live models, or mannequins as they were later called, to display his designs. In the 1870s, Worth introduced the fashion collection—at first biennial, then by the 1880s, biannual. He was able to achieve this by developing designs that were engineered with interchangeable parts; any variety of sleeve styles would fit an assortment of bodices, which themselves could fit various types of skirts. He also sold his designs wholesale to "modistes," or agents for dressmakers, who took the

Ready-to-Wear Manufacturing and Retail Fashion

The industrialization and urbanization of Europe and the Americas in the nineteenth century created an ever widening consumer middle class. From the needs and wants of this cash-endowed populace emerged new opportunities for the fashion industry. Even as early as the mid-1700s, industrious tailors in the seaports of England and its North American colonies set up "**slop shops**" in which they produced and sold ready-made men's apparel, primarily to sailors seeking civilian clothes when off duty. Basic jackets, shirts, and breeches were hand-sewn in somewhat general sizes comparable to our small-medium-large standards today. During the 1820s, the first ready-to-wear factories were founded in England, and soon afterward in the United States, mainly producing uniforms and selected standardized types of men's and boy's clothing. At the end of the 1850s, though, a greater variety of affordable women's apparel was available as ready-to-wear. In 1860, *Godey's* noted that "a ready-made garment can be purchased nearly as cheap as the cloth of which it is made." By the 1870s, women's three-piece wool suits were advertised in *Harper's Bazaar* at $3.75.

During the 1850s, production of ready-to-wear clothing quadrupled as manufacturers invested in new technologies, particularly industrial fabric cutters and sewing machines. Electrical versions of these machines were introduced in 1890, increasing the speed and precision of production even more. Other important developments in the apparel industry included the discovery of **aniline dyes** in 1856 from which a rich palette of synthetic dyestuffs were produced,

providing manufacturers and consumers with a vast array of color options. In 1868, the first commercially viable plastic was invented, called **celluloid**. This sturdy, durable product made from cotton and cellulose was used in the manufacture of collars, cuffs, shirt fronts, buttons, buckles, ornaments, and jewelry.

There was no shortage of skilled labor in the cities to work in clothing factories, especially in the United States where liberal open-door policies encouraged immigration. From these huddled masses, desperate men, women, and children were easily recruited to slave long hours in sweat shops, producing high quality goods for meager wages. Although throughout the nineteenth century numerous garment industry unions were formed to advocate changes and challenge abuses, most were ineffectual and soon disbanded. Only in the 1890s did a union achieve national status with the organization of the United Garment Workers of America (UGWA).

As mass production increased, new methods of sales distribution and marketing developed. The warehouse slop shops of the late 1700s evolved into larger specialty stores offering a wider choice of related manufactured and custom goods. From these specialized stores emerged the first grand emporiums, or department stores, in the 1840s and 1850s. The Bon Marche (meaning "great bargain") in Paris is often credited with being the first retail giant in this arena. Founded in 1838, the Bon Marche brought together under one roof full lines of apparel and accessories for men, women, and children, as well as a

wide range of household goods. The doors of these emporiums were open to the public, and all classes of society were invited to view the wondrous products of the mechanized age available for purchase.

The third wheel that drove the success of the ready-to-wear industry in the 1800s—after manufacturing and retail merchandising—was advertising. Mass media during the early Industrial Revolution consisted largely of newspapers and magazines, both of which featured limited advertising. In the second half of the nineteenth century, though, publishers discovered they could operate their periodicals at a loss, but make substantial profits on advertising—the principal business model of mass media today. As ready-to-wear manufacturers increased output and retailers faced rising competition, both turned to advertising to inspire the masses to buy. (Figure 2.4.) With the advertising barrage from newspapers, magazines, catalogs, mailers, billboards, posters, and handbills, the nineteenth-century consumer—from the meanest of the working classes to the wealthiest of the bourgeoisie—aspired to the acquisition of more variety and better quality goods.

Indeed, the very notion of fashion itself became democratized with ready-to-wear. Nineteenth-century fashion magazines such as *Harper's Bazaar*, *Vogue*, *Delineator*, and *McCall's* featured the newest styles of ready-to-wear in both advertising and editorials. In 1875, a *Harper's Bazaar* fashion column advised readers that retailers "are providing ready-made suits at such reasonable prices and of such varied designs that something may be found to suit all tastes and purses." In the 1890s, *Vogue* regularly featured a column titled "Seen in the Shops" in which ready-to-wear and accessories were described in detail, including retail prices. In addition, mail order catalogs—profusely illustrated with the latest fashions—made ready-to-wear clothing and accessories accessible wherever the post office or mass transportation delivered.

The recurring cycle of mass production, marketing, and consumption became entrenched in the socioeconomic patterns of EuroAmerican society by the end of the 1800s. The cycle survives with us today and continues to drive the ready-to-wear industry on a multibillion-dollar global scale.

FIGURE 2.4. Mass production and mass marketing of ready-to-wear democratized fashion in the late nineteenth century. Advertising instilled aspiration across a wider social spectrum, and rapid distribution quickly brought the newest trends and styles to the masses. Detail of page of ready-to-wear and retail fashion ads from *Harper's Bazaar*, 1873.

designs back to London, Rome, Vienna, Berlin, Madrid, and New York. *Godey's Lady's Book* apologized in the December 1888 issue for not having fashion plates of the coming new trends because the modistes had returned late from Paris and current styles "could not be obtained earlier in the season." In addition to the made-to-measure dress shops, the emerging women's ready-to-wear industry looked to the couturiers and their collections for models to adapt to mass production. When coupled with advertising and mass media, the easy availability of ready-to-wear encouraged an aspiration for fashion across a broader range of socioeconomic classes.

Women's Dress: The Crinoline Period 1856–1868

The bell-shaped skirt of the late 1840s continued to expand into an ever widening circle in the early 1850s. This horizontal silhouette was further enhanced in the mid-1850s by flounces, many of which were given even more expanse by trimming edges with ruffles, ruching, scallops, or vandyking. Another optical border treatment for emphasizing the breadth of flounces was a technique of fabric roller printing called "**á la disposition**" in which printed designs were created specifically for the edges of flounces.

To support the increased volume and weight of the skirt, multiple starched petticoats or heavy, horsehair crinoline petticoats were layered underneath. This additional weight and mass of fabric was uncomfortably heavy and cumbersome, especially when coupled with the added volume of capacious sleeves and the discomfort of tightly laced corsets. Simply walking was an arduous task when weighted down with an ensemble made of velvet or taffeta.

By the mid-1850s, though, relief appeared in the form of a newly constructed petticoat formed with a cage of airy hoops and tapes. Also called a crinoline, its superstructure of cane or whalebone and later, thin steel hoops, was sufficient to spread the circumference of the skirt without multiple layers of heavy, starched or ruffled petticoats.

The distinction between the two types of crinolines can be confusing. The petticoats of the late 1840s were reinforced with strips of the stiff horsehair-and-linen blended fabric called crinoline, and the undergarment came to be named after this textile. After the mid-1850s, the **cage crinoline**, serving the same purpose as its heavier predecessor, continued the name of the earlier petticoat style.

In 1856, a hooped petticoat was introduced made with bands of watch spring steel coated with rubber. In 1858, Charles Worth opened his couture salon in Paris with a collection of dresses that featured enormous bell-shaped skirts supported by the hooped crinoline. (Figure 2.5.) Worth's success, of course, was largely due to the acceptance of the crinoline by the Empress Eugenie, from whom Paris and, hence, the fashionable world, took its cue.

Throughout the early 1860s, dozens of new patents were registered for improvements in the construction of the crinoline. Equally significant was the pervasiveness of the crinoline across classes. Due to the mass production of crinolines, almost all women except the lowest classes and advocates of clothing reform indulged in wearing them, even if only for their Sunday-best dress.

Around 1861, the shape of the crinoline began to shift from a rounded, bell shape to a more conical silhouette. By 1863, the half crinoline, with only half hoops in the back, flattened the front of the skirt and concentrated the fullness at the back. (Figure 2.6.) Instead of deep gathers at the waistline, the excess fabric was folded into flat box pleats to fall more vertically

Detail of fashion plate from *Godey's*, 1857.

Lilac cotton print day dress, c. 1855–59.

FIGURE 2.5. In the late 1850s, the petticoat made of crinoline material was replaced by the structural cage crinoline. The thin hoops of whalebone or steel were lighter than layers of heavy linen petticoats.

Steel cage crinoline from *Godey's*, 1859.

in the front. Another construction method used to achieve the flattened front was **goring**, triangular or tapered pieces of cloth used to shape the bodice or skirt. Long sections of fabric that extended from the shoulders to the hemline were also shaped with a narrow, curved cut at the waistline, thus reducing excess material from the skirt front. Skirts became the widest of the era, some as much as eighteen feet in circumference. The emphasis on the back of the skirt was sometimes further exaggerated with a hemline that extended into a deep, full train.

The tightly fitted bodices of crinoline dresses were usually shaped by curved seams in the back and darts in the front. With the reduction of multiple petticoats—and their thick, layered waistbands—the contours of the bodice waistline appeared all the more slender over a tightly

FIGURE 2.6. In the early 1860s, the silhouette of the crinoline skirt shifted from a round, bell shape to that of a cone with a flattened front. By shifting the mass of the skirt to the back, the circumferences expanded to the most exaggerated widths of the era. Fashion plate from *Peterson's,* 1864.

laced corset. The most common dress construction featured the bodice sewn to the skirt with a variety of waistlines including V-fronts, U-fronts, or straightline cuts. The **princess style** was made of one long piece (or long-gored pieces) from the shoulder to the hem with no waist seam. Toward the end of the 1850s, the separate bodice and skirt became increasingly popular. The two pieces could be of the same material or mixed with contrasting colors or fabrics. Some bodices included **basques**, or short, skirt-like tabs that extended down from the waist over the hips. In the 1850s, basques were usually cut in one piece with the bodice; after about 1860, they were separate pieces sewn to the waist and often cropped at an oblique contour longer in the back. (Some fashion historians refer to these basques as **peplums**.)

Dress sleeves were created in an endless variety. Armscyes remained "dropped," or positioned off the shoulder. As a complement to flounced skirts, some sleeves repeated the tiered look with layers of ruffles or flared sleeves within sleeves. The **pagoda sleeve** was shaped like an inverted funnel with a narrow fit over the upper arm and an abrupt flare at the elbow, usually with an opening short in the front and longer in the back like those shown in Figure 2.5. A large, bell-shaped sleeve was similarly cut with a more gradual flare from the shoulder that ended between the elbow and the wrist. For more conservative tastes, though, long sleeves extending to the wrist in narrow cylinders continued from the 1840s.

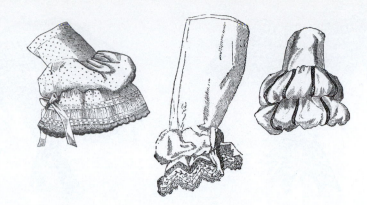

FIGURE 2.7. Bodices and jackets of the crinoline age were fashionably made with half or three-quarter sleeves. To cover bare forearms, discerning ladies attached separate undersleeves usually made of brilliant white muslin or linen. The infinite assortment of decorative treatments at the cuffs of undersleeves also added variety to a wardrobe of plain bodices and jackets. Undersleeves from *Godey's,* 1855.

Assorted variations of decorative undersleeves were made for dresses with wide sleeve styles or sleeves cropped at the elbow. (Figure 2.7.) These were usually half sleeves that were pinned or buttoned above the elbow. In 1855, *Graham's Magazine* cautioned ladies to always properly secure their undersleeves so as not to have them "come down into your soup plate at a public table."

Crinoline Dress Accessories and Outerwear 1856–1868

In skimming through the many women's magazines of the 1850s and 1860s, one might be surprised by the numerous illustrations of assorted dress accessories. Some pieces such as detachable collars, sleeves, and cuffs were devised for easy laundering, particularly since women often wore the same dress day after day, especially in winter. Victorian modesty was another factor in the layering of accessories, such as undersleeves to cover the bare arms exposed by dresses with half sleeves, or chemisette neck fillers for scoop necklines that revealed more shoulder than was acceptable in daytime. More importantly, though, was fashion variety. Then, as now, a limited wardrobe of dresses could be expanded into a wide range of looks by adding a few decorative accents. (Figure 2.8.)

The **canezou** varied from short muslin jackets to elaborate neckline fillers. Other accessories were more specifically styled and named, some new and some revivals. **Bretelles** were described at the time as a pair of "braces" made of bands of ribbons or lace that attached at each shoulder and tied together at the waist with a bow. **Fichus** of the period were cape-like or scarf-like coverings for low necklines, following the styles of the eighteenth century. Most fichus now included lappets of varying lengths that extended to the waist where they were tied, tucked into a belt, or cross-wrapped around to the back and secured in a bow. For evening dresses, **berthas** and half berthas of ribbon and lace were also popular accents for minimizing the exposure of deep decollette necklines. Plain skirts were enlivened with fanciful silk or fine linen aprons ornamented with combinations of embroidery, lace, ruching, and similar decorative elements.

The three silhouettes of outerwear of the crinoline age included various wrap garments, snugly fitted jackets and coats, and loosely fitting jackets and coats. The most popular form of outerwear, though, continued to be the wrap garment. A wide assortment of shawls, capes, and mantles were circular cut to adequately fit over the enormous crinolined skirts.

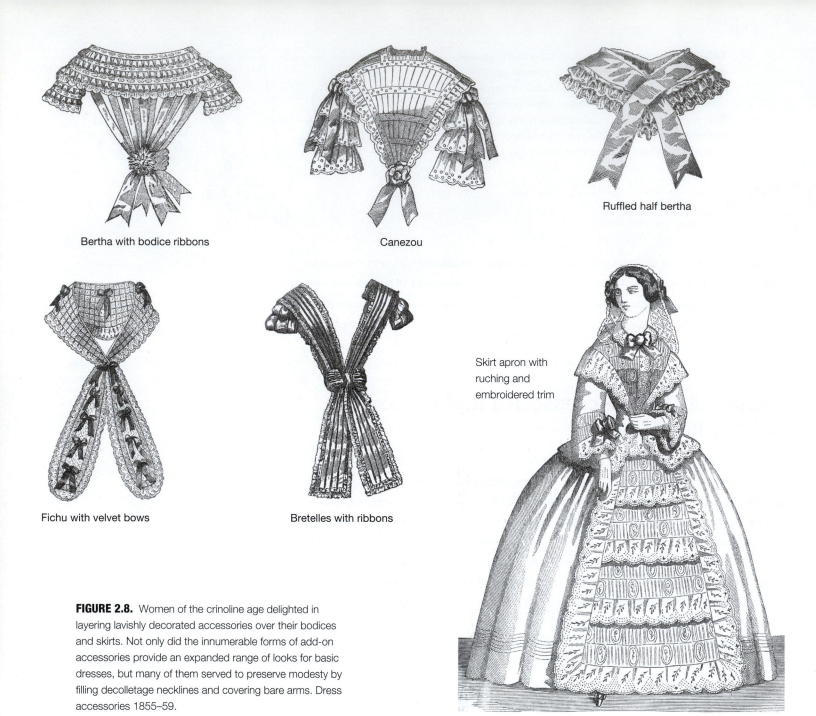

Bertha with bodice ribbons

Canezou

Ruffled half bertha

Fichu with velvet bows

Bretelles with ribbons

Skirt apron with ruching and embroidered trim

FIGURE 2.8. Women of the crinoline age delighted in layering lavishly decorated accessories over their bodices and skirts. Not only did the innumerable forms of add-on accessories provide an expanded range of looks for basic dresses, but many of them served to preserve modesty by filling decolletage necklines and covering bare arms. Dress accessories 1855–59.

Outerwear accessories included fur muffs and detachable fur cuffs that could function as a muff when the hands were tucked inside opposite sleeves. Gloves were among the easiest items to standardize for mass production so that fine quality kid gloves were widely available. An example of the subtleties of style at the time was an admonition by a fashion editor in 1856 against wearing white kid gloves in the street; white was for indoor use only.

The most prevalent form of headwear was the bonnet. (Figure 2.9.) During the 1850s and 1860s, the close-fitting styles were shaped to sit back on the head, entirely exposing the face and much of the hair in the front. Caps likewise were close fitting and usually arranged back on

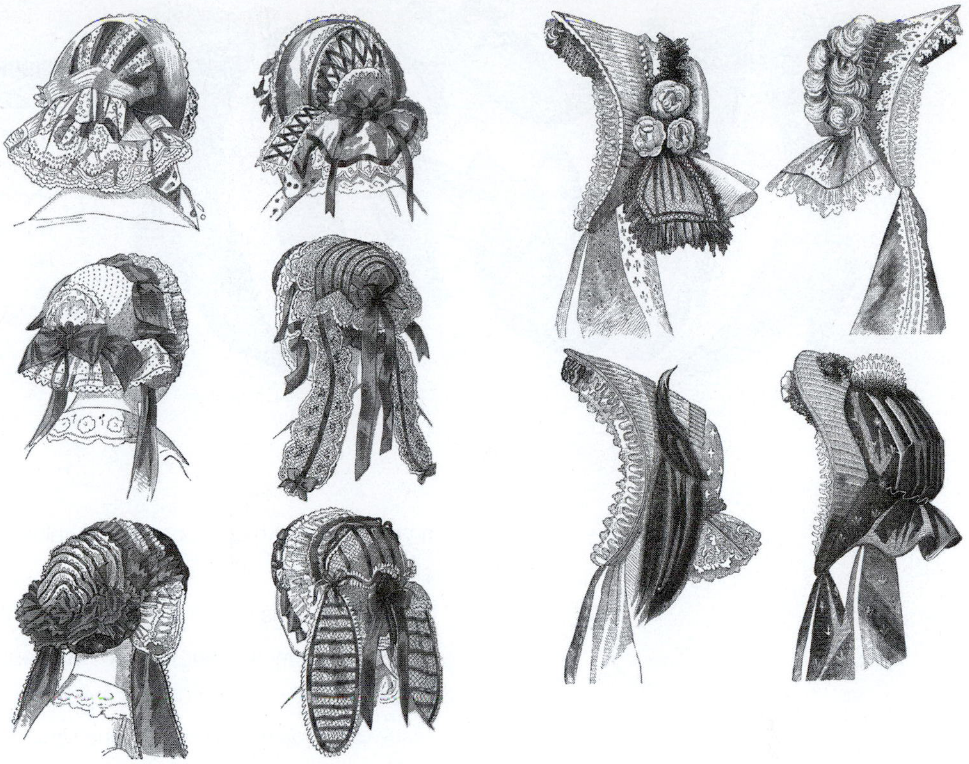

FIGURE 2.9. Bonnets continued to be the most prevalent form of headwear during the crinoline period. Styles were designed to sit back on the head to complement rather than conceal the face and hair. Left, bonnets, 1857; right, bonnets, 1861.

the head with the hair up in a chignon or plait. Chenille or silk cord hair nets called **snoods** of assorted sizes covered the knots and held false hair pieces in place. Velvet, satin, felt, beaver, and **Neapolitan** (horsehair) were the principal fabrics for winter bonnets and hats; for summer, "everything in the shape of bonnets is with straw or trimmed with straw," declared a fashion editorial in 1855. Bonnets and caps were richly adorned with an abundance of decorative treatments. Unlike designs of the Romantic Age, though, feathers, silk flowers, ribbon loops, bows, and lace ruffles on the hats of the Second Empire did not project outward in an exuberant display, but rather clung closely to the structure of the cap or bonnet in a rich surface embellishment. Bavolets of lace, ribbon, satin, or velvet at the nape of the neck remained a consistent element throughout the period.

For daywear in the home, white cotton or linen caps were most common. For matrons and elderly women, house caps were decorated with various types of lappets at each side, and sometimes in the back.

The hightop boot was still the favorite style of footwear for women. Heels became increasingly higher into the 1860s. The square-toed, button top boots shown in Figure 2.10 were typical of the era. As skirts got shorter, more attention was focused on the look of shoes, which included the revival of satin bow rosettes and vividly colored kid to coordinate with dresses. At the 1867 Paris Exposition, shoe styles featured high tapered heels and a revival of the thick, curved **Louis heel**, named for Louis XV. Extravagant trimmings of feathers, fur, jet beads, and large metal buckles were liberally applied.

Other accessories included assorted hand-carried items. Parasols were a necessity for a lady to preserve her prized alabaster skin. Handkerchiefs were embroidered by hand not only as a symbol of refinement but also as a display of sewing skills. Women's magazines were profusely illustrated with patterns and techniques for hand embroidering. Various forms of

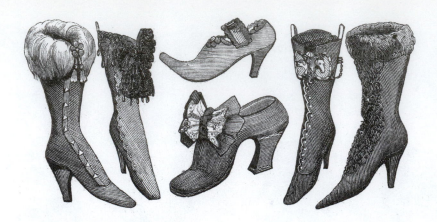

FIGURE 2.10. High-top boots were still the favorite types of shoes for street wear in the crinoline era. As hemlines became shorter, boots were more richly accoutered with ornament, texture, and color. High, tapered heels were applied to both boots and slipper styles. The Louis heel was also revived for special occasion shoes. Plate from *Harper's Bazaar,* 1867.

small purses with chain or cord handles were made of colorful plain fabrics or rich tapestries and beadwork.

Jewelry was more subdued in design than in the Romantic Age. A strict protocol of what, when, and how to wear jewelry was constantly reiterated in fashion editorials. *Graham's* insisted in 1855 that, "In summer, when the daylight and not the gaslight illumines festive doings, all jewelry should be avoided—the simplest gold bracelet, the plainest gold brooch, of evident necessity, can be allowed." Diamonds were never to be worn in daytime. Earrings were small and unobtrusive.

Women's Dress: The Bustle Era 1868–1889

In August 1868, *Harper's Bazaar* lamented the demise of the crinoline: "A little while since it was predicted that the crinoline, which had filled for so long a time such a large space in the world, was gradually slinking away, and was destined to disappear altogether. . . . That tyrant, Fashion, may issue against them his edict, which no one dare refuse to obey." But the change in silhouettes was not abrupt. The crinoline of the early 1860s had already begun to shift the emphasis of the skirt to the back in various arrangements. By the end of the decade, the **Grecian Bend profile** of the late 1780s had been revived, aided by high heeled shoes that further tilted the posture forward to balance the weight and volume of skirt in the back. (Figure 2.11.) This first of three distinct phases of the bustle silhouette lasted from 1868 until around 1876.

The skirt was the focal point of dress designs during this period. The complexity of draping and the mixed combinations of textures and colors astound us still today. At its zenith in the mid-1870s, the bustle dress featured aprons and swags of fabric that draped from the waist to the hemline in all sorts of busy lines—diagonals, curves, or zig-zags—and pleats, flounces, ruffles, ruching, tucks, and fringe trim abounded. Overskirts were variously arranged in puffs and swags revealing a separate underskirt sometimes of a different shade of the same color as the dress. Dresses were further overloaded with the addition of decorative fichus at the neckline and wide ribbon bows variously tied about the hips. Many skirts also were cut with excessive trains that extended behind in yards of material despite the street-sweeper results and the dangers of being trod upon. In 1875, *Harper's Bazaar* warned ladies about ball gowns with excessive trains ornamented with delicate trimmings: "Nothing, or almost nothing, is left of

FIGURE 2.11. The bustle treatment of skirts evolved through three phases, the first of which occurred between about 1868 and 1876. The complexity of draping the dress bustle often involved arranging aprons and swags of contrasting fabrics with all sorts of decorative treatments such as pleats, flounces, ruffles, and a wealth of lavish trimmings. Engravings from *Harper's Bazaar:* top left, 1869; top right, 1869; bottom left, 1874; bottom right, 1875.

"THE GRECIAN BEND."
Does not Tight-Lacing and High Heels give a Charming Grace and Dignity to the Female Figure?

FIGURE 2.12. Between about 1876 and 1882, the second phase of bustle dress designs featured narrow skirts with a clinging fit. Bustles were reduced to small pads, and decorative treatments were concentrated low on the back. Fashion plate from *Harper's Bazaar*, 1879.

a dress of tulle made with a full train; everybody has stepped on its trimmings, and no further account need be given of its condition on reaching home."

Bodices were most commonly separate jacket styles with basques cut in a variety of shapes and lengths. Some basques were short peplum versions and others were long enough to drape to the back like a shortened overskirt. The bodice fit was tight and smooth over a constricting corset, reinforcing the new narrowness of the dress silhouette. Necklines for day dresses were usually high and closed, most with some form of standing collar. When cut in an open square or V-shape, the neckline was filled by a lace- or frill-front chemisette. Formal gowns continued to bare the arms and shoulders. Some evening wear bodices plunged to the waist in both the front and back over a sleeveless chemisette with decorative facings.

Sleeves were much simpler than those on crinoline dresses. The armscyes were now set at the shoulder, squaring the upper bodice. Most sleeves were narrow cylinders extending to the wrists although three-quarter lengths were popular for afternoon tea gowns. The same extravagance of surface embellishments was applied to sleeves as to the skirts, particularly over the forearm and at the wrists.

Between 1876 and 1878, the contours of the bustle dress were significantly reduced, becoming ever more slim and columnar. In 1878, *Harper's Bazaar* credited Worth with popularizing the new "draped yet clinging" skirt styles. The cut of skirts became so narrow at the knees that a woman's movement was restricted to short, mincing steps. (Figure 2.12.) Decorative treatments lacked the volume of a few years earlier and were concentrated low on the back of the skirt. Trains remained long for most formal dresses. The projecting structural bustle was eliminated although petticoats were engineered with a "small pad filled with [horse] hair" at the back or a cascade of ruffles extending the full length down the back to the floor.

One of the key design elements of the tight, vertical silhouette was the **cuirass bodice**, formed by a sheath-like construction that fitted tightly and extended over the hips. To ensure the smooth, long line of the bodice or jacket, decorative treatments were less pronounced than previously, even on evening gowns. Sleeves likewise became closely fitted with minimal decoration.

The columnar skirt designs with their shallow bustles were short lived, lasting until around 1882. By the summer of 1883, *Harper's Bazaar* alerted readers that at fashionable centers such as Newport and Saratoga, dresses had exhibited "the preference for large tournures [bustles] and a tendency toward fuller skirts." The lavish use of material in gathers, folds, tucks, ruching, and similar volumetric treatments returned. "Drapery is more bouffant on the hips and back," reaffirmed *Harper's Bazaar* a few months later. The structural bustle had returned with a vengeance, thrusting the skirt out almost horizontally at the back. Dress historian Blanche Payne wrote that the look of the new bustle dress appeared "as if the wearer had inadvertently become attached to an overflowing pushcart." The long-line bodice endured, positioning the fullness of the skirt bustle treatment lower on the hips than the styles of the early 1870s. (Figure 2.13.) Evening dresses were even more exaggerated with additional

FIGURE 2.13. With the third phase of bustle dresses, the structural bustle returned in its most extreme forms. The bouffant treatment of excess fabric and decoration further emphasized the exaggerated horizontal skirt silhouette. Top left, fashion plate from *Harper's Bazaar*, 1884; top right, silk faille reception gown, 1888; bottom, fashion plate from *Harper's Bazaar*, 1884.

CRAPE AND LACE FICHU-COLLAR.

Fig. 1.—LACE COLLAR WITH JABOT.

Fig. 2.—VELVET COLLAR WITH LACE PLASTRON.

Fig. 3.—VELVET COLLAR WITH CRAVAT OF VELVET, GAUZE, AND LACE.

FIGURE 2.14. Many of the decorative dress accessories that became popular during the crinoline age were carried over into the bustle period. Ornamental neckwear, for example, served the same purposes as earlier—to provide modest concealment and wardrobe variety. Many of the styles that looked basically the same were cataloged in magazines with a confusing array of fashion terms. Illustrations from *Harper's Bazaar*, 1883.

volume fashioned from lightweight tulles or frilly trimmings such as starched lace ruffles and garlands of silk flowers. Both the long, sleek bodice and the horizontal bustle remained the fashionable silhouette until 1889.

Bustle Dress Accessories and Outerwear 1868–1889

Victorian ladies loved to layer on their ensembles an endless variety of detachable decorative accessories. As mentioned previously, the terms applied to many of these accessories are often confusing since they were sometimes used interchangeably for multiple items. A frilly lace neckpiece may have been called a fichu, jabot, cravat, or **plastron** and yet all generally resemble each other in size, shape, and placement. (Figure 2.14.) Similarly, some fichus featured in magazines of the time looked identical in shape and size to wide, cape-like berthas. Even so, all of these various forms of fabric confectionery delighted the fashionable woman and provided a wide assortment of fresh looks for plain bodices and jackets.

Outerwear categories of the bustle era were largely the same as those of midcentury: wraps, jackets, and long coats. Although new constructions were necessary for the shape of longer coats to fit over bustles, shorter types of jackets were still cut with much of the same fullness and hip treatments as those of the crinoline period. Familiar styles of long coats featured innumerable types of collars, cuffs, front closures, and trim. Most were cropped shorter than the hemline of the dress ranging from three-quarter to seven-eighths lengths.

The 1890s

Between 1889 and 1892 the drama of the bustle silhouette diminished and the emphasis shifted to the sleeves and bodice. Skirts became more conical with a smooth fit over the hips all around. During the transition some draped effects of the 1880s lingered, but by 1895, virtually all skirts fell from the hips to a flared bell-shape at the hem.

Initially, sleeves expanded into a typical leg-of-mutton style with a puffed fullness at the shoulder and upper arm that tapered to a close-fitting cylinder from the elbow to the wrist.

From 1893 to 1895 the volume of the sleeves ballooned into enormous proportions reminiscent of those of the 1830s. (Figure 2.15.) In fact, much was written at the time comparing the two eras and the styles of each. In 1895, a *Vogue* editorial conceded that "we, at the end of the nineteenth century, are copying the fashions of the early second quarter to a very marked degree." In magazines and catalogs, the gigantic sleeves were even more commonly referred to as gigot sleeves rather than leg-of-mutton. Unlike the gigot sleeves of the 1830s, though, the styles of the 1890s were not padded with feather pillows and balloons. Some

FIGURE 2.15. In the 1890s, fashion drama shifted from the bustle skirt to the sleeves and bodice. Huge leg-of-mutton sleeves, high collars, and all sorts of cape-like frills and treatments transformed the upper half of the dress silhouette into massive proportions. Left, Hilton Hughes dress, 1893; right, illustrations from *Vogue*, 1895.

support was provided by inner linings of layered crinoline or a cambric base, but upon removing a wrap or coat, women were required to fluff the crushed fullness of their sleeves back into shape.

Bodices either were smooth fitting with rigid constructions of boning and stiff linings or were full and loosely tucked into a belt or sash. New forms of constricting corsets that ended just under the bosom pushed up the fullness of the breasts and extended a sleek line over the hips, sculpting the much vaunted hourglass contours. The forward tilt of the Grecian bend from the bustle era was now supplanted by a more erect, vertical posture.

High, stiff collars reinforced the upright look. *Vogue* noted in 1893 that the woman of fashion "ransacks her mamma's, aye even her grandmamma's treasure boxes, to discover any old lace collars that might have been laid away." In addition to choker style lace collars, other types included revivals such as narrow pleated or fluted ruffs. The **cavalier collar** was a high band that flared into a shallow roll similar to styles of the 1590s. The new **Marie Stuart collar** curled out from a high-standing band into five points.

Between 1897 and 1899, the balloon sleeves were reduced and took on new shapes. The fullness remained primarily at the shoulders and upper arms, though. The **mushroom puff sleeve** fitted tightly over the full length of the arm and was capped at the shoulder by a shallow, flattened puff. (Figure 2.16.)

The short **bolero jacket** had been a recurring but tentative dress bodice enhancement since the 1830s. By the 1890s, though, the style was all the rage. "Boleros are worn by everyone having pretensions to smartness," gushed *Vogue* in 1896. The styles of bolero jackets at the end of the century were more of a cropped vest with a rounded cutaway front extending to about the edge of the rib cage. The bolero was frequently fitted with the cavalier or Marie Stuart collar during this period. Other boleros were attached to all sorts of shoulder treatments. A typical example is shown in Figure 2.16, in which a lace bolero is joined to a matching bertha with fluted frills that stand out over the mushroom puff sleeves. Some forms of the bolero were simply a front sewn at the shoulder and side seams of the bodice.

As women became more independent and sought employment in business offices and retail establishments, the tailor-made suit of a matching jacket and skirt worn with a blouse became indispensable to the modern woman's wardrobe. The tailor-made suit was not the same as a made-to-measure suit, which required fittings and custom tailoring. Instead, apparel retailers took the woman's measurements (or received them through the mail) and placed orders to a factory where the precut components were assembled. Ads for tailor-made suits often claimed that their suits were produced by "men tailors" for the cachet of a quality superior to manufactured ready-to-wear. Prices for tailor-made suits were mostly in the five- to

FIGURE 2.16. By the end of the 1890s, sleeves were reduced and reshaped. One of the most innovative sleeve styles was the mushroom puff. Fashion plate from *Delineator*, 1897.

ten-dollar range. The majority of the tailor-made suit styles were almost severely plain with obvious influences from menswear. Women often wore masculine neckwear with these suits and, sometimes, even a cropped vest of a contrasting fabric such as corduroy.

In addition to popularizing the tailor-made suit, advertising by apparel manufacturers and retailers also helped make the blouse and skirt ensemble universal. The big wish book catalogs from Sears and Montgomery Ward featured dozens of blouses called **shirtwaists**—or more commonly **waists**—priced from fifty cents to a dollar. Initially, waists were worn informally with intimate friends and family by the middle classes. For working class women, the affordable waist was ideally suitable for office or factory work or similar jobs where comfortable and easy-care garments were necessary. By the end of the century, though, waists were acceptable even for the most formal occasions.

Outerwear during the 1890s followed the top heavy silhouettes of dresses. Coats and jackets for outdoors featured huge sleeves to accommodate the volume of bodice sleeves. Shoulder-widening details and trim were applied to both coats and wrap garments. Capes, cloaks, and mantles were newly constructed with high collars and frills. In the United States, military forms of coats and wraps were made with braid and large brass buttons during the Spanish-American War.

Women's Undergarments 1850–1900

The three prevalent fashion silhouettes of the second half of the nineteenth century could not have been achieved without unique and extraordinary undergarments. The cage crinoline of the 1850s and 1860s has been discussed earlier in the chapter and is shown in Figure 2.5. During the transition from the wide, circular crinoline to the bustle, numerous varieties of experimental bustle-and-crinoline combinations appeared briefly. (Figure 2.17.) One form, the **crinolette**, was a flat front petticoat with steel half hoops at the back that widened in segments from hip to hem.

During the early 1870s, innumerable versions of bustles and bustle petticoats were marketed, some with structural supports and others laden with flounces of heavy batiste. Bustle petticoats were made in two sections that buttoned together at about mid-thigh, which allowed for easier laundering since the hems soiled easily and needed to be washed more often than the bustle pad. For dresses made of heavy materials requiring layers of petticoats with the bustle, the weight could be oppressive, requiring additional support garments fitted with suspenders.

By the late 1870s, when the silhouette of skirts became narrow and vertical, the projecting bustle was replaced by thin pads called **pannier bustles**. Petticoats were cut with the upper rear portion removed, as shown in Figure 2.17, to which could be buttoned or tied various sizes of padded bustles or a flounced petticoat extension.

In the early 1880s, the bustle look returned with a more pronounced and exaggerated profile than ever. Heavy frames called **tournures** made of steel, duck, laces, and tapes were needed to support and shape the massive volume of skirts. With ingenuity and the technology of mass production, inventors engineered light, airy wire bustles in the late 1880s that replaced the heavy structural petticoat versions. For only twenty-five cents, a woman could strap on a wire frame bustle over which was layered a light cotton petticoat for the most fashionable silhouette of the day.

Structural bustles, 1875.

Transitional crinoline and bustle combination undergarments, 1868.

For the oppressive weight of bustles, layers of petticoats, and heavy dresses, skirt supporters were fitted with suspenders. Ad 1875.

Bustle pad and petticoat, 1879.

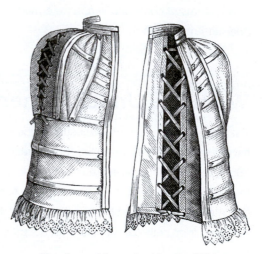

New form of the revived bustle, 1884.

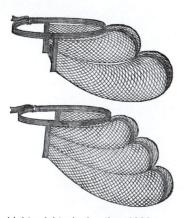

Lightweight wire bustles, 1888.

Bustle petticoat, c. 1885.

Corset and corset waist, 1899.

FIGURE 2.17. The exaggerated dress silhouettes of the 1870s through the 1890s were made possible by an amazing assortment of structural bustles, engineered corsets, and a host of other support undergarments.

The chemise of the crinoline and bustle periods remained short, at about the knees, and continued to be made of cotton or fine-gauge linen. Most chemises were short-sleeved or, for evening wear, sleeveless. In the 1870s, chemises were constructed with breast seams to prevent the fabric from bunching at the front of the corset, and gussets were added under the armscyes to ease the tightness caused by the rigidly laced stays. During the 1880s, plain white linen and cotton were replaced by colored and patterned textiles including bright red knits, luxurious silks, and **nainsook**, a woven striped cotton from India whose name means "delight for the eye" in Hindi.

The tight-fitting bodices of crinoline and bustle dresses fitted smoothly over corsets that could cinch a woman's waist measurement to as little as seventeen inches, according to contemporary sources. Through the mid-1870s, corsets were short, extending just over the hips. As the dress silhouette became narrow and vertical, the line of the corset dropped lower over the hips forming the slender hourglass figure. By the 1890s, the corset was reduced at the top to fit just under the breasts, but retained the long line over the hips. Versions of the **corset waist** fully covered the upper torso and included a constructed bosom support with shoulder straps. For full-figured women who opted for the low-cut corset, an early form of the brassiere called a **bust bodice** provided additional coverage and lift. If a woman lacked the amplitude to fill a decollete bodice, then a padded **bust improver** might be attached to the chemise.

Camisoles, also called underbodices or corset covers, and basic drawers changed little during the late 1800s. In the 1870s, the camisole and drawers were sewn together to form "**combinations**" in both knit and woven varieties. By the 1890s, these had come to be known as **union suits**, not because they were produced by union labor, but because the camisole top was united with the drawers into one garment.

Women's Sports Attire 1850–1900

As noted at the beginning of this chapter, women of the late nineteenth century became increasingly independent and self-assured with new perspectives about the traditional roles of the Victorian housewife and mother. Among the contributing factors in advancing women's ideas of self and place in society were athletics. Besides the cycling craze, other sports activities pursued by women included golf, tennis, fishing, hiking, canoeing, hunting, and swimming. Advertising saturated mass publications with sports images and messages of health and recreation in pursuing an active, outdoor life. In addition, famous artists whose work appeared regularly in popular-culture magazines such as *Life* and *Cosmopolitan* perpetuated the modernity of the athletic woman in their editorial illustrations. The epitome of this idealized woman was the Gibson Girl who was not only confident and athletic but also was a fashion style-setter. Named for the illustrator Charles Dana Gibson, the Gibson Girl was the female icon of the era. (Figure 2.18.)

The specialized clothing that emerged for women's sports activities ranged from everyday garments with simple adjustments such as shortened shirts and reengineered corsets to innovative styles like the knickerbockers shown in Figure 2.1. Women's participation in sports inspired dress reform with numerous other garments as well. Skirts that were cropped above the ankles for active pursuits or walking on rainy days came to be known popularly as "**rainy-daisies**." Split skirts that extended to mid-calf were a compromise for the cycling enthusiast who was less bold than those who donned knickerbockers. Middy blouses, usually made with

FIGURE 2.18. In the late 1890s, artist Charles Dana Gibson created the ideal American woman in his mass-media illustrations. The Gibson Girl was tall, athletic, confident, and most especially, a fashion style-setter.

FIGURE 2.19. Among the most daring and controversial forms of women's clothing in the second half of the nineteenth century were bathing costumes. Throughout the period, though, as styles changed with the fashions, bathing suits nonetheless remained cumbersome and impractical for swimming. Left, smock, swim dress, and trouser suit from *Harper's Bazaar*, 1868; right, leg-of-mutton sleeve adaptations, 1895.

a wide, flat sailor's collar, were loose through the shoulders and neckline—ideal for lunging after a tennis ball. Most significantly of all, though, was the alteration or, even elimination, of the corset for sports activities. Various types of sports corsets were widely advertised in women's magazines. The bicycle waist was cropped short and included elasticized side panels and shoulder straps that "give with every motion of the body" as an 1897 ad promised.

Second, perhaps, to women's trousers in fashion controversy and social drama were women's bathing suits. (Figure 2.19.) Although as early as the eighteenth century, women wore loose sack gowns or sack jackets with petticoats for immersion into spa pools, specific costumes for public seaside dips in the surf were not developed until the nineteenth century. In 1855, *Graham's* reported that there simply was "no *becoming* bathing costume," only "various attempts to make a pretty thing out of an ugly thing." That being asserted, the editors advised on an "appropriate" costume for those women intent on such "healthful" pursuits as swimming, but warned that it was nonetheless "morally unbecoming to seek the conspicuous or to strive to attract in the operation of bathing." The dress recommended at the time "should consist of trousers, made full and fastened round the ankle with a button . . . and a full tunic reaching to the knee." A broad straw hat was suggested to help protect against sunburn.

By the 1860s, bathing suits consisting only of the trousers and a shirtwaist were "objected to by many ladies as masculine and fast," according to *Harper's Bazaar*. "But experience proves that they do not expose the figure more than a wet clinging robe, and are much more

FIGURE 2.20. Ladies' hats of the bustle era were high and sumptuous, reflecting the vertical silhouette of the bustle dress. In the 1890s, hats were much more varied ranging from low, soft turban styles to winged leghorns. Left, fashion plate from *Harper's Bazaar,* 1874; right, fashion plate from *Delineator,* 1898.

comfortable in the water, where all superfluous drapery should be dispensed with." However, for those women who preferred a modest appearance over practicality, the wool serge or flannel "polonaise" bathing dress was recommended, even though many an unwary bather drowned from such heavy, voluminous garments when wet.

In the 1890s, bathing suits became briefer with short skirts, short sleeves, and decollete necklines, though they were just as impractical for swimming as earlier versions. The huge leg-of-mutton sleeves, full skirts, baggy bloomers, and thick wool stockings dangerously encumbered and weighed down the bather.

Women's Hats, Shoes, and Accessories 1870s–1890s

Hats of the 1870s and 1880s were high, vertical, and excessively decorated to complement the silhouette of the bustle dress. (Figure 2.20.) Brimless toques and hats with shallow, rolled, or

FIGURE 2.21. Shoes of the 1890s became narrow with long, pointed toes. Heels were lower and thicker than in the bustle period. For street wear, the high-top button boot was richly decorated. Plainer, more utilitarian boots were usually secured with laces. Slipper-style shoes for special occasions were made of opulent fabrics and ornaments. Illustrations from *Vogue*, 1897.

turned-up brims were given additional height with ribbons, rosettes, feathers, ruching, silk flowers, lace, and similar trimmings arranged in all sorts of combinations. The more commonplace bonnet was less formal than the tall toques even though some styles could be as elaborately decorated.

In the 1890s, hairstyles and dressy hats were less towering. Soft, free-form types of fabric hats like those shown in Figure 2.20 resembled small turbans that echoed the look of the tight, busy hair arrangements. Hat crowns were flattened and brims expanded in width. Brims were bent, crimped, slashed, and curled into an infinite variety of exaggerated shapes. Some hats were even made with double brims between which rolls or plaits of vividly colored fabric could be added to match any day ensemble. Wide-brimmed straw hats, called **leghorns** after the name for a type of bleached wheat straw, were fashioned in all shapes. Plain straw **boaters**, also called sailor's hats, like those worn by the Gibson Girl in Figure 2.18 were the most ubiquitous of the period. Popular decorations for street hats included pairs of birds' wings jutting up into space or even entire artificial birds appropriately covered with real feathers.

Shoes became more round-toed in the 1870s and 1880s, but returned to a pinching, long point in the 1890s. (Figure 2.21.) Heels were thicker and less high for dressy shoes, and street shoes often featured medium heels of about three-quarters of an inch high. Button-top boots were eventually replaced with lace-up models. Footwear for the tailor-made suit of the nineties was adapted from men's shoe styles, including sturdy, two-tone **oxfords** with low heels. Formal slippers were covered in fine fabrics like satin dyed to match gowns, and accented with faceted beads, pearl-encrusted buckles, and stand-up ribbon bows. For the cycling enthusiast, a type of high spats called **leggins** (not to be confused with trouser-like leggings) buttoned over the boot instep and extended to mid-calf or even the knee.

The most indispensable fashion accessory for women in the late nineteenth century were gloves. A lady never went out of her house without an appropriate pair of gloves for her ensemble—short fabric or kid gloves for summer, heavier leather for winter, and long silk styles for evening wear. Hand-carried accessories such as purses, fans, muffs, and parasols changed little in style and shape beyond colors and trimmings that coordinated with ensembles.

Women's Hair Treatments and Cosmetics 1850–1900

In the 1850s and 1860s, the Empress Eugenie was equally as influential with the fashion of hairstyles as with dress styles. She particularly preferred to wear her luxuriant, dark Spanish hair parted in the center and swept outward from the temples with ringlets over one shoulder, a look even Queen Victoria adopted. Variations of this hairstyle are shown in Figure 2.3, including arrangements with the ringlets symmetrically at each side. The chignon and assorted other forms of knots at the nape of the neck remained popular, some accented with a corded silk snood. In the 1870s and 1880s, younger women wore their hair more loosely with masses of

FIGURE 2.22. The Gibson Girl pompadour was widely copied by young women of the 1890s who preferred not to wear a hat when outdoors.

curls, plaits, and twists down the center back. Matrons wore their hair in high, almost vertical arrangements on the back of the head, sometimes with a few short ringlets to the shoulders. By the 1890s, the hair was piled atop the head in tight, close curls and coils, usually with a curly fringe at the front, to better accommodate the smaller, excessively decorated hats. For women who preferred simpler hats like straw boaters, or no hat at all, the Gibson Girl pompadour was widely copied. (Figure 2.22.)

The use of make-up in the Victorian era was possibly not as rare as we might think although it was undeniably viewed with distaste by polite society. An editorial in 1855 espoused that "artificial coloring . . . is, excepting on the stage, entirely confined to a class whose morality and principles are as false as their complexions." Beyond the moral dangers associated with cosmetics, though, there were very real health dangers, which the editor further noted. White skin foundation, made from bismuth and chalk mixed with rose water, "besides destroying the skin, destroys the play of the features and the expression of the face." In addition, "rouge, whether carmine, vegetable or liquid, is injurious, because it obstructs the natural perspiration from the pores of the skin."

Since, flawless alabaster skin was universally associated with youthful beauty and health, eventually the use of white facial powder became widely acceptable. In 1868, *Harper's Bazaar* advised that "the best of all artificial applications to the complexion is a little starch or rice powder." Manufacturers mass marketed all types of tinted face powders that claimed to be undetectable even in daylight.

Men's Clothing 1850–1900

The men's suit, comprised of a coat, vest, and trousers, continued to evolve, subtly and cautiously, in the second half of the nineteenth century. Permutations occurred without abruptness and drama, and never strayed from the easy-fitting sheath that articulated and covered almost the whole surface of the body. The classic assemblage of its three basic components, along with correct accessories, was expressive of a confident adult masculinity—purposeful, disciplined, and proper. The modern Victorian man's suit was also a uniform of official patriarchal power, largely devoid of the quixotic fancifulness associated with women's fashions of the time. Moreover, men's ready-to-wear suits leveled the class field, providing the proletariat

FIGURE 2.23. The frock coat, also called a Prince Albert coat, was the correct daytime town dress for business executives and for daytime social calls. For evening, the tail coat remained the required attire worn with a white vest and tie for balls and embassy receptions or a black vest for dinner and the theater. Photo c. 1855–60.

with a quality ensemble for Sundays and special occasions, suits that were virtually indistinguishable in appearance from custom-made versions except upon close inspection.

Men's suit coats were categorized into four principal types: the frock coat, morning coat, tail coat, and sack coat. Each one was worn for specific functions and Victorian dress protocol was strictly observed. For the most part, textiles of coats were predominantly of somber, dark colors, mostly black or navy, until the end of the century when colorful sports jackets were introduced.

The frock coat was worn as business attire or for making afternoon social calls. (Figure 2.23.) By the 1870s, the style was frequently called the **Prince Albert coat** since it had been the favorite style of Queen Victoria's consort. During the late 1850s, the cinched waist and full skirt of the frock coat were replaced with a boxy, tubular silhouette. The standardized cut featured a straight-line, double-breasted closure, loose-fitting waist seam, and knee-length skirt. Some styles were made with velvet collars and silk-faced lapels. Frock suit trousers and vests were often of a contrasting color or pattern, especially pin stripes or checks. A top hat and walking stick completed the correct look.

Morning coats were a variation of the frock coat with a cutaway front that tapered to the back. Many catalogs of the time refer to morning coats as cutaway frocks. Morning coats, too, formed a semi-formal day suit although worn mostly for social functions, particularly weddings. As with frock coats, trousers and vests were often of contrasting fabrics.

The **tail coat**, or now more appropriately, the **dress coat**, retained its cut-in front cropped above the waistline and tails in the back variously shaped as a "coffin" or "swallow's tail." The dress coat was formal evening attire worn with a white tie and white vest for balls or embassy receptions, and with a black vest and black tie for dinner parties and the theater. At the court of the Second Empire, the dress coat was still required to be worn with breeches and silk hose for high state functions. Ironically, the formality of the dress coat, sometimes with breeches, also came to be applied to certain categories of servants, such as butlers and grooms, as well as to specialized professions, such as undertaking. Even at the end of the century, *Vogue* lobbied its society readers to "find a costume which shall be included in the wardrobe of a gentleman, but not that of a servant . . . to prevent awkward mistakes."

The most significant innovation in men's suit designs during this period was the introduction of the **sack coat**. (Figure 2.24.) The style first emerged in the mid-1850s as an English "negligé" or casual day coat. It was cut to hang straight from the shoulders with no waist seam, and the shortened hemline was cropped just below the hips. The three- or four-button, single-breasted closure was usually worn with only the top button fastened. In the 1860s, the fresh new look quickly became a fad with stylish young men in London and Paris—from which the influence spread to the rest of Europe and the Americas. As with many dramatic fashion trends, the sack coat was a sartorial scandal at first, derided by social traditionalists as a "real terrorism against propriety." Nevertheless, the sack coat grew in popularity, aided by the rapid and easy mass production of this simple new style by ready-to-wear makers. Variations included subtleties such as covered buttons, lapels edged with grosgrain ribbon, and rounded front openings. During the 1860s, the vest and trousers worn with the sack coat frequently were

FIGURE 2.24. The most innovative change in men's suits was the introduction of the sack coat in the late 1850s. The cut was loose and square without the fitted waistline of the frock coat. Initially the sack coat was a casual day wear garment. By the 1860s, though, it was commonly accepted as a component of the business suit. Fashion plate from *Harper's Bazaar,* 1868.

made of the same fabric and came to be known as a **ditto suit**, a term commonly used until the First World War.

Initially, the sack coat with its matching vest and trousers was regarded as casual attire only for daytime and was even labeled a **lounge suit** in England and America. By the mid-1860s, though, the sack coat suit was more accepted as town wear and proper office dress. The ditto suit shown at the far right of Figure 2.24 is described in *Harper's Bazaar* as a "business suit." Indeed, the social protocol for the sack coat suit was in constant evolution throughout the remainder of the century. Innumerable photos from the 1870s through the 1890s show men wearing the sack coat as their Sunday best—some as ditto suits and others with trousers or vests of contrasting fabrics. (Figure 2.25.)

By the end of the century, even dress versions of the sack coat had emerged for formal occasions. The **tuxedo**, named for a style of dinner jacket first worn in New York's Tuxedo Park Club in the 1880s, married design elements of the tail coat such as silk-faced lapels with the boxy cut of the sack jacket.

Another derivative of the sack coat that first appeared in the late 1880s was the **blazer**. Among the possible origins for the casual style and its unusual name were the scarlet uniform

FIGURE 2.25. The lounge suit, comprised of a sack coat, vest, trousers, starched collar, and necktie became the Sunday-best attire for most ordinary men. Ready-to-wear makers mass produced affordable "ditto" suits made entirely of the same material although trousers or vests of contrasting fabrics were popular throughout the period. Photos c. 1885–95.

FIGURE 2.26. Vests and neckwear remained the two garments worn in public with which men could express their individuality with minimal social opprobrium. Plaid satin vest and foulard tie, c. 1865.

jackets of the Cambridge College Boat Club or, perhaps, the jersey styles worn by the sailors of the ship H.M.S. *Blazer*. Whatever its beginnings, the blazer with its loose boxy fit and patch pockets became widely popular especially as tennis attire in the 1890s.

The suit vest, or waistcoat in England, continued to be made in a great variety of styles with both single- and double-breasted closures. Necklines varied in depth from high at the throat to a deep V-cut at mid-torso. Vests with lapels were about equally popular as plain fronts. For evening dress, they were cut deep, almost to the waistline, and extended slightly longer than day suit styles. The suit vest was still a garment with which men could feel free to indulge in a bit of peacock flash with textures, colors, and textile patterns. (Figure 2.26.) Fashion plates throughout the period show a spectacular assortment of day vests in striking brocades, matelasse, printed pique, dotted velvet, and striped satins, most in vivid hues. In fact, what would appear to us today as a clash of mixed patterns between checked vests and plaid trousers, or floral vests and striped trousers, was at the time the epitome of sophisticated taste. Vests for evening dress were white for formal receptions and balls, but could be black for dinner parties and the theater.

Trousers fitted straight, narrow, and smoothly although the cut fluctuated widely from slim to full year to year. Hemlines might be pegged or even slightly flared, both of which could be seen concurrently on a city street. Patterned textiles for trousers, especially checks, plaids, and stripes, were fairly constant throughout the era. Waistbands were affixed with buttons for fastening the ends of suspenders. It is unclear when or how belt loops were revived from ancient times and reintroduced to the construction of trousers although, by the 1880s, illustrations of sports clothes depicted belted versions.

Two stylistic treatments of today's trousers—creases and cuffs—originated in the late nineteenth century. A number of sources are credited with initiating the trend of steam creasing trouser legs including England's Prince of Wales (later Edward VII). Two different methods of creasing are evident in photos of the time. The earlier form had the creases at the sides with a smooth front and back. The second, with the creases down the center front and back, became the standard, most likely because the crisp ridges helped prevent an age-old problem of baggy knees. The look was quickly adopted by style setters, and it has endured as the proper look for both dress and casual trousers.

Trouser cuffs, however, were met with resistance. Initially called "roll-ups" or "turn-ups," the practice of forming cuffs to protect the hem of trousers against damp and mud was a common practice. As a stylish innovation, though, the cuffed trouser leg originated with men's sports attire of the 1860s, particularly for cricket and rowing clubs. The hems were turned up and tacked with a couple of stitches at the sides that could easily be clipped for laundering. Even when Prince Edward appeared at Ascot wearing cuffed pants, the look continued to be criticized by sartorial purists.

Men's pullover shirts through the 1870s remained full and loosely fitting. (Figure 2.27.) By the 1880s, the construction of the shirt was largely the same as that of the Second Empire

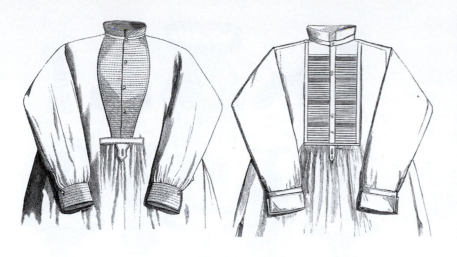

FIGURE 2.27. Through the end of the 1800s, men's shirts were made with bosom or shield fronts and had to be pulled on over the head. Left, shirt patterns from *Godey's,* 1860s; right, detail of linen shirt with mother-of-pearl buttons from the Karen Augusta Collection, c. 1850–60.

Coat Front Shirts

For centuries, men's shirts were cut as pullovers with assorted types of keyhole neck openings that tied or buttoned. In the early 1890s, a new form of shirt was introduced with a front closure that opened the full length from the collar to the hem. Since the design was modeled on the sack coat, it came to be called a **"coat front shirt."**

Fashion lore holds that the innovative style originated when a famous stage actor accidentally tore open the front of his bosom shirt while making a quick change between performances. Exclaiming that this was the way all shirts should be made, he promptly ordered a number of shirts from his tailor with a coat front closure. Demand spread quickly for the innovative style and ready-to-wear makers responded with mass production of the new shirt design. (Figure 2.28.)

QUICKPUTON SHIRTS.

TRIPLER'S NEW OPEN FRONT SHIRT.

Buttoned all the way down the front. Slips on and off like a coat. Convenient, comfortable and elegant. Cuffs attached. Different length sleeves. Perfect fitting.

— $1.19 Each —

NEW ERA IN MEN'S SHIRTS.

No more of the unpleasant, unrefined and undignified over-the-head process. No more getting into or climbing out of or fighting your way through a shirt. Tripler's Quickputon obviates all the above. Once worn a friend for life. For sale only by the maker,

GEORGE BRADFORD TRIPLER,

NEW YORK'S LEADING MEN'S OUTFITTER,

101 Nassau St., Cor. Ann (Bennett Building). | 36 Park Row, N. Y. (Potter Building).

OLD WAY | NEW WAY

FIGURE 2.28. In the early 1890s, the coat front shirt was introduced as an alternative to the traditional pullover bosom fronts. As this ready-to-wear maker's ad from 1894 avows, the new open front shirts meant "no more getting into or climbing out of or fighting your way through a shirt."

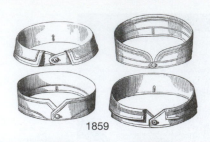

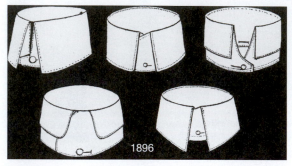

FIGURE 2.29. Easily laundered detachable collars buttoned to the shirt collar. Between the 1850s and 1890s collars became higher and more rigidly starched. Top, collars from *Godey's,* 1859; bottom, collars from *Vogue,* 1896.

FIGURE 2.30. Men's neckwear of the second half of the 1800s was greatly varied in size, shape, knot, and fabric. However, strict standards governed what type or color of tie was appropriate for any given social circumstance. Ties from *Harper's Bazaar*, 1868.

except for a more narrow, fitted cut. The long sleeves ended in a wide assortment of cuffs including turned back "**French wrists**" fastened with cuff links. Hemlines were either square or rounded with side slits. The **bosom front** of the shirt, sometimes called a **shield front** or **breastplate front**, was usually fastened by two or three buttons or, for formal shirts, by jeweled studs. Fronts were elaborately decorated with vertical or horizontal tucks, pleats, and even delicate embroidery if a wife's sewing skills were adequate. As shirt fronts disappeared beneath high vest necklines and a variety of wide neckwear, they were gradually simplified. By the 1880s, *Harper's Bazaar* advised readers that "all ornament is useless for these bosoms as they are entirely concealed by the high vest and scarf."

Negligee shirts, also called "soft shirts," featured an attached, "soft" collar. They were mostly worn as casual dress and became increasingly popular for lawn tennis, croquet, and similar leisure activities.

Shirt collars were ordinarily narrow bands to which would be buttoned any number of detachable collars. Magazines often recommended detachable collars because they could more easily be starched to a satisfactory rigidity for properly affixing neckwear. The collars shown in Figure 2.29 are examples of the change in height from the 1850s to the 1890s. By the end of the century, collars could be up to three inches high. Moreover, collars became a sort of masculine hallmark, expressing, on the one hand, a man's social position, and on the other, his personality and lifestyle. A gaping, V-front collar might represent an artist or writer of some success, whereas the rigidly starched neck-brace styles were the mark of a bourgeois gentleman or businessman.

Although most men preferred shirts bleached brilliant white, a surprising palette of colors became acceptable for Victorian men's suit shirts. In the 1890s, *Vogue* described cambric and percale shirts of blue, pink, lilac, heliotrope (purple), browns, and ecrus. Some men, noted the

THE "NEWMARKET."

JEAMES. "WELL, IF THAT HAIN'T HENOUGH TO DISGUST ONE WITH THE SERVICE! GENTLEMEN TOO, THEY CALL THEIRSELVES! TAKING THE VERY CLOTHES OFF OUR BACKS."

FIGURE 2.31. One of the popular new styles of men's outwear for the 1880s was an adaptation of the coachman's coat. The design included a fitted body, pleated skirt at the back, and capacious pockets with flaps. Left, cartoon from *Harper's Bazaar,* 1883; right, photo of coachman, 1894.

editors, daringly donned shirts in patterns of "colored hair-line stripes or pin figures," or even of "colored grounds with white stripes broad, and white lattice-work."

Types of men's neckwear and the methods of tying each were incredibly varied in the second half of the nineteenth century. (Figure 2.30.) A magazine article on men's ties in 1895 opened with: "Here we have fancy let loose." Bow ties, long ties, cravats, and scarfs were made in all sorts of fabrics from fancy silks and fine linen to colorfully patterned madras. By the 1870s, a number of preknotted ready-made ties were available that "could be affixed to the neck in a matter of seconds, with no preliminary study, and independently of any personal dexterity," as a ready-to-wear catalog noted. Yet the sophisticated and subtle conventions for how and when to wear certain forms and colors of ties were equally complex and varied. Magazine articles not only reported on the newest neckwear styles for the season but often emphasized which neckwear or colors *not* to wear. For example, in 1883, *Harper's Bazaar* warned that white satin ties were "tabooed" for dinner parties. Similarly, certain knots and shapes became recognizable by popular names just as they are today. In the 1890s, for instance, the **toreador** was a narrow four-in-hand knot and the **ascot** was a wide, scarf-like cravat that filled the open neckline of the vest.

Men's Outerwear, Underwear, and Sports Attire 1850–1900

Types of outerwear for men between 1850 and 1900 were versions of standardized, capacious topcoats in double- and single-breasted styles. The two principal types of coats were the

FIGURE 2.32. Beginning as early as the 1860s, knickerbockers were worn by men for sports activities. In the 1890s, the garment became more associated with bicycling and especially golf. Illustration from *Scribner's,* 1897.

overcoat, cropped at the knees, and the **ulster**, extending to midcalf. Both the overcoat and ulster were made with many of the same details including pocket treatments, front closures, and widths and shapes of collars and lapels. The fitted **chesterfield topcoat** featured a velvet collar and a fly front that concealed the buttons. The **Inverness cape coat** included a full, circular cape that covered the shoulders to the forearms; some versions were layered with a second, shorter capelet. A variant of the Regency long frock overcoat was the **coachman's coat** with its trim waist seam, full skirt, and multiple flap pockets, which became a trend for gentlemen of the 1880s and 1890s. (Figure 2.31.)

Through the 1880s, men's underwear was primarily two basic pieces, drawers in short or long varieties with button front closures, and an undershirt, often called the undervest. Both were made in knit or woven cotton, linen, wool, or silk. Colored underwear for men is known from the 1850s but did not become more common until the 1880s. *Vogue* reported in the mid-nineties that purple and black underwear were seen in men's shops in London and New York. The combination or union suit described earlier in the chapter was also adapted to menswear and, by the end of the century, was the most prevalent type of underwear for men.

The most common form of men's sleepwear was the nightshirt in knee- or ankle-length varieties. In the late 1870s, sophisticated men began to wear a type of trouser suit to bed called **pajamas** (pyjamas in England). The pajama suit had been introduced from India by returning British colonial officers. By the 1880s, flannel pajamas came in a number of colors and textile patterns including assorted vertical stripes and bold polka dots.

During the second half of the nineteenth century, sports and physical exercise became an obsession of all classes. The Olympics were resurrected in 1896, and numerous sports organizations like the AAU (Amateur Athletic Union) were founded during this period. In America, newly created competitive sports for the masses such as baseball, football, and basketball joined the established aristocratic activities of rowing, polo, riding, and sailing as healthful pas-

FIGURE 2.33. Victorian men rarely went out of doors without a hat or cap. New to the second half of the nineteenth century were the round-crown derby, also called a bowler, and the fedora with its deeply creased crown. By the end of the century, catalogs offered a wide assortment of specialty hats and caps appropriate for specific attire and activities. Hats from ads and catalogs, 1888–96.

times. Other sports such as tennis, golf, and cycling appealed to a broad segment of the social spectrum, blurring class boundaries. As sports became organized into clubs and intramural competitions, specialized attire for safety and ease of movement was developed. These forms of activewear became mass produced and mass marketed by ready-to-wear makers, furthering the appeal of sports for the average weekend enthusiast.

One of the earliest types of casual sports clothes for men was knickerbockers, a highly practical and comfortable garment that women later adapted for their own pursuits of outdoor fun. Men's knickerbockers first became fashionable for hunting, fishing, hiking, and canoeing in the 1860s when the Prince of Wales wore them for his trips to country estates. The typical example of knickerbockers from the 1890s shown in Figure 2.32 depicts full legs that blouson over the knee bands, side-slash front pockets, welt back pockets with flaps, and a waistband with belt loops. Worn with knickerbockers for traipsing about in the woods was the **norfolk jacket**, named for the region around Sandringham Castle where the Prince of Wales often went on hunting excursions. The jacket was loose-fitting with an attached belt and double box pleats in the front from shoulder to hem.

For swimming and some types of competitive sports, like track and field events or bicycle racing, men preferred trim, briefer garments. Knit shorts cropped above the knees were cut basically the same as drawers, and short-sleeve knit tops or sweaters were similar in construction to undervests. Wool was recommended for bathing suits since wool retained heat even when wet, but breathable knit cotton was the fabric of choice for strenuous exertion in the sports arena.

Men's Accessories 1850–1900

The most indispensable men's accessory of the second half of the nineteenth century was a hat. (Figure 2.33.) Seldom would a man go outside bareheaded. A strict code of hat etiquette could betray the ignorance of the uninformed. For instance, when greeting a lady, a gentleman should remove his hat in a manner that would not allow the inside to be seen as "a poor man would hold out his hat for charity," cautioned a Victorian etiquette guide. In addition,

FIGURE 2.34. Men's shoe styles became as varied and specialized as headgear in the late 1800s. The toe shapes might concurrently be pointed, rounded, or squared during any one season. Designs ranged from basic gaiter boots with fabric uppers and leather vamps to flashy two-tone kid oxfords. Shoes from the 1895 Montgomery Ward catalog.

the sartorially savvy man knew when and where he could wear his hat indoors, and how to dispose of it unobtrusively when making social visits.

For the upper bourgeoisie, the top hat was the requisite headgear for town. The topper was worn with the frock coat or dress jacket but never a lounge suit. The most common daytime hat was the rounded top **derby**, called a **bowler** in England, which became the prevalent headwear complement for the ditto suit. The **fedora** featured a high, conical crown with a deep crease on top front to back and a wider brim than the derby. A shorter variant of the fedora with a stiff, narrow brim edged with grosgrain came to be known as a **homburg** when the style was adopted by the Prince of Wales following his tour of a hat factory in Homburg, Germany. Men's **crushers** were low, round top hats with turned-up, saucer-like brims; the name originated from the hat's three-ounce weight as compared to the more substantial five-ounce fedora or eight-ounce top hat. For summer, the shallow, cylindrical boater of a natural, light straw was ubiquitous. Sports hats included the soft **deerstalker cap** with its turned up ear flaps—more familiar today as the Sherlock Holmes cap. Numerous other forms of hats and caps included adaptations of military styles worn for yachting, travel, and certain sports.

Men's shoes and ankle boots became more varied after 1850. It is difficult to determine precisely when round toes, square toes, or pointed toes may have been most fashionable at any given season during this period. In 1883, *Harper's Bazaar* reported with uncertainty, "There is a tendency to broaden the toes of all shoes that have been worn nearly pointed on account of the closely fitted trousers; but sensible men have never followed either of these fashions to the extreme." Twenty years later, all three toe shapes were similarly offered in the Montgomery Ward wish book. (Figure 2.34.) One of the key changes to men's footwear was a dual construction of the half-boot with leather vamps over the instep and toes but dyed-to-match canvas uppers around the ankles. This style was often described as a **gaiter boot**, named for the spats-style look of the fabric upper. Gaiter boots were both lace-up and button-topped with plain vamps or embellished with decorative perforated edging. Some walking types of gaiter boots featured elasticized insets for added comfort. So-called "low" shoes or oxfords were principally worn with dressy suits for social occasions. Except for formal patent leather slipper styles called "pumps," most low shoes were constructed as lace-ups and included assorted decorative treatments—even two-tone designs.

Among the new categories of accessories for men in the late nineteenth century were belts. As mentioned previously, belt loops were reintroduced during this period after centuries of absence. Belted waistbands were initially applied to sports pants since suspenders interfered with strenuous activities like golf swings and bicycling. In retail catalogs of the nineties, men's belts were often featured with the specific sports attire such as tennis or cycling rather than collectively in the men's accessory section. Both woven fabric and leather belts were fitted with buckles of various metals and electroplates.

Despite the comfort and practicality of the belt, though, suspenders, or braces in England, remained the most prevalent form of support for trousers through the First World War. As with neckwear and vests, suspenders were often colorful and richly decorated. An acceptable gift for a man from a lady was a pair of suspenders that she had hand embroidered.

Among the controversial accessories that emerged in the late 1800s was the **cummerbund**, a wide, vividly colored sash worn with the tuxedo in place of a vest. Like the pajama suit, the cummerbund was introduced into England by colonial officers from India where the kamarband sash was part of the Mughal military uniform. French magazines blasted the cummerbund as "grotesque" and in "bad taste" when it first appeared in the early 1870s. Only after the dinner jacket began to be accepted as evening dress in the late 1890s did the hostility toward the cummerbund ease.

Other typical accessories of the well-dressed man included walking sticks. Gentlemen carried sticks with ornately carved ivory, horn, or silver handles. In the 1890s, the Shepherd's crook cane became more fashionable. Gloves, likewise, were a required accessory of the gentleman—tan or ecru kid for street wear, white for evenings. Jewelry for the proper Victorian man, though, was largely limited to cuff links and one plain gold ring, unless he was entitled to display a heraldic or military crest. Also, tie clips and especially jeweled stickpins were popular as a dapper finishing touch to a ditto suit. "But little jewelry should be worn by a gentleman;" chided *Vogue,* "watchchains, charms, seals, etc., are vulgar." In the 1890s, most men began carrying lavishly embellished gold or silver pocket watches. (Figure 2.35.) Popularly called "turnips" from their bulbous shape, mass produced pocket watches with nickel cases were priced as low as $3.50.

Hairstyles for men remained the same short crop from the Napoleonic era. The side whiskers that had crept across the cheek or jawline through the Romantic Age expanded into all sorts of full, bushy mutton chops, mustaches, and beards through the 1880s. During the nineties the clean-shaven look of the Gibson Man made men appear more youthful, healthy, and well-groomed.

FIGURE 2.35. Mass production made precision timepieces affordable to most men. Nickel cased pocket watches sold for as little as $3.50. By the 1890s, most men carried a pocket watch popularly called "turnips" from their large, rounded shape. Western Brand pocket watches, 1895.

Clothes of Ordinary People 1850–1900

With the mass production and mass distribution of cheap, ready-to-wear clothing for the entire family in the second half of the nineteenth century, fashion became democratized. The

FIGURE 2.36. In 1873, Levi Strauss began manufacturing riveted work pants made of heavy cotton serge de Nimes, or denim. Note that even jeans were made with suspender buttons instead of belt loops. Photo of California miners from the Levi Strauss & Co. Historical Collection, c. 1890.

distinction between styles of clothing for the affluent and those of ordinary people became less apparent except in materials. Depictions of female servants of the 1850s show them wearing uniforms with crinolined skirts, and those of the 1880s have bustle arrangements. The $5 men's ditto suit replicated the customized styles of London's Savile Row and the $5 women's tailored suit was modeled on the latest silhouettes from Paris. Similarly, mass-marketed casual and sports clothing, outerwear, and underwear were based on the styles displayed in the finest dress shops and carriage-trade stores. Even fashion accessories were manufactured with inexpensive trim and decorative motifs that simulated the most current trends.

This is not to say there were not significant and evident differences between the ensembles of the privileged classes and the clothing of the working classes. Town streets were filled with factory and shop girls in shirtwaists without jackets or hats, and laboring men in shirtsleeves and soft caps without sack coats, collars, and neckties.

In addition, certain categories of work clothes were specifically identified with ordinary people. For example, the term "pantaloons" was still commonly used through the end of the century to refer to men's casual or work types of trousers. In ready-to-wear catalogs of the period, the word was often shortened to "pants" as they are known today.

A famous type of work pants that was created during this time was blue jeans. In 1853, German immigrant Levi Strauss set up a business in California to sell supplies to the gold-rush miners and other retailers. In 1872, he was contacted by one of his customers, a tailor in Nevada, with an idea for riveting the corners of pants pockets to secure them against tearing. Lacking the funds for a patent, the tailor suggested a partnership, which Strauss accepted. The following year the two entrepreneurs began to manufacture a waist-high, riveted overall made of a heavy French twill cotton called **serge de Nimes**, from which we get the word **denim**. (Figure 2.36.) The fabric—and later the pants—also came to be called **jeans** after the "genes," or Genoese sailors, whose trousers were made of the material.

Various other forms of denim work pants were also mass produced in assorted colors by other ready-to-wear makers. Through the First World War, jeans were largely sold as work pants for farmers, ranchers, cowboys, and field hands. Following the tourist boom of the 1920s, Easterners became enamored with the cachet of the Old West and began to bring jeans back from vacations for weekend casual wear.

Children's Clothing 1850–1900

As during the early phases of the Industrial Revolution in the Romantic Age, children of the second half of the nineteenth century were likewise dressed to reflect the prosperity and social prestige of the parents. This parental preoccupation with the elaborate attire of their children was an example of what the nineteenth-century economist Thorstein Veblen labeled "vicarious consumption," the degree of which was in accordance with the parents' social ambition. Victorian girls usually wore clothes very similar to those of their mothers including restrictive corsets and lavishly ornamented accessories. Toddler boys were dressed virtually identical to girls until about age three or four. Until age ten or eleven, boys wore a wide assortment of two- and three-piece suits and sometimes fantasy costumes, often of sumptuous materials, including tunic dresses, kilts, and diminutive military uniforms. The clothing of older boys were

FIGURE 2.37. During the crinoline age, girls' dresses were shortened versions of their mothers' styles with tightly fitted bodices and wide, hooped skirts. The hemlines of young girls were cropped just below the knees, and for older girls the skirt extended to the ankles. Plate from *Godey's,* 1857.

FIGURE 2.38. Girls' dresses of the 1870s and 1880s followed the same three phases of bustle treatments as adult versions. Large bustles prevailed until the late 1870s when skirts narrowed and decorative elements dropped low on the back; exaggerated bustles returned in the early 1880s and remained the fashion until around 1890. Plate from *Harper's Bazaar,* 1873.

FIGURE 2.39. In the 1890s, the gigantic leg-of-mutton sleeves and bell-shaped skirts of women's fashions were applied to girls' dresses. Illustration from *Delineator,* 1896.

FIGURE 2.40. Toddler boys were commonly dressed in frilly skirts, lace pantalettes, and an excess of overly decorated accessories. To the Victorian parent, though, the differences between the boy's attire and that of his sister were distinct. In this 1859 plate from *Godey's,* despite the ribbons and lace trim, the boy's costume is evident by the pleated bosom shirt, open jacket, and short skirt.

replicas of menswear complete with the trappings of starched collars and cravats like those worn by the boys in Figure 2.37.

During the crinoline period, small girls wore dresses modeled after those of adults with tight bodices, open necklines, and wide skirts cropped at the knees; older girls wore hooped skirts shortened to about the ankles. (Figure 2.37.) The dresses, jackets, coats, and accessories of the children of bourgeois families were often made of the same opulent materials and trimmings as their mothers' styles. Lace or ruffle edged pantalettes continued to be worn by both girls and toddler boys until the late 1860s.

By the 1870s, girls' dress styles shifted to bustle silhouettes similar to those of adults. (Figure 2.38.) The short skirts for young girls continued the conventions of previous decades. Bodices were fitted and skirts were layered with aprons, polonaise overskirts, frills, and all manner of trim. As with women's bustle dresses, girls' versions followed the same three phases of the period: large bustles until the late 1870s; narrow profiles with reduced back treatments placed low on the skirt until the early 1880s; finally, a return to large, exaggerated bustles.

When narrow, bell-shaped skirts and gigantic leg-of-mutton sleeves replaced the bustle dress around 1890, girls' styles followed those of their mothers. (Figure 2.39.) The full array of fashion accoutrement—jackets, shirtwaists, skirts, capes, coats, and accessories—were likewise made in diminutive styles for girls.

One should be cautioned, though, on thinking that the clothing depicted in fashion plates and photographs of the period represented girls' everyday wear. A more realistic view of their day dresses and playwear is famously represented by Alice of the Wonderland notoriety. In the 1865 book, she wears a plain bodice dress with a full, gathered skirt, short puff sleeves, and a narrow, turned-down collar. Six years later, in *Through the Looking Glass,* Alice has added a simple apron with frilled cap sleeves to her plain dress. Only at the end of the story when she is transformed into a queen does her costume become a fashion plate, replete with a bustle polonaise.

The clothing of boys during this period is far more confusing to understand than that of girls. Along with plain, simple suits of dark woolen jackets and pants that emulated the attire of their fathers were any number of costume eccentricities that are perplexing to our modern perspectives. In examining photographs and engravings of children, the gender of many toddlers seems undefined. In many instances, boys were recognizable by their short cropped hair—although not always—but the dresses and accessories often appear virtually identical to that of girls. The four-year-old boy depicted in Figure 2.40 wears an outfit from 1859 that included a full skirt, lace pantalettes, cape-jacket, sash, and straw hat with feathers and ribbons. Yet *Godey's* assured readers that this "outfit for boys" would "distinguish them from their sisters on the one hand, and from monkeys on the other." Among the subtle masculine differences that were quite distinct to Victorian parents was the pleated bosom shirt, open front jacket, and the shortened hemline of the skirt.

Another category of fanciful ensembles for boys was the assorted adaptations of military garb. One of the earliest types of pretend uniforms was the sailor's outfit, sometimes called the **Jack Tar suit**, variations of which endure still today. (Figure 2.41.) Costume tradition holds that the Victorian obsession with children's pretend uniforms began in 1846 when the five-year-old

FIGURE 2.41. Numerous types of military-inspired costumes were worn by boys throughout the second half of the nineteenth century. The most prevalent version was the sailor suit with its square-back collar and nautical trim. Left, illustration from *Harper's Bazaar,* 1879; right, illustration from *Delineator,* 1896.

Prince of Wales wore a miniature replica of a white naval uniform aboard the royal yacht. The portrait of the prince sailor was later painted by Winterhalter of which engravings were widely distributed. The little sailor suit was modified over the decades by new blouse and jacket styles and trouser lengths but the wide, square-back collar and assorted types of embellishments resembling naval insignia remained constant. Instead of white serge, though, blue wool and cotton twill were the most prevalent fabrics.

The sailor suit was also adapted to versions for girls. Ready-to-wear makers mass produced sailor shirtwaists, called the **middy**, after midshipman, for everyday wear. From the 1880s through the 1930s, school girls wore variants of the middy with bloomers and short skirts for athletic activities.

In addition to dresses, tunics, skirts, kilts, and military uniforms were variations of the cavalier or Stuart-inspired suit that came to be known as the **Fauntleroy suit**. Based on the outfit of the character in the children's book *Little Lord Fauntleroy* (1891) by Frances H. Burnett, the fantasy suit was usually made of dark velvet or satin and was comprised of knee breeches with a satin sash, short jacket, wide collar, and wide cuffs. The look became an absolute mania in Britain and the United States for the upper bourgeoisie until the 1910s.

Review

In the second half of the nineteenth century, the evolution of fashion was affected by three significant developments. First was the emergence of the couturier as arbiter of fashion and style. Second was the continued specialization of ready-to-wear manufacturing with its rapid advances in technology and methods of production. Third was sales distribution, supported by marketing and advertising, which led to a democratization of fashion across virtually all social classes.

By the 1850s, these three socioeconomic changes were already in play when the cage crinoline was introduced to women's fashion. Skirts had continued to widen throughout the 1850s becoming massive, bell-shaped expanses of fabric. To ease the burden of the skirt's weight, the hooped crinoline replaced layers of petticoats, allowing skirts to expand into their widest silhouettes in the 1860s.

Toward the end of the 1860s, the crinoline was discarded in favor of a bustle treatment of the skirt. The trend for large bustles prevailed until the late 1870s when skirts narrowed and decorative elements dropped low on the back. By the early 1880s, exaggerated horizontal bustles returned and remained the fashion until the end of the decade.

In the 1890s, fashion drama shifted from the skirt to the sleeves and shoulders. The leg-of-mutton form of sleeve reemerged in dimensions not seen since the gigot styles of the 1830s. The mammoth sleeves, tightly constricted waistline, and the bell-shaped skirt combined to shape the hourglass silhouette that defines the decade.

For men, fashion was principally an issue of subtle change and dress protocol. The comfortable frock coat of the late eighteenth century became the town suit coat of the Victorian era worn with a top hat. Cutaway morning coats and tail coats became reserved for formal occasions. The innovative sack coat with its straight, boxy fit was introduced in the mid-1850s. When combined with a vest, dress trousers, starched collar, and a necktie, the sack coat formed the business suit—a legacy surviving to this day. Among the subtle but significant and enduring changes to menswear of the period were pant creases and belt loop waistbands.

The variety of fashion categories for both men and women dramatically increased in the last quarter of the nineteenth century. Specialty sportswear included knickerbockers for sports activities like bicycling and swimming. Casual clothes such as the shirtwaist for women and the colorful, patterned sportshirt for men were widely adopted across all classes.

Girls' dress styles followed the vicissitudes of women's fashions through the crinoline period, followed by the three phases of the bustle dress, and finally to the revival of the leg-of-mutton sleeve. Boys' attire was far more diverse, ranging from conservative replicas of their fathers' plain, dark ditto suits to eccentricities of pretend military uniforms and fanciful cavalier costumes.

review questions

1. How did Charles Frederick Worth alter the course of fashion production? What were some of the significant contributions Worth made to fashion styles of the 1850s and 1860s?

2. Which three business components drove the success of the ready-to-wear industry in the second half of the nineteenth century? How did each contribute to the democratization of fashion?

3. Identify the distinctions between the crinoline of the 1840s and that of the late 1850s. How did the crinoline silhouette change in the 1860s?

4. When and how did the transition from the crinoline to the bustle dress occur? Which were the three phases of the bustle dress silhouette? Describe the dress design elements of each phase.

5. Which three key elements of women's dress design formed the hourglass silhouette in the 1890s? How did the new forms of corsets contribute to the hourglass contours?

6. As Victorian women increasingly participated in sports activities, especially bicycling, what were some resulting innovations in clothing?

7. Identify and describe the three principal types of Victorian men's suit jackets that continued as standard styles from the Romantic Age. Which social protocols governed how and when each style was worn?

8. Identify and describe the innovative style of men's jacket introduced in the 1850s. Which two derivatives of the style became popular in the 1890s, and how did they vary in design from the prototype?

9. Which three common elements of today's men's trouser designs were innovative features in the late nineteenth century? What were the origins of these elements?

10. How was boy's attire more diverse than girlswear? Identify and describe an example of each of the three categories of boy's suit styles.

research and portfolio projects

Research

1. Write a research paper on the House of Worth. Trace the development of the salon from its inception through the end of the nineteenth century. Explain the significance of the House of Worth in its influence on fashion of the second half of the 1800s.

2. Write a research paper on the women's movements in America and Britain and their contributions to dress reform. Identify which advocacies of change in women's clothing had broad public support and which ones were viewed as eccentricities.

Portfolio

1. Research the style and motifs of Art Nouveau and design a sketchbook set of matching women's accessories as they would have been worn in the late 1890s. The set should consist of a brooch, belt buckle, hair comb, and purse.

2. Research the construction of a cage crinoline and reproduce a life-size model made of thin strips of posterboard for the hoops and paper or muslin for the connecting tapes. Demonstrate for the class how the cage crinoline was put on.

dress terms

á la disposition printing: a technique of fabric roller printing in which patterns were designed specifically for the edges of skirt flounces

aniline dyes: synthetic dyestuffs first developed in the 1850s

ascot: a wide, scarf-like cravat that filled the open neckline of the vest

basques: short, skirt-like tabs attached at the waist of women's bodices and jackets

bertha (also half bertha): ribbon and lace covering for decollete necklines

blazer: a variant of the men's sack coat made with patch pockets and worn as casual attire, particularly for sports events

Bloomer dress: women's long, baggy trousers worn with a short skirt named for Amelia Bloomer who wore them while on tour as an advocate for women's rights

boater: shallow, cylindrical straw hats worn by both men and women

bolero jacket: a woman's short, cropped jacket or vest, often with a rounded cutaway front

bosom front shirt (also shield front or breastplate front): the front panel of men's shirts often made of fine linen and embellished with tucks or pleats; the slit closure usually fastened with two or three buttons

bowler: see derby

breastplate front: see bosom front shirt

bretelles: a pair of decorative braces for women's bodices that attached at each shoulder and tied together at the waist

bust bodice: an early form of brassiere

bust improver: padding for the decollete bodice

cage crinoline: a petticoat reinforced with hoops of whalebone or watch spring steel

canezou: various decorative tops ranging in style from short muslin jackets to elaborate neckline fillers

cavalier collar: a woman's collar designed as a high band that flared into a shallow roll similar to styles of the 1590s

celluloid: a nineteenth-century type of plastic produced from cotton and cellulose

chesterfield topcoat: a men's or women's topcoat with a velvet collar and a fly front that concealed the buttons

coachman's coat: a men's heavy overcoat featuring a fitted bodice, full skirt in the back, and large flap pockets

coat front shirt: men's shirts of the 1890s designed with a button front closure from the collar to the hem

combinations: women's underwear made with the camisole and drawers sewn together

corset waist: a form of corset that fully covered the upper torso and included breast support with shoulder straps

crinolette: a flat front petticoat with steel half hoops of widening sizes top to bottom

crusher: low, round-top hat with turned-up, saucer-like brims; named for its light, three-ounce weight

cuirass bodice: a sheath-like bodice that fit tightly over the hips, producing a long-line dress silhouette

cummerbund: a men's vividly colored sash worn with formal wear in place of a vest

deerstalker cap: a men's sports cap with turned-up earflaps

denim: a heavy cotton twill named for the French serge de Nimes

derby: a men's round crown hat with a narrow brim

ditto suit: a men's three-piece combination of lounge jacket, vest, and trousers all made of the same fabric

dress coat: men's formal suit jacket with a cut-in front cropped above the waistline and tails in the back variously shaped as a "coffin" or "swallow's tail"

Fauntleroy suit: a boy's velvet or satin suit that included knee breeches, short jacket, and a wide falling-band collar

fedora: a men's hat with a high, conical crown with a deep crease front to back

fichu: cape-like or scarf covering for open necklines

French wrists: turned-back cuffs that fastened with cuff links

gaiter boot: a style of men's and women's shoe made with leather vamps over the instep and toes and a fabric upper around the ankles

goring: triangular or tapered pieces of cloth used to shape garments

Grecian bend profile: women's silhouette of the bustle era in which the torso appeared to tilt forward as a balance to the skirt volume in the back

homburg: a shorter version of the fedora; named for a style adopted by the Prince of Wales after his visit to a hat factory in Homburg, Germany

Inverness cape coat: a men's heavy travel coat that included a circular cape that covered the shoulders and arms to the elbows

Jack Tar suit: a boy's or girl's sailor suit featuring a middy top and nautical trousers or skirt

jeans: denim work pants named after the "genes" or Genoese sailors who brought boatloads of the material from France

knickerbockers: knee breeches worn by both men and women for sports activities, especially bicycling and golf

leggins: high, buttoned spats worn by men and women over their shoes for sports activities

leghorns: wide-brimmed straw hats named for the type of bleached wheat straw used in their construction

Louis heel: women's shoe style with high curved heel similar to that popularized by Louis XV

lounge suit: see ditto suit

Marie Stuart collar: a high standing collar that curled out into five points

middy: a square-collar sailor's shirt named after midshipmen worn by both women and children

morning coat: men's semi-formal day jacket cropped at the waist in the front with a knee-length skirt that was cut away in a tapering contour of the tails at the back

mushroom puff sleeve: a tight, cylindrical sleeve capped at the shoulder by a shallow, flattened puff

nainsook: a woven striped cotton from India whose name means "delight the eye" in Hindi

Neapolitan: a smooth, horsehair fabric used for women's winter bonnets

negligee shirt: men's casual shirt with attached turn-down collar; also called a "soft shirt"

norfolk jacket: a men's loose-fitting jacket with an attached belt and double box pleats from shoulder to hem

oxford: a stout, low shoe for men and women, often designed with contrasting tones of material

pagoda sleeve: a style of sleeve cut with a narrow fit at the shoulder and upper arm and an abrupt flare at the elbow

pajamas (pyjamas in Britain): men's trouser sleepwear suit

pannier bustle: a thin, padded form of bustle worn with the narrow skirts of the early 1880s

peplum: a short skirt attached at the waist of bodices or jackets

plastron: a woman's frilly lace neckpiece often embellished with ribbon bows

Prince Albert coat: the name given to men's dressy frock coats of the last quarter of the 1800s

princess bodice: a style of dress made of one long piece (or long gored pieces) from the shoulder to the hem with no waist seam

rainy-daisies: skirts with shortened hemlines worn for walking on rainy days or for sports activities

sack coat: a men's short coat cut to hang straight from the shoulder with no seam or tapered line at the waist

serge de Nimes: a heavy cotton twill from which the word "denim" was derived

shield front: see bosom front shirt

shirtwaist: women's blouses of various styles and fabrics

slop shops: early retail tailor shops specializing in ready-made clothing for men

snood: chenille or silk cord hair net

tail coat: see dress coat

toreador: a narrow four-in-hand necktie knot

tournure: a bustle frame of steel, duck, tapes, and laces worn in the mid-1880s

Turkish trouser: a form of women's trousers from the mid-1800s featuring voluminous legs fastened at the ankles

tuxedo: a version of the men's sack coat that incorporated elements of the dress coat such as satin lapels; named for New York's Tuxedo Park Club

ulster: a capacious, mid-calf length topcoat with varying details

union suits: one-piece underwear for both men and women; so named for the union of the top and drawers

waists: another name for shirtwaists

3 Edwardianism 1900–1909

President McKinley assassinated 1901	Rayon spinning developed 1902	U.S. began Panama Canal 1904	First Paris exhibit of the Fauves 1905	First Ford Model T 1908	Peary reached the North Pole 1909
		Russo-Japanese War 1904	Norway and Sweden separation 1905	Cellophane invented 1908	First flight over English Channel 1909
First Nobel prizes 1901	First aeroplane flight 1903	Louisiana Purchase Expo 1904	Picasso's *Les Demoiselles d'Avignon* 1907		

The Edwardian Era

In January 1901, Queen Victoria died. Her successor, the Prince of Wales, became Edward VII, for whom the first decade of the twentieth century was named. The new king was an amiable, portly man, whose life had been spent indulging in gambling, dalliances, and fashionable pursuits. After decades of somberness and stifling formality during Victoria's forty-year widowhood, the British court was revitalized by Edward with a cheerful emphasis on social life and fashion. His consort, Queen Alexandra, was a tall, slender beauty whose every public appearance showcased fashions of the era.

Edward had inherited a Britain that was still the world's greatest naval power. The nation's imperial reach extended over every continent of the world and included India, Canada, Australia, and vast sections of Africa. This empire was cause of much jealousy from other European countries and resentment by many nationalists in the lands over which England held dominion.

During the last quarter of the 1800s, France and Germany asserted themselves on the world stage with colonial acquisitions through conquest, commercial investment, and political

The Changing Role of Women

During the early 1900s, technology, mass production, and consumerism had a profound impact on the role of women in industrialized nations. Electric home appliances eased the labor of housework, affording women more leisure time. Manufactured food products conveniently packaged in bottles, jars, cans, boxes, and cellophane reduced the time spent in the kitchen. Household cleaning products became more specialized and efficient ranging from granulated laundry soap powder to cleansers just for the toilet bowl. (Figure 3.1.)

The truest form of freedom for women, though, was financial independence. For the overwhelming majority of the female populace of industrialized nations, financial independence was achieved through increasingly greater opportunities for employment. During the last quarter of the nineteenth century, the mechanical typewriter caused a restructuring of office work as more and more women were hired as operators of the newfangled equipment. Other technologies such as the telephone switchboard provided work and income for women.

Politically, suffragettes in Europe and America redoubled their efforts for enfranchisement. In addition to massive parades and marches, suffragists resorted to civil disobedience, including handcuffing themselves to the White House fence, to keep up the pressure. In the United States, only two states had granted women the right to vote by 1900 so suffragists redoubled their efforts for a drive toward a constitutional amendment. Twenty-one other nations had already enfranchised women by the time the United States finally adopted the Nineteenth Amendment to the Constitution in 1920, granting American women the right to vote.

As the political and economic climate changed for women, so too did society and culture. Colleges and universities began to admit women into science and technology programs that had been the exclusive bastions of men. Women entered the public sports arena, competing in all forms of intramural events, including, for the first time, swimming at the Olympics in 1912. Sex education and methods of birth control were made available at the clinics founded by Margaret Sanger. Movies, magazines, and advertising besieged women of all socioeconomic classes with images of the modern, fashionable woman. By the 1910s, it was no longer the painted ladies of questionable reputation who reddened their lips and cheeks, and accented their eyes with kohl. The demure, reclusive alabaster lady of 1900 metamorphosed into an independent, self-confident woman of the high-tech, fast-paced "moderne" era in less than a generation.

FIGURE 3.1. Advances in technology and mass production provided the modern woman of the early 1900s with conveniences throughout the home. Electrical appliances eased burdensome tasks, and manufactured products reduced time and effort in food preparation and household cleaning.

concessions and treaties that allowed them to compete globally with Britain. The subterfuge and crises that arose from these international military and economic ventures laid the path to the First World War.

In Germany, young Kaiser Wilhelm II led the way in overcoming political resistance to economic growth and industrialization on a national scale. As in Britain and the United States, private enterprise was encouraged, financed by a strong banking system. The education of German children emphasized technology and industrial vocation so that, by the beginning of the 1900s, Germany had caught up with Britain and the United States as a world leader in the progress of science- and technology-based industries. Politically, though, Germany was governed by an elitist minority of aristocrats and industrialists whose international blunderings hurtled the country toward its disastrous fate in 1914.

France, on the other hand, struggled with internal instability as the Third Republic continued to confront right-wing monarchal constituencies. During the Dreyfus Affair in the 1890s, the French right and the Catholic Church supported a military leadership that tried to cover up a scandal in which officers had forged and concealed evidence in the conviction of a Jewish army captain wrongly charged with espionage. The republicans used the nation's sense of outrage at the miscarriage of justice as a catalyst to suspend participation of the Church in government and to wrest supervision of the educational system from Catholic control. Anti-clericism dominated France's domestic agenda in the early 1900s, leading eventually to the confiscation of Church property and the irrevocable separation of church and state.

The reform efforts were a significant drain on France's political energies, impeding the nation's efforts toward an industrial parity with the United States, Britain, and Germany. Although France's status was unsurpassed as producer of the world's finest luxury goods—couture fashion, textiles, furniture, perfume, cosmetics—there was minimal interest in developing large manufacturing operations until World War I.

The United States at the beginning of the twentieth century found itself as an imperial power following territorial cessations from Spain in 1899 that included the Philippines, Guam, and Puerto Rico. The continental expanse forged by Manifest Destiny throughout the nineteenth century had been carved into forty-five interlocking states stretching from coast to coast. At the dawn of the twentieth century, the nation's population was seventy-six million, of which almost a third were immigrants who had arrived in the years since the Civil War.

America had embraced the Industrial Revolution and thrived on the newness of technological advances. In the years before the First World War, the wider availability of electricity coupled with manufacturing mass production and mass marketing broadened the consumer base with affordable labor-saving devices for the home. The automobile, too, became more accessible to ordinary folk when Henry Ford began mass production of his Model T in 1908, and a new buy-now-pay-later concept called the finance installment plan made such high-end goods as cars and home appliances more available to the masses. Fashionable advertising campaigns by auto manufacturers especially marketed to the modern twentieth-century woman, which greatly appealed to their continued aspiration for independence and mobility. (Figure 3.2.) Telephone wires reached across the country, connecting businesses and reaching into ever more homes. In North Carolina, the Wright brothers successfully flew the first aeroplane in 1903. A

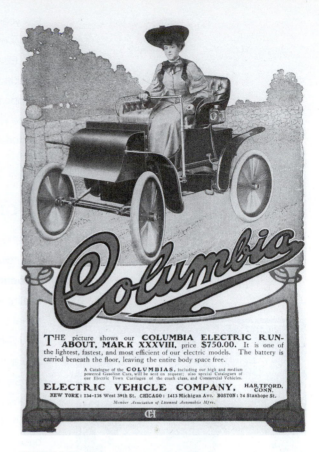

FIGURE 3.2. Early automobile manufacturers targeted women in advertising campaigns with the promise of mobility, freedom, and modernity. Columbia ad, 1903.

few years later, a group of creative filmmakers moved to a sleepy little town in California called Hollywood to establish a new industry there.

Elsewhere in the world, the stagnant, autocratic government of Russia spawned a revolutionary movement that would eventually topple the Czarist regime. In Asia, imperialist Europeans destabilized the Chinese imperial government, causing its collapse and the birth of the Republic of China in 1912. Japan came to dominate Korea after defeating Russia in a territorial war in 1905.

Women's Fashions 1900–1909

In 1900, a dramatic shift in the silhouette of women's fashions occurred with the introduction of a newly engineered corset. (Figure 3.3.) Called the "health" corset at the time—and later the "**S-bend**" **corset**—the style was designed in Paris by Madame Gaches-Sarraute as a more healthful alternative to the prevailing corset models that exerted extreme pressure on the internal organs. Instead of a curved front busk with its tightly laced indentation at the waist, the new S-bend corset featured a straight-line busk with a lowered support beneath the bosom and a longer line over the hips. (See the underwear section on pages 87–88.) Unfortunately, the S-bend corset was not the healthy solution that its makers advertised. Instead of alleviating the contortions caused by the Victorian hourglass styles, the S-bend created new stresses to the body by thrusting the chest forward in a pouter pigeon projection and by shifting the hips back into a swayback, or S-bend, appearance. In addition, the tightly cinched waistline was retained as a fashionable contour women would not abandon.

Despite the discomfort of the S-bend corset, it provided an exciting new look for the new century, even though, in general, women's clothing styles were not significantly altered from the shapes and types of the late 1890s. Bell-shaped skirts were still constructed with gores for a smooth fit, though now conforming to rounded S-bend hips instead of bustle pads. Hemlines remained at the floor, usually with a train, except for walking skirts, which were cropped to about the vamp of the shoes. Flouncing, ruffles, and pleats at the hem added flare all around to the bell shape. Dress bodices were tightly fitted. The high, stiff "**dog-collar**" **necklines** favored by Queen Alexandra were adapted to most styles of dresses, blouses, and jackets. The **bishop's sleeve** with its fullness at the wrists remained popular. Edwardian dresses were especially noted for their abundance of frills and decorative treatments. Colors were subdued neutrals for suits or soft, pale pastels for day and evening dresses. (Figure 3.4.)

The tailor-made suits that had become so popular in the 1890s remained a prevalent wardrobe option for Edwardian women. As more and more women left the home to work in offices, stores, and other businesses, the coordinating suit jacket and skirt with a crisp shirtwaist became the uniform of the urban working woman. The simple, almost stark styling of the Victorian tailor-made suit was easily adaptable to the new S-bend silhouette with only minor alterations of cut and construction. Jackets remained snugly fitted with a wide variety of closure, collar, and pocket treatments. For women of leisure, the two- or three-piece suit was often worn for afternoon social calls. These styles were sometimes as elaborately embellished as tea gowns with beading, lace panels, tassels, braid, and fur trim. Variations of suits for the upper classes included specialized styles for riding and hunting such as an adaptation of the men's norfolk jacket. Most suit coats were cropped short with narrow basques or short pep-

EFFECT OF AN OLD STYLE CORSET

THE NEW FIGURE

FIGURE 3.3. In 1900, the innovative S-bend corset revolutionized the silhouette of women's fashions. The torso was pushed forward in a pouter pigeon profile and the hips were thrust back into a kangaroo stance. Detail of Coronet Corset ad, 1900.

lums at the waist. During the second half of the decade, though, jackets were cut longer over the hips, some extending almost to the knees. (Figure 3.5.)

The S-bend look endured as the prevalent style throughout most of the first decade of the twentieth century. Variety was achieved primarily by surface embellishment. For the upper classes, lavish hand embroidery and hand beading were in abundance on almost any garment, which would include dressing gowns in the morning, day dresses at noon, tea gowns at five o'clock, and dinner or ball gowns for night. By mid-decade, this love of exterior ornamentation evolved into the **lingerie look** with its superfluity of lace and ribbons covering entire outer surfaces of dresses, blouses, evening gowns, and accessories.

The opulent and sophisticated excesses in dress by the "smart set" of the Edwardian era were often criticized by moralists of the time. The bare necks, shoulders, arms, and bosom cleavage of evening gowns were denounced as immodest and suggestive of degeneracy and immoral behavior. Similarly, tea gowns made of diaphanous pastel fabrics, often with sheer chiffons at the neckline and over half sleeves, were especially regarded as risqué since they were worn in public in daytime.

The luxurious fashions of the Edwardian era were not the exclusive domain of the elite. As in the second half of the nineteenth century, technology and mass production increasingly brought fashion to the masses in emulation of the haute couture of Paris or London. Advertising and timely fashion articles in mass media kept women informed of rapidly changing looks, infringing upon the privilege of the wealthy to differentiate the classes with the status of vogue modes. Ready-to-wear clothing with machine-made lace, machine-applied embroidery, and machine-stitched jet or glass beads filled mail-order catalogs, making sumptuous fashions available to all but the most remote populations.

FIGURE 3.4. The flouncing, ruffles, pleats, and frilly decoration of Edwardian fashion recalled the styles of the 1830s. Promenade dresses from *Delineator,* 1902.

Mass production also made the shirtwaist an indispensable wardrobe item for all classes. As in the 1890s, styles were greatly varied, ranging from plain cotton shirts for outdoor activities such as tennis and golf to opulent silk waists for evening wear richly ornamented with lace, beading, embroidery, and even hand-sculpted silk flowers. Early Edwardian day wear waists typically featured high collars and the bishop's sleeve. The straight-front, S-bend silhouette of the period was easily achieved with a combination shirtwaist and skirt. (Figure 3.6.) Later in the decade, a greater variety of collar and sleeve styles were offered in ready-to-wear and sewing pattern catalogs, including a revival of the flared Medici collar and the leg-of-mutton sleeve.

During the fashion seasons of 1908–09, three key changes in styles aligned and, almost overnight, swept away the S-bend silhouette and the frilly excesses of Edwardian ornamentation. First, Paris designers adopted a new form of corset that followed the contours of the figure without constricting the waist and bending the torso into an artificial stance. The look was more erect and natural although advertising illustrations tended to exaggerate the narrowness of the

FIGURE 3.5. The styling of Edwardian tailor-made suits was adapted to the new S-bend contours. Fitted jackets were cut longer over the hips, some of which extended almost to the knees. Left, suit with ribbon trim by Tollman, 1908; right, "French Model" tailor-made suits from Saks, 1907.

hips. (See the underwear section on pages 87–88.) Second, the Rococo extravagance of garment cut and decoration was supplanted by more simple, vertical lines. (Figure 3.7.) Third, Parisian couturiers discarded the Edwardian layers of petticoats and underskirts in favor of a simpler chemise-style slip that allowed the fabric of dresses and gowns to fall in a soft, unimpeded line.

This almost abrupt fashion drama is universally credited to the innovative leadership of Paul Poiret, whose inventiveness and modernity dominated Paris couture in the pre-World War I

FIGURE 3.6. Ready-to-wear makers produced shirtwaists in a broad range of styles for virtually all occasions. The combination of a shirtwaist and skirt was appropriate for almost everything from sports activities to formal social events. Lace and embroidered waists from Franklin Simon, 1908.

FIGURE 3.7. After the controversial hobble skirt was introduced in 1908, dress styles became more vertical and narrow within a year. Fashion plate from *Vogue,* 1909.

years. At the time he opened his salon in 1904, the Russo-Japanese War had just ended and he became enthralled with Eastern art, textiles, and costumes. Imported kimonos—modified by Japanese makers for Western wear—became all the rage as women's morning attire. Many of Poiret's designs of the mid-decade were based on the simplicity of the kimono—a presage of the narrow, straight-line styles that would dominate haute couture just a few years later.

In 1908, Poiret introduced a slim, tube skirt that was worn with a strip of material at the ankles called a hobble garter, from which the narrow style of skirts of the time got the name **hobble skirt**. Formal versions were only about twelve inches wide at the hem, forcing the wearer to take short, mincing steps, or sometimes even hopping to negotiate stairs and street curbs.

Women's Outerwear 1900–1909

Outerwear for the Edwardian woman was shaped and ornamented much differently than dresses. The **covert coat** frequently featured in magazines and catalogs of the period was

Coat and cape with matching collarettes, 1902.

Left, motorcar duster of water repellent material; right, leather three-quarter box coat, 1906.

Wool coat with fur collar and cuffs, 1909.

FIGURE 3.8. Edwardian coat styles were often plainer than dress or shirtwaist designs. Styles were constructed with ample room to fit comfortably over S-bend fashions. By the end of the decade, coats reflected the new columnar silhouette of fashions.

a loose-fitting, three-quarter overcoat made of twill (covert) wool. (Figure 3.8.) The look was masculine and usually plain without the typical Edwardian decorative trim. Coats that covered the entire skirt to the ground were less popular since a brush-down of the hem to remove mud and dust could take as much as an hour after each wearing but a skirt was easily laundered. Jackets, capes, and cloaks of varying lengths were equally popular. Capes were often richly decorated with ornamental top-stitching, embroidery, or passementerie. Wide **collarettes** in the fashion of the dog-collar look of the era were often attached to coats and capes for an extra layer of warmth over the shoulders.

Also during the early years of the twentieth century, long, durable coats, called **dusters**, made of rubberized cotton duck or twill were worn for sojourns in open automobiles. Natural-colored silk serge was another favorite fabric for motoring costumes. Leather jackets with matching goggles and visored chauffeur's hats were more preferred by younger women.

FIGURE 3.9. The Victorian bloomers gymsuit remained the prevalent sports attire for schoolgirls well into the early 1900s. Gymsuit designed by Florence Bolton, director of women's athletics, Stanford University, 1908.

In the second half of the Edwardian period, Orientalism was all the rage. Kimono style coats and capes constructed with full, T-cut sleeves were an influence from the East following the victory of Japan in its war with Russia.

By the end of the decade, coats reflected the new columnar silhouette of fashions. Lines were more narrow with detailing that emphasized the vertical look.

Women's Sports Apparel 1900–1909

As noted in the previous chapter, by the end of the nineteenth century, women of all classes had loosened their corsets and shortened their skirt hemlines to participate in all sorts of sporting activities. One of the first specialized sports costumes for women, excluding swimsuits, had been the knickerbocker suit, worn primarily for bicycling. (See chapter 2, Figure 2.1.) By the beginning of the Edwardian era, athletic women appreciated the freedom of knickerbockers and wore versions of them for other outdoor activities as well, such as canoeing and hiking.

Another specialized sports costume that continued into the twentieth century from the late Victorian period was the one-piece gymsuit, comprised of a jumper top and knee-length bloomers. (Figure 3.9.) A variation was the middy blouse worn with separate bloomers. Gymsuits were largely a school uniform for girls and college women active in intramural sports.

For the most part, though, women participating in sports wore looser fitting versions of day clothes. (Figure 3.10.) Strenuous activities such as golf, tennis, bowling, and skating (both ice and roller) challenged women's skill levels since they had to contend with volumes of fabric encumbering the legs as well as layers of undergarments, thick stockings, accessories, and even "sports" corsets. Vented jackets, box-pleated norfolks, and slit skirts provided some relief from the constriction of fashionable clothing for the female athlete.

Women's Underwear and Sleepwear 1900–1909

Corsets of the Edwardian era were more than just an undergarment, they defined the silhouette of fashion. The S-bend corset, commonly advertised as the "health" corset, was engineered to reduce the binding stress on the internal organs caused by the hourglass Victorian styles that were indented at the waist all around. (Figure 3.11.) Although the S-bend was made with a

FIGURE 3.10. For most athletic pursuits such as golf, tennis, bowling, and skating, women usually wore comfortable day clothes rather than specialized sports attire. Walking skirts were a few inches shorter than day dresses, and the daring woman might even roll up her sleeves for added comfort. Wool flannel dress, 1905.

FIGURE 3.11. The silhouettes of corsets in the Edwardian period began with the S-bend style that pushed the hips back and the bust forward. By the end of the decade, corsets were constructed with a verticality and a longer line extending over the hips. Left, S-bend corset, 1900; right, straightline corset, 1909.

straightline front, it nevertheless continued to constrict the waist. Moreover, the S-bend further contorted the body into a kangaroo stance by pushing the torso forward into a pouter pigeon contour and thrusting the hips back.

By the end of the Edwardian period, corsets were once again dramatically redesigned to a more natural, upright shape with less constriction of the waist such as those shown in Figure 3.11. The lines were longer, extending low over the hips, and more narrow with an emphasis on a youthful-looking slim figure—a significant change from the ideal looks of the curvaceous, full-figured, mature woman of earlier years.

In the early part of the twentieth century, a decently dressed woman had to layer two or three petticoats beneath her skirt. During the first years of the first decade, undergarments became exceedingly frilly, especially petticoats. Hemlines were laden with flounces, pin-tucks, ruffles, ruching, and lace trim. When the hobble skirt dispensed with the petticoat, frou-frou treatments of underwear were also minimized.

Drawers, camisoles, and chemises were the other most common components of women's underwear. Victorian styles of combinations—a camisole and drawers sewn together in one piece—continued to be worn but became particularly prevalent after skirt silhouettes narrowed and bulky underwear was abandoned. Long union suits were favored more by ordinary women until the early teens when skirt hemlines rose. **Camiknickers**, or **chemiknickers** in England, were a sort of short slip with a button and loop at the hem that could be fastened between the legs to form a divided underskirt.

Sleepwear for the Edwardian lady was primarily the silk princess style nightgown, or **negligee**, and matching robe, called a **wrapper** or **dressing sacque**. (Figure 3.12.) The simple nightshirt of linen, flannel, or cotton was preferred most by ordinary women. Throughout the early years of the period, nightgowns were as extravagantly trimmed with lace, ribbons, bows, embroidery, and ruffles as were undergarments. Following the Russo-Japanese War in 1905, silk kimonos became widely popular for the boudoir.

FIGURE 3.12. Edwardian nightgowns, or negligees, were lavishly trimmed with lace, ribbons, bows, embroidery, and ruffles. Empire revival wrappers of chambray and silk by *McCall's* patterns, 1907.

Women's Swimwear 1900–1909

The swimsuits of the Edwardian woman varied little from the bloomer suit styles that first appeared at resort beaches almost twenty years earlier. (Figure 3.13.) Tunics and overskirts still extended to the knees covering voluminous bloomers, and thick, opaque wool or silk stockings covered the legs. Bodices were the most daring with short sleeves and deep V-neck or scoop decolletes exposing flesh to the sun and to masculine gazes. The most significant design change was the adaptation of the S-bend silhouette, usually achieved by a waistline that dipped to the front and a bodice cut with the pouter pigeon contour.

FIGURE 3.13. Edwardian swimsuits were comprised of a blouse, skirt, bloomers, opaque hose, and canvas shoes. Top, from *McCall's*, 1908; bottom, from *Harper's Bazaar*, 1902.

FIGURE 3.14. The most prevalent type of women's shoes for street wear in the early 1900s was the high-top ankle boot. The beveled Cuban heel was the most popular trend for both walking boots and pumps. Left, walking boots, 1907; right, dress pumps, 1908.

Women's Shoes 1900–1909

In 1902, *Harper's Bazaar* noted that women's shoes had changed significantly from the "flat, broad" styles of the preceding years. "The heels are so much higher, there is so much more curve under the instep, and the toes are so much more pointed." These new contours of the Edwardian woman's shoes would remain the prevalent shape—or the **last** as it was commonly called in editorials—until the First World War. The high arched insole, sharply pointed toe, and high heel (at about 2 to 2 1/2 inches) were applied to all styles of shoes except utility footwear such as riding boots.

The ankle boot remained the most common form of street shoe. (Figure 3.14.) As with nineteenth-century versions, they were made of leather or with the high tops of stiff, waterproof fabric stitched to leather vamps. Both lace-up and button styles were equally popular. Following the Spanish-American War, the Cuban heel became a favorite change to the ogee-curved Louis XV heel. The thicker Cuban heel with its beveled slant looked sleek and modern. Pumps of satin or velvet were still the proper shoe for evening wear. For utilitarian purposes, such as riding, hiking, or similar outdoor activities, the design of tall boots with wide comfortable soles, low heels, and sturdy, thick leather uppers remained constant.

Shoes of all types were predominantly black, except in summer when white and pale neutrals such as sand or mushroom were acceptable. Even so, *Harper's Bazaar* further advised in 1902 that "shoes made of the same material as the dress are charming for evening wear and to wear with tea gowns." Satin, velvet, and suede shoes were dyed the soft colors favored for dresses and visiting suits in the first decade of the century: dusty blue, rose, mint green, and pale ecru.

Shoe ornamentation was minimal—punched overlays, instep straps with light beading or machine embroidery, and simple buckles and bows such as those shown in Figure 3.14. The more flashy ornamentation such as rosettes of silvery tulle or chiffon were only for house shoes and boudoir slippers.

Women's Jewelry 1900–1909

For women of the Edwardian age, the most popular types of jewelry were the richly detailed and ornamental looks that their Victorian grandmothers had worn. (Figure 3.15.) In 1907, *Vogue* advised readers that the Rococo styles of Louis XV jewelry added "the very most up-to-date air to one's costume," and "to be in the mode one should have these little trinkets among one's accessories." In addition, jewelry with a distinct look from the distant past or distant lands remained as popular as in the nineteenth century. When the affluent went on their European Grand Tours, they purchased varieties of jewelry with motifs from antiquity such as Roman cameos, Greek coin busts, and Egyptian scarabs. In addition, the Art Nouveau trend remained a powerful influence on all the decorative arts, including jewelry design, well into the 1910s.

Costume jewelry makers such as Whiting & Davis, Trifari, and Napier mass produced high quality adaptations of fine jewelry that were widely distributed through mail order and five-and-dime retailers. In considering the degree of quality of some costume jewelry, *Vogue* suggested in 1907 that the new "imitation jewels are quaintly and artistically set, which, for wear with the pretty light frocks in summer, seem much more appropriate than the costly gems used with elaborate costumes in the winter."

The wristwatch made its fashion debut during this decade. Although some experimental versions date back to the 1880s, the wristwatch became an avant-garde accessory after the British began mass producing them for their soldiers in 1901 during the Boer War.

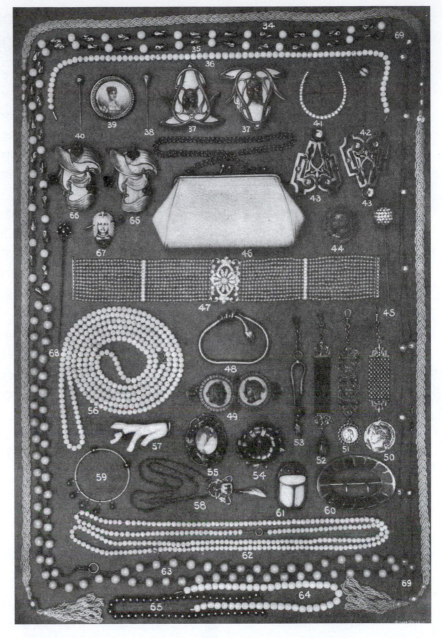

FIGURE 3.15. Edwardian jewelry design was a pastiche of Victorian neo-styles mixed with the modern look of Art Nouveau. Detail of ad from Maison Nouvelle, 1902.

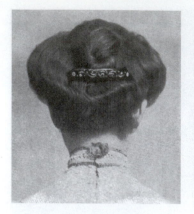

FIGURE 3.16. The Victorian sentiment that a woman's hair is her glory remained the feminine ideal for the Edwardian woman as well. Pompadour hairstyles in *Ladies' Home Journal,* 1905.

THOUSANDS OF WOMEN

Attribute their beautiful complexion to the fact that they

Use Lablache Face Powder

It softens, soothes, nourishes the skin; restores its freshness and rich color; removes all roughness and blemishes; prevents sunburn and kindred ills. Delightful to use. Invisible on application. No woman's summer equipment complete without it. Avoid substitutes.

Flesh, White, Pink and Cream Tints. 50 cents per box. All druggists, or by mail.

BEN. LEVY & CO., French Perfumers, 125 Kingston St., Boston, Mass., U.S.A.
Sold by ROBERTS & CO., 5 Rue de la Paix, Paris; 76 New Bond St., London, and KINGSFORD & CO., 54 Piccadilly, W., London.

FIGURE 3.17. Except for a touch of face powder, respectable Edwardian ladies did not use makeup. Lablache face powder in "flesh, white, pink, and cream tints," 1901.

Women's Hairstyles and Makeup 1900–1909

For the woman of the early 1900s, the Victorian cult of hair remained firmly in place. A woman's hair was her glory as haircare product advertising emphasized with its images of women displaying long, thick tresses that extended down the back to the hips or even longer. When a woman was not satisfied with the length or volume of her natural hair, she could attach any variety of hair pieces to achieve the desired effect. Horsehair pads could also be concealed under a woman's hair to add dimension and shape to hairstyles, especially for the **pompadour**, which was a high, bouffant arrangement with a chignon at the back. (Figure 3.16.)

The use of makeup likewise underwent a pronounced transition from the early Edwardian period into the 1910s. At the beginning of the century, the social stigma of the painted lady persisted from the Victorian era, and only an actress or a demimonde brazenly appeared in public wearing makeup. The ideal was the alabaster lady with pale, flawless skin. Soap and cold cream manufacturers advertised specialized products that would "assist nature" by "improving bad complexions" and "preserving good complexions," as one 1902 Ingram's facial cream promotion avowed. When soaps, skin creams, and genetics failed to result in a smooth complexion, the application of a little rice powder, sometimes tinted, or facial powders made with talc or chalk was acceptable in polite society. (Figure 3.17.) U.S. manufacturers produced such excellent quality vanity products, including fragrances, that *Vogue* advised readers in 1907: "Once, all the world turned to Paris for toilet things, as well as for shoes. Now both these things manufactured in America are often preferable."

Women's Hats 1900–1909

To most women of the first half of the twentieth century, the hat was the most important fashion accessory. A hat was a statement of social status for some women and, for others, an expression of personality or even mood. In 1902, *Harper's Bazaar* noted, "Every season the fashions show more and more that individual tastes and individual looks are to be consulted in headgear. One shape may be becoming to the majority of faces, and is consequently dubbed the leading style, and is of course copied in various modified designs, all built on the same principles, but each hat is altered to suit each wearer." The alterations that the Edwardian woman considered were not markedly different from the choices her Victorian mother had to make—the right hat for the season, the climate, and, of course, her own taste.

The hat styles of 1900 to 1909 gradually expanded in size from the compact models of the previous decade to scales not seen since the eighteenth century. (Figure 3.18.) Pompadour hairstyles added further dimension for an even more impressive silhouette. The assortment of hat designs was enormously varied. Wide-brimmed picture hats were particularly popular with younger women. One of the newest looks of the period was the **Mercedes toque** that featured a circular crown with a brim turned straight up the same height as the

FIGURE 3.18. The most important accessory for the Edwardian woman was her hat. Between 1900 and 1909, hats expanded in size from compact Victorian styles to enormous dimensions festooned with gigantic plumes and other oversized trim.

Picture hat with ostrich plumes, 1909.

Hats from *Delineator,* 1902.

Velvet turban with coque feathers, 1909.

Feather and tulle hat, 1908.

crown. Hat revivals included the "Marie Antoinette turban" and the tricorne. Straw hats, including the enduring boater, were not worn before mid-April unless travelling to a southern climate in winter.

All dressy hats of the period were lavishly decorated with an excess of Edwardian frills such as ribbons, rosettes, feathers (and entire stuffed birds usually referred to simply as "wings"), artificial fruit, silk flowers, lace, chiffon swags, beading, and all manner of other trim. Ornaments

Crocheted boa for evening wear, 1902.

Detachable collars and jabots, 1907.

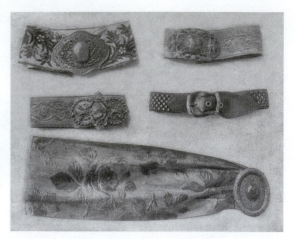

Tapestry and tooled leather belts, 1907.

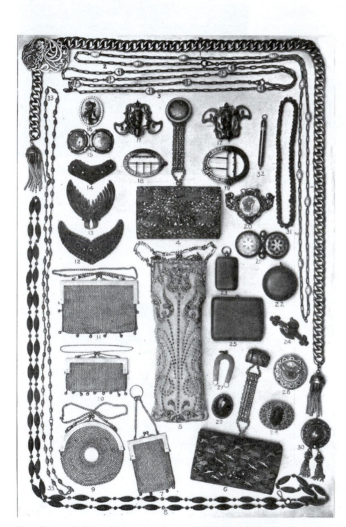

Handbags, belt buckles, and chain necklaces, 1902.

Wristwatch, handbags, combs, and jewelry from 1906.

FIGURE 3.19. "The little things of dress," according to *Vogue* in 1907, were critical to the image that a fashionable lady wanted to project. In keeping with the excessive ornamentation of Edwardian dresses, a head-to-toe display of the correct accessories was needed to complement the proper, fashionable look of the time.

included long hat pins with decorative ends and **cabochons**, which were large, rounded clasps used to hold the ends of feathers or ribbons to the hat.

From the end of the first decade through the early 1910s, hats reached huge proportions. As the shapes became larger, the decorative treatments likewise increased in size and quantity. Enormous bows spread across picture hats, feathers cascaded down the back or spread outward, and turbans were piled high with volumes of fabric and trim.

Women's Accessories 1900–1909

"The Little Things of Dress" was the title of *Vogue's* regularly featured article on accessories for the properly dressed woman of the early 1900s. One of the recurring themes of the editorials was that accessories may be small in size but they can make—or break—the image a woman wanted to project in society. Then, as now, the variety of accessories with which a woman could accent her ensemble was considerable. In addition to the hats, shoes, and jewelry shown in previous sections of this chapter, the Edwardian woman also accoutered herself with belts, collar treatments, handbags, hatpins, watches, boas, scarves, handkerchiefs, fans, muffs, gloves, parasols, and hair ornaments. (Figure 3.19.)

In the early years of the 1900s, belts were important for defining the S-bend silhouette with its angled waistline. Styles of belts reflected the Edwardian delight in lavish decoration. Belts of tapestry, embroidery, beadwork, and tooled leather were punctuated with large, ornamental buckles.

Neck dressing was an easy way to make plain shirt waists or dress bodices more fashionable and varied. High, detachable collars of the Edwardian period were machine embroidered or decorated with lace insets and scalloped edging. Jabots of lace or pleated handkerchief linen provided still more options for fashion variation.

Handbags did not change much in shape or size from those of the late 1800s. Instead, textiles and surface embellishment with Art Nouveau or Asian motifs gave the new models a modern distinction.

Fur muffs were the most fashionable and functional accessory for winter. The upper classes indulged in rare furs such as sable, but dyed opossum and fox pelts made muffs an affordable fashion accessory for middle classes as well.

In cold or warm weather, a lady always wore gloves when going out. Unlike most other accessories of the period, gloves were not richly decorated. According to *Harper's Bazaar* in 1902, gloves "should be made as simply as possible"; any "eccentricity is considered bad form."

Scarves were also a popular accessory to protect against chilly winds. Styles ranged from narrow stoles to large shawl-like sizes. A more decorative form for summer evenings was the **boa**, which came in a wide variety of materials besides the traditional feather arrangements, including lace or tulle flounces, taffeta petals, silk netting, and crochetwork.

Since hats were not worn with evening gowns, jeweled hair ornaments and especially ornate combs were important for securing the mounds of hair arranged in pompadours and other high, upswept hairstyles. For sports and other active pursuits, hair was held in place by celluloid combs blended to resemble tortoise shell or ebonized and inlaid with mother-of-pearl and silver. For rainy or snowy days, the plain, functional umbrella was a necessity to protect hats and hair from the damp. In the summer months, a sun parasol was still a popular accessory for the proper lady to prevent sunburn and to toy with coquettishly. Edwardian parasols were small, domed confections of flounces, ruffles, lace trim, pleats, and tucks. Handles were often ornamented with carved ivory or coral, faceted rock quartz, repousse metals, and inlaid woods.

Other less common accessories cited in fashion publications included corsages of artificial fruit or flowers molded of papier-mache, and canes, of which *Vogue* assured readers in 1907 that "there is not great danger of these things becoming common."

Men's Fashions 1900–1909

Although women's fashions of the Edwardian period were dramatically altered by the S-bend corset, men's clothing of the same time continued the heavy, upholstered look of the late Victorian years. The sack suit (called a lounge suit in England) was the standard everyday attire for all but the laboring classes. It had continued to gain in popularity even in urban business arenas, where it gradually replaced the long frock coat as proper day attire. By the beginning of the twentieth century, ready-to-wear makers mass produced such high-quality men's suits that, in 1902, a fashion editor was compelled to note: "There has been so great an improvement during the last few years in the general cut and finish of men's clothes, that it would be snobbish as well as untrue to say that it is not possible to buy a ready-made suit of any kind that will fit and look well." Almost every man could afford at least one ready-made blue serge suit priced about $5.00 to $8.00 in the Sears catalogs of the time.

The cut of the suit coat in the first decade of the 1900s was long, loose fitting, and bulkily padded. (Figure 3.20.) Hemlines were either cut straight across or rounded at the front closure. Some lengths also extended almost to the knees, though these were looks for young men and should not be confused with the long frock coat styles of the time. Lapels initially were narrow and placed high with a button closure to the throat. Around 1905, the neckline opening dropped slightly and lapels were widened. Single-breasted jackets more commonly had three-button closures although the Victorian four-button style persisted through the decade. Double-breasted jackets were viewed as more sporty, and were usually favored by younger men. In men's tailor-made catalogs, the jackets for **outing sack suits** were distinguished by patch pockets and bolder textile patterns such as checks, plaids, or herringbone.

Suit trousers were **pegged**—cut full around the hips and thighs and tapering to a close fit at the ankles. Belted waistbands became more popular, especially in the United States, although suspenders continued to be commonly worn. During this transitional period, trousers were made with both belt loops and suspender buttons at the waistband.

One of the subtle but significant distinctions of Edwardian menswear was the length of trousers. Two varieties are clearly evident in ads of the period, especially when both are shown together. (Figure 3.21.) Regular trousers were cut with leg hems that draped over the shoe to the sole heel. The front crease broke at a gentle angle over the instep of the shoe. Trousers with rolled cuffs were cropped high at the ankles with a front crease that fell in a straight line. Wide rolled cuffs added weight to ensure a clean leg line and minimize bagging at the knees. In addition, the shortened leg prevented cuffs from gaping and collecting dirt. Men with fashion

FIGURE 3.20. Edwardian men's ditto suits were heavily padded and loose fitting with long hemlines on sack coats and baggy, pegged trousers. More casual suit styles featured jackets with patch pockets and bold textile patterns. Left, suit styles from Tailor-Made Clothing catalog, 1908; right, Society Brand suit, 1909.

flair emphasized the high cut by wearing brightly colored and patterned socks that showed clearly at the ankles, and with shoes that were laced with eye-catching grosgrain ribbons tied in large bows.

The properly suited Edwardian male cast an imposing silhouette, appearing to possess a physique with broad shoulders, barrel chest, and massive thighs. A 1908 cartoon in *Cosmopolitan* derided the foppish dandy of the day with a costume of exaggerated dimensions and clashing patterns that were not too far from reality. (Figure 3.22.)

The other component of men's suits, the vest (or waistcoat in England) gradually became less important through the first two decades of the century. It remained integral to the business suit and formal attire but was increasingly discarded for the sake of simplicity and comfort. Most vest styles were single-breasted although the double-breasted vest was commonly

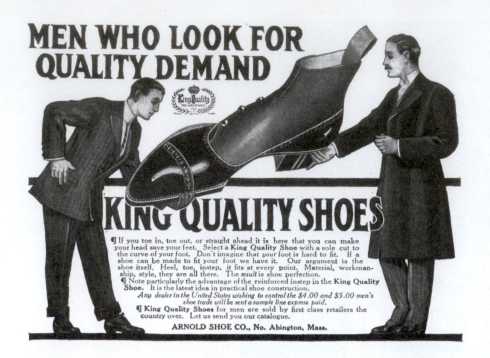

MEN WHO LOOK FOR QUALITY DEMAND

KING QUALITY SHOES

¶ If you toe in, toe out, or straight ahead it is here that you can make your head save your feet. Select a **King Quality Shoe** with a sole cut to the curve of your foot. Don't imagine that *your* foot is hard to fit. If a shoe can be made to fit your foot we have it. Our argument is the shoe itself. Heel, toe, instep, it fits at every point. Material, workmanship, style, they are all there. The *result* is shoe perfection.
¶ Note particularly the advantage of the reinforced instep in the **King Quality Shoe.** It is the latest idea in practical shoe construction.
Any dealer in the United States wishing to control the $4.00 and $5.00 men's shoe trade will be sent a sample line express paid.
¶ **King Quality Shoes** for men are sold by first class retailers the country over. Let us send you our catalogue.

ARNOLD SHOE CO., No. Abington, Mass.

FIGURE 3.21. Two distinct trouser lengths were worn by Edwardian men. Regular pant leg hems extended over the heel of the shoe with a break in the front crease over the vamp. Trousers with rolled cuffs were shortened to the ankles to prevent gaps that could collect dirt. King Quality Shoes ad, 1908.

FIGURE 3.22. The exaggerated dimensions of the Edwardian men's suit combined with the boldly patterned accessories of the dandy were a favorite topic for editorial cartoonists of the period. Cartoon from *Cosmopolitan,* 1908.

FIGURE 3.23. The vest, or waistcoat in England, remained an integral component of the business sack suit, but increasingly was abandoned in favor of simplicity and comfort. *Vogue* featured this English novelty vest in 1902 but judged it to have a "peculiar" and "not overly attractive" arrangement of buttoning.

offered in tailor-made catalogs as well. Vests were made with notched collars in a V-closure or shawl collars with a deep, scoop opening. Some novelty closures appeared periodically, like the one shown in Figure 3.23, but they never became a trend. As men replaced their pocket watches with wristwatches in the late 1910s, the utilitarian importance of the vest diminished as well.

Despite the formidable, oversized proportions and bulky fit of the Edwardian man's sack suits, evening apparel was, instead, sleek and trim. The traditional styling of the fitted tail coat and slim trousers did not change much from the Victorian cut and contours. Some shoulder padding and wider sleeves updated evening wear, and trousers were only slightly pegged. The matching black or white vest also featured the traditional deep scoop front to display the brilliantly white, starched, bosom-front shirt—the pullover type with a keyhole neckline. Increasingly, though, the tuxedo, or dinner jacket as it was more frequently called, became the uniform of formal dress where previously the tailcoat was required. (Figure 3.24.) As a menswear catalog noted of the tuxedo in 1907, "There's not much variation of style possible." One subtle departure from the standard was to elevate the appearance of the tuxedo by wearing a stiff, bosom-front shirt instead of the usual starched, pleat-front version if the social event was more formal than a business dinner or the theater.

The coat cut or open front shirt that was introduced in the 1890s continued to gain in popularity. The bosom front shirt, though, remained a favorite of many traditionalist men who were reluctant to surrender the comfort of the familiar. Ready-to-wear makers continued to manufacture bosom front shirts in as many colors and textile patterns as their coat cut lines. Although numerous varieties of "fancy percale shirts" with an attached turned-down collar had been sold by ready-to-wear catalogers and retailers for decades, these types of shirts were largely regarded more as ordinary work or casual shirts. Proper dress shirts, though, worn to offices or for dressy social occasions, were made with narrow, banded collars to which stiff, bleached white detachable collars were affixed by a button in the back. (Figure 3.25.)

FIGURE 3.24. The tuxedo, or dinner jacket, increasingly replaced the tail coat as the accepted formal dress. Tuxedo from Hart, Schaffner and Marks, 1907.

Men's Sports Attire and Outerwear 1900–1909

Specialized sports attire and playwear were primarily worn only by the sports professional, varsity athlete, or the avid enthusiast. Uniforms for baseball, football, track and field, and other competitive sports had become fairly standardized by the early 1900s. (Figure 3.26.) Olympic committees and amateur athletic associations strictly regulated the design and materials for competition clothing. Comfort and unrestricted movement were the principal tenets of athletic wear. The non-binding elastic comfort of knitwear was particularly welcomed by the athlete. Not only was the weight of knitwear variable for warmth or coolness, but the knitted fabrics were adaptable to a broad range of garment types and functions.

ARROW COLLARS

The new Arrow Collar for summer—high enough in the back for good appearance, low enough in the front for comfort, and there's room for the cravat to slide and tie in. It's the Concord with the Ara-Notch and the Evanston with the usual buttonholes. *15c., 2 for 25c.* In Canada, 20 cents, 3 for 50 cents. Arrow Cuffs, 25c., in Canada 35c.

(Patented, Aug. 3, '09)

Send for Ara-Notch Folder   CLUETT, PEABODY & CO., Troy, N. Y.

Cluett SHIRTS

are made to meet the wants of men who have heretofore been unable to secure satisfaction in ready-made shirts. They are shirts that you can wear without a coat, and yet know and feel that you do not appear at a disadvantage. *$1.50 and more.* In Canada, $1.25 up.

Send for Booklet, "Proper Dress"   CLUETT, PEABODY & CO., Troy, N. Y.

FIGURE 3.25. During the Edwardian period, the open-front coat cut shirt gradually replaced the pullover bosom-front styles. Until the First World War, though, both types of men's dress shirts were worn with a high, stiff detachable collar. Cluett-Peabody ad, 1910.

For the weekend golfer or tennis player, ordinary street clothing continued to suit their sportswear needs. For the most part, men simply rolled up the long sleeves of their shirts for easier movement although illustrations and photos of the era show collars buttoned and neckties firmly knotted in place. For the serious golfer, knickerbocker suits remained a common outfit. Hunters and fishermen might also wear knickerbockers for ease of putting on tall boots.

Riding costumes of the early 1900s were still the prerogative of the elite. The English "pink" (actually scarlet) frock coat with white stock about the neck, white breeches, and black boots remained the proper attire for a fox hunt. For urban park riding, the black cutaway coat, dark blue saddle trousers, and top hat lingered as the correct dress of the elite in Europe, but in America, the upper classes opted for the more casual ditto riding habit with its short sack coat, jodhpurs, gaiters, and derby.

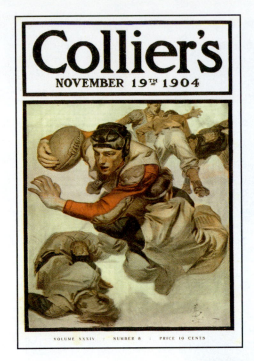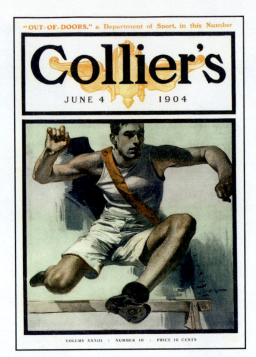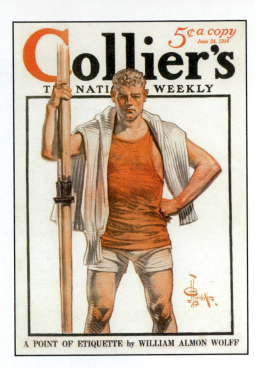

FIGURE 3.26. By the early twentieth century, varsity and professional athletic uniforms had become fairly standardized. Most garments were styled for ease of movement and comfort. Knit shirts, shorts, and sweaters were particularly popular for their elastic give and versatility.

During the first decade of the 1900s, men's outerwear had to be capacious enough to adequately cover the bulky, oversized sack suit. Hemlines were long, usually from mid-calf to just above the ankles. (Figure 3.27.) Most Edwardian overcoat styles changed little from the Victorian versions except in volume. Ulsters often came with a detachable hood or cape. The chesterfield featured a velvet collar and a fly front closure that concealed the buttons. The mackintosh became a generic name for almost any style of raincoat.

Also in the early years of the century emerged a new outerwear costume—the motoring ensemble. (Figure 3.28.) In 1902, *Vogue* illustrated the correct automobile dress to wear when driving the large, open touring cars of the period. (For driving a small runabout, the editors noted, "there is no distinct dress.") The ankle-length belted duster shown here is made of a checked, lightweight silk although other varieties were usually of more durable, weather-resistant materials like rubberized cotton duck or leather. As covered cars became more common, the motor costume became redundant.

Men's Underwear and Swimwear 1900–1909

Men's undergarments varied little in style from those of their Victorian fathers. (Figure 3.29.) The form-fitting knit union suit—so named for the uniting of the shirt and drawers into one piece—remained the most common type. Long-sleeved and ankle-length winter versions, called longjohns, were made of soft lamb's wool that was nonetheless maddeningly itchy

FIGURE 3.27. Men's outerwear of the Edwardian era was cut wide and long to fit over the padded, oversized suit styles of the time. Wool greatcoats from Hart, Schaffner & Marx, 1905.

FIGURE 3.28. For a few years at the beginning of the century, varieties of waterproofed motorcar dusters were added to men's outerwear wardrobes. Motorcar duster with driving gauntlets and visored cap from *Vogue*, 1902.

in the overheated offices and parlors of the time. Summer styles were of lightweight wool or cotton knits, including a new form of cool, mesh fabric, branded as Porosknit. Separate tops and drawers in woven cotton, linen, or silk were also popular although these were cut fuller and looser than the union suits. Knee-length drawers and short-sleeve or sleeveless tops were primarily for warm seasons. The new open-front cut was adapted to undershirts.

Fine wool or silk knits were also used in manufacturing men's socks. Perhaps surprising to many today is the wide assortment of colorful and patterned socks that men of the early 1900s popularly wore. "Fancy silk embroidered socks" were even offered in the Sears catalogs of the time—at the pricey thirty-five cents a pair compared with eight cents a pair for solid color cotton socks. For men who wished to avoid rumpled socks bagging about the ankles, especially considering that cuffed trousers of the period were cropped high, elasticized garters were strapped about the calves just below the knees to secure their silk knit "half hose" for a smooth fit. Knee-high hose and leggings for sports were also knitted in bold patterns such as plaids and vibrant primary colors like bright red or yellow, many with contrasting "fancy colored roll tops."

FIGURE 3.29. The Victorian union suit remained the most prevalent form of men's underwear. In warm weather, short sleeve or sleeveless tops and knee-length drawers in cotton, linen, or silk were preferred. Left, union suit by Munsing, 1902; right, coat cut undershirt and knee length drawers from B.V.D., 1909.

Swimwear also remained basically the same as late nineteenth-century styles and still resembled forms of men's underwear. (Figure 3.30.) Knit pullover tunics with placket button fronts or tank styles were cut long to the upper thighs for modesty. The matching knee-length drawers—sometimes called tights—were secured with a drawstring waist. Dark blue wool flannel was the most common fabric for men's swimsuits. Competitive swimmers, though, wore the regulation wool knit **racer**, a sleek, one-piece tank-style suit with legs cropped to the upper thighs.

Men's Accessories 1900–1909

The most important accessory for the Edwardian man was a hat. Seldom would a man go out of doors bareheaded. The assortment of hat styles available through the early decades of the 1900s was enormously varied although not much changed in shapes, materials, or dimensions

FIGURE 3.30. Styles of men's swimwear varied little from those of the late Victorian years. Assorted types of long tunics cropped to mid-thigh were worn over knee-length drawers. Drawstring drawers with short sleeve or sleeveless tunic by *McCall's* patterns, 1909.

FIGURE 3.31. The great variety of Edwardian men's hat styles reflected social status, age, and, at times, even the wearer's mood. On most any urban street of the time, the assortment of hat styles would be as diverse as depicted here.

1901

1908

1909

FIGURE 3.32. The hightop shoe was the most common men's footwear of the Edwardian period. Versions included all leather or a combination leather vamp with fabric upper. The Edwardian dandy might opt for oxfords with 1 1/2 inch heels and fancy ribbon laces. Bulb toe shoes featured raised, rounded ends.

from designs of the late Victorian years. In any urban crowd of men, a vast array of hat types would be ordinarily mixed, depending upon the season. Even men of limited means or sartorial interest knew not to wear a straw hat in winter. Most importantly, each style of hat bespoke the social status—and perhaps even mood—of the wearer. (Figure 3.31.) The high, shiny silk top hat, when worn during the day, asserted the dignity of a politician, professor, or businessman of some importance. Smooth felt derbies were the hat of choice to complement the ditto suit of the serious executive. The soft, creased fedora proclaimed a bit more flair and personality—the hall-mark of dashing youth. The office boy or mature working man preferred the easy casualness of the low, visored cap, sometimes called a golfer's cap or a newsboy's cap. Other men expressed their personality or regionalism with high domed stetsons, military-styled fatigue hats, or light-weight porkpie "crush" hats. In the summer months, low straw boaters were everywhere, from city streets to resorts. During the years the United States built the Panama Canal (1904–14), a wide variety of high crowned straw hats became popular and were collectively called **panamas**.

Men's footwear was also basically a continuation of nineteenth-century styles. (Figure 3.32.) The shape most commonly illustrated in shoe ads and catalogs featured wide, rounded toes. A raised "**bulb-toe**" styling became increasing popular after the turn of the century, particularly since it was regarded as the correct shape to wear with high-cropped cuffed trousers. The high-topped shoe we would call an ankle boot today was the preferred style for every day, including with business suits. Versions featured all-leather uppers or combination leather vamps with fabric tops. Both types were made with or without pull tabs at the back of the heel. The low, lace-up oxford was styled by the Edwardian dandy with wide laces that formed broad, decora-tive bows. For a short period around 1905–09, trendy young men stepped out in oxfords with a high heel of about 1 1/2 inches. For formal dress a patent leather slipper with a low throat and a grosgrain ribbon bow was proper.

Neckwear in the early 1900s was as varied as styles of the late Victorian period. (Figure 3.33.) The type of flared, pointed tip tie familiar to us today was usually called a cravat at the time. Unlike our contemporary styles, though, once knotted the lengths were short, sometimes extending only to mid-abdomen rather than to the belt—just long enough to tuck into a vest. The four-in-hand knot was the most prevalent. The term "ties" usually applied to bow ties, which could have flat, rounded, or pointed ends. Ascots were wide,

FIGURE 3.33. The variety of men's neckwear types, colors, and patterns in the early twentieth century was extensive. Left to right from 1902: four-in-hand knotted tie, ascot, imperial tie, and bow tie.

FIGURE 3.34. With the aid of mass marketing, Gillette sold millions of his safety razors and disposable blades within the first decade of production. The images of smooth-shaven young men promoted the whiskerless face as the preferred modern masculine look. Gillette ads, left 1907, right 1910.

scarf-like neckwear that were folded over at the throat and fastened with a stickpin. Most forms of neckwear were woven silk although some knit varieties were listed in catalogs of the period. Instructions on tying ties and affixing detachable collars were frequently featured in catalogs, men's furnishings brochures, and advertising.

Gloves were more of a seasonal accessory than they had been in earlier decades. The gentleman and dandy still wore or carried their softly dressed kid gloves when in public or making social calls. Colors were usually gray, tan, or brown. Heavier calfskin or buckskin gloves were worn for motoring or winter protection.

Jewelry remained an accessory of limited use for men. Besides the wedding ring, the gold pocket watch and fob were the most common masculine jewelry. A matching watch chain usually extended across the front of the vest or looped from the vest watch pocket to the trouser pocket. Cuff links, collar buttons, shirt studs, vest buttons, and tie stickpins were the other forms of jewelry permitted men, and then only if subtle and subdued. Even wealthy men were cautious on diamond stickpins or oversized cuff links. *Vogue's* long-running editorial, "The Well-Dressed Man," frequently chided men for excessive jewelry or flamboyance. When grudgingly the *Vogue* editors acknowledged some new trend, such as the "fad" of jeweled vest buttons in 1901, they usually also included the caveat, "if not too conspicuous to be bad style."

Walking sticks were still a status symbol that no gentleman would go into the street without. Whereas men eschewed flashy jewelry, they could indulge in fanciful excess with the handles of their walking sticks. Some handles were gold, sterling silver, or carved ivory sculptures of animals or allegoric heads; others were inlaid with large gems, mother-of-pearl, cloisonne, contrasting metals, or other decorative treatments from the jeweler. In summer, cane, bamboo, and wood carved to simulate exotic woods were acceptable alternatives to formal, bejeweled types.

Rounding out the accessory wardrobe for men were handkerchiefs and scarves of varying knits, colors, and patterns. Mail order catalogs offered Irish linen handkerchiefs monogrammed with a single initial for the inside jacket pocket. For the outside breast pocket, colorful Japanese silk squares were available with richly patterned borders.

Men's Grooming and Hairstyles 1900–1909

For most of the second half of the nineteenth century, facial hair of all kinds was common to men young and old. Around the turn of the twentieth century, though, two disparate influences contributed to the return of the clean-shaven face—one from technology and the other from popular culture.

In 1903, an enterprising traveling salesman, King Gillette, collaborated with a professor from the Massachusetts Institute of Technology to invent a safety razor with a disposable razor blade. The idea was an instant success. With the aid of mass marketing and advertising, Gillette sold a half million blades within the first three years of production. (Figure 3.34.) During World War I, the U.S. government ordered 3.5 million Gillette razors and 36 million blades, which were sent overseas to American doughboys who introduced the concept around the world.

In addition to images of smooth-shaven young men in Gillette ads, a new ideal of masculine aesthetic appeared in the mass media that promoted the whiskerless face. Depictions of handsome, square-jawed young men created by the famous artists Charles Dana Gibson and J. C. (Joseph Christian) Leyendecker were featured by the hundreds in magazine editorials and advertising. So popular were these images that the shirtmaker Cluett-Peabody received thousands of fan letters from women—including several proposals of marriage—addressed to the Arrow shirt men illustrated in Leyendecker's ads such as those depicted in Figure 3.25.

Besides the successful marketing of the safety razor and a media saturation of compelling images of clean-cut young men, a barrage of magazine and newspaper editorials also urged the "cleanly fashion" of shaving for health reasons. In 1907, for example, *Harper's Bazaar* affirmed that the clean-shaven face was "peculiarly gratifying and should be encouraged in all proper ways." The editors further reported on "scientific experiments" in which the lips of a woman were "sterilized" before she kissed a man with a moustache; afterwards, her lips were tested and discovered to be "literally swarming with malignant microbes."

Men's hairstyles remained closely cropped around the sides with the volume on the top—a necessity of grooming for a proper fit of a hat. Most men parted their hair on the left. The center part was more common with boys and college men. Hair coloring products were available but only actors, politicians, or other men in the public eye indulged in the use of hair dyes. The greatest fear was baldness. Since the genetic causes were not understood at the time, many massaging devices and restoration treatments were sold to balding men with promises of reversing hair loss. (Figure 3.35.)

FIGURE 3.35. The Edwardian man who suffered from male pattern baldness was susceptible to advertised promises of hair restoration. Scalp massager, 1905.

Children's Clothing 1900–1909

Although the swaddling of infants had largely been discontinued in industrialized nations, except in remote, rural regions, babies of the early 1900s were nevertheless weighed down with layers of multiple garments. In 1902, the superintendent of the New York Babies Hospital wrote in an article for *Harper's Bazaar,* "There is no reason why the baby of today should not have just as dainty, as fine and expensive a wardrobe as the one of a few years ago, and there is every reason why he should not have all the weight and discomfort of the old one." She then lists an eleven-part layette that actually varied little from the Victorian ensemble except in the shorter lengths of the dresses.

Childcare experts recommended that, to ward off colds and other ailments, an infant should be wrapped chest to hips in a warm flannel band or cotton webbing before dressing. This differed from swaddling in that the baby's arms, legs, and head were left free to move at will. Over the binding was then layered the full layette—diaper, gown, petticoat, vest or sacque, socks, knit booties or moccasins, knit bonnet, and shawl. If the child were to be taken out of doors or if visitors were expected, additional layers might include frilly, starched aprons, bibs, detachable collarettes, tall caps, mitts, and lace-up fabric or kid shoes, all usually lavishly embellished with embroidery, lace, flounces, pin tucks, ruching, ruffles, and other decorative trimmings. (Figure 3.36.) Such Edwardian excesses for babies were not confined solely to the upper classes. Proud, aspiring parents of the middle classes equally indulged in ornamenting their children with superfluous clothing, especially with the increased availability of mass-produced infants wear from ready-to-wear makers.

Edwardian girls were subjected to the same types of restrictive clothing that their Victorian mothers had endured in their childhood. Heavily boned corsets were still common for girls as young as four or five. Teen girls were expected to reflect the fashionable taste of their mothers and consequently were harnessed into S-bend corsets for the proper profile. (Figure 3.37.) Dress lengths continued the conventions of the late nineteenth century with toddlers and girls through about age twelve wearing hemlines at the knees, teen girls of about thirteen to fifteen with crops at mid-calf, and young misses of age fifteen to seventeen with skirts to the ankles. Waistlines were the fashion news for girls. Belts and waist seams for young girls dropped low on the hips, almost to the upper thighs. The waistline contours of teen girl's dresses and skirts fitted snugly over S-bend corsets and dipped to the front. In keeping with the trends of the Edwardian era, girl's frocks were as lavishly decorated with assorted forms of trim as were their mothers' styles.

Toddler boys of the Edwardian period suffered the same torments of fashion traditions as had their Victorian fathers as youngsters. Until about the age of four, depending upon the child's growth, boys wore dresses or short, kilt-like skirts with shirts. Unlike the childhood of their fathers, though, most boys in the early twentieth century did not have to be bothered with long, curled tresses although the tradition lingered primarily with the leisure classes until the First World War.

Older boys had the advantage of trousers for comfort and maneuverability. From about the age of four or five through their mid-teens, boys wore knickerbocker suits with a variety

FIGURE 3.36. The Edwardian infant was layered with multiple garments and accessories in a misguided attempt to safeguard the baby from chills that most parents still thought caused all sorts of illnesses. A layette from *Harper's Bazaar,* 1902.

FIGURE 3.37. In the early 1900s, the waistline was the fashion focus for girls' fashions. Toddler and young girls wore dresses with a dropped waistline low on the hips. Teen girls wore S-bend styles that emulated women's silhouettes. Fashion plate from *Delineator,* 1902.

Sailor suit from De Pinna, 1907.

Belted knickerbocker suit from De Pinna, 1907.

Corduroy knickerbocker suit from *Vogue*, 1907.

FIGURE 3.38. Some form of the knickerbocker suit was the principal attire for the Edwardian boy.

of jackets. (Figure 3.38.) The sailor suit also remained a perennial favorite for boys throughout the era, some styles of which were depicted in magazines of the time with long, bell-bottom trousers instead of knickerbockers. For special occasions such as weddings, boys might wear long pants with a vest and a tuxedo jacket or a short, cropped Eton coat. Once boys were in high school, they began to wear the same styles of ditto suits and sports clothes as adult men.

Review

As the twentieth century dawned, women's fashions were transformed by the invention of a new form of corset that altered the silhouette from the Victorian hourglass contours into the Edwardian S-bend stance. Gored skirts fitted smoothly over rounded hips in a flared bell shape and bodices and blouses projected forward into a pouter pigeon fullness. Frills and lavish surface embellishment abounded.

Affordable tailor-made suits were mass produced for working women. Similarly, ready-to-wear shirtwaists and skirts became increasingly popular alternatives to dresses and suits.

At the end of the first decade of the new century, three key fashion changes occurred that swept away the S-bend silhouette. First was a change in the configuration of the corset, which became more vertical with a longer line extending low over the hips. Second was the introduction of the narrow, columnar hobble skirt by Paul Poiret. Third was the discarding of layers of petticoats in favor of a simpler slip-style chemise.

Menswear of the Edwardian period also had a distinctive look that differed from the Victorian styles. The sack suit became even more prevalent, replacing the frock coat as the preferred business attire. The cut of the Edwardian sack coat was long, loose fitting, and heavily padded. Pegged trousers were full about the hips and tapered to a close fit at the ankles.

Children's clothing continued the regressive practices of the Victorian age. Babies were weighed down with excessive layers of clothing. Girls wore adaptations of women's S-bend styles, including constricting corsets. Preschool boys were still dressed as girls, and school-age boys donned knickerbocker suits.

review questions

1. In 1900, which innovation dramatically altered the silhouette of women's fashions? How did the Edwardian woman's silhouette differ from that of her Victorian predecessor of the 1890s?

2. Identify the key characteristics of the Edwardian woman's dress designs.

3. Which three key changes in women's fashions of 1908 and 1909 helped sweep away the S-bend silhouette?

4. Who is credited with designing the hobble skirt? Describe the style and how women adapted to the fit.

5. Compare and contrast the cut and line of men's everyday sack suits of the Edwardian period with those of the Victorian age.

6. During the Edwardian period, how did the dress designs of young girls differ from those of teen girls?

research and portfolio projects

Research

1. Write a research paper on the revivalisms of women's fashions of the Edwardian period. Compare and contrast the twentieth-century adaptations with the period originals.

Portfolio

1. Research the construction of S-bend corsets and replicate a life-size version of one in papier-mache. Include details of panels, seams, and laces.

dress terms

bishop's sleeve: women's sleeve with a fullness between the elbow and wrist

boa: a decorative scarf made of feathers or materials cut or knit in a feathery treatment

bulb-toe shoe: men's shoes with a wide bulbous-shaped toe

cabochon: large rounded clasps or pins used as ornaments on women's hats

camiknickers (also chemiknickers): a type of short slip with a button or loop at the hem that could be fastened to form a divided underskirt

collarettes: wide capelets with a dog collar neckline used as an attachment to Edwardian women's outerwear

covert coat: a women's loose-fitting, three-quarter length overcoat made of twill (covert) wool

dog-collar neckline: high, stiff collars of Edwardian women's fashions

dressing sacque: a woman's loose dressing robe

duster: long, waterproofed coats for men and women initially used for motoring in open cars

hobble skirt: a slim, tube skirt that tapered to a narrow opening at the hemline, some with a strip of material at the ankles called a hobble garter

last: industry term applied to the shape of a shoe; also, shoe-shaped forms, usually of wood, inserted into shoes for storage to preserve the shape

lingerie look: the excessive use of laces and ribbons as decoration for Edwardian women's fashions

Mercedes toque: a woman's hat with a circular crown and a brim turned straight up the same height as the crown

negligee: a woman's loose nightgown or dressing robe

outing sack suit: men's suits made with a sack jacket with patch pockets and bold patterned textiles

panama hat: a high crowned straw hat that became popular during the construction of the Panama Canal

pegged trousers: men's trousers cut full around the hips and thighs and tapering to a close fit at the ankles

pompadour: women's hairstyles arranged up on the head in a high bouffant shape with various knots at the back

racer: a sleek, one-piece tank-style swimsuit initially worn by men in competition sports

S-bend corset: corset designed with a straight-line busk and long hipline that thrust the chest forward and shifted the hips back into a kangaroo stance

wrapper: a woman's loose dressing robe

4 The End of Innocence and World War I 1910–1919

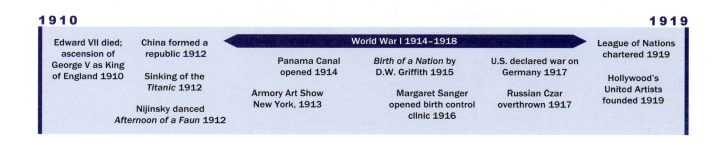

1910					1919
Edward VII died; ascension of George V as King of England 1910	China formed a republic 1912		World War I 1914–1918		League of Nations chartered 1919
		Panama Canal opened 1914	*Birth of a Nation* by D.W. Griffith 1915	U.S. declared war on Germany 1917	
	Sinking of the *Titanic* 1912				Hollywood's United Artists founded 1919
		Armory Art Show New York, 1913	Margaret Sanger opened birth control clinic 1916	Russian Czar overthrown 1917	
	Nijinsky danced *Afternoon of a Faun* 1912				

The World at War

The road that led to the First World War (1914–1918) was paved by decades of European jealousies, rivalries, and dynastic resentments: France's surrender of territory and loss of its 200-year supremacy in Europe following the Franco-Prussian War in 1870; the growing pains of nationalism in Germany, a newly unified nation in 1871; political maneuverings in the Balkans by Russia and its rival, the Austro-Hungarian Empire; and the naval arms race with Britain, which expanded beyond the emerging European powers to include Japan and the United States.

The powder keg finally exploded in 1914 when the heir to the Austro-Hungarian throne was assassinated in Serbia. An outraged Vienna government declared war on the tiny Balkan principality, setting off a chain reaction of conflict all across Europe. Russia mobilized its army to aid its Slavic ally, Serbia. Germany became alarmed at a perceived military threat on both its eastern border by Russia and its western border by long-time enemy, France. The Kaiser decided to knock France out of the war early and then deal with Russia. Germany marched

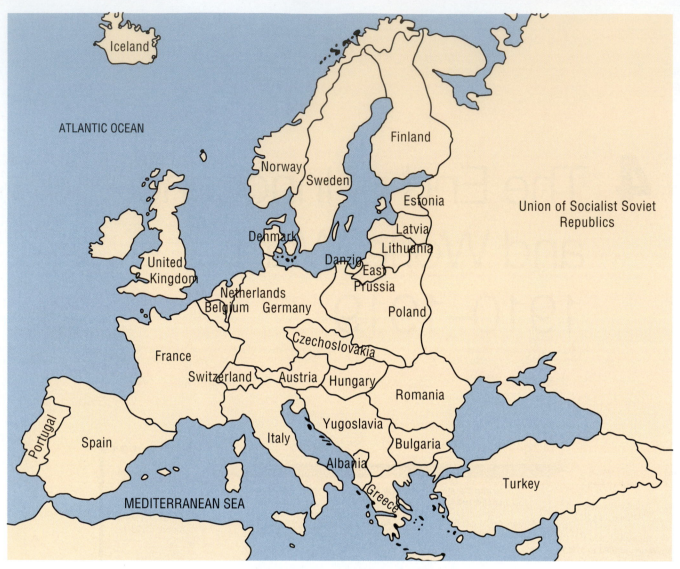

Map of Europe after World War I.

on France through Belgium, whose neutrality had been assured by treaty with England, thus drawing the British into the war on the side of France. Germany was halted by Allied forces just inside the northern French border, and the war settled into a deadly trench warfare for the next four years in which less than ten miles of devastated landscape repeatedly changed hands.

The United States managed to remain neutral until 1917 when Germany declared that all merchant ships entering waters blockaded by the Allies would be subject to submarine attack. After the United States lost four unarmed ships to German U-boats, America declared war and joined the Allies.

Most Americans had been sympathetic to the British and French anyway, pouring millions of dollars in aid to war causes. The Allied propaganda drive in the United States had been highly successful, spreading reports and rumors of German barbarism and blood-thirsty savagery (while suppressing accounts of similar atrocities committed by the Allies). Everyone in the United States participated in the war effort either by fighting "over there" or working toward service and production goals on the home front.

Because of the global empires of these warring nations, the conflict truly became a world war on a scale never seen before. Moreover, technology had redefined warfare in the early twentieth century—machine guns, barbed wire, armored tanks, mammoth cannons, and lethal gas killed more than 10 million young men and wounded another 20 million by the armistice in November 1918.

After the war, economies around the world were in ruins. Population growths declined. The map of Europe was once again dramatically redrawn as the Austro-Hungarian Empire broke into the republics of Austria, Hungary, and Czechoslovakia, and Russia surrendered Poland, Finland, and the Baltic states to their independence.

Whole societies changed as well. The French and British were exhausted victors. The Germans lost their fervor of nationalism and destiny. The Russians struggled with the transition to communism. In the United States, doughboys returned with different views of culture and society to discover that the women they had left to tend home and hearth had changed as well with a new-found independence and self-determination of their own.

American Culture and Society

Many historians view the 1910s as the end of innocence for the United States. During the first half of this decade, the progressive idealism of the Roosevelt years collided with the realism of business greed, extremist social conservatism, and power politics. In the second half of the decade, a world war and a deadly pandemic shattered the optimism and confidence most Americans had felt at the beginning of the new century.

The early 1910s was a period of labor unrest marked by thousands of strikes and lockouts and violence from both workers and corporations. The great masses of the poor who labored in factories, mills, and mines suffered the hardships of twelve-hour shifts, six days a week in unsafe, unhealthy working conditions for low wages. More than two million children worked in hazardous jobs for as little as fifty cents a day. When workers went on strike to seek improvements from management, strikers and union organizers were often brutalized by company guards, many times aided by local police and state militia.

One of the turning points for the U.S. garment industry was the Triangle Shirtwaist factory fire in March 1911. The New York ready-to-wear maker operated production facilities on the upper floors of a ten-story building in which more than 200 women and girls crowded into the sweatshop, sewing piecework. When one of the mountains of discarded fabric remnants caught fire, the panicked workers found they could not escape because the exits had been locked and the fire doors chained by management to prevent theft. In horror, Manhattan pedestrians watched as more than 40 women leaped to their deaths from blazing windows. Another 100 perished in the fire. Firefighters were helpless since ladders only reached to the sixth floor.

From this tragedy, 1800 factories were subsequently investigated, and 56 reform bills were enacted, including new safety codes, worker's compensation, and a reduction of the work week to 54 hours. In addition, the International Ladies' Garment Workers' Union (ILGWU), founded in 1900, grew more powerful with the support of union leagues and national labor leaders whose collaboration strove to set safety standards for clothing manufacturers across the country.

Our Boy Is Uncle Sam's Boy Now

FIGURE 4.1. From small towns and farms all across America, millions of wide-eyed young men registered for military service when the United States entered World War I. Illustration from *Life,* 1917.

HER NEW EASTER MILLINERY

FIGURE 4.2. To ease the labor shortage caused by so many young men in the military, the U.S. government encouraged women to join the workforce as their patriotic duty. Illustration from *Life,* 1918.

Among labor's most vocal support groups were women's organizations. It was during the 1910s that women crusaders began to call themselves feminists. A growing solidarity of American women demanded the vote and other changes to laws that limited their opportunities for education and employment. In 1910, the first suffragette march in New York drew only a few hundred participants; by 1915, the procession numbered more than 40,000. At the end of the decade, Congress passed the Nineteenth Amendment granting women the vote.

Although the First World War had erupted in Europe in 1914, the United States remained neutral until drawn in by German aggression against American shipping in 1917. Almost immediately, American society was upended as 10 million young men registered for the draft and the U.S. government shifted to a wartime footing. (Figure 4.1.) Rationing was immediate, from fuels and medical supplies to food and raw materials for clothing.

With so many men in military service, the labor shortage was immediately acute. Women stepped in to help wherever they could. Soon women were working as telegraph messengers, auto mechanics, streetcar conductors, traffic cops, and postal carriers. (Figure 4.2.) They operated complex heavy equipment in shipyards and farms, and they labored in dangerous munitions factories. More than 11,000 women also provided clerical work to the armed services as Navy "Yeomanettes" and Marine Corps "Marinettes." Women who could not leave the home rolled bandages, collected bushels of peach pits used to make gas mask filters, and taught children to knit socks for soldiers.

The labor shortage also initiated a migration of tens of thousands of African-Americans from southern plantations to northern factories. Though the emigrés found jobs that paid better than those in the Old South, they still faced racial inequalities and new problems with assimilation that eventually led to riots in Chicago, Philadelphia, St. Louis, and Washington, D.C.

One of the lasting results of wartime rationing was the passage of Prohibition in 1917. From the view of many in Congress, breweries and distilleries unnecessarily used up grains critical to war needs. In addition, as the antisaloon leagues had asserted for decades, drinking impaired clear thinking and clean living—both of which were vital to the nation in crisis. When the war was over, most Americans thought the experiment was worth continuing and the Eighteenth Amendment was passed in 1919 making Prohibition permanent.

Just as the war was winding down in the fall of 1918, the world was hit with another calamity that killed millions globally. A virulent flu pandemic swept into Europe from Asia with deadly results. Because Spain was especially hard hit, the outbreak was labeled Spanish Influenza. During the winter of 1918–19, America was ravaged by the disease, killing more than 500,000.

Postwar America was radically different from that of the early 1910s. Organized labor had made great strides in improving working conditions. Advances in technology made mass production faster and more efficient than ever. The New Woman was enfranchised and more self-assured and independent, having earned a paycheck. Prohibition was the law of the land. The doughboys who went abroad to do their duty to make the world "safe for democracy" returned as changed men. Besides having faced the trauma of a horrific war, they had been exposed to sophisticated foreign cultures and mores.

FIGURE 4.3. The controversial hobble skirt was introduced in 1908 and became an international trend by 1910. The design was a slim, tubular shape that tapered to a narrow opening at the hemline. To walk in the hobble skirt, women had to take short, shuffling steps. Left, velvet suit by Paquin; fur-trimmed dress by Paul Poiret; velvet suit by Francis, 1910; right, hobble skirt styles from *Delineator*, 1911.

Women's Fashions 1910–1919

Almost immediately upon Paul Poiret's introduction of his tubular hobble skirt in 1908, virtually all the other couture houses in Paris presented adaptations of narrow, columnar skirts in their collections. Within a year, the trim, hobble skirt silhouette had completely transformed fashion. Initially, hemlines rose from the floor about four inches, but soon dropped again to about two inches above the floor. By the beginning of the 1910s, the slim, vertical look had become universal. (Figure 4.3.)

FIGURE 4.4. At the end of the Edwardian era, the S-bend silhouette was replaced by a more natural, upright look. Skirts narrowed and the volume of layered, frilly petticoats was eliminated. Revivals of the high-waisted, columnar Directoire styles especially reinforced the narrow, vertical contours. Left, striped pekine chiffon dress with lace inset and panniers by Maria Guy, 1911; right, dress of blocked polka dot foulard by Margaine Lacroix, 1911.

For many designers, the narrow, columnar silhouettes recalled the styles of the Directoire era (1795–99), and revivals were widely adapted to all types of clothing from day dresses and evening gowns to outerwear. (Figure 4.4.) The high-waisted Directoire style remained popular until the beginning of World War I in 1914.

Ready-to-wear makers and retailers instantly made the new styles available to the masses. Versions of the tubular hobble skirt were easy to make and required less fabric and production time to manufacture than the bell-shaped Edwardian skirts. For the middle and working classes, though, makers omitted the hobble strap and, instead, developed various flat or box pleats for a less restricting hemline. Their budget-minded customers wanted affordable fashions, but the styles had to be wearable and functional.

For dancing, narrow overskirts with slits to the knees or even to the hips were worn over gathered or pleated underskirts. This practical alteration preserved the slim tube shape, but allowed greater freedom of movement that was especially necessary after the lively tango was introduced from South America in 1911. Tunic-style overskirts also became a popular alternative to the restrictive hobble skirt with hemlines ranging from mid-thigh to seven-eighths lengths—some with multiple tiers of varying lengths.

Diametrically opposite to the hobble skirt were the **jupe-culottes**, or **Turkish trousers**, that Poiret created in his collections of 1910 and 1911. Whereas the designer had shackled women's legs with his hobble skirt, which he had proudly claimed in his 1931 autobiography, he completely freed women's locomotion with the jupe-culotte designs—a freedom that was only available at the time to outdoor enthusiasts who donned knickerbockers or jodhpurs for cycling, hiking, and horseback riding. Three variations of the jupe-culottes were designed for women of varying degrees of self-confidence. Wide-legged pantaloons were worn under a skirt that was shortened to just above the ankles. A second style was a full, baggy skirt stitched at the hem between the ankles to form trousers. The third was a skirt with a long train cut in the shape of a fish tail that could be pulled between the legs to the front and fastened to fashion a sort of trousers. Only the most adventurous women dared don the jupe-culottes. Both the jupe-culottes and the hobble skirt were mightily condemned from pulpits and conservative social organizations around the world. In 1911, *Vogue* hastily predicted, "The jupe-culotte had been relegated to oblivion, where it belongs." In reality, the jupe-culotte was just the beginning of fashion trousers for women, which would continue to gain in popularity through the war years and into the twenties.

In 1913, Paul Poiret broke more new ground when he designed costumes for the ballet *Les Minarets.* He adapted the short, panniered tunics he created for the dancers into fashionable evening wear versions that he combined with a slim skirt for a striking contrast of silhouettes. (Figure 4.5.) Although stunning and innovative, the **minaret tunic**, also called a **lampshade tunic**, was a brief and limited trend on the eve of the First World War.

Two other significant changes in fashion became pervasive as the Edwardian era came to a close. First, skirt hemlines got shorter, initially rising from the pools of fabric about the feet to a length level with the floor, and then to a crop of about four inches by 1914. Second, necklines also underwent major alterations. The high, stiff collars of Queen Alexandra's preference were succeeded by low, rounded necklines, many with the petal-like **Peter Pan collar**. For evening wear, plunging decolletes had remained a prevalent holdover from the previous century. During the early 1910s, though, crisp, fluted Medici collars and lacy ruffs were revived from the Renaissance and attached to wide, open necklines.

A notable shift in color palettes occurred at the beginning of the 1910s. In addition to sweeping away the S-bend silhouette with his hobble skirt, Paul Poiret dispensed with the soft, pale colors that dominated Edwardian fashions. His love of vivid color was particularly inspired by the artistic revolution that occurred in Paris during the pre-World War I years. The Fauves, Expressionists, and Abstractionists shocked the art world with their brilliantly hued paintings. In 1908, Poiret found further inspiration from the richly colored and ornamented costume and set designs of the Ballet Russe, which presented performances of *Scheherazade* and *Cleopatra* in Paris. His designs of these early years featured ensembles of vibrant, contrasting colors that were fresh and dazzling. Instead of the basic black or white stockings of the period, Poiret's showroom models even wore vividly dyed hose and shoes that provided startling accents of color from beneath shortened hemlines.

The heady tempo of fashion change that occurred in the early 1910s did not subside as the first cannons of World War I began blasting. Practical need supplanted the vagaries of hobble skirts and minaret tunics. Busy women doing their part in the war effort needed ease of movement and comfort. The slim lines of the hobble skirts and the tight boning of fitted bodices quickly disappeared. Skirts became fuller, even voluminous, and hemlines rose a few more inches above the ankles. (Figure 4.6.) Many people thought the war would be brief and few in the fashion industry anticipated fabric shortages. Designers were uncertain where to put the waist so a variety of placements were shown in the Paris collections of 1915 to 1917, though most remained slightly raised.

Suits likewise were released from their rigidly tailored construction. Jackets became boxy and shapeless with minimal trim and decorative treatments. Elements of military garb were adapted to women's styles—capelets, epaulets, big patch pockets, gauntlet cuffs, brass buttons, braid, and tassels. Suits were even made of durable cotton corduroy to conserve wool for soldiers' uniforms and blankets. Some women wore jacket, tunic, and skirt coordinates made of soldier blue or khaki broadcloth as an expression of their patriotic support for the boys in uniform.

Tea dresses and evening apparel were more subdued during the war years. The lavish use of decorative trimmings was considered unpatriotic and commonly associated with war profiteering. Colors also were less varied and vibrant because of the ban on imports from Germany, a major source of dyes and textile chemicals.

By the last two years of the war, shortages of fabric were severe, even in the United States, which had only entered the conflict in April 1917. When French government regulations restricted the use of fabric to no more than 4 1/2 yards, skirts and sleeves narrowed once again,

FIGURE 4.5. The panniered minaret tunic, or lampshade tunic, was derived from the ballet costumes designed by Paul Poiret in 1913. Gowns with minaret or lampshade tunics by Paul Poiret, 1913.

FIGURE 4.6. At the beginning of World War I, narrow hobble skirts and boned bodices still prevailed. By 1916, however, fuller, loose fitting fashions better suited busy women in their active war support efforts. Left, tunic dresses from *Delineator,* 1914; right, dresses with short hemlines and full skirts from *Delineator,* 1916.

almost to pre-war styles. (Figure 4.7.) Silk and cotton were more available than wool for civilian clothing. One of the social dilemmas created by the fabric shortages was the advent of short sleeves for day dresses. "Just how these are to be worn is the question," posed *Vogue* in 1918. "One can scarcely picture the American woman going out during the daytime hours with the upper part of her arm uncovered, and of course, shoulder-length gloves are unthinkable for day wear and also an extravagance not to be considered in war times." As with the concerns about women wearing trousers, exceptions in the name of wartime duty became the norm and changed forever long established protocols of style.

The fashion industry further demonstrated its cooperation with war efforts by reducing the variety of models and limiting the assortment of fabrics used. In 1918, one U.S. ready-to-wear maker advised women in an ad to buy clothing that was serviceable and practical because "we can make under war conditions only enough for eight women in every thousand." Other fashion advertisers promoted the idea of patriotic sacrifice to counter customers' discontent with the shortages. "Save the waste of promiscuous styling; save the waste of adulterated

FIGURE 4.7. Due to shortages of fabric and other materials, fashion designers narrowed the silhouettes of dresses and coats. Unlike the slim hobble skirt contours, though, the wartime styles were softer with a generous fit. Dresses with narrow, short skirts and military influences from *Delineator*, 1918.

Women's Trousers

During the war years, practical needs forced social changes on all fronts, including fashions. Although Poiret had introduced Turkish trousers for women years earlier—and women's dress reform advocates had campaigned for feminine trousers for decades—it was the necessity of women working outside the home in factories and in public services that finally dispelled the social stigma of women in trousers. As men marched off to war, women filled their job vacancies in record numbers, working as streetcar conductors, auto mechanics, shipyard steeplejacks, operators of industrial equipment in munitions factories, house painters, and carpenters, to name but a few. (Figure 4.8.) The common types of overalls and trousers for women were made for ease, comfort, and safety, not as a fashion statement. Even though ads by ready-to-wear makers of the time promised a fit "made along lines that are essentially feminine," the look was anything but flattering to the female figure.

Nevertheless, once the door was opened for women to be seen in public wearing work overalls and trousers, other forms of the bifurcated garment were soon adopted for the feminine wardrobe. In 1918, a *Vogue* editorial expounded upon the "paradoxical trousers" and how women had quickly appropriated various forms of the masculine garment for themselves: the pajama trousers for loungewear at home, the pajama suits for sleepwear, and even men's swimsuits. "Perhaps it is because she realizes the charming betrayal of her feminine quality that woman is finding so many excuses nowadays for taking to trousers," concluded *Vogue.*

FIGURE 4.8. As a considerable number of women entered the labor force during the First World War, the need for safety and function in dress provided opportunities for female workers to wear various forms of trousers in public. Photos, 1917–1918.

FIGURE 4.9. In the fashion seasons following World War I, Paris couturiers were largely uncertain what to design for the modern woman. Hemlines, waistlines, and shirt shapes varied widely with a confusing array of revivalisms and contrived silhouettes.

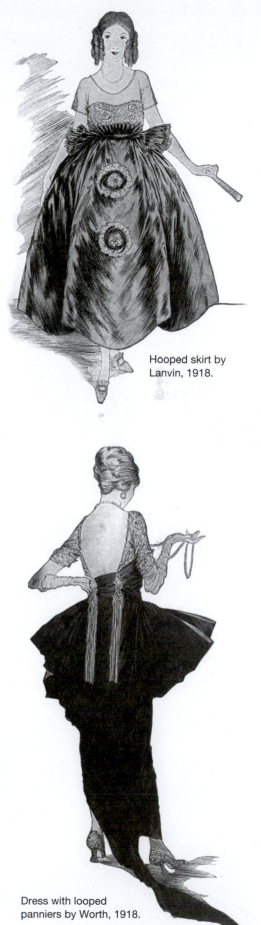

Hooped skirt by Lanvin, 1918.

Dress with looped panniers by Worth, 1918.

fabrics and careless tailoring," declared a wartime Wooltex ad. Similar messages filled editorials of the fashion press.

Despite all the restrictions and limitations with materials, labor, shipping, and finance, Paris couturiers continued to produce collections on time each season throughout the war. Although some designers, notably Poiret and Molyneux, closed their salons and enlisted in the military, the other houses did all they could to provide for the export demands. A French correspondent for *Vogue* wrote in 1918, "The manufacture of materials and articles of luxury is so very much on the decline that we must watch over it and support it in every possible way. This is a national duty." Even though there were movements in the United States and England to take this opportunity to establish their own couture industry, all eyes around the world still turned to Paris for fashion direction, and the mass media continued to report excitedly on the French collections.

Open-front frock with chemisette and a pleated skirt and jacket with high collar from *Vogue*, 1918.

In the first years after the war ended, couturiers seemed uncertain how to design for the modern woman. Since shortages persisted as industries converted to peacetime manufacturing and international trade recovered, designers continued to face limited options with fabrics and materials. Skirts varied widely in width and shape as well as in length—from mid-calf to just at the ankles. All sorts of panniers, hoops, and bustle treatments were tried. Waistlines were more confusing than ever, ranging from the raised Empire line to the dropped "Oriental" line just below the hips, and several points in between. (Figure 4.9.) Attempts were made to revive the restricting corset, but women overwhelmingly refused them. Poiret failed to connect with the new woman and repeatedly tried to revive styles that were richly ornamented casings of the body, which were rejected by all but the nouveau riche.

Although some women were ready for a return to the glamour, indulgence, and femininity of prewar fashions, by and large, most women of the postwar years wanted modernism—clothes with comfort and ease, and a look that was a clear departure from the frilly, corseted Edwardian or hobbled styles. A few designers—Molyneux, Patou, and Chanel, in particular—were forward thinking enough to focus on the straight, simple chemise that would be the prevalent look of the coming decade.

Women's Outerwear 1910–1919

By the beginning of the 1910s, coats narrowed in keeping with the trend of the hobble skirt. Much of the outerwear at the time was designed with an unmarked waistline. Hemlines were more varied than a few years earlier, ranging from just above the knees to ankle length. Decorative treatments were minimal. Wrap coats became the fresh trend just before World War I, especially styles with cutaway tulip hemlines. (Figure 4.10.)

When skirts widened during the war, coats were cut full and loose to accommodate the new dress silhouettes. Military accoutrement such as epaulets, braid, oversized patch pockets, and gauntlet cuffs were adapted from masculine uniforms. When dress hemlines began to rise, coats were cropped shorter as well, usually a few inches above the skirt edge like the one shown in Figure 4.10. Quilted hoods were revived from the previous century. Since buildings were often unheated to reserve fuel supplies and women had to walk more due to a shortage of taxis, the use of fur increased during the war years—including an abundance of pelts from opossums, foxes, and other more common varieties. Similarly, as wool and leather became scarce for civilian apparel, heavy cotton corduroy was frequently used for coats and jackets.

As the war entered its fourth year in 1918, shortages of fabric and other materials needed by the fashion industry led to narrower designs in outerwear. In addition to the simplicity of cut, the austerity in surface adornment remained in effect for women's coats. After the war ended in November 1918, coat and jacket proportions remained narrow but hemlines dropped several inches, some to the ankles.

Women's Sports Apparel 1910–1919

In the years just before World War I, women of the leisure classes began to play polo, which, unlike hunting and jumping, required them to ride astride the horse. Although some feminine equestrian costumes had begun to include jodhpurs just after the turn of the century, they were almost completely hidden by long jacket skirts extending to the ankles. By the early teens, though, some jacket hemlines had been cropped to mid-thigh for the polo equestrienne. (Figure 4.11.)

As with their Edwardian counterparts, most women participating in sports simply wore loose fitting versions of day clothes. Where the challenge for women in the previous decade had been to contend with the heavy volume of skirts and petticoats, in the early 1910s, the effort was movement in the confining, narrow styles.

One notable change that occurred in the 1910s was the acceptance of daytime short-sleeve tops in public. Even though some women in the Edwardian period had rolled up their long sleeves to the forearms or even the elbows to better swing a tennis racket or golf club, the etiquette at the time still prohibited bare arms in public before evening, particularly if men were present. The social and stylistic evolution of short sleeves in the 1910s was subtle but significant.

Overcoats from Franklin Simon, 1912.

Narrow contours from *Delineator*, 1918.

Wartime ease and comfort from Montgomery Ward, 1917.

FIGURE 4.10. Coat styles of the early 1910s followed the narrow, columnar contours of the hobble dresses. After World War I began in 1914, outerwear became looser and shorter. As the war dragged on, shortages of material led to narrower cuts.

FIGURE 4.11. Specialized sports attire like jodhpurs was worn by women for certain activities like polo or hunting, but for the most part, they wore loose fitting versions of day wear. Left, hobble skirt and waist, 1913; center, doe-skin polo jodhpurs, long cheviot coat, and silk shirt, 1915; right, short-sleeve blouse with gingham skirt, 1916.

Women's Underwear and Sleepwear 1910–1919

As noted in the previous chapter, orsets were dramatically redesigned at the end of the Edwardian period. A more natural, upright shape with less constriction of the waist was developed with longer lines to define and emphasize a youthful-looking figure. The construction of corsets of the 1910s continued the straightline control of the waist and hips. (Figure 4.12.)

During the hobble skirt years, petticoats were discarded in favor of lightweight chemise-type slips. However, when skirts became full again during World War I, petticoats were revived, though no longer with the multiple-layering nor the excessive, frilly decorations.

With the new styles of narrow skirts and longline corsets, short combination drawers became particularly favored. Similarly, long union suits were abandoned as hemlines rose. (Figure 4.13.)

Since the tops of corsets were cut lower, a camisole-type of the **brassiere** became a more comfortable and practical alternative to the old forms of bust bodices. (Figure 4.14.) The first designs constructed specifically for an articulated support of the breasts were patented in the mid-1910s.

FIGURE 4.12. Illustrations in magazines and advertising for the new style of corset in the early 1910s exaggerated the look of a trim waist and narrow, youthful-looking hips. Lyra corsets, 1911.

FIGURE 4.13. The narrow hobble skirt required less bulky forms of undergarments than the Edwardian styles of full, flounced petticoats and long, voluminous drawers. Lightweight chemises and short combination drawers were more suited to the trim fit of pre-war fashions. Lingerie of nainsook and Cluny lace from Bonwit Teller, 1912.

FIGURE 4.14. As the shape of corsets shifted lower under the bosom in the 1910s, variations of camisole-type brassieres became popular. From DeBoise: left, Irish linen brassiere, 1912; right, silk bandeau brassiere, 1919.

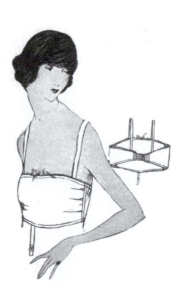

LE COUCHER DES INGÉNUES

OU LES DÉSHABILLÉS DE BON GOUT.

FIGURE 4.15. The variety of women's sleepwear in the 1910s expanded to include shorter nightgowns and pajama sets. Left, kimono robes from National, 1916; right, French lingerie and sleepwear by Premet: two embroidered chemises, striped silk "travelling" nightgown, satin camisole, and silk print pajamas, 1919.

Silk princess style nightgowns with matching robes and the basic nightshirt of linen, flannel, or cotton remained the most prevalent forms of sleepwear in the 1910s. Although women's pajamas were available by the late Victorian years, the style only became widely adopted during World War I when large numbers of women experienced the comfort of overalls and trousers while working outside the home. (Figure 4.15.)

Women's Swimwear 1910–1919

By the beginning of the 1910s, the proliferation of affordable, mass-produced autos made weekend excursions to lakes and beaches possible for a broader spectrum of socioeconomic classes. Ready-to-wear makers tapped into the resulting demand for beachwear and swimsuits, producing inexpensive knock-offs of chic couture styles seen at the fashionable resorts. In 1912, *Vogue* insisted that it was "absolutely compulsory to have a bathing suit as charming and becoming as an evening gown." Swimwear overskirt designs became as varied as day

FIGURE 4.16. In the early 1910s, the narrow silhouette of dresses was also applied to swimwear, thereby reducing the volume and contours of sleeves, bloomers, and skirts. By the end of the decade, swimwear had sleeveless tops, shorter hemlines, and close-fitting menswear pantalettes. One-piece swimsuits shocked Edwardian sensibilities and were even prohibited at many public beaches. Above left, Paris designs, 1912; above right, swimsuits from Bonwit Teller, 1917; bottom, one-piece styles from Jantzen, 1918.

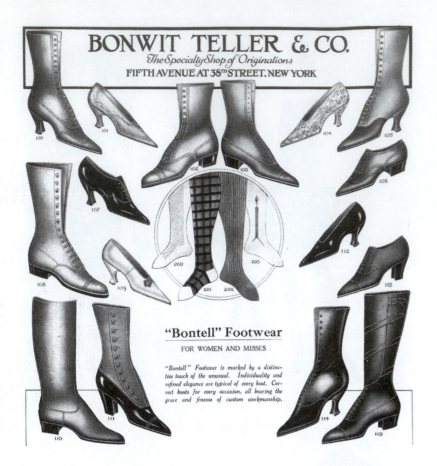

FIGURE 4.17. Women's shoes of the 1910s largely continued the variety of styles of the previous decade. Bontell pumps, street shoes, and boots featuring Louis heels, Cuban heels, and low or flat heels, 1917.

dresses with all the same complexities of cut and line. The new narrow silhouette of dresses was also adapted to swimwear, forcing a reduction in the volume of bloomers although skirt hemlines remained at the knees, and bodices were still sleeved. (Figure 4.16.) At the same time, colorfast silks and taffetas were the most popular fabrics for swimwear. Women on the Continent even began to scandalously appear in public without stockings.

During the war years, women adopted various forms of men's trousers for work clothes, sleepwear, and swimwear. The sleeveless jersey tunic and cropped trunks that had been a standard swimsuit for men for decades were appropriated by women with little modification for a feminine fit or decorative treatments. The menswear influences of the short, sleeveless tunic and close-fitting trunks (usually attached at the waistline of the tunic in the feminine form) such as those shown in Figure 4.16 were also applied to other versions of women's swimwear by the end of the 1910s.

Women's Shoes 1910–1919

As hemlines rose, shoe makers began to offer more varied designs and colors of shoes. By the early 1910s, pumps were increasingly more common for street wear than ankle boots except in inclement weather, although the high-top button shoe remained common into the early 1920s. (Figure 4.17.) For street pumps, the vamp was usually high, covering the instep to the ankles with a tongue for lace-ups or a variety of strap treatments for buckle styles. For evening wear, pumps were cut lower with a throat opened to the toes and even pierced sides. In 1917, *Vogue* noted with a play on words that "the last [the industry term for the shoe upper] is the first in footwear . . . slim and squared at the tip is the new last." The sharply pointed toe that had continued since the beginning of the century was now reshaped with a subtly chiseled square tip.

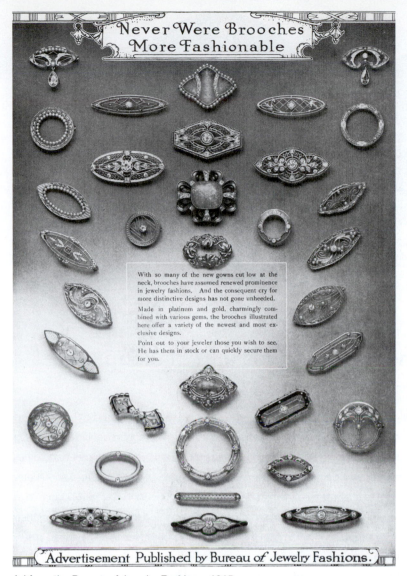

Ad from the Bureau of Jewelry Fashions, 1915.

Seed pearl jewelry by Frederick, 1912.

Costume jewelry by Henry Fishel, 1918.

Women's Jewelry 1910–1919

In the pre–World War I years, a favorite jewelry style was the lustrous look of seed pearls arranged in aggregate forms for earrings, brooches, pendants, and hair ornaments. Another popular trend was the exotic Eastern motifs made with colorful stones or enameling—an influence from Poiret's vividly hued fashion designs. By the second half of the teens, jewelry began to reflect the influences of art movements such as the Jugenstil in Germany and the Viennese Secession—precursors of the art deco style of the twenties. Jewelry was scaled down in size compared with Edwardian pieces, and designs were geometric and clean-edged. (Figure 4.18.)

FIGURE 4.19. Wartime safety needs and influences from movies inspired many woman to sheer their long tresses for a modern look. Short hair cuts: left, 1916; right, 1918.

FIGURE 4.20. In the 1910s, social mores toward makeup changed and women expanded their beauty regimens to include eyeliner, eyeshadow, cheek rouge, and lipstick. Rigaud's ad depicting lipstick and the purse compact, 1918.

Women's Hairstyles and Makeup 1910–1919

By the early 1910s, some French and English women in the vanguard of high fashion began to experiment with short hairstyles. American women lagged behind in escaping the Victorian cult of hair. The compromise was the much reduced pompadour and other coiled or knotted arrangements that kept the hair piled up off the neck and shoulders. When fashionable stars of the cinema adopted the trend of short hair and appeared in contemporary-themed films, women around the world copied the modern looks of their movie idols. (Figure 4.19.) During the First World War, practical needs inspired many women working in factories to shear off lengthy locks for convenience and safety.

In the early 1910s, social mores began to change toward makeup. Movies exalted women made beautiful and glamorous with eyeliner, eyeshadow, cheek rouge, and lipstick. Even "beauty patches" were revived from the eighteenth century. Cosmetics makers saturated women's magazines with ads depicting famous and beautiful women in full makeup. (Figure 4.20.) Five-and-dime department store chains like Woolworth's began to stock a wide assortment of makeup that office girls and salesclerks could afford. In 1915, Maurice Levy made lip-tinting more convenient with his invention of the metal tube dispenser for lipstick. The application of makeup had become such a high art that publishers and women's magazines commonly offered advice on how to achieve the best results with cosmetics. Facial powder, for instance, was no longer merely applied to eliminate a shiny nose. In 1918, the Women's Institute published a fashion and beauty guide, *The Secrets of Distinctive Dress,* in which the editors suggested methods of blending tinted powders to emphasize various skintones and hair colors or to minimize facial features such as a prominent nose or receding chin. By the end of the First World War, the use of makeup was so pervasive that women felt at ease to touch up their lipstick or face powder in public, previously a private function of the boudoir toilette.

As short sleeves became more accepted for daytime dresses during the fabric shortages of the war years, razor manufacturers began to target women with messages about shaving arms and especially underarms. "The woman of fashion says the underarm must be as smooth as the face," cajoled a 1915 Gillette ad.

Women's Hats 1910–1919

The massive sizes of late Edwardian hats remained popular until the mid-1910s. (Figure 4.21.) The fit of the huge hats, as *Vogue* observed in 1912, caused brims to "brood low and darkly over the face." A cartoon of the time suggested that milliners cut eyeholes in the descending brims for practicality. As the shapes became larger, the decorative treatments likewise increased in size and quantity. Enormous bows spread across picture hats, feathers cascaded down the back or towered upward, and turbans were piled high with volumes of fabric and trim.

During World War I, hats were much reduced in size and decoration. "Doubtless it is the war," commented a fashion editor upon seeing the "frugal trimmings" of Paris hats in 1915. Instead of mass and piles of trim defining the contours of hats, designs of the late 1910s were sculpturally linear. Wide picture hats remained popular, though now with crisp, aerodynamic looking brims and minimal trim. The most striking look of the period was the verticality of hats. Tall toques and turbans rose closely from the sides of the head, and the crowns of other models were high cylinders, somewhat resembling the Victorian man's top hat with a wide brim. Feathers or the tips of bows often pointed sharply skyward to reinforce the vertical lines. The **cloche** at this time was a high crowned hat with a shallow brim that angled downward over the brow. Women who cropped their hair to work in factories and wartime services needed a hat that did not require pins to stay on.

Women's Accessories 1910–1919

Despite the narrow, streamlined hobble look of the prewar years followed by the simplified austerity of wartime dress, a full accoutrement of accessories was as necessary for a woman in the 1910s as it had been for the Edwardian lady. In addition to attention to her selection of hat, shoes, and jewelry, a woman also carefully considered: a variety of gloves depending on the season and time of day, decorative hosiery for the shortened skirt hemlines, hair ornaments, assorted types of handbags, parasols and umbrellas, evening fans, and detachable collars and cuffs. (Figure 4.22.)

Although machine-made lace was affordable and greatly varied in design, the snob appeal of handmade lace for collars, cuffs, neckline fillers, and bodice embellishments led to a "fascinating fad" of collecting antique lace, according to *Vogue* in 1911. "Gowns may become priceless creations when encrusted with rare old laces from milady's cabinet." Even as fashions became more simplified during the war years, lace remained a favorite accent for dresses and accessories.

Handbags of the 1910s retained the small dimensions and shapes of the Edwardian styles. Colors, though, were more vibrant, and surfaces were decorated with stylized geometric motifs inspired by the avant-garde art movements in Europe at the time.

Parasols were still a necessary accessory for ladies venturing out into the sun although types of the 1910s had abandoned the frills and excessive decoration of Edwardian versions.

FIGURE 4.21. Hats in the prewar years of the 1910s were enormous and decorated with bold, oversized trimmings. During the First World War, hats were reduced in scale and decoration. By the end of the decade, sleek contours reflected the modernity of the machine age.

Rose trimmed picture hat by Weiss, 1911.

Turban with wings by Madeleine Lechat, 1911.

Wide-brim leghorn hat with silk roses by Lewis, 1912.

Straw hat with velvet bow by Hennard, 1912.

Straw hat with taffeta ruffles by Carlier, 1912.

Cloche by Jeanne Lanvin, 1916.

Tailored straw hat by Lucie Hamar, 1916.

Close turban of chenille by Joseph, 1918.

Velvet hat with ostrich plume by Joseph, 1918.

Velvet hat by Thurn, 1918.

"Aircraft" hat by Bendel, 1918.

Braided turban by Jeanne Duc, 1918.

FIGURE 4.22. Despite the practical austerity of wartime clothing in the 1910s, the "necessaries of dress," as noted by the B. Altman ad, included a wide range of accessories for the correctly dressed woman.

Fox muffs and scarves from Charles Williams, 1916.

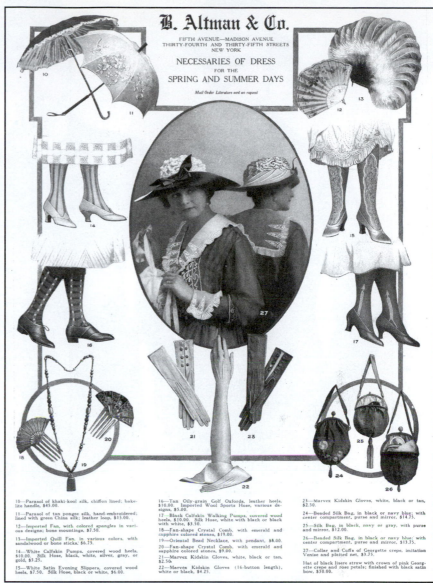

Parasols, collars and cuffs, fans, hair pins, gloves, handbags, and hosiery, 1917.

Combs, 1913.

Beaded bags by M. Markel, 1919.

Flat satin hair bow, 1914.

Detachable collars and matching jabots, 1912.

FIGURE 4.23. As women's fashions became narrow and slim in the early 1910s, men's styles also adopted a more trim, youthful look. Bulky padding was eliminated from jackets and waistlines were more fitted. Trousers narrowed for a longer, leaner look. Three-piece suits in patterned wool cassimere from National Suits, 1916.

Men's Fashions 1910–1919

By the early 1910s, the silhouette of men's clothing changed to follow that of women's with an emphasis on trim, youthful contours. (Figure 4.23.) Young men were at the forefront of the civilized world's consciousness as a world war erupted and vast armies of youths were sent off to fight each other in distant lands.

Even though during the late Edwardian period men's suits had begun to show some contouring at the waist, the new look of the 1910s was a marked contrast. Jackets were snugly fitted and waistlines were raised "in the new military tendency" as one menswear ad noted. Skirts were shortened, emphasizing the longer, leaner look of trouser legs. Shoulders and sleeves were stripped of their excessive padding for a natural shoulderline. The five yards of fabric that had been required for a suit of 1905 was reduced to 3 1/2 yards by 1915.

Sport jackets were likewise contoured to the new slender masculine ideal. Belted varieties of jackets flattered the youthful, narrow waist. During the 1910s, the sport jacket became more integrated into the masculine wardrobe and was often substituted for the sack suit jacket at business or social functions. According to the copy in a 1917 Kuppenheimer ad, from which the artwork is shown in Figure 4.24, sport jackets were "as much sought after for general wear as for sports and the country."

When the war ended and droves of young men returned to civilian life, they were eager to discard their military uniforms for "civvies" (civilian dress). Menswear designers continued to emphasize youthful, slender styling that was well-suited to the lean builds of the returning war heroes. The fitted, natural-shoulder jacket and slim, leggy trousers continued as the prevalent silhouette—a look that would dominate the subsequent decade as well.

The coat cut shirt with its center front button closure had become the standard style by the 1910s. During World War I, governmental regulations required manufacturers to find ways of conserving commodity materials, and the superfluous detachable collar was a style casualty of war needs. When the war ended, men who had become accustomed to the comfort and ease of the turned-down collar of the uniform shirt refused to return to the high, stiff, detachable collars.

FIGURE 4.24. Sport jackets with half belts in the back defined the narrow waistline and reinforced the trim youthful looks of the time. Kuppenheimer sport jacket, 1917.

Men's Sports Attire and Outerwear 1910–1919

The sports attire of the athlete and outdoor enthusiast of the 1910s changed little from the previous decade. Advances in knitting processes improved the fit and comfort of many types of manufactured sports clothes.

As with the Edwardian man, for golfing, hunting, or hiking, the knickerbocker suit remained the most prevalent attire. For the weekend golfer or tennis player, though, everyday street clothes were worn. The first half-sleeves began to appear at club competition. In 1911, *Vogue* reported an innovative new "tennis shirt" made with short sleeves and attached drawers cut as a single piece to prevent the shirt tail from coming undone during a game.

FIGURE 4.25. Men's outerwear of the 1910s became narrow and more fitted with natural shoulderlines and shorter hemlines. Fitted topcoat by Kuppenheimer, 1913.

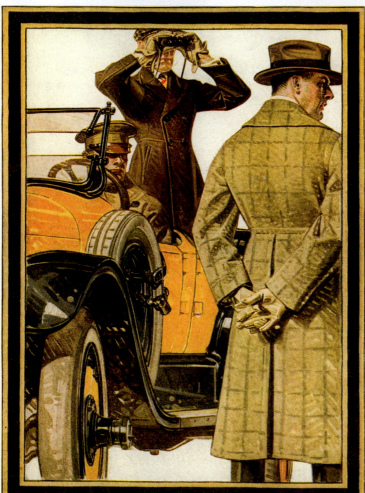

FIGURE 4.26. During World War I, men's outerwear designs were influenced by military styles. Trim waistlines were raised and skirts became fuller. Sleeves were widened for greater ease of movement. Kuppenheimer coats, 1918.

FIGURE 4.27. Men's underwear continued the trend toward lightweight fabrics and briefer cuts in the 1910s. B.V.D. athletic union suit and coat cut undershirt with knee-length drawers, 1915.

Men's outerwear of the early 1910s adopted the slender, fitted proportions of suit jackets. Sleeves were narrow and hemlines were shortened to about the knees. Waistlines were trim, often emphasized by half belts in the back that defined the youthful silhouette like the style shown in Figure 4.25. As with suit jackets, the natural shoulderline was applied to outerwear as well.

From about 1914 until the end of the decade, the design of men's outerwear was influenced by the ease and comfort of military apparel. (Figure 4.26.) Sleeves were fuller, armholes deeper, and collars wider. The raglan sleeve afforded more freedom of movement and was applied to many types of outerwear. Waistlines remained slim but were raised above the natural position. On belted styles, skirts flared fuller.

Fur coats became especially popular with men in the late 1910s. As with cloth coats, fur styles were fitted to the slender masculine contours. Fur coats with half belts in the back were the favorite.

Men's Underwear and Swimwear 1910–1919

Men's underwear of the 1910s continued the same basic forms of the previous two decades. The assorted variants of the union suit remained the most popular types. New knitting technologies made possible the "double body" longjohn made with a double thickness over the torso, and a single thickness over the legs and arms. The new "athletic" cut of the union suit featured a tank-style top with shorts cropped above the knees. (Figure 4.27.) During the war years, when wool was strictly rationed, some men's underwear was made of one-third wool blended with combed cotton.

FIGURE 4.28. Men's swimwear of the 1910s continued the Edwardian tank style tunics with thigh-length modesty skirts and long trunks. Belted knit trunks with tank swim shirt and two-piece knit swim suit from Clement Company, 1915.

Swimwear also changed little in the 1910s. For young men, sleeveless tank tops became more popular than the half-sleeve and short-sleeve styles. Tops of contrasting colors or, particularly, white, added new flair to otherwise redundant looks of men's swimwear. The length of the tops with their long modesty skirts continued to extend to the upper thighs, and drawstring-waist drawers were still knee length. (Figure 4.28.)

Men's Accessories 1910–1919

The hat was still the most important accessory for men. The assortment of Edwardian hat styles shown in chapter 3, Figure 3.31, was typical of the 1910s as well.

Men's footwear, likewise, was basically a continuation of previous styles. High-top street boots with sharply pointed toes remained the most prevalent until the end of the decade when the ease of lace-up oxfords became increasingly favored for the fast-paced war years. The

Bulb toe street shoes with fabric uppers, 1915.

Army officer's dress shoe, 1918.

Razor toe street shoes, 1918.

FIGURE 4.29. Edwardian styles of men's shoes continued into the 1910s. Sharp pointed high top boots were the most common street shoe although wide bulb toe styles were a favorite fashion statement for younger men.

wide bulb toe shoes were equally popular with young dandies through to the end of the decade. (Figure 4.29.)

The wide, pointed-tip tie secured with a four-in-hand knot was the most popular neckwear of 1910s. Vivid colors and bold prints offset the somberness of the navy or charcoal suit. (Figure 4.30.)

Stiff, detachable shirt collars were still common through the war years. (Figure 4.31.) By the end of the decade, though, shirts with attached collars were in greatest demand since millions of ex-soldiers sought the convenience and comfort of the soft shirt styles of their uniforms.

During the First World War, the wristwatch gained in popularity and gradually made the pocket watch and chain duo a quaint anachronism. Other acceptable forms of men's jewelry, provided they were not too flashy, included cuff links, collar buttons, shirt studs, vest buttons, and tie stickpins.

FIGURE 4.31. Stiff, detachable collars were required dress for business and special occasions. Makers provided instructions in flyers and ads for attaching collars without damaging them. Arrow ad, 1910.

FIGURE 4.30. The most popular neckwear of the 1910s was wide with a pointed tip secured with a four-in-hand knot. Boldly patterned silk ties with stitched-on easy-slide bands on the backs, 1916.

Men's Grooming and Hairstyles 1910–1919

During the 1910s, men were further encouraged to be clean shaven when menswear and images in popular culture, particularly movies, began to emphasize youthful looks. Facial hair became more associated with men of mature years and bygone Victorian times. Men's hairstyles remained closely cropped around the sides with the volume on the top and parts on the left.

Children's Clothing 1910–1919

By the First World War, the exigencies of materials shortages impacted even the lingering Edwardian obsession of overdressing babies. Layettes were reduced to a full, loose dress—long for newborns and shortened to the ankles once the child could sit up—combined with a short, loose vest or wide sacque, and booties. (Figure 4.32.) Even bonnets were now reserved primarily for chilly days and outings. Decorative trim, too, was greatly simplified.

FIGURE 4.32. During the First World War, shortages of materials led to fewer components of the layette. Garments and accessories were also more simply made with less frills and decorative treatments. Macy's ad, 1918.

FIGURE 4.33. At the end of the 1910s, girls' dresses were comfortably loose-fitting and full. Girls could move more freely in the high-waisted or chemise styles. Girl's dresses from *Vogue,* 1918.

In glancing through pictorial magazines of the early 1910s, one will notice that the hemlines of some young girls' dresses were thigh-high short, many hardly more than a band of fabric or a ruffle attached to the edge of the hip-line waist. Yet this was not a pervasive trend judging from the illustrations in mass market catalogs and the several editions of *Vogue*'s "Children's Fashions Number" at the time. Instead, hemlines of girls' dresses during the 1910s remained constant with those of the preceding three decades: toddlers and girls through about age twelve with hemlines at the knees, teen girls of about thirteen to fifteen with crops at mid-calf, and young misses of age fifteen to seventeen with skirts to the ankles. (Figure 4.33.) Even when the vertical, columnar look of the hobble skirt was applied to all forms of women's fashions in the early 1910s, young girls' dresses remained full and loose.

For boys in the 1910s, knee-length short pants were widely adapted from active sports-wear costumes and applied to young boys' suits although older boys continued to dress in

FIGURE 4.34. During the First World War, boys' clothing featured many elements adapted from military uniforms. For young boys, short pants replaced knickerbockers and long, heavy stockings were discarded in favor of bare legs. Macy's ad, 1918.

knickerbocker suits. Legs were bared with the new cropped pants styles, but long, thick stockings, usually in black, continued to be required for knickerbockers. During the war, elements of military uniforms were adapted to boys' clothing, including the raised waistline, epaulets, braid, and insignia. (Figure 4.34.) Hightop shoes remained more common with boys than with girls into the late teens.

Playwear for both girls and boys afforded the first real freedom for children since the clothing of the late eighteenth century. School uniforms had helped ease the transition to loose, comfortable clothes throughout the child's wardrobe. Boys could romp in easy fitting overalls and short sets. Girls enjoyed the comfort of nonbinding, high-waisted dresses, some with Empire waists or shoulderline yokes, and full, chemise styles that hung loosely from the shoulders. Heavy, black hose and high, button shoes were discarded in favor of short, knit socks and low, strappy shoes.

Review

By the beginning of the 1910s, the narrow, vertical silhouette that Paul Poiret had introduced with his hobble skirt designs became the universal look. The contours recalled the styles of the Directoire era, which were a favorite inspiration for designers until the start of World War I.

Throughout the prewar years, Poiret's designs were innovative and influential. His jupe-culottes, or Turkish trousers, forecasted a trend of trousers for women that would become increasingly common in subsequent decades. His minaret tunics inspired fresh new looks by his peers and ready-to-wear makers alike.

When World War I erupted in Europe, fashion reacted with an abrupt shift in the fit and shape of clothes. Busy women active in war efforts needed clothes that provided comfort and ease of movement. Fitted bodices and long, narrow skirts disappeared in favor of loose-fitting, full skirts with shorter hemlines. Waistlines were raised. Jackets and coats became full and shapeless. Colors were more subdued and decorative treatments were minimal. Women went to work outside the home wearing trousers for practical and safety needs. As wartime shortages of fabric and other materials became acute, fashions once again narrowed, though with a softer and easier fit than the hobble skirt looks of the early part of the decade.

After the war, Paris couturiers seemed unsure how to design for the modern woman. In the midst of all sorts of revivals and exaggerated silhouettes, a few designers focused on the simple straight chemise—the look that would dominate the post-war decade.

When women's styles adopted a more youthful, slim silhouette in the early 1910s, menswear likewise became trim and more shaped. Jackets were shortened and fitted with an emphasis on a natural shoulderline and a slender waist. Trousers were cut narrow. The sport jacket became an acceptable substitute for the suit jacket as business dress.

Another important shift in menswear during the 1910s was the increased popularity of the open-front soft shirt that would soon eclipse the old bosom-front styles. In addition, the high, stiff detachable collar gradually disappeared as dress shirts with attached turned-down collars became the preferred type.

During the war years, military styling influenced the looks of men's knitwear, coats, and shoes.

Children's clothing began an evolution toward freedom and comfort in the 1910s. For young girls, the Edwardian dresses with dropped waists and frilly excesses were replaced in the 1910s by simple, loose-fitting styles. The young miss now enjoyed the natural fit of the youthful women's fashions, which better suited the trim, adolescent figure. Boys' clothing also began to shift more toward ease and comfort with the adaptation of playsuits with shorts as an alternative to knickerbockers.

1. Identify and describe two of the innovative fashion looks created by Paul Poiret in the early 1910s. What were his sources of inspiration for his designs and color palettes?

2. How did World War I impact the design of women's fashions?

3. What were three different forms of trousers worn by women in the 1910s?

4. What were two notable distinctions about couture fashions in the first years following World War I?

5. Compare and contrast the cut and line of men's everyday sack suits of the 1910s with those of the Edwardian period.

6. How did children's fashions evolve toward freedom and comfort in the 1910s?

research and portfolio projects

Research

1. Write a research paper on how women's changing roles in society between 1910 and 1919 impacted fashion. Identify the causes of social change and which types of clothing were altered by the changes.

Portfolio

1. Create modern adaptations of Paul Poiret's jupe-culottes and minaret tunic in your sketchbook. Imitate the couturier's use of color, textile pattern, and texture in a modern version, retaining the essence of the pre-World War I silhouette, but updating the concepts with today's fit, accessories, and hairstyles. Include color photocopies or digital scans of the Poiret designs used as models with a written description of each.

dress terms

brassiere: various forms of bust support garments

cloche: women's close-fitting, high-crowned hat with shallow brim

jupe-culottes (also called Turkish trousers): women's wide-legged pantaloons of the early 1910s

minaret tunic (also called a lampshade tunic): short, panniered tunics that flared into a funnel shape from the waist

Peter Pan collar: low, rounded neckline with a petal-shaped collar used on women's and children's clothing

5 The Jazz and Gin Age 1920–1929

1920							1929
First meeting League of Nations 1920	Tutankhamen's tomb discovered 1922	Death of Lenin 1922	Paris Decorative Arts Expo 1925	Stalin assumed power in USSR 1927	Penicillin discovered 1928		U.S. stock market crash 1929
U.S. women granted right to vote 1920	Italy's Mussolini became "Duce" 1921	First Nazi congress in Munich 1923	Fitzgerald's *Great Gatsby* 1925	Lindbergh's solo flight across Atlantic 1927	Hirohito made Emperor of Japan 1928		First Academy Awards 1929
Prohibition began in U.S. 1920	Valentino in *The Sheik* 1921		Gershwin's *Rhapsody in Blue* 1924	First talking movie *The Jazz Singer* 1927			Thomas Wolfe's *Look Homeward, Angel* 1929

Politics and Nations of the 1920s

In the aftermath of World War I, central Europe was entirely reshaped. Following their capitulation, Germany, Russia, and the Austro-Hungarian Empire were carved into new countries or ceded vast territories to existing nations. Among the new countries were the republics of Austria, Hungary, Czechoslovakia, Finland, and Yugoslavia, along with a reconstituted Poland and Lithuania. Democracy was further expanded across Europe when all three of the defeated imperial powers replaced their monarchies with other forms of government.

One of the primary concerns that the newly formed League of Nations had dealt with in redrawing the map of Europe was the fear of revolution. In the last years of the war, Russia had been torn apart by its civil war, which ultimately resulted in the seizure of power by communists. The League tried to make the new democratic nations as large and strong as possible to resist the expansion of communism. It was this "Red Scare" that gradually empowered the fascist parties and governments that emerged in Italy, Germany, and Spain during the 1920s and 1930s. Totalitarianism seemed to be the most certain method of extinguishing the violence and dangers of communism. Demagogues such as Benito Mussolini of Italy and Adolf Hitler of Germany ascended to power largely through the promise of resisting communism.

Even in the United States of the 1920s, fear of the Red Menace was pervasive. Perceived alien Reds were deported to Russia, and more than 6,000 suspected radicals were jailed by the U.S. Attorney General.

More significant for the United States in the postwar years than the communist threat was its shortsighted isolationism. Despite President Wilson's herculean efforts, the U.S. Congress refused to allow America to join the League of Nations. Americans had entered the war with an idealism and enthusiasm "to make the world safe for democracy," but at the end, they were disappointed that the Allies did not march to Berlin, did not hang the kaiser, and did not occupy Germany. Almost three years after the Armistice, the Harding administration finally negotiated separate peace pacts with Germany and Austria that deliberately excluded the types of obligations and ideas for nation building Wilson had proposed.

In the Middle East, the decaying Ottoman Empire, which had entered the war on the side of Germany, was divided up into "mandates" by the League that were parceled out between France and Britain. These territories were not colonies but became protectorates, which Europe would help modernize until they could stand alone as independent nations. Even as the mandates concluded in the 1930s, Britain and France continued to exercise indirect rule through treaty rights for another generation.

In Asia, Japan rose to supremacy during this time by a rapid modernization modeled on the industrialized economies of the West. By the beginning of the 1920s, Japan had a powerful army and the third largest navy in the world.

China, however, still struggled with unification following the establishment of a republic in 1912. Well into the 1930s, much of China was under the dominion of local warlords who controlled the regional armies to their own purposes. It was during the 1920s, also, that an alliance with Russia laid the groundwork for a Chinese communist party.

Culture and Society in the 1920s

When the Great War ended, soldiers and home front citizens alike wanted more than anything for a return to normalcy. But the extreme circumstances of the war had so utterly shattered the comfortably familiar that the pieces of everyday life as it once had been could not be put back together again. During the war years, changes in technology, economics, and social order had been so enormous and dramatic that, even as they happened, the effect on society was palpable to its very core. The war had not ended as most Europeans and Americans had hoped. U.S. doughboys returned stateside to a postwar recession, prohibition, and the New Woman who was financially independent and now enfranchised. The political idealism of Wilson and his Democratic administration had been supplanted by the rancorous Republicans, led by Harding and the most corrupt administration since Grant. It was anything but normalcy. In 1920, F. Scott Fitzgerald captured the spirit of the day in his novel, *This Side of Paradise*: "All gods dead, all wars fought, all faiths in man shaken."

The disillusionment and cynicism of the postwar period only gradually eased when the economy turned around. The famous bull market of the twenties began its joy ride of boom-

FIGURE 5.1. The booming economy of the 1920s was fueled by the robust mass production of new consumer goods and by mass marketing that inculcated a broader socioeconomic class of consumers with aspiration and materialism.

or-bust stock trading and wild speculation in 1922. Everyone from barbers and office girls to dowager socialites and captains of industry seemed to be buying stocks "on margin"—that is, with a small down payment—and cashing in quick.

The dam of pent-up needs and wants that had accrued from the privations and shortages during the war years burst in an orgy of consumerism in the prosperous 1920s. Materialism was the new idol of the jazz and gin era. Enticing advertising was everywhere, from the magazines and direct mail pouring into homes daily to billboards, posters, and store window displays, urging consumption. (Figure 5.1.) The newly devised payment installment plans

The Flapper

The flapper has come to epitomize the young woman of the 1920s Jazz and Gin Age. In 1921, *Vanity Fair* editors wrote of the flapper as "always on the watch, eager, unafraid, insatiable, and ready to spring." The following year, *Vogue* was more prosaic: "This is that strange product indigenous to this generation—the flapper—hair bobbed, lips reddened, cigarette in hand—everybody knows her."

There are many suggestions by historians and scholars for how the term "flapper" came to be applied to young women of the 1920s. One of the most common is from the way women wildly flapped their arms while dancing the Charleston. Another is from the nickname for young women who brazenly road astride the flapper bracket of a motorbike. Yet another is a derivation of British slang for a juvenile partridge.

However, the origin of the term as a label for unconventional young women actually predates the era by as much as a generation. In 1914, a *Vanity Fair* editor recalled that the flappers of circa 1902 were a "certain type of peach-skinned little English girls with blonde braids hanging down their backs." "F-l-a-a-p! F-l-a-p! FLAP! went their feeble little wings," as these young women danced on the stage of London's Gaiety Theatre or played lawn tennis in the English countryside. On the eve of World War I, noted *Vanity Fair*, the flapper of 1914 delighted "in shocking one by a studied worldliness": by taking great pains to render a fine natural complexion unnatural with makeup, by smoking cigarettes, and by eating toffee in public. By the time the daughters of the original Edwardian flappers came of age in the raucous days of the twenties, the notion of the flapper was not as radically new as we might think looking back today.

World War I flapper by Florrie, 1914.

Jazz Age flapper by John Held, Jr., 1928.

enticed consumers to buy beyond their means—new and bigger cars, refrigerators, radios, phonographs, and similar high-end goods. The binge of spending further fueled the blazing economy and the decade came to be called the Roaring Twenties.

This insatiable consumerism also had a profound impact on social change. The affordable, mass-produced automobile opened new worlds for previously isolated rural folk. In the reverse, the automobile made possible suburbia and a commuter lifestyle for urban workers. The automobile is also credited (or blamed) for the revolution in sexual morality. As many social cartoonists of the time depicted, the car was an ideal, mobile parlor where a boy and girl might escape from chaperoning elders.

The rapid erosion of traditional values was further aided by the radio. The first commercial radio station began broadcasting in 1920. Within five years, consumers spent $400 million on radio equipment. Small town America was exposed to a world of popular culture they may not otherwise have known. Over their "wireless" radio, listeners heard instantaneous news reports, political speeches and debate, and new forms of music. Dramas and sophisticated comedies brought new ideas of social diversity and change into their living rooms night after night.

Motion pictures similarly had a significant influence on changing social values. In the 1920s, movie palaces proliferated across the landscape. Upon silver screens flickered the images of the beautiful people of the era, wearing the latest fashions, hairstyles, and makeup. Hollywood stars demonstrated modern behavior and social trends, including the new, permissive rituals of romance. By the millions, women and men of all ages emulated their movie idols in dress, appearance, and mannerisms.

The decade was especially a youth-oriented era—the first youth rebellion. The young drank hard and played hard. Sheiks and shebas danced the Charleston to the cacophony of jazz bands, drank bathtub gin in speakeasies, and necked in the backseats of flivvers. Girls, in particular, embraced change and all that modernism had to offer. The flapper wore her skirt to her knees, smoked cigarettes, painted her lips and rouged her cheeks, and experimented with premarital sex. The heady Great Euphoria of the 1920s, sustained by its blend of materialism, consumerism, and social change, continued to soar frenetically right through to the end of the decade.

Influences and Technologies of Fashion in the 1920s

During World War I, Paris had remained the arbiter of fashion and style despite the shortages of materials and restrictions on shipping and communications. In the months after the armistice, couture shops that had been converted to uniform manufacturers were quickly refurbished and salons that had closed for the duration reopened. Molyneux, Patou, and Poiret returned from military duty to energetically resume fashion design. The fashion press and retail buyers flocked to Paris season after season to see and buy the fresh collections.

Although U.S. designers had received more press coverage during the war years than ever before, as a group, they were unable or unwilling to take advantage of the publicity and name recognition to emerge from beneath the shadow of Paris as innovative fashion leaders. Most American designers traditionally worked for ready-to-wear manufacturers producing seasonal collections based on trends from Paris. Similarly, some "carriage-trade" department stores had custom shops that also provided copies or adaptations of Paris originals. American designers continued to comfortably maintain the convention of following Parisian dictates.

However, the American ready-to-wear industry came into its own during the twenties. Between 1918 and 1921, a group of investors and about fifty clothing manufacturers built a complex of showrooms and workshops on Seventh Avenue in New York to serve as a one-stop buying center for clothing merchants. The co-op also addressed the concerns of garment workers' organizations for fire safety and improved working conditions by setting high

The Zipper

An especially important American invention that eventually impacted fashion worldwide was the **zipper**. The slide closure design of today with its interlocking teeth affixed to fabric evolved from various types of mechanical hook-and-eye fasteners first introduced in the 1890s. In the 1920s, the rubber manufacturer, B. F. Goodrich, produced galoshes with an improved form of the "hookless fastener" and christened the zipper with its onomatopoetic name. The zipper was soon applied to all sorts of accessory items like purses, luggage, shoes, money belts, tobacco pouches, and some utilitarian garments such as outerwear and children's playwear. (Figure 5.2.)

A broader fashion application of the zipper occurred in the 1930s when tailors and designers began to add the zipper to couture styles and made-to-measure clothing. Charles James' famous spiral zippered dress was designed in 1933, and Elsa Schiaparelli used oversized and colored zippers as decorative accents in 1935. The Prince of Wales requested his first pair of zipper-fly trousers in 1934.

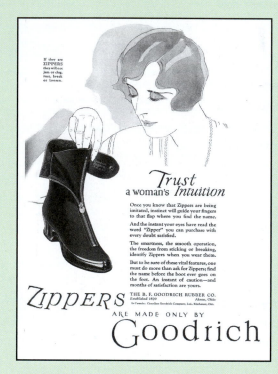

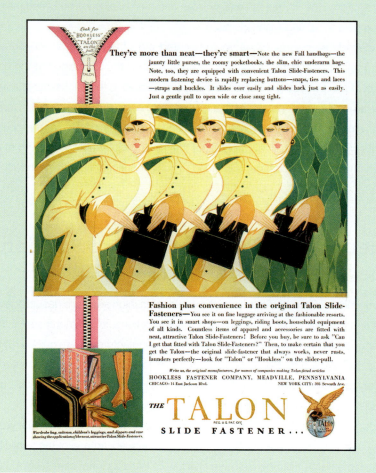

FIGURE 5.2. Initially the zipper was used primarily for accessories, luggage, and utilitarian garments like jackets. Goodrich ad, 1926; Talon ad, 1928.

standards of building construction and shop layout. As the leases were sold, apparel makers filled the suites with modern, high production equipment that could more efficiently keep pace with the booming consumer demand of the era. Today Seventh Avenue—better known as **"Fashion Avenue"** or simply the "market"—is still the central hub of American ready-to-wear.

As in the 1890s and early 1900s, one key influence that flowed from America to Paris was sportswear designs. During the 1920s, women broke through the barriers of competitive sports setting records, winning Olympic medals, and excelling in highly publicized championships. Increasingly women were encouraged to participate in all forms of athletics for which designers created comfortable, easy-care clothing. These active sportswear styles soon became integrated into everyday wardrobes. As *Vogue* observed in 1924, "It has been said, with more or less truth, that the ultramodern woman wears only two types of clothes in summer: sports things all day and dance frocks all night." Paris recognized that the New Woman of the twenties not only wanted the ease and comfort of sports clothes, but delighted in the youthful look of the styles. Gabrielle (Coco) Chanel especially recognized this change in women's attitudes and designed comfortable jersey knit suits that were widely copied.

Another American influence on Paris fashions came from technology. Although synthetic silk made of cellulose had been invented by the French in the 1880s, early forms of the filament produced textiles with too much sheen to be a convincing substitute for real silk. Over the subsequent decades, U.S. firms refined the processes of synthetic yarn production and weaving, patenting numerous improvements. Two different forms of artificial silk, both of which came to be known as **rayon**, were developed in the early part of the century: **viscose rayon** and **cellulose acetate**. By the end of World War I, artificial silk fabrics—popularly referred to as "art silk" at the time—could be produced supple and fine enough to be used in women's lingerie and hosiery. In 1924, the term rayon was first used commercially by a U.S. manufacturer for its synthetic silk. (Figure 5.3.)

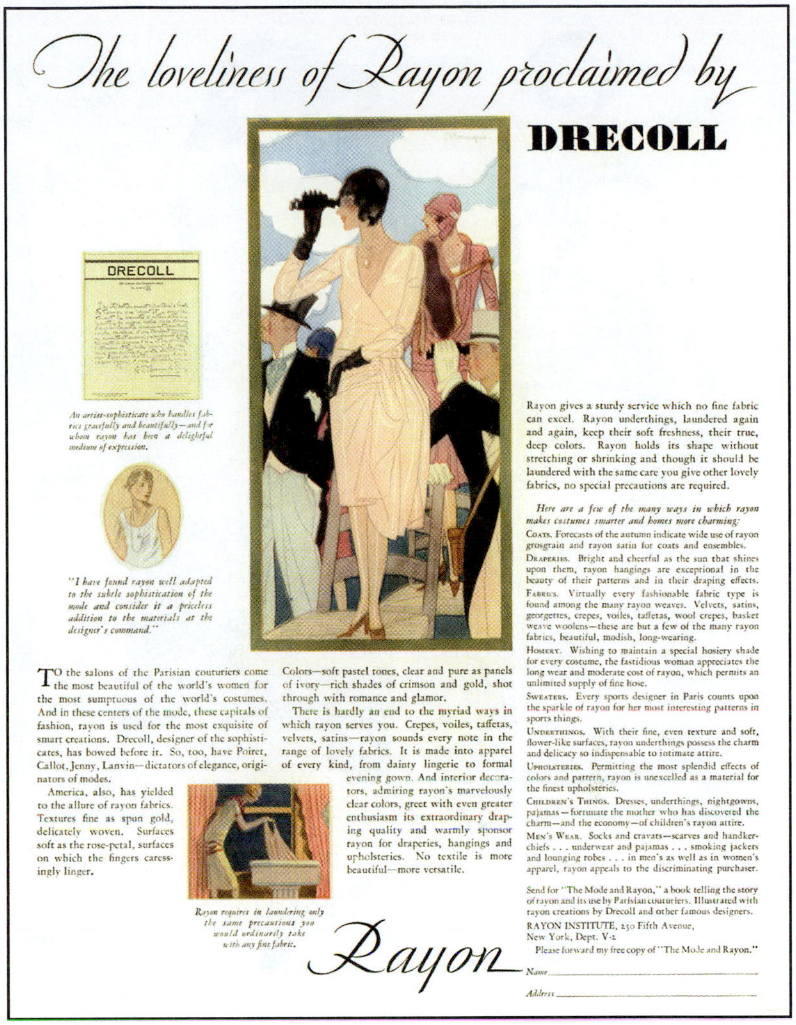

FIGURE 5.3. After decades of production refinement, the synthetic substitute for silk, named "rayon" in 1924, at last could be produced with a high quality suppleness and finish to be widely used for apparel. Rayon Institute ad, 1928.

Women's Fashions 1920–1929

In the first few seasons following the end of the First World War, Paris designers continued to produce a myriad of looks that seemed to have few things in common. In 1920, *Vogue* reported that "straight lines will be the rule of daytime, and fantasies from all parts of the world and all periods of the mode will prevail for evening." The straight silhouette that *Vogue* had observed was achieved by the dropped waistline—a look that would prevail throughout the decade and come to define the fashions of the era. Initially the waistline was lowered only slightly, but after the high placement of the waist throughout the mid- and late-1910s, the effect was dramatic. (Figure 5.4.) Between 1922 and 1924, the line further shifted downward to mid-hip where it remained till the end of the decade.

Despite the dominance of the loose, straight cut of dresses, some designers offered other styles as well. The Empire waist had continued throughout the war years and was still making its appearance into the early twenties. Panniered and bustle enhancements with a placement of the waistline at its natural position were also favorite looks of the early years. Even hooped skirts and infanta revivals continued as options. In 1922, the discovery of King Tutankhamen's

FIGURE 5.4. In 1920, the silhouette shifted the waistline low on the hips, a harbinger of the styles that would dominate the decade. From 1920: left, three dresses by Polly Francis; right, silk crepe dress by Cheruit.

tomb also inspired designers to sprinkle their collections with interpretations of costume styles from ancient Egypt, Persia, and China.

Hemlines became the most newsworthy topic of design throughout the first half of the decade. In the spring of 1920, *Vogue* assured readers that "street clothes remain short," which at that time were at mid-calf. Barely ten months later, though, hemlines descended almost to the ankles—about "eight to ten inches from the floor," advised *Vogue*—which is where designers tried to keep skirt lengths over the next couple of years. (Figure 5.5.) The problem was that women did not like the long skirts. A survey of readers by *The Flapper* in 1922 concluded that "of the hundreds of votes on modern styles . . . all but one was in favor of short skirts." As Paul Nystrom noted in his 1928 landmark study *The Economics of Fashion,* not only did dress sales drop when hemlines dropped, but "alterations expenses mounted rapidly" as women demanded shorter skirts. By the end of 1923, sagging sales and a flood of complaints from retailers convinced designers to shorten hemlines—first, returning them to about where they were in 1920, at mid-calf, and then up to the knees by 1925. (Figure 5.6.)

FIGURE 5.5. From 1921 through 1923, couturiers persisted in designing long skirts—some barely eight inches from the floor—despite resistance from consumers. Left, serge dress with lingerie collar by Worth and gabardine dress with muslin collar and beaded belt by Jenny, 1922; right, cropped waist styles by Pacific Mills, 1923.

Besides the lengths, the treatment of skirt hemlines was equally important to the styles of both day dresses and evening wear of the early twenties. **Handkerchief skirts** were cut with uneven, pointed hemlines all around. Other treatments included scalloped and tulip-edged hems. Asymmetrical overskirts and off-center gathers or pleats added further hemline interest.

The most popular forms of evening wear in the 1920s were lavishly decorated versions of the short, sleeveless chemise. Some styles even featured the barest of deep decollete necklines with thin, spaghetti shoulder straps. In the early twenties, after-six dresses often included a long, trailing panel, sometimes split in two or lined with contrasting fabrics, that dropped from the back of the bodice, waistline, or hips. In the later part of the decade, these extensions were often simplified into a longer hemline in the back although some designs retained the train-like effect. (Figure 5.7.)

FIGURE 5.6. By the end of 1924, designers responded to demands from consumers and retailers by shortening skirts. The following year hemlines rose to knee length. Left, dresses from Carolyn Modes, 1925; right, short chemise dresses from Darbrook Silks, 1926.

Suits adapted the long, lean silhouette of dresses by dropping design elements of jackets low on the torso. Buttons, especially for double-breasted styles, fastened at the hips rather than at the waist and bust. Lapels descended in long lines and deep openings. Patch pockets were placed low in the front, sometimes at the hemline. Jacket belts encircled hips. Wide box jackets were worn open to display the dropped line of blouses underneath.

To apply the dropped waist look to sportswear separates, many types of blouses were designed to be worn untucked. Some were long tunics and others were fitted with belts at the hips. One of the most popular blouses featured banded hems at the hips. (Figure 5.8.) Loose, comfortable knit versions were especially popular with active, young women. Certain styles of soft, bow front tops called **jabot blouses** were made to be tucked but were cut wide and full to allow a deep blouson over the skirt waistband.

Lanvin, 1921.

Evening dresses from Shelton Mills, 1928.

Lanvin, 1928.

Lelong, 1928.

Chanel, 1928.

FIGURE 5.7. As hemlines rose in the 1920s, floor-length evening gowns were abandoned in favor of shorter styles. During the early part of the decade, after-six dresses were often embellished with trains or trailing panels of fabric. In the late twenties, this treatment evolved into a longer hemline that dipped in the back.

FIGURE 5.8. The long line of the dropped-waist chemise was carried over to separates with tunic-style blouses that mostly were designed to be worn out over skirts. The dropped waist was emphasized with belts and banded hemlines at the hips. Blouses from Fashion Service, 1927.

By 1925, the look that represented the twenties had been perfected. The ideal feminine figure was that of a young boy—virtually devoid of curves of any form except for the legs. Skirt hemlines cropped at the knees now exposed more of a woman's legs than at any time in the history of the Christianized West. If a woman possessed a full bosom, she compacted the contours of her breasts within tight-fitting bandeaus. Any hint of a waistline was obscured by boxy, straight bodices. "This is our ideal today, gone are the busts, the hips, the curves of yesteryear," asserted a fashion editor in 1923; "Woman's figure is the exclamation point of the world!"

The squared, straightline silhouette of fashions in the 1925 to 1929 period was further emphasized by **art deco** textile patterns and graphical treatments of fabrics. (Figure 5.9.) The geometric shapes and purity of line that characterized the art deco movement embodied the dynamism and modernity of the machine age. Many of the designs, color palettes, and motifs of art deco were derived from prewar art movements such as Cubism, Futurism, Viennese Sezessionism, and German Jugenstil, as well as ethnic and folk art influences. Called "modernistic" or more commonly "moderne" at the time, the style culminated in the Exposition Internationale des Arts Decoratifs et Industriels Modernes hosted by Paris in 1925 (from which the term "art deco" was coined in the 1960s). There, architecture, painting, sculpture, and, particularly, the decorative and applied arts—including fashion—exhibited the cohesive, comprehensive look of the era. From this international expo, Paris reclaimed preeminence as the world's leader of style and fashion.

Women's Outerwear 1920–1929

Outerwear of the early 1920s was a mix of modern looks and revivals. (Figure 5.10.) Adaptations of eighteenth-century styles such as the fitted redingote and caped pelisse were the

FIGURE 5.9. Virtually all types of garments and accessories of the late 1920s were variously produced with geometric cuts, textile patterns, or surface embellishments influenced by the art deco movement. Dress designs by Magdeleine des Hayes, 1926.

result of a flurry of period plays and historical movies popular in those years. Long, straight overcoats, though, were the most prevalent through about 1924. By the mid-twenties, coats were as short as skirts. The dropped waistline of dresses was applied to coats by lowering closures and lengthening lapels. Large fur collars were ubiquitous from the second half of the 1920s into the mid-1930s. Cape coats were popular as transitional outerwear for fall and spring. Wrap coats, called **clutch coats**, were favorites of college girls.

FIGURE 5.10. Coats of the early 1920s were capacious and shorter than dress hemlines. In the second half of the decade, knee-length wrap coats with plunging, oversized collars became one of the most distinctive looks of the flapper. Left, camel's hair coat from College Club, 1923; right, wool coats with fox collars by House of Swansdown, 1927.

FIGURE 5.11. Pleated skirts were especially favored for the freedom of movement they provided when playing exerting sports. All white ensembles became the uniform of country club tennis courts. White pique tennis dresses from Wanamaker's, 1927.

FIGURE 5.12. Knickerbocker suits continued to be common on golf greens of the 1920s. Tweed knicker suits from Golftex, 1923.

Women's Sports Apparel 1920–1929

Throughout the 1920s, the New Woman discovered new arenas for expressing her independence and self-confidence. Sports particularly provided opportunities for women to compete and demonstrate youthful agility and athletic skills. Knit garments of all kinds were the recommended clothing for active sports. Track and field competitors wore form-fitting one-piece short suits with modesty skirts extending to the upper thighs. (See also women's swimwear, page 163.) Bloomer suits and middy blouses were still the most common attire for school athletics. In place of cumbersome coats for winter sports, pullover sweaters, cardigans, and vests of all types were layered to peel away as exertion warmed the active body.

For weekend recreation, women primarily wore everyday casual clothes to neighborhood tennis courts and community golf ranges. Pleated skirts were favored for the ease of movement they provided, especially the short styles of the late twenties. Split skirts, now more commonly called **culottes**, remained a comfortable, practical alternative to flying hemlines when lunging for a ball or traipsing over windblown golf greens. White was the correct color for skirts and tops at country clubs although soft colors like peach and pale yellow were acceptable at sunny resorts where suntans were fashionable. (Figure 5.11.)

FIGURE 5.13. The corset of the 1920s was engineered to compress the figure into the slim, boyish shape of the flapper. P. N. Practical Corset, 1923.

FIGURE 5.14. Silk or rayon step-ins called singlettes were the underwear of choice for the clingy chemises of the 1920s. Rayon step-ins and camisole and bloomers from Montgomery Ward, 1927.

Knickerbocker suits for women remained a common outfit for golfing, hiking, canoeing, camping, hunting, and other country activities. Jodhpurs and short jackets were still the preferred trouser uniform for riding. A similar ensemble was trendy for skiing at winter resorts. Jodhpurs also became a fashionable pant style for women when hunting was a mixed social event, such as shooting grouse. (Figure 5.12.)

Women's Underwear and Sleepwear 1920–1929

During the 1910s, women had begun to free themselves from constricting, heavily boned corsets, replacing them instead with more comfortable, elasticized foundation garments that smoothed more than shaped the figure. By the 1920s, corsets were engineered to compress the feminine form into the fashionable boyish contours of the era. (Figure 5.13.) All-in-one **corselettes** that encompassed the bust and hips were preferred by full-figured women, but most women opted for the abbreviated girdle styles that could better slim the hips and buttocks. Younger women, especially the flapper, discarded the corset altogether.

From World War I through the 1920s, a myriad of drawers, panties, and combination undergarments were developed by manufacturers. Styles ranged from full-length knit union suits of the early twenties to diaphanous step-ins called **singlettes**. (Figure 5.14.) Fine lingerie was made of crepe de chine, silk tricot, or voile, and cheaper varieties were of linen, cotton, or the new "art silk," rayon.

FIGURE 5.15. In the 1920s, brassieres were constructed for better support and articulation. Bra from G. M. Poix, 1927.

The camisole type of brassiere that had developed in the 1910s was gradually pared down in the 1920s and constructed for greater articulation of the breasts. (Figure 5.15.) However, bandeau bras of elasticized fabrics that concealed and flattened the bosom were particularly popular for the correct draping of the boxy chemise dresses of the time.

Other basic types of intimate apparel included assorted styles of petticoats and chemises, now called **slips** in this era because they were a mere "slip" of their former volume and weight. Camisoles were also a common covering over bras and corsets to smooth telltale seams and fasteners.

Sleepwear became widely varied in design and fabric. Negligee ensembles were lavishly trimmed with machine-made lace and embroidery. As skirt hemlines rose, shorter nightgowns became popular. Empire waist and princess-line gowns were most common. The kimono and other wrap robes remained favorite cover-ups for the boudoir or dressing room. The most important change in women's sleepwear, though, was the increasing popularity of pajamas, which, since the 1890s, had been selectively appropriated from menswear. By the 1920s, women's sleepwear pajamas and lounging pyjamas were widely advertised by ready-to-wear makers. (Figure 5.16.)

Women's Swimwear 1920–1929

During the 1920s, the automobile made vacations and weekend excursions to lakes and seashores available to the masses. Ready-to-wear makers happily mass produced chic, affordable beachwear and playwear modeled on the latest styles worn by the leisure classes at the resorts. At the beginning of the 1920s, briefer versions of the Edwardian full tunic, bloomers, and hose lingered as the most prevalent bathing suits for women. (Figure 5.17.) Adaptations of men's swimwear that had emerged during World War I increasingly became the feminine standard. In 1920, knit manufacturer Carl Jantzen introduced skintight, stretch swimsuits for both men and women "that changed bathing to swimming," as their logo floorline of the era advertised. "A Jantzen suit always fits trimly—and with scarcely the sign of a wrinkle," promised the copy in the 1926 ad shown here. But initially not all women were eager to reveal so much of themselves on a public beach. In fact, in some areas of the United States and Britain, women wearing the second-skin, one-piece swimsuits were arrested for indecent exposure. Only in the later part of the twenties did the sexy, new look gain popular acceptance. By then, the trunks had been trimmed from the knees to the upper thighs, armholes had become deeper, and hose had been discarded. When tanning became the rage at the end of the decade, swimsuits with low backs and even baring midriff cutouts made tentative appearances on the beach.

Woven Crepe Blue Bird Design 24H660 $1.79

Satin Stripe Radium 24H661 $1.69

2-Piece Pajama Blue Bird Flannel 33H216 $1.98

FIGURE 5.16 Pajamas steadily increased in popularity for women's sleepwear in the 1920s. Pajama suits from Bellas Hess, 1925.

Jantzen made it smarter to get right in and *swim!*

SMART FOLK—active swimmers—delight in wearing the trim fitting Jantzen swimming suit. It allows such a world of vigorous in-the-water fun.

Jantzen with its original improvements is so fashioned that *it must fit* . . . never stretching out of shape . . . never binding . . . never sagging.

Virgin wool and an improved knitting process known as "Jantzen-stitch" result in lively, springy fabric of marked flexibility. Hence a Jantzen suit *always* fits trimly—and with scarcely the sign of a wrinkle.

This is the suit that changed bathing to swimming—making it smarter to get right in and *swim*. In or out of water, wet or dry, a Jantzen always lets you look your best . . . trim, chic, smooth; but with the grace and modesty of tightly woven wool.

Jantzens are favored by smartly-clad folk at the beaches everywhere, here and abroad. Indeed, they're famed around the world.

Going abroad? In case you didn't pack in a Jantzen, you'll find your size at Selfridge's or Irette's in London; or Grande Maison de Blanc, Grands Magasins du Louvre, La Samaritaine and the smarter Parisian shops. In America the best stores have Jantzens for men, women, children. *Your weight is your size.*

Write for style folder. Jantzen Knitting Mills, Portland, Oregon. Jantzen Knitting Mills of Canada, Ltd., Vancouver, Canada.

Jantzen
**The suit that changed
bathing to *swimming***

Jantzen ad, 1926.

FIGURE 5.17. In the span of just a few years, swimwear dramatically evolved, shedding the last remnants of the Victorian tunic skirt and bloomers, into a sleek, formfitting one-piece design.

Taffeta bloomer suit by Plage and chambray bathing frock by Rivage, 1922.

Bradley Knitwear
swimsuits, 1922.

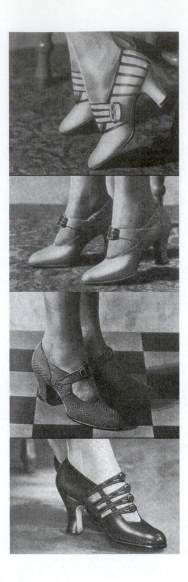

FIGURE 5.18. The typical shoe of the 1920s featured the curved Louis heel and a variety of instep straps. After 1925, shoes became even more varied with art deco influences, vivid colors, and a wide assortment of textures. Left, colorful, two-tone deco shoes from Goodyear-Welt, 1926; right, "Replicas from the famous bootiers of France" as claimed in a Best Company ad, 1927.

Women's Shoes 1920–1929

During the war years of the late 1910s, the availability of shoe styles and colors had been limited due to war rationing and production restrictions. By the 1920s, a pent-up demand for fashion coupled with a robust economy and a surge in ready-to-wear manufacturing led to a tremendous assortment of new shoe designs. The utilitarian high-top walking shoe was widely advertised still, but finally disappeared around 1923. Versions of flat-heeled boots remained a necessity for riding and outdoor enthusiasts. With more leg showing as hemlines rose, new fashion emphasis was placed on the shoe. Except for sport shoes, most styles were high-

Oreum ad, 1928.

FIGURE 5.19. The geometric art deco styling, called moderne in the 1920s, dominated jewelry design.

Wristwatches by Elgin, 1928.

Bracelet and facial powder compact by Mauboussin, 1927.

heeled with pointed toes. The curvy Louis XV heel was dominant throughout the era although straight heels and the tapered Cuban heel were also typical. Straps crossed the instep in single strips and crisscrossing arrangements of multiples. (Figure 5.18.)

Shoe materials were equally varied in the 1920s. In addition to dyed kid, suede, or patent, the different types of leathers were often appliqued in cutwork layered one over the other, or even over textiles like velvet or silk, for contrasting effects. Genuine reptile skins or leather textured to resemble lizard or alligator were a favorite dressy look. Exotic fabrics such as machine embroidered or beaded silk and gold or silver lamé were popular for evening shoes.

Ornamentation included a vast array of buckles, ranging from simple squared metal forms to elaborately jeweled medallions. After 1925, art deco motifs were applied to all types of footwear both as surface embellishment and as decorative attachments.

Color was especially important for footwear in the 1920s with virtually every hue available ranging from vibrant jeweltones to soft pastels. No longer did the tints of shoes have to match precisely the color of a gown as with the Edwardian lady. A fad of Flapper Jane even included brightly colored galoshes worn unzipped as street shoes, rain or shine.

Women's Jewelry 1920–1929

Throughout the 1920s, art deco (called "moderne" at the time) was the predominant design style of jewelry. The sleek, geometric look of art deco evolved from influences of modern art movements such as Cubism and Futurism, blended with visual elements derived from the technology of the Machine Age. (Figure 5.19.) Following the discovery of Tutankhamen's tomb in 1922, the stylized, flat patterns of ancient Egyptian art and similar motifs from other distant, exotic cultures also influenced jewelry designs of the period. Through mass production and mass distribution of chain stores, moderne jewelry was available to all socioeconomic classes.

During the 1920s, the flapper emphasized the long lines of the dropped-waist chemise and her short, bobbed hair with dangling earrings and long ropes of beads. Ankle bracelets

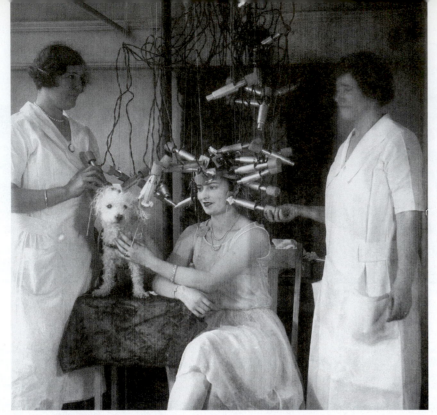

Electric tentacles of the marcel permanent wave system, 1928.

FIGURE 5.20. The sculpted bob or shingle haircut epitomized the look of the flapper. Faces were defined with linear applications of makeup that shaped crimson lips, kohl-blackened eyes, and pencil-drawn eyebrows.

Hollywood starlets, 1927.

glittered above the strappy Louis-heel shoes. For evening wear, chain and pendant necklaces were sometimes worn backward to accent dresses cut with low, open backs. Chanel popularized piling on mounds of costume jewelry necklaces and adorning both wrists and several fingers with numerous bracelets and rings.

FIGURE 5.21. Cosmetics makers influenced the sexual revolution of the 1920s with a marketing saturation of ads, depicting the New Woman as an alluring vamp. The flapper shaped her lips with lipstick, rouged her cheeks, arched her eyebrows, and enlarged her eyes with mascara, eyeliner, and eye shadow. She even brazenly applied makeup in public. Left, flapper with lipstick, 1928; right, Vivaudou ad, 1924.

Women's Hairstyles and Makeup 1920–1929

The stigma of the painted lady had begun to diminish during the war years of the late 1910s when women began to enjoy a greater independence and self-confidence. They had shorn their long Edwardian tresses to work outside the home, and they took their cue from Hollywood movies and fan magazines on how modern women looked with makeup.

Short hair became the hallmark of the flapper. "The cut's the thing—whether the hair is straight or waved," declared a *Vogue* editorial in 1927. Young women flocked to barber shops rather than beauty shops to have their hair sheered into bobs or shingled into a close crop with a straight razor. (Figure 5.20.) Hair salons opened by the thousands to provide "permanents"—waves and curls made long-lasting with chemicals electrically heated by the tentacles of the **marcel**.

In the years after World War I, cosmetics makers saturated mass media with ads promoting the tinted face powders, cheek rouge, and the lipstick in a metal tube, newly invented in 1915. The image of women in cosmetic ads changed from the demure Edwardian user of rice powder to the sexually alluring vamp. (Figure 5.21.) Her lips were shaped into a crimson cupid's bow with lipstick. Her eyes were enlarged with kohl liner and eyelash mascara, and given depth with colored eye shadows. Her eyebrows were plucked to a fine arc and defined with a penciled line. Her nails were oval shaped and polished with a pink wax. Her underarms and legs were shaved. Mass distribution of cosmetics through chain stores and mail order catalogs provided office girls and shop clerks everywhere with easy access to inexpensive beauty regimens.

Women's Hats 1920–1929

The cloche is the hat style most associated with the 1920s. As noted in the previous chapter, though, the close-fitting cloche had emerged during the First World War when working women cropped their hair and needed a hat style that did not require pins to stay on. As the bell-shaped cloche evolved in the mid-twenties, some styles lost their brims entirely and others extended the narrow brims well down over the brows. (Figure 5.22.) Milliners referred to this type of cloche as "skull helmets." By the end of the decade, the fronts of cloches receded back from the brows or were turned up to reveal the trendy makeup looks of the flapper.

A close second to the cloche in popularity in the 1920s was a variety of toques. In the early part of the decade, the toque was the favorite base for milliners to design fanciful embellishments with ribbons, feathers, flowers, and lace. In the second half of the twenties, the toque was ornamented with deco trimmings and geometric surface treatments.

For special daytime events, the wide picture hat remained the favorite style. Brims were sometimes made of contrasting, semitransparent materials. For evening wear, befeathered and beaded bandeaux or low turbans of sumptuous materials were preferred. Hollywood influences included occasional revivals such as the cavalier hat of 1923 when the *Three Musketeers* was released. The tricorne hat also reappeared periodically.

Women's Accessories 1920–1929

The accessories of the well-dressed woman of the early 1920s continued to be basically those of the late Edwardian period—only updated in design and color. Just as with high-top button shoes, though, some categories of accessories became obsolete during the decade, including walking sticks, parasols, and evening fans.

However, some new accessories reflected the changing social mores and status of women at the time. During the twenties, tobacco companies aggressively and successfully targeted women in their marketing efforts. The cigarette case became a new addition to the handbags of many women. Similarly, the flapper's beauty regimen expanded beyond facial powder to include rouge, lipstick, mascara, eyeliner, eyeshadow, and eyebrow pencils. Not only did handbags become more capacious to accommodate all of these feminine accoutrements, but compact **vanity cases** were created to hold all the necessities for touch-up, including a mirror. (Figure 5.23.) In addition, as an increasing number of women went to work after World War I, accessories for the office girl or career woman could include small leather items such as appointment books, notepads, pencil holders, day journals, and business card cases.

FIGURE 5.22. The bell-shaped cloche that first developed during World War I became the hat style most associated with the 1920s. For women who did not opt for a bob haircut—virtually a prerequisite for wearing the close-fitting cloche—toques and wide-brimmed picture hats remained popular traditional looks.

Straw hat from De Marinis, 1920.

Sport hat draped with Roman scarf from Dobbs Hats, 1922.

Cloches by Ritzcroft, 1927.

Picture hat with feathers by Molyneux, 1922.

Beaded cloche by Mallory Hats, 1924.

Felt cloche with ribbon band from Dobbs Hats, 1927.

Cloche with turned-back brim from Catalina, 1928.

FIGURE 5.23. New types of accessories for the modern postwar woman included cigarette cases and cosmetic vanity sets. Left, cosmetics vanity set from Tre-Jur, 1924; right, International Sterling cigarette cases, 1926.

FIGURE 5.24. Long scarves and shawls with geometric patterns complemented the straightline cut of chemise dresses in the 1920s. Amalfi batiste scarf from Brightwood, 1925.

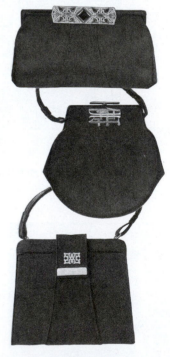

FIGURE 5.25. The high-style modernity of art deco design and motifs was applied to all types of accessories. Left, gloves by Grewen, 1926; right, handbags by Isakof, 1926.

FIGURE 5.26. Flappers delighted in affixing their silk or rayon hose with colorful, eye-catching garters that could be easily glimpsed beneath shortened hemlines. Left, Nufashond shirred garters, 1925; right, Photo of flapper, c. 1928.

Neckwear in the early twenties included a variety of jabots and collar treatments that disappeared as the dropped-waist chemise became the standard style. Instead, long scarves and shawls were preferred for accenting the straightline cut of fashions. (Figure 5.24.)

Belts were a key accessory for defining the fashion silhouette. Thin variations were worn at the hips to emphasize the long torso of dresses and blouses.

For a polished look, ladies seldom went out without gloves. Simple, plain types had been preferred by the Edwardian woman, but in the 1920s, art deco styling was applied to all accessories, including gloves. (Figure 5.25.) Gauntlet styles with long, flared cuffs, sometimes worn turned down over the wrist to display a contrasting color, were a favorite. Long gloves for evening wear disappeared temporarily in the late twenties.

As skirt hemlines rose to the knees (and hiked higher when a flapper danced the Charleston or was seated), garters became an important eye-catching accessory. (Figure 5.26.) Not only did the colorful bands draw attention to bared, shapely legs, but they also served as handy repositories for cigarettes, flasks, and makeup compacts.

In winter, fur muffs remained a popular and useful accessory. Coats often featured huge fur collars and sometimes matching cuffs, which were complemented by an oversized muff.

Notched lapels, 1926.   Variant of peaked lapels, 1928.   Rounded notch lapels, 1928.   Cloverleaf lapels, 1928.

39F 1662
$23⁰⁰~

Youth's Suit
Chest 31 to 36 in.

39F 1932
$15⁰⁰~

39F 1128
$22⁰⁰~

FIGURE 5.27. The dominant silhouette of men's business suits of the 1920s was the trim, natural-shoulder jacket with narrow, leggy trousers that had developed in the previous decade. New features included the return of bold textile patterns and varied lapel treatments. Sterlingworth suits, 1927.

FIGURE 5.28. The wide-legged trousers, called Oxford bags, originated with college men at Oxford and Cambridge in England in the mid-1920s. Among the college fads of the period in the United States were variations of the trouser with legs ranging from twenty-five inches up to forty inches in circumference at the bottom. Left, photo of young man in Oxford bags, c. 1925; right, Oxford bags from Duchess Trousers, 1926.

Men's Fashions 1920–1929

The young men who returned from the Great War wanted to distance themselves from the trauma, disillusionment, and privations of that time. As the 1920s heated up, they danced hard to jazz music, drank bootleg whiskey, smoked too much, drove too fast, and indulged in all the hedonistic and carnal pleasures so readily available to them with the surplus of women. Flaming youth of the twenties also used fashion more aggressively than in any previous period to assert their independence from the older generations. The emphasis on the trim, youthful look in men's clothing during the 1910s evolved into a virtual fetishistic obsession—a youth cult—in the 1920s.

The two- and three-button, natural shoulder suit with its trim V-line jacket, snug vest, and narrow, leggy trousers was the proper attire for both young and mature businessmen of the 1920s. Jackets with notched lapels were the most common although some dapper lounge models featured rounded **cloverleaf lapels** or **peaked lapels** with the points angled upward. (Figure 5.27.) The greatest sartorial debate of the time seems to have been the proper way to button the jacket. Catalogs of the period show all variations: on a two-button jacket, the top or bottom button, or both, fastened; on a three-button jacket, the top only, the center only, or all three.

By mid-decade, though, college youths traveling to London brought back with them a look that differentiated their suit styles from those of their fathers. The suits of the Oxford and Cambridge students featured new lines and proportions that were fresh but still emphasized the slender, youthful ideal. Jackets were cut with straight-hanging lines for a close fit over the hips. Most jackets were unvented, or only had a short, overlapping vent in the back. Hemlines were shortened slightly. Lapels were high and narrow, especially on the three- and four-button styles, which were often worn fully buttoned. The most distinctive change in the cut of the college man's suit, though, was the trousers. **Oxford bags**, as they were called at the time, were cut with bottoms at about twenty-two to twenty-five inches in circumference. The trousers of the businessman were still made at a slim seventeen to eighteen inches at the cuffs. Fashion lore holds that the students at Oxford and Cambridge were forbidden to wear the loose-fitting, comfortable knickers on school grounds, so they simply wore the wide-legged flannel trousers over the knickers when on campus for a quick change after classes. As the look evolved into a fad, the cuffs of Oxford bags expanded as much as forty inches around. (Figure 5.28.)

FIGURE 5.29. Golfing knickers of the 1920s, called plus fours, were cut full and baggy enough to blouson over the kneebands about four inches below the knees. The style was also commonly worn by young men as casual daytime wear. Tweed plus fours in a glen plaid by Charles Merton, 1927.

FIGURE 5.30. Flare-thighed jodhpurs were introduced from India as riding attire by nineteenth-century British colonial officers. Following the first World War, the comfortable, durable style became a favorite of sportsmen and working men who spent much of their time outdoors. Corduroy and moleskin jodhpurs from Montgomery Ward, 1927.

During the 1920s, the influence of sports attire on day dress was significant. The ease and comfort of clothing worn for active sports greatly appealed to the postwar generation, who assimilated many types of garments from the sports arena into their everyday wardrobes. For example, the Victorian knickerbocker suit that was primarily worn for bicycling, hiking, or golf at the turn of the century became casual attire for young men not only for a weekend in the country but also for leisure time in the city. The Ivy Leaguer who returned from London with Oxford bags in the second half of the twenties also brought home a new type of knickers: the **plus fours**. These were a longer form of golf knickers with wide, baggy legs that would blouson about four inches over the kneeband. (Figure 5.29.) The plus fours suit was usually worn with a dress shirt and tie, and either a sport jacket sometimes with a vest, or a pullover sweater.

Jodhpurs, likewise, became more proletariat after the First World War. Originally, the flare-thighed form of knee breeches had been introduced into England as riding attire by nineteenth-century colonial officers who had adopted the style from East Indian military dress. Although jodhpurs remained a component of equestrian costume, the style was also broadly adopted by working men who spent much of their time outdoors. Construction foremen, aviators, field archaeologists, and sportsmen especially favored the comfortable fit, the reinforced construction, and the durable fabrics of jodhpurs. (Figure 5.30.)

Instead of tailored suits, young men in the twenties increasingly preferred sport jackets for leisure time and informal social events. The most notable form of sport jacket, the blazer, had been a perennial favorite since the second half of the nineteenth century. Now, the blazer was a conservative fixture in the wardrobe of the upper class male. Most blazers were usually in navy, although other somber colors such as chocolate brown and slate gray were acceptable if worn with the obligatory dress shirt, necktie, and white or cream flannel trousers. For the more rebellious youth of the era, though, sport jackets provided new opportunities for self-expression. Besides vivid colors, sport jackets were made in a wide array of weaves and textile patterns from more subtle honeycomb patterns to bold awning stripes. (Figure 5.31.)

In keeping with the quest for greater comfort and ease in dressing, men of the 1920s abandoned the stiffly starched detachable shirt collar in favor of the "soft shirt"—still commonly referred to as a negligee shirt—with an attached, turn-down collar and coat front opening. (Figure 5.32.) Many styles of the new forms of dress shirts also had attached French cuffs to keep them from too closely resembling casual sport shirts. After the success of using rayon as a textile substitute for natural fiber yarns during the First World War, the fabric

FIGURE 5.31. Sport jackets were a popular alternative to the tailored suit jacket for informal social gatherings. Textile patterns and colors became bolder in the postwar years. Awning stripe jacket with pin stripe flannel trousers by Palm Beach Suits, 1927.

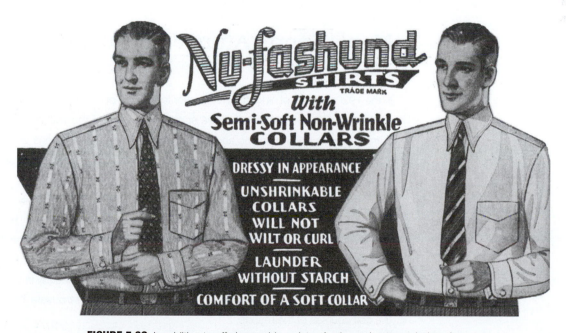

FIGURE 5.32 In addition to offering a wide variety of color and pattern choices for men's shirts, mass market catalogs of the 1920s featured styles in assorted fabrics, including cotton madras and English broadcloth, pongee, silk, and rayon. Men's "soft collar" shirts from Nu-fashund Shirts, 1928.

became more commonly used for men's shirts. A variety of madras and English broadcloth prints were featured in the ready-to-wear catalogs by the mass merchandisers of the period. In the second half of the 1920s, color and pattern were key elements of dress shirt designs. The wardrobe of F. Scott Fitzgerald's Jay Gatsby was punctuated with "shirts with stripes and scrolls and plaids in coral and apple green and lavender and faint orange."

The pullover bosom shirt, however, did not vanish completely but, instead, remained the preferred style for formal attire. As the ready-to-wear maker Cluett Peabody noted in a 1923 ad, the variety of shirt options for the well-dressed man ranged from "the immaculate bosom shirt of the Ball Room to the good looking oxford of the [golf] links."

As noted previously, young men of the 1920s often made fashion selections with one of two purposes in mind—as a distinction from the older generations, and for easy, comfortable dressing. From these tenets a burgeoning sportswear industry rapidly expanded, offering a broad range of casual style options. Many types of active sports clothing that once had been worn only for athletics were adapted for everyday dress during this transition period. Menswear catalogs provided some guidance in putting together these various garments but, for the most part, there was not a dress protocol for sportswear.

Knit shirts also became mainstream apparel from the late 1920s onward. The appearance at resorts of the short-sleeve **polo shirt** with its knit Eton collar and placket front was duly noted in the fashion press of 1928. Some polos were made with banded bottoms, but most were worn tucked. The comfortable, easy-care polo shirt quickly became a favorite of all men of all ages.

Other forms of knit sportswear that were adapted from active sports clothing (and also from the working man's attire) became staples in men's wardrobes. Throughout this period, pullovers, cardigans, twin sets, and sweater vests were often worn as a substitute for sport jackets or in place of tailored suit vests. (Figure 5.33.) Knicker suits, especially, were often topped with sweaters—with and without ties—that usually included stockings of the same pattern to match.

Men's Sports Attire and Outerwear 1920–1929

In the 1920s, sports of all kinds were a favorite pastime of men of every age and socioeconomic standing. The radio broadcasted live sporting events and movie theater newsreels featured current reports on champions and championships. A surge in college enrollment of demobilized doughboys attending university, often with their younger siblings, expanded interest in varsity sports.

Among the fastest growing sports of the period was golfing. Virtually every community of any size had a country club or public links by the end of the twenties. The standard apparel for playing golf was the full-cut plus fours, stockings, and a loose-fitting shirt, often worn with a pullover such as that shown in Figure 5.29. A necktie was required for the country club set, but most men preferred the comfort of an open-throat shirt, especially in warm weather. News from Palm Beach in 1928 reported on the increasing trend of trousers instead of knickers on the golf courses of the resorts.

The other sport that had widespread appeal and a correctness of dress was tennis. The Edwardian look of crisp white trousers and shirts with white, tan, or buckskin shoes remained the constant throughout this period. To break the monochrome of tennis whites, some men

FIGURE 5.33. Knitwear was not only comfortable and versatile casual wear, but the wide variety of types, vivid colors, and striking patterns provided men with the opportunity to express their personal style. Cardigans and pullovers from Tom Wye, 1926.

with fashion flair wore a vividly colored silk scarf at the waist instead of a belt. The obligatory blazer in blue, slate, or bottle green was a welcome dash of color as well.

As winter sports gained in popularity, fashion and "physical culture" periodicals recommended how to dress for strenuous activities on snowy slopes. Throughout the 1920s, plus fours with thick woolen stockings and layers of knit tops were the most prevalent winter playwear. Knits of all kinds also continued to be the preferred types of garments for most warm season athletics, including track and field events, team ball games, and swimming and diving. Knitwear was nonbinding and comfortable yet warm and lightweight enough to be layered for easy removal as the body heated up during exertion.

Men's outerwear of the early 1920s still reflected the military influences of World War I. The fit of overcoats was slender, high waisted, and kept taut to the body by a belt, half belt at the back, or waist seam with a tapered bodice. (Figure 5.34.) After 1923, the hemline dropped from knee length to mid-calf. The single-breasted, fly-front topcoat with the natural shoulderline

FIGURE 5.34. Military styling still influenced the design of men's outerwear in the 1920s. Coats were usually fitted, often with a half belt in the back, or snugly secured with a full belt. Coats from Kuppenheimer, 1921.

FIGURE 5.35. Everyday, functional types of coats were made of heavy "weather-proofed" materials and thickly lined with sheepskin. Moleskin coat with fleece lining, 1928.

was the most popular throughout the twenties although double-breasted styles were featured in all the menswear catalogs. The exception was the fur coat, which was preferred full, long, and opulent with a massive collar and sleeves. The fad of **raccoon skin coats** among Ivy League sheiks and shebas was a favorite theme of cartoonists in the twenties. For the most part, though, coat makers and retailers took their design cue from London. Tweeds abounded on all types of outerwear. When the Prince of Wales was photographed in a raglan sleeve overcoat in 1929, demand for the style instantly swept America and Paris. For everyday winter wear, serviceable coats of "weather-proof" cotton moleskin or thick merino wool, usually with heavy sheepskin linings, were common. Most styles were cropped to mid- or upper-thigh to allow freedom of movement. (Figure 5.35.) In wet, snowy climates, coats made of leather or Leathertex—a branded form of rubberized fabric that resembled leather—were often preferred for their water resistance and durability.

Men's Underwear and Swimwear 1920–1929

The union suit was still the most common form of men's underwear throughout the 1920s. Younger men, especially those who had been in the military during World War I, had come to prefer the briefer and more comfortable boxer shorts and the tank style undershirt, both similar in cut to swimwear at the time. (Figure 5.36.) Increasingly, the long union suit—with or without long sleeves—was more often reserved for winter wear. Similarly, the button front undershirt

FIGURE 5.36. Boxer shorts and tank style undershirts were the more popular forms of underwear for young men of the 1920s. By the end of the decade, boxers had been shortened from the knees to the upper thighs, and pullover undershirts were more popular than button front versions. Topkis underwear, 1920.

became less favored than the easy, pullover versions. By the end of the decade, boxer shorts had been shortened from knee-length to the upper thighs. As improvements were made in the production of woven rayon in the mid-twenties, the silky, durable fabric was applied to all types of men's undergarments.

The other bare necessity that almost all men had in some form was a swimsuit. As noted in the section on women's swimwear, the formfitting knit suits produced by Jantzen in the 1920s "changed bathing to swimming." (Figure 5.37.) The heavy flannel trunks and tank top of the prewar era were abandoned in favor of the snug, knit one-piece, often advertised as a "**speedsuit**" since it was favored by U.S. swim teams at the Olympics. During the second half of the 1920s, Jantzen introduced the "**twosome**" swimsuit, which was a one-piece suit that looked like two pieces with short trunks and a tank of a contrasting color or horizontal stripes. The design of the speedsuit and twosome was a radical leap

FIGURE 5.37. Although the modesty skirt persisted with some styles of men's swimsuits through the 1920s, most swimwear makers introduced ever briefer cuts with shorter trunks and tank tops with deeper armholes and open backs. Jantzen's "twosome" was a one-piece design with solid colored trunks and a tank top of a contrasting color or stripes. Photo c. 1928.

Leghorn boater, 1926.

Snap-brim fedora, 1927.

Camel's hair beret, 1926.

FIGURE 5.38. Men's hats of the 1920s included new varieties such as the snap-brim fedora and the beret. Traditional forms like the straw boater were given dash and vitality with wide, colorful grosgrain ribbon hat bands.

since it eliminated the modesty skirt of previous styles. In addition, with the fad of suntanning that emerged in the late 1920s, swimsuit armholes were extended much deeper, and some versions had cutout backs and sides, called "crab backs," to expose as much skin as possible to the sun. Although topless swimming was prohibited at most public beaches, in the 1920s, young men at resort spots like the Riviera and Hawaii began to wear trunks with no tops for the first time.

Men's Accessories and Sleepwear 1920–1929

The wardrobe of the well dressed man of the 1920s included an even wider array of accessories than his prewar predecessor. The style-conscious man paid as much attention to the little details of dress as he did to the newest cut of a suit jacket. He knew when, where, and with what to wear the correct accessory in the right style, color, and material.

Hightop style from Hanover Shoes, 1923.

Two-tone art deco styling from Wescot, 1926.

Wide-toe "balloon" shoes from Selz brand shoes, 1927.

FIGURE 5.39. The hightop street boot remained a prevalent form of men's shoes throughout the 1920s. In the second half of the decade, wide-toe "balloon" construction was applied to all varieties of men's footwear.

Subtle changes in men's hats made for fresh new looks in the 1920s. (Figure 5.38.) One of the most popular hats with flaming youth was a soft fedora with a wide brim and high, tapered crown. Called a **snap-brim fedora**, its pliable brim could be "snapped" down in the front or up at one side or in the back. Older men still preferred the stiffly blocked homburgs with a curled brim and center creased crown. A variety of the fedora with a pair of dents on each side of the front was called a **pinched-crown hat**. For summer, broad-brimmed panamas were modeled on the new shapes of fedoras. For young men who wanted to express themselves differently than the older generations, there was the beret, brought back by soldiers from France after World War I. Many times, newspapers reported on the Prince of Wales sporting a beret angled to one side of the

FIGURE 5.40. Neckties of the Jazz Age were designed with vibrant colors and bold, art deco patterns. Blade lengths still only extended to the middle of the shirt front rather than to the belt. Knit ties from Berkley Knitwear, 1926.

head. The soft, flat golf cap with a stiff visor covered with the same fabric was still popular with the young set although it was also recommended headwear for the casual knicker suit for men of all ages. The classic straw boater also remained a favorite of young and old alike. Color provided drama in the look of men's headwear. The brown derby became so common that a restaurant by that name opened in Hollywood. Dark green fedoras were commented on in fashion reports from Alpine resorts. Striped grosgrain hat bands added color and panache to natural leghorn panamas.

Men's shoes of the early 1920s changed little from those of the war years. The high-top styles were still common through the decade. Footwear of the second half of the 1920s reflected two style trends of the era. As young men's trouser legs expanded in width and volume, shoes also were widened to balance the look. Broad, square-toed oxfords, bluchers, and brogues—collectively called **balloon shoes** at the time—were favorites of college men who put in a lot of mileage hiking across campus to classes. (Figure 5.39.) The second style trend was the influence of art deco on men's shoe designs. Although two-tone oxfords had appeared in the 1890s, the geometric shapes of the contrasting layers were ideal for moderne styling. For business attire, though, traditional rounded-toe wingtips were preferred throughout the 1920s.

Neckwear in the 1920s was transformed on two fronts—first by a new technique of construction with an interlining of bias cut wool that kept its shape after unknotting, and second by men's demands for striking hues and modern, Jazz Age patterns and prints. (Figure 5.40.) Vividly colored and patterned knit ties of wool and wool/silk blends were particularly popular with college men throughout the decade. More subdued silk foulards were standard for business attire. The length still only extended to about the middle of the shirt front rather than to the belt. Bow ties were at opposite ends of correct dress—white or black for formal attire and flashy prints for golf suits and casual sportswear.

As comfort and casual elegance came to dominate men's dress in the twenties, day gloves and walking sticks were gradually abandoned as cumbersome accoutrement of bygone times. Utilitarian purposes still necessitated stylish gloves for winter and for sports, especially golfing.

Jewelry became a more important accessory for men after the Great War than in previous decades. That men of the 1920s enjoyed a wide variety of jewelry was noted in a trade magazine of the time: "Given the chance, and if fashion indicated, they would wear earrings and nose rings." In fact, new types of jewelry created for changing styles of clothing added even more options for men. (Figure 5.41.) As shirts with stiff detachable collars were abandoned in

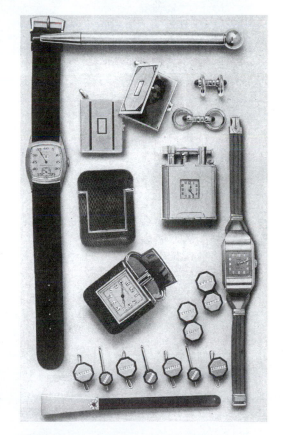

FIGURE 5.41. In the prosperous postwar years, men increasingly wore a greater variety of jewelry, including cuff link and tiebar sets and even chain bracelets. Art deco-styled wrist watches, photo locket, cigarette holder, cigarette lighters, and cuff links from Brand-Chatillon Jewelers, 1929.

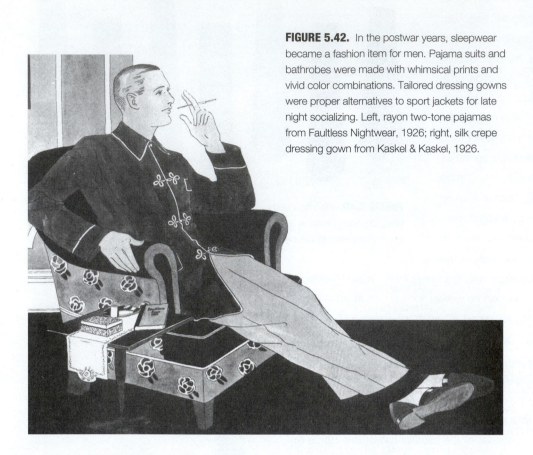

FIGURE 5.42. In the postwar years, sleepwear became a fashion item for men. Pajama suits and bathrobes were made with whimsical prints and vivid color combinations. Tailored dressing gowns were proper alternatives to sport jackets for late night socializing. Left, rayon two-tone pajamas from Faultless Nightwear, 1926; right, silk crepe dressing gown from Kaskel & Kaskel, 1926.

favor of the soft-collar shirts, collar pins, collar bars, and **collar grips** became an important jewelry accessory for holding soft collars smoothly in place. A renewed interest in tie clasps was inspired by jewelers when they replaced ornate Victorian designs with die cuts and engravings of horses, game animals, and sports motifs such as tennis rackets. Wristwatches continued to be preferred over pocket watches although the pocket model with a gold chain was an elegant accent for formalwear. Art deco styling of cuff links added a smart touch to French style shirts. Men even clasped on gold chain bracelets in emulation of Hollywood sheik, Rudolph Valentino.

Another accessory that became more significant was the belt. During the youth-oriented twenties, men with slender waists preferred belts to suspenders, which became associated with men of more rotund proportions. As with shoes, belts were designed to coordinate correctly with the clothing depending upon purpose and season.

Sleepwear for men became much more of a fashion item in the 1920s than it had been for the prewar generation. (Figure 5.42.) Although pajamas had been a common type of night wear for decades, designs in the twenties featured a huge assortment of collar and sleeve treatments, and fabrics in fun, allover prints and wild color combinations. Some pajama styles were modeled after exotic costumes of the Far East that included mandarin collars, passementerie trim, and braid frog closures. The **cossack pajama suit** blended the stand-up Chinese collar with an off-center closure and a sash modeled after a Russian officer's tunic.

FIGURE 5.43. The well-groomed man of the 1920s was clean shaven and kept his hair closely cropped. Various hair oils were applied for a slicked-back, shiny helmet look.

Robes came in two forms—a bathrobe to accompany pajamas as sleepwear or a dressing gown worn over regular clothes. The basic wrap bathrobe was a utilitarian garment for a warm coverup out of bed in the morning or a wrap for lingering around a late night radio program. Varieties of collar treatments were the principal distinction on the standard, T-shape cut of bathrobes. Fabrics included terrycloth, waffled cotton, seersucker, quilted wool, or patterned heavy flannel called **blanket cloth**. Dressing gowns, also called **house coats**, were worn in the intimacy of private moments at home with family or the closest of friends. These were not sleepwear garments, like those worn with pajamas, but were loungewear, worn over trousers and a shirt, often with a tie or a silk scarf like the example shown in Figure 5.42. Styles were usually more tailored than robes, some with fitted contours and others modeled after foreign costumes such as kimonos and kaftans. Fabrics were often luxurious—satins, brocades, embroidered silks, and rayon.

Men's Grooming and Hairstyles 1920–1929

Men's hairstyles of the 1920s were of two varieties: cut long or cut short. The more common long cut was cropped close around the ears and back, but left full and long enough on top to be brushed straight back or parted to the side or center. Pomades and hair oils were worked into the hair, which was slicked back into a fixed, shiny helmet. (Figure 5.43.) In the youth-oriented mood of the era, older men more frequently colored their hair than a generation earlier.

Children's Clothing 1920–1929

The trend toward greater freedom and comfort in children's clothing that had begun during the Edwardian era continued to develop in the 1920s. Whereas Paris dictated women's fashions and London set the looks for men's attire, America was the principal leader in childrenswear. While European garment and textile industries rebuilt after World War I, U.S. ready-to-wear makers expanded and modernized businesses that had flourished during the 1910s. Among the vast volumes of manufactured goods exported to a recovering Europe were shiploads of children's clothing, Americanized.

FIGURE 5.44. Simple, loose-fitting dresses allowed small girls comfort and freedom. Dresses for older girls of the 1920s adopted the boxy, dropped waist styles of the flapper. Left, short, shoulder-yoke summer dresses, 1922; right, dropped-waist chemises, 1928.

Infants were at last freed of the remaining forms of Victorian shackles of constricting, excessive clothing. The smothering layers of garments that comprised the layette were reduced to gown, diaper, and blanket—with a loose jacket, booties, and bonnet if weather was chilly. Even headcoverings were largely discarded except for outdoors. Gowns were reduced from about twenty-eight inches long in the pre-war years to a standardized twenty-four inches. The frills and flounces that had been common on virtually all infant's clothing now were reserved for christening gowns and accessories.

Little girls continued to wear simple, shoulder-yoke dresses cropped at just above the knees. (Figure 5.44.) Shorter versions, at about mid-thigh, were worn with bloomers, often of the same fabric as the dress. Older girls of the early 1920s wore longer dresses—to mid-calf for teenagers—styled with the new dropped waists. By the second half of the decade the boxy chemise with its hipline waist and knee-length skirt was the most prevalent look.

Small boys of this era were no longer dressed as girls although many toddlers of the upper classes often still endured long hair. The tunic and shorts outfits of the Edwardian era were now standard forms of boys' wear. Variants included revivals of the eighteenth-century skeleton suit with separate tops and bottoms that fastened together into a one-piece. (Figure 5.45.) Toddlers enjoyed the additional comfort of being free of long stockings, which their older siblings still wore. School-age boys continued to wear the knicker suit. As with the cut of adult styles

FIGURE 5.45. Clothing for toddler boys continued the trend toward greater freedom with easy, comfortable short sets and skeleton suits. Older boys adopted the baggy forms of plus fours and knitwear for school and play. Teenage boys donned scaled down versions of men's styles.

Skeleton suit, 1922.

Sailor suit, 1923.

Schoolboy's knicker suit, 1922.

Teenage boy's suit. 1921.

of the time, the knickers were loose and baggy, worn with assorted types of matching jackets, blazers, or sweaters. For teenage boys, one of the rites of passage was a graduation from knee britches to long pants. The suit styles of older boys were principally those of adult men. Teenage boys also wore scaled-down versions of men's overcoats, formalwear, swimwear, and other categories of clothing.

Review

Following World War I, women's fashions were transformed on ever shorter cycles of change. In the early 1920s, the short, high-waisted dresses of the war years were narrowed into long, straight lines emphasized by a lowered waistline and hems dropping nearly to the ankles. When women resisted the long skirts, designers responded with the boxy, dropped waist chemise and shorter hemlines to the knees by 1925—the flapper look. Evening wear became shorter as well with a myriad of revivalisms and asymmetrical hemlines.

Women now smoked and put on makeup in public, which filled handbags with new forms of accessories such as cigarette cases, compacts, and vanity cases. Hair was sheared off into bobs and shingle cuts allowing the redesigned cloche to hug the head like a helmet without hat pins.

New technologies also significantly impacted fashion design. Designers experimented with the high quality synthetic fabrics produced at the time, including the new artificial silk, rayon. The improved zipper provided new methods of closure for selected garments and accessories.

For men, a youth-oriented casual style influenced changes in their postwar wardrobes. Shirts with stiff, detachable collars were gradually abandoned in favor of versions with attached soft collars. Trouser legs were widened, some to the extreme dimensions of the Oxford bags. Full, baggy plus fours became a casual style adapted from golf knicker suits for everyday leisure wear. The variety of sportswear styles exploded into exciting new forms of shirts, jackets, trousers, shorts, knitwear, and athletic attire. Swimwear became ever briefer and more form-fitting. At some sophisticated resorts at the end of the decade, the tank-style one piece with a modesty skirt was reduced to thigh-high trunks without a top.

Childrenswear continued to evolve toward its own versions of casual comfort. Short sets and skeleton suits were ideal for active boys. Older boys enjoyed the ease of baggy knickers and soft-collar shirts. For small girls, the loose, short, shoulder-yoke dress styles allowed comfort and ease of movement. Older girls were dressed in scaled down versions of women's fashions, particularly the dropped-waist chemise. Clothing for teenage boys replicated adult styles.

review questions

1. Which were the key features of the silhouettes of women's dresses between 1920 and 1924, and 1925 and 1929?

2. Describe the chief characteristics of the ideal feminine figure and look of the flapper.

3. What influence did the Paris Exposition Internationale des Arts Decoratifs et Industriels Modernes of 1925 have on men's and women's fashions?

4. How did the silhouette of young men's dress suits evolve in the 1920s?

5. How did the young man's demand for casual elegance and distinction from older generations alter the course of menswear and masculine style in the 1920s?

research and portfolio projects

Research

1. Write a research paper on the emergence of New York's Seventh Avenue ready-to-wear market and the impact it had on American fashions of the 1920s. Identify the key labels of the era and their chief designers.

Portfolio

1. Choose a colorful art deco brooch from the 1920s and design in your sketchbook matching earrings, necklace, bracelet, ring, beaded handbag, and leather belt. Write an accompanying paragraph explaining the art deco elements or motifs used to coordinate all the pieces.

dress terms

art deco (also known as moderne): a decorative art style featuring geometric shapes and a pure linearity

balloon shoes: men's broad, square-toed shoes of the 1920s

blanket cloth: thick, flannel fabrics in bold plaids and patterns used for men's bathrobes

cellulose acetate: a cellulose-based fiber used in the production of rayon

cloverleaf lapels: the rounded points on notched lapels

clutch coat: a wrap style of coat popular with the flapper

collar grips: a metal clasp affixed to the tips of the collar behind the knot of the necktie to hold the collar smooth on men's dress shirts

corselette: an all-in-one corset style of the 1920s that encompassed the bust and hips

cossack pajamas: men's sleepwear suit with tunic top cut with an off-center closure and a stand-up round collar

culottes: short styles of the split skirt

Fashion Avenue: the name generally applied to the New York City apparel market located on Seventh Avenue

handkerchief skirt: skirt style draped with uneven, pointed hemlines resembling handkerchiefs

house coat: men's dressing gown worn over regular clothes during late night or early morning hours

jabot blouse: women's blouses of the 1920s with frilly neck treatments and a wide cut that could form a deep blouson over the skirt waistband

marcel: a hair curling device used in salons of the 1920s and 1930s for "permanent" waves

Oxford bags: trousers with wide legs worn by young men of the 1920s

peaked lapel: the wide, pointed style of lapel first popular on suit jackets of the 1920s

pinched-crown hat: men's brimmed hat with a pair of dents in the front of the crown

plus fours: loose, baggy knickerbocker trousers worn by both men and women in the 1920s and 1930s for sports activities, and by men as casual country attire

polo shirt: short-sleeve knit shirt with placket button closure and knit Eton collar

raccoon skin coat: long, voluminous fur coat with large collar worn by collegiate men and flappers of the 1920s

rayon: a synthetic fabric commonly known as artificial silk

singlette: lightweight step-in underwear favored by young women of the 1920s

slip: the generic term usually applied to petticoats and chemises since the 1920s

snap-brim fedora: men's hat with a pliable, wide brim and high, tapered crown

speedsuit: men's one-piece swimwear with short trunks and a tanktop

twosome swimsuit: men's one-piece swimwear with short trunks and a tank of a contrasting color or pattern

vanity case: handbag cosmetic containers with small, touch-up amounts of makeup and a mirror

viscose rayon: fabric made from synthetic yarns produced with viscous cellulose

zipper: a slide closure of interlocking teeth affixed to fabric or other material

6 The Great Depression 1930–1939

Great Depression began 1930	**Hitler named German chancellor 1933**	**Italy invaded Ethiopia 1935**	**England's Edward VIII abdicated; George VI ascended throne 1936**	**Du Pont patented nylon 1937**	**Germany invaded Poland; start of World War II 1939**
Empire State Building completed 1931	**Franklin Roosevelt's "New Deal" program 1933**	**Cole Porter's *The Gay Divorcee* 1934**			**Germany annexed Austria 1938**
Jean Harlow in *Platinum Blonde* 1931	**Prohibition ended in U.S. 1933**		**Spanish Civil War 1936–1939**	**Disney's *Snow White* 1937**	**Clark Gable in *Gone with the Wind* 1939**

The Great Depression of the 1930s

In October 1929, the soaring, decade-long prosperity came to an abrupt and ruinous end when the U.S. stock market crashed. In one day, the value of shares on the New York Exchange dropped 14 billion dollars. The speculative bubble had finally burst. The economic disaster caused a calamitous chain reaction around the world, plunging global economies into a deep and sustained business depression.

In the three years from 1930 to 1932, 86 thousand U.S. businesses failed, 9 million savings accounts were wiped out, and wages fell by sixty percent. More than 5,000 banks collapsed. Unemployment spiked sharply from less than 1 million in 1929 to almost 12 million in 1932. Countless thousands lost their homes and farms to foreclosure.

Because President Hoover had been slow to act in providing decisive measures of relief for the hard times, he lost the election of 1932 to Franklin Delano Roosevelt. In his first 100 days, Roosevelt pushed through Congress many of the essentials of his New Deal program aimed at the three R's: relief, recovery, and reform. An "alphabet soup" of federal agencies was developed to provide employment such as the WPA (Works Progress Administration) and the PWA (Public Works Administration). Government relief prevented mass starvation and eased suffering, but economic recovery was slow. Only with onset of the Second World War did the Great Depression finally come to an end.

In Europe, the Depression further fanned the fears of revolution and communism. Germany yielded democracy for the perceived stability of fascism. In 1933, Adolf Hitler became chancellor, and within a year had established a Nazi Party dictatorship. Almost immediately Hitler began rearming Germany. In 1938, he seized Austria and part of Czechoslovakia. A year later, he sent German troops into Poland, instigating the start of World War II.

Italy, too, was subjected to a totalitarian government headed by Benito Mussolini. In a quest to revive the glory that was the Roman Empire, Italy attacked Ethiopia in 1935 and occupied the territory as a colony.

The emergence of fascism in Spain resulted in a brutal civil war between 1936 and 1939. Aided by Hitler and Mussolini, General Francisco Franco overthrew the republican government in Madrid and established his own iron-fisted dictatorship.

In Asia, Japanese imperialists took advantage of the West's preoccupation with the Depression to conquer Manchuria in 1931. By 1937, Japan had expanded its aggression to all of China. This full-fledged war was a proving ground for Japanese militarists who would enter the Second World War in 1941 by attacking the United States at Pearl Harbor, Hawaii.

America in the Lean Years

During the worst years of the Great Depression, 1930–1933, more than 40 million people learned the misery of poverty as a way of life. In manufacturing, the last hired—usually unskilled whites and African-Americans—were the first fired as consumer sales dropped and factory production slowed. White collar workers went from being home owners to homeless as banks failed, wiping out their life's savings. Farmers lost everything as crop prices plummeted and a series of natural disasters struck—droughts, dust storms, and floods. Everywhere there was real hunger and despair. (Figure 6.1.) These bewildered Americans were the desperate souls so poignantly captured by John Steinbeck in his novel *The Grapes of Wrath* (1939).

President Hoover had stood firmly against a government "dole," convinced instead that the independent, pioneer spirit of the American people would enable them to overcome the hardships, and free enterprise would once again bring prosperity. But as the Depression deepened, those hopeless, displaced millions blamed Hoover, and his name became an adjective for many of the manifestations of the prolonged disaster. Hoover blankets were old newspapers used as bedding by the urban homeless. Hoover hams were the squirrels and rabbits caught for food by destitute country folk. And most notorious of all, Hoovervilles were the many shantytowns constructed of scraps of wood and cardboard in city parks and vacant lots across the nation.

In 1933, Franklin Roosevelt became president and inaugurated his "New Deal" program of government action for relief and recovery. His campaign slogan had been "Happy days are here again!" and the American people felt a renewed sense of hope and optimism. In addition

FIGURE 6.1. The 1930s was marked by a prolonged economic depression that lasted the entire decade. Times were hard for millions of Americans who lost their jobs, homes, and farms. Left, displaced farm family migrating westward, 1934; right, "Free Soup, Coffee, and Doughnuts for the Unemployed," 1932.

to new legislation for jobs programs, wage regulations, social security, banking reform, and child labor restrictions, the much-hated Prohibition was also repealed.

Although many millions of Americans suffered hard times during the 1930s, the great majority had been able to get on with life fairly much as always. In their 1937 study of middle America, social researchers Robert and Helen Lynn noted, "The fact that Middletown does not regard the depression as in any sense 'its own fault,' or even the fault of the economy by which it lives, makes it easy for the city to think of the confusion following 1929 as 'just a bad bump in the road,' one of those inevitable occurrences that spoil things temporarily but do not last." To muddle through, the average American postponed buying that new car one more year, and made due with fixing the washing machine and having their shoes resoled. As a result, jobs in the repair service sector actually increased.

Among the diversions that helped ease the gloom of the era were movies. Depression weary Americans could escape into the cinematic fantasies produced by the dream factories of Hollywood to laugh at W. C. Fields and the Marx Brothers, or delight in the musicals of Shirley Temple and Busby Berkeley, or cringe at the crime dramas of James Cagney and Edward G. Robinson. By many accounts today, the greatest single year in movie making history was 1939, hallmarked by *Gone With the Wind, The Wizard of Oz, Mr. Smith Goes to Washington,* and *Goodbye, Mr. Chips* among the gems. Radio programming expanded to fill the entire day beginning with "soap operas" in the morning for the housewife and, in the evening, all varieties of family shows from concerts and comedy "sketches" to dramatic serials and nightly news reports.

The Influences of Hollywood on Fashion

One of the most often cited examples of American influence on fashion of this period was the movies. Previously, film studios had commissioned Paris couturiers such as Molyneux, Lanvin, and Chanel to design costumes that were exaggerated and theatrical, not necessarily the mode of the season. As costume historian Jane Mulvagh noted, to remark on a 1920s look with "Whew! Pretty Hollywood" was an insult. In the 1930s, though, movie studios established wardrobe departments headed by some of America's most talented designers: Edith Head and Howard Greer at Paramount, Adrian at MGM, Orry Kelly at Warner Brothers, and Walter Plunkett at RKO to name a few. The costumes they designed for both historical and contemporary themed movies often broadly influenced mainstream fashions. The designers themselves even came to be as famous as film stars and frequently designed freelance for fashion firms or, as with Adrian, established their own salons and labels.

In 1930, the Modern Merchandising Bureau in New York began selling replications of hats and dresses from popular movies. Under the label Cinema Fashions, designs of clothing and accessories were licensed from the studios and sold exclusively by selected stores such as Macy's. Hollywood studios and movie stars benefitted from the additional publicity, and licensed retailers enjoyed promotional advantages over competitors.

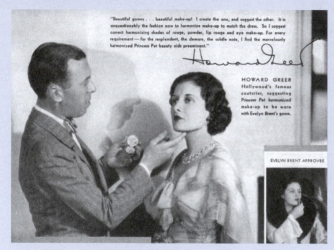

Howard Greer, detail of Princess Pat Cosmetics ad, 1931.

Edith Head, detail of a Johnson and Stevens Shoes ad, 1938.

The Depression at long last came to an end at the close of the 1930s when the U.S. economy geared up for war production. Despite the ominous clouds of war on the horizon in Europe and Asia in 1939, Americans celebrated the promise of the World of Tomorrow with a World's Fair in New York. Fairgoers crowded into 300 futuristic pavilions to wonder at thousands of exhibits from U.S. businesses and 60 foreign nations. Among the marvels of the future on display were television, nylon stockings, talking robots, and a model rocket airport for the city of 1960. *Vogue* sponsored a fashion show with style predictions for the year 2000 in which clothing was made of high-tech materials like Lucite, Plexiglass, cellophane, and glass filaments. The "magnificent spectacle of a luminous world," as the fair was described in the guide book, was a huge success. But with America just coming out of a ten-year depression, and the threat of a world war looming, was there "any validity to the theme: the World of Tomorrow"? asked the *Ladies' Home Journal*. Absolutely, concluded the editors. The fair portrayed for Americans "what lies ahead by showing the accomplishments in science and industry and art of today." America was back on its footing and the future was bright.

Women's Fashions 1930–1939

As the economic conditions of the industrialized world worsened in the first years of the 1930s, the fashion industries of Paris, London, and America suffered significant losses in sales and numerous business failures. Some Paris houses such as Doucet and Doeuillet merged to survive, while other salons, notably Poiret's, went bankrupt and closed permanently. Innumerable ready-to-wear operations on both sides of the Atlantic folded. Designers presented fewer models in their collections as there were fewer couture clients and merchant buyers.

One of the misconceptions today of fashion change during the period between the World Wars was that the onset of the Great Depression was the catalyst for the shift in silhouettes from the flapper's short, straightline chemise to the curvaceous contours and long skirts of the 1930s. In actuality, the change had already begun well ahead of the catastrophic collapse of the U.S. stock market. Reporting on the autumn collections of 1929, the Paris editor of the *Ladies' Home Journal* advised readers that the "vast majority of the leading dressmakers" now designed a "normal waistline," thus allowing "a smart figure to follow nature's curves in the outlines of dress." In addition, the editor noted, hemlines for street dresses had dropped "a few inches below the knees," and for afternoon dresses, skirts were now "well down, at least half way to the ankle." The following year *Vogue* was more specific, citing measurements of hemlines "from thirteen to fifteen inches from the ground." By the worst period of the Depression in 1932, many fashion depictions showed hemlines almost to the ankles. (Figure 6.2.)

The new interest in feminine curves, though, did not extend to a renewal of the voluptuousness and mature proportions of the Edwardian woman. The feminine figure of the 1930s was delineated but not exaggerated by the shape of clothing. The waist was defined but not cinched, the bust was shaped but small, and hips were rounded but slender. Legs may have vanished beneath longer hemlines but the narrow cut of the skirts contoured the hips and thighs redefining feminine sensuality. The slim, form-fitted silhouette was reinforced with snug bodices, blouses, and sweaters, and with skirts made with the addition of gores and bias-cut sections set into hip-line yokes.

In the opening years of the Depression, fashions were simplified and conservative. The flash and dazzle of the flapper were left behind. Shimmering materials such as taffeta were replaced with matt fabrics like satin-faced silk or rayon, and the lavish use of beading, fringe, and embroidery largely disappeared. Colors were more somber to reflect the mood of the moment. Long sleeves were more prevalent, even in warm weather.

One reason for the more simple, subdued clothing designs during the early thirties was economy—clothes were meant to last for several seasons without appearing to be out of style. Women's magazines devoted many pages to thrift and frugal shopping. Even upscale *Vogue* introduced new feature articles such as "Tips on the Shop Market" to keep readers informed of affordable styles in ready-to-wear.

By the mid-thirties, a slow but perceptible economic recovery had begun. The darkest days of the Depression were over and people once again dared hope for better times. Designers began to reflect the renewed optimism with a return of opulence and a touch of frivolity of style and color.

Leading the charge out of the doldrums of the Depression was Elsa Schiaparelli, whose association with the Surrealists, particularly Salvadore Dali and Jean Cocteau, inspired her to design many quirky, eye-catching fashions of the period. "Shocking Elsa," as she was nicknamed, thrust vibrant color into the fashion arena reminiscent of Poiret a generation earlier.

FIGURE 6.2. When the 1930s opened, hemlines had dropped below the knees and the waistline returned to its natural position. Within two years, skirts had descended almost to the ankles. Above left, worsted jersey dress from Durene, 1930; above right, wool knit dresses from Marinette, 1932; below, print dress by Echarpe Fabrics, 1932.

She introduced exposed colored zippers as decorative accents. (Figure 6.3.) Her trademark hue was a vivid pink appropriately called "shocking pink." Later, when she launched her house perfume, she labeled it "Shocking." Among her most memorable creations were hats sculpted like upside down high heels or lamb chops, purses shaped like desk telephones or giant padlocks, and costume jewelry of crawling, lifelike insects. More importantly, though, Schiaparelli's fashions were very wearable. Her suits with bolero jackets were widely copied and remained popular through the Second World War. Equally significant was her persistent use of wide, exaggerated shoulders, an influence that endured until the mid-forties. (Figure 6.4.)

The fancifulness and opulence of movie costumes also influenced both mainstream styles as well as Paris couture during the 1930s. For instance, among the most popular styles of evening gowns of 1932–33 were replicas of Adrian's ruffle shoulder organdy gown worn by Joan Crawford in *Letty Lynton* (1932) and his white satin gown worn by Jean Harlow in *Dinner at Eight* (1933). Historical films such as the *Merry Widow* (1934), *Mary of Scotland* (1936), *Camille* (1937), *Marie Antoinette* (1938), and *Gone with the Wind* (1939) inspired various revivals of bustles, crinolines, Medici collars, and panniers.

Despite the occasional exaggerated revival and the persistence of broad shoulders and big sleeves, the silhouette primarily remained trim and fitted to the feminine curves. Skirts hugged hips and thighs, with a flare at the hem for added fluidity of motion. Hemlines began to rise in 1933 to about fourteen inches from the floor, and gradually continued upward about another four inches by the end of the decade.

FIGURE 6.3. "Shocking" Elsa Schiaparelli added oversized colored zippers as contrasting accents to her dress and evening gown designs, beginning in 1935. Crown Zipper ad, 1938.

The exception to the rule of curves were some styles of women's tailored suits. Many suit designs adopted strong masculine lines that were further enhanced by boxy jackets with padded shoulders and wide lapels and slim skirts. (Figure 6.5.) The squared shapes of bolero suits particularly disguised the feminine form, especially when jackets were worn opened or draped around the shoulders like a cape. As Europe's war machines began to mobilize in the second half of the decade, military details like metal buttons and grosgrain ribbon or braid trim became popular embellishments for women's suits. Firm, durable fabrics and strong textile patterns such as houndstooth checks, glen plaids, and pin stripes reinforced the menswear look.

Evening wear of the 1930s was especially enhanced by the redefined waistline and natural proportions. (Figure 6.6.) Sweeping floor-length gowns returned, often with flowing trains. Opulence was concentrated on fabric and cut rather than the lavish surface embellishments favored in the previous two decades. Most dramatic of all, though, were the backless gowns, many of which were open fully to the waist. To emphasize the expanse of bare flesh, designers sometimes added all types of eye-catching, fussy trim and detailing to the back openings. As

FIGURE 6.4. As global economies eased out of the Depression during the mid-thirties, fashion designers reintroduced flair and fancifulness into fashion. Shoulders were broadened by new, exaggerated interpretations of puffed and padded sleeves. Left, pagoda sleeves from Grossman & Spiegel, 1936; right, suit styles by Carolyn, 1936.

legs disappeared beneath longer skirts, the bare back became the new displayed erogenous zone. Patou's dramatic halter styles of 1933 daringly laid bare the entire back, shoulders, and arms. Such open designs challenged couturiers to develop innovative constructions of internal bras and bodice boning to hold the garments in place. By mid-decade, exaggerated sleeves provided a fresh look to evening wear. Shoulderlines ranged from wide, leg-of-mutton revivals to the **pagoda sleeve** with its high, peaked shoulderline. The deep dolman cut, commonly called the **batwing sleeve**, with its fullness extending beneath the arm to the waist, was a softer alternative to the top-heavy, puffed construction.

Women's Outerwear 1930–1939

In the 1930s, coats were reshaped to follow the natural contours of the feminine form. (Figure 6.7.) Waists were defined with belts or by tapered cuts on princess lines, though

not tightly cinched, and hemlines grazed just above the ankles by 1931. Large fur collars were a carry-over from the twenties and remained popular throughout the decade. Military detailing began to appear in the early thirties, primarily influenced from Schiaparelli's "soldier" collections. As the war machines of Italy and Germany became constant headlines in the news, military looks for women's outerwear such as epaulets and padded shoulders gained in popularity. Wide shoulders and exaggerated, oversized sleeves—including leg-of-mutton and pagoda styles—dominated mid-decade. Fuller cut, three-quarter lengths were more common as hemlines shortened in the second half of the thirties.

A new form of vividly colored rainwear was widely promoted in the 1930s. Transparent coats, hooded capes, and matching umbrellas were made of "Philofilm," a transparent rubber that resembled our modern synthetics like vinyl.

Women's Sports Apparel 1930–1939

By the 1930s, when New Deal programs built parks, sports facilities, and community swimming pools, sports that were previously regarded as activities for the affluent, such as tennis and golf, became more popular with the middle classes. Winter sports, like skiing, ski jumping, and ice skating, also extended from the resorts into suburbia, especially following the highly publicized 1932 Winter Olympics in Lake Placid, New York.

Comfortable knit garments continued as the favored clothing for both summer and winter active sports. All types of pullover sweaters, cardigans, and vests were layered to peel away as exertion warmed the active body.

For backyard recreation or golf and tennis games at the community park, women most often wore everyday casual clothes. Pleated and split skirts remained popular for sports activities despite the longer hemlines of the thirties. Shorts and three-piece playsuits comprised of matching short-sleeved shirts, shorts, and thigh-high wrap skirts were increasingly commonplace in public. (Figure 6.8.)

The category of resort sportswear—trousers, shorts, culottes, knit tops—had continued to grow in popularity throughout the 1920s and, in the 1930s, increasingly became standard, everyday casual attire for most women across all demographics. Trousers—now usually referred to as **slacks**—were particularly adapted to women's wardrobes for leisure activities and relaxing at home. Hollywood stars such as Katherine Hepburn and Marlene Dietrich became trendsetters by appearing in movies wearing slacks and being photographed wearing various trouser styles in public. Ready-to-wear makers, especially those from California, mass produced slacks tailored to the female form with a more flattering fit than Poiret's Turkish trousers or the functional work pants of the World War I years. Similarly, shorts migrated from active sports arenas to the playwear wardrobes of women where colorful and patterned variants were worn for summer leisure.

The transition from knickerbockers to slacks for sports was gradual throughout the early 1930s. By the end of the decade, the knickerbocker suit had disappeared from the mass merchandising catalogs. Jodhpurs and cropped jackets were still the accepted costume for

FIGURE 6.5. As a contrast to the contoured, curvaceous fit of dresses, many suits adopted the look of menswear that altered or disguised the feminine form. Suits from Carolyn, 1936.

FIGURE 6.6. Evening wear elegance in the 1930s was hallmarked by a return of the flowing, floor-length gown and sumptuous, fluid fabrics. Fashion drama was achieved with daring open backs, some of which plunged to the waistline.

Backless gowns from Symphonie, 1932.

Pagoda sleeve gown by Nettie Rosenstein, 1936.

Tiered gown by Jo Copeland, 1936.

Fringed gown from Jay Thorpe, 1937.

FIGURE 6.7. Coats of the 1930s followed the long lines of dresses with hemlines dropping to a few inches above the ankles. In the second half of the decade, exaggerated sleeve shapes and dimensions defined the silhouette. Left, princess line coats from Printzess, 1933; right, wool coat with karakul collar from Fashion Firsts, 1936.

FIGURE 6.8. Sportswear for weekend recreation became more diverse in the 1930s, including slacks and short sets. Left: rayon slacks suit, three-piece skirted playsuit, and sharkskin culotte suit, 1938; right, cuffed slacks and contrast placket polo shirt, 1938.

FIGURE 6.9. For skiing and other winter sports, the most prevalent form of dress was the pant suit. Comfortable, baggy pants of heavy wool were lined with cotton flannel and secured at the ankles with knit cuffs. Jackets were short for easy maneuverability outdoors and came in a wide variety of coordinating styles. Kerrybrooke Togs, 1937.

riding. For winter skiing and sledding, wool pant suits lined with cotton flannel were the most common. Ski suits were made with a variety of short jackets and baggy pants with wide, high waistbands and knit cuffs. (Figure 6.9.)

Women's Underwear and Sleepwear 1930–1939

In the 1930s, foundation garments, as the category of corsets, girdles, and bras came to be known in retail, were revolutionized by changes in fibers, finishes, and fasteners. The fashionable silhouette was now curvaceous but slim. Corsets once again became substantial, not only to shape the figure, but also to smooth any bulges and sagging of the natural form. Advances in knitting technologies allowed for elasticized yarns to be knitted into seamless tubes for corsets

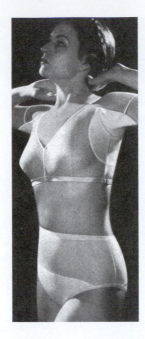

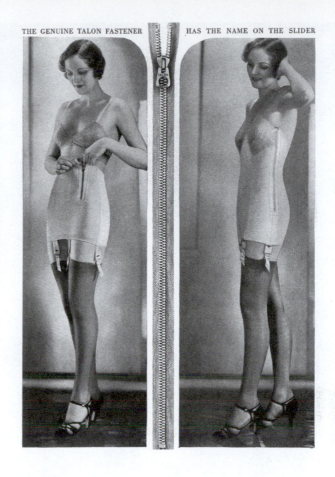

FIGURE 6.10. Intimate apparel of the 1930s became briefer and more formfitting to minimize show-through with the clinging dresses of the time. Left, bra and "scant" panties from Kleinert's, 1936; right, girdle and corset featuring the new zipper closures, 1932.

that could be rolled on. Particularly important was the introduction of the zipper to foundation garments, which eased the strain of squeezing into corsets and girdles. (Figure 6.10.)

When feminine curves returned in the 1930s, new emphasis was placed on the bust, and bras were reengineered into cup models to shape and delineate the contours of the breasts. In 1935, Warner introduced the alphabet cup sizes to ensure the best fit.

Women's intimate apparel of the thirties was scaled down in size and bulk. Lightweight rayon step-ins and the new brief-style "**skanties**" were ideally suited for the clinging dresses of the period.

During the late twenties, the U.S. chemical manufacturer Du Pont began experimenting with molecular engineering to create polymers that would form the basis of numerous synthetic materials. In 1938, they introduced durable, resilient **nylon** yarns. A year later, nylon stockings created a sensation at the New York World's Fair. Because nylon became an important war material during the Second World War, the widespread application of the material in fashion was deferred until the late 1940s.

As with intimate apparel, sleepwear also continued to be reduced in bulk and scale. Long gowns and pajama sets of rayon, silk, cotton crepe, and batiste filled the pages of retail catalogs. (Figure 6.11.) New varieties included delicate shortie pajamas and backless styles. In the late 1930s, assorted puff sleeves and ruffled or gathered shoulder-cap treatments reflected the sleeve interest of dresses, suits, and coats.

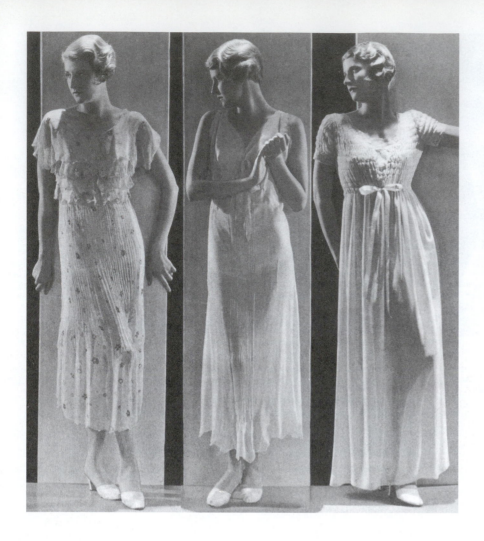

FIGURE 6.11. Nightgowns of the 1930s were widely varied in style, many of which were designed with the elegance and sumptuous detailing of evening gowns. Nightgowns from Franklin Simon, 1931.

Women's Swimwear 1930–1939

During the 1930s, swimwear continued to evolve ever briefer lines for the maximum exposure of skin. Halter styles and backless racers were favorites. By the mid-thirties, the first two-piece swimsuits bared midriffs in public. (Figure 6.12.) Fabrics made of Lastex and other elasticized yarns held their shape and color better than knitted wool for a flattering delineation of the female curves. Although swimwear continued to become more revealing, social prudery still dictated that, for two-piece suits, bottoms must be cut high to conceal the navel, and many other styles continued to be made with modesty skirts that extended over the hips to the upper thighs.

Women's Shoes 1930–1939

In the first years of the Great Depression, comfort and durability were key considerations in shoe designs. Heels were lower and more solid with less pronounced curves than the Louis ogee. Toes were more rounded and wider but became squared after 1935. The shape was higher over the instep and lace-ups returned as an alternative to buckle straps. (Figure 6.13.)

Halter suit by Mabs, skirted maillot by Kohn, tank suit by Ocean, 1936.

Two-piece swimsuit from Sacony, 1936.

Kool-Tex reversible rubber swimsuits, 1935.

FIGURE 6.12. Swimwear increasingly became more revealing. Among the daring innovations were halter styles and bared midriffs.

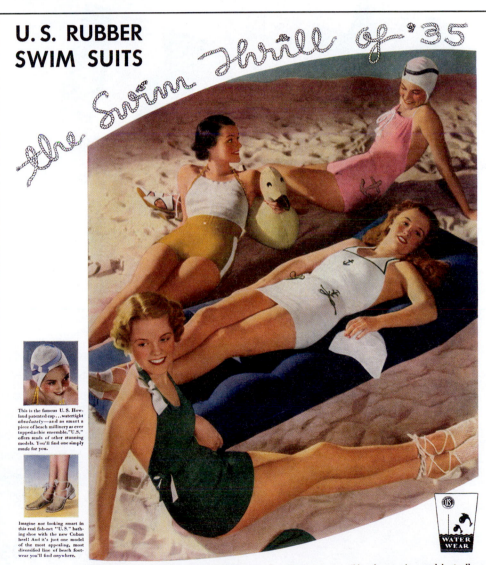

Walk-Over Brand Shoes, 1936.

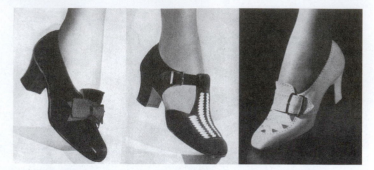

FIGURE 6.13. Everyday shoes of the Depression era were usually lower, more solid, and subdued in color than the strappy styles of the twenties. In casual footwear, thick, cork platform "Lido" shoes were fresh and exciting.

Vitality Brand Shoes, 1938.

Patent leather, suede, and gabardine shoes from Montgomery Ward, 1938.

Lido platforms, 1938.

When the global economic outlook appeared to improve in the mid-thirties, fashion began to exhibit the fun and frivolity of big sleeves and fanciful revivals, and sportswear—including culottes, shorts, and slacks—became common everyday wear. Footwear also developed some of the most dramatic eccentricities since the seventeenth century. Open-toe shoes and slingbacks for daytime made their debut. Sandals and the rubber-soled "**tennis shoe**" were now seen on the street. In 1937, cork platform "**Lido shoes**" first appeared at the resorts. Overall, colors were less vibrant than a decade earlier but still came in a huge variety of deep, rich tones such as burgundy, hunter green, russet, and deep blue.

Women's Jewelry 1930–1939

Throughout the 1930s, the linear, geometric look of the moderne style dominated jewelry design. (Figure 6.14.) Novelty plastic jewelry provided women with affordable and fun adornment

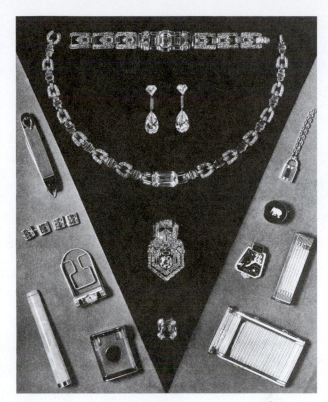

FIGURE 6.14. Moderne (later known as art deco) styling dominated jewelry design in the 1930s. When revivals of historical costumes became fashionable in the second half of the decade, jewelry makers complemented the looks with replicas of period pieces. Left, ad from Leo Glass depicting "replicas of exquisite jewelry worn by historical beauties," 1938; right, jewelry by Cartier, 1937.

for many of the drab fashions of the time. Early **phenolic plastics** like **Bakelite** and **Catalin** were used in the mass production of colorful jewelry, hair and hat ornaments, shoe attachments, belt buckles, buttons, and other accessories.

As historical revivals became more popular in fashions of the mid-thirties, jewelry makers also replicated designs from earlier eras, especially Rococo styles from the eighteenth century. Sparkling jewels were once again favored. Large brooches with clusters of faceted stones were worn with menswear suits to feminize the look. Small-link chain necklaces and bracelets of precious metals complemented the fluid draping of fashions.

Women's Hairstyles and Makeup 1930–1939

In keeping with the softer, curvaceous femininity of women's fashions, hairstyles became more wavy and curvilinear as well. (Figure 6.15.) Short hair remained the most popular look although the cuts were often fuller than the flapper's bob with soft curls over the ears and at the back of the head. By the end of the decade hairstyles became more sculptural with greater mass, though still predominantly worn up.

1933

1936

1938

FIGURE 6.15. Hairstyles of the Depression era remained short and wavy. Clusters of curls were arranged at specific parts of the head rather than in an all-over pattern like the flapper's bob. Cosmetic regimens were more refined with palettes of facial powder, lipstick, eyeshadow, and nail polish complementing the woman's features and natural coloring.

The application of makeup in the thirties became more refined and sophisticated, especially with the advent of color movies in which women could see up close how Max Factor and other professionals accentuated different face shapes and features. The caricatured mask of the 1920s was replaced by the sculpted, refined face of the 1930s. A dual layer of tinted foundation and powder was applied and then accented with eyeshadows and lipsticks that suited the woman's hair color and skin tones. Rouge was used to shape and define cheekbones rather than rose tint the surface. The beauty regimen that was advertised by cosmetics mass marketers like Helena Rubinstein, Elizabeth Arden, and Dorothy Gray became a daily routine for women of all ages and classes in the 1930s.

Women's Hats 1930–1939

Since hairstyles largely remained short in the early 1930s, hats also continued to be made close fitting although now they sat back away from the face. Most notable about hats of the era was that, despite the style, virtually all varieties were worn at a sharp angle. (Figure 6.16.) By the end of the decade when hairstyles increased in volume, but were still worn up, hats were pushed forward onto the brow. When fashion designers began to show fantasy and frivolity in their collections of the mid-thirties, milliners joined the creative fun. Schiaparelli's famous upside-down shoe hat and other surrealistic sculptural headwear made fashion headlines, but most women, instead, opted for any of numerous hat styles laden with exuberant arrangements of feathers, ribbons, flowers, and other colorful trimmings. Also, in the latter part of the decade, verticality dominated the newer looks. Toques, fedoras, and turbans were shaped with tall crowns. Even low hats such as pillboxes and tams were given a vertical line by the addition of a feather or bow pointing skyward. Verticality was further achieved by the extreme side angle of a wide brimmed picture hat. Other popular styles of the late 1930s included the so-called "**toy**" hats—miniaturized

"The Watteau" by Gage Hats, 1931.

Hat from Germaine Millinery, 1932.

Felt turban from Stetson, 1932.

Straw broad-brim hat by Jane Engel, 1935.

Turban with petite plumes by Maria Guy, 1938.

Felt sailor with wings by Rose Valois, 1938.

Hat with "corkscrew" crown by Peck & Peck, 1938.

Straw tricorne with veil by Daché, 1938.

Felt hat with swirled crown and rope band from Stetson, 1938.

Toy hat from Carolyn, 1939.

Styles from the Chicago Mail Order Company, 1936.

FIGURE 6.16. At the start of the Depression, hats were close fitting and worn at sharp angles. By mid-decade, touches of fancifulness were reintroduced, including imaginative shapes, vivid colors, and unusual trimmings.

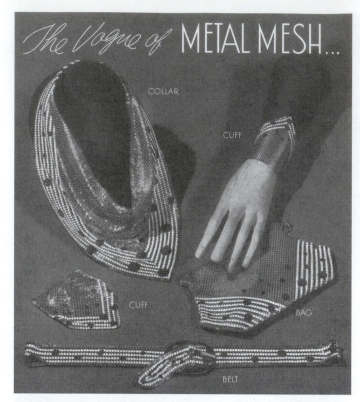

The Vogue of METAL MESH...

COLLAR

CUFF

CUFF

BAG

BELT

Metal mesh accessories by Whiting & Davis, 1935.

Schiaparelli handbags designed for Whiting & Davis, 1938.

Glentex silk scarves and clips, 1937.

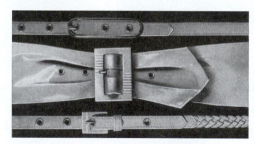

Patent belts from Slote & Klein, 1931.

Gloves from Van Raalte, 1937.

Evening bag with vanity and matching cigarette case and compact from Gold Seal, 1938.

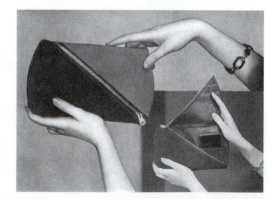

Talon handbag, 1932.

FIGURE 6.17. The shapes and embellishments of accessories of the Depression era were largely influenced by moderne styling. In addition, innovative uses of the zipper, metal mesh, rayon, Bakelite, and other new materials provided fresh looks to traditional types of accessories.

versions of contemporary styles—that were tied with wide ribbons under the chin or in the back anchored by knots of hair. Veils of all sorts of netting were the epitome of elegance and were attached to almost all types of hats. In 1939, the snood reappeared and would become a practical form of headwear during the Second World War when women working in factories needed to protect their hair from the dangers of machinery.

Women's Accessories 1930–1939

As with jewelry designs of the Depression era, the shapes and surface embellishments of accessories were predominantly influenced by the flat pattern geometry of moderne styling. (Figure 6.17.)

Belts had a renewed importance when the natural waistline was redefined after 1930. Styles ranged from ultra-thin to oversized and dramatically sculptural.

Handbags began to increase in size as women needed more space to carry an increasing assortment of accessories. Varieties of bags on frames with pouch containers remained a common form from the previous few decades. The zipper was imaginatively applied to create new types of closures for handbags, totes, and other small leathers. Beading and metal mesh were popular for evening bags.

Silk and rayon scarves were affordable fashion accents for the Depression era woman on a budget. Patterns and colors were vivid to set off the more subdued dresses and suits of the early years. Scarf makers provided instructional flyers on ways to tie scarves for fresh looks.

Gloves were worn with all dressy day outfits. Gauntlet styles were often detailed with topstitching, piping, ruffled edges, and other trimmings. Women owned a number of pairs of gloves in colors to match ensembles and other accessories. Wide cuff bracelets were sometimes worn over the glove. For evening wear, long gloves were worn to offset the bareness of sleeveless and backless gowns.

Men's Fashions 1930–1939

By the beginning of the 1930s, the wave of Anglomania in menswear that had begun after the First World War was further bolstered by two significant influences from Britain that reshaped and redefined the masculine wardrobe into much of what it is today: the personal style of the Prince of Wales (later King Edward VIII, and after his abdication, the Duke of Windsor), and the drape cut of men's suits developed by the Savile Row tailor Frederick Scholte.

The style leadership of the Prince of Wales paralleled that of his grandfather as a young man, later Edward VII, whose every nuance of dress had been equally influential on men's attire at the end of the Victorian era. In the 1920s, the young prince had been instrumental in the change to "soft" dressing for men. Instead of high, stiff detachable collars, the prince preferred the soft, turned down styles. He opted for roomy trousers with belts rather than suspenders— or he even went beltless if the trousers were made with an adjustable-tab waistband. In the 1930s, the prince was in the vanguard of men's fashion with his unlined, unconstructed sport jackets and his zipper fly front trousers. He dared bold pattern mixing of glen plaid jackets and striped or print ties. He shocked old-guard society with his colorful shirts, including a pink one worn on an official visit to France.

FIGURE 6.18. The drape cut suit of the 1930s featured a jacket with broad, unpadded shoulders, a tapered waist, and narrow hips worn over wide-legged trousers. Suit styles from Krafft & Phillips, 1937.

But the Prince of Wales was more of an advocate of style rather than a menswear innovator. That distinction belonged to Frederick Scholte, who, like Giorgio Armani fifty years later, deconstructed the men's suit with innovative new cuts and master tailoring. Scholte had been the tailor for the elite officers of the royal guards. He admired the lean, athletic image projected by the guards, and developed three principles of cut from the construction of their tunics and greatcoats: wide shoulders, slim waists, and roomy armholes. Scholte did not resort to padding to achieve the athletic contours of his jackets. Instead, by masterful draping, he broadened the shoulders with a full sleevehead and tiny tucks that aligned the tip of the jacket shoulder with the triceps, and then subtly tapered the sleeve to the wrist. Additional material at the armhole filled out and softly draped over the shoulder blades and chest for greater ease of movement. It is from this feature that the style came to be called the **drape cut** (also **London cut** or **blade cut**). Finally, lapels were rolled rather than pressed flat, adding dimension to the chest. (Figure 6.18.)

The drape cut suit particularly appealed to men of the 1930s because it reflected the new classical ideal of the athletic masculine silhouette. Throughout the 1920s and 1930s, sports of all forms were immensely popular with young men. Hollywood also projected this new ideal of the athlete with movies like the Tarzan series, depicting the nearly nude Johnny Weissmuller displaying the well-toned physique of an Olympic champion. The slender, natural shoulder contours of the previous men's suit styles now seemed almost effeminate or, at best, juvenile, compared to the new athletic profile.

FIGURE 6.19. One of the technological advances in men's suit construction in the 1930s was the replacement of gaping, button fly fronts on trousers with the zipper fly front. Detail of a Talon Fastener ad, 1936.

FIGURE 6.20. Sport jackets were a popular alternative to the tailored suit jacket both for informal social gatherings and as business dress. Double- and single-breasted sport jackets by John Maly, 1937.

FIGURE 6.21. Men's trousers in the 1930s became full and heavy with high waistbands, baggy legs, deep pleats, and wide cuffs. Ferris wool sports trousers, 1938.

Technology also aided the new fit and construction of suits in the 1930s when zipper fly fronts were introduced as an alternative to gaping, button closures. (Figure 6.19.) Although tailors were initially reluctant to experiment with the device—some claiming the inherent dangers of its location—when the Prince of Wales began to have his trousers fitted with zipper flies in 1934, the new standard was set.

An American variant of the drape cut suit made of lightweight tropical fabrics came to be called the **Palm Beach suit** after the Florida resort. In the mid-1930s, **seersucker**, a puckered textile that derived its name from the Persian "shirushakar," especially became a favorite summer suit fabric as a substitute for linen and shantung, both of which wrinkled badly in hot, humid climates. *Esquire* declared in 1935 that men should "sail for a seersucker for a cool change."

Blazers and sport jackets continued to be an important substitute for the suit jacket, mostly for informal social gatherings, but also increasingly as business dress. During the early years of the Depression, colors and patterns of sport jackets became more somber and subdued. In the second half of the decade, though, some of the frivolity of clothing design that affected women's fashions similarly appeared in menswear, including pattern mixing of jackets and trousers, and experimental jacket styles like the **weskit**, a fitted jacket cut with a short, vest-like hemline. (Figure 6.20.)

Despite the trim, athletic fit of suit coats and sport jackets, trousers became fuller through the seat and hips with wide legs that almost resembled the faddish Oxford bags of the previous decade. (Figure 6.21.) Deep, multiple pleats, sometimes set in reverse (opening inward toward the fly) added volume that flapped about the legs when walking. Wide, high waist bands—called "high waisters" in menswear catalogs—and wide cuffs contributed to the heavy appearance of trousers.

A shift in men's formal wear also occurred during this era. The tuxedo continued to gain in popularity, replacing the tail coat at many high social events. The white dinner jacket, made with a variety of front closures and non-satin lapel styles, became a favorite of Ivy Leaguers. In the 1930s, the dinner jacket was ubiquitous, and ready-to-wear makers mass produced versions to be worn for everything from high school proms to wedding suppers. Also in the 1930s emerged the short **mess jacket**, resembling a naval officer's dinner dress. The requisite for the mess jacket was a youthful, slim waistline since the style was cropped high and fitted snugly. The tail coat continued to be worn for selected special occasions, particularly by older men in urban settings. "The usual question is 'black or white tie?'—meaning tail coat or dinner jacket," observed *Vogue* in 1936. But the editors conceded, "Requirements differ, depending on locality." Similarly, the cutaway morning coat suit endured for formal day events like England's Ascot or weddings although it, too, was worn less frequently in the thirties.

As color and bold stripes became more prevalent in dress shirts, a look especially popular with the Prince of Wales, men had to put more thought into their clothing selections by coordinating ties, jackets, and trousers more assiduously. (Figure 6.22.) As evidence that men in general had become more style conscious, even those of the working classes, *Esquire* was launched in 1933 to advise on men's dressing, among other topics of masculine style.

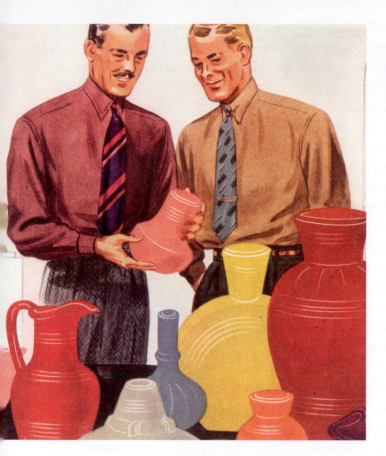

FIGURE 6.22. Fabrics for men's shirts of the Depression era expanded the vivid color palettes of the 1920s to include deep, rich hues and bold vertical stripes. Neckties were wider than Jazz Age styles but still worn a few inches short of the belt. Graphical art deco designs, called "moderne" at the time, of neckwear complemented the bold colors and fabrics of shirts. Left, earthtone colors for dress shirts by Jayson, 1937; right, dress shirts and ties by Arrow, 1937.

Casual sportswear as general day wear continued to gain in popularity. In 1936, *Vogue* advised, "With clothes of this sort, there are no rules except those dictated by a man's own good taste." More importantly, though, was *where* men wore these new forms of clothing. Even into the late thirties, magazines like *Esquire* and *Vogue* tried to stem the tide of casual sportswear indecorously appearing in the wrong places. For example, *Vogue* insisted that men must never appear in the city dressed in "country wear" such as "rough tweed suits—sometimes of a loud pattern—white flannel trousers or the still more popular grey flannels, polo shirts in wool or cotton, flannel shirts with collars attached, pullovers of every variety, careless-looking corduroy slacks, rubber-soled brogues, golf shoes, soft felt hats, windbreakers, leather jackets, cardigans, and what-nots." Yet these "what-nots" were exactly what men increasingly wore at public events and in town. The Prince of Wales, especially, led the change from staid sartorial correctness to personal style, with the emphasis on comfort.

Among the changes seen on city streets and in public places like race tracks and urban parks were the many new designs of the sports shirt, worn without a tie and the collar throat open. (Figure 6.23.) When worn with a sport coat or even a tweed or seersucker suit, the collar of the shirt would be spread over the lapels, much to the chagrin of traditionalists.

Just as the color palettes of dress shirts exploded into every conceivable variation, sport shirts likewise were produced in hues that only the most confident of men might wear. In the

FIGURE 6.23. Casual shirts worn with an open collar became increasingly acceptable to wear in public places where previously a necktie and jacket had been required. Sport shirts from Wilson Brothers, 1935.

late 1930s, vividly colored **Hawaiian print shirts** appeared at the resorts and were quickly copied by ready-to-wear makers for mass distribution. By the end of the decade, most men had at least one pineapple or palm print shirt for vacation picnics and backyard barbeques.

Versions of the short-sleeve polo shirt continued to be a favorite for home recreation as well as at resorts. (Figure 6.24.) In the 1930s, a variant, the **dishrag shirt**, featured a torso, and sometimes sleeves, in an open-mesh weave, somewhat resembling the textiles used for household cleaning cloths.

Improved techniques in commercial knitting led to an enormous variety of affordable knitwear. Men's wardrobes were populated with a wide assortment of pullovers, cardigans, twin sets, and sweater vests. (Figure 6.25.) The V-neck pullover was by far the most popular, having been prevalent as tennis wear for more than fifty years. In the mid-1930s, zippers were added to cardigans and sweater vests for an updated look.

In addition to the diversity of nontraditional looks such as Hawaiian shirts, weskits, and patterned knit tops, the cowboy look gained popularity in the 1930s. The proliferation of affordable automobiles and New Deal highways made long-distance travel more accessible to the masses. As the middle classes from east of the Mississippi River vacationed in the Old West, they returned home with jeans, Western cut shirts, fringed jackets, Stetson hats, and fancy cowboy boots as novelty items for their casual wardrobes. In 1938, *Esquire* avowed, "We can't figure out whether it is in spite of their flamboyancy or because of it, but these [cowboy] outfits come highly recommended by those who know as being the

FIGURE 6.24. Another type of active sports clothing that became mainstream attire was the knit short-sleeve polo shirt with a placket front closure and knit Eton collar. Numerous variations of the style were common by the mid-1930s. Knit polo shirts from Minerva, 1934.

FIGURE 6.25. Knitwear of the 1930s became ever more varied in designs and specialized in purpose.

Bateau neckline sweater, 1934.

Twinset cardigan and pullover, 1934.

Patterned Shetland sweater, 1934.

Sweater vest, 1934.

McCoy." Few Easterners went for the whole cowboy look on the streets of Philadelphia or Boston, but the popularity of jeans and dropped-yoke denim jackets revealed the influence of Western style that would remain a recurring theme in menswear to the present day.

Men's Sports Attire and Outerwear 1930–1939

In 1932, the United States hosted both the Summer Olympics in Los Angeles and the Winter Olympics in Lake Placid, New York, from which the youth of America were introduced to exciting new forms of sports and advances in sports equipment and correct attire. Moisture-repellent rayon fabrics were used to make new types of skiwear, including long trousers with elastic knit bands at the ankles, and jackets or pullover tops with knit cuffs and waistbands as a barrier against snow. (Figure 6.26.) Thick knit gloves, goggles, and wool caps with ear flaps or knit "helmets" protected the body's extremities.

Although in the 1920s white flannel shorts were frequently seen on collegiate tennis courts, it was not until British champion Bunny Austin wore them in the 1932 U.S. National Championship that the style became widely accepted. Another change that altered the tennis costume in the 1930s was the introduction of the tennis shoe, made with a crepe outsole and white duck upper with white laces.

Throughout the 1930s, both plus fours and trousers were equally prevalent for golfing. By the mid-thirties, fashion magazines were reporting on knee-length shorts seen on the greens at resorts. Worn with knee-high stockings, the cool and comfortable shorts became the alternative to plus fours.

FIGURE 6.26. Winter sports became especially popular with the middle classes in the United States following the 1932 Winter Olympics in Lake Placid, New York. By the end of the decade, moisture repellent, colorfast rayon replaced thick, heavy knits for winter active sports attire. Puritan Sportswear ad, 1938.

As suit shoulders widened to the new athletic silhouette, overcoats and outerwear jackets reflected the delineated V-line profile. Raglan sleeves provided capacious shoulder room to adequately fit over the drape cut suit. (Figure 6.27.) Lengths shortened somewhat to just below the knees. Easily removed zipper linings provided overcoat versatility for transitional weather in autumn and spring when heavy linings were not needed.

A popular urban style in America was the dark blue **guards coat**, modeled after the uniform outerwear of the British Grenadiers. It featured a double-breasted closure, a half belt in the back, wide lapels, and center back pleat that extended the full length from collar to hem.

FIGURE 6.27. Men's coat styles of the 1930s were often tailored to complement the athletic silhouette of suits. The raglan coat sleeve especially provided ample room to fit over the wide shouldered, drape cut jackets. Raglan sleeve coats by Oliver Woods, 1937.

Also in the 1930s, fingertip-length leather coats became a trend among the American collegiate set, particularly in the Midwest and West. Suede was usually preferred to that of smooth, finished leather. The cropped sheepskin coats that had become prevalent in the twenties continued to be best sellers for mass merchandisers. For the working classes who could not afford leather sheepskin coats, variants were made of "imitation leather"—a rubberized, waterproof fabric with the look of leather.

Men's Underwear and Swimwear 1930–1939

Dramatic change in the cut of men's underwear styles occurred during the 1930s, principally influenced by newly engineered swimwear designs. (Figure 6.28.) In 1934, the ready-to-wear maker Cooper's introduced "**Jockeys,**" a knit cotton brief with a "Y-front" opening and elasticized waistband. "Jockeys are snug and brief," declared the copy in a 1936 ad, "molded to your muscles." Men's underwear had suddenly become erotic although advertisers heavily

FAMOUS Y-FRONT CONSTRUCTION

OPENING HERE

NO-GAP OPENING
WEARING KEEPS IT CLOSED
SUPPORT FROM THE BELT

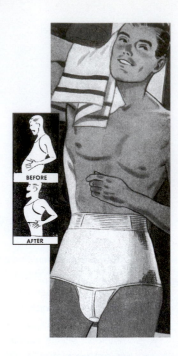

BEFORE

AFTER

FIGURE 6.28. In 1934, the form-fitting Jockey brief was introduced by Cooper's, based on young men's swimwear styles that had appeared at European resorts in the early thirties. Competitors quickly produced their own versions, including reinforced types for figure control. Left, Jockey briefs, 1936; center, athletic union suits, 1938; right, support briefs by Bracer, 1938.

airbrushed photos that were too revealing. The new look was a sensation and an instant success. Other underwear makers followed suit with their own versions of briefs that "fit like your skin," as a Scandal's ad promised in 1935. Still other new types of brief, formfitting underwear were influenced by the dominance of the youthful, athletic suit silhouettes of the period. "Bracer" underwear was made with the improved two-way stretch Lastex yarns to provide older men with a defense against "a growing waistline bulge."

Mail order catalogs still abounded with long johns in the winter editions. "Athletic" union suits combined long boxers and tank tops into one piece as shown here. Candy-striped short boxers worn with white ribknit tank undershirts were equally common.

The transition of swimwear from tank or crab back one-piece styles to thigh-high trunks without a top of any kind was gradual in the 1930s, as community ordinances changed and athletes began to compete in trunks alone. As a contingency for either circumstance, Jantzen even produced a swimsuit with a zipper at the waistband that separated the tank top from the trunks.

The brief-style trunks with its oval leg openings first appeared around 1932 although some one-piece suits with high-cut leg openings had been worn for several years by competitive collegiate and Olympic swimmers. As with the bottoms of women's two-piece styles, the waistbands had to be high enough to cover the navel. (Figure 6.29.) By the end of the decade, the knit brief style was commonly offered in mass merchandising catalogs. Colorful patterns and prints provided an endless variety of swimwear options. Some experimental forms of the brief were made with such high-cut leg openings that they resembled the men's bikinis that first appeared in the mid-1950s, although this look did not become a trend and was primarily

FIGURE 6.29. Dramatic changes in men's swimwear occurred in the 1930s. The topless brief form of men's swimwear first appeared at resorts in the early years. By the second half of the decade, the style was common at all public beaches and pools.

Lastex briefs from Jantzen, 1938.

Catalina tropical print brief, 1938.

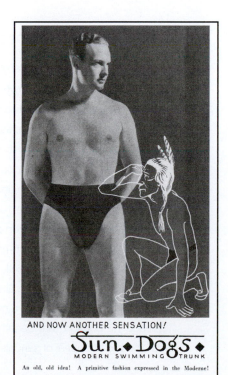

Sun Dogs high-cut brief, 1935.

FIGURE 6.30. Bound-edge fedoras and the Tyrolean with its corded band and feather accent were among the fresh looks for men's hats of the 1930s. Mallory hats, 1938.

FIGURE 6.31. Among the popular new shoe styles of the 1930s was the monk with its single strap and buckle in place of laces. Top, shoes from Montgomery Ward, 1938; bottom, two-tones by Nunn-Bush, 1939.

limited to the upscale Mediterranean resorts. For many men, though, less revealing styles of swim shorts in solid colors and bold prints and plaids became the preferred style.

Men's Accessories and Sleepwear 1930–1939

In 1935, when the Prince of Wales visited Vienna, he bought several Austrian hats fashioned with a wide brim, tapered crown, and a feather in a corded band. Adaptations of the Austrian style came to be called **Tyroleans** and remained popular into the 1960s. (Figure 6.30.) Other typical hats of the 1930s were the pinched-crown fedora, with and without bound edges, and the straw boater. Visored newsboy caps of wool or wool blends remained the sportsman's and working man's preferred headcovering. For winter, styles of the cap were made with ear flap extensions that could tuck up under the band when not needed.

Men's dress shoes of the 1930s were not significantly different from those of the twenties with one exception: the hightop street boots that had been so prevalent for several decades increasingly disappeared from men's wardrobes, replaced, instead, by a variety of oxfords. (Figure 6.31.) In the second half of the decade, a moccasin style slip-on, later called **loafers**, was introduced from Norway, first to London and then to the United States by returning tourists. Similarly, the **monk** was a new look with its single strap and buckle instead of laces. The demand for comfort that began in the previous decade continued in the Depression years with the broad appeal of sandals and other casual styles of shoes, especially **huaraches**, an

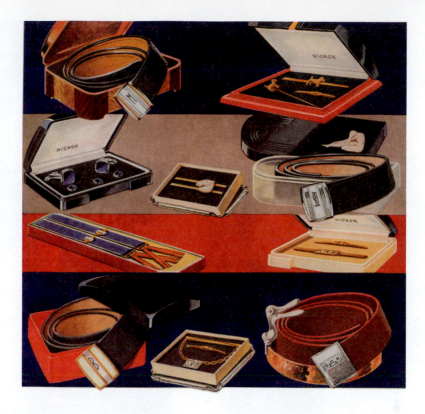

FIGURE 6.32. Men continued to wear assorted types of jewelry and related items such as tie bars, cuff link sets, keychains, money clips, signet rings, identification bracelets, detachable belt buckles, shirt studs, and wrist watches. Left, monogram jewelry by Swank, 1936; right, jewelry sets and belt from Hickok, 1936.

adaptation of Mexican peasant sandals made of woven strips of leather over the toes and a single strap at the heel.

Jewelry continued to be an important accessory for men during the thirties. Tie bars, cuff link sets, keychains, cigarette lighters and cases, money clips, signet rings, identification bracelets, shirt studs, detachable belt buckles, and wrist watches were among the types of jewelry featured in men's catalogs and ads. (Figure 6.32.) The geometric designs of art deco were favored by the man of style, while animal and sports motifs were common for traditionalists.

The colors and patterns of neckwear in the thirties were more dazzling than ever despite the gloomy economic conditions. Neckties became wider, but the length remained shorter than today, still ending a few inches above the belt. Prints and patterns were bolder and more vividly hued to complement the strong color palettes of

FIGURE 6.33. Men's ties of the Depression era were vividly hued and boldly patterned with moderne graphics and stripes. Silk foulards by McCurrach, 1938.

FIGURE 6.34. Men's sleepwear of the early 1930s was a continuation of the types from the preceding two decades. In the late thirties, bolder patterns and masculine prints such as hunting scenes and nautical themes became popular again. Left, Clover Club print pajamas and robe, 1939; right, flannel robe and broadcloth pajamas from John David, 1935.

shirts. Graphical art deco design, called "moderne" at the time, dominated. (Figure 6.33.) New in the period was the wash-and-wear cotton tie for summer in both long and bow tie styles. Reversible ties made of the same material on both sides stitched with hidden side seams provided longer wear in the event one side got soiled.

Sleepwear for men ranged from basic cotton pajama sets and knee-length nightshirts to silk lounge ensembles. (Figure 6.34.) In addition to commodity types of flannel shirt and bottoms in the usual vertical stripes, Sears catalogs offered red or black "Russian Cossack" styles with asymmetrical front closures, imperial patches on the chest, and fringed sashes. With the athletic influence of menswear in the 1930s came pajama prints with hunting scenes, nautical themes, and sports motifs in addition to bold tartans, awning stripes, and white polka dots.

Men's Grooming and Hairstyles 1930–1939

Men's haircuts of the 1930s were not much different from those of previous decades back to the Victorian era. The most common cut was cropped close around the ears and back with a fullness on top that was combed straight back or parted at the side. Hair oils were advertised as healthy treatments for the hair. (Figure 6.35.)

Faces were mostly clean shaven in keeping with the emphasis of youth and athleticism of the times. In 1931, Schick introduced the commercial electric razor. Mustaches returned in the late twenties and lasted through the thirties. Instead of the full, bushy, brush-like versions of the Edwardian man, though, new styles were small and waxed into sculpted comma shapes

FIGURE 6.35. The well-groomed man of the 1930s was clean shaven and kept his hair closely cropped. Various hair oils were applied for a slicked back, shiny helmet look. Makers of haircare products capitalized on men's terror of baldness with ads promising prevention or restoration. Vitalis ad, 1937; Kreml ad, 1935.

with curled ends or trimmed into narrow, pencil mustaches like that favored by Clark Gable. Massive Victorian beards, sideburns, vandykes, goatees and the like were still worn by elderly men or eccentrics such as bohemian artists and poets.

Children's Clothing 1930–1939

The infant's basic layette was the long gown, diaper, and blanket—with a front-closure shirt, wrap undervest, knit bootees, and bonnet for cold weather. For the twelve- to eighteen-month-old, long-sleeve wrap shirts, called vests, that extended over the diaper were made of soft ribbed cotton or waffle-weave rayon. Waterproof panties with snap-front flaps were made of rubberized silk or rayon.

Little girls of the 1930s continued to wear short, shoulder-yoke dresses. Older girls continued to be dressed as smaller versions of adults and wore the same soft dressing, knitwear, and playwear as their mothers. Waists returned to the natural position and exaggerated puff sleeves were adapted to all forms of girls' wear. (Figure 6.36.) Costume styles of clothing, such as sailor suits that included trousers for girls, were a particular influence from Hollywood in the thirties. Films and advertising images of petite Darla of the "Our Gang" serials and especially of Shirley Temple wearing trendy fashions inspired millions of mothers to dress their daughters similarly. (Figure 6.37.) In England, mothers modeled the dress of their daughters after the clothing worn by Princesses Elizabeth and Margaret.

Toddler boys continued to enjoy the ease and freedom of short playsuits. School-age boys still wore the knicker suit and thick, knee-high stockings. (Figure 6.38.) Dress suits and sport jackets for older boys were

FIGURE 6.36. In the 1930s, girl's dresses followed the new silhouettes of women's styles with an emphasis on femininity and sleeve interest. Flock dot frocks, 1938.

FIGURE 6.37. Mothers and daughters alike were influenced by the fashions and hairstyles worn by Hollywood's child stars such as Shirley Temple. Testimonial ad featuring Shirley Temple, 1937.

FIGURE 6.38. The knicker suit, worn with thick, knee-high stockings, remained the prevalent year-round dress for schoolboys of the Depression era. Knicker suits, 1938.

modeled on the new triangular drape cut of men's suits. Adaptations of men's styles also included versions of the knit polo shirt. Jeans were largely viewed as work pants and were bought by thrifty parents to be worn with the cuffs turned up several inches to allow for growth spurts. When Jockey briefs were introduced for men in 1934, underwear makers produced sizes for boys as well. Brief style swimsuits were also scaled to boys' sizes.

Review

Simultaneous with the onset of the Great Depression, the fashion look again shifted dramatically. Feminine curves returned with a renewed focus on the hips and bust. The waistline moved back to its natural position, or sometimes slightly higher, and hemlines dropped almost to the ankles. Floor-length evening gowns also returned, now with emphasis on open backs and bare shoulders. By middecade, exaggerated sleeves and wide shoulders prevailed in the design of dresses, evening gowns, suits, coats, and playwear. The modern woman was confident in her new wardrobe options that included slacks, shorts, and two-piece swimsuits.

New technologies also significantly impacted fashion design. The convenient zipper was applied to everything from accessories and outerwear to couture gowns and intimate apparel. Plastics were used in jewelry and fashion ornaments. Nylon was introduced and became an instant success in the manufacture of sheer hosiery.

For menswear, Anglomania dominated suit styling. The contours of men's suit jackets shifted from the trim, natural shoulder silhouette of the previous decade to the athletic drape cut, sometimes called the London cut. Trousers with the new zipper fly front solved the age-old problem of gaps in button closures. New textiles such as seersucker were introduced for summer suits. Blazers and sport jackets were increasingly substituted for the suit jacket even as business dress.

The Prince of Wales led the way to greater comfort and casualness in men's dress. Men began to wear unconstructed jackets and open-throat shirts to public events and went hatless at resorts. Bermuda shorts appeared on golf courses. Versions of the polo shirt, the Hawaiian print shirt, and a wide variety of knitwear became ubiquitous weekend wear.

Children's wear continued to emphasize casual comfort. Shoulder-yoke dresses were still the preferred style for little girls. Their older sisters dressed in diminutive versions of women's fashions, including exaggerated sleeve styles. Shorts sets remained prevalent for little boys and knicker suits were the most common attire for school-age boys. Teens wore the athletic drape cut suits of their fathers.

review questions

1. What impact did the Great Depression have on the color palettes and decorative treatments of fashions in the early 1930s?

2. How did the election of Franklin D. Roosevelt impact fashion?

3. Describe the transition of women's silhouettes from the end of the 1920s into the early 1930s.

4. How did movies of the 1930s influence mainstream fashions?

5. How did the zipper impact women's and men's fashions? Give specific examples of how couturiers and tailors first used the zipper in the 1930s.

6. How did Anglomania of the 1930s change the silhouette of men's suits?

7. How did the Prince of Wales (later Edward VIII) influence menswear fashions of the 1930s?

8. What were the dramatic changes in women's and men's swimwear of the 1930s?

research and portfolio projects

Research

1. Write a research paper on the key fashion design innovators of Hollywood's movie studios in the 1930s. Include brief biographies of the leading designers and identify their movie costume designs that influenced mainstream fashion.

Portfolio

1. Compile a reference guide of art deco (moderne) accessories from the 1930s. Photocopy or digitally scan 10 examples each of jewelry, handbags, shoes, and hats. Include a written description of each with designer or maker, materials, date, and the design elements that define the items as art deco.

dress terms

Bakelite and **Catalin:** brand names of phenolic plastics used for costume jewelry, buttons, and ornaments

batwing sleeve: a deep, softly draped, dolman sleeve style, wide at the shoulder tapering to a close fit at the wrist

blade cut suit: see drape cut suit

dishrag shirt: men's short sleeve knit shirt with mesh bodice

drape cut suit: men's jacket style of the 1930s featuring broad, unpadded shoulders, a smooth fit across the shoulder blades, roomy armholes, a tapered waistline, and rolled lapels; also called London cut and blade cut

guards coat: an adaptation of the dark blue, double breasted greatcoat of the British Grenadiers with center back pleat and half belt

Hawaiian print shirt: casual, short sleeve sport shirts in vividly colored, tropical motif prints

huaraches: an adaptation of Mexican peasant sandals with woven leather toes and a strap at the heel

Jockey briefs: men's formfitting knit underwear cut with high leg openings, an elasticized waistband, and a Y-front closure; introduced in 1934

Lido shoes: any variety of women's thick, cork soled shoes of the 1930s

loafers: a moccasin style of slip-on casual shoe introduced from Norway in the 1930s

London cut suit: see drape cut suit

mess jacket: men's dinner jacket cropped at the waist and resembling a naval officer's dinner dress

monk: men's shoe style with a single strap and buckle over the instep rather than laces

nylon: an amide synthetic used to produce resilient yarns used in textiles

pagoda sleeve: wide, exaggerated sleeves with a high, peaked shoulderline

Palm Beach suit: men's lounge style suit made of lightweight tropical fabrics; named for the Florida resort in the 1930s

phenolic plastic: a resinous plastic made from benzene used in the manufacture of jewelry, accessories, and trimmings

seersucker: a puckered textile that derived its name from the Persian "shirushakar"

skanties: women's brief style panties of the 1930s

slacks: the generic term applied to women's or men's tailored casual trousers

tennis shoe: sport shoe with rubber sole and canvas upper originally worn on tennis courts

toy hat: miniaturized versions of women's hat styles popular in the late 1930s

Tyrolean: men's hat of the 1930s with a wide brim, tapered crown, and feather in a corded hatband

weskit: a men's jacket with a short, vest-cut hemline

7 The Second World War and a New Look 1940–1949

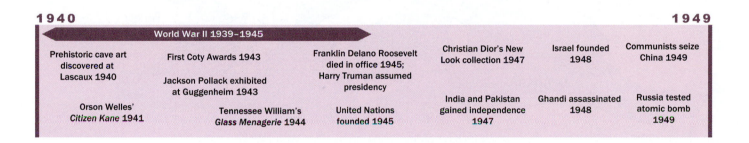

1940

1949

World War II 1939–1945

Prehistoric cave art discovered at Lascaux 1940

First Coty Awards 1943

Jackson Pollack exhibited at Guggenheim 1943

Franklin Delano Roosevelt died in office 1945; Harry Truman assumed presidency

Christian Dior's New Look collection 1947

Israel founded 1948

Communists seize China 1949

Orson Welles' *Citizen Kane* 1941

Tennessee William's *Glass Menagerie* 1944

United Nations founded 1945

India and Pakistan gained independence 1947

Ghandi assassinated 1948

Russia tested atomic bomb 1949

The Second World War

Unlike the First World War, which came almost as a surprise to the Europeans who had been drawn into the conflict, World War II was an inevitability that had been brewing for years. After Germany had seized Austria and Czechoslovakia in 1938, Western democracies did nothing, preferring appeasement of Hitler over war. In September 1939, though, Germany resumed its aggression by invading Poland, at which Britain and France declared war. While Europe erupted into a conflagration, in Asia, Japan extended its war with China into a conquest of resource-rich territories around the Pacific rim. Despite the neutrality acts passed by the U.S. Congress, America shipped millions of dollars worth of equipment and supplies to Europe through the Lend-Lease program, and hindered Japan's aggression by embargoes. In December 1941, Japan attacked the U.S. fleet at Pearl Harbor, Hawaii, and America declared war. A few days later, Germany declared war on the United States, and Americans also entered the conflict in Europe.

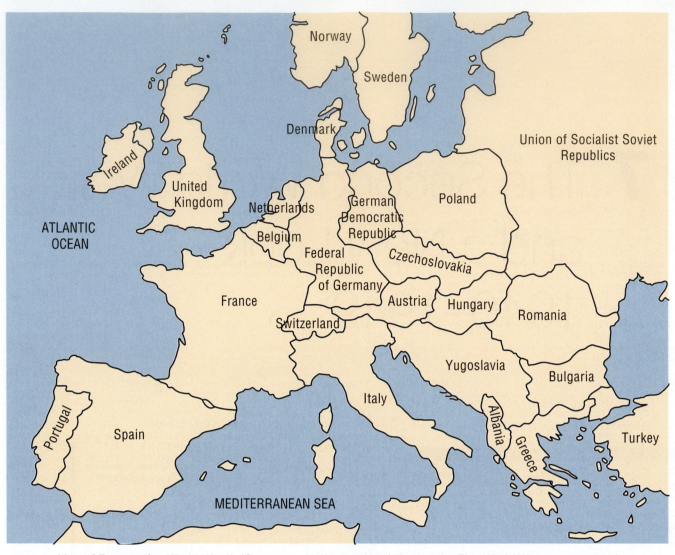

Map of Europe after World War II. (Compare with the borders following the First World War on page 114.)

Changes on the homefront for Americans recalled those of 1917. As fifteen million men joined the armed services, huge numbers of women went to work outside the home filling those critical positions in manufacturing, agriculture, and services left vacant by enlisted men. (Figure 7.1.) The Great Depression was clearly and finally at an end as unemployment dropped to 1.2 percent. Labor unions agreed to no-strike pledges. Retired folks volunteered for civil defense duties. Rationing was immediate for food, rubber, metals, gasoline, and heating fuels. To supplement food shortages, Victory Gardens were cultivated in backyards and city parks nationwide. Price controls were put in place to stem inflation.

Even with the powerful economic might of the United States behind the Allies, the tide of the war turned with agonizing slowness. In 1943, the Allies began their invasion of fortress Europe from the shores of North Africa across to Italy. D-Day, or the cross-channel invasion of France from England, was June 6, 1944. Meanwhile the Russians pushed westward into Germany meeting up with the Americans just south of Berlin the following spring. Hitler committed suicide in his bunker, and on May 7, 1945, Germany surrendered.

Women in the Work Force During World War II

During the Second World War, labor shortages became critical enough for governments around the world to call upon women to fill the vacancies left by men going off to military service. In the first few months after the bombing of Pearl Harbor, 750,000 American women volunteered to work in armaments factories; at its peak in 1944, the U.S. labor force included six million women. (Figure 7.1.) The U.S. government at last endorsed equal pay for equal work, and bans on hiring married women or women more than thirty-five years old were rescinded. Women adeptly operated complex and dangerous machinery in factories, welded heavy metal parts with acetylene torches, and handled sensitive explosives. They drove tanks off assembly lines, flew fighter planes to deployment airfields, and operated heavy farm equipment. They also worked as truck drivers, train conductors, auto mechanics, gas station attendants, policewomen, postal carriers, and lumberjacks. Of 1,900 war jobs categorized by the U.S. Department of Labor, only 56 were classified as "unsuitable for women."

To work in many of these dangerous conditions, women altered their standards of dress. Trousers of all kinds were worn not only for comfort but for safety reasons. "Slacks have become a badge of honor," wrote columnist Max Lerner at the time. Compared to the functional and unflattering cut of pant styles worn by working women during the First World War, slacks and jeans of the early 1940s were tailored to the feminine form. Short hair was also encouraged for safety purposes. Women who preferred to keep their hair long pinned up their tresses in colorful bandanas or netted snoods.

FIGURE 7.1. During World War II, women by the millions stepped into trousers and went to work in factories, farm fields, and civilian services in answer to the nation's call for help with the labor shortage. Ads 1942 and 1943.

In Asia, the turning point in the war with Japan came in 1942 at the Battle of Midway Island in the Pacific in which the Japanese fleet was badly crippled. The U.S. strategy of "leapfrogging," or bypassing certain heavily fortified islands to set up airfields and then return to neutralize enemy bases, effectively moved the Americans within easy roundtrip bombing of Tokyo by 1944. Fanatical resistance on many of these outer islands convinced President Truman to unleash the atomic bomb on Hiroshima in August 1945. Only after the second atomic bomb annihilated Nagasaki three days later did Japan capitulate, at last bringing an end to World War II.

The Postwar United States

When the Second World War ended with the awesome awfulness of an atomic explosion, the United States was confronted once again with demobilization. Despite the threat from communism, the United States began dismantling its massive war-production machine and rapidly brought home millions of service men and women to resume civilian life.

Because of war rationing, little new housing had been built during the first half of the 1940s. Immediately after the war, every American city contended with a sprawling suburbia partitioned with endless rows of new development homes. The housing boom assured plenty of jobs for returning ex-soldiers. A more notable boom was the surge in births from 1946 through 1964. As more houses went up and the population increased, demand for consumer goods soared. In addition, those who had remained on the home front had made high wages but had little to buy during the war. The pent-up demand for new cars, furniture, appliances, clothes, and luxury items contributed to the most robust consumer economy since the 1920s.

American Fashion on Its Own

Not only was the American fashion industry pinched by shortages of leather, wool, silk, and nylon during the Second World War, but the innovative guidance of Paris came to a halt as well. In the face of a German invasion in the spring of 1940, Parisian couturiers moved their operations to Biarritz in southwestern France where they struggled with shortages of labor, equipment, and materials to produce limited collections. Despite the dangers of travel, American retailers and ready-to-wear makers made significant purchases. When the Germans marched into Paris in June, the borders of France were closed, and for the next four years, Americans received little information about what Paris couturiers were designing. Even the French edition of *Vogue* shut down for the duration. Despite their isolation, the couturiers continued to create abbreviated collections only for the French and German market. At one point, Germany's ministry of culture even considered relocating the entire couture industry to Berlin, but Lucien Lelong, as president of the Chambre Syndicale de la Couture, courageously persuaded the Germans of the inadvisability of such a venture.

For the first time, American designers were on their own without any creative guidance from Paris. "The fashion spotlight turns on New York," declared *Vogue* in 1940. Many designers who had achieved notoriety in the thirties gained greater prominence as they took up the mantel of fashion leadership. The fashion press and ready-to-wear makers cast an anxious eye to Hattie Carnegie, Henri Bendel, and Adrian, as well as to the new labels of Norman Norell, Adele Simpson, Claire McCardell, and Clare Potter.

These, and numerous other U.S. designers, created fashions during the war years that reflected the ease and casualness of the American woman. Claire McCardell's sportswear, especially, led the way in dispensing with exaggerated shoulder pads and restrictive foundations. Many styles of suits and dresses were made with a duality in mind—comfortable for day time and elegant enough for evening.

When the United States entered the war in December 1941, a long list of raw materials and manufactured goods were immediately rationed for war needs. The U.S. War Production Board instituted the **L-85 regulations** that restricted the kinds and quantities of materials that could be used in apparel manufacturing. Most American designers, though, went one step further and created fashions that were even more narrow and trim than L-85 measurements required, saving an estimated 15 million yards of fabric by war's end.

Women's Fashions During World War II

Before Germany had occupied France and closed its borders in June 1940, American and British journalists, retail buyers, and consumers took away from the Paris spring showings fashions that reflected the mood and needs of wartime. The cinched-waist and long skirts that had briefly appeared in 1939 were abandoned for trim, easy-fitting lines. Dresses retained the defined waist of the thirties, but bodices and sleeves were looser and skirts were shortened to the knees. Suit jackets were less fitted and armholes were roomier although the occasional peplum added a touch of feminine flair to otherwise tubular bodices.

Behind the fortress of occupied France, Parisian couturiers continued to design seasonal collections with about two-thirds fewer models than previously. Fewer designers also remained in business. Schiaparelli and Mainbocher went to New York, but Schiaparelli worked as ambassador for French couture, writing for fashion publications and making personal appearances rather than reopening her salon. Molyneux and Worth moved their ateliers to London. Chanel remained in Paris but ceased designing, becoming mistress to a German Nazi officer instead, for which she would suffer a ten-year exile as a collaborator after the war.

The styles that Paris couturiers created during the war years featured excesses that were forbidden to American and British designers. Gathers, pleats, shirring, flounces, and other construction details that required excessive amounts of fabric were in abundance on French fashions. In 1943, when a collection of French haute couture arrived in New York in the wardrobe of a visiting French aviator's wife, American journalists were perplexed by what they saw. *Life* reported that the styles were hardly more than "vulgar exaggerations of famous silhouettes." For many couturiers, though, the excessive use of fabric meant less yardage available to the Nazi occupiers, and for French women, wearing these fashions was a gesture of patriotism.

In Britain, the Utility Scheme was introduced in the spring of 1941. Government restrictions on the use of materials and the making of apparel largely dictated the fashion silhouette of the time. Measurements for everything from collar widths to hemlines were regulated. Not only was the intent to reduce the amount of fabric used by the clothing industry, but by standardizing garments, retooling of machinery and retraining the limited labor force were eliminated. From these dictates, fashion inventiveness was largely shackled, and the usual cycles of innovative change ceased. In place of fashion choice emerged a nationalized, functional war costume. In essence, the **utility look** was one of squared shoulders, narrow hips, and skirts at the knees—

Enka Rayon dress, 1942.

but not above the kneecaps. Trimmings disappeared, and substitutes for many scarce materials had to be found. Simplicity was the objective of the day with no fussy details to suggest a squandering of precious resources.

In the United States, the War Production Board introduced similar utility restrictions with the L-85 regulations. Measurement specifications included limiting skirts to seventy-two inches at the hem, pant legs to nineteen inches in circumference, and suit jacket lengths to twenty-five inches, which was just at the hips. Turned-back cuffs, double yokes, and multiple patch pockets were among the details now prohibited. The use of certain materials was rigidly controlled, particularly wool needed for uniforms and blankets, silk and nylon needed for parachutes, and leather needed for military boots. As with the British silhouette, the American austerity look was trim and narrow. Shoulders remained wide and squared, bodices were loose with natural waistlines, and skirts were slim and cropped to the knees. (Figure 7.2.)

FIGURE 7.2. During the war, U.S. and British government restrictions on the use of materials and the construction of clothing determined the fashion silhouette. Women's dresses and suits featured squared shoulders, narrow hips, and skirts at the knees.

L-85 suit by Mandelbaum, 1943.

L-85 suit by Adele Simpson, 1943.

Sportswear continued to gain wider acceptance for everyday town dress. As huge numbers of women went to work outside the home, slacks were more commonly seen on city streets and in public offices as war workers rushed about taking care of personal business during lunch hours and after work.

Not all clothes were restricted to the L-85 specifications. Textile manufacturers were encouraged to produce plenty of materials not needed for the war, especially cotton and rayon, that could be used for casual sportswear, playwear, and evening wear. Luxurious velvets, taffetas, and silky rayons were fairly plentiful for special occasion dressing. Although most designs of after-six dresses followed the slim, vertical lines of day wear, some styles offered a contrast with full skirts or revivalisms such as bustle treatments, large back bows, overskirt swags, or deep peplums. (Figure 7.3.) However, ostentation was viewed as an unpatriotic display of extravagance that disregarded the austerity needed to win the war. Hence, excessive use of sequins, beading, embroidery, and similar embellishments were largely eschewed.

FIGURE 7.3. Fabrics not needed for the war effort such as velvet, taffeta, and rayon were in sufficient supply for designers to create opulent evening wear.

Rayon gown by Rémond Holland, 1944.

"Finger Silhouette" gown by Adrian, 1943.

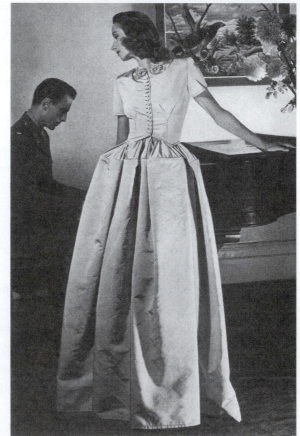

Taffeta gown by Henri Bendel, 1942.

Despite limited resources and the hazards of shipping abroad, Britain's fashion industry continued to export apparel to the Americas. Woolen knitwear was especially in demand as home heating fuel shortages and rationing forced everyone to turn down thermostats and close off furnace vents. Americans were encouraged to help support the fight for democracy by buying British-made clothing. "A new sweater puts another nail in a plane for Britain," wrote a journalist in 1942. Competing American knitwear makers also extensively advertised the practical and fashionable new looks of their styles. For GIs far from home, photos of Hollywood sweater girls like Lana Turner, Betty Grable, and Rita Hayworth were favorite pin-ups. Sweaters made with silk lamé or trimmed with fur collars such as the designs by Mainbocher became popular evening wear. (Figure 7.4.)

When Paris was liberated in the fall of 1944, couturiers abandoned the frilly and frivolous fashions they had created during the German occupation and, instead, adopted the narrow, simpler silhouettes of American and British austerity styles. Even in the months following the end of the war in August 1945, materials were scarce and official restrictions on clothing designs remained in effect. By 1947, though, women were more than ready for a dramatic change in fashion. After years of privations and the monotonous austerity styles, almost everyone was anxious for a new look.

the sweater dines out . . . shimmering and beautiful in silk lamé that shines like cloth-of-gold. Back and sleeves knitted of very fine all wool yarn. Exclusive with Altman's. In white or black with gold. Sizes 14, 16, 18. Each, 29.95 Altman sweater fashions, third floor

FIGURE 7.4. Sweater dressing was extended to evening wear during the war as theaters, nightclubs, and restaurants turned down thermostats to conserve heating fuels. Knits were luxuriously embellished with silk lamé or trimmed with fur for a formal, sumptuous look. Evening wear sweaters of silk lamé from Altman's, 1943.

The New Look

During 1946, Paris designers began to experiment with elements that were contrary to the utility styles of the war years—full, long skirts, natural shoulderlines, and a small waistline. The "**spool torso**" was a fitted bodice attached to a shapely fullness at the hips formed by a peplum, pannier, or hoops. Swags of fabric and bustle treatments were also used to emphasize the hips and smaller waist.

The pivotal change, though, came with the debut collection of Christian Dior in the spring of 1947. The couturier had left his chief designer post at Lelong the year before to open his own salon at the urging of a wealthy textile magnate. Dior's "Corolle" collection crystallized the postwar woman's fantasies of graceful and elegant fashions into a cohesive, ultrafeminine look—the "**New Look**" as *Harper's Bazaar* christened it. (Figure 7.5.) The common denominators of the clothes Dior designed, he later wrote, were "rounded shoulders, full, feminine busts, and hand-span waists above enormous spreading skirts." His fashions were meticulously constructed and detailed, very much in the traditional haute couture approach to design. Many dresses had built-in corsets and boning, and all were lined with cambric or taffeta. To these fundamentals of construction, Dior added head-to-toe accessories—the right hat and handbag, earrings, necklaces and many bracelets, gloves, opera pumps, and even parasols.

As revolutionary as Dior's fashions seemed to be at the time, the New Look was actually a rejuvenation of the mock-Edwardian revivals that had emerged just before the outbreak of the Second World War. Dior's timing, though, could not have been more perfect. Amidst the

FIGURE 7.5. In 1947, Christian Dior launched the New Look with his pivotal debut collection. Fashions of the following fifteen years would emphasize the cinched waist, rounded hips, and a full bustline. Left, Christian Dior's debut collection, the Corolle, that launched the New Look in 1947; center, ready-to-wear adaptation of the New Look from I. Magnin, 1948; right, ready-to-wear adaptation of the New Look from Enka Rayon, 1948.

confusion and intensity of the Cold War, coupled with the still raw memories of the cataclysmic death and destruction of the world at war, women overwhelmingly embraced the nostalgia the New Look engendered. The safety and security of a conventional lifestyle was all many women (and men) now wanted. The New Look provided the trappings of traditional femininity that women sought to secure society's illusory ideals of normalcy. The new silhouette was that of a fertility goddess, and the postwar baby boom confirmed its effectiveness.

Dior's many variations of the New Look were sensational. Each collection had a youthful vitality that appealed to women of all ages. From the start, the impact of Dior's New Look on the entire fashion industry was immediate. Few designers were impervious to its influence. Ready-to-wear makers were ecstatic with the market's unceasing demand for New Look styles, even if mass-produced adaptations required significant compromises on the perfection of the couturier's craftsmanship.

Almost overnight, Paris was once again the preeminent center of style. But competition from London, Rome, and New York now forced changes that the prewar Chambre Syndicale de la Couture had viewed with disdain. Although some couturiers, such as Patou, Lelong,

FIGURE 7.6. Suit designs of the late 1940s adopted the ultrafeminine silhouette of Dior's New Look. Fitted jackets emphasized cinched waists, and flared peplums created the illusion of full, rounded hips. Skirts were either pencil slim or gathered and full. Left, New Look peplum suit from Bloomingdale's, 1948; right, bolero jacket, linen vest, and pencil skirt from Izod of London, 1949.

and Chanel, had begun producing ready-to-wear boutique collections as early as the 1920s, the French fashion industry only began a consolidated effort toward mass production in the late forties. At that time a group of French businessmen went to the United States to study American ready-to-wear expertise. The result was French **prêt-à-porter**— high quality and high style ready-made clothing tailored to the U.S. and British mass market.

The success of the French prêt-à-porter collections were indicative of the international fashion market that emerged in the postwar years. London's premier couturiers, Norman Hartnell and Hardy Amies, had begun expanding their interests in ready-to-wear during the early 1940s as a financial life line to the Americas. After the war, the member firms of the Incorporated Society of London Fashion adopted American sizing, and set a calendar of showings the week before the Paris openings to attract U.S. buyers on their way to France.

Women's suits of the New Look era were infinitely varied, often with an exaggerated femininity as a reaction to the dowdy, menswear styling of the war utility styles. Rigidly tailored jackets followed the body-conscious tenets of the New Look with fitted bodices that rounded the bosom and short, flaring peplums or wide, hip-length hemlines. Many jackets were belted to emphasize the cinched waistline. Both pencil-thin skirts and full, gathered or pleated skirts worked easily with the new, shapely jackets. (Figure 7.6.)

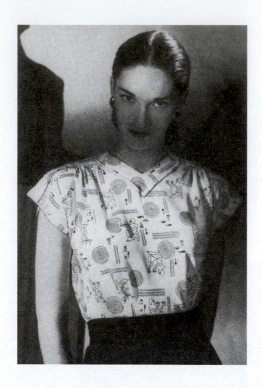

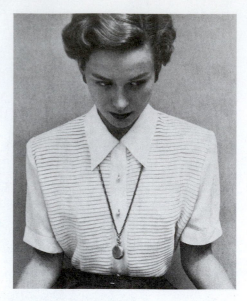

FIGURE 7.7. New emphasis was placed on blouse designs for career women who chose to continue working in offices after the war. Synthetic fabrics such as nylon and rayon, combined with improved garment cutting and construction techniques, made possible an endless variety of blouse designs to pair with many styles of New Look skirts. Left, rayon crepe blouse with Egyptian hieroglyphics print by Alice Stuart, 1946; center, rayon crepe blouse with decorative slashing by Bates, 1946; right, tuck-pleated blouse of rayon tissue faille by Adelaar, 1948.

After the war, many women who had enjoyed the self sufficiency and financial independence of working gave up their heavy industry jobs to returning veterans and found employment in offices. In the postwar years, *Glamour* magazine even included the tagline "for the girl with a job" as part of its cover title. For the workday wardrobe, the many varieties of New Look skirts were paired with a wide assortment of blouses, including styles made of new, easy-care synthetics such as nylon and reformulated rayons that held dyes and prints better than natural fibers. Improved garment cutting and construction techniques likewise made possible the mass production of complex styling such as fabric piercing, machine embroidery, lace inserts, and delicate pin tucks. (Figure 7.7.)

The ultrafemininity and fullness of the New Look were also extended to evening wear with the addition of panniers, crinolines, and hip pads. (Figure 7.8.) Greater fullness was added with bustle treatments, wired overskirts, and flounces. Sumptuous fabrics once again were in abundance and designers lavished their creations with yards of material, including matching evening coats, capes, and wraps. Bodices, though, were tight with natural shoulderlines or with deep decollete necklines.

Women's Outerwear 1940–1949

During the Second World War, utility regulations restricted the lengths of coats and the dimensions of collars, lapels, pockets, and sleeves. Shoulders were still squared but without the

FIGURE 7.8. New Look evening wear of the late 1940s exhibited the demand for abundant, opulent fabrics following the privations of the war years. Left, taffeta flounced gown by Adrian, 1948; right, post-World War II silk opulence by Rémond Holland, 1948.

expanse of sleeves popular in the years before the war. Prohibited were big patch pockets, turned-back cuffs, wide Napoleonic collars, and excessive detailing that wasted materials. Fabric blends noted in wartime catalogs included equal parts of wool with cotton and rayon or wool combined with "reprocessed" and "reused" wool. Masculine, military styling, particularly the belted trench coat, was the prevalent look for women's outerwear by 1943. (Figure 7.9.) The tubular **cigarette silhouette** was popular in both fingertip and knee lengths and was easy to mass produce with the limited labor available. Three-quarter length coats and even hip-high reefers were two solutions to the fabric shortages.

By the end of the decade, the silhouette of the New Look was applied to coats and jackets with molded, fitted bodices and full, flaring skirts or peplums. The fitted cut was usually the shoulder-to-hem princess line that was often cinch-belted. Short **toppers** cropped to about mid-thigh were preferred over wide, full skirts. Most coats, though, were cut full from the shoulders with a variety of wide sleeves, including roomy raglan and kimono styles.

FIGURE 7.9. Women's coats of the war years were narrow and short with squared shoulders and minimal trimmings. Left, military inspired L-85 coat by Donnybrook, 1944; right, box coat, reefer, and cigarette coat by Craftmoor, 1943.

Women's Sports Apparel 1940–1949

The line between active sports attire and casual, everyday sportswear continued to blur during the 1940s. There still were fine distinctions in many specialty quarters, though. Of the numerous forms of trousers worn by women for war work, most would not have been appropriate attire for skiing, tennis, or golf. At resorts and country clubs, tailored slacks and shorts were a must on the links or courts. Jodhpurs remained the preferred trousers for riding.

Clothing for other active sports such as bicycling, hiking, and neighborhood ball games included a wide assortment of comfortable playwear, particularly knit tops, shorts, culottes, one-piece playsuits, and cropped pant styles. During the war years, women discovered the comfort and easy care of jeans when they began to wear them to work in the factories. In the postwar years, jeans, called **dungarees** at the time, were featured in catalogs as a fashionable alternative to slacks and shorts for outdoor activities. (Figure 7.10.)

For winter sports, the ski suit with its baggy pants and assorted short jackets remained the prevalent outfit through the war years. By the end of the decade, though, the knit pants narrowed and were worn tucked into the boots.

FIGURE 7.10. Options for sports clothing of the 1940s continued the diversity that had developed in the thirties, including slacks and play sets of shorts, skirts, and matching tops. In the postwar years, jeans became more common attire for neighborhood sports and other social activities. Left, rayon sharkskin trousers, shorts, sport skirt, and sport shirts from B. Altman, 1942; right, jeans and wool shirt jacket, 1948.

Women's Underwear and Sleepwear 1940–1949

Functionality was the keyword for women's undergarments during the war years. The attempted return of the cinched-waist corset in 1939 faded as materials shortages and wartime restrictions preoccupied underwear makers. The amount of rubber used in textiles was greatly reduced by the War Production Board so that girdles and bras had to be made with panels of elasticized yarns that were inserted into knit rayon or cotton. (Figure 7.11.) Disclaimers in catalogs advised of the wartime restrictions on rubber and of the changes in the manufacture of foundation garments. "While less flexible than before, our garments still give good support and control," claimed the copy in a Montgomery Ward catalog in 1943. Advertisers depicted lingerie models in active poses to emphasize the flexibility of the new forms of undergarments, but the fit was much more stiff and uncomfortable than prewar versions.

Simplification and freedom from constraint were the focus of lingerie makers during the war. Slips and petticoats were narrowed and shortened to the knees. Panties were cut with higher leg openings; some were even made with elasticized control panels to replace girdles. In addition, as supplies of imported lace were quickly depleted and stocks of silk were needed for parachutes, lingerie became plainer. Nylon, too, which had only been introduced in yarns for hosiery in 1939, was scarce as supplies were diverted to war production. Instead, women

FIGURE 7.11. Wartime restrictions limited the amount of rubber that could be used in foundation garments. Styles were reengineered with elasticized insets and panels, but the results were noticeably less flexible. Wartime girdle with elasticized sides and rayon front panels from Carter's, 1942.

How slim...
How lovely
your legs will look
clad in this beautiful
Velva Leg Film
soft... smooth...
water-resistant ...it
lasts until
washed away.

Elizabeth Arden

FIGURE 7.12. Because nylon was one of the materials restricted to war use by L-85 regulations, nylon hosiery was scarce. As a compromise, women resorted to applying skin tints that simulated the look of nylons. Ad for Elizabeth Arden's Velva Leg Film, 1943.

painted their legs with various commercial skin dyes to simulate hosiery, often with a seam drawn up the back with an eyebrow pencil. (Figure 7.12.)

With the conclusion of the war and the launch of Dior's New Look, greater emphasis was placed on undergarments. The constricting **guimpe**, or **waspie** as it was commonly called, was a bust-to-hip corset that reappeared to provide the necessary contours for the ultrafemininity in fashion. Some versions even included old-fashioned forms of laces and hooks. (Figure 7.13.) Improved girdles made with better elasticized yarns were the preferred foundation garments for most women.

During the war, sleepwear was often designed with the same plain practicality as other intimate apparel. Nightgowns and wraps ceased to resemble formal evening wear as they had in the thirties, and, instead, were sometimes even cut like men's nightshirts, many with high necks and long sleeves. Square-shouldered housecoats replicated functional men's versions. Flannel pajamas and thick cotton chenille robes were preferred for chilly nights when thermostat settings were lowered in fuel-rationed homes. Military and patriotic motifs were often applied to sleepwear. (Figure 7.14.)

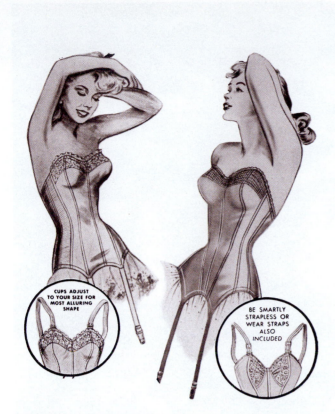

FIGURE 7.13. The bust-to-hip, waist-cinching guimpe, or waspie, was the essential undergarment for ultrafeminine New Look fashions. Some of these revived corsets included boning and even old-fashioned laces and hooks. Rayon and Lastex Waspies by Wilco, 1949.

FIGURE 7.14. Sleepwear of the early 1940s was plainer than the sumptuous styles of the thirties. Military and patriotic motifs were especially popular. In the postwar years, sleepwear was made with an abundance of fabric and lavish trim. Left, sailor suit pajamas from Spiegel, 1942; right, chenille robe from Spiegel, 1948.

In the postwar years, feminine curves were accentuated by gowns with the Empire waistline and billowing skirts of pleated or gathered nylon. Lace and ribbon trim, satin rosettes, ruffles, and other frills abundantly embellished nightgowns, pajamas, and robes.

Women's Swimwear 1940–1949

The swimwear industry was hit with the same restrictions and shortages as all other apparel makers during World War II. Rayon crepe and sharkskin, waffled linen, and cotton velour replaced the preferred silk and wool. As with undergarments, rubberized yarns such as Lastex were in short supply for swimsuits, so new techniques of construction had to be developed. Side lacings and horizontal shirring offered some of the snug fit of prewar styles. One-piece maillots were the most common swimsuits, usually still made with the thigh-length modesty skirt. The two-piece that had developed in the 1930s continued to be made with the same bandeau or bra-cut top and high-waisted bottom that covered the navel, though the style was not popular in the United States because it too closely resembled underwear to most women. (Figure 7.15.)

The great leap forward in women's swimwear design occurred immediately after the war when Jacques Heim and Louis Reard independently of each other designed the **bikini** in 1946.

FIGURE 7.15. In the early 1940s, swimwear makers were subjected to the same restrictions on materials as all other apparel manufacturers. As with undergarments, swimsuits were redesigned with new methods of construction that included inset panels of elasticized fabric. In the postwar years, elasticized fabrics ensured formfitting contours. Left, two-piece "Aleutian Flower Print" suit by Mabs of Hollywood, 1944; right, Lastex maillots with modesty skirts from Sea Goddess, 1948.

Because of the atomic bomb tests that the United States was conducting near the Bikini Islands in the Pacific, Heim named his swimsuit the "**Atome**" since it was the tiniest swimsuit of the time. Reard called his design the bikini possibly because of the many beach and poolside "bikini parties" that were popular during that summer. The drama of the bikini was its lowered waistline that exposed the navel; otherwise, the style was hardly different from other two-piece designs. American women who had clamored for everything French and New Look after the war resisted the bikini until the late 1950s, and even then, the style was still viewed by many as shocking in public.

With the availability of nylon, rubber, and elasticized materials again, swimsuits of the late 1940s became formfitting and trim. However, even as bared midriffs now expanded to five or six inches, the navel was still commonly covered and many styles still featured a modesty skirt.

Wartime utility shoes from Montgomery Ward, 1943.

Multicolored fabric shoes from Montgomery Ward, 1943.

High heels, platform soles, slingbacks, and open-toe styles from Alden's, 1948.

FIGURE 7.16. War Production Board restrictions limited the manufacture of leather footwear for non-military purposes. Ration coupons were required to buy leather shoes when they were available. Fabric shoes were not rationed so women could enjoy some colorful variety of footwear in their wardrobes. In the postwar years, materials were once again in full supply as reflected in the higher heels and platform soles of shoes.

Women's Shoes 1940–1949

Wartime utility regulations applied to shoes as well as clothing. Leather particularly was needed by the military since soldiers wore out a pair of boots about every month. In the United States and Britain, civilian leather shoes were rationed, requiring coupons when a supply became available. The English had to "make do and mend" much more than Americans. As with clothing, the emphasis on shoe designs was practicality as well as conservation. Heels were limited to two inches. For women working in plants and services, open-toe and strapped styles were banned as unsafe. Trodding about in sturdy, masculine-looking lace-ups confirmed a woman's patriotic duty. Since fabric uppers and synthetic or wooden soles were not rationed, some variety in footwear was still possible. (Figure 7.16.)

FIGURE 7.17. In the early 1940s, materials such as semiprecious stones and metals like sterling silver were used to make jewelry in place of base metals and plastics that had been reserved for war use. Top, Mexican jade set in sterling by Imperial Gem, 1943; bottom, patriotic red, white (diamonds), and blue jewelry by Rubel, 1944.

In the postwar years, high heels and ankle straps returned. Sandal toes and other open-toe styles, also called peep-toes at the time, were everywhere. With the availability of materials again, platform soles and three-inch heels were a distinct contrast to L-85 utility footwear styles.

Women's Jewelry 1940–1949

During World War II, metal-based jewelry became more costly and scarce. As cheap base metals became reserved for war efforts, jewelry makers used more sterling silver, which was plentiful and not rationed. The designs of the period were a mix of moderne high style and retro-Victorian and Edwardian revivals. Patriotic motifs such as the letter "V" for victory and adaptations of military insignia were especially popular. Also pieces made with a combination of red, white, and blue enamels or rhinestone settings were everywhere. (Figure 7.17.)

At the end of the decade, New Look fashions required a full regalia of accessories, including an abundance of jewelry, real or costume. Complete ensembles of matching necklace, earrings, bracelet, brooch, and sometimes even rings, wrap and stole clips, or shoe and hat ornaments were not uncommon.

Women's Hairstyles and Makeup 1940–1949

Hairstyles of the war years were longer than in the thirties despite the urging of safety organizations to cut it short. Even when Veronica Lake cut her blond tresses on camera "for the duration," most women preferred the longer styles. Bandanas were a practical solution to managing long hair while at work in the munitions factory. Netted snoods were a more fashionable option for other jobs. Whatever the length, the style usually was arranged high, whether in bilateral twin rolls or huge curls on top or in asymmetrical waves and pompadours that pushed forward onto the brow. (Figure 7.18.)

Of all the shortages women endured during the war, cosmetics were among the most missed. Many key ingredients used in the manufacturing of cosmetics, especially alcohol and petroleum, were restricted by the War Production Board even though lipstick and face powder were classified as "necessary and vital products." In addition, availability was reduced when some cosmetics factories were converted to the production of war needs such as manufacturing medical ointments and sunblock creams for desert fighting. Although more women were working and had disposable incomes, there was less to buy. A resourceful GI could capture the attentions of a pretty girl with the gift of a tube of lipstick or a scarce pair of nylon stockings. But despite the shortages of raw materials, cosmetics makers did not shut down operations. Wartime advertising actually promoted the need for women to use makeup. "America expects its women to keep busy—and keep beautiful," cajoled one 1943 ad. In contrast to the drab colors of utility clothing and accessories, makeup was bold and bright. Lipsticks with names like "Flame Swept Red" and "Dragon's Blood Ruby" emphasized

FIGURE 7.18. Hairstyles of the early 1940s were longer than in the thirties despite the publicity of safety concerns for factory workers. Coiffures of the war years were sculptural with vertical masses of waves and curls.

the strong reds for lips and fingernails. (Figure 7.19.) The pencil thin "surprised" eyebrows of the 1930s were replaced by the wider, more strongly angled eyebrows exemplified by Joan Crawford.

Women's Hats 1940–1949

As with cosmetics during World War II, women's hats were integral to the nation's morale—keeping women pretty for the fighting boys. Hats also provided some degree of individuality for women in the face of the monotonous utility clothing of the time. (Figure 7.20.) The two primary millinery tenets of the war years centered on the hairstyle. If the hair was worn down or full in the front, the hat sat back on the head. If the hair was worn up in the back then the hat sat forward, some pushing low onto the brow at a forty-five-degree angle. This latter style has come to be most associated with hats of the war years.

After the war, the Edwardian grand hat was revived with its great expanse and piles of fabric and trimmings. Feathers became popular again, adding not only dimension but also sumptuous texture.

Women's Accessories 1940–1949

Superfluous accessories for most women during the war years were discarded in keeping with the national call for utility, simplification, and conservation. Fashion editorials and ads still featured women dressed in the full accouterment, including matching handbag, shoes, belt, hat, jewelry, and gloves, but such ensembles were largely reserved for special daytime occasions or evening wear. (Figure 7.21.) To be decked out in so much finery suggested a flouting of patriotic duties.

New Look accessories, though, were vital for the correct finishing touches on almost everything a woman wore, whether dressy or casual.

FIGURE 7.19. Vivid reds dominated wartime cosmetics as a contrast to the drab colors of L-85 clothing and utilitarian factory work clothes. Red lipsticks for the "chic woman of 1944" from Chen Yu Cosmetics, 1944.

Military inspired hats from Spiegel, 1941.

Toy hat from Swansdown, 1943.

Netted velvet hat by Reine, 1943.

Combination snood and netted veil by Lilly Daché, 1944.

Dobbs pinched crown felt hat, 1945.

Wartime varieties from Stetson, 1944.

Feather picture hat by Lilly Daché, 1948.

FIGURE 7.20. The key emphasis for hats of the early 1940s was the angle. If the hair was worn up, the hat tilted forward onto the brow; if the hair was worn down, the hat sat back on the head. During the war years many hat styles featured military embellishments such as braid, stars, and insignia. Other hat styles were lavishly adorned with trimmings to offset the plainness of most utility fashions. In the postwar years, hats were designed with new shapes and varied dimensions to complement the drama of the New Look.

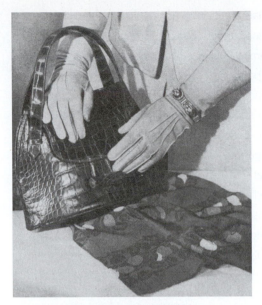

Silk scarf, alligator handbag, and doeskin gloves from Georg Jensen, 1944.

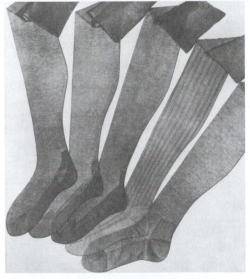

Wartime utility hosiery of reinforced cotton and rayon, 1943.

The abundantly accessorized and color-coordinated New Look, 1948.

Military motifs on wartime handbags and gloves, 1941.

FIGURE 7.21. During the war, accessories were mostly worn for special occasions since excesses of any kind were viewed as unpatriotic. The New Look ensemble, though, required a full accouterment of accessories, including an abundance of jewelry, hat, gloves, handbag, and even parasol.

FIGURE 7.22. The athletic look of the English drape cut remained the preferred suit silhouette through the 1940s. From Montgomery Ward: left, three-button suit in Donegal tweed; right two-button suit in rayon/wool blend, 1943.

Magazine editorials and fashion ads depicted women with head-to-toe accessories carefully chosen to coordinate perfectly with the New Look dress, suit, or evening gown. It was the total look more than the parts that was so critical. The properly attired woman of the period carefully matched her shoes, belt, and handbag, which sometimes included assorted matching small leather items like change purse, checkbook cover, key holder, compact, and cigarette case. Equal attention was devoted to coordinating her hat and veil, gloves, necklace, earrings, bracelets, wristwatch, handkerchief, the occasional scarf, and possibly a parasol. Even casual wear required special attention to accessories, whether simply by coordinating shoes, belts, and purses, or by adding other touches like sunglasses or a neckerchief.

Men's Fashions 1940–1949

During the Second World War, men's suit styles retained the English drape cut that had become the standard in the 1930s. The athletic silhouette with its broad shoulders, roomy armholes, tapered waist, and narrow hips remained the preferred masculine look. (Figure 7.22.) The three-button jacket with its rolled notch lapels was the most common for mature men, and the two-button jacket with the long line lapels was favored by younger men. Peaked lapels were usually for double-breasted styles. Since wool was strictly regulated, rayon blends became acceptable alternatives. Military influences included fabrics in "air blue" based on the color of U.S. Army Air Force uniforms and variations of khaki such as tans and olive browns. Because of the trim, pared-down simplicity of men's drape cut suits, few design changes were imposed by the War Production Board—primarily limitations on trouser cuffs and pleats, and elimination of patch pockets and back belts on jackets. Still, some streamlining occurred with trouser leg widths reduced a half inch at the hem, jackets shortened slightly, and lapels narrowed a bit.

Although the obsession with youth that dominated men's suit styles of the 1910s and 1920s had been replaced with the mature masculine styling of the English drape cut, many young men sought styles that provided some individuality to distinguish their generation from that of their elders. In France, the new Incroyables of the wartime years came to be called the **zazous**. The term may have originated from American swing music such as Cab Calloway's popular "Zah Zuh Zah" or similar refrains by the French crooner Johnny Hess. Contrary to the tailored looks of the conventional drape cut suit, the zazous, instead, donned fingertip-length jackets with sloping shoulders and pegged sleeves worn with baggy stovepipe trousers pegged at the leg bottoms and cropped three or four inches above the ankles. Thick soled shoes and brightly colored socks emphasized the shortened pant length. For the zazous, everything American was a fad—cigarettes, movies, novels, and especially music. The zazous trend was short-lived, though, lasting but a few years in the early forties due primarily to hostility from Vichy government officials who resented this influence of American pop culture.

FIGURE 7.23. The zoot suit was popular with segments of urban, young Latino and African-American men in the early 1940s. The exaggerated look featured an oversized coat, high-waisted pegged trousers, and a long watch chain. Photo 1943.

FIGURE 7.24. Mainstream variations of the youthful zoot suit, called swank suits, included jackets with huge, padded shoulders and a fitted waist worn with pegged trousers cropped at the ankles. Young men's swank suit by Pioneer Tailoring, 1942.

In the United States, the swing generation also expressed their individuality and youthful vigor with fashions all their own. The **zoot suit** was a uniquely American creation that emerged from the Harlem nightclub scene at the end of the thirties. (Figure 7.23.) The outfit featured an oversized jacket, usually double-breasted, with enormous, overly padded shoulders and huge lapels. The waists were tightly fitted, and hemlines extended to mid-thigh. Baggy, pegged trousers often had a long crotch that was pulled up high by suspenders or a cinch belt so that the waistband fitted just under the ribs. Accessories included bold print ties, a long watch chain that hung to the knees, and a wide-brimmed fedora. Less extreme versions of the zoot suit, called **swank suits**, were adopted by white suburban teens to wear to swing dances. (Figure 7.24.) When the War Production Board L-85 restrictions went into effect in mid-1942, young men who continued to wear swing style suits were viewed as being unpatriotic in their

FIGURE 7.25. At the end of the 1940s, the athletic draped cut suit transitioned into a loose, straight hanging silhouette. Summer weight suits from Haspel Suits, 1947.

Two-tone twin set, 1941.

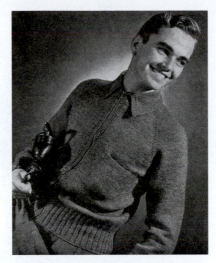

Zipper-front raglan style, 1941.

FIGURE 7.26. Fashionable knitwear was one way to combat home heating fuel shortages and lowered thermostats in winter.

Wartime motif, 1943.

Jacquard pattern, 1948.

excesses. In 1943, violence erupted between uniformed Marines and zoot-suiters on the West Coast that lasted for weeks, bringing the trend to its end.

After the war, men's suits began a transition away from the English drape cut. Jacket shoulders remained wide and hips were still snug, but instead of a tapered waist, the lines became more straight hanging, which eliminated the drape cut back. (Figure 7.25.)

In addition to the beginning of a new look in suits, bolder accessories and new dress shirt collars hallmarked men's business dress in the late 1940s. The Windsor-knot tie, socks with wide ribbing and decorative clocking, colorful pocket squares with wide borders, and assorted types of jewelry were key to the new masculine style of the late forties, referred to at the time in fashion journalism as the "**bold look.**" Shirts featured the "command collar," with its bold top stitching a half inch in from the edge instead of the traditional one-eighth inch.

Formalwear for men during the war was more strictly affected by L-85 restrictions than day suits. The excesses of the double breasted dinner jacket and the tail coat were prohibited. Instead, the one-button, single-breasted dinner jacket was the approved look. Black was the conventional choice for evening wear although younger men with fashion flair adopted the new midnight blue styles, especially with the grosgrain shawl collar.

Men's sportswear continued its extensive diversification from the 1930s. Knit tops and sweaters that had been adapted from athletic wear to everyday wardrobes became even more important during the war. Comfortable and casual knit shirts made wartime activities easier, such as working in victory gardens or running scrap metal and paper collection drives. Indoors, the chill of minimally heated rooms was offset by thick sweaters in all sorts of variations, including traditional cable stitch pullovers and cardigans, as well as new zipper front windbreaker styles. (Figure 7.26.) With the L-85 restrictions on wool usage, yarns of rayon and rayon/cotton blends were substituted for making knitwear.

FIGURE 7.27. Military influences on civilian outerwear of the Second World War included adaptations of the bomber's jacket and the duffle coat. Left: civilian bomber's jacket, 1943; right, shortened topcoats from Kraft & Phillips, 1942.

Sport shirts of the 1940s featured the broad range of colors and prints from the previous decade. The tropical motifs in Hawaiian print shirts even expanded into a unisex look with matching his-and-her sets. Military influences appeared in "campaign stripes"—colors and alternating widths inspired by service ribbons.

Casual trousers of the war years were also subject to L-85 restrictions. Cuffs were less common and leg widths were pared down. Straight, plain front pants increasingly replaced multiple-pleat styles. Even with wartime shortages and rationing, cotton fabrics, especially corduroy and denim, were plentiful for manufacturing pants and shorts.

After the war, GIs headed off to college and vocational schools in casual pant styles most familiar to them: khaki-colored cotton twill **chinos**. The styleless uniform of chinos and the button-down oxford has remained the ubiquitous American male dress for the last sixty years. Cuffs and pleats returned.

Men's Sports Attire and Outerwear 1940–1949

As with women's wear, the distinction between men's active sports attire and casual sportswear had become less clearly delineated by the beginning of the 1940s. Some specialty outfits continued to be associated with specific sports throughout the war years such as jodhpurs for riding and knickers for golfing. On most fairways, though, almost any variety of casual tops and slacks was acceptable. For tennis, white flannels or shorts, white shirt, white cotton socks, and white or blue canvas sneakers were typical. The cool and comfortable polo shirt remained a favorite for virtually all sports activities.

Skiwear of the war years primarily continued the styles of the previous decade. Moisture-resistant rayon fabrics were used to make jackets and wide-legged ski pants with elastic cuffs at the ankles and wrists. Heavy knit sweaters in winter-theme motifs and moderne patterns were most common on the slopes as well as around the fireplaces at resorts.

Outerwear for men became narrower and shorter during the early 1940s. (Figure 7.27.) Buttons on double-breasted styles were set closer together, and hemlines rose to just below the knees. When available, English tweeds were used for almost every style of outerwear. Four military inspired civilian coats of World War II were the U.S. battle jacket and bomber's jacket, a revival of the canadienne, and the introduction of the duffle coat. Adaptations of the U.S. **battle jacket** were made with the same big pockets, buttoned waistband, and fly front as the original military version. The **bomber's** (also bombardier's) **jacket** was a short, leather style with high pockets and snug-fitting knit waistband and wrists; corduroy and gabardine variants were mass produced in lieu of leather for civilian wear. The **canadienne** was a rustic, goat skin jacket with fleece lining that originated in Canada during the First World War and was revived in the 1940s. The three-quarter length **duffle coat**, or **toggle coat**, featured a hood, square shoulder yoke, huge patch pockets, and rope frogging that hooked over wooden peg buttons.

FIGURE 7.28. Through the 1940s, the two most popular forms of men's underwear were the basic white cotton brief and the patterned boxer. Athletic suit, briefs, and boxers from Spiegel, 1948.

Men's Underwear and Swimwear 1940–1949

Short boxers and formfitting knit briefs remained the two most prevalent types of men's underwear during the forties. (Figure 7.28.) Boxers were made in assorted colors and patterns but briefs were only in white, at least for the time being. Mass merchandise catalogs still offered longjohns as winter wear. Both the tank-style and T-cut undershirts were equally common.

Short boxers and formfitting knit briefs were also the two principal forms of men's swimwear. (Figure 7.29.) Both styles were made with concealed built-in supporters. During the war, knit briefs were made with various blends of yarn, including rayon with wool or cotton. Under L-85 restrictions, the amount of rubberized yarns used in knit swim briefs was reduced to as little as eight percent or eliminated entirely.

Formfitting Lastex briefs by Jantzen, 1949.

Boxer swim trunks with support liner from Cooper's, 1948.

The Secret!

FIGURE 7.29. The high waisted brief and short, baggy boxer were the most common forms of men's swimwear in the forties.

Knit swim briefs and woven boxers, 1943.

Men's Sleepwear and Accessories 1940–1949

Striped broadcloth cotton pajamas were standard men's sleepwear through the 1940s. Fly-front bottoms with elasticized waist and one-pocket, button-front tops were the most popular. Collarless V-neck and placket-front pullover tops were more prevalent for younger men. Knit athletic pajama sets with pullover crewneck tops and ribbed sleeve and ankle cuffs to prevent bunching up were also favorites of teenagers. (Figure 7.30.) Shortie pajama sets with knee-length bottoms and short-sleeve tops were for warm weather.

Robes were shortened to the knees during the war and became only slightly longer in the postwar years. Styles of robes made of terrycloth or cotton blanket cloth were a sleepwear accompaniment for pajamas while silk, rayon, and seersucker robes, sometimes advertised as **pullman robes**, were for travel or late evening and morning loungewear worn over regular clothing—with dress shirt and tie if entertaining close friends. Clashing pattern mixing of robes and pajamas were the norm.

The correct hat was still as indispensable as correct shoes for any particular outfit. Hats of the war years took on greater dimensions with wide snap brims turned down in the front and up at the back. Dress hats were made from two forms of felt: wool and fur. Soft-textured fur felt was mostly made from rabbit and hare although beaver was used in more expensive made-to-measure hats. Wool felt was heavier than fur felt and did not retain its shape as well. The two most popular colors of felt styles in the 1940s—deep blue and sand—reflected the influence of military uniforms. Hat bands were also sometimes embellished at the side with a military-inspired ornament such as an insignia or fighter plane. The studied casualness of men's wardrobes in the early 1940s inspired the **slope-crown hat**, which was blocked higher in the front than in the back. (Figure 7.31.) The sloped silhouette was also applied to the varieties of resort hats such as the pinched-front panamas and coconut palm hats. The traditional homburg with its rolled brim and center crease continued to be the recommended headwear for business suits although the style was worn primarily by older men.

Footwear for men during the war became strictly rationed due to the amount of leather and rubber used in their construction. Even so, the assortment of styles was greatly varied. (Figure 7.32.) Available to men with the correct ration coupon was his choice of slender two-tone wingtips with fancy perforated treatments, buckle strap monks, square-toe lace-ups, military ankle boots, officer's oxfords, or moccasin-style loafers called **loungers**. Unlike with women's shoe options, though, men had fewer nonrationed casual shoe styles to add variety to their wardrobes.

Neckwear in the 1940s featured some of the most flamboyant prints and colors since the influence of art deco in the twenties. Handpainted designs were a particular fad during the

FIGURE 7.30. Striped two-piece pajamas were the ubiquitous sleepwear for men of the era. Knitwear styles featured banded wrists and ankles that did not "creep up" during the night. Pajama varieties in cotton flannel, cotton knit, and cotton shirting, 1948.

FIGURE 7.31. Men's hats of the early 1940s were reshaped with a sloped crown, which was blocked higher in the front than the back. Fur felt hats, 1943.

FIGURE 7.32. Shoe styles of the 1940s became more widely varied than in the thirties. During the war years, standard oxfords and ankle boots were given military names like "grenadiers" and "officer's chukkas." Shoes by Herald Square, 1943.

FIGURE 7.33. The vivid colors and wild patterns of postwar men's ties and accessories were labeled the "bold look" by journalists and advertisers. Left, silk ties from Haband, 1947; right, suspenders by Hikkok, 1948.

FIGURE 7.34. Although wartime restrictions on certain metals made jewelry for men less favored or abundant than previously, tie clips and cuff links continued to be accessory essentials for the well-dressed man throughout the 1940s. Tie clips, tie chain, key chain, belt buckle, and cuff links from Hadley Jewelry, 1947.

FIGURE 7.35. Men, young or mature, were mostly clean shaven throughout the 1940s. Hair styles remained cropped short, but the top volume steadily increased with pompadours becoming the most popular look. By the end of the decade, makers of men's toiletries extended product lines to include after-shave lotions and colognes, and even tinted skin talcs for the face. Left, Vaseline Hair Tonic ad, 1946; right Tawn ad, 1947.

war years. End points of ties were up to four and a half inches wide, which balanced the thick Windsor knot that was so popular. Bow ties declined in popularity. As silk and wool supplies diminished during the early forties, men's ties were made with rayon or rayon blends. In the postwar years, men's ties and accessories continued the use of striking colors and patterns, labeled as the "bold look" by journalists and advertisers. (Figure 7.33.)

Men's jewelry was less important as an accessory in the war years than it had been in the 1930s. Metal shortages made scarce the usual variety of tie clasps, watch chains, cuff links, key rings, and identification bracelets. After the war, jewelry was redundant to the flamboyance of "bold look" accessories, except for the occasional tie clip or requisite cuff links. (Figure 7.34.) Cigarette cases, lighters, and even studded wallets were often advertised as forms of men's jewelry.

FIGURE 7.36. Girls' dresses and suits of the war years followed the short, narrow utility lines of the time. In the postwar period, the New Look influenced girls' clothing by replicating fitted bodices, full, sweeping skirts, and a complete ensemble of accessories. Left, utility dressing from Montgomery Ward, 1943; center, playwear from Spiegel, 1948; right, New Look dressing for girls from Celeste, 1949.

Men's Grooming and Hairstyles 1940–1949

In the 1940s, American men were clean shaven. In Europe, though, various forms of the mustache remained common. The eccentricity of Adolf Hitler's lobbed-off cut and the waxed artifice of the British male's mustache are notable examples. Similarly, only short hair was the accepted look of the era. Almost all hair cuts were cropped close at the sides around the ears but full on top and back. The top fullness was combed back or parted at the side to shape the volume of pompadours. Hair tonic manufacturers heavily promoted the shiny oiled look as good grooming for healthy hair. By the end of the decade, makers of men's grooming toiletries expanded product lines to include colognes and even skin toned talcs. (Figure 7.35.)

Children's Clothing 1940–1949

Infant's clothing of the 1940s retained the simplicity that had developed following the First World War. The layettes of the period usually included a long-sleeve cotton wrap shirt cropped

FIGURE 7.37. Boys' clothing was primarily miniature versions of menswear—from the draped cut suit of the 1940s to replications of military uniforms. Mass merchandisers featured casualwear and playwear with licensed screen prints and logos from movies.

Army officer's uniform for boys, 1943.

Boys' single- and double-breasted suits, 1943.

to about the hips, a long gown to cover the feet, and a matching open-front wrapper. Diapers, socks, and a receiving blanket completed the dressing necessities.

The design of children's clothing in the early 1940s was largely guided by the American L-85 and Britain's utility restrictions. Just as with men's apparel, boys' suits lost patch pockets, multiple pleats, and trouser cuffs. Girls' dresses were narrowed and shortened, and full-around pleats or excessive trimmings were forbidden. Shirt tails for both boys and girls were reduced to save every inch of material possible for the war efforts.

The styles of girls' dresses remained largely unchanged from those of the 1930s. (Figure 7.36.) Bodices were fitted with a high waist and short, puffed sleeves. Loose fitting princess styles featured shoulder to hem gores. For toddler girls, skirt hemlines were about mid-thigh, and for school-age girls the hemline was at the knees. During the war, silhouettes were narrow and suits were cut with the same utility plainness as women's styles. Playwear for little ones was often unisex shorts and knit tops, creeperalls, and one-piece jumpers, differentiated by gender-specific colors and decorative motifs.

Following the launch of Dior's New Look in 1947, girls' clothing adopted an ultrafeminine emphasis. Skirts were full, bodices fitted, and waistlines at the natural position. Frills and fussy detail abounded. As with her mom's total New

Licensed Lone Ranger playwear, 1948.

Look, a properly dressed little miss also wore an abundance of accessories, especially gloves, hats, and handbags that matched shoes and belts.

Boys' wear was largely miniature versions of men's clothing, even to outerwear, underwear, shoes, and accessories. (Figure 7.37.) During the war, uniforms of virtually every branch of the military were replicated in diminutive proportions for boys. The knicker suit, though, disappeared even though it remained a country squire style for adults into the 1950s. This fundamental social change, suggests historian Perry London, was because the wartime boy "was expected to mature earlier, assume more responsibilities, and devote less time to living in a state of hibernation." Boys' casualwear and playwear increasingly featured assorted licensed screen prints and branded logos from famous Hollywood movie serials and cartoons—a portent of the TV era just ahead.

In the postwar years, tons of used and new children's clothing were shipped from the United States to bombed-out families in war-ravaged Europe. As ready-to-wear industries in Britain, France, and Germany rebuilt and resumed production, they began to adopt many of the comfortable playwear styles from America in response to homeland consumer demand for "Yank" childrenswear.

Review

During the Second World War, America and Britain were cut off from the fashion dictates of Paris. In addition, homegrown and exiled designers were further challenged by materials shortages and governmental utility restrictions on clothing construction. Women's dresses and suits were narrow and simple in silhouette with squared shoulders and short, knee-length skirts. Men's suits continued the athletic look of the English draped cut although details such as multiple trouser pleats or jacket patch pockets were prohibited.

For both women and men during the war years, sportswear became ever more important. Women wore a wide variety of slacks and casual tops to work in factories and the service sector as well as for leisure time on weekends. Jeans became a fashion item rather than merely a commodity work garment. Men similarly dressed down, preferring sport jackets and knitwear when business and social protocol permitted.

With the conclusion of the war, Paris once again reclaimed fashion preeminence with the launch of Christian Dior's New Look in 1947. After several years of austerity clothing and privations, women adored Dior's high style, yards of fabric, and head-to-toe accessories. The ultrafeminine New Look silhouette with its rounded shoulders, full bosom, cinched waist, and wide, spreading skirts over curvaceous hips would dominate women's fashions in various forms for the following fifteen years.

Fashions for girls and boys of the forties were largely miniature versions of adult styles. Girls' dresses and suits of the war years were narrow and simplified. Boys' suits were cut on the English drape line, and the knicker suit for preteen boys finally disappeared. Following the war, girls' fashions reflected the influence of the New Look with fitted bodices, full skirts, and all the correct feminine accessories.

review questions

1. What were the three purposes of the wartime utility restrictions?

2. How did utility restrictions affect the design of women's clothing during World War II? What was one key exception to the restrictions and how was it applied to women's fashion?

3. What were the principal elements of Dior's New Look?

4. What was the basic look of men's suits in the 1940s? Which changes in men's clothing resulted from wartime utility restrictions?

5. Identify the time, place, and look of the zazous and zoot suiters.

research and portfolio projects

Research

1. Write a research paper on the emergence of American fashion design without the influence of Paris during the Second World War. Identify the key U.S. designers and their innovative contributions to fashion.

Portfolio

1. During World War II, shortages of materials inspired French designers to create new ways of fastening garments without standard buttons, toggles, or zippers. Design five different ways for fastening the front closure of a jacket without the usual type of buttons, toggles, or zippers. Construct individual sample cards with each closure type mounted, and demonstrate to the class how they function.

dress terms

Atome: the name given to the 1946 bikini swimsuit design by Jacques Heim

battle jacket: civilian version of the military jacket with big pockets, buttoned waistband, and fly front

bikini: women's two piece swimsuit of the late 1940s with a bandeau or bra-cut top and low waisted bottom

bold look: the term applied to menswear of the late 1940s in which accessories were vividly colored and patterned

bomber's jacket: men's short leather or fabric jacket with high pockets and banded bottom

canadienne: men's goatskin jacket with fleece lining

chinos: khaki-colored cotton twill trousers

cigarette silhouette: the slim, tubular cut of women's outerwear during World War II

duffle coat: men's hooded, square-shoulder coat with patch pockets and rope frogging that hooked over wooden pegs

dungarees: jeans

guimpe: a bust-to-hips corset; see also waspie

L-85 regulations: restrictions and guidelines for making clothes instituted by the U.S. War Production Board in 1942

loungers: men's moccasin style slip-on shoes

New Look: the term applied by the fashion press in 1947 to describe Christian Dior's debut collection; the look featured rounded shoulders, full busts, cinched waists, and spreading skirts

prêt-à-porter: French high-style, high quality ready-to-wear tailored to the U.S. market

pullman robe: men's tailored dressing robes

slope-crown hat: men's styles of hats in the 1940s that featured a crown blocked higher in the front than the back

spool torso: a fitted dress bodice of the early post World War II years

swank suit: a less extreme variation of the zoot suit, featuring a jacket with broad, padded shoulders, trim waist, and wide lapels

toggle coat: another name for duffle coat

toppers: women's loose fitting coats usually cropped at the waist or high on the hips

utility look: the simplified, utilitarian styles of World War II fashions

waspie: a constricting corselette popular in the early years of the New Look

zazous: young Frenchmen of World War II who dressed in long jackets with baggy, pegged trousers

zoot suit: an urban American men's suit of the early 1940s with an oversized, padded jacket and baggy, pegged trousers

8 The Jet Age 1950–1959

1950   **1959**

| Korean War 1950–1953 | | | | | | |

| Color TV tube developed 1950 | Death of England's George VI; Queen Elizabeth II assumed throne 1952 | Polio vaccine discovered 1953 | Warsaw Pact established Communist bloc 1955 | Grace Kelly married Prince of Monaco 1956 | Soviets launched Sputnik satellite 1957 | Alaska and Hawaii became states 1959 |

| J.D. Salinger's *Catcher in the Rye* 1951 | | U.S. Supreme Court ordered school integration 1954 | Marilyn Monroe in *Seven Year Itch* 1955 | Hungary occupied by Soviets 1956 | Leonard Bernstein's *West Side Story* 1957 | Fidel Castro seized power in Cuba 1959 |

The Cold War

In the aftermath of the Second World War, the newly founded United Nations struggled to establish itself as a guarantor of a warless world. Instead, Russia, having been granted one of five seats on the kingpin Security Council, vetoed scores of resolutions that they regarded as an interference with their schemes for world revolution. Immediately after the war, the Soviet Union dropped the Iron Curtain of communist dominion over the nations of central Europe. In China, the communists took over in 1949. The Cold War between democracies and communism had begun.

In 1949, the Russians further shocked the world by successfully testing its own atomic bomb. The arms race intensified when the United States responded with the thermonuclear hydrogen bomb in 1952, which was matched by the Russians in 1955. Submarines were armed with nuclear warheads and jet aircraft flew faster than the speed of sound. It was the Jet Age. For a moment in the war of wills, the Russians outpaced America by being first into space with the Sputnik satellite in 1957. The United States entered this new phase of the Cold War with its first satellite the following year.

FIGURE 8.1. In the postwar years, suburban family living and a preoccupation with materialism and consumerism became the American dream. Advertising and television programming of the 1950s perpetuated a sanitized myth of the nuclear American family.

A shooting phase of the Cold War erupted not in Europe, where tensions were continually high along the Iron Curtain, but in Korea. After the world war, the Allies had divided up the nations formerly occupied by the Axis powers into zones of reconstruction. In Korea, Russia administered the northern half, which became communist, and the United States accepted the southern half, which was democratized. Less than a year after U.S. troops withdrew in 1949, belligerent communists invaded the south. Although the United Nations voted to defend the south, the bulk of the air and naval materiel, and most of the men, except for the South Koreans, were supplied by the United States. The Chinese joined the North Koreans and the conflict was fought to a stalemate at the 38th parallel. An uneasy truce was finally negotiated in 1953, leaving one of the most heavily fortified and armed borders in the world.

Throughout the 1950s, the global expansion of communism threatened French Indochina (Vietnam), Greece, Turkey, Egypt, and even France and Italy. One counter measure against the Soviet Union was the Marshall Plan, named for U.S. Secretary of State, George Marshall, which pumped tens of millions of dollars of economic aid into nations that agreed to resist communism. Another deterrence against the spread of communism was the formation of the North Atlantic Treaty Organization (NATO) in Europe and, later, the South East Asia Treaty Organization (SEATO), both of which assured member nations that an attack against anyone of the member nations would be regarded as war against them all.

In the Middle East, the Arab League was formed in 1945 to advance national interests in the Near East against European imperialism. When the British abandoned its Palestine mandate in 1948, an Arab-Jewish war ensued in which Egypt and Jordan suffered humiliating military reversals. With the truce agreement the following year, an independent Israel was founded.

Television

One of the most potent and pervasive influences on American pop culture of the 1950s was television. (Figure 8.2.) Programs often depicted an illusory representation of the ideal American family, which was perpetuated in long-running series like *The Adventures of Ozzie and Harriet* and *The Donna Reed Show.* "Mr. Television," Milton Berle, kept millions of viewers home Tuesday nights to see if he would appear in drag, and everyone loved Lucy on Mondays.

With the expansion of television stations across the continent during the 1950s, marketers capitalized on this new medium for advertising. Sponsors of television programs controlled virtually every aspect of production. Scripts for talk shows were interwoven with dialog promoting the sponsor's products, and game show sets were plastered with product brand logos at every camera angle. Ready-to-wear makers and clothing retailers vied with each other to provide wardrobes for the program characters or hosts with the promise of an acknowledgement in the credits or a mention on the air. Only with the quiz show scandals of 1959—when it was revealed that many contestants had been given the answers ahead of time—were television networks able to wrest control of programming from sponsors.

FIGURE 8.2. Television became an integral part of family life in the postwar years. Commercials fueled aspirational consumerism, and programming idealized the American home and family. Ad, 1952.

American Culture and Society in the 1950s

In the years following the Second World War, millions of American families moved into suburbia, eager to put the trauma of the war behind them and get on with life. (Figure 8.1.) Weekends became a ritual of lawn mowers, car washes, and backyard barbecues. Sales of patio furniture quadrupled between 1950 and 1960. Bowling leagues and little league baseball teams gave neighbors a sense of community. Teenagers went to sock-hops at school gymnasiums and danced the Bop, the Stroll, or the Calypso to the new sounds of rock and roll.

Among the most prevalent social issues that challenged the contentment and conformity of American society were economic inequalities and racial injustices. In 1954, the Supreme Court finally reversed the "separate but equal" doctrine that had been in place since the 1890s by ordering public school integration. Compliance was tied to federal funding of education. Despite efforts by regional demagogues, most Southerners accepted integration rather than no public schools for their children. Encouraged by this and similar decisions by the courts, African-American leaders such as Martin Luther King, Jr., effectively organized marches, "sit-in" demonstrations, and boycotts to further voting rights, desegregation of public transportation and facilities, and nondiscrimination in jobs. In 1957, Congress acted with the first civil rights legislation since Reconstruction.

Buy wash-and-wear!

A sport shirt has to put up with some pretty strenuous wear and frequent washings. That's why good wash-and-wear cottons are a special blessing. They're easy to care for . . . cut ironing time down to almost nothing . . . and keep their fresh appearance throughout an active day.

Not wash-and-beware!

No shirt is fun if it shrinks up, binds the shoulders and sours the mood. Some wash-and-wear does shrink, too . . . right out of fit. So be sure you look for "Sanforized" on wash-and-wear just as you do on other cottons. Then you'll *know* the shirt will wash and wash and keep its fit.

·SANFORIZED·

FIGURE 8.3. Among the technological advances in textile manufacturing during the 1950s was the improvement in shrink-resistant wash-and-wear fabrics.

Other rifts in the comfortable conventions of postwar American society occurred when the children of this "silent generation" began to rebel against the complacency of their elders. In 1953, Marlon Brando represented the rebellious leather-clad biker and his antisocial view of America in *The Wild One.* Two years later, James Dean portrayed the quintessential modern adolescent struggling for his own identity, free of conformity, in *Rebel Without a Cause.* Another counterculture movement was that of the Beats—a term alternately used as a contraction of "beatitude," since they felt they had been blessed with mystical qualities, and also as a symbol of those who had been "beaten down" and excluded from the American dream. These first voices of dissent and disillusionment paved the path for a more vocal and activist generation in the 1960s and 1970s.

Technology and Textiles

By the beginning of the 1950s, textiles had become the second largest industry in the United States with more than 6,000 manufacturers employing about one and a quarter million people. During the decade following the war, numerous textile makers relocated to the South where not only labor and land were cheap but labor unions were largely unwelcome, resulting in a twenty-two percent decline in the northeast textile industry.

Advances in technology expanded the varieties and availability of yarns well beyond those made with natural fibers to include a host of new synthetics and treated materials. In 1947, the Dan Rivers Mills began production of cotton fabrics prepared with a synthetic resin that made them wrinkle-resistant. In 1949, Dynel was introduced as a fire-resistant, moth- and mildew-proof fiber used in fake furs and later for wigs. Du Pont launched Orion acrylic in 1950, and Dacron in 1953. In 1958, Eastman Chemicals produced the Kodel polyester fiber. Synthetic yarns and treated fabrics made possible a wide array of shrink-resistant, **wash-and-wear** apparel, sales of which leapt from $45 million in 1952 to $285 million just four years later. (Figure 8.3.)

Women's Fashions 1950–1959

With Christian Dior at the forefront of couture design, Paris reigned supreme as the world's center for fashion leadership throughout the 1950s. Season after season, Dior led the way with innovative collections that subtly evolved from the previous season's styles into a fresh variation on the New Look theme. (Figure 8.4.) In the spring of 1950, he launched the "Vertical Line" collection, which reintroduced the trim, fitted sheath—"the single most important day for fashion," avowed *Vogue* at the time. Between 1954 and 1956, he introduced his influential alphabet lines. The **H Line** featured a dropped waist (an adaptation of Balenciaga's **middy** styles of 1953), which differed dramatically from the 1920s dropped-waist looks in that the bodice snugly contoured the figure, emphasizing the cinched waist, rounded hips, and defined

FIGURE 8.4. Throughout the 1950s, Christian Dior presented innovative creations season after season, including the alphabet line collections.

H Line dress, or middy, by Nelly Don, 1956.

Y Line sheath by Karen Stark, 1955.

A Line suit by Christian Dior, 1955.

bosom. The **Y Line** was a slender body with shoulder details like puffed sleeves, pelerine collar, or decollete necklines that visually formed the converging top of the "Y."

Between 1955 and 1957, Dior explored fresh shapes and styles that were antithetical to his original concept of the New Look. His **A Line** silhouette was narrow and fitted at the top and widened from the bust or waist in a straight line to the hem. The triangular contours were successfully applied to dresses, evening gowns, suits, and outerwear such as the ready-to-wear adaptation shown in Figure 8.4. The crossbar of the A was variously centered between the bustline and hips, providing an ingenious assortment of design possibilities. The look was so well received that the term "A line" immediately became a part of fashion vocabulary and has been replicated and interpreted by fashion designers ever since.

Among those interpreting the A line silhouette was Yves St. Laurent whose **trapeze** collection in 1958 was applauded in the press as having saved French couture, following the sudden death of Dior from a heart attack the previous year. The twenty-one-year-old St. Laurent had been a protégé of Dior and was catapulted into the head designer role at the House of Dior with the success of his trapeze designs. The trapeze line—short for trapezium, a quadrilateral with two parallel sides—featured a full, tent shape with a high bust and back that fell from

FIGURE 8.5. At the end of the 1950s, Yves St. Laurent introduced the trapeze line, the most extreme counter to Dior's original concept of the New Look. Trapeze dress by Nelly Don, 1958.

FIGURE 8.6. The silhouette of the enduring shirtwaist dress reflected the influences of the New Look styling with its fitted bodice and full skirt. Shirtwaister in acetate taffeta by Jeanne Carr, 1955.

the shoulders. Ready-to-wear makers easily made variations of the trapeze for mass market distribution. (Figure 8.5.)

Italy, too, entered the international fashion arena in the 1950s, achieving widespread acclaim primarily for its resort wear, knitwear, and leather goods. Emilio Pucci, Donna Simonetta Fabiani, Roberto Capucci, and the Fontana sisters were among the innovative designers who brought an exciting inventiveness and bold use of color to fashion. Italy especially became the fashion leader in footwear during the fifties with the popularity of the four-inch stiletto high heel. A decade later, Italian boots similarly were in demand around the world.

After four years without influence from Paris during the Second World War, American designers continued at the forefront of fashion with an endless variety of casual dressing. Year after year in the 1950s, the elements of the New Look—delineated bust, cinched waist, and rounded hips—were easily adapted to comfortable mix-and-match separates and the ubiquitous **shirtwaister** that were in every American woman's wardrobe. (Figure 8.6.)

Part of the American youth look also included crinolined **circle skirts** decorated with three-dimensional appliques of stylized poodles, music notes, hearts, and even actual vinyl

FIGURE 8.7. After years of masculine, austerity suit styles during World War II, women overwhelmingly embraced the ultrafeminine variations of New Look fashions. Above, cinched waist suits from House of Swansdown, 1953; right, bolero jacket dress by Herbert Sondheim, 1954.

records or Christmas ornaments. Teen girls, called **bobbysoxers**, wore scuffed black-and-white saddle oxfords or penny loafers with turned-down white cotton socks, and hung out at music stores or drug store soda fountains.

Hollywood continued to exert influence on the fashion and beauty industries, though it was less pronounced than it had been in the 1930s. Audrey Hepburn was first among equals of the great Hollywood beauties of the era, which included Elizabeth Taylor, Grace Kelly, Natalie Wood, and Lauren Bacall. Her large, captivating eyes, sharply drawn eyebrows, and pouty lips were the composite for a new ideal in beauty. Clothes of any type fitted her slender angularity beautifully. *Vogue* wrote of Hepburn in 1954, "Nobody ever looked like her before World War II. Yet we recognize the rightness of this appearance in the relation to our historical needs. And the proof is that thousands of imitations have appeared."

Women's suits of the New Look era were as widely varied as dresses. (Figure 8.7.) Throughout the 1950s numerous versions of the cropped bolero remained popular, including fitted Edwardian revivals and capacious A Line cuts. In 1954, Chanel returned to Paris after

William Rose, 1951.

Christian Dior, 1952.

Von Marek, 1957.

Gothe, 1953.

FIGURE 8.8. New Look styling was applied to evening wear either through the sumptuous abundance of fabric or with formfitting sheaths that accentuated the curvaceous line of the female form. Teen girls' spring prom dresses were conically shaped with layers of stiff crinolines.

FIGURE 8.9. Although the ultrafeminine silhouette of the New Look with its fitted bodices and flowing skirts was also applied to coats and jackets, one of the most popular outerwear styles was the capacious flare coat. From Lassie Maid coats, 1954: left, fitted coat; right, flare coat.

a fifteen-year absence from fashion during her exile in Switzerland. She reintroduced the ease and softness of the boxy suit styles that had been her staple before the war. Despite criticism from the fashion press that Chanel offered nothing new, many of her contemporaries appreciated the nonchalant lines and simplicity of her designs. At about the same time, other designers concentrated on fresh variations of the long, straight suit lines that had appeared in 1951. Balenciaga created tunic suits, and Dior launched his loose-fitting A Line suits. New attention on English tweeds resulted from the highly publicized coronation ceremonies of Elizabeth II in 1953. In the second half of the decade, skirts became shorter and, by 1958, were nearly at the same knee-length they had been during the war. Also at the end of the decade, Yves St. Laurent's trapeze-line suits provided fresh options for the modern women's wardrobe.

Evening wear of the 1950s similarly reflected the changing trends in New Look styling. (Figure 8.8.) After 1950, versions of the narrow, form-fitting sheath were adapted to evening dresses and gowns although bouffant skirts dominated throughout the decade. At the end of the decade, innovative evening wear styles included adaptations of St. Laurent's trapeze line as well as avant-garde silhouettes such as puffball skirts.

Women's Outerwear 1950–1959

Although the ultrafeminine silhouettes of New Look styling influenced many outerwear designs, for the most part, women's coats and jackets were capacious and full without a marked waistline. (Figure 8.9.) With the increased variety of fabrics, especially synthetics such as nylon and orlon, coats and jackets featured an endless array of opulent details such as pleats and tucks, large turned-back cuffs, detachable capelets, deep saddlebag patch pockets, and expansive collars and lapels. Other new fabrications such as **poodle cloth**—a nubby, deep pile wool resembling poodle fur—provided fresh looks for wide **flare coats** and short **toppers**. Wrap coats, called **cocoons**, had appeared soon after the war, but remained a favorite look for younger women with slender, angular figures. **Martingale coats** with half belts in the back were made with both fitted and wide cuts in the mid-1950s. **Umbrella backs** featured triangular gores set into the back collar that flared into deep organ pipe folds. Furs continued

FIGURE 8.10. Postwar suburban living inspired a proliferation of casual pant styles and shorts. Increasingly, the wide variety of colorful and patterned sportswear was preferred to the traditional white athletic uniforms for golf, tennis, and other regulation sports activities. Top left, sportswear ad from Ship 'n Shore, 1958; top right, corduroy tunic top with matching cropped pants, and corduroy shorts with popcorn knit shirt from Fligelman, 1956; bottom left, Orlon acrylic sweater twinset from Blairmoor with tailored Orlon/wool slacks from Davenshire, 1955.

to be every woman's dream, whether a simple evening fox stole or a full-length wild mink. American ready-to-wear makers capitalized on this market with high quality fake furs made of new synthetic materials, especially those dyed to replicate exotic skins like leopard and tiger. As with suits, English tweeds became especially popular for outerwear following the coronation of Elizabeth II in 1953.

Women's Sports Apparel 1950–1959

In the 1950s, slacks became more narrow than the styles of the thirties and forties. Thigh-high short skirts became common for tennis, many of which were made as wrap skirts to fasten over matching shorts. Most

FIGURE 8.11. In the 1950s, denim for women ranged from weekend wear for suburbanites to rebellion dress for teen girls. By the end of the decade, though, tailored denim in assorted colors was promoted as mainstream fashion. Colored denim jackets and jeans from Wrangler, 1959.

tennis leagues continued to require all whites for play although pastels were favored by weekenders for leisure time tennis. The knit polo top was ubiquitous. Golfers were increasingly less restricted on the proper attire for the courses although jeans, short shorts, playsuits, and similar casual playwear were often prohibited. Winter sports clothing became more lightweight and snugly fitting. Improved stretch yarns and knitting technologies made ski pants fit smooth as a second skin. After the war, nylon jackets in vibrant colors were especially popular on the ski slopes. Attire for other active sports such as bicycling, hiking, and neighborhood ball games included a wide assortment of comfortable playwear, particularly knit tops, shorts, one-piece playsuits, and cropped pant styles. The California casual style that had begun to expand eastward in the 1930s was ideal for postwar suburban living. (Figure 8.10.) In addition to assorted types of tailored trousers, women's pant styles now included slim **capris** cropped just above the ankles, **pedal pushers** extending a few inches below the knees, and shorts at lengths from long **bermudas** to thigh-high cuts.

Jeans were still called dungarees in catalogs and were shown with the cuffs rolled to mid-calf as a fashion look such as those shown in Chapter 7, Figure 7.10. Some jeans were lined with striking plaid flannels that created a decorative cuff when rolled. During the 1950s, jeans were transformed into a teen look and made fashionable with colored denim and matching jackets. (Figure 8.11.)

Women's Underwear and Sleepwear 1950–1959

The constricting corset continued to be one of the most important undergarments for achieving the New Look contours. Varieties even included revivals of lace-up forms to ensure the tiniest waistline. (Figure 8.12.) Some foundation garments were reduced to only an eight-inch waistband to more comfortably cinch the waist for women who did not need full figure control.

As the 1950s progressed, undergarments continued to reshape the female form into ultrafeminine silhouettes. The waist remained tiny and the hips full and sloping, but the bosom was sculpted into exaggerated proportions and shapes by the mid-fifties. The **torpedo bras** with their spiral cup stitching and padded linings enlarged and separated the breasts into a stylization of the bosom that remained popular until the end of the decade. Fashion colors were featured in mass merchandising catalogs, ranging from pastels to red and black. Nylon replaced rayon as the more common synthetic for bras.

Strapless nylon slips by Mojud, 1951.

Merry Widow corselette by Warner's, 1956.

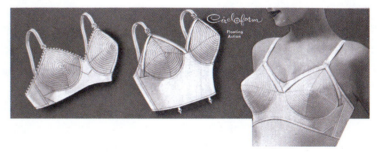

"Torpedo" bras with concentric stitching from Circloform, 1954.

Lace trimmed nylon tricot panties from Montgomery Ward, 1952.

Warner's Cinch-Bra "makes your waist more diminutive, more appealing," promised ad copy in 1951.

FIGURE 8.12. The ultrafemininity of New Look fashions required undergarments that shaped and controlled the figure. Constricting corsets cinched waists and the torpedo bra exaggerated busts.

FIGURE 8.13. Varieties of nightgowns ranged from fitted, frilly New Look ensembles to short and sexy baby doll sets. New synthetic yarns made possible a wider assortment of fabrics for sleepwear, including fluid acetate tricot and soft, warm nylon fleece. Left, peignoir and gown by Vanity Fair, 1954; center, baby doll set by Rogers Lingerie, 1956; right, print flannel pajamas by Pat Hilton, 1957.

Frilly treatments and lace and ribbon trimmings returned to slips and petticoats in abundance. Stiff mesh net crinolines were layered under the full, New Look skirts to hold the shape, some as smooth and conical as sixteenth-century Spanish court styles.

For sleepwear, feminine curves were accentuated by gowns with the Empire waistline and billowing skirts of pleated or gathered nylon. (Figure 8.13.) Lace and ribbon trim, rosettes, ruffles, and other frills embellished nightgowns, pajamas, and robes. Shortie pajamas, called **baby doll sets**, with hip-length tops and matching shorts or bloomers were a favorite of teen girls in the 1950s. Thigh-high versions of nightshirts and sheer nylon negligees likewise became popular with young women. Robes were similarly varied in styles and fabrics. New Look robes featured fitted bodices with full, ankle-length skirts of cotton percale or rayon satin. Wrap robes with matching sashes were of terrycloth, pinwale cotton chenille, or cotton flannelette. Knee-length housecoats, called **dusters**, were of textured or quilted nylon.

FIGURE 8.14. Swimwear of the New Look era was constructed with internal devices and surface treatments to emphasize a cinched waist, full bust, and rounded hips. Many styles retained the modesty skirt. Constructed swimsuits with modesty skirts by Catalina, 1955.

FIGURE 8.15. The shape of shoes was the news of the 1950s. The important New Look styles featured high, thin stiletto heels with shallow lasts and low throats.

Stiletto pump by Pandora Footwear, 1957.

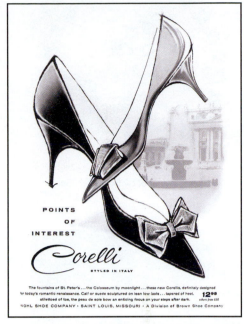

Italian "décolleté" lasts and low, spiked heels by Corelli, 1957,

Women's Swimwear 1950–1959

In keeping with the idealized femininity of New Look fashions, swimwear makers of the 1950s produced the **constructed swimsuit**, engineered with all types of clever devices to sculpt, control, and idealize the female body. (Figure 8.14.) Bodices were boned to cinch waistlines, peplums emphasized the hips, and bras were molded, wired, and padded to shape the bust. Ruffles, bows, beading, and even fur trim embellished the New Look swimsuits of the decade. Modesty skirts were still prevalent on American swimsuits. Colors were vibrant and textile patterns were bold, including exotic animal skin prints.

Women's Shoes 1950–1959

In the early 1950s, the shape of the shoe was everything. Four-inch Italian **stilettos** were all the rage. (Figure 8.15.) Heels became more slender, almost spiked. The thick, round **spool heels** of 1952 were one of the exceptions. The heel of the foot also became more exposed with strappy sling-backs and open-toe mules. Platform soles continued to be popular for dress shoes of the early fifties, though less thick than the designs of the forties. Durable nylon lace and mesh insets added elegance to evening shoes. By comparison, younger women opted for tomboyish flats that featured wider, **egg-point toes**. **Ballet slippers** were completely without any heel and became a favorite of high school girls. Saddle oxfords remained a trend for bobbysoxers. **Kilties** featured turned-down fringed tongues, and **back-straps** had a tab of material across the heel that buckled.

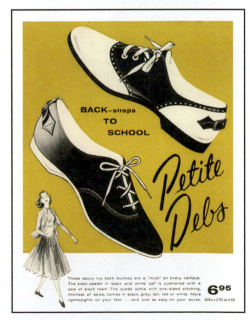

Saddle oxfords and back-straps for teens by Wohl Shoes, 1957.

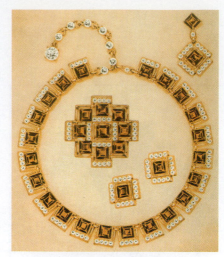
Faux topaz jewelry set by Bogoff, 1954.

White plastic and goldtone necklaces from Coro Jewelry, 1956.

FIGURE 8.16. Matching sets of jewelry, especially collections made of the new jet-age plastics, were a key component of the correct New Look ensemble. Jewelry fads of the 1950s included oversized charm bracelets and boyfriend ankle bracelets.

Charm bracelets from Bergère, 1954.

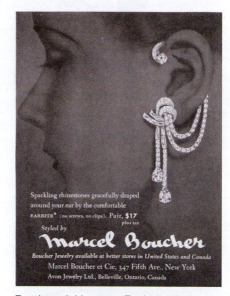
Ear-draped rhinestone Earrite earrings from Marcel Boucher, 1950.

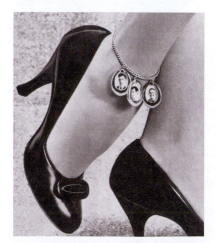
Beaux ankle bracelet, 1956.

Women's Jewelry 1950–1959

Throughout the fifties, the complete ensemble of jewelry continued to be integral to the required full accessory regalia of the New Look. To meet the surge in demand, jewelry makers developed cheaper methods of mass production. Casting processes were replaced by high-speed stamping methods, and stones were glued in instead of set with prongs. Glittery rhinestone pieces were especially popular throughout the period. The topaz was one of the most favored jewels; so popular was the topaz in the fifties that Avon launched a line of fragrances and cosmetics called Topaze, which featured bottles and jars adorned with faux topaz gems. Plastics provided jewelry designers with infinite choices of shapes and colors. (Figure 8.16.) Fun, casual jewelry was even created for playwear such as colorful plastic pop-beads that could be made into necklaces of varying lengths or bracelets with an infinite variety of bead color combinations. As the space age got underway at the end of the 1950s, comets and atomic motifs for pendant necklaces, charm bracelets, and pins became favorites of teen girls.

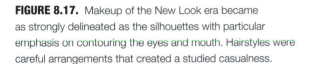

The studied casualness of hairstyles in the late fifties. Prom Home Permanent ad, 1955.

Soft, swept-over hairstyle, 1955.

Linear makeup by Coty, 1958.

Pancake powder compact from Angel Face, 1954.

FIGURE 8.17. Makeup of the New Look era became as strongly delineated as the silhouettes with particular emphasis on contouring the eyes and mouth. Hairstyles were careful arrangements that created a studied casualness.

Women's Hairstyles and Makeup 1950–1959

Hairstyles were carefully coiffed into a myriad of styles, long and short, curled and straight, that created the look of a studied casualness. (Figure 8.17.) Home permanent kits were perfected after the war, which encouraged women to vary their hairstyles more frequently. One distinctive look of the period was short bangs cut in a sharp, straight line high above the eyebrows. Mamie Eisenhower and Edith Head were among those noted for this cut. Another fifties look was what *Vogue* called the "rat nibbled hair" of Audrey Hepburn with its short crop and errant wisps framing the face. In unprecedented numbers, women experimented with hair dyes, not so much to conceal aging as for a change of fashion. "Does she, or doesn't she?" was the big question of the era posed in mass advertising by Miss Clairol hair coloring.

Makeup for the New Look emphasized the eyes with heavy liners, thick mascara, and rich colors of eyeshadow. Layers of foundation creams and powders provided a smooth mannequinesque uniformity over which soft cheek blushes and scarlet lipsticks were applied.

Sculpted hat by Mr. John, 1951.

Red velvet broad brim hat by John Fredericks, 1951.

"Coolie" hat by Hattie Carnegie, 1951.

Skullcap with veil and pinfeather by Harryson, 1952.

Open crown hat by John Fredericks, 1953.

Lampshade hat by John Fredericks, 1954.

Button hat from Forstmann, 1954.

Safari hat by Emme, 1956.

Cartwheel straw hat from Bonwit Teller, 1957.

Flowered straw tam by Sally Victor, 1957.

FIGURE 8.18. Hats of the 1950s were dramatically varied in their sculptural shapes, dimensions, textures, and colors. The "more hat" advocates preferred large shapes often with an abundance of trim; the "less hat" contingency wore smaller varieties like pillboxes and skullcaps, usually with minimal adornment.

Mushroom hat by Rex, 1958.

High straw toque by Emme, 1959.

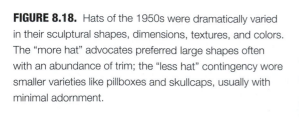

FIGURE 8.19. New synthetic materials, especially nylon and the new thermoplastics, provided wider options for accessory makers to simulate luxury items. With the mass production of accessories made of inexpensive synthetics, a broader socioeconomic spectrum of women could afford the wide assortment of coordinated accessories for New Look fashions.

Simulated leopard bag, belt, and hat, 1956.

Plastic calf-grain box bags, 1952.

Dark Accent nylon hosiery, 1951.

Sheerio nylon gloves, 1950.

Hat-to-heel accessories for the total New Look, 1952.

Copper cinch belts by Renoir of California, 1958.

Calf handbag with matching cigarette case, lighter, compact, and lipstick from Evans Case. 1954.

Women's Hats 1950–1959

To complement the New Look fashions of the 1950s, hats were created in one of two camps. The "more-hat" contingency encouraged large hats adorned with swathes of tulle and netting, mounds of flowers, large bows, ribbon rosettes, and even fur trim. The "less-hat" advocates preferred diminutive headwear such as pillboxes, half turbans, skullcaps, and soft berets, each with minimal trim, if any at all. Regardless of the dimensions, though, millinery styles were often cut with sharp, sculptural silhouettes inspired by the exaggerated lines of New Look fashions. (Figure 8.18.)

Women's Accessories 1950–1959

Key to successful and correct dressing in the New Look era was the total head-to-toe accouterment of accessories. Dressy ensembles were accented with hats, veils, gloves, jewelry, scarves, matching shoes, belts, and handbags, and sometimes parasols. Even for casual wear, accessories mattered.

The use of many new synthetic materials of the 1950s expanded options for accessory makers to produce affordable simulations of luxury items. (Figure 8.19.) Orion or rayon pile was used in faux furs such as leopard and tiger skins for handbags and belts or Persian lamb for stoles, muffs, and hats. Stretch nylon was used for lacy or machine crocheted gloves. Colorful plastics were used for a variety of handbags, ranging from soft, "calf-grained" satchels and clutches to molded Lucite box bags. Rare reptile skins also were replicated in plastic. Oversized totes for the baby boom moms were covered with prints and patterns in easy-care acetate fabrics or plastic bead work.

Men's Fashions 1950–1959

In the 1950s, two new suit silhouettes appeared—the American Ivy League look and the Italian look.

The emergence of the conservative **Ivy League style** during the first half of the decade paralleled the cult of conformity that Americans embraced in the face of the Korean War, McCarthyism, racial unrest, and global communist aggression. The look was that of a shapeless, tubular sack. Columnar jackets were cut with natural shoulders, no waist, narrow lapels, and single-breasted three-button closures. Trousers were slimmer and usually pleatless with narrow, tapered legs. "That undraped, unpadded, unpleated silhouette in the tradition of Bond Street and Brooks Brothers," noted *Vogue* in 1953. (Figure 8.20.) Easy care rayon and rayon blends continued to be popular for men's suits. In addition, a plentiful supply of **silk shantung** was imported from Italy, setting the trend for other slub yarn fabrics. For the first time in American menswear, silk suits and sports jackets were no longer exclusively for the upper-income classes.

FIGURE 8.20. The conservative Ivy League suit featured a columnar jacket with straight hanging lines and natural shoulders. The shaped, slim Continental suit, according to the copy in the 1958 ad shown here, was designed with "flattering subtleties" such as "narrowed peak lapels, gently angled pockets, side vents and a shorter, rounded-front coat." Above, Ivy League style suit of silk shantung by Surretwill, 1953; bottom, Continental suit styling from Eagle, 1958.

FIGURE 8.21. Dinner jackets of the 1950s largely followed the conservative silhouette of the Ivy League look although the Italian cut became popular at the end of the decade. Vividly colored or boldly patterned ties and cummerbunds added flair. Shawl collar jacket in white silk shantung by Rudofker, 1959.

Of greater significance to menswear, both in the United States and Europe, was the entry of Italian designers into the fashion spotlight. In 1952, Italy sponsored its first Men's Fashion Festival at which the distinctly Italian style suits—often called the **Continental look** in the press—were presented to an international audience. Jackets were slightly shorter than the Ivy League models and were shaped with a more fitted line, including tapered waist and sloping, natural shoulders. Styles included one-, two-, and three-button closures although the two-button model with semipeaked lapels shown in Figure 8.20 became the most popular in the United States during the second half of the 1950s.

Italian suit trousers were close-fitting with plain, straight fronts and narrow legs. In his study of men's fashions, Farid Chenoune suggests that the slim Italian trousers were derived from the trim jeans and chinos worn by American GIs stationed in Europe in the postwar years. This trim fit of American menswear produced a "certain swagger"—an exaggerated masculine look that was adopted first by Italian teenage boys and then applied to

FIGURE 8.22. Advances in commercial knitting technologies and new synthetic yarns widened the range of sweater styles for men. Left, Orlon wash-and-wear sweaters by McGregor, 1958; center, shawl collar bulky knit pullover from Catalina, 1958; right, trompe l'oeil pullover with simulated cardigan front, 1958.

business suits by tailors. From the Italian influence, men's trousers became increasingly narrow until at the end of the decade leg openings were barely fourteen inches in circumference.

Although English tailored menswear lost market share to the success of mass-produced Ivy League and Continental looks, a portent of sartorial things to come for Britain developed in London during the mid-fifties. Just as American youth had regressed into the comfortable conservatism of the Ivy League look and Italian young men adopted a more masculine exhibitionism, British adolescents began to develop their own unique fashion identity in the 1950s. The **Teddy boys** were working class teenagers who adopted a sort of neo-Edwardian dandyism with dress. Named for the cockney sobriquet for Edward VII ("good Ol' Teddy"), these young men preferred fingertip-length boxy jackets cut with no center back seam so the line fell long and straight. Some styles featured velvet collars and cuffs adapted from the chesterfield overcoat preferred by the upper classes. Ted dress trousers were narrow, without cuffs, and cropped short at the ankles. Accessories included thick, crepe soled oxfords and bluchers called "**beetle crushers**" and string neckties called "**slim jims**." Ted boys shopped for their unique styles in specialty shops far from the upscale Savile Row—a forecast of the emergence of Carnaby Street boutiques in the mod sixties. By the late 1950s, though, the Ted dress became associated with hoodlum street gangs and racist violence, and the style movement rapidly declined. Even so, the Teddy boys, who had numbered in the tens of thousands, reinforced the economic significance of teenage consumerism in the 1950s.

In the postwar years, the single-breasted dinner jacket followed the development of daytime suit coats. (Figure 8.21.) For semiformal events, style-conscious men wore a pale **French blue** or white double-breasted jacket. Similarly, after-six jackets for warm weather and resorts became vividly colored in the mid-1950s, ranging from soft "parfait" hues to palettes of jeweltone colors. During the same time, the short, white mess jacket, that came to be called the **Janeiro jacket**, was popular with young men possessing trim waistlines. With the Italian influence of the Continental look in the second half of the fifties, formalwear often adopted the shorter, shaped jacket and narrow, plain front trousers. Matching sets of thin bow ties and wide cummerbunds appeared in striking colors and patterns such as bold tartans or paisleys.

Despite the onset of a conservatism in men's suit styles during the postwar period, the variety of knit sportswear expanded with new shapes, textures, patterns, and colors. The polo shirt in all hues was a perennial Father's Day gift. A variation, the Lacoste knit shirt with its distinctive cuffed sleeves and long back tail, was introduced in 1953. New techniques in high-speed commercial knitting made possible mass-produced sweaters with colorful, graphical insets and complex border designs. (Figure 8.22.)

Sport shirts of the 1950s were one of the exceptions to the conservatism in menswear. Wash-and-wear synthetics made possible a wide array of brilliant colors, bold patterns, and vivid prints. (Figure 8.23.) Textured weaves with nubby surfaces such as India madras and silk shantung became fashion staples for sport shirts. For the reserved Ivy Leaguer, though,

FIGURE 8.23. In the staid, conservative 1950s, men could indulge in fashion flair and flamboyance with the vibrant colors and striking prints of sport shirts. Van Heusen shirts, 1952.

FIGURE 8.24. In the 1950s, jeans were associated with pop-culture segments, ranging from the clean-cut cowboy myth to the inner city teenage hoodlum. Left, James Dean in *Rebel Without a Cause,* 1955; right, cowboy styling from Arrow Casual Wear, 1954.

button-down collars and subtle petite-prints or baby blue and mint green solids were the most daring choices.

Trouser pleats and cuffs continued to be a standard construction element both for suits and casualwear. With the increasing popularity of the Continental look in the second half of the decade, plain-front styles became increasingly prevalent. New treatments of waistbands included self-belt styles and elastic insets at the back for added comfort. Backstraps with buckles were a popular trend with teenagers in the mid-1950s.

Shorts were the constant fashion news for menswear throughout the 1950s as the style increasingly appeared in public arenas other than resorts, golf courses, and community parks. The protocol for this social infringement, though, was length and cut. Tailored bermuda styles were acceptable for some restaurants, museums, and government buildings, but thigh-high sports shorts were not. "Why it's easy for a man to look smart in shorts," advised *Vogue* in its 1953 menswear edition, "there's only one length to consider, just above the knee." For a brief time in the mid-fifties, tailored bermuda shorts were even worn with suit jackets, dress shirts, and ties to some downtown offices in the heat of summer before air conditioning became more common.

The cachet of jeans ranged widely during the 1950s, depending upon brand advertising and popular culture. Previously, jeans mostly had been promoted as a durable, impermeable work pant for both men and women. In the fifties, counterculture groups adopted jeans as the foundation of their distinct image. Bikers, as exemplified by Marlon Brando in *The Wild One* (1953), opted for tight-fitting jeans with long legs turned up or rolled into deep cuffs over thick soled boots. Rebellious youth differentiated themselves from conformist Ivy Leaguers in faded jeans as worn by James Dean in *Rebel Without a Cause* (1955). (Figure 8.24.) There was also the cowboy look, or "dude" clothes, as advertised by Levis, Wrangler, and Lee, and personified by mass marketing of the Marlboro man.

Men's Sports Attire and Outerwear 1950–1959

Despite the increased popularity of colorful and patterned sport shirts, the tennis uniform of white trousers or shorts, white shirt, white cotton socks, and white or blue canvas sneakers remained a preferred look in competition. The comfortable, easy-care Lacoste knit shirt was introduced in 1953. Tennis shorts were cropped a few inches above the knees at the beginning of the fifties and climbed to mid-thigh by the end of the decade. Knee-length bermuda walking shorts even became widely popular for golfing in the second half of the 1950s. Fashion journalists repeatedly emphasized that short shorts versus knee-length walking shorts should only be worn as active sports attire or beachwear but not as street clothes.

Skiwear in the 1950s became sleeker and more trim. Nylon knit fabrics were used for slim, fitted ski suit trousers. By the end of the decade, formfitting knit skipants and one-piece jumpsuits lined with nylon fleece were developed to minimize wind drag. (Figure 8.25.)

With the expansion of suburban sprawl in the fifties, an increased reliance on the automobile led to shorter varieties of overcoats, sometimes called **car coats** or **suburbans**. Most styles, such as the examples shown in Figure 8.26, were cropped at fingertip length to allow free range of motion for the legs to operate the floorboard pedals. The short bomber's jacket and duffel coat also remained favorites throughout the decade.

Tweed variations of the fly-front chesterfield and ulster topcoats were preferred by businessmen. The traditional wide, straightline fit was conservative and an ideal complement to the gray flannel suit. By mid-decade, the full-cut raglan coat featuring a **bal collar**—a banded type of turned-down collar derived from the Scottish **balmacaan topcoat**—slash pockets, and sleeve tabs became a stylish outerwear option. Tweeds reflected men's renewed interest in color and were often interwoven with blue, ochre, or red nubs. At the end of the decade, a revival of the 1920s bottonless wrap coat with a broad sash belt became a trendy look for collegiates.

The most common form of rainwear was the oyster-colored trench coat, made with a variety of water repellent fabrics. In the early 1950s, clear vinyl raincoats were introduced, and although the style was truly waterproof, not just moisture resistant, men did not like the look. Instead, **rain topcoats** made of lightweight nylon, the new polyesters, or other synthetic textiles appealed to men because of their all-weather, ali-season versatility.

FIGURE 8.25. Many of the new synthetic fabrics, especially stretch nylons, made possible lighter weight and more comfortable winter sportswear. One-piece skisuit by John Cobb, 1958.

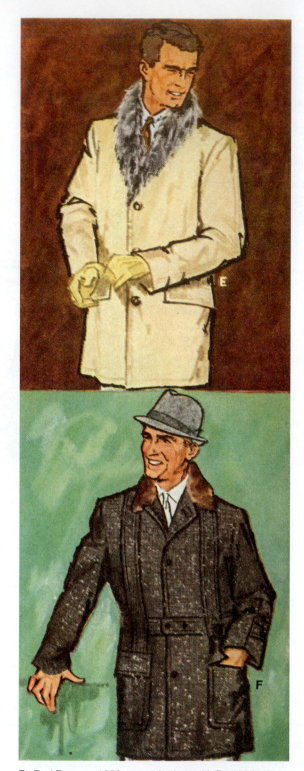

By Bud Berman, 1959: top, suburban with Dynel fake fur collar; bottom, tweed suburban with Dynel fake fur collar.

FIGURE 8.26. By the 1950s, suburban living inspired cropped car coats that were easier to drive in than long styles. For urbanites and commuters, knee-length all-weather topcoats were preferred.

...YOUR PASSPORT TO FASHION FOR '59!

McGREGOR

Toggle or duffle coat and suburban from McGregor, 1959.

Kneebreaker all-weather topcoats by Aquascutum, 1958.

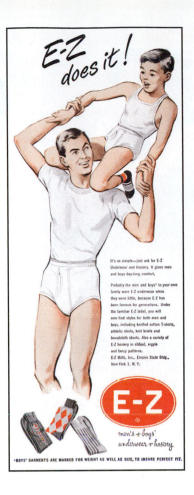

FIGURE 8.27. Through the 1950s, the two most popular forms of men's underwear were the basic white brief and the patterned boxer. In the late fifties, underwear designs adopted the briefer cuts of swimwear, including the introduction of the bikini for men. Left, briefs and athletic T-shirts for men and boys from E-Z, 1951; right, bikini Skants in fashion colors from Jockey, 1958.

Men's Underwear and Swimwear 1950–1959

The two most prevalent types of men's underwear during the fifties were still boxers and briefs. (Figure 8.27.) A variation of the patterned boxer, called the **gripper**, featured a fly front with snap closures. Longjohns remained a common catalog item for winter wear, and shorter athletic-cut union suits were common in warm weather. During the 1950s, underwear manufacturers began to experiment with some of the new synthetic fabrics for men's underwear. Dacron, Durene, rayon, and nylon yarns were blended with cotton. Even the ubiquitous white brief, T-shirt, and tank were made entirely of Helanca, a stretch nylon. In the second half of the decade, as men's swimwear began to be reduced in cut, inching down from the waist and higher up on the hips, underwear styles also began to reflect this briefer look. In 1958, Jockey introduced the Skants brief made of stretch nylon in fashion colors, including red, yellow, blue, and black. The advertising copy in the Skants ads emphasized that the nylon fabric "molds to your body . . . with minimal coverage."

As with underwear, short boxers and formfitting knit briefs were the two primary types of men's swimwear. Despite the conservatism of much of men's clothing in the 1950s, swimwear designers explored a wide assortment of eye-catching prints and revealing cuts that allowed men to express their personal style. (Figure 8.28.) The fashion press first reported the appearance of the men's low cut bikini at North American resorts in 1955. In contrast to the briefer forms of swimwear, in the second half of the fifties, new types of longer, fuller cut swim trunks were introduced. In 1957, the knit bermuda-length **swim-walker** made fashion news although

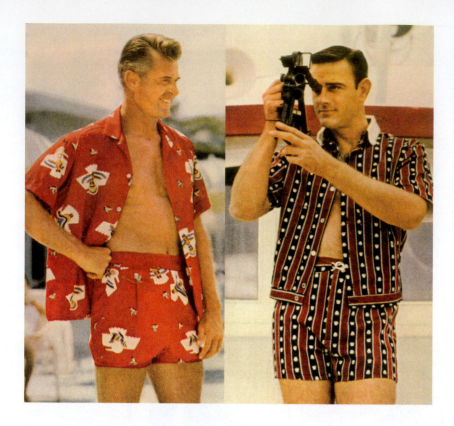

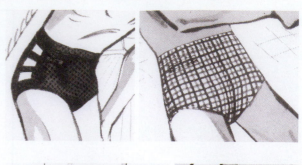

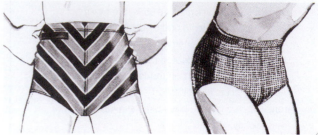

FIGURE 8.28. The high-waisted brief and the short, baggy boxer were the most common forms of men's swimwear until the 1950s. Gradually brief styles were reduced in cut and boxers became more trim. Left, cabana sets from Catalina, 1958; right, knit Lastex brief style swim trunks by Gantner, 1954.

the look was not especially popular since it resembled the old-fashioned Edwardian drawer styles. A compromise between the snug brief and the baggy boxer appeared in the mid-fifties with fitted boxer styles made either of stretch knits or woven fabrics. Most boxer and brief styles were still designed with high waists that concealed the navel.

Men's Sleepwear and Accessories 1950–1959

Sleepwear styles changed little in the 1950s from those of the previous two decades. Pajamas and robes made of the new wash-and-wear synthetics and blends were bestsellers for catalog retailers.

The 1950s was the last period in which the propriety of accessories was still a concern of the well dressed man. As the trim, youth-oriented Ivy League and Italian Continental looks came to dominate men's clothing, hats were reshaped to complement the slender new fashions. Sloped crowns were tapered and brims narrowed to give the illusion of slimness. (Figure 8.29.) Fur felt remained the preferred material for blocking dress hats. The snap-brim fedora—with or without a pinched front—was the most prevalent style. The businessman wore the new styles of demi homburgs with wide grosgrain bands and a flat bow at the back. A more sporty style was the shallow brim porkpie that looked right with sport jackets and tweed suits. Casual types of headwear also were reduced in size. The Tyrolean sported a low crown, narrow rope band, and tiny feather or brush. Newsboy caps fitted the head closely with a tapered back band to give it depth and a narrow front visor concealed by the soft fabric.

FIGURE 8.29. As suits and sport jackets were reshaped in the second half of the 1950s to a trim silhouette with reduced details, hats were similarly proportioned with tapered crowns and narrow brims.

Summer straw hats from Knox, 1952.

Wool sports cap from Lakeland, 1958.

Demi homburg with back bow band from Mallory, 1957.

Round porkpie hat from Mallory, 1958.

Crepe and rubber cleated collegiate shoes, 1952.

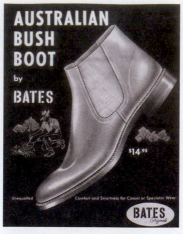
Australian bush boot by Bates, 1956.

Suede chukka or desert boot from Evans Casuals, 1953.

Two-tone summer dress shoes with insets of nylon mesh by Roblee, 1952.

FIGURE 8.30. Among the new footwear styles for young men were the thick-soled bluchers and oxfords and ankle-high bush boots. Makers began to apply the new synthetics such as nylon to the construction of men's casual and dress shoes.

Dress shoe designs varied little except in their slimness and lighter treatments such as finer topstitching and leaner soles and heels. The Italian influence inspired a more pointed tip and curved vamp. The fifties collegiate crowd opted for thick crepe-soled bluchers and ankle-high **Australian bush boots** with contrasting elastic insets at the sides. (Figure 8.30.)

As a reflection of the materialism and consumerism of the 1950s, monogrammed small leathers such as wallets, key rings, cigarette lighters, and belts were common. (Figure 8.31.) Colorful woven and knit belts were favorite complements to bold patterned sport shirts, bermuda shorts, and golf trousers.

Neckwear in the early 1950s continued the vivid colors and patterns of the Bold Look of postwar styles with widths remaining broad at about 4½ inches. As the trim Ivy League suit became the dominant look in menswear, ties began to diminish in width—to about three inches

FIGURE 8.31. Monogrammed belts and other small leather accessories reflected the materialism and consumerism of the 1950s. Colorful woven and knit belts were popular complements to the vividly hued and patterned sportswear of the era. From Paris Belts: left, leather belts with initial buckles, 1956; right, elastic woven belts, 1952.

wide at mid-decade, narrowing to about two inches wide in 1959. The squared-off skinny ties for young men were at a slim 1½ inches wide by the end of the decade. (Figure 8.32.) Basic petite foulards and traditional stripes best suited advocates of the Ivy League look. With the advent of the Italian Continental suits, though, vibrant colors and striking prints returned to neckwear although the widths remained thin. Knit varieties of neckwear made from the new wash-and-wear synthetics were novelty alternatives to the typical silk or wool dress styles.

Smaller and plainer jewelry replaced the large moderne designs of the previous two decades. In the second half of the 1950s, though, Italian influence inspired the reintroduction of

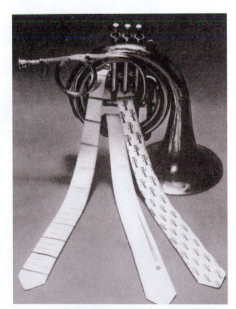

FIGURE 8.32. During the 1950s, ties narrowed gradually from 4½ inches wide at the beginning of the decade to only 2 inches wide by 1959. Squared-off skinny ties for young men were 1½ inches wide. Left, woven acetate neckties from Cutter Cravat, 1951; center, poodle cloth knit ties from Wembley, 1957; right, skinny ties from Herbert Bergheim, 1958.

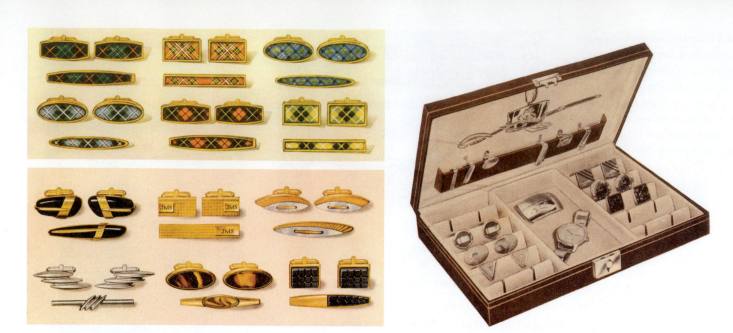

FIGURE 8.33. Despite the conservative, conformist trends in most masculine business dress in the 1950s, men could indulge in some subtle self-expression with colorful, jeweled cuff links and tie clips. Left, cuff links and tie clips by Anson Jewelry for Men, 1956; right, Collector's Case by Babcock, 1956.

color in men's jewelry—enamels, mother-of-pearl, and precious or semiprecious stones like lapis lazuli and tiger's eye. (Figure 8.33.) Pinkie rings and thick chain ID bracelets were part of the Continental look. When ties became narrow, collar pins were also revived and shaped as a miniature golf club, polo mallet, or tennis racket.

Men's Grooming and Hairstyles 1950–1959

The youth-oriented fashions of the 1950s continued to deter facial hair, which was associated with mature men. Even the long-running ad campaigns of the Hathaway shirt man, which featured a model with a mustache (and eye patch) did not encourage men to revive the Edwardian trend of lip adornment. Only counterculture groups like the beatniks adopted goatees, vandykes, or pencil mustaches as their nonconformist identity. Earlobe-length sideburns were part of the look of the Teddy boys, bikers, and other fringe youth groups.

Haircuts were cropped close at the sides around the ears with a fullness on top that was combed straight back or parted at the side and combed over. Exceptions were the military-styled crew cuts, which in the late fifties were often precision cut flat tops that were gelled into a spiky perfection. Teenage boys had the greater variety of hairstyles, ranging from assorted lengths of soft bangs over the forehead to the slicked back "D.A.," meaning "duck's ass" (also "ducktail"), with its swept-back point at the nape of the neck. (Figure 8.34.) The high rounded front of the pompadour was popularized by young rock celebrities like Elvis Presley and Ricky Nelson.

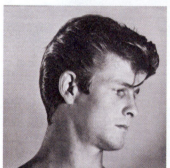

FIGURE 8.34. Hair styles were greatly varied in the fifties, especially among teenagers, and ranged from buzz-cut military flat tops to well-oiled pompadours and slicked-back ducktails. Top, collegiate crewcut, 1957; bottom, ducktail, 1959.

New Look influence of fitted waists and full skirts from R.A.R. Moppets, 1956.

Matching hats, handbags, and gloves, 1957.

Circle skirts with attached nylon net crinolines, 1957.

FIGURE 8.35. The New Look influenced girls' clothing by replicating the fitted bodices and full, sweeping skirts of adult styles. Head-to-toe accessories completed the New Look ensemble just like mom's.

Wrangler jeans, 1956.

Children's Clothing 1950–1959

With the baby boom of the postwar years, innumerable types of easy-access, wash-and-wear garments were designed for babies, including one-piece footed sleepers and zip-front sleeved sleep sacks. Print fabrics and appliques with licensed images such as Disney and Warner Brothers cartoon characters were especially popular in this marketing-driven period.

Girl's dresses reflected the New Look influences with fitted waistlines and fuller skirts. Even adaptations of Dior's H line middy and the triangular A line were made in girl's sizes. The full head-to-toe assortment of New Look accessories were also made for girls. (Figure 8.35.) In imitation of big sister, girls wore long circle skirts with attached nylon net crinolines and appliques or screened motifs on the front. Jeans were rolled to mid-calf, just like mom wore hers. Mother-and-daughter sets of matching dresses and sportswear were especially popular in suburbia.

When the Ivy League and Italian Continental looks became the trend for menswear in the 1950s, boys' suits were similarly cut and tailored with the details that made each style

Lone Ranger shirt, 1956.

Jeans and T-shirts, 1957.

5-way Suit

Really 3 Pieces!
● Check Coat
● Solid Slacks
● Reversible Vest

3-Pc. 16.95 or $5
Suit monthly

WEAR MANY WAYS

√ Suit plus check vest
√ Suit plus solid color vest
√ Solid vest and slacks
√ Check vest and slacks
√ Wear suit without vest

Or you can combine the 3
pieces with other suits to
stretch your clothes budget!

5 WAYS
TO WEAR
Suit plus check vest / Suit plus solid vest / Check vest-solid slacks / Solid vest and slacks / Suit worn without vest

Sports jacket, reversible vest, and solid slacks from
Spiegel, 1952.

Screenprints of licensed TV program
characters, 1956.

Tab-back trousers, 1957.

FIGURE 8.36. Boys' clothing was primarily miniature versions of
menswear—from the Ivy League and Continental suits to sportswear.
Fun and personal style could be expressed with a wide assortment of
costumes and licensed images from TV programs.

distinctive. (Figure 8.36.) Sport jackets, too, were modeled on adult styles and textiles. Boys'
wide, patterned ties of the early fifties were replaced by skinny rayon and knit varieties by the
end of the decade. Licensed logos and images from TV programs were screenprinted, appliqued, or embroidered on all types of children's garments. Among the most popular for boys
was the fringed suede jacket and 'coonskin cap of Davy Crockett fame in the mid-1950s.

Review

The ultrafeminine New Look silhouette with its full bosom, cinched waist, and rounded hips continued to dominate women's fashions through much of the 1950s. Year after year, Dior led the fashion way with innovative variations that evolved gradually and decisively from the formfitting debut Corolle line, through the alphabet lines of the mid-fifties, and finally culminating at the end of the decade in the freedom of the trapeze line of his protege and successor, Yves St. Laurent.

For men, fashion was almost counter to that of women's styles. The Ivy League look was a conservative style that shifted away from the draped cut. Suits featured natural shoulder jackets with straight hanging lines and smooth, unpleated trousers with narrow legs. In the second half of the 1950s, the Continental suit jacket became a stylish alternative to the Ivy League look. Influenced by Italian designs, the Continental suit was shaped with a more fitted line, including a tapered waist and sloping shoulders; trousers were trim and straight.

Among the important news for men's fashions were the new wash-and-wear synthetic fabrics used in sportswear. With the wide array of vibrant colors and bold prints, men were able to break out of their conservatism and express themselves sartorially with vividly hued sport shirts, sweaters, swimwear, and weekend clothes.

Fashions for girls and boys of the fifties were largely miniature versions of adult styles. Girls' dresses and suits replicated the fitted bodices and full skirts of the New Look silhouette. Boys' suits were modeled on the boxy straight lines of the Ivy League look. The influence of TV added fun and flair to children's fashions with licensed logos.

review questions

1. What were Christian Dior's New Look alphabet lines? Describe the key design elements of each.

2. What were the contributions of the Italian fashion designers in the 1950s?

3. What was the style and significance of the Teddy Boys?

4. How did technological advances in the production of textiles affect clothing of the 1950s?

5. Compare and contrast the men's Ivy League suit with the Italian influenced Continental styles.

research and portfolio projects

Research

1. Write a research paper on the development of the prêt-à-porter segment of the Paris fashion industry in the 1950s. Compare the influences of prêt-à-porter collections versus couture on American ready-to-wear of the time.

Portfolio

1. Select a dress style from any of today's fashion catalogs and recreate that dress in your sketchbook in the Dior alphabet lines (A line, H line, Y line). Keep the fabric color or textile pattern and trimmings of the modern dress. Add New Look accessories from the 1950s to complement each design. Attach a color photocopy, digital scan, or tearsheet of the catalog image.

dress terms

A Line: one of Dior's 1955 collections that featured dresses, suits, and coats that were narrow and fitted at the top and widened from the bust or waist in a straight line to the hem

Australian bush boots: men's short ankle shoes with side elastic panels

baby doll pajamas: women's pajama sets with hip-length tops and bloomer bottoms

back-strap shoes: women's shoes with a tab of material stitched across the heel that buckled

bal collar: banded type of turned-down collar derived from the Scottish balmacaan topcoat

ballet slippers: women's wide, flat slip-on shoes

balmacaan: raglan sleeve overcoat with narrow, turned-down collar

beetle crushers: men's thick, crepe-soled shoes

bermuda shorts: tailored, knee length shorts for both women and men

bobbysoxers: teenage girls who wore turned down white cotton socks with saddle oxfords or penny loafers

capri pants: women's and men's casual pants cropped just above the ankles

car coat: any variety of men's or women's coat cropped between the upper thighs and hips to allow greater freedom of motion for driving

circle skirt: fully round skirts usually worn with crinolines by girls and teenagers

cocoons: slim wrap coats worn by young women in the early postwar years

constructed swimsuit: women's swimwear with various engineered devices to sculpt, control, and idealize the female body

Continental suit: a variety of Italian inspired looks, including shortened jackets with natural shoulders, shaped waistlines, narrow lapels, and rounded fronts

duster: women's knee-length housecoat

egg-point toes: women's flat shoes with wide, rounded toes

flare coat: a capacious coat that flared from the shoulders to the hem without a marked waistline

French blue: a pale shade of blue popular for men's suit jackets and dress shirts of the early 1950s

grippers: men's boxer style underwear with a snap-closure fly

H Line: one of Dior's 1954 collections that featured dresses with a dropped waistline

Ivy League style: conservative men's suits with columnar, straight hanging jackets and unpleated, narrow trousers

Janeiro jacket: the 1950s adaptation of the mess jacket

kilties: shoes with a turned-down fringed tongue

martingale coat: a variety of women's wide or fitted coats with half belts in the back

middy: dress silhouette of the mid-1950s with a dropped waistline and fitted torso

pedal pushers: casual pants cropped just below the knees for women and men

poodle cloth: a nubby, deep pile wool fabric resembling the texture of poodle fur

rain topcoats: outerwear made of moisture-resistant nylon or polyester fabrics

shirtwaister: the 1950s version of the shirtwaist dress with a fitted bodice and full skirt

silk shantung: a nubby silk weave

slim jims: men's string neckties

spool heels: women's shoes with thick, rounded heels resembling a spool of thread

stilettos: women's shoes with thin, high spiked heels

suburban: another name for car coat

swim-walker: men's knit, bermuda-length swim trunks

Teddy boys: British working class teenagers of the early 1950s who dressed in a mock Edwardian style with long, boxy suit jackets, string ties, and cuffless trousers cropped at the ankles

toppers: women's loose-fitting coats usually cropped at the waist or high on the hips

torpedo bra: bra with spiral cup stitching and padded linings that enlarged and separated the breasts into a stylization of the bosom

trapeze line: a dress or coat cut featuring a full, tent shape with a high bust and back that fell from the shoulders

umbrella-back coats: women's outerwear with triangular gores set into the back collar that flared into deep organ pipe folds

wash-and-wear: clothing made from synthetic or chemically treated fabrics that were shrink- and wrinkle-resistant

Y Line: one of Dior's 1955 collections that featured dresses with balloon sleeves and other shoulder emphasis over slim skirts

9 The Space Age 1960–1969

1960   **1969**

| | | | | U.S. Vietnam War 1965–1975 | |

First manned space flights by U.S. and Soviet Union 1961

John F. Kennedy assassinated 1963

Khrushchev ousted as Soviet Premier 1964

First U.S. space walk 1965

First heart transplant 1967

U.S. moon walk 1969

Construction of Berlin Wall 1961

Assassinations of Martin Luther King, Jr. and Robert Kennedy 1968

Birth control pill approved for use in U.S. 1960

Cuban missile crisis 1962

Beatles appear on U.S. television 1964

Julie Andrews in *The Sound of Music* 1965

Israeli-Arab Six-Day War 1967

Woodstock music festival 1969

Nations and Powers 1960–1969

Three giant powers dominated events of this era: the United States, the Soviet Union, and China. The modern ideologies of each drove global economies, altered regional politics, and transformed ancient cultures almost overnight.

The Cold War intensified in hot spots around the world and, in 1962, teetered on the brink of nuclear conflict. When Russia installed ballistic missiles in Cuba, the United States "quarantined" the island and threatened to sink Soviet ships that crossed the blockade. War was narrowly averted when Russia offered to remove the missiles if the United States would agree not to invade Cuba and would withdraw American missiles from bases in Turkey.

Only the year before the Cuban missile crisis, the Soviets and Americans had faced off in divided Berlin, where the United States had retained the western sector in the heart of Communist East Germany since the end of the Second World War. The most tangible symbol of the Iron Curtain was a concrete and barbed-wire wall constructed by the Russians in 1961 to stem the flood of East Germans into the U.S. sector. Hundreds were killed over the following decades trying to escape to the West over the wall.

At the opposite side of the globe, the United States also challenged communism in Asia. In 1961, the Kennedy administration began sending "military advisors" to aid the South Vietnamese army in their battles against the Communist North Viet Cong. By 1965, though, American combat units were fully deployed to southeast Asia, and the United States sank into the mire of the Vietnam War that expanded to encompass Cambodia, Thailand, and Laos by the end of the decade.

Although China had supported the expansion of communism in Asia, the governing leadership had far greater concerns internally. In 1966, Chairman Mao Tse-tung inaugurated what came to be known as the Cultural Revolution, during which the entire country was subjugated by a harsh, totalitarian regime whose policies were violently enforced by the zealous Red Guards.

The great divide that bisected Europe into the prosperous west of the democracies and the blighted east under communist dominance remained a hard line of reality throughout the sixties. The European Common Market continued to expand in which member countries enjoyed common agricultural policies and an end to internal tariffs. The nations of the Soviet bloc, though, struggled with repressive communist governments and inefficient state-run industrialization. When Czechoslovakia began to initiate some modest democratic reforms in 1968, Soviet tanks and troops clamped down.

In the Middle East, the tensions between the Arab nations and Israel once again erupted into war in 1967 in which the Israelis defeated Arab armies and made significant gains in territory.

All across the gigantic continent of Africa, national liberation movements led to an end of exploitative colonialism and the birth of dozens of new countries. In some of the newly formed nations, the native populations had gained some experience in government administration before independence, making the transition to statehood less difficult. For others, tribal strife led to civil war, which, many times, encouraged intervention from non-African governments.

Camelot to Woodstock: American Culture 1960–1969

As noted in the previous chapter, the American obsession with youth that had begun in the 1950s was different from that of the 1920s, when youth was collegiate rather than adolescent. By the beginning of the 1960s, the first baby boomers were in high school, and by the end of the decade, almost one-third of the U.S. population was under the voting age. In the fifties, marketers had quickly recognized teenagers as a unique and economically viable segment of the population, and aggressively targeted them with mass advertising and mass merchandising. These multimillion dollar marketing efforts grew exponentially as the youth market continued to expand throughout the sixties. (Figure 9.1.)

Reinforcing the youth-oriented shift in American culture was the election of America's youngest president, John F. Kennedy, in 1960. His beautiful and cultured wife, Jackie, possessed a sense of fashion that set the standards for a casual, yet elegant, American style that was emulated around the world. With their two young children, the First Family projected the epitome of youthful optimism and vitality for the new era. Their cachet was the magical romance of Camelot—a legacy perpetuated by the popular press after the president's assas-

1967   1968   1969

FIGURE 9.1. Mass marketing and advertising in the sixties directly targeted the young: left, Polaroid's camera named the "Swinger" reflected the sexual revolution of the sixties; center, the Campbell's Soup kids became psychedelic teenagers; right, the economic power of young career women was a focus of car makers.

sination in 1963 when it was disclosed that Kennedy used to play a soundtrack recording of that musical for his children at bedtime.

Unlike the silent generation of the post-World War II years, the youth of the 1960s wanted to be heard. They were not complacent about America as it was and set about to make changes. Almost from the instant the Vietnam War began in 1965, antiwar protests and student demonstrations rocked campuses across the land. Civil rights activists participated in pickets and sit-ins throughout the South to force desegregation and advance other issues of the civil rights movement, including voting rights and equal opportunities in education and employment. Young women revitalized the feminist movement with the founding of NOW (National Organization of Women) in 1966 and demanded an end to sex discrimination. The gay rights movement emerged from the 1969 Greenwich Village riots against police harassment and began a quest for equal protection under the law. Many thousands of America's young also joined the Peace Corps and went to far-flung communities around the world to help in education, health care, and civil engineering.

In addition to the young advocates of political and social change, American youth across all walks of life in the 1960s rejected the values of their parents and grandparents. To many, the older generations had made a mess of America—and the world—by perpetuating war, social injustices, and environmental pollution. "Trust no one over thirty," was a popular refrain of the young. The hippies—a name derived from the word "hip," meaning aware or "with it"—epitomized the disaffected youth who disavowed the materialistic and societal baggage of their elders. "Do your own thing," was the mantra of the hippies that became universal for the youth of the era. By degrees, teenagers celebrated the freedom and exhilaration of youth. They experimented with recreational drugs and explored new and open sexual experiences, freed from unwanted pregnancies with the introduction of the birth control pill in 1960. They gathered

Technology and Textiles

Throughout the 1960s, new and improved synthetic fibers continued to be introduced in great varieties. Among the innovations of the time were spun-bonded polyesters with soil-release properties, non-static tricots, and permanently textured, crimped, or "**crepeset**" monofilament nylons. Fabric fasteners called **velcro** were made of nylon strips of material with a filament nap of hooks that held fast when pressed together. The first **permanent press** garments were commercially marketed in 1964. In 1968, Du Pont launched **Qiana** with its look and feel of silk combined with the performance of nylon. That same year, the consumption of synthetic fibers surpassed that of natural fibers, aided in part by millions of dollars in marketing by chemical and textile makers. Manufacturers of synthetic fabrics were just as relentless as other consumer product makers in targeting the youth market with advertising in the 1960s. (Figure 9.2.)

FIGURE 9.2. The fashion-conscious youthquake generation of the 1960s was a prime target of marketing efforts by chemical and fabric makers. Du Pont ad, 1969.

by the tens of thousands for the Summer of Love in San Francisco in 1967, for a peace rally in Chicago in 1968, and for a rock festival at Woodstock, New York, in 1969. Flower power became an image and a credo of the antiwar advocates who wore flowers in their hair and inserted blossoms into the rifles of police and national guardsmen who were often deployed to antiwar rallies. Symbolic flowers of peace were painted on faces and cars, embroidered on clothing, and shaped in various materials into jewelry, belt buckles, and assorted other ornaments. From this street trend, fashion makers adapted a colorful assortment of flower power motifs to women's, men's, and children's fashions and accessories.

The sixties was an intense, invigorating, and traumatic decade. Youth around the world was in revolt. The arms race between the Soviet Union and the United States escalated, especially after the triumph of America's moon landing in 1969. The fabric of Southern society was repatterned as institutional segregation was dismantled. Race riots destroyed communities in Los Angeles, Detroit, Newark, and Washington, D.C. National leaders were assassinated: John F. Kennedy, Robert Kennedy, and Martin Luther King, Jr. The Vietnam War dragged on.

Women's Fashions 1960–1969

Despite the bold proclamations of "change" and "new" on the covers of fashion magazines of 1960, in actuality, Dior's New Look still largely prevailed. *Vogue,* for instance, reported in its January 1960 edition of cinched waists and fitted clothes made with the "female-feminine" look of "gently curved proportions." Hemlines remained at knee length. What added a fresh touch to the lingering New Look silhouettes, though, was sleeve interest. Rather than exaggerated, constructed styles like those of the 1930s and 1940s, sleeve drama of the early sixties was created by the three-quarter length that was cut in various shapes and applied to virtually all types of garments from casual sportswear and dresses to evening gowns. (Figure 9.3.)

Innovative style leadership in the United States was conspicuously absent during the early 1960s. The icon of American style and fashion at the time was First Lady Jackie Kennedy, whose look was quietly elegant for public functions and unassumingly casual in her private role of wife and mother. Even her designer of choice, Oleg Cassini, tempered his usually flamboyant designs with a simpler, more conservative feel. Other top names in American fashion, such as Claire McCardell, Adele Simpson, Norman Norell, Oscar de la Renta, and Pauline Trigére, likewise focused on traditional silhouettes and a simplicity of line.

Coinciding with the escalating youth movement of the 1960s was the emergence of the **mod looks** (short for "modern" or "modernist") from London. Mary Quant and her protege Kiki Byrne adapted the looks of street-scene youth to their collections of simple chemises, tunic dresses with flounced or pleated skirts, and tweed cardigan dresses—all with hemlines cropped about six to eight inches above the knee.

The debate over who created the **miniskirt** has continued unabated since the early sixties. Mary Quant is often credited with the innovation although she denied it in interviews, stating instead that she merely popularized a youth look that was common in the streets of London at the time. On the other hand, Andre Courrèges frequently claimed to have originated the miniskirt—a style he first presented in his 1962 collections.

Despite the fresh and imaginative miniskirt designs from London, Paris, and Italy, the huge American ready-to-wear market initially resisted the radical look. Instead, for most young women, hemlines only gradually rose to just slightly above the knees by the mid-sixties before finally climbing thigh high in the second half of the decade. (Figure 9.4.) Even then, few women over thirty wore skirts cropped above the knees.

In 1964, international fashion headlines were made by Andre Courrèges with his "Space Age" collection. The futuristic looks were based on the perfect cut and clean, minimalist lines. For some of the more abbreviated garments, Courrèges added one-piece knit **body stockings** popularly called **catsuits** because of their sleek fit. The influence of the **space age style** was widespread, ranging from smooth, A line dresses and coats to high-domed space helmet hats like the one by Samuel Robert shown here. Synthetic and metallic materials used in textiles added to the space age styling. (Figure 9.5.) In addition, the short white boots that Courrèges' models wore on the runway sparked the "**go-go**" **boot** fad that lasted several seasons in the mid-sixties.

FIGURE 9.3. The ultrafeminine New Look silhouette that endured into the early 1960s was revitalized with a fresh focus on sleeves, particularly half and three-quarter varieties. Worsted suit by Lilli Ann, 1961.

FIGURE 9.4. Although the miniskirt had become commercially popular with urban teenage girls in the early years of the 1960s, most hemlines had only risen slightly above the knees by middecade. By the second half of the sixties, hemlines were thigh high. Top left, space age influenced kidskin coat and short skirt by Samuel Robert, 1964; top right, A line miniskirt and mini-tent with shorts by Robbie Rivers, 1967; bottom, red and white collection by Andre Courrèges, 1968.

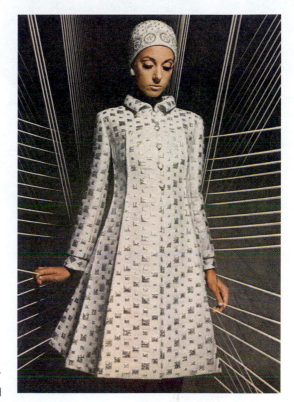

FIGURE 9.5. Shimmering synthetic metallic fabrics enhanced the futuristic space age fashions of the 1960s. Left, knit top and hose from Knoll Textiles, 1968; right, flared evening coat with side pleats of Qiana by Mila Schon, 1968.

Fashion designers of the mid-sixties also found inspiration from the three key art movements of the decade. The graphical images of American pop culture, such as soup cans and the Sunday comics, were a source of imagery for paintings and prints by Pop artists Andy Warhol, Roy Lichtenstein, and Peter Max, among others. Textile makers produced endless varieties of prints and patterns based on the Pop artists' stylizations of everyday images. The Op artists experimented with the optical illusions of bold flat patterns and vivid, clashing color combinations—another favorite source of design for fabric makers. (Figure 9.6.) A precursor of the Pop and Op artists was Piet Mondrian, whose paintings of bright, primary colored rectangles were adapted to the rectilinear chemise by Yves St. Laurent in 1965. In the second half of the decade, the Kinetic artists created visual dynamics through motion, which fashion designers adapted to modern clothes with the use of surface embellishments such as fringe, metal plates, crushed cellophane, or plastic tiles.

Like short skirts, the new cuts of women's pants were designed for the young, slender figure of the teenager. *Vogue* had observed in 1964 that **flamenco pants** were "riding low on the hips and flared below the knees." Within the year, all types of casual pants, tailored trousers, and even jeans sported the new low-rise cuts with **bell bottoms**. By the end of the decade, some forms of **hiphuggers** featured wide waistbands for three-inch belts while other styles were made with a simple facing without belt loops at the top for a smooth fit across the hips.

FIGURE 9.6. Pop, Op, and Kinetic art provided textile manufacturers and clothing designers with fresh fashion looks throughout the sixties and seventies. Left, Oscar de la Renta dress and matching tights, 1967; top right, Op art miniskirts by Emilio Pucci, 1968; bottom right, "Souper" dress inspired by Andy Warhol's Pop art paintings of Campbell's soup cans.

FIGURE 9.7. The self-styled looks of the sixties flower children were both statements of youthful rebellion as well as expressions of personal styles. Cast of *Hair,* 1969.

The youthquake—a term coined by a *Vogue* editor in 1963—came to full fruition in the second half of the 1960s. A myriad of counterculture looks sprang from the assorted groups of restless young people who gathered in city parks and urban bookstores or set up communes where they could do their own thing. The self-styled looks of the flower children were widely and wildly varied, ranging from pattern-mixed gypsy costumes that featured colorful print peasant blouses and long dirndl skirts to everyday ready-to-wear miniskirts or bell bottom hiphuggers, all accented with leather fringe vests, patterned scarves, floppy suede hats, love beads, and flowers in the hair. (Figure 9.7.) Tie-dyeing and flower power prints and textures were favorites of both women and men, looks that were appropriated by mass merchandisers for mainstream clothing and accessories.

Social changes within ethnic populations also influenced fashions of the 1960s. The plight of the American Indians and the substandard conditions of the federally regulated reservations were among the social injustices many young folks took up as a cause. The American Indian look of fringed leather jackets and skirts or pants worn with buckskin boots and beaded headbands became popular on high school and college campuses not only as fashion but as a social statement. (Figure 9.8.)

Black women in both America and Europe began to commemorate their cultural identity by wearing adaptations of traditional African costumes. Long, T-cut tunics called **dashikis** were made of brilliantly hued kente cloth or fabrics printed with motifs evocative of African heritage. Tall, meticulously arranged **headwraps** were particularly expressive of the emergence

FIGURE 9.8. To express their support for improving conditions on federally regulated Indian reservations, many socially conscious young people began to wear fringed leather jackets, skirts, and pants with buckskin boots and belts and beaded headbands. The Indian look was quickly adapted to mass market fashions by ready-to-wear makers. "Comanchero" buckskin miniskirt jumper with suede blouse by Jean Louis, 1969.

FIGURE 9.9. Hollywood movies of the late 1960s inspired numerous fashion revivals, including adaptations of the flapper looks of the twenties. Silk crepe chemise from Leslie Faye, 1969.

of the new black consciousness in the sixties. Black celebrities such as Aretha Franklin wore flowing tunics, voluminous wrap garments, and elegant headwraps for interviews and concert performances. The Pan-African celebration of Kwanzaa was established in the 1960s, and blacks were encouraged to wear combinations of the three colors—black, red, green—of the horizontally striped Kwanzaa flag.

Commercially successful revivalisms of the 1960s were principally inspired by two sources—the romantic dress of the flower children and the period movies from Hollywood. A street scene reaction to the ultramodern space age styles of Andre Courrèges, Paco Rabanne, and Pierre Cardin was manifested in **Victoriana** looks that adapted elements from late nineteenth-century fashions. Ankle-length calico **granny dresses** were made with high collars, puff sleeves, and ruffled hemlines. Teen girls wore them with soft, high boots or strappy sandals and wire framed eyeglasses with small oval or circle lenses in yellow, pink, or blue glass. In England, Laura Ashley opened her first shop in 1968, selling similar dress styles and smock tops for a look that later came to be called "**milkmaidism**," a reference to the simplicity of rural life of a bygone era.

Revivalisms of Edwardian styles stemmed from the theatrical costumes that became popular with rock bands in the late 1960s. The Beatles went from the cohesive but drab

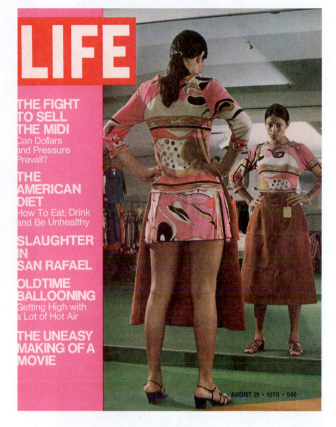

FIGURE 9.10. Revivals of thirties styles included longer hemlines introduced in the late 1960s as the mid-calf midi and the ankle-length maxi. Left, fall 1968 collection from Ossie Clark and Alice Pollock featuring a silk dropped-waist miniskirt, silk Empire miniskirt, and asymmetrical leather jacket with midi skirt; below, *Life* cover, August 21, 1970.

uniform-like suits worn in their movie *Hard Day's Night* (1964) to an individu-alism expressed with the neo-Edwardian looks of Sergeant Pepper's Lonely Hearts Club Band in the animated film *Yellow Submarine* (1968). Young women and men began adding to their wardrobes velvet jackets, lace collars, ruffled shirts, brocade vests, and awning striped pants.

In 1966, an arts exposition in Paris called *Les Années '25* celebrated the birth of the art deco style forty years earlier. A renewed interest in the high style of art deco design (called moderne in the 1920s and 1930s) greatly influenced the graphic arts, architecture, decorative arts, and fashion of the sixties. The following year when Julie Andrews starred in the movie *Thoroughly Modern Millie,* she wore adaptations of flapper looks that became widely copied by ready-to-wear makers. The innumerable varieties of dropped-waist chemises with mini-skirt hemlines already had been popular for a few years but now were accessorized with soft cloches, long strings of beads, and interpretations of art deco jewelry and scarves. (Figure 9.9.)

Probably one of the most controversial fashion trends of the second half of the sixties was the **midi** with its hemline at mid-calf. In 1967, the hit movie *Bonnie and Clyde* starred Faye Dunaway who made fashion news with the sexy, curvaceous styles of thirties dresses and skirts she wore in the film. After several years of skirts cropped above the knees, fash-ion designers relished the idea of a fresh, contrasting silhouette and introduced the midi. (Figure 9.10.) Women, though, rejected the midi and continued to prefer the leggy look of

After-six caftan by Bill Blass, 1968.

Brocade evening gown from Simplicity Patterns, 1969.

Empire miniskirt from McCall's Patterns, 1967.

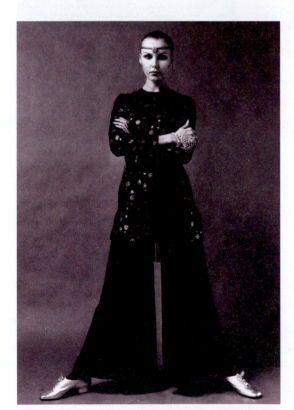

Sequined silk tunic and crepe palazzo pajamas, 1966.

FIGURE 9.11. Evening wear fashions of the 1960s ran the gamut from traditional ball gowns to trendy miniskirts and the increasingly popular pantsuits.

Floral cotton jumpsuit by Adele Simpson, 1967.

the miniskirt. Nevertheless, throughout the late sixties and into the early seventies, designers repeatedly produced variations of the midi as well as the ankle-length **maxi**. Some skirts were even made with button or zipper front closures that could be worn open up to mid-thigh, but the longer hemlines continued to be regarded as eccentricities by most women. The one form of the midi and especially the maxi that had moderate commercial success was in outerwear. The longer lengths were a practical solution to the miniskirt's exposure of knees and thighs in winter.

Despite the excitement and drama of the 1960s revivalisms and counterculture looks, the overwhelming majority of women wore less extreme clothing. Dresses in the mass merchandise catalogs of Sears, Penney's, and Spiegel in the late sixties showed hemlines fairly uniformly at just above the knees. The designs of tailored suits particularly were more reserved in cut and skirt length. Young career women began to break the dress code barriers in corporations by wearing tailored menswear-styled pantsuits or blazers and trousers of varying widths.

Evening wear of the 1960s provided women with the widest range of options since the 1920s. (Figure 9.11.) Just as short dresses were more popular than long gowns in the flapper era, the mod woman of the sixties went to cocktail parties and discotheques in dressy miniskirts. Fabrics and trimmings rather than silhouette usually determined after-six styles. Similarly, like the evening pyjamas of the twenties that had been worn by women in the vanguard of fashion, luxurious wide-legged pantsuits called **palazzo pajamas** became a popular evening fashion of the confident and assertive woman of the sixties. Concurrent with pantsuits and miniskirts for nightlife were opulent evening gowns in the New Look tradition often made of the newest synthetic textiles such as silky nylon Qiana or richly textured Trevira polyester.

Women's Outerwear 1960–1969

Through the first half of the 1960s, the favorite silhouette of coats continued to be the straight-line shapes of the New Look years, which could be worn loose and free or cinch belted. The flared A line cut was particularly popular. As skirts steadily climbed above the knees, the hemlines of coats were shortened as well. (Figure 9.12.) By 1966, coats were cropped as thigh-high as miniskirts. A year later, though, midi and maxi coats appeared. Even though women largely rejected the longer lengths for dresses, the midi and maxi coats were popular in winter with the miniskirt wearer for practical reasons. Some maxi coats were designed with zip-away bottom sections that could instantly change to a mini.

Women's Sports Apparel 1960–1969

Beginning with the youthquake of the 1960s, a cult of the body developed as millions of women joined the emerging fitness craze. Mature women who wanted to wear the sixties miniskirt or hiphugger jeans obsessively jogged and swam laps, and young women who wanted to retain their trim, youthful figures avidly played tennis and racquetball, roller skated, and cycled on ten-speeds. Specialized workout apparel in the 1960s was primarily based on functional,

Leather cape and pants by Nina Ricci, 1967.

A Line miniskirt coat by Pat Sandler, 1968.

Glen plaid maxi coat by Ali, 1969.

FIGURE 9.12. As dress hemlines climbed to mid-thigh in the late 1960s, coats were similarly cropped short. At the end of the decade, the mid-calf-length midi and ankle-length maxi coats were introduced. Space Age styling also inspired innovative new looks for outerwear.

Women's fur trimmed poncho and pants, men's fur kneebreaker, and women's leopard midi trimmed with arctic fox, 1969.

FIGURE 9.13. Ready-to-wear makers were slow to respond to the fitness craze that emerged during the youthquake of the 1960s. Exercise wear was viewed as basic functional clothing. On the other hand, sports clothes for resorts and clubs such as skisuits, tennis wear, and golf ensembles continued to follow fashion trends. Left, basic leotard and tights from Danskin, 1968; right, nylon skiwear, 1968.

school gym styles—unitards and opaque tights, knit shorts and T-shirts, or fleece sweatpants and sweatshirts. (Figure 9.13.)

Downhill skiing grew in mass popularity during the 1960s with the extended TV coverage of the 1964 and 1968 Winter Olympics. The sleek look of nylon and polyester skipants, jackets, and coats that developed in the late fifties continued to dominate the slopes. Mod color and pattern mixes updated the styles. Despite their bulk, thickly quilted jackets, vests, and coats filled with down or synthetic materials were preferred by cross-country skiers.

Tennis wear retained its uniform look. Shorts, culottes, little wrap skirts, and camp shirts in crisp, white fabrics were a must for most tennis clubs. Soft pastels, especially knit polo shirts, were more common at resort courts.

Women's Underwear and Sleepwear 1960–1969

Through the first few years of the 1960s, the styles and construction of women's lingerie continued the forms of the New Look. Torpedo bras and waist-cinching corsets or girdles defined the fashion silhouettes. As the youthquake movement began to influence mainstream fashion, the ideal feminine figure somewhat reverted to that of the flapper—tall, slender, and boyish. With hemlines at mid-thigh and dresses with cutouts and cutaway midriffs, bras and panties became ever briefer and lighter. The bikini brief followed the reduced cut of swimwear. (Figure 9.14.) Bras softly contoured the breasts rather than reshaping them. In 1965, Rudi Gernreich created the sheer nylon "No Bra" bra. Teenage girls with small bosoms even discarded the bra altogether with the help of BandAids to prevent nipple show-through. Bulky garter belts and garters were also abandoned in the second half of the decade after

Bra, bikini, slip, half slip, and mini-nightgown by Kayser, 1968.

Sheer body stocking by Emilio Pucci, 1969.

**FIGURE 9.14.** Undergarments and sleepwear of the sixties replaced the engineered construction of the New Look styles with lightweight fabrics and softer, briefer contours.

Print bra, pantie-girdle, and shortie robe from Artemis, 1963.

The sheer, nylon tricot "No Bra" bra designed by Rudi Gernreich in 1965.

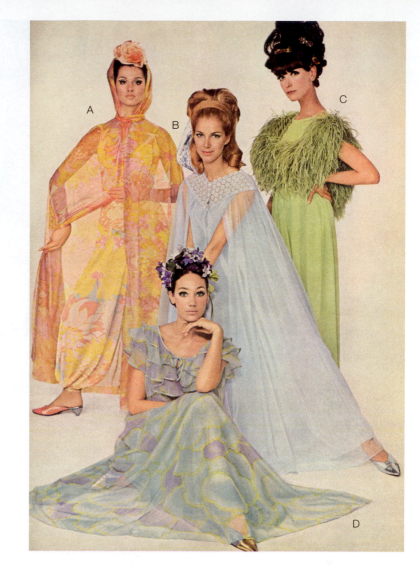

FIGURE 9.15. The styles of women's sleepwear gowns and robes in the sixties largely retained the traditional full, flowing cuts trimmed with lace, ruffles, and bows. The drama was in the application of new silky, sheer synthetics and vividly hued big prints. From 1966: A. Harem pajama and cape by Rodriguez. B. Norman Hartnell nightgown. C. Cape and nightgown by Fontana. D. Fontana's ruffled nightgown.

control-top **pantyhose** were introduced. Colorful and textured body stockings served as both underwear and fashion accent. Half slips were hardly more than a snip of nylon tricot with a thin elastic waistband.

New lightweight synthetic yarns like Lycra were widely used for lingerie and sleepwear. The flexible knits produced with these synthetics were three times stronger than earlier elastics and were more resistant to damage by perspiration and detergents. Colors and prints were vibrant. Lingerie collections were color or pattern coordinated—especially vivid flower power prints.

Sleepwear of the sixties had a less dramatic evolution than underwear. The primary advances were in the application of new synthetics, wash-and-wear fabrics, and vibrantly colored big prints. Knee- and ankle-length nightgowns continued to be the most common—almost all with coordinating wraps or robes. (Figure 9.15.) The **baby doll gown** with its short, hip-length top and bloomers remained a favorite of teens. Many women opted for any type of easy, comfortable garment for bedtime, including men's shirts or pajama tops, long T-shirts, or simply their underwear.

Women's Swimwear 1960–1969

At the beginning of the 1960s, women's swimwear retained much of the construction rigidity that shaped and accented the rounded, mature female figure. By middecade, though, the slim, angular, boyish figure of Twiggy and the surfer girls in the popular beach movies epitomized the mod ideal of feminine beauty. Swimwear was redesigned without boning, wires, padding, and modesty skirts. The new spandex nylon fabrics were sleek and formfitting. The bikini became the preferred style of youthquake girls. (Figure 9.16.) By the end of the decade, bikini bottoms had been pared down from about five inches wide at the sides to thin straps of fabric barely a

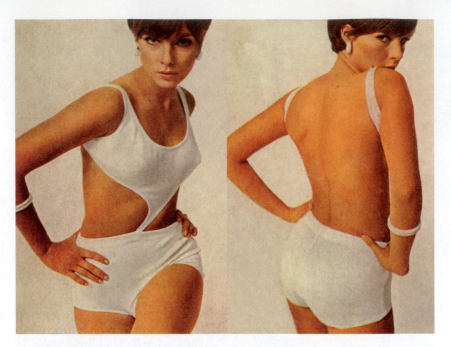

FIGURE 9.16. As with underwear, swimsuits of the 1960s lost the rigid constructions of the New Look styles. The bikini became the favorite swimwear of youthquake girls due in part to the surfer movies. Left, cut-out maillot by Bill Blass, 1965; right, polka dot bikini from Catalina, 1968.

half inch wide. Tops ranged from strapless bandeaus to small triangles of fabric. In 1964, Rudi Gernreich made fashion headlines worldwide with his monokini—a topless one-piece with a high waist and a pair of straps at the center front that fitted over the shoulders, forming a V between the exposed breasts. Other one-piece styles of the sixties reflected the influence of space age theme fashions with geometric cut outs and necklines. Psychedelic prints and acid colors were particularly popular with teens.

Women's Shoes 1960–1969

The heel and toe shapes of shoes in the early 1960s were primarily the same as those of the late fifties. The stiletto had been lowered but was still finely chiseled and toes were sharply pointed. British mod designers such as Mary Quant changed the shape of women's shoes by pairing wide, rounded little girl styles with the miniskirt. (Figure 9.17.) Variations in the second half of the decade became more square toed and square heeled. Some broad heels were flared wider at the base than the top like an inverted Cuban heel. Revival fashions of the 1960s, such as the flapper or the Bonnie and Clyde look, inspired retro shoe styles from those eras. Both the Louis heel from the 1920s and the strappy, thick heeled silhouette of the Depression period reappeared. At the end of the decade, adaptations of the forties-styled platforms set a trend

Go-go boots from Desco, 1966.

FIGURE 9.17. Boots were the most important footwear fashion of the 1960s. Little girl shoes with low heels and toe ornaments were a popular complement to the miniskirt.

Little girl shoe styles from Auditions, 1967.

30-inch thigh-high stretch vinyl boots, 1968.

that would last through the mid-seventies. The most important footwear news of the 1960s, though, was the enormous popularity of boots. Courrèges' short white kid boots shown with his 1964 Space Age collection launched a go-go boot mania. Boots were designed in every imaginable color and texture of leather, suede, plastic, rubber, and fabric. Frosted and metallic finishes coordinated with similar lipsticks and eyeshadows. As hemlines became shorter, boots climbed higher, to mid-thigh in some instances.

Women's Jewelry 1960–1969

Jewelry in the early 1960s was understated and classic. Pearls, real or simulated, were especially popular because they were a favorite of First Lady Jackie Kennedy. By the middle of the decade, though, the brevity of clothes with cut-outs, decollete necklines, and above-knee hemlines were balanced by heavy boots below and big hair and oversized jewelry

Mod watches from Vendome, 1967.

Oversized mod earrings, 1966.

Jewelry and chain hip belt from Swarovski, 1966.

Mod wrist and ring watches from Old England Watches, 1967.

FIGURE 9.18. To balance thigh-high miniskirts, low-rise pants, and short coats, mod jewelry was oversized and sculptural. Psychedelic colors and patterns were rendered in mass-produced plastics.

above. The sculptural, geometric shapes of mod jewelry were inspired by two key sources—the hard-edged looks of space age fashion collections, such as those by Courrèges and Cardin, and the revival of art deco design. Huge, dangling earrings, wide cuff bracelets,

FIGURE 9.19. Hairstyles of the early and mid-sixties were teased and piled high into assorted bouffant arrangements firmly fixed in place with hairspray. Left, lacquered hairstyles from 1964; center, singer Roberta Flack's full afro, 1969; right, Cher's straight tresses, 1967.

and dome rings of plastic in psychedelic color combinations were the quintessential sixties look. (Figure 9.18.) Counterculture groups opted for jewelry that made a personal statement such as the peace sign, horoscope symbols, or mystical emblems like the Egyptian ankh and the yin-yang circle.

Women's Hairstyles and Makeup 1960–1969

As with shoes and jewelry in the 1960s, hair too became an oversized compensation to the cropped and shortened proportions in fashions. Big boots, oversized jewelry, and piled-up hair seemed to balance the miniskirt and slim fit of clothes. (Figure 9.19.) The teased and lacquered bouffant of Jackie Kennedy (adapted as the "bubble cut" on millions of Barbie dolls at the time) was a presage of things to come. By the mid-sixties fashion news was made by the **beehive hairstyle**, created by the spiral twist of tresses into a cylindrical arrangement atop the head. In the second half of the decade, though, youthquake girls rejected the artifice of the teased, hair-sprayed mounds and curls and opted for natural, flowing hair. The preferred look was the soft, straight hair of pop celebrities like Cher and Candice Bergen, which for many women required a great deal of maintenance with hair relaxers or ironing. Also in the late sixties, African-American women began wearing their hair in its natural state rather than chemically straightening it. The full, bushy **afro** became a potent statement of black identity for both women and men.

Makeup in the 1960s emphasized the eyes above all else. The boldly colored and glittery accented eyeshadows worn by Elizabeth Taylor in *Cleopatra* (1963) revolutionized the cosmetics industry. By the time big-eyed, waif-like models, such as Twiggy, came to represent the ideal in feminine beauty in the second half of the decade, cosmetics makers were producing eyeshadows and liners in a wide variety of vivid colors. Mascara and false eyelashes were huge sellers. (Figure 9.20.) On the other hand, lipstick colors either became softer and more natural

FIGURE 9.20. Emphasis on large eyes was achieved with thick false eyelashes, heavy eyeliner, and vividly colored eyeshadows. At the extreme, mod looks inspired body painting, especially around the eyes. Ad for Twiggy false eyelashes, 1967.

Pillbox from Arthur Jablow, 1961.

Silk grenadier's cap by Georgia Bullock, 1962.

Houndstooth British Bobbie's helmet by Tannél Jomana, 1964.

Adaptation of the Nureyev cap from McCall's Patterns, 1966.

Space age helmet hat from Thayer, 1965.

Bonnie and Clyde beret by Simplicity Patterns, 1968.

Visored skull cap from Cole of California, 1969.

Javanese-style plantation hat by Chester Weinberg, 1969.

FIGURE 9.21. In the early 1960s, hats were as varied as those of the New look era. As bouffant hairstyles increased in scale and complexity, hats were often abandoned. In the second half of the decade, hats reflected the mod and space age look.

or, for youthquake girls, were emphatically unnatural. White, silver, and even stark shades of blue and green were options of body paint for the lips that were often blended with the warm earthtones of commercial lipsticks for frosted looks. Nail polish also came in palettes of frosted shades to coordinate with the shimmer of lips and eyes. Mod fashions were sometimes accentuated with eyes that were painted with psychedelic colors and patterns, especially flower power motifs. In 1967, Twiggy appeared on the cover of *Vogue* with the surround of one eye painted as a lavender and red flower to match a similar motif on her sweater.

Women's Hats 1960–1969

With the advent of the high bouffant hairstyles of the early 1960s and the youthquake-inspired styles of the second half of the decade, hats ceased to be the crowning accessory for the fashionable woman. Increasingly, women abandoned wearing hats except for special occasions like Easter Sunday or weddings. As a result, many upscale retailers closed their millinery departments and focused on casual headwear that the accessory industry mass produced.

During the transition years of the early sixties, hat designs were shaped tall and full, mirroring the hairstyles of the period. Decorations were often exuberantly horticultural with masses of silk flowers, fruit, and foliage. The height was retained in middecade but the styles were streamlined with space age silhouettes such as the round domed British Bobbie's helmet that had a futuristic look of a space helmet. (Figure 9.21.) Stetsons were given a modern look with wide chin straps, often of contrasting colors.

In the second half of the 1960s, mod looks and revivals prevailed. The **Nureyev cap**—named for the famed Russian ballet dancer who popularized the style—was made in bold colors and prints to coordinate with mod fashions. Floppy, wide brimmed hats with flower power prints were fun styles for the young. Soft cloches were revived from the twenties and thirties, and snap brim fedoras recalled the smart looks of the forties. Fake fur caps and toques were inspired by the costumes in *Dr. Zhivago* (1965) and berets from *Bonnie and Clyde* (1967).

Women's Accessories 1960–1969

With the lingering New Look, styling of fashions in the early 1960s remained the full accoutrement of head-to-toe accessories. Handbags, belts, and shoes had to match, or at minimum, coordinate. An abundance of understated, classic styles of jewelry were an important finishing touch. No well-dressed woman would leave the house without her hat and gloves, both of which had specialized styling depending upon the time of day, season, and type of suit or dress worn.

In the wake of the youthquake, though, accessories took on a different meaning from that of fashion complement. Besides abandoning hats and gloves, young women also disregarded the traditional tenets of coordinating accessories. Instead, accessories in any combination were an expression of personal style. (Figure 9.22.) The gypsy look with its piling on of accessories of mixed styles had wide appeal even for mainstream dress. The clean lines of space age design met the retro-geometric styling of art deco in small leathers, handbags, and scarves. Ethnic influences included American Indian beaded belts, headbands, wristlets, and purses. Chain belts for dresses fastened low over the hips, emphasizing the lowered waistbands on hiphuggers. Exotic versions of chain belts ranged from harem coin skirts to mock cache-sex styles reminiscent of African adornment.

Men's Fashions 1960–1969

As with women's fashions of the early 1960s, men's clothing was largely a continuation of fifties styles. The ubiquitous gray flannel suit of either the straightline Ivy League cut or the more fitted Continental style evolved only minimally. London's Savile Row recaptured preeminence in men's suit tailoring with a subtly new jacket silhouette that featured lightly padded shoulders, slightly wider rolled lapels, and a more flared skirt. The deep V-line of the opening exposed a greater expanse of the shirt and gave men the appearance of possessing a broad, athletic

Striped tights, 1968.

Art deco print scarves, 1969.

Beaded headband, 1967.

Flower power hosiery from Hanes, 1968.

FIGURE 9.22. Accessories of the 1960s were worn with less emphasis on the correct complement to a fashion look and more of an expression of personal style. Mixed motifs might include psychedelic mod patterns, flower power motifs, and art deco graphics.

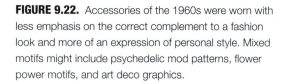

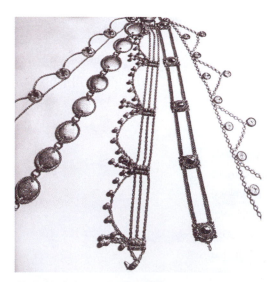

Chain hip belts by Napier, 1969.

Metal jewelry and accessories by Vendome, 1969.

FIGURE 9.23. During the early 1960s, London's Carnaby Street became famous as the center of the peacock revolution in menswear. Young men flocked to the numerous mod boutiques to buy fashions that shattered the conventions of masculine dress. Photo, 1965.

chest. The new suit silhouettes created a look of the mature man somewhat reminiscent of the 1930s draped cut, though without the exaggerated padding and shaping. The two-button front closure was the favorite style of the time, made especially popular with American men by President Kennedy.

Meanwhile, not far from the long-established traditionalist businesses of Savile Row, a cultural phenomenon was gaining momentum with its nerve center along a few short blocks of Carnaby Street in Soho. (Figure 9.23.) Throughout the early 1960s, throngs of teenage boys migrated to the numerous menswear boutiques there seeking the newest styles of mod clothes that collectively came to be called the **Carnaby look**: skinny-rib knit body shirts vividly colored in cherry red, fuchsia, yellow, pink, and lavender; dress shirts in bold prints and stripes; pastel hued jeans and skin tight knit or suede hiphuggers; and fitted Edwardian jackets in silk or velvet.

FIGURE 9.24. Men's suit styles were transformed during the peacock revolution of the 1960s. Mod modes featured new shapes and contours, vivid colors, and bold textile patterns. Left, 10-button double-breasted suit jacket with contrasting lapels and pocket flaps, 1967; right, square front suit jacket and collarless suit jacket from Blades, 1969.

Accessories for young men now included scarves, ascots, and ties in vivid floral or art deco revival prints. Shoes and belts were embellished with oversized buckles and chains. Necklaces and bracelets adorned throats and wrists. Men also began to grow their hair long—first over the ears, then to the collars, and finally down to the shoulders.

By middecade, even the mainstream press was commenting on the "**peacock revolution**"—a hedonism in masculine dress that shattered the prosaic conformity of menswear. It was fashion from the bottom up—youth on a budget setting the trends that soon transcended age and income. High society and the realm of the couturier no longer set the dictates of style; fashion followed the street. (Figure 9.24.)

The mod mode was further bolstered by the enthusiastic adoption of peacock styles by rock and roll bands such as the Beatles, the Rolling Stones, The Who, and numerous other top pop groups. In the early part of the sixties, the Fab Four, as the Beatles were called, dressed alike in mod styled suits inspired by the avant-garde designs of Pierre Cardin. Beginning in 1960, Cardin had transformed the traditional male suit by dramatically reconstructing jackets with a collarless, high jewel neckline, shortened hemline, vented cuffs, and slim fit. In the second half of the decade, though, the Beatles were completely immersed in the peacock revolution and opted for individuality and self-expression through the **Sergeant Pepper suits**, which blended Edwardian dandyism with psychedelic-patterned fabrics and color combinations. Similarly, Pete Townsend, lead guitarist for The Who, made famous the controversial

Union Jack jacket constructed with red, white, and blue panels stitched together to resemble the British flag. In the United States, adaptations of the jacket made of the Stars and Stripes sparked their own controversy, and sometimes even incited violence against the wearer.

For most American men, though, mod suit styles were a remote, teenage fad. Fashion editorials and menswear ads largely focused on the traditional suit styles of the mature businessman rather than the teenager. Even the male models used for suits depicted in *GQ* and *Esquire* during the sixties, whether in photographs or illustrations, mostly looked fortyish rather than collegiate. In the second half of the decade, though, the peacock influence began to manifest itself in several ways. In 1967, *GQ* examined the "mod aftermath" and the resulting fashions designed "with little concern for traditional concepts of what men's clothing should look like." The three predominant influences on American suit styles, according to *GQ*, were color, textile pattern, and "the new love of sport coatings." Colors of sport coats became vibrant, especially turquoise, orange, royal blue, and assorted shades of gold and yellow. Bold windowpane checks, oversized houndstooth patterns, and complex plaids were combined with these intense colors for more visual dash. Some sport jackets were even produced in paisley and flower power prints for the truly flamboyant male. As a result of this new patterning of the sport jacket, the tailored business suit, too, began to appear in stronger glen plaids and gangster pin stripes, particularly following the movie *Bonnie and Clyde*.

Of the radical changes in men's suit silhouettes, the most widely accepted was the Nehru collar styling. In 1965, French designer Gilbert Féruch presented a collection of men's suit designs that included a fitted tunic jacket with a stand-up mandarin collar, which the pro-Chinese French called the "**Mao collar**," named for Chinese Communist leader Mao Tse-tung. In English-speaking countries, though, the style was adapted as the **Nehru suit**, named for the peace advocate Jawaharlal Nehru, prime minister of India, who, for decades, had worn a similar tunic that was a native male garment. (Figure 9.25.) As a substitute for the conventional business suit, the Nehru style was made of flannel or woven worsted in subdued colors. Fancy versions were cut with an off-center closure, and collars and cuffs were edged with embroidery or grosgrain piping. Evening wear styles were made of rich brocades, silks, and velvets. Young men of the "in-crowd" often wore jeweled or zodiac pendants or even long strands of love beads with their Nehru jackets.

As men's tailored suits evolved during the sixties, evening wear kept pace with the dynamic shifts in style. The straightline Ivy League tuxedo was replaced by the English cut with its lightly padded shoulderline, wider lapels, and slightly flared skirt. In the second half of the sixties, though, richly colored and patterned versions were alternatives to the black-and-white penguin tradition in formalwear. (Figure 9.26.) An elegant Edwardian opulence was revived in the sumptuous jeweltone velvets and brocades of jackets and in the frilly jabot-front shirts. At the same time, modernism further eroded convention when sophisticated men appeared at formal events dressed in silk or velvet Nehru suits.

As in the 1950s, men's sportswear of the sixties was widely diverse. Knit and woven sport shirts were designed with all sorts of collar, sleeve, and pocket treatments. Shirt jackets were

FIGURE 9.25. The round collared Nehru suit was named for the prime minister of India, who usually dressed in a traditional native tunic of similar design. Shaped Nehru jacket from Schwartzman of Sweden, 1968.

FIGURE 9.26. For the peacock male of the 1960s, formalwear was enriched with opulent fabrics and vivid hues. Floral silk brocade dinner jacket with contrasting shawl collar from First Nighters Formalwear, 1968.

cut with straight hems and vented sides so as not to resemble the careless appearance of an untucked shirt. Sport shirts had continued the vivid prints and colors of the fifties. New additions to the fabric maker's repertoire were international motifs and patterns taken from Aztec, Persian, American Indian, East Indian, and Asian traditions. Paisleys especially were hugely popular.

The peacock revolution first made inroads into American culture in the second half of the 1960s with the hippies. Young men wishing to express their rebellion against the staid conventionality of their elders found the ideal solution in flamboyant, snug-fitting clothing that their parents—and many editorials—viewed as effeminate or homosexual. (Figure 9.27.) Shirts and pants in paisley or flower power prints, fringed jackets and vests, embroidered ponchos, tight jeans, bell bottom hiphuggers, kaftans, beaded headbands, brightly colored scarves and

FIGURE 9.27. The mod looks in menswear of the 1960s were a frontal assault on the conventions of masculine dress. Young men donned flowered shirts, vividly hued jackets, tight hiphuggers, and a colorful abundance of accessories. Left, peacock revolution color and bold pattern in men's shirts by Vera, 1969; right, hiphuggers and print shirts by London Gear accessorized with Nureyev caps and Chelsea boots, 1966.

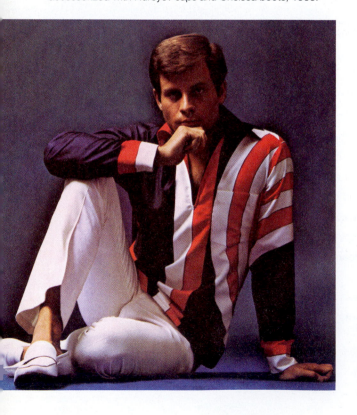

bandanas, love bead necklaces, and painted sandals were all assembled into a hodgepodge tapestry of pattern, texture, and color that expressed the personal style of the wearer. Portions of the American flag were used as patches on ragged jeans and jackets as a visual protest against the Vietnam War or social injustices. Tie-dyed everything replicated the psychedelic, color-blurred LSD trip that many young people experienced while listening to the Beatles' *Lucy in the Sky with Diamonds.* Unpleated pants retained the trim cut of the fifties but became increasingly slimmer in the second half of the decade with straight-leg cuffs, called "**broom-sticks**," at a narrow seventeen inches in circumference. Levi's "13s" were even more narrow with hemlines measuring 13 inches around the ankles.

The defiant, hip, anti-fashion style of the hippies coupled with the Carnaby Street looks of the rock and roll bands gradually filtered into ready-to-wear for the youthful masses to selectively adopt piecemeal—just enough to be a part of mod culture without appearing to wholly rebel. Bell bottom hiphuggers, colorful body shirts, commercially tie-dyed T-shirts, and the occasional Nehru top were fashion forward enough without seeming radical, especially when mixed with, and diluted by, the conventional khakis, Levis, oxford button-downs, and similar everyday apparel of typical young men.

Men's Sports Attire and Outerwear 1960–1969

Vibrant color and bold patterns had become standards of golf apparel in the 1950s. Throughout the sixties, the big plaids and checks of shorts and trousers, and the combinations of colors like kelly green and pink or fire-engine red and yellow seen on fairways were often the punch line of many jokes. Nylon zipper jackets, also in brilliant hues, were constructed with a lightweight hood that could be rolled up and tucked into a snap or zipper collar pouch. Sweaters for golfing were capacious and long, some covering the hips. In the late sixties, trousers were made with a velcro-flap pocket for golf balls and a detachable terrycloth towel for drying wet equipment.

Tennis wear was more resistant to change than other sports attire. White shorts, white knit tops and sweaters, white socks, and white canvas top shoes remained the most common ensemble for exclusive tennis clubs. A hint of navy, hunter green, or maroon was acceptable as a collar stripe, for piping on shorts, or as a solid color for blazers. For the most part, except for the tighter fit and briefer, thigh-high cut of the shorts, the tennis outfit was basically that of the 1930s. At the end of the sixties, though, tennis clothes exploded with color. Shorts and polo shirts in bold primary solids and stripes were fashionable, but not strong plaids or prints.

On the ski slopes of the early 1960s, fashion trends for men continued the nylon quilted parkas and jackets with formfitting stretch pants that had developed in the late fifties. As with golf wear, color in skiwear and winter knits included such vibrant combinations as royal blue with orange or lime green. Since the late 1950s, the Italians dominated knitwear with innovative new shapes and detailing of sweaters and luxurious knit patterns like complex **intarsias**, meaning inlaid. (Figure 9.28.) For the youthquake male, though, parkas made of neon colored fake furs of Orion pile were a fad in the mid-sixties. Another trend of the same time was Western-styled outfits made of tan stretch denim; leather and jeans jackets sported dropped V-cut yokes of contrasting colors or piped seams.

The newest look for men's outerwear of the early 1960s was actually a fresh take on a fifties favorite—the raglan sleeve. Modified variations included the **split raglan**, which had a

FIGURE 9.28. Italian knitwear set the pace for innovation and exceptional design in the sixties. Intarsia cardigan from Gino Paoli, 1963.

FIGURE 9.29. Standardized coat hemlines remained at the knee-breaker length throughout the 1960s. Revivals of norfolks and safari jackets appeared at the end of the decade. Left, kneebreaker coat from Italian Fashion Imports, 1968; right, wide wale corduroy norfolk jacket from Europe Crafts, 1968.

set-in sleeve effect in the front but diagonal raglan seams in the back. By the mid-sixties, the men's topcoat silhouette began to reflect the hemline changes in women's apparel. The **knee-breaker coat** was cropped at or slightly above the knees. (Figure 9.29.) Simultaneous with the shortened hemline, coats began to follow the shaped and fitted contours of the tailored suit. In the second half of the decade, men's coat lengths were adapted to the styles of women's outerwear. Some men's coats were cropped short at mid-thigh, more resembling jackets than topcoats, while others were cut with the midi length below the knees and the maxi length that varied from mid-calf to almost at the ankles. The most popular style of the midi and maxi was the military greatcoat look with a double-breasted closure, large flap pockets, and wide Napoleonic collar. Nehru collars were also adapted to outerwear for a couple of years.

Of particular appeal were coats and jackets of leather, suede, or fur. Unlike the black leather-and-chain versions of the 1950s biker, the mod leather coats were in rich colors and finishes, including suede and patent leather. A favorite variety of the hippies was the fringed cowboy jacket or long duster with dropped shoulder yokes inspired by the wardrobe choices of Texas native President Lyndon Johnson. Revivals of belted safari and norfolk jackets in wide wale corduroy or waterproof gabardine appeared in the late sixties.

Furs of all kinds, too, made a comeback with wealthier men in the 1965 to 1969 period after an absence since the 1920s. Fur enthusiasm ran the gamut from mink collars to full-length muskrat maxis. For a brief transitional period at the end of the decade and into the early sev-

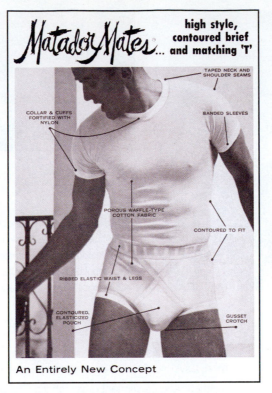

FIGURE 9.30. Basic white briefs and print boxers remained the most prevalent men's underwear styles of the period. Some peacock males, though, opted for the exhibitionism of underwear in revealing cuts and formfitting fabrics. Left, brief and T-shirt from Matador Mates, 1961; right, nylon mesh torso shirt and bikini from Ah Men, 1969.

enties, fun furs made of synthetic pile fabrics were widely promoted as substitutes for the real thing, but the fakes matted and soiled easily. Trench coat styles, in both all-weather fabrics and heavy worsteds were the most ubiquitous. Suburbans, peacoats, and similar fingertip-length coats retained the look of the fifties, only now made in durable synthetic materials.

Men's Underwear and Swimwear 1960–1969

The reduced silhouettes of underwear and swimwear that had developed at the end of the fifties became ever briefer during the youth-oriented 1960s. The low-rise hipster and bikini underwear complemented the trim contours of trousers, casual pants, and summer shorts. The white cotton brief, though, remained the best-selling style of underwear. (Figure 9.30.) Boxers were a more common undergarment for the older businessman whose looser suit trousers could adequately conceal the excess volume of fabric.

On the beaches of Europe and the Caribbean, men indulged in an exhibitionism years ahead of American men. Hipster swimsuits, some belted to emphasize the low-rise cut, and the tiniest of bikinis were made of formfitting nylon spandex and other synthetic knits. (Figure 9.31.) Despite these trends, though, the most common swimwear for men globally continued to be loose-fitting cotton or nylon shorts or, for teens, the baggy, bermuda-length surfer jams in wild tropical or floral prints.

Men's Sleepwear and Accessories 1960–1969

Since the 1890s, the varieties of fabric prints used in making men's pajamas and robes had always included a wide assortment of whimsical patterns and prints. During the sixties, the

FIGURE 9.31. As with underwear styles, new forms of men's swimsuits of the 1960s became exhibitionistic with ever briefer shapes and contouring materials. Most men, though, preferred traditional boxer styles. Left, "Surfer" collection by Catalina, 1966; right, French bikini and hiphugger boxers, 1967.

mod, psychedelic, and art deco revival motifs were made even more intensely vivid by the new synthetic and permanent press fabrics. The pajama short set that had been popular as summer sleepwear for decades became the preferred year-round nighttime wear for young men in the second half of the sixties. Ensembles often included matching short-sleeve top, boxers, and a kimono style robe cropped at the knees. At the same time, the sleepshirt made a comeback, only now shortened above the knees and often screen printed with bold graphical images or pop captions.

The protocol of the correct accessories for the well dressed man had already become a thing of the past by the mid-1960s. The peacock revolution dismantled the predictable traditions of masculine attire. The self-expressive fashion and personal style of the Carnaby look men and the hippies had a widespread influence on menswear conventions, including the finishing details of accessories.

Prior to the Kennedy years, men regarded a hat as an essential part of an outfit. The young president, though, seldom donned headwear of any kind, even in cold weather. In addition, young men began to grow their hair longer and fuller, an expression of youthful style they wished to display, not conceal beneath a hat. For those men who tenaciously clung to the tradition of headwear, the British influence dominated hat shapes of the sixties. Crowns were tapered, and narrow brims had deep rolls in the back and sides but only a slight turn-up at the front. Mod-look hats for young men included the Nureyev cap, a fashionable adaptation of the Soviet

FIGURE 9.32. Famed ballet dancer Rudolf Nureyev popularized the proletariat worker's cap he continued to wear in the early sixties following his defection from the Soviet Union. Versions of the Nureyev cap were worn by both women and men. Photo, 1963.

FIGURE 9.33. Among the fashion footwear trends for men in the sixties were Chelsea boots with Cuban heels and elastic gussets. In the second half of the decade, shoes were squared off with a wider vamp. Left, Chelsea boots, 1965; right, square-toe styling, 1968.

proletariat worker's hat named after the Russian ballet dancer who defected to the West in 1961 and was frequently photographed wearing the style. (Figure 9.32.) Despite the long hair of hippies, the flower child of the late sixties often wore variations of floppy wide brimmed hats of felt, suede, or patchwork leather.

The most important footwear news for men in the 1960s was the boot in all its variations. In the early part of the decade, **Chelsea boots**—short ankle boots with pointed toes, elastic side gussets, and Cuban heels—became a must-have for teenage boys when the Beatles wore them. (Figure 9.33.) The hippies adopted lace-up knee-high boots of soft suede or pliable, pieced leather, often trimmed with fringe around the top. Also a favorite of flower children were moccasins and sandals, the latter of which were worn in cold weather with socks of wild patterns and colors. During the second half of the sixties, toes for both boots and traditional forms of footwear became squared.

The skinny tie that complemented the Continental and Ivy League suits of the late fifties remained the most prevalent neckwear of the early 1960s. (Figure 9.34.) Ties gradually widened to about 3½ inches at the widest point by the end of the decade. Vividly hued shirts and suits of the era were adorned with equally colorful neckwear. Floral prints in pinks, lavenders, and similar vibrant colors shattered the conventions of men's ties. In addition, the Carnaby look men revived the ascot, also in the bright shades. In the late sixties, American

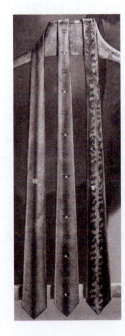

FIGURE 9.34. Neckties of the early 1960s retained the slim two-inch width and gradually widened to about 3½ inches by the end of the decade. The mod male opted for neckwear with flamboyant prints and brightly colored patterns. Left, skinny ties from Wembley, 1962; right, wide ties from King's Road, 1969.

FIGURE 9.35. For the peacock male, long hair was an element of the new male aesthetic. For hippies and other counterculture men, long hair was an anti-establishment protest. The Who, 1969.

men wore adaptations of the ascot, called **Apache scarves**, tied around the neck with an open-throat collar or tucked under the collar and secured with an ornamental ring. Bow ties had largely vanished in the early 1960s—relegated to the image of the styleless professor or civil servant. With the fashion revival influences of movies like *Bonnie and Clyde,* butterfly bow ties were rediscovered at the end of the decade.

The narrow range of gender appropriate jewelry for men that had become standardized in the fifties was disregarded as young men slipped on multiple chain and cuff bracelets, necklaces of all kinds, and oversized ornamental rings. Costume jewelry pendants with flashy faux jewels or mystical emblems and sociopolitical symbols such as peace signs were the fashion accent for Nehru collar jackets and shirts. Hippies doubly expressed their social views with strings of handmade love beads that not only avowed their make-love-not-war philosophy, but also rejected the commercialism of mass-produced jewelry.

Men's Grooming and Hairstyles 1960–1969

The youthquake of the 1960s sent powerful shockwaves through grooming and haircare businesses as well as the fashion industry. In droves, young men began to do the unthinkable; they grew their hair long. (Figure 9.35.) Since the Napoleonic era, long hair for men had been the peculiarity of eccentric musicians and symphony conductors (Leopold Stokowski), bohemian artists and aesthetes (Oscar Wilde), and "egg head" scientists (Albert Einstein). Now, young men undermined the very foundation of gender-role social order by adopting hair lengths and styles that, for generations, had been exclusively women's. "Is that a boy or a girl?" queried the caption of a 1964 *Sunday Times Magazine* photo, featuring a back view of a young man with shoulder-length hair. For hippies, long hair was an anti-establishment protest; for teenagers and collegiate young men, it was an affirmation of the youthquake generation.

As more men grew their hair long, two key industries keenly felt the impact. Hair oils suffered a significant drop in sales. Ads for shampoos in the late 1960s proclaimed "the wet head

Miniskirts, 1968.

FIGURE 9.36. Girls' fashions of the 1960s followed the trends of adult styles from miniskirts to pantsuits.

Mondrian dress, 1966.

is dead." On the other hand, makers of hair dryers and styling implements enjoyed a boom. In addition, long hair required more specialized care than the neighborhood barber could provide. Just as the flapper had invaded men's barber shops in the 1920s, now men made appointments for shampoos and styling at beauty salons.

Facial hair also returned. Sideburns inched down to the earlobes in the early 1960s and finally to the jawline at the end of the decade. Full mustaches, untrimmed beards, and goatees were social statements exhibited by counterculture groups.

Children's Clothing 1960–1969

Changes in infants' wear were primarily in the application of the many new miracle fabrics developed during the 1960s. Garments made of knit or woven blends of Orlon, acetate, acrylic, and nylon yarns were comfortable, durable, and easy to clean. Clothes in pink for girls and blue for boys continued to be best sellers although parents increasingly opted for gender-neutral colors and prints. The snap-front coverall made of soft, stretch terrycloth remained the prevalent form of infants' wear. The sleeved sleeping bag with its easy access zip front or drawstring bottom was the modern equivalent of swaddling clothes but without the restrictive binding. For an outing, parents might dress their babies in sacque sets, which featured full, hip-length smock tops with matching snap-closure panties lined with moisture-repellent vinyl.

Just as in previous decades, girls' clothing of the 1960s reflected the drama of women's fashions. (Figure 9.36.) The mod look of the sixties translated easily into the diminutive girl's

Mod melton pantsuit and go-go boots, 1968.

Beefeater jacket, "granny" print shirt and matching belt, hiphugger pants, 1967.

Continental blazer, 1966.

Space age pullover and hiphuggers, 1967.

Corduroy Nehru suit, 1968.

FIGURE 9.37. The peacock revolution of menswear significantly impacted boys' clothing styles as well. Makers of boys' ready-to-wear produced diminutive versions of colorful hiphuggers, Nehru jackets, paisley print shirts, and slim pants.

styles. Hemlines rose above the knees by middecade and to thigh-high by the close. Textured and patterned tights matched knit tops and kept legs warm in chilly weather. Go-go boots were mass-produced in miniature sizes for school girls who wanted to emulate their teen sisters. Psychedelic prints, art deco motifs, and vibrant neon colors abounded on all types of girls' wear. As women began to adopt the pantsuit for the workplace, girl's versions gradually became acceptable for school. Peripheral trends for girls included ankle-length granny dresses with the same Victoriana details as adult versions.

Boys' wear was similarly transformed in the 1960s. The peacock revolution in menswear inspired a transition of boy's attire from basic clothing into fashion during this period. (Figure 9.37.) The ubiquitous short sets and short jumpsuits that had been the everyday year-round playwear for toddler boys since the 1920s were now reserved primarily for warm weather. Preschool boys, instead, more often dressed in long pants that replicated adult styles in miniature. Hiphugger bell bottoms were produced for boys in the same colors, textures, and prints as those of their teen brothers. Wild prints, particularly vividly colored paisleys and florals, were favorites for the new permanent press shirts. Color blocked tops reflected the designs of men's space age looks. Scaled-down versions of the Nehru jacket were made in boys' sizes. In addition, as the baby boomers became parents, they dressed their children in the branded jeans and denim jackets they had preferred to wear as children.

Throughout the sixties, the television generation as young as preschool age was persuaded by advertising to demand certain types of clothing. Makers of licensed clothing advertised heavily on TV promoting their products and inculcating children with brand awareness and the notion of style. The colorful Muppets from Sesame Street became perennial favorites for everything from screen-printed T-shirts to appliqued tennis shoes. School-age boys and, to a lesser degree, girls as well, were swept up with images from the TV space fantasies *Star Trek* and *Lost in Space*. Comic book super heroes had never waned as favorite icons on clothing. Sleepwear and underwear sets imprinted with emblems and images to resemble the costumes of Superman, Spiderman, and Batman were hugely popular.

Review

The 1960s was a decade of dramatic social and fashion change. As the baby boom generation came of age, they sought fashion looks that not only differentiated them from their elders but also were evocative of the modern, space age era. Swinging London became the hub of youthful mod fashions. Key to the new looks of youthquake women was the miniskirt with its above-the-knee hemline that climbed to thigh-high by middecade. Fashion fads that complemented the miniskirt included textured tights or catsuits, go-go boots, especially short, white versions, and oversized pendant earrings. During the second half of the sixties, several revivalisms provided variety and excitement in fashion. Romantic Victoriana featured long granny dresses, wire-framed eyeglasses, and wide picture hats. Influences from movies included 1920s flapper looks, replete with dropped waist chemises and soft cloches, and thirties style skirts, called midis, with hemlines at mid-calf. Counterculture styles of street scene youth ranged from the pattern-mixed gypsy looks of the hippies to the protest ensembles of altered military garments and adaptations of American Indian dress.

Men's fashions underwent an even more dramatic change with the peacock revolution of the 1960s. Decades of staid conformity in menswear were overthrown by young men who donned the mod styles of flowered shirts, slim hiphugger pants, and flamboyant accessories like ascots and psychedelic print ties. Suits were reshaped and vividly colored and patterned. The conventions of gender were further dismantled as men grew their hair long. For the hippie, dress was a statement of protest against society, commercialism, or events of the time. The "peacenik" flower child layered on love beads, scarves, headbands, and fringed vests, belts, and boots; the militant dressed in altered military garments mixed with street clothes appliqued with the American flag or protest emblems.

Children's clothing reflected the trends of adult styles. Girls wore miniskirts, mod pantsuits, flower power accessories, and go-go boots. Boys donned Nehru jackets, paisley print shirts, hiphuggers, Chelsea boots, and Nureyev caps.

review questions

1. Describe women's mod looks of the 1960s, including accessories.

2. What three contemporary American art movements of the 1960s influenced fashions, and how?

3. What were four key revivals of women's fashions in the 1960s? Describe the modern adaptations inspired by them.

4. Where is Carnaby Street and what was its influence on men's fashions in the 1960s?

5. What was the peacock revolution? How did it transform men's fashion and masculine style?

research and portfolio projects

Research

1. Write a research paper on the space age designers of the 1960s. Explore the influences of technology on the cut and line of their designs. Include details of the designers' use of non-traditional textiles and materials.

Portfolio

1. Research movies of the 1960s that influenced mainstream fashions of the era. Compile a reference guide with a photocopy or digital scan of a period costume featured in the movie on one page and a corresponding fashion adaptation on the facing page. Write a description of each outfit, including the name of the film, costume designer, and date for the movie, and the name of the maker or designer and date of the fashion adaptation.

dress terms

afro: full, bushy hair worn by African-American men and women

Apache scarf: American adaptations of the ascot worn by men in the late 1960s

baby doll gown: women's smock-like shortie nightgown with short, ruffled bloomers

beehive hairstyle: high, cylindrical arrangement of long hair popular in the mid-1960s

bell bottoms: pants with flared cuffs

body stocking: long sleeve, one-piece knit suit; also called a catsuit

broomsticks: men's tight fitting pants cut with leg hems between thirteen and seventeen inches in circumference

Carnaby Street looks: young men's mod styles that included vividly colored shirts, tight hiphugger pants, and brightly hued ascots, scarves, and neckties; named for the shopping district in London's Soho section

Chelsea boots: men's short ankle boots with pointed toes, elastic side gussets, and Cuban heels

crepeset: permanently textured or crimped monofilament nylon fabric

dashiki: long, T-cut tunics made of kente cloth or fabrics evocative of African heritage

flamenco pants: women's pants of the mid-1960s with a low-rise waistline and flared legs below the knees; a precursor to bell bottom hiphuggers

go-go boots: any of a variety of boots, but usually the short white styles with flat heels and wide uppers; named for the wild go-go dancing of the period

granny dress: ankle-length calico dress often made with Victorian details such as high collars, puffed sleeves, and ruffled hemlines

headwrap: a cloth headcovering worn by black women as an expression of their African heritage

hiphuggers: men's and women's pants cut with a low waistline that fitted tightly about the hips

intarsia: Italian word meaning inlaid applied to complex knitwear patterns that appear to have inset panels

knee-breaker coat: men's outerwear of the 1960s and early 1970s cropped at or slightly above the knees

Mao collar: the French term for the rounded stand-up collar on men's jackets and shirts of the late 1960s; named for Chinese Communist leader Mao Tse-tung

maxi: a skirt or coat with a hemline near or to the ankles

midi: a skirt or coat with a hemline at mid-calf

milkmaidism: the English term applied to women's Victoriana revivals

miniskirt: dress or skirt with a hemline above the knees

mod look: short for "modern" or "modernist" fashions for women and men of the mid-1960s

Nehru suit: menswear style of the late 1960s that featured a tunic-style jacket with a rounded stand-up collar; named for Indian prime minister Jawaharlal Nehru

Nureyev cap: Russian worker's cap with short visor and wide headband; named for ballet dancer Rudolf Nureyev

palazzo pajamas: women's wide-legged evening pants

pantyhose: seamless, one-piece knit hose, combining stockings and panty, introduced in the mid-1960s

peacock revolution: the hedonistic changes in menswear in which men adopted colorful clothes and styles that broke with conventional masculine dress

permanent press: treated fabrics that resist wrinkling, introduced in 1964

Qiana: Du Pont synthetic silk introduced in 1968

Sergeant Pepper suits: menswear of the mid-1960s that blended a form of Edwardian dandyism with psychedelic patterned fabrics and color combinations; named for the costumes of the mythical band in the Beatles' *Yellow Submarine*

space age style: sleek, minimalist women's and men's fashions of the mid-1960s with clean, smooth lines and simple shapes

split raglan coat: men's outerwear with sleeves that featured a set-in effect in the front but diagonal raglan seams in the back

Union Jack jacket: mod sport coat constructed with red, white, and blue panels stitched together to resemble the British flag

velcro: nylon strips of material with a filament nap of hooks that held fast when pressed together

Victoriana: clothing and accessories that featured revivalisms from the age of Queen Victoria (1837–1901)

10 The Me Decade 1970–1979

1970   **1979**

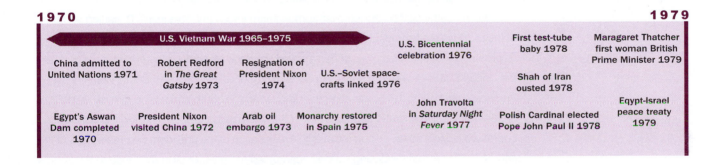

U.S. Vietnam War 1965–1975

China admitted to
United Nations 1971

Robert Redford
in *The Great
Gatsby* 1973

Resignation of
President Nixon
1974

U.S.–Soviet space-
crafts linked 1976

U.S. Bicentennial
celebration 1976

First test-tube
baby 1978

Maragaret Thatcher
first woman British
Prime Minister 1979

Shah of Iran
ousted 1978

John Travolta
in *Saturday Night
Fever* 1977

Egypt-Israel
peace treaty
1979

Egypt's Aswan
Dam completed
1970

President Nixon
visited China 1972

Arab oil
embargo 1973

Monarchy restored
in Spain 1975

Polish Cardinal elected
Pope John Paul II 1978

Nations in Transition 1970–1979

During the 1970s, the countries of Europe began to assume a more cohesive identity and
unity despite the continued tensions between the communist East and democratic West. The
European Economic Community admitted Great Britain, Ireland, and Denmark in 1973. The
two Germanys signed an agreement in 1971, allowing travel and mutual traffic access; two
years later, both were admitted to the United Nations. Spain became a constitutional monarchy in 1975 after forty years of a military dictatorship. In 1978, a Polish cardinal was elected
Pope John Paul II, the first non-Italian Pope in more than 400 years. A renewed nationalism
swept Poland and inspired a trade union movement that set the stage for democratic reforms
throughout central Europe in the 1980s.

Russia continued its global efforts toward detente (a relaxing of hardline policies) with
non-communist countries. Significant progress was evidenced by the dissident minorities
in countries like Poland, Czechoslovakia, and Hungary who became increasingly visible and
vocal. All that progress and goodwill, though, was undermined in 1979 when Russia invaded

Afghanistan and entered into a costly guerrilla war. As a result, the United States and other countries boycotted the Moscow Olympics in 1980.

In the Middle East, the tensions between Arab nations and Israel once again erupted into another full-scale war in 1973 over the lands that Israel still occupied from the 1967 conflict. Though Israel prevailed, the Sinai was eventually returned to Egypt and, in 1979, the two countries signed a peace accord.

Between 1978 and 1980, world attention focused on Iran. The secular government of the pro-Western Shah collapsed from internal pressures, and a revolutionary committee headed by the Ayatollah Khomeini established an Islamic republic. During the chaos, the U.S. embassy was occupied by militants, and Americans were held hostage for 444 days.

In China, Mao Tse-tung died in 1976. The hardline Red Guards were ordered to cease their violence and repression that, for the ten years following the Cultural Revolution in 1966, had fastened a harsh, totalitarian grip on the entire country. Subsequent regimes opened the doors to international contacts, notably with the United States and Europe.

Cambodia to Disco Fever: American Culture 1970–1979

By 1970, there was a palpable relief felt by most people that the turbulent sixties had ended. But a new decade did not mean a clean slate and a fresh start as so many had naively hoped. The war in southeast Asia spilled over from Vietnam into Cambodia in 1970, setting off some of the most violent campus demonstrations yet—the worst being at Kent State where National Guardsmen shot and killed or wounded a dozen unarmed student protesters. Three years later, the United States brokered a cease fire agreement between North and South Vietnam. When America pulled out in 1975, the communists overran the south amidst the turmoil. In 1972, a break-in at the Democratic headquarters in the Watergate complex by Nixon administration operatives led to a cover-up and the eventual resignation of the president two years later. At the end of 1973, Arab oil producing nations quadrupled the price of oil in response to the West's support of Israel during the Yom Kippur War, setting off a global economic crisis.

From the continued social unrest of the early seventies came significant progress, though. In 1972, the Equal Rights Amendment (ERA) was passed by Congress, and in 1973 the women's movement cheered the Supreme Court's decision overturning state laws against abortion. Science offered new hope for women wanting children when the first test-tube baby was born (from an "in vitro" fertilized egg) in 1978. Environmentalism brought millions of supporters into the streets nationwide for the first Earth Day in 1970, followed by legislation to protect habitat and endangered species. The National Gay Task Force lauded the 1973 decision by the American Psychiatric Association to remove homosexuality from its clinical list of mental disorders.

By the mid-seventies, Americans prepared to celebrate the bicentennial of the birth of their nation. A feeling of introspection swept the country. The second wave of the baby boomers (1956–1964) came of age. Their generation was less idealistic than their older siblings had been in the sixties. The 1970s became the "Me Decade," meaning "What's in it for me?" College men took business courses and eschewed the humanities. Women discarded their miniskirts and donned pantsuits to pursue corporate careers.

In popular culture, the glittery glam rock of the early seventies gave way to a Saturday night fever and the hedonistic disco era in the second half of the decade. Punk rock inspired an iconoclastic look and a lifestyle of revolt against all social conventions. The sexual revolution of the 1960s evolved into an uninhibited casualness toward sex in the 1970s. The search for novelty—in lifestyle, fashion, personal relationships, sex—was a driving force that crossed all generations and incomes.

Technologies and Textiles

In the seventies, sophisticated laboratory research continued to improve the quality and performance features of synthetic fibers. The development of new, high-speed textile production machinery greatly increased output and reduced the cost of fabrics. In 1972, Congress established the Consumer Product Agency to conduct research and develop testing methods for textiles and other materials used in consumer goods. In 1975, the **Kevlar** aramid fiber was first used in protective clothing called "soft body armor." By the end of the 1970s, the world production of synthetic fibers exceeded 28 billion pounds, compared to only 3 billion of wool.

Women's Fashions 1970–1979

As the 1970s opened, the seeming confusion of fashion styles that developed at the end of the sixties became even more pronounced. The couturiers and fashion leaders of Paris, London, and Milan had long since ceased to provide the dictatorial style leadership of the Dior era, and that most potent barometer of the latest trends, the hemline, was at varying lengths up and down the leg. (Figure 10.1.) "There are no rules," conceded *Vogue* in 1970. "Let's relax, wear whatever length—or as many lengths—as we want." Ready-to-wear advertising and retail catalogs perpetuated the confusion by showing hemlines at most every length: thigh-high, above the knee, at the knee, covering the knee, mid-calf midi, and ankle-grazing maxi.

For young women, the preferred skirt length remained thigh-high short. Responding to the demand of the market for short, European designers in 1970 experimented with tailored varieties of short shorts in upscale fabrics and materials such as linen, lamé, and suede. The following year, **hot pants**, as they came to be labeled, were a fashion phenomenon. (Figure 10.2.) Most hot pants were worn with textured and colorful body stockings or ribbed tights and, especially, tall boots. The trend was short lived, however, and vanished from daytime wardrobes because the look quickly became associated with prostitutes.

One of the most important developments of women's fashion in the early 1970s was the emphasis on pant styles. The pantsuit that had begun to emerge as a career woman's option in the late sixties increasingly became accepted business attire as corporations dismantled archaic dress codes. Instead of the traditional menswear jacket styles, pantsuits were made with comfortable, loose-fitting tunic tops, cardigans, and long vests. (Figure 10.3.) The new suits of the seventies also were made with easy-care polyester knits in vibrant colors such as turquoise, kelly green, royal blue, and burnt orange that would not fade. In addition, advanced commercial knitting techniques made possible durable jacquards and other richly textured surfaces for an added feminine touch to pantsuits.

Bring back the thirties.

FIGURE 10.1. In the early 1970s, hemlines were at varying lengths from thigh-high miniskirts to ankle-sweeping maxis. Left, thigh-high mini, 1972; top right, knee-length skirt, 1972; bottom right, mid-calf midi, 1971.

Besides pantsuits, other forms of trousers provided women of the seventies with comfortable and varied alternatives to the miniskirt. Midi-length versions of culottes, called **gauchos**, and tweed knickers were worn with the requisite knee-high boots. Even the jodhpur was reintroduced from the equestrienne costume to street wear suits, usually topped with a bolero jacket. Variants of gauchos and knickers made of velvet or satin were similarly worn with brocaded jackets or vests and patent leather or embroidered suede boots for evening wear. Wide-legged trousers also continued to be favorites for the theatre and cocktail parties. By 1970, leg widths were so enormous that the bifurcation was swallowed up in the voluminous fabric, and the trousers looked more like long, full skirts. In the mid-seventies, Japanese designers, notably Kenzo and Miyake, presented loose, baggy variations called **kimono trousers** that draped somewhat like harem pants. In the second half of the decade, the Japanese experimented with totally new approaches to the construction of trousers such as cropping one pant leg at the knee and leaving the other at the ankle. More traditional pant styles included adaptations of the men's straightline Oxford bags with wide cuffs. For casual wear, hiphugger bell bottoms remained popular with slender teenagers. The fit was snug around the hips and thighs but the legs flared out to enormous widths—a style marketed in boutiques as **elephant bells**.

Teenagers coming of age in the 1970s sought to define their own identity that was distinct from that of their older youthquake siblings. Although many hippies and flower children lingered on into the early seventies, teens viewed the Age of Aquarius as passé and irrelevant to the times. As with their predecessors of the sixties, young people of the 1970s found inspiration for new looks and new attitudes from rock and roll. In 1972, "**glam**" or "**glitter rock**" burst onto the pop culture landscape when David Bowie went on tour with his Ziggy Stardust show. Bowie performed with crimson-dyed spiked hair, thickly applied glittery makeup, and lavish costumes. At the same time Mick Jagger, Elton John, and other rock stars similarly developed concert images centered on gender ambiguity, more commonly referred to in the press as androgyny. For young people emulating their pop idols, the lines of gender fashion often became blurred. Many basics became unisex glam, from rhinestone-studded elephant bells and sequined skinny-rib shirts to platform high heels and feathered shag haircuts.

In the mid-1970s, edgy punk rock groups such as the Sex Pistols and the Ramones gathered substantial followings of urban teenagers who were disillusioned with their personal lives and the values of a class-conscious society. In addition to their iconoclastic music, these bands and their fans expressed their rebellious discontent through antisocial looks, which included jackets and T-shirts embellished with obscenities, pornographic images, swastikas, cultist symbols, and anything else that could create shock value. The **punk look** especially

FIGURE 10.2. For a few seasons in the early 1970s, tight short shorts, called hot pants, were acceptable town attire. Hot pants by Bonnie Doon, 1971.

Hiphugger jeans from Sears Junior Bazaar, 1972.

Rayon gabardine elephant bells from FBS, 1973.

Jacquard knit knicker suit from FBS, 1971.

Double knit polyester pantsuit from Spiegel, 1973.

FIGURE 10.3. Pants of all varieties were the key fashion emphasis throughout the 1970s. Styles ranged from polyester double knit suit trousers to the exaggerated elephant bells.

Jacket, vest, and baggies in vibrant colors from Bobbie Brooks, 1972.

Cuffed baggies from Simplicity Patterns, 1973.

FIGURE 10.4. In the second half of the 1970s, women dressed for success in longer hemlines, mix-and-match coordinates, and layers of accessories such as scarves and wraps. Separates by Kasper, 1977.

featured clothes that were slashed or ripped and then pinned together with rows of safety pins or patched with duct tape. Other garments were inventively constructed with the discards of industry such as bits of colorful plastic, rubber, or other high tech synthetic materials. Their hairstyles were flamboyant and distinct, ranging from short, spiked cuts dyed magenta, purple, or green to wildly exotic crests such as Mohawks and rooster's combs.

British avant-garde designer Vivienne Westwood led the front for punk-influenced high fashion in London, while French designers Jean-Paul Gaultier, Claude Montana, and Thierry Mugler selectively found inspiration for their haute couture collections based on the drama of both the punk looks and glam rock style.

As the youth of the seventies defined their niche looks, mainstream fashions also began to shift dramatically. In 1975, the thigh-high miniskirt finally faded from fashion—but only for a few years. Hemlines for ready-to-wear dresses and skirts that had been above the knees for almost ten years now universally dropped to below the kneecap. By 1977, hemlines were commonly at mid-calf and some even to the ankles. (Figure 10.4.)

Throughout the decade, designers on both sides of the Atlantic constantly searched for ways to combine novelty with versatility. When Richard Nixon made his epochal trip to China in 1972, designers rediscovered the mandarin collar, kimono sleeves, and the **qi pao dress**— an Asian sheath style usually with a mandarin collar and slits at the sides or front of the skirt.

FIGURE 10.5. In 1972, Richard Nixon made an epochal visit to China and began the normalization of relationships that had ceased with the Communist takeover in 1949. Soon afterward, many Western designers were inspired to incorporate Asian motifs and silhouettes into their collections. Left, silk chiffon wrap skirts by Hanae Mori, 1974; right, silk floral damask tunic with mandarin collar by Yves St. Laurent, 1976.

Fabric makers reproduced endless varieties of traditional Asian motifs and textile patterns. (Figure 10.5.) In 1978, Yves St. Laurent presented an entire collection of Chinese inspired fashions and, two years later, launched his Opium fragrances and licensed bamboo logo for home furnishings. Ready-to-wear makers capitalized on the mass market's continued interest in the East by producing innumerable adaptations and interpretations of Asian garments and accessories.

Another source of novelty for designers was the Russian peasant look. Among St. Laurent's series of ethnic collections during the second half of the seventies were his Cossack collections of 1976 and 1977, which included "rich peasant" styles like gold lamé dresses adorned with passementiere or trimmed with fur, and everything layered with sumptuously patterned shawls and scarves. Although most of St. Laurent's ethnic designs were largely theatrical drama, the collections repeatedly made international fashion headlines, influencing popular trends such as the layered "**folklorica**" looks shown in Figure 10.4 and especially textures, patterns, and color palettes of knits.

Despite all the excitement and theatricality of the counterculture or ethnic inspired fashions from St. Laurent, Gaultier, Mugler, Montana, and Westwood, working women could not wear these styles to the office. For them, a closet full of polyester pantsuits and double knit coordinates provided variety, functionality, and ease of dressing. In 1977, this comfort zone of professional attire was reinforced by the bestselling fashion guide *Dress for Success* by John Molloy. Career women were advised of wardrobe do's and don'ts for succeeding in a corporate world dominated by men. Subtlety and simplicity were key to that success. American designers like Calvin Klein, Anne Klein, Geoffrey Beene, Bill Blass, Liz Claiborne, and Ralph Lauren provided collection after collection of wearable fashions with a simplicity of silhouette that fitted the criteria of dressing for success. These and numerous other American designers produced an endless array of masterfully tailored suits and suit separates, especially blazers—the single most important component of a career woman's wardrobe in the 1970s. Besides the basic menswear styles, some blazers featured subdued but elegant touches such as grosgrain piping, ornamental buttons, or braid trim. The day-into-evening versatility of the blazer was especially appealing to busy career women. The transition from the colorful polyester double knit pantsuits of the early 1970s to the tailored powersuits of the 1980s had begun. (Figure 10.6.)

Dressy suit jackets may have been appropriate for many after-six social events, but luxurious evening gowns were still the preferred look for most formal affairs. (Figure 10.7.) Bold prints and textile patterns especially dominated evening wear in the early seventies. The striking graphics of the Op and Pop art movements and the renewed interest in art deco design continued to influence fabric makers. Revivalisms also abounded in the 1970s. Historical details such as ruffs, leg-of-mutton sleeves, and bustle treatments were reinterpreted with new fabrics and modernist construction by Cardin, Capucci, and Givenchy. The corset bodice was freshly reengineered as bustiers by St. Laurent, Westwood, and Mugler. The Empire waistline was everywhere. American designers delighted in slinky, sexy, bias-cut styles reminiscent of the 1930s.

One of the most significant impacts on nighttime fashion glamour in the late seventies was the disco phenomenon. In 1977, the hit movie *Saturday Night Fever* showcased John Travolta gyrating to the pulsating music of the Bee Gees across a strobe-lit dance floor in a dazzling white suit. Disco was an instant hit and became the ideal hedonistic party for the conclusion of the me-decade. Sex, drugs, and rock and roll all merged into the wild club scene of New York's famed (or infamous) Studio 54—and hundreds of hometown versions scattered around the globe. Few young people of any industrialized nation were impervious to the throbbing beat of disco music and the lure of the boogie night life. Disco fever dressing, according to *Vogue* in 1978, had to show "a lot of body." Designers and wearers alike were obliging. Pencil slim pants and skintight designer label jeans were worn with halters, tube tops, or at least shirts with a few buttons strategically opened. Anything that shined and glittered was right for night. (Figure 10.8.) Shoes and hose shimmered with metallic allure. Sparkling jewelry accented the body in motion.

FIGURE 10.6. Tailored suits and suit separates became integral to the career woman's wardrobe of the 1970s. Tweed suit by Ferragamo, 1979.

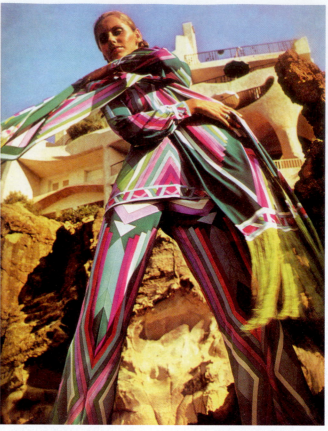

Op art evening gown and pyjamas from Leonard, 1972.

Revival leg-of-mutton sleeves and velvet evening skirt by Yves St. Laurent, 1979.

FIGURE 10.7. Revivals dominated evening wear of the 1970s. Sleek, bias-cut thirties gowns and adaptations of historical silhouettes such as the empire waist were revitalized with the sumptuous synthetic fabrics of the time.

Bias cut satin gown by Halston, 1976.

Folklorica vest over lamé gauze gown by Oscar de la Renta, 1976.

Branding, Logos, and Jeans

Until the Second World War, denim clothing was largely viewed as work clothes. Mass merchandising catalogs emphasized the strength and durability of jeans. Hollywood used denim as a visual reference for class distinction.

Following World War II, though, jeans increasingly became a fashion garment. Called dungarees at the time, jeans had been worn by millions of women who went to work in armaments factories. They had softened the image of the commodity work pant by rolling the cuffs to mid-calf and by accessorizing their jeans with matching belts and shoes or coordinating tops. Some jeans makers had even added linings of vividly colored plaids as a fashion accent for rolled up cuffs. Having come to appreciate the comfort and easy care of denim, women continued to wear jeans as playwear in the postwar years. By the 1960s, jeans were the preferred garment of the youthquake generation.

During the 1970s, the basic denim pant was redefined and transformed into a high fashion garment. In keeping with the sexuality of disco fashions, jeans were cut to fit skintight. Patch pockets were reduced in size and raised to contour the buttocks, thighs, and crotch. Designers used slick marketing methods to brand ready-to-wear jeans with designer logos and distinctive top-stitching. Calvin Klein featured a fifteen-year-old Brooke Shields in TV commercials in which she avowed that nothing (meaning underwear) came between her and her Calvin Kleins. On weekends, discos often refused entry to anyone wearing jeans without the requisite designer label on the back; admission was summarily declined to those in commodity brands such as Levi's, Lee, or Wrangler.

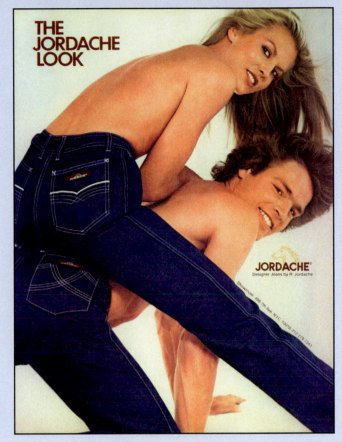

Jordache jeans ad, 1978.

Women's Outerwear 1970–1979

In the early 1970s, outerwear featured Asian influences such as kimono sleeves and mandarin collars, following the renewal of U.S.-China diplomatic and economic relationships. At about the same time, the Big Look of the Japanese designers inspired voluminous styles of coats, wraps, and jackets with full skirts, rounded shoulders, capacious sleeves, and patch pockets. (Figure 10.9.) At the other end of the spectrum, wrap styles, called **dressing-gown coats**, were made of luxurious fabrics and were worn as a snugly belted cocoon. Leather jackets and coats were everywhere, many of which were constructed in a multicolor patchwork. Denim was equally popular for both jackets and long coats. During the mid-1970s, synthetic fake fur jackets and coats were heavily promoted as an alternative to real fur, which had become socially unacceptable in light of new laws protecting endangered species. In the second half of the seventies, both skirts and coats were well below the knees, some almost to the ankles.

FIGURE 10.8. At the end of the 1970s, disco fashions were designed to display a lot of body and to attract attention with glitter, shimmer, and shine. Body revealing nightlife looks by Valentino, 1978.

The Russian peasant looks of St. Laurent and the many folklorica derivatives inspired an interest in rich textiles such as tapestries for outerwear. The modern look at the end of the decade ranged from the oversized quilted **duvet coats** by de Castelbajac, which were widely copied, to the simple, finely tailored dress coats of Halston and Ralph Lauren.

Women's Sports Apparel 1970–1979

Throughout the seventies, women of all ages joined one of the many private membership clubs and spas that invaded the suburbs. Magazine editorials and apparel marketers advised women to think fashion even when exercising. Makers of active sports clothes such as Jantzen and Danskin expanded speciality lines with colorful mix-and match leotards, shorts, tanks, tights, leggings, warm-up fleece, jackets, and coordinating accessories like totes, gym bags, caps, and wrist and head bands. (Figure 10.10.) Many women opted to wear active sportswear as casual attire for weekends and vacations.

Winter resorts enjoyed a boom during the 1970s as career women began to take both winter and summer vacations. The fit of ski pants, jackets, and coats was trim. The one-piece unitard became the trendy skiwear, especially in stretch metallic fabrics. Thickly quilted jackets, vests, and coats were filled with down or synthetic materials that retained body heat.

FIGURE 10.9. In the second half of the seventies, coat styles reflected the longer hemlines of dresses and the layered looks of suits and separates. Left, coat-on-coat styling by Calvin Klein, 1975; right, patchwork leather coat by Skin Gear, 1978.

FIGURE 10.10. Makers of active sportswear in the 1970s developed mix-and-match collections of coordinates that many women wore as casual attire as well as workout clothes. Cotton jogsuit and sportswear by Jantzen, 1978.

FIGURE 10.11. The bright white tennis uniform remained the preferred dress for many leagues and clubs throughout the 1970s. Tennis shorts, skirt, jacket, and tops from Vogue Patterns, 1976.

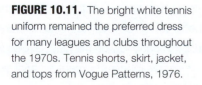

FIGURE 10.12. Undergarments became briefer and more luxurious in the 1970s. Lacy bra and bikini by Donald Brooks for Maidenform, 1978.

FIGURE 10.13. Following the reopening of economic relations between China and the United States in 1972, ready-to-wear makers mass produced adaptations of Asian garments as sleepwear and robes. Asian motif print kimono from Kasper, 1973.

For tennis, bright white shorts, little skirts, and camp or knit shirts were still often the required uniform for leagues and clubs. (Figure 10.11.) Color and even prints gradually became acceptable after 1972 when women were permitted to play in color attire at Wimbledon.

Women's Underwear and Sleepwear 1970–1979

Undergarments were in their briefest forms by the beginning of the 1970s. As the fitness boom increased, a subcategory of sports bras became big business for manufacturers. Bikini panties were further reduced to barely more than a thin band low on the hips. Girdles were only worn by women needing figure control. Slips largely disappeared except for midi skirts until about middecade when dress hemlines dropped below the knees.

In the second half of the seventies, luxurious natural fabrics such as silk crepe de chine and satin returned. Colors were more subdued but rich—apricot, teal, olive, coffee, burgundy. All types of undergarments were lavishly adorned with lace insets, trimmings, or appliques.

FIGURE 10.14. Swimsuits of the seventies were cut to the briefest ever, including the first string bikinis and thongs. Left, cotton voile bikini and beach wrap from Jean Patou, 1975; right, the "Chain Suit" by Marc Vigenron, 1977.

(Figure 10.12.) During the disco craze, sleek, glossy lingerie complemented the glittery, body-conscious fashions for night clubbing. Sexy corsets, garters, and frilly underthings made a comeback. One-piece body briefers that looked like racer swimsuits and fitted like a second skin eliminated panty and bra lines beneath clinging nylon and silk dresses.

Most sleepwear of the seventies changed little from styles of the sixties. The baby doll became a minigown with matching bikini panties rather than bloomers. Zip-front kaftans, some with oversized hoods, were comfortable alternatives to wrap robes. A number of revival styles were popular in the seventies, including bias cut nightgowns and flowing robes modeled on 1930s originals. Instead of silk or rayon, though, nylon tricot was the most common fabric. Similarly, flapper era pyjamas in sumptuous silk or nylon were substituted for the utilitarian cotton pajama. Following the reopening of relationships between China and the United States in 1972, Asian-styled kimonos and mandarin collar pajama suits became especially popular. (Figure 10.13.) Traditional robes and gowns were made from textiles printed all over with vividly colored reproductions of Asian woodblock prints and silk scroll paintings.

Women's Swimwear 1970–1979

Swimsuits of the seventies were cut to the briefest ever. (Figure 10.14.) The string bikini, called a "**rio**" because it first made its appearance on the beaches of South America in the early 1970s, allowed the maximum exposure to the sun. In 1974, Rudi Gernreich launched the thong for both women and men. At the opposite end of the swimwear spectrum, one-piece

FIGURE 10.15. In the early seventies, footwear became dramatic with the exaggerated shapes and heights of platform shoes. By the end of the decade, natural materials such as wood or cork soles and rope or canvas coverings were a prevalent look. Left, platforms from Sole Shoes, 1973; center, pumps in assorted heel heights, 1977; right, wood sole wedges, clogs, and sandals from Brazil, 1978.

suits and similar maillots covered more but were made of contouring Antron nylon and Lycra without any darts for a smooth, sleek fit. Many simple one-piece suits were given a new look with retro details such as skirted styles and swimdresses. At the peak of interest in art deco in the early seventies, the tank necklines and straight-cut leg openings of the flapper era were among the revivals.

Women's Shoes 1970–1979

In the first years of the decade, platform shoes and boots rose to exaggerated heights and shapes—some with heels as high as five inches. (Figure 10.15.) Many variations of platform shoes were molded of new age materials such as acrylic, aluminum, synthetic rubber, or plastics. Thigh-high boots worn with miniskirts in the sixties were adopted to hot pants in the early 1970s. Throughout the seventies, the innumerable eclectic looks of fashions inspired one of the most varied assortments of shoe designs of the century. Women's closets were crowded with mules, sandals, flats, wedges, high heels, moccasins, and boots of all heights in all sorts of materials and colors. Vamps remained wide with ovoid or bluntly squared toes. At the end of the decade, tall, sculpted wedges replaced the towering high heel platforms. Natural materials such as cork and wood—or plastic simulations—were sculpted into heavy solid soles that were difficult to walk in. Stacked heels of thin, laminated strips of wood offered the same trendy look of natural materials only with flexible leather or crepe soles. Along the same lines, canvas espadrilles featured wedge soles covered in braided or basket-weave rope or macrame. By contrast were the beaded, sequined, or metallic disco shoes with spiked heels and open, strappy designs that bared much of the foot, complementing nightlife fashions that bared shoulders, cleavage, and legs. The footwear industry also responded to the seventies fitness boom with branded active sports shoes in designer colors and materials.

Torques by Van Cleef & Arpels, 1975.

FIGURE 10.16. The diverse looks of jewelry in the seventies ranged from finely crafted art deco revivals to the arts-and-crafts varieties of natural materials like sculpted ceramics, handwrought metals, and carved wood.

Handcrafted porcelain jewelry by Capri, 1978.

Women's Jewelry 1970–1979

Oversized costume jewelry in vivid colors remained popular through the early 1970s. Licensed designer logos were increasingly incorporated into the designs of jewelry. (Figure 10.16.) Replications and new interpretations of art deco jewelry continued to be in such huge demand that makers like the 1928 Jewelry Company produced full lines of matching sets each year. After Nixon's visit to China in 1972, jewelry with Asian motifs became trendy, particularly jade, carved cinnabar, and luminous cloisonne. In the second half of the seventies, patriotic jewelry in red, white, and blue were prevalent in America for the celebration of the U.S. bicentennial in 1976 and in Britain to honor the Queen's Silver Jubilee (twenty-fifth anniversary) in 1977.

Toward the end of the seventies, jewelry in natural materials and earth tones complemented the resurgence of natural fibers in clothing and the wood, fiber, and raw leather prevalence for shoes. Terracotta and glazed stoneware ornaments, wooden beads, handwrought metals, and fiber crafts provided a fresh look after the polished machine-perfect plastics of the previous two decades.

In contrast to the return to nature was the high gloss style of the disco divas who required eye-catching jewelry that glittered and shined but did not overwhelm. Thin rhinestone necklaces and diamond tennis bracelets or finely wrought gold chains added just the right sparkle to accentuate the body in motion on the dance floor. Zodiac pins and pendants served as a conversation opener for the opposite sex.

Art deco revival necklace by David Weber, 1972.

FIGURE 10.17. Hairstyles of the 1970s became softer and longer, complemented by natural tones of makeup. Ethnic looks included variations of the afro cut from the late sixties. Left, soft, natural make-up and fuller hair styles of 1977; right, the "super Afrique" cut and "afro puffs," 1972.

Women's Hairstyles and Makeup 1970–1979

Hairstyles of the 1970s were predominantly soft and long. (Figure 10.17.) The fluffy, feather cuts of the actresses on the TV series *Charlie's Angels* epitomized the easy casualness of hairstyles of the era. In addition, the carefree pageboy crop of 1976 Olympic gold medal skater Dorothy Hamill became a favorite cut for teen girls with thick, straight hair. Retro-fifties chic fashions also inspired some women like Liza Minelli to trim their hair to the close crop of Audrey Hepburn, circa 1955. Ethnic styles featured variations on the full, rounded afro that had developed in the late sixties. For women who wanted a variety of hairstyle options, including changes in lengths, textures, and colors, wigs and falls were widely promoted. Synthetic filaments such as Dynel modacrylic made wigs affordable to a mass market.

Make-up continued the natural look with soft-toned lipsticks and negligible eyeshadows. For the career woman, dressing for success meant understated makeup—coral lipsticks and, perhaps, just a touch of a mauve blend of eyeshadow for depth. For the disco nightlife, though, makeup was applied for seduction. Wet-looking lip glosses in deep shades of red, glittery cheek blushes, and softly blended smoky eyeshadows enhanced feminine features to stand out in the dim lighting of night spots.

Women's Hats 1970–1979

Hats largely vanished from most women's wardrobes in the seventies. Mass merchandise catalogs that once featured multiple pages of millinery now only included a few versatile and easy-care utilitarian hats. (Figure 10.18.) Soft, knit caps of all shapes and colors were particularly popular. As a fashion statement, many women in the early seventies wore scarves as headwear, an influence from the dress of the Rhoda character on the *Mary Tyler Moore Show*.

Felt "swinger brim" hat with paisley scarf band, 1970.

Singer Aretha Franklin in African-inspired headwrap, 1970.

Tweed Eton cap from Blassport, 1971.

Feathered pillbox, 1974.

Mass-produced netted hat in polyester, 1976.

Ethnic peasant turban by St. Laurent, 1977.

Sueded poly/cotton newsboy cap from Thornes, 1978.

FIGURE 10.18. In the 1970s, hats ceased to be the critical accent to a fashion look they had been in the New Look era. Most hats were worn for utility. Exceptions included the occasional special event like a wedding, funeral, or Easter Sunday.

Unrelated to the scarf fashion trend was the headwrap adopted by some urban black women as a statement of their African heritage. During the second half of the seventies, richly decorated and patterned folklorica fashions inspired a renewed interest in hats, especially exotic shapes and ornamentation. Women who dressed for success opted for tailored fedoras to complement their menswear coats and blazers in daytime, and small retro styles with sophisticated touches like veiling and Edwardian cabochons (jeweled pins) for evening.

Women's Accessories 1970–1979

Simplification and functionality were the guides for accessorizing in the early 1970s. (Figure 10.19.) The predominance of the perfectly coordinated separates collections, often with matching self belts, detachable collar bows, scarves, or dickies, removed the uncertainty of choosing accessories. Neutral woven fabric, knit, or leather totes went with almost

FIGURE 10.19. Accessory options of the 1970s included art deco styling, patriotic Bicentennial motifs, designer logos, and a host of thematic looks from European peasant to American Western. Left, retro art deco scarf, belt, jewelry, and beaded handbag by Walborg, 1974; right, scarf, handbag, jewelry, and sunglasses in Bicentennial red, white, and blue by Lanvin, 1976.

everything, regardless of season. Art deco pieces worked well with contemporary fashions as well as revivals.

With the layered looks of the second half of the seventies, accessories once again became important fashion details that required thought and planning. Retro fashions, Western wear, and peasant looks were also more purist than in the sixties with accessories as important accents to the thematic looks. In addition, dressing for a corporate career in the late seventies involved a lengthy checklist of right and wrong wardrobe choices for business attire. Bicentennial red, white, and blue accessories were everywhere during middecade. Designer logos were licensed for virtually every category of accessory manufacturing.

Men's Fashions 1970–1979

In the early 1970s, Hollywood exerted a powerful influence on men's suit designs. Movies like *Cabaret* (1972), *The Sting* (1973), and especially *The Great Gatsby* (1974) featured period suits with the English drape cut silhouettes of the 1930s. Ralph Lauren achieved international fame with his menswear costumes for *Gatsby*, styles which were universally adopted by tailors and ready-to-wear makers. In the spring of 1974, *GQ* devoted an entire edition to "the movie that's influencing what you wear." Unlike the meticulously tailored drape cut of the thirties, though,

FIGURE 10.20. The classic look of the English drape suit was revived in the early 1970s. Adaptations were shaped with padding and inner lining construction rather than meticulously cut as in the original 1930s styles. Gatsby style suit from St. Laurie, 1976.

Gatsby style jackets were shaped with rigid padding and inner lining construction to achieve the illusion of an ideally proportioned, athletic male. (Figure 10.20.) Lapels were huge, spreading across most of the expanse between the V-front opening and the shoulder seam. The vest was back. Colors were rich—not in vibrant peacock flamboyance but in the taste of F. Scott Fitzgerald's era: caramel, cream, slate blue, and even the softest peach or dusty rose.

Concomitant with the stiffly tailored Gatsby look in the early seventies was the persistent demand in the menswear market for greater ease and comfort in suiting. The durable, easy-care synthetic knits that had continued to gain popularity throughout the sixties became integral to suit and sport jacket designs of the 1970s. The polyester double-knit or stretch denim **leisure suit** was a casual alternative to the sport jacket or blazer. (Figure 10.21.) The shirt-like jackets with big patch pockets and wide collars were unconstructed—without the fixed lining and padding of tailored suit jackets. Some were cropped bolero style, but most

FIGURE 10.21. The leisure suit was a popular alternative to tailored sport jackets in the 1970s. Polyester double knit leisure suit from Jockey Sportswear, 1973.

FIGURE 10.22. Variations of the leisure suit included the vest suit for young men and styles with mixed historical details preferred by African-Americans. Tweed vest suit with matching peacoat by Jon Jolcin, 1970.

GIORGIO ARMANI

FIGURE 10.23. In the late 1970s, Giorgio Armani led the way in redefining the men's suit silhouette by eliminating padding and shifting proportions for a more fluid, sensual fit. Giorgio Armani ad, 1979.

were worn like an untucked shirt, often with the front unfastened. Flared cuff trousers were of the same material as the jacket with sharp, permanently pressed creases and, often, detailing that matched the tops such as contrast top stitching or buttoned pocket flaps.

Variations of the leisure suit included the **vest suit**, featuring a variety of long, sleeveless tunic-like jackets, usually belted. (Figure 10.22.) The vest suit was worn with a colorful print or vibrant hued shirt with a wide pointed collar either open throated or with a broad necktie. Ethnic varieties of the leisure suit were some of the most imaginative styles of the decade. Inspired by so-called "blaxploitation" movies like *Shaft* (1971) and *Superfly* (1972), African-American men expressed their urban modernity in smoothly fitted polyester suits that blended vivid colors and textile patterns with a mixed styling of historic details such as Napoleonic collars, pagoda shoulderlines, pelerines, frock coat lengths, and gathered Renaissance sleeves.

At the end of the 1970s, the idiom of the classic male suit underwent a profound reworking that set the path for men's suit and sport jacket design ever since. The new look came not from London, Paris, or New York, but from Italy, led by the innovative Giorgio Armani. With his first menswear collection in 1975, Armani revolutionized men's suit silhouettes. Through several iterations in subsequent years, Armani deconstructed the rigidly shaped Gatsby jackets

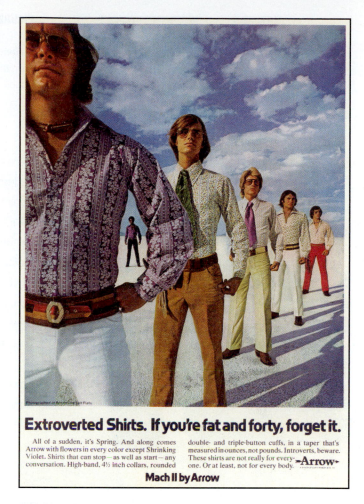

FIGURE 10.24. New variations of colorful Op art and art deco prints for men's shirts were enhanced by the silky, shimmering surfaces of synthetic fabrics such as nylon, acetate, and polyester. Op art nylon shirt from Mr. Henry, 1975.

FIGURE 10.25. For the extroverted peacock male of the early 1970s, shirts were constructed with tapered side seams and darted backs to fit snugly. "If you're fat and forty, forget it," advised this 1971 Arrow ad.

by removing padding and shifting proportions. Lapels were elongated and buttons pushed low for a longer, leaner look. Jackets were cut with a plenitude of drapery that fell fluidly from natural shoulders and glided with the wearer as he moved. (Figure 10.23.) The Armani suit redefined masculinity with a nonchalance and sensuality that culminated in the styles he created for Richard Gere in *American Gigolo* (1980).

Men's evening wear of the early seventies expanded on the peacock flamboyance of the previous decade. In addition to vibrantly colored brocades and other textured fabrics, bold plaids became a trend. By the middecade, though, the Gatsby look inspired a return of the traditional black mohair dinner jacket of the 1920s and 1930s, now updated with a broad expanse of peaked satin lapels spreading across to the shoulder seams.

The significance of men's sportswear designs in the 1970s was in the fabrics. Catalogs and retailers were well stocked with knits and wovens in acrylic, polyester, nylon, Orlon, Ban-Lon, Kodel, Dacron, and numerous synthetic blends. Texture was all important. All categories of sportswear were manufactured in assorted jacquards, crochets, bouclés, and other textured surfaces. In the first half of the decade, colorful Op art patterns and art deco graphics

FIGURE 10.26. The seventies versions of the Oxford bags were produced in a wide assortment of colors and textile patterns. Baggies fit smoothly about the hips and widened from the thighs to the deep turned-up cuffs. Polyester double knit baggies by Williamson-Dickie, 1973.

were reproduced in light, silky nylon, acetate, and polyester fabrics for shirts. (Figure 10.24.) The popularity of glitter rock music inspired rhinestone studded denim jackets, jeans, and T-shirts. Reptile skin prints were applied to men's tops, pants, and accessories. New shirt styling included wide pointed collars and stretch materials that molded to the youthful, slim torso. Shirts made with an "athletic" cut indicated side seams and sometimes back darts tapered to fit snugly at the waist. "If you're fat and forty, forget it," advised an ad in 1971. (Figure 10.25.) In addition, shirts were often worn open several buttons down the front to display a hairy chest—the epitome of machismo sexuality in the seventies—usually accented with chains and pendant necklaces.

Men's hiphugger pants in the early seventies were also cut to fit with a trim smoothness that emphasized the young physique. Despite the tight fit of trousers around the hips and thighs, pant legs became more varied. In addition to the usual straight leg cut, the bell bottoms were expanded into a wide assortment of dimensions, especially when high platform shoes became a trend. Most flared pants measured about twenty inches in circumference at the hem. At the extreme end were twenty-eight-inch elephant bells that were worn completely covering the shoes and dragging the ground. As a contrast to the slim fit of hiphuggers, retro high-rise **baggies** were introduced in 1972. The fit, too, was still smooth about the hips but

FIGURE 10.27. Knitwear of the 1970s continued to be dominated by Italian makers, which produced innovative new shapes and knit patterns for sweaters and accessories. Layered sweater styles by Valentino, 1976.

widened higher on the thigh and dropped to a wide, cuffed hem about twenty-two inches around. (Figure 10.26.) By middecade pleats reappeared with the new high-waist styles.

At the end of the 1970s, menswear lost much of its peacock flair. Natural fibers and earthtones replaced the vibrant hued nylon skins of early shirt styles. Shirt collars narrowed. A revival of the banded-collar shirt from pre-1920s styles (without the detachable spread collar) became a popular look for casual dress in 1977.

Natural fiber knits reclaimed fashion status in the late 1970s. Front-button sweater vests worn with sport jackets became favorite alternatives to the tailored three-piece business suit. Richly textured raw silk and Shetland cardigans and twinsets replaced the leisure suit for casual elegance. The layered look of women's fashions in the late seventies was adapted to menswear with knitwear. (Figure 10.27.)

At the end of the seventies, pants were cut fuller with a high waistband. The hiphugger and bell bottoms vanished. Pleats were on almost every type of pants from casual gabardine khakis to suit trousers.

Men's Sports Attire and Outerwear 1970–1979

Throughout the seventies, men became as interested in fitness as women. Men's workout clothes, though, were largely limited to nylon jogging shorts, T-shirts, fleece warm-up suits, and sweatshirts. In the second half of the decade, color palettes became more intense and varied with neon and bright primary hues added to the usual assortment of muted shades and the ubiquitous gray.

On the golf course, polyester double knit trousers, shorts, and shirts were comfortable alternatives to cotton and nylon styles. Preferred colors and textile patterns remained vivid and bold for high visibility to other players ready to tee off at a distance. Knit knickers reappeared for a few years in the early seventies, only trimmed down to a plus-twos fullness rather than the archaic plus-fours bagginess.

Tennis wear continued to be produced with a wide assortment of colors, ranging from vibrant to pastel. (Figure 10.28.) Thigh-high shorts were constructed with front slash pockets with contrasting terrycloth facings. Knit polo shirts and T-tops were striped or color blocked to coordinate with solid colors of shorts. Fabric visors and knit wrist bands were likewise dyed to match.

For winter sports, skisuits and hooded jumpsuits of colorful nylon shells were insulated with polyester fiberfill or down. Bib snow pants resembling overalls were cut with a deep U-front

FIGURE 10.28. By the 1970s, bold primary colors and strong stripes and plaids replaced conventional tennis whites at even the most traditional clubs and leagues. Gant sportswear, 1973.

Knee-breaker trench coat in melton cloth from F.B.S., 1973.

Burberry trench coat, 1974.

FIGURE 10.29. Standardized coat hemlines remained at the knee-breaker length through the end of the seventies when lengths dropped below the knees.

Wool velour overcoat from St. Laurie, 1978.

and narrow shoulder straps for greater freedom of upper torso movement. The slim knicker styles that had been revived for the golf fairways were also seen at ski resorts.

During the early seventies, most coat lengths remained at just above the knee, but then dropped to mid-calf lengths in the second half of the decade. (Figure 10.29.) The midi and maxi great-coat styles of the late sixties were still popular boutique fashions but not mass market trends. Trench coat styles, in both all-weather fabrics, heavy worsteds, and even leather were the most ubiquitous of the decade. Suburbans, peacoats, and similar fingertip-length coats looked the same as the fifties' versions, only now made in durable synthetic materials. Split cowhide bomber's jackets and short ranch jackets were accented with wide collars and linings of warm acrylic pile that replicated fur or shearling.

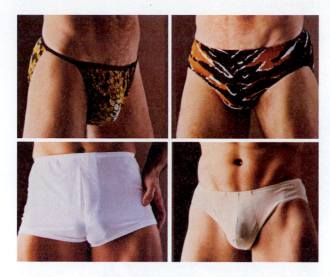

FIGURE 10.30. Underwear of the 1970s ranged from silk boxers to fashion and novelty styles in a variety of colors and wild prints. Underwear by Adam International, 1978.

FIGURE 10.31. The line between men's swimwear and fashion underwear became blurred in the 1970s. The same colorful prints and abbreviated cuts of underwear were applied to swimwear. Left, swimshort from Barak, 1977; right, nylon bikini and brief from Ah Men, 1978.

Men's Underwear and Swimwear 1970–1979

In the 1970s, the demarcations between the silhouettes, colors, and prints of fashion underwear and swimwear were confusingly blurred. In many cases, the only distinction was that underwear was made of more lightweight or sheer fabrics such as nylon tricot. (Figure 10.30.) In addition, the briefest forms of underwear that had developed in the 1960s became more mainstream in the 1970s as men discovered that women enjoyed the sexual objectification of the young male physique. (*Playgirl* magazine made its debut in 1973 and completely sold out its first run of 600,000 copies.) Even mass retailers like Sears and Penney's included numerous varieties of fashion and novelty underwear in their annual wish book catalogs. During the disco era at the end of the decade, both underwear and swimwear were reduced to their barest essence with the microbikini and thong styles. Novelty underwear, a favorite Valentine's Day gift to men, featured screen prints of sexually suggestive graphics or messages such as allover prints of lipstick kisses or licensed cartoon characters. For the man who wanted to do the Hustle or the Bump at the disco without his shirt tail coming loose, the **turtlesuit** was a one-piece, fitted body shirt with a snap closure pouch for the crotch—an adaptation of swim shirts from the 1920s.

The same colorful prints and abbreviated cuts of underwear were applied to swimwear. (Figure 10.31.) Versions of the rio, or string bikini, and the thong for men were adapted from women's styles in the mid-1970s. As a result of the fitness craze of the era, many men opted for the briefer, revealing forms of swimwear to exhibit the results of hours in the gym and on the racquetball court. Tropical print surfer trunks remained a favorite of teen boys.

FIGURE 10.32. New forms of sleepwear for men such as jumpsuits, kaftans, and pajama suits were designed to serve also as loungewear. Embroidered kaftan by Rudolph Moshammer, 1971.

FIGURE 10.33. Ties of the early seventies expanded to 4½ inches wide. The butterfly bow tie was revived as an influence of movies like *Bonnie and Clyde* in the sixties and *The Great Gatsby* in the seventies. Wide necktie, ascot, and butterfly bow tie from Butterick Patterns, 1973.

Men's Sleepwear and Accessories 1970–1979

The line between sleepwear and loungewear became less distinct in the 1970s. Exotic kimonos and kaftans were not only sleepwear but also replaced the lounge robe for intimate evening social gatherings. (Figure 10.32.) Pajama suits were made with shirt tops, sometimes belted, in a variety of prints with contrasting solid bottoms, and jumpsuits often featured elements of day clothing such as hiphugger styling and bell bottoms. Traditional pajamas and sleepshirts were made of "no-iron" fabrics like polyester/cotton blends and nylon tricot. Many men preferred to simply sleep in their favorite school gym shorts or the new forms of fashion underwear.

FIGURE 10.34. The extremes of men's footwear in the 1970s included high heel platforms and "negative heel" Earth Shoes. For most men, though, basic styles of oxfords or loafers were the most common. Left, two-tone platform shoes from Italia, 1972; right, Earth shoes, 1974.

Hats for men enjoyed a resurgence with the popularity of Gatsby revival looks. The snap fedora with a wide brim and wide hatband complemented the wide jacket lapels, big shirt collars, and broad ties.

At the beginning of the seventies, ties were about 3½ inches wide but within a couple of years had expanded to 4½ inches wide. (Figure 10.33.) With the fashion revival influences of movies like *The Great Gatsby,* butterfly patterned bow ties were rediscovered for day wear. Instead of silk, textured synthetics and polyester double knits were the new fashion for neckwear. At the end of the decade, a renewed interest in natural fibers brought back silk foulards and even wool knit ties in narrower widths of 3½ inches.

Men's footwear of the seventies reached extremes not seen since the eighteenth century. High-heeled platform shoes and thick-soled wedges came in a variety of heights and thicknesses. (Figure 10.34.) A famous scene at the beginning of *Saturday Night Fever* featured a close-up of the high-heeled platforms worn by John Travolta as he strutted down the street to the music of the Bee Gees. At the opposite end of the spectrum were **Earth Shoes**, or "negative heel" shoes, which were constructed with molded soles shaped with a lowered heel and elevated toe that, according to the ads, allowed the wearer to "walk in a gentle rolling motion." For most men, though, classic low-heeled oxfords and loafers were preferred, especially designs from high-end branded makers like Gucci.

Jewelry for men continued to break the boundaries of gender traditions in the 1970s. Necklaces and bracelets came in matching sets that included gemstones, pendants, and combinations of metals like gold with silver or chrome with brass. (Figure 10.35.) Gold chain necklaces were important for sexual display as men opened their shirt fronts a few buttons to reveal hairy chests. The punks further broke masculine traditions by piercing their ears and wearing studs, hoops, and dangling chain earrings.

With the exception of long hair on men in the sixties, few cultural and fashion changes were as alarming to conventional men (and conventional women) as the man bag. Shoulder bag styles that first emerged in Europe in 1970 looked more like women's carry-on luggage or utility camera bags. Gradually, though, the practicality of the man bag became

FIGURE 10.35. Men's jewelry of the 1970s ran the gamut from ordinary matched necklace and bracelet sets to symbolic paraphernalia such as a curvilinear bull's horn, a razor blade for cutting cocaine, and a bondage rope noose.

Pantene. Because great looking
hair doesn't just happen.

What does "just happen" to hair is usually more like this...
It looks like it just spent a month on safari.
It feels like it just came off a ski slope.
And it never does just exactly what you want it to.
Unless of course you use Pantene.
Pantene is full of imported Swiss conditioners.
Pantene cleans, conditions and controls your hair.
Just a quick shampoo in the shower, a little conditioner,
a touch of the spray, and you'll stop wishing you could
do something about your hair. You just did it.
Pantene. The shampoo, the conditioner, the spray.
Because great hair takes a little time, a little effort,
and a little Pantene.

PANTENE® FOR MEN.

FIGURE 10.36. By the 1970s, traditional hair grooming tonics and oils had been replaced by haircare regimens that included specialized shampoos, conditioners, hair dryers, and hairspray. Manicured mustaches returned, and hairy chests were displayed with open shirt fronts often accentuated by gold chain necklaces.

FIGURE 10.37. The snap-front all-in-one suit continued to be the most common infants' wear throughout the seventies. Short-sleeve poly/cotton coverall, 1977.

evident in the late 1970s. Pants pockets had been an effective solution for carrying a wallet, keys, comb, and excess change for decades, but the accoutrement of the modern male was expanding far beyond those few essentials. Address books, organizers, pocket calculators, pen sets, business card cases, manicure implements, hair brushes or picks, breath mints, and business receipts could all be effectively stored in a sectionalized shoulder bag. American men only began to carry shoulder bags and envelopes in the late 1970s when styles were made more to resemble business cases.

Men's Grooming and Hairstyles 1970–1979

The variety of hair lengths that had developed in the late sixties continued throughout the 1970s. Although long hair had been the trend for the youthquake generation, by the seventies, men of all ages grew their hair long. Men's haircare products now included regimens of specialized shampoos, conditioners, and hairspray. (Figure 10.36.)

The bushy mustaches that had been an expression of rebellion in the sixties became a well-manicured symbol of machismo sexuality in the 1970s. Long sideburns to the jawline remained common, but disappeared by the end of the decade.

Flower power pant suit, 1970.

Bicentennial motifs, 1976.

Licensed screen-printed sweatshirts, 1977.

FIGURE 10.38. Girls' clothing of the seventies reflected the fashion trends of adult styles, including pantsuits, longer skirt hemlines, and denim dressing.

Denim skirts and jeans, 1978.

Children's Clothing 1970–1979

In the seventies, U.S. consumer advocacy groups succeeded in getting federal regulations enacted that prohibited children's wear from being treated with flame-retardant chemicals. Mass merchandising retailers like Sears and J. C. Penney placed disclaimers on garment tags and within the children's wear sections of their catalogs to assure consumers that they were compliant with these regulations.

The all-in-one terry knit suit with snap-front closure remained the most common form of infants' wear. (Figure 10.37.) Other forms of playwear and sleepwear included long-sleeve footed sleepers in pastel polyester or nylon knits. Sacque sets featured hip-length gowns with full, gathered necklines and matching snap-on panties lined with vinyl.

Girls' clothing of the seventies followed the trends of adult styles. As women increasingly adopted the pantsuit for business attire in the early 1970s, girls' versions became more acceptable for school. (Figure 10.38.) Denim, too, became a fashion look, including jeans with designer logos emblazoned on patch pockets just like teen sister's disco jeans. In the second

Polyester double knit leisure suits, 1975.

Poly/cotton blazers, vests, and slacks from J.C. Penney, 1978.

FIGURE 10.39. Boys' wear makers produced scaled down versions of men's styles, including leisure suits, belted vest suits, and padded three-piece Gatsby suits.

Belted vest suits, 1972.

half of the decade, dress hemlines dropped and the layered look was adapted to girls' wear. Folklorica motifs and prints were applied to all categories of girls' apparel. Among the most popular licensed images for apparel were Holly Hobbie and cartoon characters by Warner Brothers and Disney.

Boys' wear also continued to be modeled on the trends of adult fashions. Belted vest suits of the early seventies were worn with bell bottom pants and wide-collar print shirts. (Figure 10.39.) The shaped Gatsby suit style with its padded shoulders and spread lapels was scaled to boys' sizes in polyester blend textiles. Leisure suits in aqua, spring green, and yellow polyester double knits replicated men's versions. Full-color photo print T-shirts were screen-printed with gender-typical sports, car, and super hero images. Stretch denim was introduced in the mid-seventies. The shoulder yokes of Western-style shirts were redesigned with wallpaper print florals and machine-made embroidery. Favorites with boys of all ages were the assorted sports jerseys of nylon mesh and poly/cotton tees with licensed team insignias and giant player numerals.

Review

In the early 1970s, the emphasis in women's fashion was on pants. As more women entered the corporate workplace, pantsuits became acceptable business attire. Varieties of pantsuits in opulent fabrics also were popular for evening wear. Sophisticated styles of city trousers included culottes, gauchos, jodhpurs, and knickers. For casual wear, hiphuggers, baggies, and elephant bells were mass marketed. Urban short shorts, called hot pants, were a brief trend.

In the second half of the seventies, all hemlines dropped below the knee, some almost to the ankles. The miniskirt vanished. Career women dressed for success in layered separates and tailored menswear suits. For nighttime play at the discos, skintight jeans, tube tops, halter dresses, and any form of body-conscious fashions that glittered and shined under the dance floor strobe lights were requisites.

For accessories of the late seventies, natural materials were prevalent such as carved wood, cork, and raw leather for shoes; ceramics, glass, and wood for jewelry; and woven or braided fibers for totes, bags, and belts. Hats and gloves ceased to be requirements for correct day dressing.

In the early 1970s, a duality of men's suiting emerged. The demand for comfort led to the leisure suit with its unconstructed shirt-like jacket and sharply creased trousers of polyester double knits. Young men opted for belted vest suits with vividly colored shirts. Business attire, though, revived the look of the English drape cut of the Great Gatsby era, except that seventies' adaptations were rigidly constructed with padding and stiff linings. Casual clothes were refreshed with boldly colored Op art patterns and art deco motifs in shiny nylon and polyester blends. Trousers came in a wider assortment of styles, ranging from tight hiphugger elephant bells at the beginning of the decade to high-rise cuffed baggies in the late seventies.

In the second half of the decade, Italian suit styles dominated menswear. Padding was removed and proportions were shifted for a more fluid, sensual fit. The colorful peacock flair subsided in favor of more subdued earthtone palettes and natural fibers.

Children's clothing reflected the trends of adult styles. Girls wore miniskirts and polyester pantsuits in the beginning of the seventies, and layered looks with longer hemlines in the second half. Boys donned scaled down versions of menswear, including leisure suits, belted vest suits, and shaped Gatsby suits.

review questions

1. Which social changes in the early 1970s led to a fashion emphasis on pant styles for women? Identify and describe three varieties of women's pantsuits popular in the early seventies.

2. How did mainstream women's fashions change in the second half of the 1970s?

3. What book influenced fashions for the career woman of the late seventies and how?

4. Compare and contrast the Gatsby men's suit of the early 1970s with the Italian deconstructed styles at the end of the decade.

5. Which key trends in adult fashions of the seventies were replicated in children's wear?

research and portfolio projects

Research

1. Write a research paper on how the revitalization of the women's movement in the 1970s impacted the traditional ideals of beauty and fashion. Examine how the ready-to-wear industry focused on fashions for the career woman.

Portfolio

1. Compile a swatch book of textiles influenced by Pop, Op, and Kinetic art from the seventies. Make color photocopies or digital scans for the swatches from bound periodicals or books. Write a description of each textile design, identifying the art style of influence and its characteristics.

dress terms

baggies: men's and women's high-waisted trousers with wide legs

dressing-gown coat: women's wrap coats of the 1970s

duvet coat: women's oversized quilted jacket or coat of the late seventies

Earth Shoes: "negative heel" styles of low shoes made with molded soles shaped with lowered heels and elevated toes

elephant bells: women's and men's pants of the early 1970s that fitted snugly about the hips and thighs but flared into enormous bell shapes over the feet

folklorica: women's fashions and accessories of the late 1970s that featured peasant or folk art motifs and decorative embellishments

Gatsby suit: men's suit styles of the mid-1970s with jackets that were padded and shaped in the style of the English drape cut of the 1930s

gauchos: midi-length versions of culottes

glam or **glitter rock styles:** androgynous looks of the early 1970s that included sequined or rhinestone-studded tops and pants, platform shoes, and feathery haircuts for both women and men

hot pants: city short shorts of the early 1970s often made of upscale materials

Kevlar: aramid fiber used in protective clothing as "soft body armor"

kimono trousers: women's baggy, Japanese inspired trousers resembling harem pants

leisure suit: casual menswear of the early 1970s that featured shirt-like jackets with wide collars and matching trousers, usually of polyester double knits or stretch denim

punk look: the self-styled look of disaffected youths of the mid-seventies, such as clothes and accessories slashed and pinned together or embellished with images and found objects that could create shock value

qi pao dress: an Asian sheath usually with a mandarin collar and slit skirt

rio: women's string bikini introduced on the beaches of South America in the early 1970s

turtlesuit: men's one-piece fitted body shirt and underwear with a snap closure crotch

vest suit: a women's or men's long, sleeveless top with matching trousers or skirt popular in the early 1970s

11 A New Gilded Age 1980–1989

First Space Shuttle flight 1981	**First artificial heart transplant 1982**	**Apple introduced the Macintosh computer 1984**	**Gorbachev became Soviet premier 1985**	**Statue of Liberty Centennial 1986**	**U.S.–Soviet INF Treaty to reduce nuclear arsenals 1987**	**Poland, Bulgaria, Hungary, East Germany, Czechoslovakia, Romania ousted Communist rule 1989**
AIDS virus identified 1981	**Michael Jackson's *Thriller* 1983**			**U.S. stock market crash 1986**		
Iran-Iraq War 1980–1988	**Debut of MTV 1981**	**Madonna's *Like a Virgin* 1984**				

The End of the Cold War

In the four decades following the end of World War II, global politics were dominated by the Cold War—an ideological conflict between capitalist nations led by the United States versus the Soviet Union with its communist allies. During this period, the efforts of the United States to oppose the expansion of communism by military action had led to the stalemate of the Korean War and the quagmire of the Vietnam War. By the 1970s, such costs had compelled President Nixon to seek friendlier relations with the Soviets—a relaxing of tensions called *detente.*

However, when Ronald Reagan took office as U.S. president in 1981, the Cold War was reignited by the "Reagan Doctrine" of aggressively containing communism worldwide. His administration initiated a massive arms race with the Soviets, including a plan for a space-based, computer controlled program referred to as "Star Wars" that was not only impossible to build but threatened to destabilize the fragile mutual deterrence.

When reformer Mikhail Gorbachev became Soviet premier in 1985, he initiated two key policies: *glasnost,* the Russian word for openness, and *perestroika,* meaning economic restructuring. Among the first steps toward glasnost was a series of arms summits with Reagan. Much to the chagrin of the president's hawkish administration and Soviet hard-line bureaucrats, Reagan and Gorbachev signed the 1987 INF (Intermediate Nuclear Forces) Treaty to reduce missile arsenals.

Gorbachev's many internal reforms had a more far-reaching impact than even he could have foreseen. When he publicly denounced the Stalin regime, Soviet citizens dared to experience the freedom to dissent. Most important of all, though, in 1989, when Gorbachev announced that the Soviet Union would no longer prop up the communist leaderships of the east European satellite states, the power structures within those countries collapsed. In that one year, communist governments were ousted in Poland, Bulgaria, Hungary, East Germany, Czechoslovakia, and Romania. Perhaps the most poignant symbol of the "Year of Miracles" was the toppling of the Berlin wall.

In the Middle East, turmoil continued as Iraq and Iran went to war in 1980 over ownership of adjoining oil-rich territories. In 1982, Israel invaded Lebanon against the Palestine Liberation Organization (PLO). As retaliation for U.S. support of Israel, Islamic terrorists bombed the American embassy and Marine headquarters in Beirut, killing more than 300. Because of the instability of the region, OPEC struggled to maintain oil prices, which negatively affected global economies of the 1980s.

In Asia, China marked the thirty-fifth anniversary of its communist regime in 1984 by announcing a move toward capitalism in which some state-owned enterprises were permitted to set prices according to supply and demand in the market. Japan became a world economic power through aggressive competition in manufacturing, particularly autos and electronics.

In the United States, the 1980s was the Reagan era. The American people wanted to believe the Reagan campaign slogans of a new "morning in America"—promises of a renewed prosperity, following the failed economic policies of the Ford and Carter administrations, a re-establishment of U.S. preeminence in the world arena after the hostage stand-off in Iran, and a revitalization of the presidency after the scandals of Nixon and Ford (who was tainted by his pardon of Nixon).

Reagan had become the standard bearer for the Republican base of conservatives in the 1960s and 1970s. He projected a personable style and a confidence in the nation's destiny that was reassuring to many Americans. He was highly effective in shaping broad themes for his administration and keeping staffers focused on them. Reagan's view of the economy was grounded in a laissez-faire "supply-side" theory in which deregulation coupled with tax cuts for the wealthy would increase investment in productive enterprises, thus creating new jobs and economic growth. Despite more than tripling the national debt, this plan, often labeled Reaganomics, gradually led to an economic recovery by middecade. But the "trickle-down" effect to middle and lower income families had not been realized. At the end of Reagan's second term, the middle class had shrunk and one in five Americans was living in poverty, a twenty-four percent increase during Reagan's eight years in office.

Also under Reagan's aegis, a New Right came of age in the 1980s. With open support by the administration, a conservative coalition of unlikely allies flourished: libertarians who wanted to dismantle government and slash taxes; social paleoconservatives who pushed an agenda of antiabortion, anti-ERA, antiwelfare, antigay, anti-immigration, and antiaffirmative action issues; and militant Christian groups who demanded school prayer, book bans, and an end to sex education. On the national level, the women's Equal Rights Amendment (ERA) was defeated in the state legislatures; on the state and local level, countless legislative acts chipped away at access to abortion, affirmative-action policies, and equal protection regulations.

One of the most notable societal products of the decade was the yuppie (young urban professional) whose self-absorption and obsession with financial success became the new work ethic. "Greed is good," evangelized the protagonist in the 1987 movie *Wall Street.* The yuppies drove themselves hard to make money quickly and to buy the most expensive material goods to reflect their achievements. Madonna's song *Material Girl* became an anthem of the era.

In technology, the IBM personal computer made its debut in 1981, and three years later came the revolutionary graphical interface of Apple. Sophisticated video games, both for home and the mall arcade, became the entertainment of choice for all new-agers.

Also in 1981, a pernicious virus was identified as the cause of the Acquired Immunodeficiency Syndrome, or AIDS—a pandemic disease for which no cure could be found. The epidemic spread through unprotected sexual contact, use of infected needles by drug addicts, contaminated blood transfusion, or from mother to unborn child. Among the top fashion designers who died of AIDS were Halston, Perry Ellis, and Willi Smith.

The Business of Fashion

Since the 1970s, fashion has become increasingly pluralistic—many widely diverse styles, silhouettes, and branded labels in each wardrobe. Personal style became a catch phrase used incessantly by fashion marketers, meaning an individual's look of the moment to suit one's mood or a total lifestyle look. Ready-to-wear makers focused on producing clothing for niche consumer groups whose preferences ranged from safe "classics" of style represented by a continuum of standardized garments like polo shirts, cableknit sweaters, chinos, and trench coats to the antifashion tribalist looks of punks, goths, and other youth groups. In the modern industrialized societies of today, writes Anne Hollander, "fashion has claimed its place in a new mutable optical world where no one view of anything is acknowledged to be the true one. . . . Everyone is essentially talking to himself, like a poet. . . . Designers merely provide the vocabulary." From this pluralism of postmodern fashion developed specialized marketing strategies and economies for the designer, manufacturer, and retailer.

As noted in the previous chapter, couture did not vanish in the wake of the social revolution of the 1960s despite dire predictions by the fashion pundits. The adaptation of ready-to-wear programs (prêt-a-porter) by the top names in couture ensured economic stability for the house while allowing the seasonal couture collections to demonstrate the designer's creativity and innovation. Logo branding became a key component in the marketing strategy of major design labels. With this shift to a pluralism of fashion trends and away from the supremacy of haute couture as style-setter, two divergent approaches developed for designing clothes. For classicists like Giorgio Armani and Ralph Lauren, the design objective was a perfection of existing styles, not unlike the preoccupation of the dandies of the nineteenth century. The other perspective was inventive and capricious, such as the avant-garde designs of Vivienne Westwood, Jean Paul Gaultier, and Thierry Mugler. "What I am trying to say with extravagant clothes is that everything is possible," asserted Mugler. "I create clothes women will wear in imaginary adventures." Some exceptional designers such as Gianni Versace succeeded in

Haute Couture in the New Gilded Age of the Eighties

When Cristobal Balenciaga retired in 1968, many in the fashion world proclaimed that true haute couture was dead. Throughout the sixties and into the seventies, a global cultural shift had significantly impacted the clothing industry. No longer did the dictates of Paris set the direction for fashion around the world.

In her book, *The End of Fashion,* Teri Agins suggests several reasons for this dramatic change. First, style trends emerged from the streets up rather than trickling down from the couturiers. The looks of urban teens, rock and roll icons, and counterculture movements provided new vitality and inspiration for fashion design.

Second, people stopped dressing up. Men and women abandoned hats, gloves, and other accoutrement of dress that had, for decades, defined fashion. Casual attire continued to gain ground as the dominant wardrobe options. Comfortable and inexpensive ready-to-wear was made in such a wide variety that people migrated toward clothing that reflected their lifestyle rather than anything they saw on the runways of the design houses or in the fashion press. One's "Sunday best" ensemble differed little from that of a work day.

Finally, women "let go of fashion." As women scaled the corporate ladders, many of them followed Molloy's *Dress for Success* advice and adopted unimaginative business uniforms such as menswear pantsuits and standardized blazers and skirts.

With the affluence of the New Gilded Age of the eighties, though, couture enjoyed a resurgence as the nouveau riche, as well as those of old money, indulged in an exhibitionism of their wealth. (Figure 11.1.) The client lists of the couturiers expanded once again. In 1987, Christian Lacroix opened a new couture salon. Fresh blood was sought by staid operations such as the house of Chanel, which signed Karl Lagerfeld as head designer in 1983.

At the end of the New Gilded Age, a stock market crash followed by a severe downturn in the global economy once again impacted couture. Design houses reoriented themselves along two avenues. Foremost was to maintain the profitable businesses of ready-to-wear and licensed products like accessories, perfume, and home decor. Secondary was couture, which increasingly became a laboratory for testing innovative fashions. Linked with drama of the couture fashion collections was public relations and

the notoriety—good or bad—which, in turn, added value to branded logo products and ready-to-wear lines.

FIGURE 11.1. The 1980s was a New Gilded Age in which the rich flaunted their wealth and social status. As a result, couture enjoyed a resurgence with demands for opulent fashions that reflected the exhibitionism of the new robber barons. Beaded gown and opera jacket by Bob Mackie, 1984.

creating both—fantasy fashion that extended a wider name recognition for the label and real-world styles that achieved mass appeal.

Merchandising fashion in the 1980s primarily expanded upon marketing tactics first developed in the early twentieth century. Licensed products peripheral to the designer's apparel collections—particularly accessories, lingerie, and fragrances—added substantial income to the house accounts as well as broadened brand recognition. Designer name awareness percolated through the socioeconomic strata to the middle and working classes through advertising and logo branding. Large retailers expanded upon the 1950s idea of boutique floorsets to attract niche consumers who shopped for certain styles or specific designer labels. Visual merchandising was tailored to those specialty shoppers, even at the cost of a cohesive look of the store as a whole. A proliferation of outlet malls and off-price retailers throughout the 1980s provided opportunities for a mass market to indulge in high style with designer labels at a discount.

Among other marketing strategies of fashion makers and retailers was the sophisticated use of demographics for defining and targeting customers. By the mid-1980s, the baby boomers—75 million individuals born in the United States between 1946 and 1964—all were over the age of thirty. As such a large segment of the population aged, clothing preferences and needs changed considerably. By the end of the eighties more than one-third of Americans were overweight. In response to these changing demographics, clothing makers extended product lines to include large size fashions constructed with contours and details that suited the fuller figure. Similarly, businesses relaxed dress codes and allowed casual Fridays or business casual attire every day. The boomer who grew up wearing jeans and sportswear abandoned tailored dresses and suits for a wider variety of comfortable, casual clothes. Apparel makers modified traditional cuts of garments and produced "relaxed-fit" versions. Stretch fabrics were adapted to jeans, jackets, trousers, and other forms of rigidly constructed garments. At the other end of the spectrum, stretch velvet and similar hybrids of "noble" materials (silk, linen, and wool) inspired designers to create body-conscious fashions for the fitness-obsessed consumer.

Women's Fashions 1980–1989

The 1980s are often viewed as a New Gilded Age, comparable to the original Gilded Age of the 1880s during which robber barons of the Industrial Revolution became immensely wealthy and flaunted their status in opulent displays of grandiose mansions, magnificent collections of art and antique treasures, and lavish dress. As with their nineteenth-century predecessors, the affluent of the 1980s unashamedly indulged in opulence, ostentation, and exhibitionism. Conspicuous consumption became the social norm. "You can have it all!" proclaimed a bold headline in the 1985 ads from Anheuser-Busch. Armani suits, Gucci footwear, Rolex watches, and Lacroix evening gowns were more than status symbols for the yuppie; they were badges of achievement.

Another symbol of personal accomplishment for the yuppies was a svelte and well-toned body. The fitness boom that had begun in the 1970s exploded into a national obsession in the eighties. Billions of dollars were spent on fitness club memberships, exercise guides and videotapes, home physical training equipment, vitamin regimens, and health foods.

As a result of the swelling ranks of the nouveau riche worldwide, couture enjoyed a rebound in sales during the 1980s. European designers delighted in creating luxurious, body-conscious fashions for a daring new clientele willing to proclaim their self-confidence and status through their wardrobes. Azzedine Alaia's "Mermaid" gowns were made of sea-green acetate knit that clung to every contour of the body like a second skin. At Chanel, Karl Lagerfeld "**deconstructed**" the classic boxy tweed jacket suit with new, softer forms of jackets in denim and stretch materials, and with skirt hemlines that grazed the ankles or rose to mid-thigh. Christian Lacroix created the definitive yuppie dress of the 1980s—a strapless pouf dress that cinched the waist and exaggerated the hips in a voluminous meringue of fabric. Vivienne Westwood integrated elements of theatrical costume into her designs to produce collections based on

FIGURE 11.2. For those women of the eighties who aerobicized their bodies into a svelte healthiness, designers created body-conscious fashions. Garments were made of clinging knits, stretch materials, and other fluid fabrics, or were superbly crafted to be form-fitting. Among the more exaggerated body-conscious designs was the red molded plastic bustier by Issey Miyake from 1983.

whimsical themes such as "Pirates," "Witches," and an urban cowgirl look called "Buffalo." Jean Paul Gaultier focused on gender bending and other aspects of sexuality with fashions that included sculptural corsets and similar form-fitting fetishistic components. One of the most exaggerated body-conscious innovations of the 1980s was the red plastic molded bustier by Issey Miyake with its indentation of a navel and protrusions of nipples combining the form-fitting look of spandex with a high-tech sleekness. (Figure 11.2.)

Such avant-garde fashions were fun to look at in magazines but were seldom worn outside of narrow, high-style circles. In the United States, designers were selectively inspired by the innovative directions of the couturiers of Paris and Milan. Most significantly, the an-

FIGURE 11.3. The most prevalent look for career women of the eighties was the powersuit, which emulated men's styles with broad, padded shoulders, a tapered waistline, and narrow hips. Left, plaid suit with bow blouse by Escada, 1984; center, menswear pin striped trouser suit by Ralph Lauren, 1984; right, peplum suit from Christian Dior, 1988.

drogynous looks of many European styles were translated into masculine **powersuits** that became the quintessential emblem of the eighties career woman. Broad, padded shoulders, narrow hips, and a trim waistline emulated the ideal physique of the youthful, vigorous male—the Darwinistic top of the food chain in a corporate hierarchy. The 1980s silhouette of the inverted triangle was applied to both women's business suits and dresses. (Figure 11.3.)

Although the androgyny of European designs was a strong influence on American versions of the powersuit, the look and attitude were actually an evolution of style that had been emerging since the early 1970s when women first donned pantsuits for the office. In 1977, the significance of the powersuit became the gospel for millions of career women who were guided by John Molloy's best-selling *Dress for Success*. "The executive suite is an upper socio-economic business club, and in order to get in you must wear the club uniform," asserted Molloy. In 1988, at the height of the yuppie prestige, Molloy advised that, ten years earlier, he had said that "the suit was the most effective outfit a woman could wear, [and] that statement is still true."

As women of the early 1980s took Molloy's checklist shopping for a power wardrobe, they discovered that the traditional blazers and bolero jackets of the previous thirty years had been dramatically recut and reshaped. Tailored suit jackets were constructed to resemble men's versions with shoulder-broadening pads and stiff sleeve interlinings. Classic details such as notched lapels, straightline pocket flaps, and plain buttons were appropriated from menswear. However, despite Molloy's recommendation that "serious" suits for women should be limited to the same gray, blue, or brown wool as men's styles, many women instead asserted their femininity by wearing suits and jackets made in bold, new color palettes of vivid jeweltones like sapphire, emerald, ruby, and topaz. Variations of bolero jackets in feminine textile patterns and softer, lighter colors became a prevalent component of jacket dresses and business separates.

FIGURE 11.4. A renewed emphasis on the chemise by designers provided busy career women with a versatile day-into-night wardrobe option. Cashmere chemise with matching shawl by Laura Biagiotti, 1987.

Another alternative to the stiffly tailored business suits was the softly draped jackets of Giorgio Armani. "I altered the way jackets were buttoned and radically modified the proportions," Armani told author Marshall Blonsky in 1987. "What used to be considered a defect became the basis for a new shape, a new jacket." This new jacket shape featured a longer lapel, lowered buttons, and shoulders that dropped yet remained broad and powerful. Armani also used softer luxury fabrics like cashmere and silk/wool blends for a more fluid, sensual fit. He expanded the repertoire of neutral colors by warming or cooling grays and beiges with hints of teal, olive, ecru, and sienna, or by creating his own colors, like "greige," a smooth, clear puree of gray and beige. The Armani suit was a superlative symbol of a career woman's self-assurance and elegance.

The top-heavy, angular silhouette of the powersuit was also applied to both daytime and evening dress styles. In fact, it was a particular challenge for designers at this time to create versatile dresses that provided a day-into-night look for the busy career woman who rushed from the office to a cocktail party or dinner engagement. One solution was a renewed emphasis on the chemise. (Figure 11.4.) Although the silhouette had remained a wardrobe staple since the 1950s, the basic dress had been eclipsed by the popularity of coordinates and separates

FIGURE 11.5. The ultrafeminine Romantique looks of the 1980s were a reaction to the severity of the powersuit silhouette. Frilly details such as lacy cuffs, ruffled fichus, puffed sleeves, and similar revivalisms from the Romantic Age appealed to many women who preferred femininity over corporate power images. Ralph Lauren tunic with lace collar and cuffs, 1982.

in the 1970s. In the eighties, though, the chemise not only worked as a dressy, feminine alternative to the powersuit, but its classic elegance was equally suitable for a wide range of social occasions. In addition, the soft draping of the chemise flattered the feminine form and accentuated the results of all those hours at the gym.

Besides the adaptation of the powersuit contours to dresses, one of the most notable changes of the 1980s was the shortening of hemlines. After almost a ten-year absence, hemlines above the knee reappeared in the mid-eighties, even in the workplace. By the end of the decade, short skirts were ubiquitous, including thigh-high miniskirts.

In spite of the warnings by John Molloy that "fashionable clothing" (especially short skirts!) sent a message that a woman was a "lightweight, not the kind of person who can be trusted with important matters," many women sought alternatives to the severity of the masculine powersuit. **Romantique modes** provided one option in the early 1980s. (Figure 11.5.) Designers like Valentino and Yves St. Laurent created whimsical new takes on ruffs, gigot sleeves, fichus, engageantes, and similar Romantic Age revivals. Ralph Lauren added paisley or lace cravats and gold watch fobs to velvet suits. Laura Ashley achieved new prominence with the Victoriana details and motifs of her fashions. In 1981, Britain's Princess Diana's much publicized wedding gown and bridal trousseau inspired millions of women worldwide to add a touch of frou-frou femininity to their wardrobes.

Opulent court fashions, of sorts, also provided women with opportunities of ostentatious display and conceits. In the United States, the First Families of the 1970s—the Nixons, the Fords, the Carters—had conspicuously lacked extravagance and glamour. The Reagans, however, were from Hollywood and understood the significance of image. For eight years, the White House court of the Reagans sparkled brilliantly with the glitterati of A-list society that projected a public image of style, wealth, and privilege.

Popular culture of the eighties provided a second arena of court fashions. Movie stars and the elite of the rock and roll music industry attended well publicized soirees, movie premieres, and awards ceremonies dressed in sumptuous couture fashions and jewels. The line between fantasy and reality was further blurred by prime-time TV soaps such as *Dynasty* and *Dallas* in which beautiful people dressed in an endless variety of luxuriant clothes with perfectly coordinated accessories.

Across the Atlantic, a genuine court of the Old World revived its pre-eminence as a fashion leader when Lady Diana Spencer became the Princess of Wales in 1981. Throughout the decade, the world watched with fascination as the tall, beautiful young princess experimented with hairstyles and sophisticated wardrobes.

The wealth, glamour, and exhibitionism of these various courts of style inspired fashion designers—most especially European couturiers—to extraordinary excesses. The rich look fashions of the 1980s were dazzling expressions of wit and fantasy combined with extravagant historical revivalisms, luscious fabrics, and a carnival of color mixes. Haute couture once again epitomized conspicuous consumption, class distinction, and style leadership. (Figure 11.6.) For the aspiring bourgeoisie, ready-to-wear makers found an eager market of women willing to buy an adaptation of their favorite designer's creation, even if only for limited wear on special occasions like a wedding, reunion, or community charity ball.

Pouf dress by Louis Feraud, 1985.

Crinoline cocktail dress by Oscar de la Renta, 1987.

Evening wear by Yves St. Laurent, 1987.

FIGURE 11.6. During the 1980s, conspicuous consumption was once again socially acceptable after a twenty-year hiatus. Designers responded with dazzling rich look fashions that proclaimed the wearer's affluence and social status.

FIGURE 11.7. The sculpted body look of the mid-1980s featured strong silhouettes of architectural garment construction. Large, sculptural belts and oversized accessories complemented the commanding statements of the look. Left, Maryll Lanvin suit, 1986; center, Albert Nipon suit, 1988; right, peplum dress by Vakko, 1986.

At the forefront of the rich look was Christian Lacroix, whose famous bouffant cocktail dress of 1986, called the **pouf** or **bubble**, epitomized the era's fantasy fashions. Said Lacroix of his work, "The trick is to add precisely the right dose of fantasy without falling into le gag."

The other great proponent of rich look fashions was Karl Lagerfeld, whose iconoclastic modernizing of the House of Chanel in 1982 contributed significantly to reviving haute couture. By many accounts in the fashion press, the most beautiful dress of the mid-1980s was Lagerfeld's extravagant "Atys" evening dress made of red satin and lavishly embellished with gold embroidery.

In the second half of the 1980s, the rich look extended beyond fantasy cocktail poufs and evening gowns to provide sophisticated alternatives to classic, conservative powersuits with sculpted body fashions. (Figure 11.7.) *Vogue* announced in 1985 that "This is a year of newly shaped and fitted clothes, day, night, across the board . . . with a shape that starts right at the shoulder—a shoulder defined by cut or by padding . . . And you'll see a small waist, held or belted; a gentle roundness over the hips." Slim skirts, often short, and soft fabrics such as wool jersey and cashmere knits contoured and flattered the hips and thighs. Large, sculptural belts defined and cinched waistlines. Bold, oversized accessories balanced the strong silhouettes and proclaimed the aplomb of a woman who could confidently wear them.

FIGURE 11.8. In the 1980s the second wave of avant-garde Japanese designers presented diverse collections of loose, oversized clothing with deliberate textile imperfections such as rips and frayed edges. Slashed and tied top with matching skirt by Rei Kawakubo for Comme des Garçons, 1983.

FIGURE 11.9. Knitwear was especially influenced by the Japanese big look. Sweaters, jackets, and other knit garments were shaped with big shoulders, oversized collars and cowls, big sleeves, and bulky mass. Sweater by Vivienne Pay, 1985.

In Paris, the second wave of Japanese designers made a significant impact on established concepts of fashion. Whereas in the 1970s, Issey Miyake initiated his designs from the abstract shape of the traditional kimono, the avant-garde Japanese designers of the 1980s, instead, introduced clothing that owed nothing to conventions of fit and construction. Rei Kawakubo and Yohji Yamamoto presented collections of loose, oversized clothing in which asymmetry and imperfections of rips, slashes, fraying, and irregularities in the fabric weave were key elements. (Figure 11.8.) Black, with its many shades, was the preferred color of Japanese designers, a portent of the monochromatic mania of the late eighties.

The Japanese big look especially influenced EuroAmerican knitwear designers. Sweaters, tunics, jackets, and other knit tops were dramatically shaped with broad shoulders, oversized collars and cowls, big sleeves, and bulky mass. Knit surfaces reinforced the big look with large gauge yarns knitted into deep, three-dimensional patterns of knots, openwork, intarsias, and sculptural trimmings. (Figure 11.9.)

Throughout the decade, several subculture looks were adapted by couturiers and ready-to-wear makers. The antifashion style of punk from the 1970s appealed to many young people

FIGURE 11.10. The antifashion style of seventies punk continued to thrive into the 1980s with new interpretations that inspired couture designers. Street punks, 1982.

of the sybaritic eighties. (Figure 11.10.) Along with the spiked hair, pierced body parts, and tattoos of the disaffected youth were added ripped clothing held together with rows of safety pins or duct tape, tight T-shirts, underwear layered on the outside, and oversized leather or denim jackets. Vivienne Westwood and Malcolm McLaren, the self-proclaimed originators of punk fashion, expanded on the theme with fetishistic leather corsets and shirts with leather strap harnesses. Other designers likewise experimented with subculture attitudes and influences. The biker's leather jacket adorned with chains and other metal hardware inspired sculptural variations by Claude Montana, Katherine Hamnett, Sonia Rykiel, and Gianni Versace. Karl Lagerfeld introduced Chanel combat boots and Fly Girl Lycra bra tops. In fact, the corset as an outer garment became so popular that many ready-to-wear makers produced versions in leather, suede, and assorted fabrics. (Figure 11.11.)

Among the more traditional and enduring subculture themes that surfaced in eighties versions was the look of the American West. Cowboy (and cowgirl) styles and motifs were immensely popular with the French and Italian designers. Fringed leather jackets and cowboy hats, boots, and leather vests repeatedly appeared in collections. (Figure 11.12.) "Down the runways of Europe sashay an assortment of cowboys and Indians as designers engage in a

FIGURE 11.11. In the late 1980s, the revival of the corset appeared not only as a constricting undergarment but also as an outer top similar to versions of the sixteenth century. Cotton corset tops by Dina, 1987.

FIGURE 11.12. The allure of the American West was irresistible for designers of the 1980s. Western style and the prairie look were a constant fashion subtheme throughout the decade. In the late 1980s, fringed pants. skirts, and especially leather jackets were widely popular in both haute couture and ready-to-wear. Western inspired suede jacket by Perry Ellis, 1988.

range war of unabashed camp," reported *Vogue* in 1989. On the U.S. home front, the Western theme was more palatable to ready-to-wear makers than most other subculture looks, and hence was marketed to a broader segment of consumers in various forms year after year. Its recurring popularity peaked when hit movies like *Urban Cowboy* (1980) and TV programs like *Dallas* featured traditional Western costumes and glamorized the interpretations.

One other trend in fashion and youth style that carried over into the eighties from the previous decade was androgyny. Unlike the 1970s glam look of rock and roll stars like David Bowie for men and the menswear replications for women, a truly unisex style became widespread in the 1980s. Unisex clothes defied conventional notions of the cut, color, and fit of gender-based designs. Loose, bulky clothing like sweaters, T-shirts, and sweatshirts, or layered, oversized garments like jackets and big shirts disguised rather than defined the physique of the wearer. Pants, in all their numerous varieties, were as much an ordinary garment for women as for men. Vivid colors and textile patterns were subject to gender bending by designers and ready-to-wear marketers like Benetton, Banana Republic, and the Gap. (Figure 11.13.) Fashion advertising often emphasized the new asexual androgyny by featuring male and female models with similar facial types and hairstyles.

At the end of the 1980s, the high-flying times seemed to come to an abrupt end. Reaganomics led to a stock market crash in 1987, followed by a recession and prolonged high unemployment and then another recession in 1990. The trickle down economic theory had failed. Jobless numbers rose, statistics on crime were alarming, AIDs became an epidemic. During this period of socioeconomic anxiety worldwide, a sense of nostalgia undulated through Western industrialized societies. As we have seen in previous eras of crisis, a nation's people sometimes looked to their past as an imagined simpler, easier time. The fashion industry responded by stepping back from the excesses and modernity of the eighties for revivals of styles from recent decades, particularly those of the New Look years. (Figure 11.14.) Designers on the threshold of the 1990s, noted *Vogue*, "fall for fifties chic, Audrey Hepburn nights." Shirtwaists with full circle skirts recalled the TV mom look of the 1950s. Christopher Morganstern rediscovered the simplicity and classic lines of the sheath. The traditional preppie look of Ralph Lauren gained new ground with young people. Perry Ellis inspired a resurgence of 1940s navy-and-white nautical styles with his sailors collection of separates. These and numerous other fashion revivalisms of the recent past closed out the eighties and rolled over into the 1990s.

Women's Outerwear 1980–1989

In the 1980s, the designs of women's coats and jackets were influenced by the Japanese Big Look and by the prevailing inverted triangle silhouette of other fashions. Outerwear was massive; shoulders, sleeves, collars, and bodices had to be capacious enough to fit adequately over the broad shoulders of powersuits and dresses. (Figure 11.15.) Details like epaulets, box-pleated backs, patch pockets, pocket flaps, and capelets added dimension. Even standardized forms of outerwear, such as trench coats and peacoats were reconfigured with widened

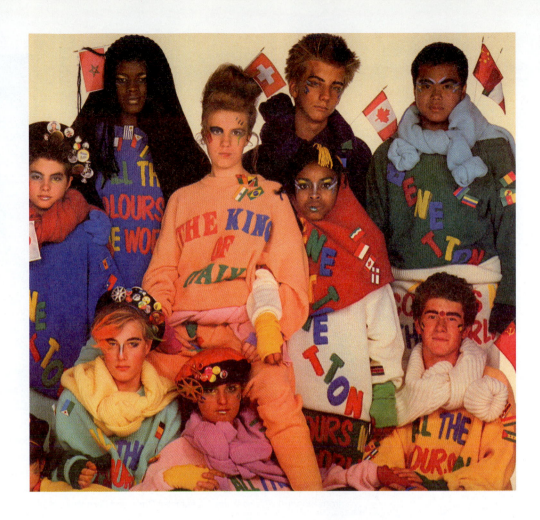

FIGURE 11.13. The androgyny of the 1980s was less glam and more conventionally unisex than a decade earlier. Basic sweaters, sweatshirts, T-shirts, pants, and accessories like knit hats, mufflers, mittens, and big socks were plied with gender bending colors that denied the usual linearity of women's and men's clothing. Benetton collection, 1985.

and padded shoulders. Lengths of outerwear extended to almost every point from the hips to the ankles. In keeping with the prevailing attitude of conspicuous consumption, fur coats were more popular than any time since the fifties. Furriers offered long, luxurious coats with massive sleeves and collars. Similar looks for the ready-to-wear market were mass produced in faux furs, some in brilliant jeweltone colors.

Women's Underwear and Sleepwear 1980–1989

The diverse categories of women's undergarments became ever more extensive in the eighties. (Figure 11.16.) Panties, garter belts, stockings, pantyhose, tights, slips, teddies, camisoles, bras, corsets, and girdles filled up large sections of floor

FIGURE 11.14. Fashions at the end of the 1980s found relief from the excess of earlier years in retro-styles, especially revivals of the fifties New Look. Adolfo suit with matching bag and lampshade hat, 1988.

FIGURE 11.15. Outerwear of the 1980s was massive with huge, padded shoulders and exaggerated details like oversized collars, sleeves, epaulets, and belts. In keeping with the age of conspicuous consumption, furs once again became as popular as they had been in the fifties. Left, leather jacket by Vakko, 1986; center, coat and sweater from Mondi, 1987; right, mink coat from Carol and Irwin Ware, 1986.

space in department stores. Specialty chains like Victoria's Secret and makers like Calvin Klein marketed fashion underwear not only as little private indulgences but also as erotic enhancements for intimate moments. Varieties of designs, colors, and fabrics were infinite. When short skirts returned middecade, cropped versions of slips and half slips revived the lengths of the early seventies.

Innovation, though, occurred more with engineering than with style. In the mid-1980s, Bali introduced the Fit Dimension line of bras that fitted both the woman's body size and the breast shape. Cinching corsets and even padded bustle panties were integral to the fitted contours of many fashions.

Sleepwear ranged from long, lacy gown and robe ensembles to footed jammies. Menswear pajama tops with boxer shorts became especially popular. Oversized T-shirts and ankle-length T-cut nightshirts were favorite dorm sleepwear for teens.

Women's Sports Attire 1980–1989

The trend for exercise and fitness continued to grow throughout the eighties as more baby boomers crossed those critical thresholds of age thirty and forty. The Jazzercize classes of the seventies became dance aerobics, which in turn evolved into step aerobics.

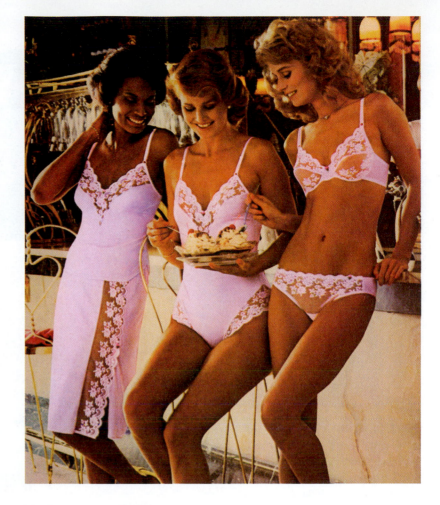

FIGURE 11.16. Intimate apparel of the eighties varied little from the previous decade. Categories were diverse and colorful. Maidenform bra camisole, petti, teddy, underwire bra, and bikini panty, 1982.

To dress for sports activities, women abandoned bulky sweatshirts, sweatpants, and big tees for formfitting spandex tank tops, shorts, and pants engineered to fit like a second skin. The sleek fitted jumpsuit eclipsed knit pants and tops on ski slopes. Lightweight synthetic blends and technotextiles supported muscles during warm-ups, and cooled and dried the skin during intense workouts. (Figure 11.17.) Leotards and unitards were fitted with internal support to eliminate the need for binding undergarments. Neon colors and wild pattern combinations were particularly popular in the 1980s. "Women are putting a lot of thought into what they wear for working out," noted *Vogue* in 1982. Shoes were also engineered for specialized activities to provide proper support and prevent injury. Both women and men might have several pairs of expensive athletic shoes for different workout programs.

For traditional sports such as tennis and golf, sports clothing largely remained conventional. Many clubs and associations retained archaic rules of conduct and appearance, including decades-old dress codes. Tennis skirts and shorts were worn with polo shirts usually machine embroidered on the chest with a tiny logo of an alligator, polo player, mounted knight, or abstract swoosh.

Headbands, wristbands, visors, sunglasses, ski goggles, canvas totes, towels, duffles, and socks were design and color coordinated by activewear manufacturers to match sports clothing collections.

Women's Swimwear 1980–1989

The pluralism of fashion was especially evident in the extensive variety of women's swimsuit options. Traditional maillots—some with skirts—and the bikini continued to be the standard forms of swimwear with infinite variations of colors, textile patterns, and decorative treatments that reflected the times. (Figure 11.18.) Kinetic application of leather, fringe, and beads occurred

FIGURE 11.17. Sleek technotextiles and synthetic fabrics made active sportswear of the eighties more functional and comfortable. Left, "Babe Sport Suit" of cotton/acrylic blend from Faberge, 1982; top right, nylon racer's skisuit, 1982; bottom right, spandex tank and biker shorts by Nike, 1988.

FIGURE 11.18. From simple maillots to string bikinis accented with fringe and other kinetic trimmings, swimwear of the 1980s was widely diverse. Among the new contours was the French cut, which featured a high arc of the leg openings. Left, string bikini by La Lail, 1980; center, bandeau bikini swimsuit by Edith Thais, 1987; right, French cut bikini by Oscar de la Renta and men's Speedo, 1988.

FIGURE 11.19. Spiky high heels were the preferred complement to the powersuits and wide-shoulder dresses of the eighties. Boots of all types remained popular for hemlines of all lengths. Left, high heels from Susan Bennis/Warren Edwards, 1986; center, thigh-high boots by Maud Frizon, 1985; right, "Buttons" sandal by Jean Paul Gaultier and "Apollo" sandal by Thierry Mugler, 1985.

throughout the eighties. The microbikini and variant, the thong, both introduced in the 1970s, became more daring with even less fabric coverage. "The bikini has been around since the days of Pompeii," said Gianni Versace, "it will *never* go out of style." In the mid-eighties, the leg openings of swimsuits were cut in a high arc or V-shape, often called a French cut, which for the bottoms of two-piece suits required the waistband to shift much higher on the hips, almost to the waistline. Also new in the 1980s was the cropped athletic top that simulated the look of a sportsbra.

Women's Shoes 1980–1989

In 1985, Imelda Marcos, wife of the deposed president of the Philippines, fled the country, abandoning a shoe wardrobe consisting of over 1000 pairs. Since hats virtually disappeared from most women's wardrobes, shoes were, arguably, the most important accessory. After all, women with a sense of style could wear the same watch and basic earrings, and carry the same neutral handbag day after day, but not wear the same shoes.

During the early 1980s, high heels remained the ubiquitous footwear for the longer dresses of the period. (Figure 11.19.) By the end of the decade, as hemlines rose, a wider variety of low heels were produced. In keeping with the big silhouettes and oversized accessories of the eighties, shoes were often sculpted with large cutouts, wide straps, contrasting appliques, and curvaceous heels. The glitz and glitter of beading, sequins, metallic finishes, and lace adorned the entire outer surface of evening shoes. The conspicuous consumption attitude of the era inspired a renewed popularity in reptilian skins for shoes and other accessories, irrespective of the endangered status of many of the species. For daytime, detachable shoe ornaments such

FIGURE 11.20. Jewelry of the New Gilded Age was worn to impress. Styles of the eighties were bold and dramatic in form, size, and color. Oversized pieces, often worn in abundance, complemented the big look of sculpted silhouettes, padded shoulders, and oversized details.

African inspired silver and ebony bracelets by Dinny Hall, 1987.

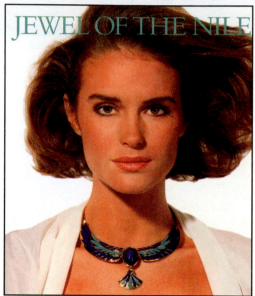

Egyptian necklace from Franklin Mint, 1988.

Necklace, bracelet, earrings, and ring set with turquoise and diamonds in 18-karat gold by Black, Starr and Frost, 1981.

Deco revivalism from Louis Bartholomew, 1986.

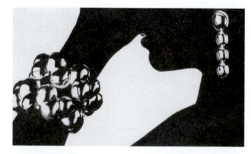

Oversized gold necklace and earrings from Polly Bergen, 1986.

as velvet and satin bows, metal and tortoise shell buckles, or faux jewels were clipped onto the throats or sides of shoes for added variety and fashion interest. Boots for both dresses and pants were a wardrobe staple. For casual wear, vividly colored Converse sneakers were adapted from hip-hop street looks—worn with laces undone or removed entirely. The urban career woman often laced up comfortable athletic shoes to trek to and from the office, and carried her dress shoes in an oversized tote.

Women's Jewelry 1980–1989

That most ancient form of body ornamentation—jewelry—reached an apogee of variety and splendor in the 1980s. From golden Byzantine opulence to colorful plastic watches worn in multiples, jewelry in the decade of conspicuous consumption was designed to complement

FIGURE 11.21. Big hair complemented the big shoulders, big jewelry, and other big looks of the eighties. At the other extreme, short crops were part of the androgynous look that was so popular in fashion marketing of the day. Left and center, big hair looks of the mid-eighties; right, androgyny, 1985.

the exhibitionism of the era. (Figure 11.20.) "Jewelry—and more jewelry—is a focal point of all [runway] collections," reported *Vogue* from Paris in 1988. "Nothing succeeds like excess," declared the banner headline of a jewelry ad that same year. Art deco revivalisms and retro fifties New Look abundance resurfaced. Just as the design of clothes, shoes, and accessories of the eighties became bold and sculptural, jewelry too developed into substantial three-dimensional forms of fashion art worn in excess.

Fads of the 1980s included quartz jewelry of all kinds since crystals were thought to have mystical powers and could ward off bad karma. Baroque fresh water pearls were a popular novelty. Ankle bracelets and toe rings adorned the feet. The punks expanded their counterculture repertoire to feature small hoops or studs inserted through pierced eyebrows, lips, tongues, upper ears, nostrils, navels, and nipples. Safety pins, paper clips, and found junk worn as jewelry were a street statement of antifashion.

Women's Hairstyles and Makeup 1980–1989

Most hairstyles of the 1980s followed the trends of clothing and accessories: big and eye-catching or styled with deliberate self-expression. (Figure 11.21.) Whether long or short, though, hair of the decade was decidedly big—bouffant on top for most lengths, and mane-like for longer styles. Despite the soft look of the teased out tresses, most big hair was heavily lacquered into shape against humidity and wind.

Also in keeping with the pluralism of fashion during this period, many women opted for a variety of hairstyles to suit the mood of the moment. Mousse and gels made possible sculpted hair to match sculpted clothes. Many black women in Europe and the Americas adopted bouffant styles that required hair straightening treatments, which had largely been abandoned a decade earlier. Similarly, manageable shorter cuts of naturally curly styles for blacks replaced

Picture hat from Tatters, 1986.

FIGURE 11.22. Big hair was more important in the 1980s than hats. Even so, many women rediscovered the elegance and glamour of hats in the New Gilded Age of affluence.

Box hat from Yves St. Laurent, 1988.

Silk crepe turban by Louis Feraud, 1986.

the massive afros of the 1960s and 1970s. Many cross-cultural hairstyles became mainstream during the eighties. Following the 1979 release of the movie *10* in which Bo Derek wore a cornrowed and beaded fringe hair arrangement, many younger women in the early 1980s experimented with variations that ranged from beading a few strands to braiding the entire head. Punk and androgyny influences inspired close crops and spiked crests. Bright, nonpermanent hair colors allowed young women to experiment safely and temporarily with street looks.

Makeup of the eighties strongly delineated and accented facial features. Eyeliner was thick and eyeshadows were dark and applied over more surface beneath the brows. Lipsticks were deep reds and berry colors. Blush was used to sculpt the cheekbones and narrow nose bridges. Fingernails were long, squared, and polished with brilliant colors. A weekly salon trip for new false nails was a must for most yuppie women.

Women's Hats 1980–1989

Between the end of the 1960s and the beginning of the 1980s, hats largely had been utilitarian, worn as accoutrement of winter wear or summer protection from the sun. By the mid-eighties, though, many women rediscovered the glamour and class distinction of fashion hats, which

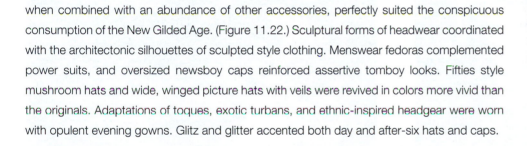

FIGURE 11.23. In the 1980s, head-to-toe accessories became almost as important as they were during the New Look era. Particularly popular were upscale collections of branded logo accessories. Left, Givenchy sunglasses, scarf, umbrella, jewelry, and perfume, 1983; right, Yves St. Laurent hat, handbag, belt, gloves, and jewelry, 1984.

when combined with an abundance of other accessories, perfectly suited the conspicuous consumption of the New Gilded Age. (Figure 11.22.) Sculptural forms of headwear coordinated with the architectonic silhouettes of sculpted style clothing. Menswear fedoras complemented power suits, and oversized newsboy caps reinforced assertive tomboy looks. Fifties style mushroom hats and wide, winged picture hats with veils were revived in colors more vivid than the originals. Adaptations of toques, exotic turbans, and ethnic-inspired headgear were worn with opulent evening gowns. Glitz and glitter accented both day and after-six hats and caps.

Women's Accessories 1980–1989

In the 1980s, accessories reached a new level of importance not seen since the height of Dior's New Look in the fifties. The utility of belts, handbags, gloves, sunglasses, and scarves was often secondary to the style statement provided by their shape, color, texture, or logo. (Figure 11.23.) Applying superfluous accessories for the sake of fashion was an important component of conspicuous consumption, which was reinforced in pop culture by the sophisticated exhibitionism shown on TV programs like *Dynasty* and *Dallas,* and the extravagance of the glitterati in the court of the Reagan White House. In 1985, *Vogue* reported that accessories were "displaying remarkable character to a dazzling effect—for ornamentation, for special effects, for pure glamour." Women once again dressed head to toe with an attention to fashion detail. Large sculpted belts complemented the architectonic silhouettes of the era. Sculptural handbags did not necessarily match belts and shoes. Daytime gloves returned in vibrant colors to be worn or carried as accent pieces. Scarves added dimension to the big shoulders of suit jackets and dresses or were tied to handbags as a decorative treatment.

Men's Fashions 1980–1989

The dual influences of Italian style and English tailoring continued to dominate men's suit designs into the eighties. Emphasis was on the Italian lead, notably that of Giorgio Armani and Gianni Versace. "Italian fashion is changing the man," affirmed the header of an advertising campaign in 1985. To Italian designers, the body should inhabit the garment, not be defined by it. The fluid naturalness produced by cut, workmanship, and soft fabrics was a new concept in the design of men's suits. At the same time, the Italian style was often labeled classic because of its closed, unified form as opposed to the ambiguous, open form of the Japanese Big Look.

American designers gradually merged Italian style with techniques of British tailoring for a polished look with a relaxed fit. (Figure 11.24.) In 1984, *GQ* identified the "big four" American menswear designers as Perry Ellis, Ralph Lauren, Calvin Klein, and Alexander Julian, each of

FIGURE 11.24. In the 1980s, menswear designers redefined the business suit by innovative construction, exquisite tailoring, new fabrics, and a looser, softer fit. The scale was big and the details were fresh and eclectic. The strong silhouettes of the eighties powersuit were a statement of the wearer's self-confidence and assertiveness. Left, single and double breasted suits by Hugo Boss, 1987; right, young men's trim suiting from Cotler, 1984.

Cropped wool jacket from Hardware, 1980.

FIGURE 11.25. Sport jackets offered a variety of alternatives to the suit coat. The eighties looks ranged from oversized, sculpted silhouettes to a *Miami Vice* casual sportiness.

Plaid sport jackets by Enrico Coveri, 1986.

Silk blend sport jacket from International Male, 1985.

whom looked to traditionalism as their point of departure for suit designs. Lauren commented that his suits captured "that particularly British custom-tailored look that always begins with very rich, expensive fabrics and ends with easy yet precise tailoring." Ellis noted that his suits "fit well on the body yet look easy; therefore, they're cut fuller and looser."

This fuller and looser deconstruction of the men's suit jacket was key to the transformation of business attire in the 1980s. The scale was big, and an eclecticism in the proportions of details kept such looks variable and fresh: both wide and narrow lapels (and corresponding neckwear), fluctuating collar sizes, and shifting button count. As with women's powersuits of the decade, men's professional dress was assertive in its strong profiles and linear details. Rich fabrics in bold plaids, checks, houndstooth, and other powerful patterns reinforced the unabashed self-assuredness of the wearer.

The sport jacket was an important alternative to the suit coat. Sport jackets were often designed with the same emphasis on oversized scale and bold patterns as that of suits. (Figure 11.25.) Similarly, the variety of new-wave jackets and suits that had first emerged in menswear in the 1960s continued to be popular for younger men through the eighties. Short crops, besom pockets, sculpted shoulders, and novel textiles characterized the experimental looks of the decade. In the mid-1980s, the TV crime drama *Miami Vice* inspired a casual, but

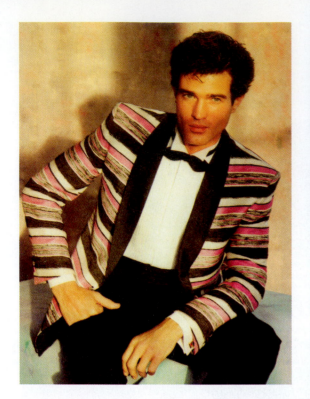 

FIGURE 11.26. The tuxedo jacket of the 1980s was designed in a wide array of colors and textile patterns, many of which were worn with contrasting trousers. Left, Pierre Cardin tuxedo, 1983; right, Canali white dinner jacket and tuxedo, 1983.

well-put-together sportiness in men's suits. Notably for the **Miami Vice look** were unconstructed sport jackets in ice cream colors, which were worn open and with the sleeves pushed up to the elbows.

The tuxedo continued to be the most prevalent evening wear. (Figure 11.26.) The diversity of colorful solids and patterns that first emerged in the 1960s and the trend of contrasting jackets and trousers that developed in the 1970s provided men with innumerable options for formal dress. The continuing nostalgic interest in the 1950s, due in part to TV programs like *Happy Days* and *Laverne and Shirley,* inspired the return of the crisp white dinner jacket. Ruffled and pleated shirts, often in vivid colors, added flair to the starkness of plain jackets. The only significant debate about tuxedo style was "between straight and wing collars" for shirts, both of which, *GQ* concluded in 1985, "are eminently suitable."

Men's Sports Attire and Outerwear 1980–1989

Men's sportswear and playwear of the eighties were as varied as women's styles. In the 1980s, designers began to experiment with new technofabrics for men's clothing. Tight-fitting parachute pants made of silky nylon blend textiles were introduced in the early eighties. (Figure 11.27.) Sleek satin trousers were popular with young men for nightlife. Snug, leather

FIGURE 11.27. In the 1980s, new textiles were applied to men's trousers, such as silky nylon blends used for parachute cargo pants. Nylon jacket and pants from Gabrielle, 1984.

FIGURE 11.28. Influenced by the street looks of the 1960s and 1970s, denim makers of the eighties began to produce distressed jeans with faded, worn finishes and even threadbare and frayed holes. Distressed Levi's, 1984.

pants were shaped and textured to differentiate the look from plain biker styles. All sorts of "distressed" varieties of jeans were produced, from acid and stone washes that faded the dyes to versions with threadbare spots and shredded knees. (Figure 11.28.)

The Japanese-inspired Big Look—reinforced by the yuppie desire for a statement of power through their wardrobes—particularly influenced the silhouettes of most sportswear. Padded shoulders, wide yoke constructions, and other lateral designs of shirts, sweaters, and tops adapted the inverted triangle look from suit coats. Equally bold and strong were textile patterns and colors. (Figure 11.29.)

For traditionalists, clothing branded with logos offered a safe haven of style choices. In addition to designer signature labels, categories of logos ranged from sports and consumer product brands to pictorials and messages on T-shirts and sweatshirts. (Figure 11.30.) Sports logos were particularly important to men who wanted to publicly demonstrate their support for their favorite sports team. Many men had seasonal logo attire embellished with various team colors and emblems for fall (football), winter (basketball and hockey), and spring and summer

FIGURE 11.29. The big look of men's sportswear in the 1980s not only featured exaggerated shoulder silhouettes, but also included bold textile patterns, powerful colors, and strong textures. Sweater by Claude Montana, 1984.

FIGURE 11.30. In the 1980s, the proliferation of logo fashions was dramatic. Every category of men's sportswear was subject to some form of logo or branding treatment. From 1986: Reebok activewear and Armani jacket.

FIGURE 11.31. In the 1980s active sportswear makers introduced new forms of athletic wear. Garments were engineered for better support and to work with muscle exertion; new fabric technologies enhanced physical performance. Spandex bicycle shorts, 1987.

FIGURE 11.32. For winter sports at popular ski resorts, yuppies opted for high style skiwear made of sleek technofabrics in vivid hues. Nylon Thinsulate jackets and knit skipants from Roffe, 1987.

(baseball). Men who might never otherwise wear certain colors, such as kelly green or bright orange, enthusiastically layered garments in the hue that matched their favorite pro team's logo or college colors, especially during championship playoffs.

For the athletic male of the period, the fit and effectiveness of the activewear were more important than a brand or team loyalty. For a jog outdoors on chilly mornings, fleece warm-up tops and pants were often worn with an indifference to color and logo combinations—despite the marketing efforts of makers and retailers to promote color coordinated mix-and-match collections. During the 1980s, active sportswear manufacturers responded to men's increased interest in workout regimens with new garment engineering and innovative fabric technologies. Spandex bicycle shorts, influenced by European designs, were made with reinforced seats and seams that smoothly contoured the muscles. (Figure 11.31.) T-tops, tanks, and similar athletic garments were likewise re-engineered for a more accommodating fit for strenuous activities. On the slopes of the ski resorts, however, the look of the outfit was still all-important for the yuppie who wanted to proclaim his affluence. Upscale winter apparel makers combined technotextiles and high-style design in collections of brightly colored skiwear coordinates. (Figure 11.32.)

Men's outerwear styles retained most of the classic versions that had remained standard for more than a century. The yuppie businessman often complemented his powersuit with the appropriate chesterfield overcoat or Armani greatcoat. The lateral expanse of shoulder silhouettes in the 1980s was equally applied to men's outerwear. The armscyes were often set off the shoulder and constructed with details that reinforced the sculpted shape. (Figure 11.33.) Much was written in fashion press at the time about the influence of the Japanese in reinterpreting classic styles of men's coats. Yohji Yamamoto and Mitsuhiro Matsuda reworked classic silhouettes with harmonious geometric cuts that softened the typically

FIGURE 11.33. Classic styles of men's outerwear in the eighties were reinterpreted by the Japanese with new geometric cuts and sculpted shapes. Italian designers softened the look of traditional outerwear with soft, luxury fabrics. The British modernized men's coats with tweeds in new textures and weaves. Left, leather jackets from Tannery West, 1983; right, wool greatcoat from Kenzo, 1986.

rigid contours of men's outerwear. From the Italians came an endless array of new luxury fabrics in subtle but distinctive patterns. Similarly, the British reinvented traditional tweeds with innovative textures and fluid weaves that set apart men's outerwear from earlier styles.

Men's Accessories 1980–1989

Among the categories of men's accessories, the most significant drama occurred with neckwear. (Figure 11.34.) In the early 1980s, ties continued to narrow. Younger men wore **skinny ties** that were usually about two inches wide at the flared end. Since this narrow cut had been prevalent in the early sixties, many men bought vintage silk ties from thrift shops. In response to this trend, neckwear manufacturers produced innumerable varieties of ties in retro textile

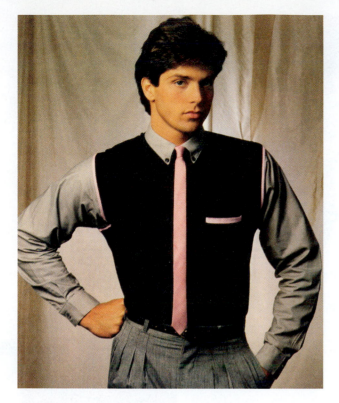

FIGURE 11.34. By the early eighties, men's ties had evolved to narrow strips of fabric barely two inches wide. During the same time, the string tie, or bolla, was adapted from the cowboy costume. Left, rayon skinny tie from Merry Go Round, 1983; right, braided leather bolla with silver clasp by Shady Character, 1985.

patterns and prints from the forties, fifties, and sixties. The skinny ties of the 1980s, though, often were made of distinctly modern fabrics such as synthetics, leather, and knits. The ultimate skinny tie was the **bolla**—an appropriation of the cowboy string tie with metal **ferrule** tips and an ornamental fastener.

Shoes and boots of the 1980s changed little from the traditional styles that had returned after the extreme platforms, wedges, and sandals of the seventies. Upscale Italian labels such as Gucci and Bruno Magli were favored by yuppies. Also, a renewed interest in rare skins such as lizard, snake, and alligator for footwear (and a disregard for ecological concerns) suited the ostentation of the New Gilded Age. High quality cowboy boots made with designer styling was a trend inspired by the 1980 movie *Urban Cowboy* and the TV series *Dallas*. (Figure 11.35.) Branded athletic footwear became a huge business. In the mid-eighties, Adidas sneakers were worn without laces by hip-hop musicians and their fans—a style called "**shell toes**."

Except for winter wear in northern climates, hats remained an occasional accessory. Knit caps served the utilitarian purpose well although felt fedoras were worn by urban businessmen as a smart suit accent. A visor or wide brimmed panama might be worn if activities required extended periods in the summer sun. The tall, wide brimmed Stetson enjoyed a brief resurgence as a complement to urban cowboy boots.

FIGURE 11.35. High style cowboy boots were an indulgence of urban cowboys and fans of the prime time TV soap *Dallas* in the 1980s. Men's cowboy boots by Giorgio Brutini, 1988.

FIGURE 11.36. In the 1980s, men's underwear styles ranged from the most minimal cuts to the standard white knit briefs and baggy boxers. Left, Mariner bikini underwear, 1982; right, cotton boxers from ACA Joe, 1987.

FIGURE 11.37. Swimwear of the 1980s continued the trend of brevity. For traditionalist men who preferred basic briefs and boxers—underwear or swimwear—color and prints provided them some sense of modernity and fashion. Left, briefs, bikini, and boxer swimwear from Eminence, 1982; right, surfer jams and logo T-shirt from Swatch, 1986.

Men's Underwear and Swimwear 1980–1989

Men's bare necessities of underwear and swimwear continued to be influenced by European style through the 1980s. (Figure 11.36.) For traditionalists, the basic white cotton brief remained the most common style of underwear—and the industry's best seller—although briefs in colors, especially black, steadily increased in popularity from their mass market introductions in the

1970s. Loose-fitting boxer shorts also were common, particularly for ex-military men who were conditioned to wearing the style. A huge assortment of theme prints and patterns made boxers a popular novelty gift item especially for Valentine's Day. In the late 1980s, form-fitting knit boxers became a fashionable alternative to the loose, baggy woven varieties. Designers like Calvin Klein and Perry Ellis began to brand their underwear styles with bold type logos repeated around the waistbands.

On the beach, the long, loose-fitting shorts styles of the sixties were revived as **surfer jams** in retro colors and wild prints. (Figure 11.37.) Also from the sixties came revivals of the low-rise and belted boxer swimsuits, though now made of sleek spandex-blend fabrics rather than thick knit materials of the originals. Most men, though, wore the same short square-cut boxer forms in cotton or nylon that had developed in the 1930s. The bikini remained a favorite swimsuit for athletic-built men, with sales peaking during Olympic years when swimming and diving champions were publicized wearing the style. The thong that had been introduced as underwear in the seventies was adapted to swimwear in the 1980s with designer label versions produced by Gucci, among others.

Men's Counterculture Styles 1980–1989

Besides the numerous standardized categories of men's clothing styles counterculture groups and ethnic cliques developed their own distinct looks in the eighties. **Skinheads** shaved or closely cropped their hair and appropriated a working class look that included heavy work boots and wallets attached to thick belt chains. Punks extended their antifashion agenda into the realm of florescent-colored hair, excessive body piercing, and lavishly applied tattoos. (Figure 11.38.) **Rockabilly** incorporated vintage casual looks of the American 1950s with modern retro interpretations, notably bowling league shirts and pompadour hair cuts, with modern retro interpretations. The "crews" of inner city **B-Boys** breakdanced to hip-hop music in their soft Kangol hats with turned-down brims, oversized quilted jackets, big gold chains, and Adidas sneakers with no laces. The gay community, according to pop culture author Shaun Cole, split into "clone" factions that included the cowboy clone, biker leather clone, lumberjack clone, and punk clone, to name a few—each of which adopted the uniform of its prototype, but was distinguishable from the original by the fit and meticulous assemblage of the dress components.

Men's Grooming and Hairstyles 1980–1989

Men's grooming looks were as diverse and reflective of an individual's personal style as clothing. Men's personal care products and services were a multimillion dollar industry by the 1980s. Manufacturers of fragrances offered almost as many varieties of scents for men as for women. Using the same tried-and-true formulas of advertising that had appealed to women for decades, skincare marketers successfully targeted men with messages ranging

FIGURE 11.38. Counterculture groups expressed their antifashion and antisocietal attitudes with looks that often included distinct tribalistic uniforms of sorts. Punk teenager, 1987.

FIGURE 11.39. Men's hairstyles remained broadly diverse in the eighties. In addition, hundreds of men's haircare products such as fixative sprays, gels, and non-permanent colors provided even more options for distinct looks.

from preserving a healthy, youthful appearance to finding romance. Even cosmetics were developed for concealing masculine age lines and other telltale signs of advancing years.

For the most part, men remained clean shaven. The full, heavy mustaches of the late seventies lingered into the early eighties briefly as exemplified by Tom Selleck in the TV drama *Magnum P.I.* By the mid-eighties, though, the *Miami Vice* look with its neatly trimmed two-day's stubble appeared in fashion editorials, but was seldom actually seen along Main Street. The rough, casual look only worked well for men with strong, chiseled features and a dark, even growth of beard.

Also lingering from the seventies was the preference for displaying chest hair by unfastening the top two or three shirt buttons. By the mid-eighties, though, that look was derided as a disco-era holdover and men with hairy chests encountered the emergence of a new ideal of masculine aesthetic—the classically smooth, hairless torso of a Greek statue.

Men's hairstyles of the period came in every conceivable cut, length, volume, and color. (Figure 11.39.) Hair care shampoos, conditioners, hairspray, gels, mousse, and dozens of other similar products were specially formulated, packaged, and promoted specifically for men. As the baby boomers aged, hair coloring products were widely advertised. The hair restorative, Rogaine, was approved by the U.S. Food and Drug Administration in 1988 for men with thinning hair. The growing multimillion dollar hair transplant and hair weaving industries were testimony of the importance men placed on a great head of hair.

Children's Clothing 1980–1989

Clothing for infants and toddlers was designed to fit the child but appeal to the parents. Garments of all types for preschool youngsters were largely made of fabrics in pastel colors and muted tones or petite-print patterns. Traditional powder blue for boys and pink for girls remained the prevalent gender identifiers. In early 1980s, though, more vivid colors, especially bright primary hues, and bold, graphical prints became equally popular. Comfort for the children and easy access for the parents—for quick, easy clothing changes—were the principal guidelines for designers of children's wear. One-piece outfits and overalls in short or long lengths, depending on the season, best satisfied the needs of both children and parents.

FIGURE 11.40. Girls had greater options than boys in their varieties of clothing styles. Dress styles followed the silhouettes of adult women's fashions, including miniature retro-looks of the fifties and sixties. Left, Esprit sweater, pants, and accessories, 1986; right, skimps and stirrup pants, 1987.

In the 1980s, greater attention was focused on child safety, including clothing designs and textiles. Strict federal legislation was enacted and numerous new regulatory policies were put into effect to better protect children. Manufacturers faced costly recalls and retailers were slapped with stiff fines by the U.S. Consumer Product Safety Commission (CPSC). Mass marketers such as Britain's Marks & Spencer even banned pins and staples from the packaging of children's clothing. A proliferation of articles in women's magazines cautioned parents on dangers such as tie strings on hoods and mittens, buttons or ornaments that could become detached and swallowed, and especially flammable fabrics. Rather than buy sleepwear garments chemically treated with fire retardants, though, many parents dressed their children in oversized T-shirts and other loose-fitting clothing that were, nevertheless, fire hazards.

The trend of unisex types of children's clothing that developed in the 1960s and grew rapidly through the seventies had become a standard by the 1980s. Sweatshirts, tees, sweaters, pull-on pants and shorts, overalls, and dozens of other clothing styles were manufactured identically in shape, style, and colors for both girls and boys. Despite the commonality of

FIGURE 11.41. Parents of the New Gilded Age dressed their children in the branded labels they themselves wore. Left, Ralph Lauren signature collection for children, 1982; right, Christian Dior boys' suits, 1987.

unisex garments, though, parents and children's peers perpetuated gender-role socialization through certain subtleties of color and decoration of these unisex garments, particularly for boys. A purple sweatshirt might be worn by both genders, but the same garment in lavender or pink was usually taboo for school-age boys; similarly, girls might wear Batman or the Hulk images on their tees, but boys would never be seen in a shirt bearing a Barbie or Holly Hobbie graphic. Only with the increased popularity of bright primary colors and non-representational prints in the eighties was the line sufficiently blurred for social comfort. This deliberate blurring of traditional roles and stereotypes was often a central theme in the advertising of children's wear makers like Benetton and Esprit throughout the eighties.

For girls, standardized forms of unisex clothes could be conventionally feminized with embellishments such as embroidered collars, ribbon trim, lace edging, scalloped borders, and faux jewel or beaded appliques. (Figure 11.40.) Pants were variously cropped between the ankles and midcalf, and sweaters were extended into long **skimps** sometimes worn as casual dresses with colorful, patterned tights or stirrup leggings.

Although girls' wardrobes were filled with an infinite variety of casual and activewear fashions, dresses remained the preferred garment for special occasions. In the 1980s, the variable hemlines and shoulder contours followed the looks of women's dresses. During holidays, crinolined dresses of rich fabrics reinforced the nostalgia of the season.

School-age boys dressed in a diverse combination of tops and pants. (Figure 11.41.) Most styles reflected those of adult men. Preppy ensembles included typical dress shirts with button-down collars or casual polo styles, usually with an embroidered alligator or polo rider to match dad's. Boys also identified with their parent's favorite sports teams by wearing almost any apparel or accessories decorated with licensed team emblems and franchise colors. On the top of most children's clothing wish list was anything bearing images from the most current hit movie, cartoon, or TV program, especially depictions of superheroes and dinosaurs. The blue gnome-like Smurfs were a particular favorite in the eighties. For dressy occasions, diminutive three-piece suits were modeled on the adult coat, vest, and trousers.

Review

The pluralism of fashion—many widely diverse clothing styles, silhouettes, branded labels, and lifestyle looks—that had emerged in the sixties through the seventies expanded rapidly in the eighties, becoming an overarching economic signpost for the fashion industry. Fashion makers and retailers recognized that most consumers wanted clothing that suited their personal lifestyles irrespective of trends featured on the runways or in editorials of fashion magazines. Niche marketers reacted to changing consumer attitudes by promoting the idea of individuality, and specialty manufacturers and retailers responded to the growing consumer pluralism by providing clothing designs fitted to modern segmented demographics: an age group, a size range, a social status.

However, this pluralism did not preclude the emergence of key fashion themes and trends that were widely popular. In the New Gilded Age of the 1980s, a surge of worldwide prosperity inspired unabashed exhibitionism of sociopolitical power and wealth among the newly affluent classes. The inverted triangle silhouette of fashions, for both men and women, was the quintessential style image of the decade. The broad, padded shoulders of the powersuit expressed self-confidence and authority. Similarly, the big sculpted looks were adapted to almost all forms of fashions in the eighties, from sportswear to sumptuous evening gowns. Colors and textile patterns were equally bold—vibrant hues, big plaids, strong graphics. For women, the opulence of billowing pouf dresses or crinolined skirts exemplified the extravagance of the era. Skirt hemlines became widely varied from the return of thigh-high miniskirts to ankle sweeping retro-looks of the fifties.

For men, a new perspective of masculine sensuality emerged with the deconstructed suits designed by Armani and Versace. In 1980, many men were uneasy watching Richard Gere in *American Gigolo* meticulously arrange ensembles of matching garments in his bedroom, but by middecade, men were commonly doing the same thing even in public as they shopped in department stores.

Children's clothing continued the trend of generic, nongender forms of sweatshirts, T-shirts, sweaters, pull-on pants and shorts, overalls, and dozens of other basic garments for both boys and girls. Among the high-style fashions for girls were knit skimps and stirrup leggings. For boys, preppie looks dominated although anything bearing screenprints of the latest action movie, comic hero, or dinosaurs topped the back-to-school shopping list.

review questions

1. What styles of women's fashions of the 1980s exemplified the exhibitionism of the era? Give examples of silhouettes, fabrics, and accessories.

2. How did the fitness boom of the eighties influence fashions of both women and men? Identify examples of body-conscious fashions of the decade.

3. Define the qualities of the rich look in fashion of the eighties. What examples of popular culture and social "courts" perpetuated the rich look of the New Gilded Age?

4. How did couture in the 1980s change from that of the sixties and seventies?

5. How did Italian style and British tailoring change traditional men's suit jackets in the 1980s?

research and portfolio projects

Research

1. Select three couture houses and write a research paper on how the social and economic changes that occurred during the 1980s impacted them.

Portfolio

1. Research bound periodicals and catalogs of the 1980s to find examples of opulent evening wear influenced by nineteenth century styles: Empire waistline, gigot sleeves, crinoline skirts, and bustles. (See Chapters 1 and 2.) Photocopy or digitally scan three examples of each. Include a written description of each with the name of the designer and date. Specify and describe the nineteenth-century influence and how the 1980s version replicates or differs from the original.

dress terms

B-Boys: inner city street looks of the 1980s that included Kangol hats, big gold chains, sneakers without laces, and oversized quilted jackets

bolla: a string tie affixed with decorative holder

deconstruction: the rejection of conventional rules of clothing cuts, form, or fit

ferrule: the metal tips of laces and bolla strings used to prevent unraveling

Miami Vice look: a men's sporty suit look of the 1980s that included unconstructed jackets worn with the sleeves pushed up, colored T-shirts, relaxed fit trousers, and shoes with no socks

pouf dress (also called bubble dress)**:** a bouffant cocktail dress of the 1980s constructed with a voluminous, rounded skirt

powersuit: men's and women's business suits of the 1980s usually designed with an inverted triangle silhouette formed by broad padded shoulders and tapered, narrow hips

rockabilly: a youth look that incorporated vintage casualwear of the fifties with modern retro-styles

Romantique: women's fashions that featured frilly, feminine elements of nineteenth-century styles

shell toes: sneakers worn without the laces

skimp: a girl's long sweater extending to mid-thigh worn with tights or form-fitting knit pants

skinheads: a counterculture group of disaffected young men who shaved their heads and dressed in working class garb

skinny ties: men's thin neckties

surfer jams: revivals of young men's long, shorts-style swim trunks in retro colors and prints from the 1960s

12 Fin de Siècle 1990–1999

1990   **1999**

Nelson Mandella freed from prison 1980	U.S.–Iraq Persian Gulf War 1981	Balkan Wars 1992–1999	Israel–Palestinian Peace Accord 1993	Apartheid ended in South Africa 1994	Britain's Princess Diana killed in auto crash 1997	First euros minted in France 1998
East and West Germany reunited 1980	Launch of World Wide Web 1991	First McDonald's in China 1992	Spielberg's *Jurassic Park* 1993	eBay founded 1995	Dolly the sheep cloned 1997	World population exceeded 6 billion 1999

Concluding the Twentieth Century

As the 1990s opened, "the iron curtain rusted and flaked away," wrote journalist Mort Rosenblum. The Soviet Union had dissolved into fifteen independent republics. The former Warsaw Pact nations of central Europe continued to struggle stoically with a conversion to democratic self-government and to a free market economy. East and West Germany reunited. After the dissolution of Yugoslavia into six separate countries in 1992, the Balkans erupted into a war of "ethnic cleansing," in which hundreds of thousands of Muslims were killed in a genocidal purge. Through the intervention of NATO led by the United States, peace was restored and Serbian military leaders were brought before an international war crimes tribunal.

Other historic events of the 1990s included two peace accords signed by Israel and the Palestine Liberation Organization in 1993, outlining areas of agreement and a timeline for resolving issues. But two years later, a Jewish religious fanatic assassinated Israeli leader Yitzak Rabin, effectively derailing the plan and setting off years of further violence in the region. In South Africa, apartheid ended with the enfranchisement of blacks in 1994.

Emerging from the shadow of Reagan, his vice president, George H. Bush, became president in 1989. Although the free world celebrated the collapse of communism and the end of the Cold War, Bush was low-key about the dramatic events to avoid any perception of the United States gloating.

In the summer of 1990, Iraq invaded neighboring Kuwait in an attempt to gain more control of oil reserves. Over the following few months, Bush assembled a coalition of 30 nations to intervene. In January 1991, Operation Desert Storm was launched, initiating the Persian Gulf War. Though successful in liberating Kuwait, Bush was criticized for not continuing on to Baghdad and capturing the dictator Saddam Hussein.

Despite the high approval ratings Bush enjoyed for his foreign policy leadership, on the home front, his administration struggled with the aftermath of Reaganomics and the resulting recession. In the 1991 campaign war room of the Democrats, a handwritten poster read, "It's the economy, stupid." The voters agreed and Bush lost his bid for reelection, sending Bill Clinton to the White House.

Clinton's economic policies disproved the premise of Reaganomics and, in spite of tax increases and governmental expansion, the U.S. economy was the most robust in thirty years. The national debt was even eliminated. During Clinton's second term, though, a sex scandal involving the president led to an impeachment effort spearheaded by Congressional Republicans. In the end, the Senate voted not to remove Clinton from office.

American Culture and Society 1990–1999

In the world of science, the Human Genome Project began in 1990 to understand the makeup of the human species by mapping the approximately 30,000 genes of the human genome. With the aid of supercomputers, the decade-long research was successful, providing hope for diagnosis and therapy of human disease in the twenty-first century. Genetic cloning and stem cell research, though, became hot topics of debate when, in 1997, scientists in Scotland cloned a lamb named Dolly from a single cell of an adult sheep. Social conservatives clamored to ban such research despite the benefits for humanity assured by geneticists.

In 1991, the World Wide Web debuted as a global information medium available on the Internet. Between 1992 and 1995, various royalty-free graphical browsers were developed allowing users free access to search the Web. During the last half of the 1990s, the Internet evolved from an informational tool with limited capabilities into an electronic universe of communications, marketing, and sales; thousands of services and retailers established Web sites for online shopping and marketing. Book giant Amazon.com and auction site eBay.com were launched in 1995.

Despite such dramatic advances in science and technology, social issues in America almost seemed to be regressive in some respects. High-profile cases of racism and gender-bias repeatedly made national headlines. In 1992, riots erupted in Los Angeles, resulting in 52 deaths and 2300 injuries, when four white police officers were acquitted of the beating of Rodney King, an African-American apprehended after a high-speed car chase. The 1995 murder trial of football legend O.J. Simpson, watched by millions on TV over several weeks, reflected the racial divide of the nation when African-Americans cheered the acquittal and whites expressed shock.

Yet in spite of the nation's crisis of conscience on race and gender, ethnic Americans and women made significant achievements. In 1997, Tiger Woods became the youngest golfer ever to win the Masters. Michael Jordan led the Chicago Bulls to six National Basketball Association titles between 1991 and 1998. During the Clinton administration, Madelaine Albright became the first female U.S. Secretary of State, and Janet Reno became the first female Attorney General. Ruth Bader Ginsburg joined the Supreme Court as a Clinton-appointed justice in 1993.

In U.S. pop culture, electronic gadgets for both business and personal use proliferated. By the conclusion of the twentieth century, pagers, cell phones, digital cameras, hand-held video games, PDAs (personal digital assistants), and laptops were everywhere. Digitized special effects were big box office for movies such as *Terminator: Judgment Day* (1991), *Jurassic Park* (1993), and *Titanic* (1997). Popular music since 1990 was a mix of the teen pop of boy's groups like 'N Sync and the Backstreet Boys, Latin pop of Ricky Martin, cross-over country of Garth Brooks, grunge from Pearl Jam and Nirvana, gangsta rap of Ice T and Snoop Dog, and hip-hop by Salt-N-Pepa and MC Hammer. TV hits seemed to suggest a dysfunctional modern society as depicted in long-running programs like *The Simpsons, Seinfeld, NYPD Blue,* and cable channel series like the *Sopranos* and *Sex and the City.*

Women's Fashions 1990–1999

The fashion pluralism of the 1980s extended into the nineties, expanding into even more segments of style as the decade progressed. The key difference between the two decades was an attitude change of consumers. From the start in the 1990s, individualism was the buzzword among the fashion cognoscenti. More than with any preceding era, fashion was the wearer's choice—what to wear, how to wear it, and with what. "Be Yourself," declared ads by Calvin Klein. Women rejected a dogmatic fealty to what Karl Lagerfeld called the "diktats of fashion." In response to women's assertion of style individuality, designers and ready-to-wear makers offered ever more choices: a wide array of skirt lengths and widths; pleated and plain front trousers; cropped, cuffed, pegged, or flared pants legs; constructed and unconstructed jackets with all varieties of lapel and pocket treatments; dresses of every imaginable cut and fabric.

Coupled with a deep recession and a wartime mood in the early nineties, this new penchant for an individual, personal style also spelled an end to the rich look that had prevailed through much of the eighties. In addition, the political tone in America and Europe shifted. Margaret Thatcher had been deposed in Britain, and the Bushes moved into the White House as the new U.S. First Family. Instead of the nouveau riche glitz of the Reaganites and Thatcherites, Barbara Bush and the Washington social circle presented a studied, patrician elegance. In London, Princess Diana replaced her youthful glam of the eighties with a mature refinement and dignity. On both sides of the Atlantic, women of the privileged classes opted for a quieter taste in clothing. The international media maintained a constant focus on the appearance of Barbara, Diana, and the many other women of elite society who had discarded the rich look for their individual styles. From throughout the industrialized world, affluent corporate yuppies and Main Street moms alike similarly sought to simplify their lifestyles and wardrobes.

With this pluralism of fashion, the principal question of the early nineties was the relevance, and hence, survivability, of haute couture. Designers produced collections of clothing that were

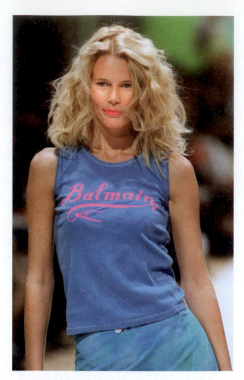

FIGURE 12.1. In the 1990s, the multimillion-dollar branding and mass marketing efforts of designer labels established images of lifestyles and attitudes that appealed to niche market segments of women customers. Wearing a specific designer logo was a form of tribalism for many women—a comfort zone that provided continuity and certainty of style. Left, Gucci logo jacket, 1994; center, Chanel logo print tunic and accessories, 1999; right, Balmain logo tank, 1998.

astonishingly unwearable, including leather bondage and biker ensembles, underwear on the outside, near-nude ethnic costumes, transparent "spiderweb" dresses, and collage garments that combined paper, plastic, and even computer chips. *Vogue* viewed these nineties couture shows as "the theatre of the absurd." As a result of the changing social climate and the declining market of couture clients in the 1990s, financial losses for the major houses were substantial. The luster of some stars of fashion design dimmed somewhat, most notably that of Christian Lacroix who seemed out of touch with the changing market. Among the fashion business fatalities was the closing of the New York salon of Carolyn Roehm, whose lavish day ensembles and sumptuous evening wear had dressed the era's nouvelle society.

Nevertheless, the extravagant haute couture collections and theatrical runway shows served two important purposes that helped sustain the industry during the transitional period of the early nineties. Foremost was fashion innovation. The high art and drama produced by so many of the haute couture designers of the early 1990s helped to urge fashion onward, past the lingering irrelevancies of the eighties styles. Second was public relations and its importance to branding the designer's label. In 1992, fashion writer Alice Mackrell suggested that haute couture had actually become "redundant for anything except PR purposes." Where once fashion houses allocated about two percent of their annual budget to marketing and public relations, that expenditure had jumped to about twenty-five percent by the close of the nineties.

The aggressive marketing of fashion labels in the 1990s provided consumers with a universal language of style. With mass licensing, mass production, and mass retailing, almost everyone could afford a number of favorite designer signature garments or accessories. (Figure 12.1.) Wearing logos expanded on the new-age tribalism that had begun in the eighties, representing a form of continuity amidst the sometimes bewildering array of ephemeral looks that filled stores, catalogs, and fashion magazines. Logo wear was a comfort zone for those women who lacked the independent bravado or time to experiment with a uniquely personal style.

Wearing logos was also a new source of consumer aspiration, particularly as the economy became robust in the second half of the decade. The brand images disseminated through mass media conveyed types of lifestyles and attitudes that appealed to specific market segments. Ralph Lauren's polo rider logo projected the cachet of country gentry. Donna Karan's DKNY acronym expressed a sophisticated urban style. The CK of Calvin Klein attested to a confident sensuality and sexuality. Tribal markings for the fashion elite included curious symbols that subtly bespoke of an affluence, and signaled the status of the wearer to other PLUs ("people like us"). Among the most visibly marketed house logos in the 1990s were Chanel's linked C's, the heraldic JPG emblems of Jean Paul Gaultier, the interlocking F's by Fendi, the Medusa head of Versace, the serif E of Escada, and the DG of Dolce & Gabbana, to name a few. The upscale fashions and accessories that sported these branded logos instilled an envious aspiration in many of those who recognized the coded language but could not afford to participate in the exclusive community.

Another segment of the market that continued to be very profitable for fashion houses in the nineties was that of the career woman. The female yuppie did not vanish with the Reagan stock market crash and recession that ended the New Gilded Age of the eighties. Although it was no longer fashionable to flaunt success through conspicuous consumption, women with high incomes indulged in clothing of subtle elegance, refined detailing, and superlative tailoring. (Figure 12.2.) Princess Diana was a fashion leader in this arena as she became more actively engaged with highly publicized daytime functions and official royal visits.

The nineties answer to the 1980s powersuit emerged in several forms. The deconstruction, or reinvention, of the Chanel suit that Karl Lagerfeld had begun when he joined the house in 1983 reached an apogee in the 1990s. Since the 1960s, the Chanel trademark ensemble—the little jacket and narrow, knee-length skirts worn with pearl ropes and chain belts—had been the standard costume of wealthy matrons in the fifty-plus age bracket. Lagerfeld, instead, brilliantly transformed the Chanel suit while staying true to the unmistakable elements of the style. He shortened skirt hemlines and varied their contours from narrow fitted types to flowing pleated variants. He even replaced the skirt entirely with tailored city shorts. Most especially, Lagerfeld experimented with fabrics. In 1991, he shocked Chanel traditionalists with a jeans look suit in which denim was combined with luxurious tweed edged in blue and pink piping. The following year he initiated a leather biker look worn on the runway by voluptuous glamazan supermodels. In the mid-nineties he created a three-piece tweed suit that featured a boned corselet that fitted snugly over a cotton logo T-shirt. (Figure 12.3.) The fresh, updated suits greatly appealed to younger women and sold well, rejuvenating the Chanel image. Ready-to-wear makers were quick to adapt Lagerfeld's many reinterpretations of the classic Chanel suit for the mass market.

FIGURE 12.2. During the recession of the early 1990s, women's fashions lost the oversized drama and showy glitz of the previous decade. Instead, quieter, classic styling became the trend of the decade. Left, wool crepe suit by J. H. Collectibles, 1993; right, wool suit from Russ Petites, 1991.

FIGURE 12.3. The Chanel trademark suit was deconstructed by Karl Lagerfeld in the eighties and nineties. By varying skirt hemlines and contours, reshaping the jackets, and experimenting with contemporary fabrics, Lagerfeld transformed the Chanel suit, thus rejuvenating the house image and appealing to a younger demographic. Chanel pink tweed suit with corselet by Lagerfeld, 1994.

FIGURE 12.4. The deflated look of soft dressing with natural shoulders and fluid fabrics like rayon and silk dominated the ready-to-wear market of the 1990s. Rayon acetate coordinates from Metroline, 1995: left, cascading jacket, shell, and sash trousers; right, shawl collar jacket, shell, and sash skirt.

Key to the new fashion attitudes of middle America in the 1990s was comfort. The over-scaled sculpted and fitted looks of the eighties were deflated, replaced by natural shoulders and fluidly draped rayon jackets, blouses, trousers, and dresses. "Soft dressing" was repeatedly emphasized in advertising and editorials throughout the decade. (Figure 12.4.) Easy knit tops and dresses dominated the ready-to-wear market. Oversized, loose-fitting sweaters and vests topped gathered skirts of varying lengths. Trousers were multipleated or gathered and cut with wide legs.

In addition to inventive avant-garde creations and deconstructionist innovations, fashion designers of the nineties often revisited styles of the past. Ransacking the past for inspiration was not new to the fin de siècle designers. In Chapter 2, we saw that a century earlier *Vogue* had wondered why fashion designers of 1895 seemed to be replicating many of the styles of the 1830s. Indeed, as has been shown in other chapters, fashion revivals were a common source of inspiration for designers, including the most innovative leaders of the time. The retro

FIGURE 12.5. In appropriating design elements from historic dress, designers stripped them of their original meaning to create modern visions of whimsy and nostalgia. Left, tricorne hat and Directoire militaire tunic and trousers by Vivienne Westwood, 1996; right, velvet hacking suit by Ralph Lauren, 1996.

fashions of the 1990s, though, were only minimally nostalgic. When appropriating the styles of the past, designers usually stripped them of their original meaning. For instance, Vivienne Westwood combined an eighteenth-century officer's tunic with striped Directoire trousers and an exaggerated tricorne hat for her 1996 "Vive la Cocotte" collection, but the result was a feeling of whimsy ("cocotte" means floozy), not a statement of aristocratic or military authority. (Figure 12.5.) Nor was Ralph Lauren's velvet hacking suit of 1996 a replication of an Edwardian carriage driver's uniform, but rather was an amusing menswear variation on women's suiting.

The two most popular decades of the recent past that designers of the nineties enjoyed revisiting were the 1950s and 1960s. "The fifties movie-star look is back," affirmed *Vogue* at the beginning of the decade. Comfortable, easy interpretations—not copies—of crisp poplin shirtwaists, cashmere sweater sets, and linen stovepipe pants were produced by Oscar de la Renta, Michael Kors, Donna Karan, Bill Blass, and scores of ready-to-wear makers. (Figure 12.6.) The biker look from American pop culture of the fifties was particularly intriguing to European designers. Hanae Mori, Thierry Mugler, Claude Montana, Yves St. Laurent, and Gianni Versace experimented with biker chic styles. Marlon Branda leather jackets were

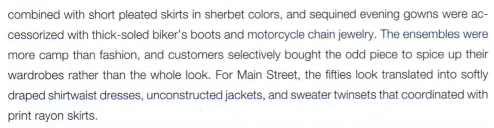

KENAR

HAPPY DAYS ARE HERE AGAIN

FIGURE 12.6. The styles of the fifties continued to intrigue designers of the 1990s, who co-opted iconic elements of the era's fashions to create comfortable, updated interpretations. Kenar ad, 1998.

FIGURE 12.7. Revivalisms of sixties Op and Pop art looks in the 1990s were a relief from the ostentatious glitz of the eighties. Top, oversized Lifesavers and Chiclets turtlenecks and cardigans, 1994; below retro-sixties geometric miniskirt from Bebe, 1996.

combined with short pleated skirts in sherbet colors, and sequined evening gowns were accessorized with thick-soled biker's boots and motorcycle chain jewelry. The ensembles were more camp than fashion, and customers selectively bought the odd piece to spice up their wardrobes rather than the whole look. For Main Street, the fifties look translated into softly draped shirtwaist dresses, unconstructed jackets, and sweater twinsets that coordinated with print rayon skirts.

Among the favorite revivals from the 1960s of both American and European designers were Op and Pop art motifs. (Figure 12.7.) These witty graphics and fun, bold colors were a relief from the extravagant glitz and excess of the eighties. Variations of Andy Warhol's prints were especially popular, including a multiple print of the Marilyn Monroe portrait on a silk gown by Versace and a take-off of Warhol's Mao prints on a nylon mesh T-shirt dress by Vivienne Tam.

Nostalgic revivals of the sixties peaked in the mid-nineties soon after Jackie (Kennedy) Onassis died in May 1994. Coffee table books filled with images of the Kennedy Camelot legacy were everywhere. The highly publicized 1996 Sotheby's auction of many items from Jackie's estate, including 1960s jewelry, period photos, artwork, and numerous mementos,

The fitted, sometimes cinching, bodice corset, bustier, and belt-like corselet remained perennial favorites of designers throughout the 1990s. Ready-to-wear makers capitalized on the popularity of the look, mass producing a wide assortment of corset-inspired tops and dresses for both day and evening. Left, bustier of nylon/spandex satin by Natori, 1995; right, bustier peplum tunic by Karl Lagerfeld for Chanel, 1993.

inspired a renewed interest in the former First Lady's elegant style. For instance, copies of her triple-strand fake pearls, the original of which sold for an astonishing $211,500, were mass marketed in costume reproductions as well as fine jewelry replicas.

Fashion elements of the more distant past, though, were among the favorite points of departure for some of the most inventive designers of the 1990s. As noted previously, Vivienne Westwood explored the eighteenth century with panniered peplums and ruffled cuffs in her 1996 "Vive la Cocotte" collection. St. Laurent's Infanta wedding gown of 1995 expanded laterally over a padded farthingale modeled on those in the seventeenth-century paintings by Velazquez. John Galliano's Empire gowns for Givenchy maintained the high waistline of the Directoire originals but brought to the front the gathered fullness from the back of the 1795 designs. And Lagerfeld's long pelisse coats of 1997 featured wide, stand-up Napoleonic collars.

The external bodice corset in its many forms also continually resurfaced throughout the nineties, just as it had in the 1970s and 1980s. The numerous wide belt corselets of Alexander McQueen were made of assorted materials and were constructed to cinch the waist. The flat front bodice corsets of Azzedine Alaia, Lacroix, Lagerfeld, and Westwood constricted the waist with laces and compressed the breasts with a cylindrical construction much as their sixteenth-century antecedents had. Other forms of the corset, such as the bustier, were cut to define and shape the contours of the breasts, and often featured the same types of front, back, or side lacing as the lingerie corset. Lainey Keogh's purple latex corset was worn under a shimmering transparent gown of metallic yarns. Galliano's Maasai inspired beaded corsets cinched slinky silk gowns. Gaultier's hook-and-eye corsets with garters secured his diaphanous Joan-of-Arc tulle dresses. The many looks of the corset were so popular throughout the period that even ready-to-wear makers mass produced versions in all kinds of materials for both daytime and evening ensembles. (Figure 12.8.)

FIGURE 12.9. The hobo chic look of grunge featured a serendipitous assembly of clothes that included layers of oversized sweaters and dresses, flannel shirts, rock concert T-shirts, and baggy pants in wrinkled, faded, and distressed materials. Left, grunge teens in a Seattle coffee shop, 1993; Ellen Tracy sportswear, 1993.

In addition to retro-looks, contemporary street style continued to be a constant source of inspiration for designers of the nineties, as has been seen by the continuation of punk and biker chic styles. From the American Pacific Northwest, though, came the first distinctive look of the decade—**grunge**. The youth culture phenomenon originated in the rock clubs of Seattle, where, observed *Vogue* in 1992, "frustrated students and minimum-wage slaves banded together and created a lifestyle, ever cynical and utilitarian, that more accurately reflected their conditions." Bands from the region such as Nirvana and Pearl Jam popularized the look internationally through their concerts, music videos, and TV appearances. Grunge emphasized a disheveled, rumpled casualness. (Figure 12.9.) Layers of ratty sweaters, faded flannel shirts, rock tour T-shirts, ripped jeans, and baggy corduroy pants were assembled with an attitude of carelessness. The ubiquitous flannel shirt—preferably with holes or patches, or with sleeves roughly cut off at the shoulders—was worn over floral pattern dresses, or simply tied around the shoulders or waist. The grunge look was accented with knit hats, baseball caps, and heavy work boots or clunky Dr. Marten's shoes.

Many designers embraced grungemania in 1993. Down the runways of Paris and New York trudged models in thick-soled boots and knit caps. Anna Sui and Marc Jacobs

FIGURE 12.10. The influence of grunge and the casualness of the collegiate youth look were adapted to the broader ready-to-wear market in the mid-1990s. Layers of unconstructed vests, distressed jeans, and crinkled fabrics became popular in the nineties. Left, soft cotton vest and crinkled rayon broomstick skirt by Zero Zero, 1994; right, rayon apron jumper by Rabbit Rabbit, 1995.

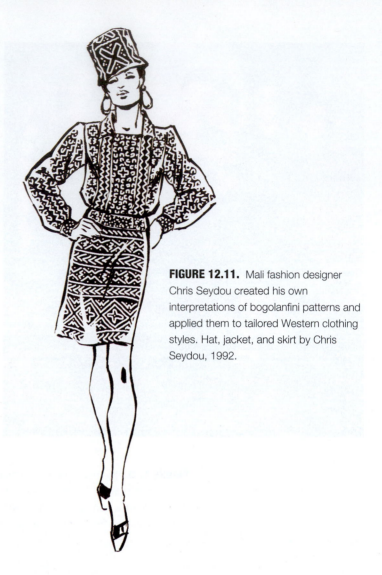

FIGURE 12.11. Mali fashion designer Chris Seydou created his own interpretations of bogolanfini patterns and applied them to tailored Western clothing styles. Hat, jacket, and skirt by Chris Seydou, 1992.

preserved the serendipitous look of grunge with layers of superbly crafted garments of fine fabrics in clashing patterns and colors. Christian Lacroix offered silk dresses that looked as worn as an old flannel shirt. Antonio Beecroft produced high-end sweaters with dropped stitches and oversized shapes that hung slightly askew.

Unfortunately for the fashion industry, both critics and consumers responded negatively to grunge. Fashion journalists savaged grunge styles because the look was viewed as ugly and impractical for any woman over the age of nineteen. Customers simply refused to buy clothing that resembled ready-to-wear "irregulars" and thrift-shop discards. Consequently, grungemania barely lasted a year.

Yet the attitude of layered grunge street wear had broadened the repertoire of many designers, in some instances bringing a more relaxed and accommodating perspective to their oeuvre. Soft, unconstructed vests were layered over silk blouses worn with distressed jeans or fuller cut poplin pants. Crinkled fabrics stylized the casualness of the 1990s youth culture, broadening the market appeal. (Figure 12.10.) Patchwork for jackets, skirts, leather goods, and shoes were revived from their heyday in the 1970s.

Fashion pluralism of the 1990s also expanded to include global influences, especially looks from Africa. In 1993, Mali designer Chris Seydou established the African Foundation of

FIGURE 12.12. In the second half of the 1990s, the futuristic look of cyberstyle combined forms of street style and historic costume with technotextiles to anticipate new-age fashions of the twenty-first century. Left, dress of Swareflex Reflectors from Swarovski, 1995; right, polyvinyl jeans by Todd Oldham, 1998.

Fashion Designers and became its first president. Seydou, who had apprenticed with Yves St. Laurent, had become internationally known for his designs of Western style clothing made with traditional African **bogolanfini**, or mud-dyed, textiles. (Figure 12.11.) Ambassadors of the Pan-Africa organization traveled the world promoting the burgeoning African fashion industry. During the late 1990s, South Africa, Kenya, and Zambia were the first African nations to sponsor regional fashion weeks to showcase designs of local talent to an international press.

From the second half of the decade into the new millennium, advances in fiber technologies opened fresh arenas for designers. Fabrics were woven with threads of metal or plastic to create surfaces that prismatically reflected light. (Figure 12.12.) Spandex was blended with cotton and wool for unprecedented comfort in slim pants and tailored jackets. David Chu of Nautica applied Teflon coatings to white cotton for greater stain resistance. Cynthia Steffe utilized computer-generated sequins in place of costly hand beading. Other **technotextiles** were made of latex, neoprene, polyurethane, nylon, and rubber. In 1999, Hussein Chalayan took the molded garment one step further than Miyake's bustier and fashioned his knee-length "airplane" dress of fiberglass. Even the nonrip paper used in making express delivery envelopes was experimentally applied to dresses by Donna Karan.

The use of technofabrics was also combined with elements of street style and historic dress to create **cyberstyle**. Like the futuristic costumes of sci-fi movies of the time, cyberstyle fashions incorporated pieces of body armor such as Mugler's metal and clear plastic "cyborg" suit of 1995 and Anela Takac's 1994 cross breastplate with 3-D holograms. Plastic CDs and

FIGURE 12.13. The silhouettes of coats of the 1990s narrowed considerably after the oversized proportions and exaggerated detailing of the eighties. The comfort and simplicity of classic styling was preferred. Left, blanket print acrylic jacket by David Wayne, 1993; right, wool coats from Evan-Picone, 1994.

computer hard drive chips were attached to garments as ornamentation. Alexander McQueen's 1999 trouser suit jacket featured an allover white-on-black pattern of a computer chip schematic. Precision slashing was produced by computer for Antonio Berardi's PVC jacket of 1997. Into the new millennium, experiments with "smart clothes" included clothing wired to receive electronic information such as email and GPS navigation guidance. Technovision and a dynamic technotextile market enabled fashion designers of the fin de siècle to exploit the properties of new materials and achieve creative innovations in cut and construction, and perpetuate that most basic element of fashion—change.

Women's Outerwear 1990–1999

Coats and jackets of the nineties became narrow and shorter, losing the huge shoulder pads, capacious volume, and ankle sweeping lengths of the previous decade. Classic styles were the most popular—a reaction to the excesses of the eighties and the unwelcomed looks of

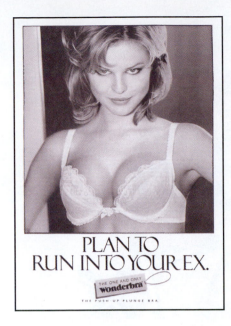

FIGURE 12.14. In the early 1990s, the popularity of the glamazon model featured in fashion editorials and advertising inspired a renewed interest in fitness and body shaping. Undergarment makers responded with a variety of engineered garments such as the Wonderbra, which enhanced the contours and cleavage of the breasts. Left, Wonderbra ad, 1995; center, foil-printed teddy from Escapades, 1992; right, Playtex Secrets underwire bra and brief, 1994.

grunge. (Figure 12.13.) Menswear wrap coats were comfortable alternatives to dressy tailored styles. Although the fur industry was impacted by animal advocacy groups, traditional styles of fur coats and jackets remained popular in the 1990s. Fur coats returned to the classic constructions of the New Look era with straight hanging silhouettes, simple flip-up collars, and cuffless sleeves.

Women's Underwear and Sleepwear 1990–1999

Styles of women's undergarments continued to be vastly diverse—from basic cotton briefs and bras to newly reengineered forms like the Wonderbra, a "push-up plunge bra" that reshaped almost any woman's breasts to form a distinct cleavage. (Figure 12.14.) To compete with highly successful niche marketers such as Victoria's Secret, department stores expanded their lingerie departments to include in-store lingerie boutiques filled with luxurious and novelty fashion undergarments in extensive color palettes. Corsets and bustiers were not worn as figure control undergarments, but rather were donned by young, slender women as sexual foreplay. Similarly, teddies and camisoles were shaped and tailored to enhance and flatter the feminine form. Despite the discomfort and inconvenience, garter belts and hosiery were enjoyed as a sexy alternative to pantyhose. As clothing became softer and more fluid in the 1990s, undergarment makers responded to consumer demands for more comfortable forms of abbreviated

FIGURE 12.15. Sleepwear of the 1990s ranged from bias-cut gowns and robes in luxurious fabrics to cozy retro chenille styles. Beaded chiffon gown with lace waistband by Flora Nikrooz, 1991.

FIGURE 12.16. Active sportswear for the athletic woman of the nineties was reengineered with new constructions and durable materials for maximum comfort and performance. Safety gear such as helmets and kneepads were the new sports accessories. Nylon spandex sportsbra and cycling pants, 1996.

figure control undergarments that included underwire bras with less binding support and panty girdles made of Lycra spandex.

Sleepwear, too, was widely varied, ranging from lacy gown and robe ensembles in sumptuous silks or satiny synthetics to commodity cotton menswear pajamas. In the early 1990s, revivals of sexy, bias-cut gowns of the thirties were inspired by the popularity of the voluptuous glamazons in fashion editorials and ads. (Figure 12.15.) In the second half of the decade, floor-length chenille robes, replicating those of the forties and fifties, reappeared along with matching bedspreads and pillow shams.

Women's Sports Attire 1990–1999

In the 1990s, women approached exercise more holistically than they had in the seventies and eighties. Look-good/feel-good factors expanded beyond the gym to include special focus on nutrition and diet, homeopathy, and even Eastern mind and body disciplines such as t'ai chi. Never before had women been more educated about health.

The reevaluation of fitness and health extended to active sports apparel as well. Most women went to the gym in nonchalant, loose-fitting garments of different mixes from favorite old sweatshirts and T-shirts to streetwear shorts and tops. Gone were the carefully coordinated separates with matching accessories of the eighties.

For serious training workouts, though, improved sports attire included compression sportsbra tops and other engineered constructions made of durable, high-performance ma-

FIGURE 12.17. Swimwear since the early 1990s has been designed more for comfort and functionality with greater coverage than in the preceding two decades. Top, polka dot maillot and cover-up from Sirena, 1993; below, notched bandeau bikini by Todd Oldham, 1997.

terials. Safety gear became all important for outdoors activities. Cyclists and skaters armored themselves with helmets, kneepads, gloves, and wrist and elbow guards. (Figure 12.16.) Garments were made with reflective patches and even battery operated flashing lights.

Many of these comfortable and colorful sports clothes continued to find their way into everyday dress. Running suits were easy to slip into for Saturday errands. Spandex tanks were worn as sexy undershirts beneath jackets and big shirts.

Women's Swimwear 1990–1999

The barest of swimwear styles were less popular in the 1990s than they had been in the previous two decades. Comfort and functionality were the more dominant factors in selecting a swimsuit. Maillots of fluidly-fitting stretch fabrics were favorites. (Figure 12.17.) Among the revivals of the 1990s was the **hipster**, with its forties-style, high-waist cut that was often paired with wide, architectonic bandeau tops. Revived from the thirties Olympics was the **racer**, with its open back, wide shoulder straps, and sleek, full-coverage front.

Still, the string bikini and thong were ever present on most beaches, especially for collegiate women during spring break in the United States and at the Mediterranean and Caribbean resorts in their respective seasons. Designers blurred the line between underwear and swimwear with the "lingerie look" that featured swimsuits cut like undergarments and made of shimmering, silky-looking fabrics. Chanel made headlines in 1996 with the micro string bikini made of cord with two small disks for the breasts and a sliver of V-shaped fabric as the bottom—each of which was embroidered with the double "C" Chanel logo.

FIGURE 12.18. Low heel comfort dominated women's footwear of the 1990s. Influenced by grunge and the youth market, revivals included thick-heeled pumps and chunky sandals reminiscent of the 1970s.

Leopard print ponyskin pump by Dolce & Gabbana, 1998.

Suede Louis heel pump from Connie, 1994.

Retro-seventies platform sandal and wedge from Aldo, 1996.

Low wedge from Life Stride; skimmer and low-heel pump from Connie, 1993.

Women's Shoes 1990–1999

The sculpted drama and glitz of footwear in the eighties were replaced by retro looks in the nineties, updated with new contours that included wide, blunted toes. More foot was exposed with plunging throats and open, strappy varieties that displayed toe cleavage. Stilettos remained favorites for evening wear, but unlike in the 1980s, less so for the office. Comfortable flats and two-inch high heels were preferred by most career women for the workday. The grunge influence of the early 1990s inspired a middecade revival of chunky straight heels and platform soles from the seventies. Even versions of the 1920s Louis heel returned. (Figure 12.18.)

Women's Jewelry 1990–1999

In keeping with the strong trend of revivalisms in the 1990s, retro jewelry from the fifties and sixties was everywhere. In 1994, when Jackie Onassis died, pearls in classic forms of jewelry were again popular after her famous three-strand necklace went on the auction block. In 1993, *Jurassic Park* launched a mania for genuine amber, which was especially prized if it contained a fossilized insect. Other natural materials such as stones, wood, cork, shells, and unglazed clay were combined with knotted cords and braided yarns, often dyed in matching earthtones. As a backlash to the massive, showy styles of the eighties, jewelry of the 1990s became more subdued—simpler in ornament and smaller in proportion and scale. (Figure 12.19.) To compensate for the smaller, lighter designs, pieces were sometimes worn in multiples, often in thematic combinations like Victoriana, art deco, or romantique.

Romantique revival jewelry, 1994.

Catherine Stein collection of wood, stone, shell, and fibers, 1996.

Cloisonne "Animalia" pins by Laurel Burch, 1991.

FIGURE 12.19. Jewelry became more subdued in the 1990s following the drama of excess and oversized sculptural scales of the eighties. Multiple pieces were sometimes worn in thematic combinations to compensate for the smaller and lighter designs.

Women's Hairstyles and Makeup 1990–1999

Preferred hairstyles of the nineties were comfortable and convenient, replacing the high-maintenance looks of the eighties. (Figure 12.20.) Revival fashions of the fifties and sixties inspired adaptations of hairstyles from those eras. The closely cropped Audrey Hepburn look returned. Instead of teased and lacquered big hair, career women chose more elegant up-swept styles such as the Grace Kelly French twist. Versions of the sixties beehive and bubble cut were softened and reduced in volume. Deep bangs were popular for both long and short cuts. The feather-edged "Rachel" cut, named for the early look of Jennifer Aniston on the TV program *Friends,* was widely copied in the late 1990s. For African-Americans, stylized ethnic braids with symbolic significance were adapted from African cultures.

Wispy Audrey Hepburn revival crop, 1994.

FIGURE 12.20. The high maintenance styles of teased and lacquered big hair of the eighties yielded to softer, easy-care styles in the 1990s. Retro looks that corresponded to the many fashion revivalisms of the decade included classics such as the pageboy and 1950s Audrey Hepburn crops. Many African-American women opted for stylized braids adapted from African cultures.

Soft, easy-care short styles, 1993.

African inspired braids called "Meet You At The Crossroads," 1998.

FIGURE 12.21. Except for utilitarian types, hats largely disappeared from women's wardrobes after 1990. Retro headcoverings included fifties style little straw hats for spring and sixties pop Nureyev caps. Left, retro adaptation of Nureyev cap, 1995; right, Liz Claiborne straw hat, 1993.

Makeup also became softer with lighter applications as well as lighter shades of lipstick, eyeshadow, and blush. Cosmetics marketing repeatedly emphasized the word "natural." Eyeliner and eyeshadows were more subtle than those of the eighties. Lipsticks were light, retro-sixties pinks and corals. In some fashion magazine editorials, the heroin drug addict look with its pale, gaunt features and circles under the eyes was used as a dramatic contrast to the healthy, girl-next-door vitality featured in cosmetic ads.

Women's Hats 1990–1999

In the 1990s, lavish hats were too integrally linked to the extravagance of the previous decade and were largely abandoned. Exceptions were traditional events such as the Kentucky Derby or England's Royal Ascot. Most models in fashion advertising and editorials, though, were predominantly bareheaded. First Lady Hillary Clinton's wide hair-bands and simple winter felt hats reflected the return to a practical utility of head dressing in the nineties. Oblong scarves, especially those with distinctive designer logos, covered the hair and wrapped about the neck for a touch of forties Hollywood glamour. Tams, berets, fedoras, and knit caps remained practical cold weather favorites. Simple straw hats were donned for spring weddings or special summer social events. Some revivals of fashion hats such as the Nureyev cap of the sixties appealed to a new generation of young women. (Figure 12.21.)

Women's Accessories 1990–1999

As the excesses of the eighties dissipated during the economic recession at the close of the decade, extraneous accessories were discarded. Instead of piling on accessories for show, women of the 1990s preferred simplicity. They wanted style combined with practicality. A single key accessory bespoke elegance and sophistication more effectively than the visual confusion of a multitude of accessories. Gone were the pretensions—and inconvenience—of carrying

Salvatore Ferragamo handbag and belt, 1995.

Chanel handbag, wallet, sunglasses, and jewelry, 1995.

Fifties style leopard print scarf, beret, and horn rimmed sunglasses, 1993.

FIGURE 12.22. The full accoutrement of head-to-toe accessories in the New Gilded Age was abandoned during the economic recessions of the late eighties and early nineties. Instead, women preferred one or two key accessories as a statement of personal style.

daytime gloves or tying a designer scarf to a handbag merely as a color extension. The exception was with haute couture shows in which many designers still exploited the theatricality of excess throughout the 1990s.

The subdued, simplified approach to accessories developed into a minimalist attitude. It was function over form, and quality over quantity. (Figure 12.22.) Accessories branded with a distinctive designer logo gained in popularity although matched sets of accessories were less important than the single item of emphasis. Colors were muted; black and earthtones were much preferred except for sportswear, where colorful accents such as disposable Swatch and Fossil watches were striking accents. Even when exaggeration was at play, particularly with fashion revivals of the fifties and sixties, the focus was usually on one component, not the full replication of the past. A Bruno Magli woven handbag (or its mass-produced knock-off) was enough punctuation for casual weekend wear, or a Judith Leiber rhinestone bag (or, likewise, a manufactured derivative) was sufficient for evening wear without the addition of glitz and glitter to the gown, neck, ears, wrists, and feet.

Men's Fashions 1990–1999

The key word in men's suit styles at the beginning of the 1990s was classic. In 1993, *GQ* forecast that "the nineties suit is a symbol of understated savvy in dress: less in-your-face than the shoulder-padded uniform that fairly proclaimed, Look at me!" (Figure 12.23.) Jacket

FIGURE 12.23. Men's suits of the nineties lost the drama of the eighties big shoulders and became trim with minimal padding. Details such as lapels and pocket treatments were subtle. Trousers were cut more narrow, losing their previous billowy fluidity. Suit separates from Haggar, 1995.

padding was minimal and high-waisted; billowy trousers were trimmed in proportion as well. Savile Row and custom British tailoring resumed prominence, although far from diminishing the menswear influences from Milan. Variety and a touch of personality were provided by the play of button treatments. Armani and Versace made the nineties jacket more open and provocative with a dropped, one-button closure. At the other end of the spectrum was Zanetti's ten-button double-breasted suit jacket that completely encased the torso throat to hem. In between were three-button revivals of the drape cut from the 1930s and five-button interpretations of the sixties space age look.

The visually jarring pattern mixing that dominated the eighties became more subdued but continued as a way to break the monotony of the pervasive traditional dark suit with its two-button, notch collar jacket. Surprising to many was the lead from Britain in the successful blending of patterns and colors that only the most daring and confident North American male might try. Catalogs and magazine editorials offered endless advice on what to wear together and what to avoid without risking "a phone call from Barnum & Bailey's." An alternative to the challenge of pattern mixing for more traditionalist men was suit separates, usually with jackets patterned in subtle checks, herringbone, or houndstooth paired with solid trousers.

At the same time, a casual dress code for Fridays became the corporate policy for businesses of all sizes around the world. Neckties were discarded and cotton gabardine or rayon blend pants replaced tailored wool trousers. (Figure 12.24.) Khaki and even denim pants that were taboo in business offices a decade earlier were common even in executive suites and boardrooms. By the end of the decade, many companies permitted a "business casual" look for the entire week, causing a significant drop in sales of professional attire.

During the 1990s, the huge consumer market of baby boomers moved into their forties and fifties, contending with expanding middle-age waistlines. Makers of sportswear, especially jeans, responded to the changing market by introducing "relaxed fit" styles of pants and shorts that were cut fuller through the hips. seat, and legs. (Figure 12.25.)

Likewise, the fit of sportswear tops and sweaters was loose and casual. The padded shoulders and sculptural styling of the eighties became a baggy, deflated look in the 1990s.

FIGURE 12.24. During the 1990s, many corporations began to allow casual Fridays where men could wear oxford shirts and gabardine pants in place of suits and ties. By the second half of the decade, "business casual" dress had been expanded to the entire workweek at most companies. Dockers mock turtleneck, railroad stripe oxford shirt, and cotton twill pleated pants, 1994.

FIGURE 12.25. As the baby boomers aged, ready-to-wear makers responded to the changing market with relaxed fit pants, cut fuller through the seat and legs. Levi's Two Horse relaxed fit jeans, 1992.

(Figure 12.26.) Colors became more muted and drab compared to the striking styles of the eighties exemplified by Cliff Huxtable's wardrobe in *The Cosby Show.* Even so, to break the monotony of basic hues and traditional textile patterns, men's wardrobes often still included the occasional pop of a strong color such as salmon or electric blue or a striking graphical print. For men with an individualistic personality, an occasional eye-catching novelty garment could help them to break out from the herd of the ordinary. Jean Paul Gaultier's muscle shirt of 1995, for example, was screen printed with a startling trompe l'oeil depiction of an athletic torso. (Figure 12.27.)

As noted previously in this chapter, the thrift store casualness of the grunge look became a youth culture phenomenon in the early 1990s. Young men emulated the dress of their pop idols Kurt Cobain, lead singer of Nirvana, and Mark Arm of the band Green River (who is credited with coining the term "grunge"). Faded flannel shirts were worn open over distressed, screen printed T-shirts—both untucked—with rumpled, shredded jeans and scuffed work boots or dirty sneakers.

FIGURE 12.26. The fit of men's sportswear in the 1990s was oversized and loose fitting for casual comfort. Sweater, rugby shirt, and shorts from Gant, 1994.

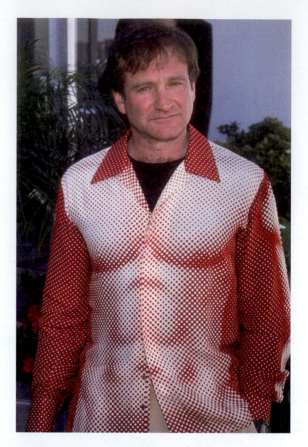

FIGURE 12.27. Despite the prevalence of bland traditionalism in menswear of the 1990s, many designers still created avant-garde fashions for men seeking to stand out from the herd. Jean Paul Gaultier's trompe l'oeil muscle shirt worn by actor Robin Williams, 1995.

A similar pop culture influence of the 1990s was the baggy, layered look of hip-hop or B-Boy bands such as the Beastie Boys, from which the label "B-Boy" is thought to have derived. (Figure 12.28.) Hip-hop fashion, assessed *GQ* in 1992, "is one of appropriation." In effect, a member of a band, or sometimes the band as a whole, would adopt an ordinary article of clothing, and by wearing it repeatedly in public and for performances, transformed the style into a hip-hop look. Among the types of clothing made trendy for hip-hop of the nineties were brightly hued nylon track suits, Adidas and Converse sneakers worn unlaced, quilted parkas, and Kangol logo hats and sweatshirts.

The way in which these pedestrian forms of clothing were worn was sometimes more important than the brand or style. Clothing had to be oversized and ill-fitting, especially pants, which were sometimes called "fifties" because of the large waist size. Baggy pants rode low on the hips, revealing the waistbands of colorfully patterned underwear, notably plaid boxers. According to a *New York Times* report in 1994, the underwear display was a bad-boy look inspired by prison inmates who were not permitted belts.

The baggy, distressed layered looks of grunge and hip-hop permeated the broader culture, influencing the dress of most young men throughout the 1990s. The comfort of old flannel shirts and long T-shirts draping over sagging, oversized jeans became the preeminent look of

FIGURE 12.28. The baggy, layered street look of teens and young men of the 1990s was derived from the antifashion dress of hip-hop or B-Boy bands. Left, hip-hop group the Beastie Boys, 1994; right, flannel and denim shirts by Union Bay with Bugle Boy jeans, 1996.

teens and young men. Ironically, what had begun as an antifashion, insurgent backlash against the over-styled aesthetic of menswear in the 1980s became, itself, the mainstream fashion at the end of the century.

Men's Sports Attire and Outerwear 1990–1999

Active sportswear followed the trend of streetwear in its looser cuts and casual fit. Big tees and oversized warm-up suits were preferred by all ages of men for workouts at the gym. The more nonchalant the look, the better; carefully matched coordinates were a thing of the past. The activewear short-shorts of the 1980s disappeared in favor of street-inspired knee-length knit shorts that were so full and baggy they often resembled a split skirt. Basketball star Michael Jordan is credited with popularizing the style. (Figure 12.29.) According to fashion lore, because Jordan wanted to wear his lucky University of North Carolina shorts under his Chicago Bulls shorts, the pro uniform had to be cut fuller and longer to conceal the school shorts. But in a 1997 interview with *Details,* Jordan claimed that the long, baggy shorts were developed to give him room to move around and, since he thought himself too thin, to project the appearance of being bigger than he actually was.

Men's outerwear styles changed little after the lateral expanse of shoulder silhouettes were deflated at the end of the eighties. As with most choices in their clothing, men sought comfort and ease over style when selecting outerwear. For many men that meant a basic jacket, or worse, relying only on their suit jacket, even in the worst winter weather. In 1996, GQ chastised

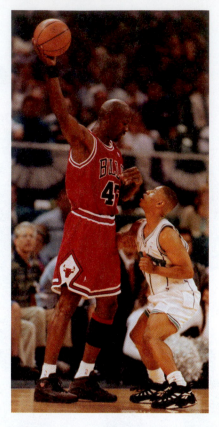

FIGURE 12.29. Michael Jordan has been credited with popularizing the long, baggy shorts for athletic wear. When he played basketball for Chicago in the 1990s, he purportedly needed a wider, longer cut of his pro shorts to conceal his lucky college shorts underneath. Photo of Jordan, 1995.

FIGURE 12.30. The easy-care casualness of leather jackets was a comfortable alternative to overcoats in the nineties. Leather bomber jacket by Kenneth Stevens, 1995.

FIGURE 12.31. In addition to traditional paisley and petit-print foulards, men's neckties of the 1990s were designed with striking multicolored prints featuring vintage graphics, old master paintings, landscapes, and exotic animals. Left, silk foulard ties by Resilio, 1995; right, graphical ties from various makers, 1990–94.

men for disregarding those "finishing touches that are the most important," particularly the overcoat. Of the "classic and always chic" styles they recommended were the cropped duffle, the trench coat in synthetic blends, knee-breaker wraps, the single-breasted reefer, and the fly front chesterfield. Comfortable and easy-care leather carcoats and bomber jackets were affordable options to overcoats. (Figure 12.30.)

Men's Accessories 1990–1999

Throughout the 1990s, neckties remained fairly uniform in width—about 3 1/2 to 4 inches at the tip—although prints, colors, and fabrics varied widely. (Figure 12.31.) As an alternative to staid foulards and paisley prints, vividly colored graphical prints were popular in the first half of the decade. Scenic landscapes, old master paintings, art nouveau posters, vintage cars, and wildlife were reproduced in large scale to fill the depth of the tie blade from shirt collar to belt. Novelty styles included cut-to-shape ties such as the fish series in the mid-nineties that were realistic screenprints of fish cut and quilted to the contours of the species.

FIGURE 12.32. Influenced by the dress of subcultures such as punk and grunge, many young men of the nineties adopted thick soled work boots and hiking boots as everyday footwear. Hiking boots from H.H. Brown, 1996.

In the 1990s, men wanted the same simplicity and comfort in their footwear that they sought in suits and sportswear. Tassel and penny loafers became as common as lace-ups for office wear. Adaptations of the heavy, lug sole utility styles that had been popular with street subcultures like punk, grunge, and bikers became mainstream for many young men. Thick soled work boots, logger boots, and hiking boots were worn as everyday footwear. (Figure 12.32.)

The principal head gear for men of all ages was the baseball cap, especially those embellished with favorite sports team logos and mascots. Boys and teens often wore their cap with the brim turned backward or at an angle to the side as a generational distinction.

Men's Underwear and Swimwear 1990–1999

Although fashion briefs and bikini styles of men's underwear continued to sell well, the trend of men's underwear in the 1990s shifted toward more coverage but still with the same formfitting smoothness. New types of **boxerbriefs** were constructed with contoured front pouches for greater fit and comfort, becoming the preferred style of young men. (Figure 12.33.) Except for the full-cut woven boxers, textile patterns and prints were less common for other styles of underwear than in the seventies and eighties. Color palettes of most underwear narrowed to the basics, primarily white, heather gray, navy, and black. Older men still opted for loose fitting woven boxers, a style also adopted by urban teen boys who wore oversized, baggy jeans pushed low on the hips to expose their colorfully patterned shorts as an anticonformity statement.

The trim fit of underwear boxerbriefs influenced swimwear with similar retro-twenties styles in the 1990s. Square-cut trunks of knit cotton and Lycra were a fresh look, especially in horizontal stripes. U.S. men were less inclined to wear the briefer forms of swimwear although the barest, most revealing styles remained ubiquitous elsewhere in the world. The

FIGURE 12.33. Although the briefest forms of underwear continued to be popular with niche segments in the 1990s, the knit boxerbrief became the favorite of most young men. Older men and teens opted for baggy woven boxers in bold prints. Top, cutaway brief from Calvin Klein, 1990; below, boxerbriefs from 2Xist, 1996.

long, baggy surfer trunks of the sixties that had been revived in the eighties as jams were once again revived in the mid-1990s as **board shorts**, becoming even longer and wider despite the discomfort when wet and the "knee socks" tan that resulted. (Figure 12.34.)

FIGURE 12.34. Long, baggy surfer trunks, called board shorts in the 1990s, became the prevalent form of swimwear for most American boys and men. Tropical print board shorts from Father of Surfing, 1996.

Men's Grooming and Hairstyles 1990–1999

Men's hairstyles came in every conceivable cut, length, volume, and color. A 1996 car ad featured the headline "Life is full of complicated decisions," and showed twenty distinct men's short hair styles, all of which were common at the time. When added with long variants and ethnic styles, the realistic list of men's hairstyle options was substantial. To add variety, assorted types of gels and mousse allowed subtle changes that required little care. The "**caesar cut**" of the mid-nineties was very short at the sides with a short fringe of bangs sometimes gelled forward in a point over the forehead. As a variation of the look, some men pushed the gelled bangs upright from the forehead in a shape called the "**slope**." (Figure 12.35.) In the second half of the decade, the fifties style pompadour of Elvis Presley and James Dean was revived by young men who combed their superbly thick hair back from the brow into a luxuriant mound. A variation of the pompadour retained the upswept volume but was fingered into a spiky fringe on top before the gel set, a presage of the millennial "bedhead" look.

Facial hair reappeared in the nineties as assorted wispy goatees, some with equally wispy mustaches. The look appealed to young men under thirty as a statement of personal style that negated clean-cut corporate traditionalism.

The hairless masculine torso that became the trend at the end of the eighties was more broadly common in the 1990s with influences from underwear ads and TV programs like *Baywatch* where the frequently shirtless male cast and guest stars displayed smoothly shaved chests and abdomens.

FIGURE 12.35. Among the retro hairstyles for men of the 1990s was the very short, fringy crop called a caesar and its variation with upright bangs called the slope. In the second half of the decade, men with thick, full hair adopted fifties style pompadours combed back from the brow into high, luxuriant mounds. Left, the slope cut, 1995; right, new wave pompadour, 1998.

Children's Clothing 1990–1999

Among the social controversies of the era was the issue of mandated public school uniforms. Some educators and social scientists believed that school uniforms reduced violence by eliminating economic class distinctions between students, and, in some inner city districts, eliminating the dress symbols of gang members. In addition, school uniforms eased the financial burden on parents. According to *USA Today,* in 1998, parents spent an average of $185 per child for school clothes compared to $104 per child for school uniforms. On the flip side, opponents of school uniforms suggested that uniforms forced conformity, hindering creative abilities and limiting personal expression. By the end of the decade less than three percent of U.S. public schools had instituted mandated school uniforms.

Children's wear of the nineties reflected the pluralism that dominated adult clothing. Ready-to-wear makers expanded categories of garments to follow the varied trends of women's and men's fashions. As with adults, children demanded casual comfort. (Figure 12.36.) In response, public schools relaxed dress codes. Jeans, paired with an endless variety of tops, prevailed for both genders. Joining established brands of children's wear like Oshkosh B'Gosh, designer labels such as Versace, Byblos, Simonetta, and Diesel entered the children's wear market.

Girls who preferred dresses could choose from the same array of hemlines as their moms, ranging from thigh high to mid-calf lengths. (Figure 12.37.) Jumper sets, split skirts,

FIGURE 12.36. Parents chose clothing for their infants and toddlers that successfully combined comfort and safety for the child, ease of quick change, and visual appeal. Bib overalls and knit mockneck top by Oshkosh B'Gosh, 1990.

FIGURE 12.37. Girls dresses of the 1990s were miniature versions of adult styles, including silhouettes with hemlines at all lengths. Catsuits, pant sets, and oversized T-shirts and fleece tops met the demand for comfort and colorful style. Left, dresses from Peach Soda, 1993; center, pant sets from Buster Brown and Health-tex, 1994; right, catsuit from Bonnie Jean, 1995.

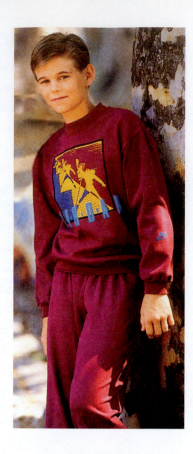

FIGURE 12.38. For boys, urban looks of layered oversized garments met the demand for casual comfort. Bold screenprints of dinosaurs and famous sports logos abounded in the 1990s. Left. flannel shirts and Bugle Boy twill pants, 1994; center, Dynokids fleece set, 1991; right, Nike Air Jordan fleece set, 1992.

and catsuits provided comfort and school week fashion options. Clothing emblazoned with designer and branded logos were as popular with children as with their parents.

For boys, urban wear styles satisfied their demand for casual comfort. The layered oversized street looks with shirttails untucked and wide pant legs bunched up around the ankles became universal. To meet the market demand, manufacturers produced boys' clothing with dropped shoulders and fuller cuts. (Figure 12.38.) Raglan baseball tees with sleeves made of contrasting colors became a favorite revival from the sixties. Nike T-shirts and sweatshirts were screenprinted with the famous caption "Just Do It" from the long-running ad campaign. College and pro-team fleece and T-shirts replicated those worn by dads. Any clothing with dinosaur prints, patches, and especially the T-Rex logo from the hit movie *Jurassic Park* were hugely popular with preteen boys. When required to dress up for a special occasion, boys preferred sport jackets and blazers with chinos rather than a suit and tie.

The ubiquitous accessory for all ages of children (and collegiates) was the backpack. Makers engineered bags with assorted multiple pockets, adjustable straps, and padding. Brightly colored nylon and vinyl backpacks appealed to gradeschoolers; fashion styles made of patterned sweater knits accented with corduroy or suede detailing served as a combination purse and book tote for teen girls.

Review

At the beginning of the 1990s. a global economic recession and the Persian Gulf War crisis caused a backlash against the excesses of the eighties and led to the end of the artificial, sculpted looks for both women and men. The broad shouldered power suit, padded sportswear, and oversized coats were deflated and narrowed. Fashion pluralism expanded to fill the vacuum. Individuality and personal style became more significant than dictates from the fashion industry. Comfort and casualness dominated even the workplace as businesses relaxed dress codes. For those who were uncertain of their individuality, at least with fashion, logo wear provided a form of group identity—from couture house brands to licensed sports team emblems. In addition, a plethora of revivals from the fifties and sixties continued to offer some refuge of comfort for the fashion-wary woman or man. Youth culture looks such as grunge and punk influenced the mainstream dress of young people with antifashion styles that included layered thrift shop discards and lug soled work boots. Hip-hop inspired new ways to wear ordinary clothing from neon hued track suits to unlaced sneakers.

review questions

1. As fashion became more pluralistic and niche-oriented in the 1990s, what two principal purposes did haute couture serve?

2. Why was logo wear particularly popular in the 1990s? What were some key designer logos that achieved mass recognition?

3. What were some of the 1990s revivalisms from the fifties, sixties, and the more distant past? Identify at least one designer with each retro-style.

4. Compare and contrast the grunge and cyberstyle looks of the 1990s. What cultural changes influenced the emergence of each style? Identify three designers whose fashions were influenced by these pop culture styles, and explain how.

5. What were some of the key changes in fashion and society that inspired a change in women's career dress from the tailored powersuits of the eighties to softer, more casual styles of the nineties?

research and portfolio projects

Research

1. Write a research paper on the emergence of hip-hop dress and how the looks filtered into mainstream fashion. Identify the music groups that led the way and which styles they popularized. Also give examples of adaptations of hip-hop fashion produced and marketed by ready-to-wear makers and couture houses.

Portfolio

1. Produce three paperdoll sets of fashions for a teen boy and girl. Each set must include ten changeable garments and accessories rendered in full color. Choose from:
   - grunge
   - hip-hop
   - cyberstyle
   - logo brand
   - African inspired
   - retro-fifties

dress terms

board shorts: men's long, baggy swim trunks modeled after the surfer jams of the eighties

bogolanfini cloth: African-inspired textiles made of cotton cloth painted or handstamped with patterns of geometric symbols in a mixture of black, mineral-rich mud, sometimes intensified with vegetable dyes

boxerbriefs: men's underwear that combined the snug fit of knit briefs with the square cut and longer legs of traditional boxers

caesar cut: men's hairstyle of the mid-nineties cropped very short at the sides with a short fringe of bangs combed forward in a point over the forehead

cyberstyle: a futuristic look of the late 1990s that combined technotextiles with street looks and elements of historic dress

grunge: a youth pop culture look of the early 1990s that emphasized a disheveled casualness and ensembles of distressed and mismatched clothing

hipster: a women's high-waist swimsuit bottom of the 1990s that was a revival of a style from the forties

racer: a women's one-piece swimsuit with an open back and wide shoulder straps modeled on Olympic swimsuits of the forties

slope: men's hairstyle of the late 1990s with a short fringe of bangs gelled to rise vertically from the forehead

technotextiles: synthetic materials produced in the 1990s that were applied to apparel and accessories

13 The New Millennium
2000 to Present

2000   **PRESENT**

U.S. War in Afghanistan began 2001

U.S.–Iraqi War 2003–2011

Y2K global computer
conversions 2000

Eight Harry Potter
movies 2001–11

Hurricane Katrina
devastated New
Orleans 2005

Al Gore's documentary
film on global warming
An Inconvenient Truth
won Oscar 2007

Collapse of U.S.
banks started global
financial crisis 2008

Facebook.com
launched 2004

Muslim terrorists
destroyed New York
World Trade Center
2001

First Euro coins
and notes
2002

Pluto designated
a dwarf planet
2006

Phoenix spacecraft
confirmed water on
Mars 2008

Barack Obama
elected first
African-American
U.S. President 2009

The Digitized New Millennium 2000–Present

The election of 2000 was one of the most contentious and divisive in decades. For weeks after election day, the results were inconclusive whether Vice President Al Gore or former Texas governor George W. Bush was duly elected. Although Gore had received 500,000 more popular votes than Bush, neither candidate had received the requisite number of electoral college votes. As ballots were recounted by hand in Florida, whose electoral votes would determine the outcome, the U.S. Supreme Court intervened with a controversial decision that favored Bush.

On September 11 the following year, a group of Muslim terrorists highjacked U.S. planes, crashing them into the Pentagon and the New York World Trade Center, killing thousands. The Bush administration immediately launched military action against the terrorist organizations by invading Afghanistan and destroying the bases that supported such groups. In 2003, the Bush administration expanded its military objectives in the region by invading Iraq to depose the regime of Saddam Hussein.

Shopping the Internet 2000–Present

By 2010, nearly 85% of U.S. households had a home computer, a leap from just 15% in 1990. In the new millennium, the World Wide Web became the "information superhighway" with its e-mail, cyber chat rooms, blogs, and billions of Web site pages. The number of online retailers and service businesses, called "dot-coms" after the period ("dot") and domain name ("com") of their Web addresses, was explosive. (Figure 13.1.) All categories and price ranges of fashion were instantaneously accessible around the globe. Designers and fashion houses such as Dior, Chanel, Versace, Gaultier, and most others posted their newest collections on their Web sites almost as soon as the runway shows ended.

In the 2000s, the Internet continued to gain ground over bricks-and-mortar retail operations as the destination for shoppers. All major retailers had robust Web store fronts with extensive online merchandise catalogs. E-commerce shopping malls gathered these Web stores together into one portal under an affiliates program in which they received a percentage of every purchase made at the e-tailer from the mall's visitors. Browser search engine marketing and e-mail programs enticed savvy Web users to the online stores with loyalty rewards programs and discount offers exclusively for the Web. Where, for decades, the day after Thanksgiving was called Black Friday (the busiest shopping day of the year in which sales for many retailers put their balance sheets into a profitable black vs. deficit red), the Monday after the holiday became known as Cyber Monday, during which millions of office workers continued their weekend of shopping online from their desks. By 2010, retailers such as J.C. Penney, Walmart, Gap, and Victoria's Secret each reported online sales topping a billion dollars.

FIGURE 13.1. During the first decade of the new millennium, the Internet made fashion easily accessible worldwide. From the comfort of their homes, consumers could shop online malls for all their favorite retailers. Ad for fashionmall.com, 2000.

Despite the unpopularity of the president and a bitterly polarized electorate, Bush was narrowly reelected in 2004. His second term was defined by the prolonged war in Afghanistan and a U.S. military occupation of Iraq. In addition, he instituted a Reaganesque tax cut for the wealthy and implemented deregulation policies that led to a financial crisis and a stock market crash in 2008, which many viewed as the worst since 1929.

In the presidential election of 2008 a record 132 million Americans went to the polls, electing Barack Obama, the first African-American President of the United States. "Change has come to America," Obama declared in his election night speech. Although Obama was sent to the White House on the promise of a fresh direction for the nation, the new president first had to deal with significant unfinished business left by the Bush administration, including a severe recession, a trillion-dollar deficit, a financial crisis on Wall Street, the highest unemployment in thirty years, and the costly wars in Iraq and Afghanistan. Even with so much demanding his immediate attention, Obama made good on one of his key campaign promises by signing into law health care reform in 2010, a need proposed by presidents since Teddy Roosevelt. Health care in America was established as a right, not simply a privilege.

American Culture and Society 2000–Present

American society continued to make progress with racial and gender issues. Venus Williams won her first Grand Slam at Wimbledon in 2000. Halle Berry became the first African-American to win a Best Actress Oscar in 2002. Condoleezza Rice was at the forefront of the Bush administration's security council during the 2003 U.S.–Iraqi War and, in 2005, became Secretary of State. In 2009, Sonia Sotomayor became the first Latina to sit on the Supreme Court. Nancy Pelosi became the first Speaker of the House of Representatives in 2006 when the Democrats regained control. And in 2009, Barack Obama became the 44th President of the United States, appointing campaign rival Hillary Clinton as his Secretary of State.

FIGURE 13.2. A digitized, wireless electronic world of information and entertainment was available at the fingertip of a cell phone user any time, any day. Left, Apple iPhone, 2009; right Alp Horn earphones from WESC, 2010.

On other social fronts, the gay community made headway in its efforts for equal rights. In 2003, the U.S. Supreme Court reversed its 1986 ruling that had allowed states to criminalize acts of intimacy between consenting same-sex adults even in the privacy of the home. Hate-crime laws were broadened to include acts against gays with the Matthew Shepard and James Byrd, Jr. Hate Crimes Prevention Act of 2009. Major corporations such as Disney and Xerox extended benefits to same-sex domestic partners. Massachusetts was the first state to grant same-sex marriage in 2004. In 2011, the ban on gays serving openly in the military was lifted with the repeal of the 1993 "Don't Ask/Don't Tell" law.

In American pop culture, the Internet evolved from an informational tool with limited capabilities into an electronic universe of communications, marketing, and sales. By the end of the new century's first decade, millions of blogs (contraction of "Web logs") around the world shared information and became public forums for sociopolitical expression. Cell phones included digital cameras and hundreds of applications for the Internet, games, news and weather updates, personal banking, and GPS mapping. (Figure 13.2.) Millions of books were digitized and made available through online libraries and ebook reader devices. Vast music and video collections were downloaded to palm-sized MP3 players. Electronic communications became both remote and personal at the same time as text messaging virtually replaced phone conversations with a new language of abbreviations and acronyms. Tweeting short messages on Twitter.com became a daily ritual for millions of users including celebrities, politicians, institutions, and retailers.

The entertainment industry was at the forefront of digital technology. In Hollywood, highly sophisticated techniques in digitized special effects garnered billions of dollars in movie ticket sales for films such as *Avatar* (2009) and especially franchise series like *Harry Potter* (2001–10), *Pirates of the Caribbean* (2003–07), and *Lord of the Rings* (2001–03). Millennial movie makers competed with HDTV (high-definition television) and DVRs (digital video recorder), which encouraged more people to seek entertainment at home. Among the top rated TV programs were an assortment of "reality" shows with staged competitions pitting ordinary people against each other to sing, dance, cook, lose weight, marry a bachelor, and design fashion. Popular music in the new century, usually accompanied with a high production video for TV and download,

FIGURE 13.3. The 1960s was one of the most popular eras for fashion designers and retailers to revisit in the new millennium. In-store visual merchandising by the Gap, 2006.

ran the gamut from hip-hop and rap by Jay Z, Lil Wayne, and Kanye West to dance hits from Lady Gaga and teen bubble gum from Miley Cyrus.

A new aspect of the sexual revolution evolved in the new century—the advent of the "cougar," a woman over forty who preferred much younger men. When 42-year-old Demi Moore dated, and later married, 27-year-old Ashton Kutcher in 2005, the idea of the cougar went mainstream. In 2007, the movie *Cougar Club* explored the idea of the older woman/younger man sexual relationship from the perspective of young men, who, rather than being considered the victims of predatory females, instead, actively pursued more mature women. That same year, an Elizabeth Arden ad featured a forty-something woman with the large type header: "Actually, he's my boyfriend. My son is slightly older." Even Web sites with the word "cougar" in the site address were established to connect young men and older women. In 2009, *GQ* presented a four-page report on the "American Cougar" as "an evolutionary leap from Anne Bancroft in *The Graduate*" to "the Older Seductress" with "claws."

Women's Fashions 2000–Present

In the spring of 2000, *Vogue* ventured on a quest for the new millennium's NBT (Next Big Thing) in fashion. The editors interviewed designers and retailers but eventually concluded that "if you look for it, you won't find it." Part of the uncertainty about the NBT in fashion was the continued fragmentation of the market, which was even more balkanized than in the nineties. The pluralism of fashion had become the standard, and most women were content to find their own personal style with, perhaps, only negligible advice from fashion journalism and marketers. No one designer, atelier, or syndicate could dominate the fashion industry as had Poiret in the 1910s or Dior in the 1950s—eras when daughter, mother, and most likely even grandmother all wore the same silhouette. Designers and ready-to-wear makers of the twenty-first century instead focused on their niche target market, usually the daughter *or* mother, seldom both.

One significant impact on the fashion market was a depressed world economy that began with a recession in 2001 and became severe following the U.S. banking crises of 2008. Many "re-" words appeared in print and on TV style shows: *recycle, revamp, rethink, reconstruct,* reconfigure, and recuperate. "Don't abandon the classics," suggested one editorial header, "reconceive them." This broadly publicized notion of recycling impacted both the fashion industry and consumers.

Designers stocked up with vintage textiles, linens, clothing, and accessories to reuse the materials in truly unique fashions. A recycled garment often ensured that no one else would be wearing the identical thing. Miguel Adrover presented dresses made from elaborate antique tablecloths. London's Kerry Seager introduced halter tops that tied in the back with sleeves cut from men's button-down dress shirts. Retro patchwork clothes and accessories were abundant. The Internet, especially online auction sites like eBay with its more than 200 million registered users, provided easy access to vintage clothing and textiles. The thrift shop look of mixed, layered styles that emerged with grunge and hip-hop looks of the nineties continued to be popular with high schoolers and on college campuses in the twenty-first century, repackaged with new cuts and proportions of garments and new arrangements of layers.

As in the 1990s, designers of the new century continued to look to the past. "Whoever buys my clothes appropriates their past," summed up Parisian designer Marc Le Bihan. Instead of the term retro or revival, though, designers and fashion editorials emphasized "heritage." In 2010, WWD's review of the fall runway collections asserted that "everyone touted heritage as a way to reassure and seduce consumers spooked by the recession." Even mass-market Main Street makers revisited their branded history. When Patrick Robinson took the design lead for the Gap in 2008, his objective was not so much to "reinvent the quintessentially American label" as it was to make the classic clothes of the brand more "of the moment because the fit and colors were right." "Since I came to the brand," Robinson concluded, "all I've done is bring that heritage back."

The sixties remained a favorite era to revisit because its range was so dramatic—from the remnants of the New Look at the start of the decade to the Age-of-Aquarius youthquake styles in its second half. In 2005, Vogue looked at "the designers who've gone absolutely mod," among whom included Dolce and Gabbana, who hung iconic photos of sixties supermodel Jean Shrimpton backstage at their runway show. Even chain retailers such as the Gap celebrated the sixties revival styles with in-store displays and merchandising. (Figure 13.3.)

One of the most pervasive revivals from the sixties—a look that has recurred every succeeding decade since—was the dress over pants ensemble. (Figure 13.4.) Marni's side slit floor-length dresses revealed the surprise of a boldly patterned pajama pant. Veronique Branquinho matched horizontal striped trousers with a diagonal striped short dress. Similar retro-duos were on the runways of John Galliano, Marc Jacobs, Jean Paul Gaultier, Damir Doma, Richard Nicoll, Zac Posen, and Richard Chai, among many others.

Also sixties-inspired were leopard print pants from Tom Ford, A-line miniskirt chemises from Marc Jacobs, and sleeveless shifts in acid colors by Prada, all of which were modernized with new technofabrics, deconstructionist cuts, and anachronistic accessories. The 2000s heir to Emilio Pucci's vividly hued, geometric Op art looks of the sixties and seventies were the textile giants Etro of Milan and Vlisco of the Netherlands. Dynamic retro Pop art fashions included giant silkscreened faces on miniskirted sheaths by Alber Elbaz and Belle Sauvage, and on logo T-shirts by Jean Paul Gaultier, reminiscent of Andy Warhol's oversized polaroid portraits. (Figure 13.5.)

Sixties hippie chic was revived as **boho (bohemian) style** in the 2000s, which, like its youthquake predecessor, was characterized by layers and mixtures of peasant and ethnic clothing that looked thrown together. (Figure 13.6.) Especially favored were colorful, richly

FIGURE 13.4. In the new millennium, designers continued to find inspiration in the looks of the past. The dress over pants ensemble appealed to a new generation of designers and wearers as much as it had throughout the previous four decades. Chanel logo print dress over corded patched-knee pants, 2001.

FIGURE 13.5. One of the favorite eras of inspiration for millennial fashion designers was the 1960s. Throughout the '00s, retro-sixties looks included every variation of miniskirt, Op and Pop art fabrics, psychedelic tie-dyes, and vibrant, neon color palettes. Above, Op art revival dresses from Vlisco, 2009; left, tie-dyed chemise by Cris Barros, 2010.

patterned tunics, skirts, sarongs, camisoles, vests, and jackets that replicated traditional clothing of India and Central Asia. Garments and accessories were lavishly enhanced with embroidery, fringe, beads, and mirrors. Pashmina wraps, batik scarves, slave bracelets, chandelier earrings, crocheted totes, and platform sandals or lace-up boots completed the look.

In 2008, the era of Dior's New Look was revived, inspired in part by the critically acclaimed TV series *Mad Men,* a drama about Madison Avenue that takes place in the early 1960s when lingering ultrafeminine styles still dominated fashion. Period costumes for the program, recreated by Emmy winner Katherine Jane Bryant, inspired designers such as Michael Kors, whose 2009 spring/summer collection reflected the vernacular of Jackie Kennedy and the early sixties.

New romantique styles of the decade, sometimes called "romance novel" looks as a tribute to the continuous movie remakes of Jane Austen classics, included an abundance of lace, velvet, rosettes, ruffles, puff sleeves, and tiered skirts. At middecade, the Empire waist was a particularly favorite silhouette for designers. (Figure 13.7.) Oscar de la Renta, Marc Jacobs, John Galliano, and J. Mendel created Empire dresses worn by high profile personalities including Princess Caroline, Melania Trump, and Sarah Jessica Parker (for her fortieth birthday party). Also at middecade, bows of all sizes appeared on everything from dresses and blouses to belts, handbags, and shoes.

Besides a host of revivalisms throughout the '00s, women also found innumerable options for expressing their individualism with some fashion basics, especially that staple commodity of ready-to-wear, jeans. In the twenty-first century, jeans became more varied than ever before: painted-on tight, hip-hop baggy, logo-branded, tie-dyed, bleach splattered, cropped, low-rise, flared, fringed, sueded, faded, distressed, and embellished with all manner of detailing. (Figure 13.8.) Numerous new labels in the denim market challenged established brands with fresh interpretations of jeans. Rogan Gregory's jeans featured triple-needle stitching and four-piece waistbands. Parasuco denim was embroidered and pierced with grommets. Stephen Hardy jeans were cut apart and repieced like a mosaic with gutters of leather between each denim section. Established brands countered the onslaught of fashion jeans with new takes of their own, such as "dirty denim" from Calvin Klein, camouflage patterns by Donna Karan, and capri length crops by Sergio Valente. Ralph Lauren embellished the entire surface of his white wide-leg jeans with beaded embroidery. Guess, Seven 7, and Not Your

FIGURE 13.6. The thrown-together hippie look of layered, mismatched peasant and ethnic styles of clothes was revived in the new century as the boho (bohemian) look. Jess "Boho Girl" of Girl Authority, 2007.

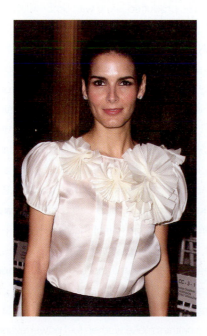

FIGURE 13.7. The new romantique styles, called "romance novel" looks, were inspired by the numerous movie remakes of Jane Austen classics. Designs included an abundance of lace, velvet, rosettes, ruffles, bows, and puff sleeves. Left, Oscar de la Renta blouse, 2008; right, lace chemise by Marc Jacobs, 2008.

FIGURE 13.8. The hiphugger pants of the sixties were revived in the 2000s as "low riders." Some ready-to-wear makers offered retro-treatments like tie-dyed patterns and embroidered motifs; others presented totally new approaches to cut and fit such as short crops and reconstructed waistbands. Left, distressed skinny jeans from Express, 2009; right, low-rider elephant bells from J Brand, 2011.

Daughter's Jeans produced jeans with embroidered detailing that ranged from small decorations on back pockets to elaborate, multicolored tattoo designs covering the entire thigh. The Gap and DKNY lined slashed and frayed jeans with patches of colorful prints or contrasting shades of blue denim, advertised as the "romantic hippy" look. Levi's added Lycra to their Slouch Straight 504 Jeans for an even more contouring, skinny look. Pop stars like Britney Spears and Jennifer Lopez squeezed into a revitalized form of hiphugger jeans called **low riders**, which were cut so shallow from inseam to waistband that when the wearer sat down or bent over, the requisite red or black silk thong (called a "whale fin") was visible in the back.

To complement the tight, leggy look of jeans and pants, tops likewise were reduced in proportion and fit for a **shrunken look**. (Figure 13.9.) Many tops featured short crops. Tight-fitting **shrunken cardigans**, also called **shrug sweaters**, became a trend with teens and young women in the second half of the decade. The short knit tops were usually worn open or fastened with one button at the throat.

Menswear styling became the "**borrowed**" **look**, which also provided opportunities for fashion individualism. "We've all had that moment of looking into a closet full of clothes and finding nothing to wear," related *Vogue* in 2010. "What to do? Nick something from the boyfriend's! Men's clothes make women feel powerful and sexy and leave a lot to the imagination." If boyfriend (or dad, hubbie, or big brother) objected to having his clothes borrowed by the women of the house, designers offered alternatives with a distinction. Martin Margiela folded over the waistband of men's baggy pleated trousers at the center front, creating a hybrid split skirt look. Ralph Lauren combined a men's black tailcoat and a white U-front vest with a long flounced skirt. Marc Jacobs kept the same boxy cut and shape of men's wrap coats from the forties, but added big square metal buttons as a vital new detail. Gucci offered men's skinny suits with shortened jackets and hiphugger trousers in vibrant colors. (Figure 13.10.) By the end of the decade, ready-to-wear makers and retailers began to label all sorts of menswear looks as a "**boyfriend**" **style**—jeans, khakis, blazers, suits, shorts, sweaters, and boyshort swim bottoms and underwear.

Similarly, because of the prolonged wars in Afghanistan and Iraq, women's sportswear adopted masculine military influences from service uniforms. Camouflage jeans have already been noted. A double-page spread of military looks in the January 2010 issue of *Vogue* included army green jackets from DKNY, Charlotte Ronson, Tory Burch, Nicholas K, Ralph Lauren, and Juicy Couture. Some of the featured jackets were made with brass buttons, pocket flaps, and epaulets; others were accented with sergeant stripe patches and embroidered flag insignias. (Figure 13.11.) Button fall front sailor's pants were produced by Helmut Lang, Tommy Hilfiger, and the Limited. Double-breasted **admiral jackets** with metal buttons and grosgrain trim were offered in a variety of cuts by ready-to-wear makers and couture houses alike.

Not surprising, logos and licensing continued to be a boon to house profits. The effectiveness of multimillion dollar marketing budgets for label branding was undeniable in the twenty-first century. A new approach to logo fashions was to cover every inch of the garment or accessory with a repeat pattern of trademark initials. "If you've got it, flaunt it!" declared *Vogue* on the subject of high-end fashions covered with logos. In popular TV programs like *Sex and the City*, characters regularly bandied about their favorite famous brand fashion names in dialog and prominently displayed designer logos on clothing, accessories, and shopping bags. Tom Ford wallpapered jackets, pants, hats, shoes, bras, and bikini underwear with a diamond

FIGURE 13.9. Shrunken look tops, with their cropped hems, shortened sleeves, and tight fit that appeared to pull button closures and strain the fabric, complemented the slim, snug silhouette of young women's fashions. Shrunken look by Valeria Marini, 2009.

FIGURE 13.10. Menswear influences came to be called the "borrowed look," as in clothing borrowed from a boyfriend's closet. In the second half of the decade, designers and retailers began to apply "boyfriend" to any women's fashions with menswear styling. Left, boyfriend tennis sweater and boyfriend khakis from Lucien Pellat-Finet, 2009; right, boyfriend suit from Gucci, 2008.

pattern of the Gucci double G. A new calligraphic Dior logo was strung together in repeat lacy stripes for denim vests, skirts, and matching stiletto boots. Ralph Lauren supersized the embroidered polo player logo on his polo shirts, advertised as the "big pony." At the more extreme edge of brandishing logos, the linked C's of Chanel were bleached into hair extensions.

Because logo-branded fashions and accessories had become such an enormous segment of the fashion industry, counterfeiting became rampant. In 2006, an awareness ad campaign sponsored by *Harper's Bazaar* and the New York City Police Foundation warned that "Profits from counterfeit sales fund organized crime including drug cartels, child labor and even terrorist organizations. It's estimated that more than $500 billion worth of counterfeit goods are sold annually." Unfortunately, many consumers continued to pursue their favorite logo branded fashions and accessories, even if the sidewalk vendor or eBay source was questionable.

Among the branded logos that were made into political statements were those of the 2008 Obama and McCain campaigns. For Democrat Barack Obama, the blue circle with three red stripes represented not only the letter "O" but also was symbolic of a new dawn, a visual graphic of the campaign's theme of hope. "Yes we can" and "change" were also favorite captions on Obama T-shirts by Alexander Wang and Narciso Rodriquez, among others. For supporters of Republican John McCain, a naval star on a gold bar representing his war hero credential was worn as oversized campaign buttons, visors, and T-shirts.

Despite all the demands and niche marketing of retro styles, logo fashions, and commodity clothing, the innovation and fantasy of fashion design did not diminish in the new millennium. (Figure 13.12.) Designers became fascinated with the idea of culture collisions: punk

Dior, 2004.

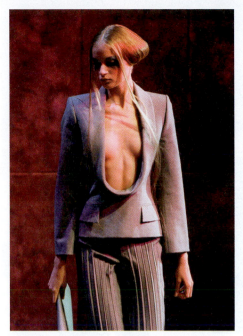

Alexander McQueen, 2000.

Jean Paul Gaultier, 2002.

Junya Tashiro, 2009.

Riccardo Tisci, 2008.

FIGURE 13.12. Through relentless and passionate experimentation and innovation, designers of the new millennium continued to produce high drama in fashion.

Christopher Kane, 2009.

Vivienne Westwood, 2008.

FIGURE 13.13. Through the support and promotion of newly founded organizations like African Fashion International, African designers received global notoriety in the new century. Many EuroAmerican designers were influenced by African culture and dress, reinterpreting and integrating ethnic looks and textiles into their collections. Left, Afrocentric styles by Oumou Sy, Senegal, 2000; right, brass, bone, and bead jewelry from Maro Designs, Nairobi, Kenya, 2004.

meets *Showgirls*; olde Hollywood mixed with Mexican religious imagery; *Dr. Zhivago* crossed with Scheherazade. In Paris, the self-named "**absurdists**" produced dramatic, experimental art school styles, which included sleeves that extended over the hands to the knees, high collars that covered the face up to the eyes, and exaggerated cowboy boot poulaines. Junya Watanabe constructed coats and cocktail dresses with volumes of honeycombed fabric somewhat resembling gigantic fold-up paper Halloween ornaments. Hussein Chalayan's "topiary" dress was a sleeveless mass of dense ruffles looking like well-manicured lawn shrubbery. Versace's thigh-high corset dresses from the "RocKoko" collection were luxuriously adorned with antique silver lace. Lagerfeld's twenty-first century iteration of the Chanel suit featured meticulously tailored jackets with frothy skirts of embroidered tulle. Galliano replaced traditional substructures like whalebone and crinolines with foam to reshape contours. Gaultier revisited the grandeur of the Viennese Hapsburgs with his three-tiered wedding cake skirt adorned with swirling hussar trimmings and hip epaulets.

High fashion from big names also came with high prices. In 2006, *Harper's Bazaar* asked "How much is too much?" when buying fashions in the twenty-first century. Among those "covetable pieces" for that autumn were a beaded velvet bell dress from Balenciaga, $101,370; a silk mousseline evening gown from Rochas, $34,547; an Hermès Fair Isle cardigan, $5,300; a hand embroidered Napoleonic military coat from Dolce and Gabbana, $85,000; platform pumps by Nicolas Ghesquière, $1,175; and Ralph Lauren's cashmere leggings, $1,098.

Throughout the decade, global influences continued to be a key element in fashion innovation. In 2010, *Vogue* referred to the "world-beat harmony of alternative visions and multicultural choices" in millennial fashions as the "tribe vibe." "**Tribal** is a convenient catchall term for a trend that encompasses almost anything that looks pre-industrial or aboriginal: clamourous colors, primitive prints, and truly funky accessories . . . especially exuberantly patterned homages to the kente cloth of Ghana and ikat fabrics of Indonesia. There was joyous ornamentation with feathers and blossoms, à la the artistic Omo people of Ethiopia. Loincloths and breastplates, Gobi desert robes, and armloads of beads."

African fashion, particularly, came of age in the new century. In 2008, African Fashion International (AFI) was founded in Cape Town, South Africa, with the aim "to improve the quality of fashion design output from Africa, to promote African brands, and to dramatically raise the profile of fashion designers from the continent." The Internet also opened the world to African style, contributing to the commercial success of designers such as Ann McCreath of Kenya, Guenet Fresenbet of Ethiopia, Estrella of Cameroon, Angy Bell of Cote d'Ivoire, and Oumou Sy of Senegal, to name a few. Working from London, Nigerian-born Duro Olowu became famous for his high-waisted patchwork boho dresses—known as the "Duro"—which became a cult item.

The twenty-first-century generation of African designers continued to explore the cross-cultural possibilities of merging Western clothing styles with traditional African textiles, or the reverse, with adaptations of African garments made of Western fabrics and materials. (Figure 13.13.) As Jean Loup Pivin wrote for *Revue Noire*, African designers "draw their modernity from the source of their countries, for Africa is not just a reservoir of a living age-old tradition, it is also rooted in the now commonplace modernity of Lycra and knitwear, anchored in the hazy identity of urban culture."

Western designers also enjoyed inspiration from African style and culture. For the June 2008 issue, *Vogue* shot an editorial in Mali. Among the African-inspired fashions featured were brightly colored and geometrically patterned dresses from Jenni Kayne, Alexander McQueen, Nicolas Ghesquière, and Missoni. Cargo harem pants from Phillip Lim and a revival seventies safari suit from Diane Von Furstenberg recalled colonial era looks. Dutch textile and design house Vlisco specifically targeted African women consumers not only with fabric prints and fashions inspired by African culture and dress, but also by opening boutiques in Benin, Togo, Côte d'Ivoire, and Nigeria.

Technology increasingly factored into fashion designs of the twenty-first century. In **nanotechnology**, the size and properties of molecules were reconfigured and engineered to attach themselves to one another, and then attach to any yarn, including synthetics, without affecting the look and feel of the woven textile. The results were "**smart fabrics**" that wick moisture away from the body, repel insects, block the sun's UV rays, and resist stains. In addition, wearable computer systems, or **electronic clothes**, were developed with electrically conductive textiles interwoven with microscopic wires. (Figure 13.14.) In 2004, the MP3 Bluetooth Jacket was introduced, which featured an impact-resistant textile keyboard on the left sleeve, attached headphones, and a microphone in the collar. Similarly, the Know Where Jacket from the German firm Interactive Wear included a GPS "eye" wired into the shoulder epaulets that

FIGURE 13.14. Electronic clothes of the new millennium included wearable computer systems such as GPS tracking devices and L.E.D. light circuits. Computerized "smart clothes" by M.I.T. students, 2003: left, Red Roadster with solar panel hat that powers a cell phone and a vest with a GPS navigation device; right, coat wired to receive e-mail that projects onto sunglasses.

FIGURE 13.15. Cybertech fashions of the new century ranged from dazzling L.E.D. lit clothing to sculpted futuristic concept designs. Materials included polypropylene, stretch synthetics, and leather treated to shine with plasticized surface. Left, leather pauldron, collar, and gauntlets by Ùna Burke, 2009; center, quilted vinyl jacket and visored cap by Jean Paul Gaultier, 2009; right, leather stomacher dress by Hussein Chalayan, 2008.

could locate people during their remote activities such as sailing, skiing, mountain climbing, or distance biking.

Technology also provided eyecatching drama in the many applications of **L.E.D.s** (a type of lighting that uses semiconductor light-emitting diodes) to garments. In 2009, the Museum of Science and Industry in Chicago displayed the Galaxy Dress by Cute Circuit, which was made with 24,000 2mm-by-2mm L.E.D.s woven into silk chiffon and organza crinoline fabrics and powered by several iPod batteries concealed beneath the garment. Lumalive Event Gear made possible flashing light messages and images on L.E.D. canvases applied to garments and accessories. The most famous application of Lumalive L.E.D. technology was the "lighting" outfit for Michael Jackson's planned O2 Arena tour in 2009, which included the "Billie Jean" costume of a jacket, tuxedo pants, ankle socks and a single white glove designed to light up to the rhythm of the song and be synchronized with the choreography.

In addition to the functionality of electronic fibers, textiles, and clothing, millennial fashion designers looked to technology for new inspiration and creative direction. The new cybertech fashions of the second half of the decade were made from "silicone-slick, metallic, shiny fabrics," looks which *Vogue* called "alternative-futurist" for lack of a better term. (Figure 13.15.) In

FIGURE 13.16. Clothing makers responded to the changing demographics of the market by extending product lines to include well-made and stylish fashions for large size women. Lane Bryant fashion show, 2001.

2007, Nicolas Ghesquière's segmented patent leather dress was inspired by the 1982 movie *Tron*. Narciso Rodriguez cut apart fiberglass body casts and inserted them into dresses, recalling the robotic storm troopers of *Star Wars*. Amy J. Thompson's 2008 "Plastic Analogue" collection of bodywear was sculpted with interlocking polypropylene pieces fitted over formfitting garments patterned with quirky textile prints. Ùna Burke devised a conceptual collection of wearable art pieces made of vegetable tanned leather, resulting in a color simulating human flesh. And Ara Jo, who has designed for Lady Gaga, created armored mermaid dresses with radiating pieces that resembled scales and gills.

Among the technical challenges for twentieth-century designers and ready-to-wear makers were fashions for the large-sized woman. According to a 2008 report from the Centers for Disease Control and Prevention, almost two-thirds of American women were overweight or obese. Specialty chains such as Lane Bryant, Avenue, and August Max offered plus size clothing in standardized sizes 12 to 28. (Figure 13.16.) Niche retailers such as Torrid targeted younger women with trendier styles in plus sizes. Even larger sizes up to 44W were readily available from many online retailers. In-store consultants and online style guides provided advice to large women on how to dress for their proportions. Typical recommendations included:

- Scale prints to the body; choose prints that have overlapping images.
- Choose body-conscious clothes that hint at your curves, without being clingy or tight.
- Add small shoulderpads to sweaters and other knit tops to make them hang better.
- Play up your best features such as shapely legs with a knee-length skirt.
- Use accessories such as scarves and earrings to draw attention to your face.

For designers and ready-to-wear makers, adapting current trends to larger sizes involved more than simply expanding the cut of a silhouette and using stretch fabrics. For comfort, fit, and sometimes even figure control, specialized engineering was often needed in producing fashions in large sizes. For example, in 2008, Not Your Daughter's Jeans developed a "lift and tuck" construction of denim jeans that featured a concealed criss-cross panel that promised to flatten the tummy and lift the buttocks.

As the second decade of the new millennium opened, the fashion establishment, with its big business perspective, continued identifying and aggressively marketing to its many niche consumer groups. The designers and retailers in the pluralistic global market of the 2000s continually fulfilled women's demands for versatile and modern clothing that suited their quest for individualism and personal style. In spite of a declining market, haute couture nonetheless endured and thrived with imaginative and passionate designers at the helm. And into the ateliers of Paris, London, Milan, and New York have continued to enter the future new guard of fashion—talented and inspired young designers eager to make fashion magic.

Eco- and Ethical-friendly Fashions and Accessories 2000–Present

In 2006, former Vice President Al Gore released his documentary *An Inconvenient Truth* to educate people about global warming. The Academy Award winning film has been credited with raising international public awareness of climate change and reenergizing the environmental movement.

Green, eco-friendly, and ethical consciousness permeated the twenty-first century fashion industry. For millennial women who wanted to reduce their carbon footprint, **green fashions** made of **sustainable fabrics** were increasingly available globally. Organically grown cotton from Japan, soy and wild silk from China, and alpaca from Peru were among the natural fibers popular with green designers. But eco fashions were not the "stereotypical homespun-looking peasant tops or hippie-dippy dresses," reported *Vogue* in 2007. New millennium eco fashions included sophisticated cowl neck dresses of soy knits from the design studio Sans; Diane Von Furstenberg's wrap dresses of cashmeres, linens, and wools without chemical dyes; 100% bamboo knit suits by Carole Wang; and water repellent raincoats made of bees-waxed organic manila by Rauffauf.

The green fashion press encouraged women to wear their jeans stiff and dark instead of the ubiquitous stonewashed, distressed, and softened finishes made with chemicals and millions of gallons of water. New York's Barney's Department Store led the way for American retailers with Barney's Green, a collection of organic cotton denim, tops, and sportswear. Even grocery shopping became an opportunity to make a fashion and a green statement with designer totes such as Anya Hindmarch's canvas carryall appliqued with the slogan "I'm not a plastic bag." (Figure 13.17.)

In addition to using pesticide-free natural fibers, some eco designers also opted for recycled polyesters, old denim, and rags. "**Trash fashion**" (also "trashion') included garments and accessories sewn, woven, or crocheted from recycled plastic bottles, food packaging, inner tubes, soda can pop top chainmail, and plastic grocery bags.

Related to the green trend in clothing was an eco-ethical conscientiousness. Makers sought sweatshop-free environments for fashion production. Globally, makers were encouraged to use local, quality materials, such as Brazil's Veja sneakers, which were made from locally farmed rubber, thus preserving rainforest trees from being cut down. Designers who wished to join So Ethic, a division of Pret-à-Porter Paris, were admitted "based on environmental sensitivity, social consciousness, or recycling and reuse."

Part of the ethical trend also included donating a portion of sales to organizations like Al Gore's Climate Project or the U.N. World Food Program. For example, with the purchase of a faux coral-decorated compact, the cosmetic maker Chantecaille donated a percentage to the Pew Institute for the Reef of Hope Fund. Similarly, 50% of profits from the sales of malachite Green Bracelets from Simmons Jewelry went to educational programs in Africa.

FIGURE 13.17. Green fashions and accessories made of organic ("sustainable") materials became increasingly popular in the new millennium. Canvas grocery tote from Anya Hindmarch, 2006.

Women's Outerwear 2000–Present

A coat is "the one piece you don't buy on a whim," advised *Harper's Bazaar* in 2005. Throughout the first half of the '00s, fur trim was everywhere on outerwear—leather coats, knit wraps, denim jackets. Shearling was favored for coats and jackets of all designs. (Figure 13.18.) Revivals of New Look styles such as cinched waist princess coats and circular swing coats were popularized by TV programs like *Mad Men, The Hour,* and *Pan Am.* A century-old tradition of conservative simplicity ended at Burberry's in 2002 when they began offering made-to-measure trench coats with the customer's choice of vividly dyed cashmere linings.

FIGURE 13.18. Outerwear of the new century included a renewed interest in furs, revivals of fifties New Look silhouettes, and military inspired detailing. Left, shearling maxi coat by Dominic Bellissimo, 2002; center, fingertip coat from Marella, 2009; right, luxe coat by Lorenzo Riva, 2010.

In the second half of the decade, the luxe printed coat was a popular option to traditional beige camel hair or black wool. Rich paisley patchworks were offered by Miu Miu, Tudor rosettes from Tocca, oversized Op art checks from Trina Turk, and allover patterns from Diane Von Furstenberg. Sumptuously soft leather luxe coats from Bottega Veneta and Derek Lam were even recommended by *Harper's Bazaar* as a double for a cocktail dress, with the right pumps, opaque hose, and handbag.

Military influences became strong in both short and long coats as the decade progressed. Double- and single-breasted jackets of army green wool were accented with brass buttons, chest and hip pockets with flaps, and epaulets. Other military inspired outerwear featured combinations of grosgrain trim, frogging, and braid. Long greatcoats were made all the more impressive with large Napoleonic or upright cowl collars.

Women's Underwear and Sleepwear 2000–Present

Lingerie makers continually reengineered bras, foundation garments (more commonly called shapewear today), briefs, camisoles, and pantyhose to improve fit, support, comfort, and

Tanga panty and bra from Biatta, 2009.

Lily of France bra and bikini, 2006.

Thong "whalefin" by Verde
Veronica, 2011.

Boyshorts by Hurley, 2009.

FIGURE 13.19. Among the new forms of lingerie for women in the new century were the tanga, cut high over the buttocks to eliminate pantyline, and thongs embellished with fancy "whalefins" at the back. The appropriation of boyfriend looks included boyshorts modeled on men's boxerbriefs.

durability. Laser-cut edges and flat seams reduced garment pinching, binding, and bulging. Other constructions were seam-free to prevent show-through beneath clothes.

Some styles of undergarments were developed specifically for what some women regarded as body "flaws," such as bra bulge across the back, stomach "pooch," "muffin tops" over waistbands, or "saddlebag" hip bulges. The Vanity Fair Beautiful Benefits bra had specially designed wings that smoothed back bulges. The Bali signature Comfort-U Back bras were introduced in 2009 with the promise that the bra straps and back stayed in place while providing a superior fit and full support. Victoria's Secret constructed each cup size of their Biofit bras with shaping and padding to feel custom made. Online blogs about shapewear often provided experts' reviews and ratings of the many varieties of undergarments, and invited consumer feedback to be posted. Among the top rated makers of compression type shapewear of the decade were Lipo in a Box and Spanx.

Intimate apparel makers such as Victoria's Secret, Pampered Passions, and Seductive Instincts also promoted lingerie as fashion for sexual allure. "Very Sexy" and "Sexy Little Things" were registered trademarks of various types of lingerie by Victoria's Secret.

Among the new forms of women's underwear were hipster panties cut below the navel to sit low on the hips. Tangas were a type of low-rise panty between a bikini and a thong cut high on the buttocks to eliminate pantyline show-through. (Figure 13.19.) The menswear influence included square-cut **boyshorts** cut along the lines of men's low-rise boxerbriefs without the

FIGURE 13.20. For many millennial women, comfort rather than sex appeal was key to their choice of sleepwear. Left, nylon trico pajamas from Vanity Fair, 2006; right, cotton knit sleepshirt from Victoria's Secret, 2008.

engineered genital pouch. The back of thongs, called a "**whalefin**," were embellished with all sorts of trim for display when the wearer was seated in low rider jeans.

To determine the type of sleepwear that was best for a woman, *Vanity Fair's* Web site asked: "What type of sleepwear are you most comfortable in? What types of women's pajamas are best suited to the climate where you live? Is there someone you want to impress when you come into the bedroom?" But sleepwear was much less about sex appeal than comfort for most millennial women. (Figure 13.20.) Long T-shirts and tanktops over baggy boyfriend pajama bottoms were a favorite look for young women. Teens preferred cotton boyfriend boxer shorts, fitted boyshorts, and camis. Traditionalists could find wide assortments of terry and velour robes, nylon tricot gowns, cotton/poly blend sleepshirts, and pajama sets at the local mall and through mass merchandiser catalogs.

Women's Sports Attire 2000–Present

New forms of exercise regimens were developed in the new century for Gen X and Gen Y women. Spinning classes were group workouts on stationary bicycles at fitness centers. Pilates (named for German physical therapist Joseph Pilates) were hugely popular programs of variable exercises for all ages of women to develop core body strength and torso stability. In the second half of the decade, Chaos classes at fitness centers became a favorite new training method that involved high intensity cardio and strength workouts involving teams and props ranging from medicine balls and free weights to balloons and orange traffic cones. Rock climbing and cliff rappelling added variety for outdoor enthusiasts.

FIGURE 13.21. The improved synthetic fabrics and garment engineering of women's active sportswear provided greater support, comfort, and safety. Traditional attire for sports such as tennis and golf was infused with new vibrant color palettes and high style options. Left, belted tennis skirt and yoke front shirt by Stella McCartney, 2008; right, Casall tank and shorts, 2007.

The preferred form of activewear for many women was spandex running pants in cool weather and nylon shorts for summer, paired with a sports bra top or racer back tank. (Figure 13.21.) Black and gray were the most common colors for bottoms, but tops were often in neon brights. The capri pant length became ubiquitous in the second half of the decade. The Lycra blend fabrics were nonbinding and stretched easily under the stress of any level of activity. Improved nylon and polyester textiles were lightweight and retained body warmth while wicking away moisture from the skin.

Even in the new century, activewear for tennis and golf was often determined by strict dress codes implemented by country clubs, community leagues, and professional organizations. Tennis "whites" remained the preferred dress of traditionalists on the court. Some millennial pros, though, broke with convention where possible with colorful versions of tennis dresses, skirts, skorts, shorts, campshirts, and polos. Wimbledon champions Serena and Venus Williams each developed and wore their own lines of vividly colored tennis clothes, and Maria Sharapova made headlines with her beaded black "night dress" worn at the 2006 U.S. Open. Expanding beyond typical pleated skirts and polos, Stella McCartney offered tennis players flutter sleeve shirts and hiphugging tiered ruffle skirts.

For winter activities like snowboarding and skiing, advances in the development of polyamide textiles improved moisture repellency and wind resistance for outdoor sports clothes. Insulated jackets and pants made with microporous, breathable polyamide shells and linings padded with polyester Thermax were lightweight and durable.

Among the new forms of safety wear for hikers, off-road bikers, cross country skiers, and others who ventured into remote wildernesses, were portable GPS tracking devices. In 2007, the British company Covert Asset Tracking Systems developed a postage stamp-sized, solar powered GPS device for clothing that was waterproof and machine washable. For urban runners and cyclists, L.E.D. safety clothing included vests, jackets, and armbands that flashed to alert motorists.

Women's Swimwear 2000–Present

The variety of swimwear for millennial women was greater than ever. In 2008, *Vogue* ran a four-page grid of eighty-seven current styles ranging from the tiniest string bikinis to full-coverage

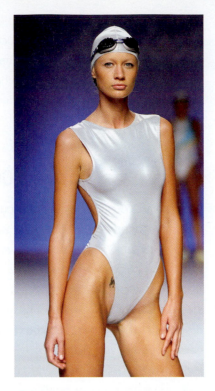

FIGURE 13.22. Among the fresh trends in swimwear were cutaways, asymmetry, and neoprene scuba looks. Left, asymmetrical cutaway by Emilio Pucci, 2005; center, French cut racer by Vives Vidal, 2004; right, boyshorts swimsuit by Hurley, 2012.

maternity styles. French cut maillots were constructed with high leg openings requiring an extreme bikini wax. Asymmetry gave swimsuits of the decade a fresh look. Designers applied the look to bikini tops or bottoms separately or to both pieces, and to one-piece swimsuits by cutaways, assorted strap treatments, and details like bows and skirts. (Figure 13.22.) Trina Turk's cutout one-piece was open in a wide oval along one side only. A bikini from ThreeAsFour included a top with a halter spaghetti strap on one side and a wide shoulder strap on the other. The barest of rio string bikinis, "influenced by Brazilian beaches," reminded a DKNY ad in 2005, replicated the looks of the 1970s in new prints and beaded detailing. In the early 2000s, the **tankini**—a tank top and bikini bottom—was introduced and appealed to a broader age range of consumers than the maillot. Similar to the tankini was the **tubini**, a two-piece swimsuit with a bandeau "tube" top, some of which extended to the hips in a short skirt. Some tubini tops came with halter straps that could be tucked into the bra. Tubini bottoms varied from bikini to square-cut boyshorts.

New takes on animal prints blended the spots of leopards and giraffes with swirls of blues and golds. Michael Kors snakeskin print was a vivid mix of iridescent peacock greens and blues. Pop and Op art prints ranged from sixties Peter Max graphics by Eley Kishimoto and Alice+Olivia to psychedelic swirls, giant dots, and inkblot splashes from GapBody, Guess, and Letarte. At resorts, swimwear reflected the romantique bow trend of middecade including eschelle bodices by Tomas Maier and bikini hip bows from Eres and Betsey Johnson.

High tech styling became a trend for swimwear at the beginning of the 2010s. Neoprene scuba looks of matte black color blocked with neon brights were accented with hardware buckles and zippers. The sleek fit of these swimsuits functioned like a second skin for women who wished to do more than sunbathe pool- or surfside. Even string bikini styles by Body Glove were promoted as high performance swimwear that did not come off during extreme water sports.

Women's Shoes 2000–Present

In the early 2000s, high heels were pushed to the back edge of the sole and flattened into a two-by-four proportion. Toes were widened and squared off at the end, requiring a longer vamp. Geometric shoe silhouettes were often decorated with art deco inspired shapes in contrasting colors. By middecade, versions of medieval **poulaines** appeared with narrow, razor-pointed toes that extended beyond the end of the foot an inch or more, usually with thin, stiletto heels. By contrast, platforms with thick heels and chunky, steep wedges reminiscent of seventies styles returned. Updated versions in the second half of the decade included the **skyscraper pump**, with platforms at two to three inches and spiked heels at five inches or more. (Figure 13.23.) One of the decade's most popular names in footwear was Jimmy Choo, whose styles ranged from classic New Look slingbacks and open toe pumps (now called "**peep toes**") to sculptural body art platforms with lucite heels, studded buckle straps, and wooden soles. A particular favorite of red-carpet celebrities—and counterfeiters—were the distinctive red-sole styles by Christian Louboutin.

Boots similarly soared with high heels varying from chunky thick to pencil thin. At the end of the decade, the eleven- to thirteen-inch mid-calf boot was a favorite, many with architectural detailing such as quilting and multiple buckles. Prada's 2008 three-part boot, which included bronzed leather lace-up leggings, laced spats, and sculpted heel pumps, received a full-page editorial photo in *Vogue*. Among the fad boot brands of the decade were Australian sheepskin Ugg boots, lined with wool on the inside and with a tanned outer surface. Sherbet color Uggs for spring and summer were introduced in 2005.

In the second half of the decade, some shoe designs reached extreme proportions and shapes. In 2009, Martin Margiela produced "split" or hoof shoes that featured a sort of mitten toe construction resembling a goat's hoof. The same year, Alexander McQueen created a sensation with his version of "hoof shoes" (also called "lobster claw" or "armadillo" shoes), which bowed outward in a ten-inch arc from the ankle to the toe, concealing the inside platform. Women were not only often perplexed how to wear and walk in these new forms of chunky, towering shoes, but also with what to wear with them. Magazine photo editorials sometimes seemed to have selected these avant-garde shoes as a contrast rather than a complement to the fashions. "When choosing chunky shoes, keep in mind that a hefty heel is best balanced with a full-shaped dress, skirt, or trouser," advised *Harper's Bazaar* in 2006. "Anything too tight or slim will look disproportionate."

As shoe designers continued to push the boundaries of shapes and heights, health and fitness editors urged caution, warning fashionistas about the dangers of hammertoes, knee joint degeneration, and torn Achilles tendons, not to mention falls. To take a break from teetering atop stiletto platforms and hoof boots, trendsetters opted for Repetto lace-up flats in deep,

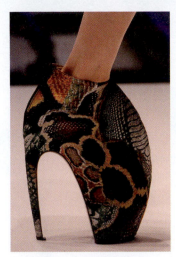

Hoof shoe from Alexander
McQueen. 2009.

Buckle poulaine by Steve Madden, 2006.

Hoof ankle boot from Martin
Margiela, 2009.

Skyscraper pumps from Salvator
Ferragamo, 2010.

Cube ankle boot from Andreia
Chaves, 2009.

Stacked heel tassel kiltie from
Alexandre Herchcovitch, 2010.

Open toe high heel from Heavy
Machine, 2010.

Crocs, 2008.

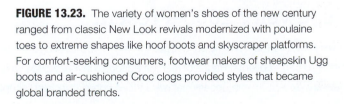

Bouley button
Uggs, 2009.

FIGURE 13.23. The variety of women's shoes of the new century
ranged from classic New Look revivals modernized with poulaine
toes to extreme shapes like hoof boots and skyscraper platforms.
For comfort-seeking consumers, footwear makers of sheepskin Ugg
boots and air-cushioned Croc clogs provided styles that became
global branded trends.

Charm bracelet watches from Anne Klein, 2007.

African beadwork jewelry by Mickael Kra, 2005.

Jewelry collection from Guess, 2002.

Native American chokers and pendants from Billy Martin's, 2003.

FIGURE 13.24. Jewelry was lighter and more diminutive in the new century than in previous decades. The occasional large impact pieces were worn selectively and singly rather than in multiples. Jewelry inspired by African, Asian, and Native American cultures complemented boho and eco looks.

rich shades of teal, burgundy, and violet, declared by *Vogue* in 2008 as "the new ballet flat." From Geox came tassel flats with a microperforated rubber sole that allowed perspiration to wick out, keeping the feet cool and dry. For casual comfort, plastic Crocs in crayon colors were everywhere. Riccardo Tisci offered a high-end use of plastic for molded shoes with his 2009 lace-up gladiator sandals priced at $170.

Women's Jewelry 2000–Present

In the 2000s, jewelry was further minimized except for the most flamboyant haute couture shows and celebrity red carpet events. Pages of fashion editorials in magazines were conspicuously devoid of jewelry except for the occasional retro fifties charm bracelet, simple strand of pearls, or small chain necklace or pendant. However, at the end of the decade, the 1980s were revisited with oversized, sculptural pieces by Alber Elbaz and Nina Ricci, except, for millennial women, a single impact piece sufficed rather than multiples worn together as in the Reagan years.

Charm bracelets were a favorite of the decade. Burberry's "Brit Charm" and Anne Klein's AK collection included a pendant watch. (Figure 13.24.) A gift with purchase from Moschino fragrance was a bracelet with colorfully enameled cloisonne charms. A sterling silver charm bracelet by Dean Harris was ringed with 1960s peace symbols. Margherita Missoni's charm bracelet included a miniature solid-fragrance compact of her perfume. Carolyn Rafaelian of Alex and Ani designed a bangle set with Charm 4 Life logo charms to raise awareness of cervical cancer; a portion of the proceeds from sales went to the Prevent Cancer Foundation. A charm bracelet was even added as a hip ornament to a string bikini from Jo De Mer and to clutch bags from Kathy Van Zeeland.

With a new emphasis on eco styling, insects and flower motifs were abundant. Dior's "Diorette" collections of 2007–08 featured clusters of three-dimensional jewel-studded flowers swarming with high-relief butterflies and ladybugs attached to huge cuff bracelets and dome rings. Jennifer Herwitt created diamond encrusted spider pendants, scorpion earrings, and fire ant chokers. Ricky Boscarino's bronzed sterling cicada brooches were made all the more lifelike with moveable wings. On the extreme side of the trend was live insect jewelry such as the "pet" Giant Madagascar Hissing Cockroach Brooch encrusted with Swarovski crystals and a tiny chain that allowed the insect limited roaming on a bodice or sleeve. (Well-fed roaches could live up to a year.)

Vintage costume jewelry provided the variable complements and contrasts to the many pluralistic fashions of the new century. Women searched vintage clothing shops and competed on eBay for the best pieces from the fifties and sixties by Eisenberg Ice, Trifari, and Coro. Also from the 1960s (via the 1920s) were boho revivals of the slave bracelet—a ring for the middle finger attached to a bracelet by a decorative chain. Jewelry designer Alyssa Norton modeled her 2009 slave bracelets on Indian panjab styles made with an abundance of rhinestones.

Among the fads of school-age teens were Silly Bandz (and their many imitators) introduced in 2008. Sold in packs of twenty-four for $5, the brightly colored rubber band-like bracelets were cut into assorted theme shapes ranging from animal and "princess" designs for girls to cowboy and sports motifs for boys. The popularity of the jewelry reached a national craze when several states banned the bracelets because they were distracting students and causing disruptions in classrooms.

Women's Hairstyles and Makeup 2000–Present

Gels, or "glues" as they were marketed, and other stylers returned in the early 2000s to add volume and textural interest rather than artificially sculpt the hair as in the eighties. The mussed **bed head** look was named for "stylizer" products from Tigi Haircare. Irregular and asymmetrical cuts became popular by middecade. African-American women experimented with honey-blonde hair following the lead of celebrities like Tyra Banks, Rihanna, and Beyonce. In 2005, Paul Mitchell celebrated its twenty-fifth anniversary with multipaged magazine inserts in which the "modern incarnations" of the best "hair couture" were depicted. Among those represented were the "sleek chic," slicked back with a quick-drying glaze; a sixties revival bubble cut; "retro-romantic" glamour of 1940s Hollywood; and several versions of eighties big hair from towering pompadours to "waves" of long cascades of curls. To complement the romantique bow look in fashion, some women with long, straight hair tied their tresses into looped bows at the top or back of the head.

The fresh-scrubbed, no-makeup look that emerged in the 1990s extended into the early 2000s. The clean, youthful look projected in the images of cosmetics ads induced many aging baby boom women, the first of whom turned sixty in 2006, to try Botox muscle relaxant injections for smoothing crows' feet and frown lines. Other women explored new appearances with less painful efforts, such as colored contacts.

Strongly colored eyeshadows returned in the second half of the decade, but instead of accenting the eyelids and underbrow, the new eyeshadows were applied beneath the bottom eyelashes in a soft, narrow band. The quest for thick, long eyelashes was fulfilled by mascara made of a "fibrestretch" formula by Lancome, which assured "instant lash extensions up to 60%," or "Expansyl-rich" volumizer by L'Oréal that promised "12 times more volume."

Pale, natural shades of lipstick dominated the decade although, for attending fashionable events, bright reds returned. (Figure 13.25.) To achieve the favored "perfectly plumped, full-out pout," LipFusion developed "lip plumpers" that caused a "mild swelling" of the lips that lasted up to forty-eight hours.

Among the biggest beauty trends of the decade was teeth whitening. For severe discoloration, bleaching was achieved by infrared lasers administered by a dentist. Most people though opted for whitening toothpastes and products for home application. Ads from whitening toothpastes such as Rembrandt promised to whiten teeth "five full shades." Over-the-counter peroxide solutions could be put into bite trays that the consumer applied to the teeth for a length of time. In 2004, Crest introduced transparent whitening strips that folded over the teeth and were worn for thirty minutes.

In addition to the continuing popularity of body piercing throughout the first decade of the new millenium, tattooing proliferated with young people. Large numbers of Gen Y teens and twenty-something women and men in both cities and suburbia used tattoos to express themselves and the distinction of their generation. As one social commentator noted at the time, "**tats**" were one of the few opportunities for young people to rebel since their parents had already thoroughly exploited sex, drugs, and rock-and-roll. For women who preferred variety, temporary tattoos—also called "body art"— were applied with transfer decals affixed to the skin with isopropyl alcohol that faded after a few days. Other temporary tattoos were achieved with stencils airbrushed on in salons or with home tat kits. And the **tantoo** was made by an adhesive-backed decal attached to the skin prior to sunbathing, resulting in a light silhouette of the shape or initial.

Dolce and Gabbana Fire lipstick, eyeshadow, and mascara, 2009.

Pluralistic looks of the new millennium.

FIGURE 13.25. In the new millennium, hairstyles ranged from spiky bed head looks to beribboned schoolgirl crops. Retro hairstyles that corresponded to the many fashion revivalisms included classics such as the pageboy. Lipsticks and eyeshadows were soft, light, and natural until the second half of the decade when strong colors returned.

FIGURE 13.26. Except for utilitarian types, hats largely disappeared from women's wardrobes. Small scale forms of headgear, such as knit caps, boyfriend fedoras, and berets were favored for winter wear. Left, mass produced knit cap, 2007; center, wool beret, 2007; right, boyfriend trilby, 2009.

Women's Hats 2000–Present

The emphasis on simplicity and ease in dress in the early 2000s further diminished hat wearing. Models in fashion advertising and editorials were predominantly bareheaded. Hats were incompatible with the frayed hair cuts and gelled bed head styles of the decade.

Knit caps were a favorite urban look to complement hip-hop styling. (Figure 13.26.) Soft felt fedoras in deep, rich colors, edged in black grosgrain, were practical winterwear that dressed up city looks. A narrow brimmed variation called a **trilby** was a favorite of young women, especially when accented with a leather band, buckle, or oversized antique coat buttons stitched to one side of the crown.

At the end of the decade, hairbands of all types became popular again. As First Lady, Hillary Clinton had made the look famous in the early 1990s. Nearly twenty years later, a new generation of young women opted for the look ranging from Coach logo patterned bow styles to jeweled double strands for red carpet celebrities.

Women's Accessories 2000–Present

In the early 2000s, the subdued, simplified approach to accessories developed into an even more minimalist trend. For most, the idea of accessorizing was function over form, and quality over quantity. Colors were muted; black and earthtones much preferred. Even when exaggeration was at play, particularly with fashion revivals of the fifties and sixties, the focus was on one component, not the full replication of the New Look past: the Audrey Hepburn *Breakfast at Tiffany's* sunglasses or the architectural go-go earrings of *Hullabaloo*.

Eyewear from Tory Burch, 2008.

Max Mara logo sunglasses, 2009.

Luggage handbag by Ralph Lauren, 2008.

Coach logo handbag, 2006.

Dooney and Burke logo handbag, 2007.

FIGURE 13.27. Rather than the full accoutrement of head-to-toe accessories, millennial women preferred one or two key accessories as a statement of personal style. The idea of what *Vogue* disdained as "matchy-matchy" accessories was abandoned in favor of a complement, rather than a coordination, of accessories.

Handbags became brand billboards with multicolored wallpaper repeat patterns of logos. (Figure 13.27.) In the second half of the decade, handbags became enormous carryalls, hallmarked with logo patches or dangling logo pendants. The age-old tenet that handbags, belts, and shoes should match—what *Vogue* disparaged as "matchy-matchy"—was largely discarded in the 2000s.

Twenty-first-century technology also provided fashion designers with new opportunities for marketing their branded logos. Designers such as Anna Sui, Giorgio Armani, and Dolce and Gabbana created designs for mobile phones, most with matching signature phone cases. Vivienne Tam created a scarlet and pink peony cover for the 2009 Hewlett-Packard laptop. Apple's iPods were offered in a rainbow assortment of iridescent hues, accessorized with matching neckband earphones and cords.

The shape of eyewear narrowed to small rectangles, often with thin, lightweight frames. Sunglasses, though, remained oversized, becoming huge goggles by the end of the decade, all the better to upsize logos along the temple arms by Fendi, Chanel, Gucci, and Prada, among many others. Ed Hardy added colorful tattoo designs embedded with Swarovski crystals to the frames of his sunglasses.

Men's Fashions 2000–Present

Despite a seemingly generic, styleless approach to dress by most men through much of the nineties, a new breed of image- and fashion-conscious male emerged at the dawn of the new millennium. The fashion press dubbed him a "**metrosexual**," or sometimes simply metro man, who, according to pop culture author David Coad, is a young, urban man for whom "attention to appearance and self-care are central . . . shopping for clothes, accessorizing, and using body products." Numerous style guides were published in the early 2000s advising the metrosexual on fashion and taste. The media's favorite metrosexual was the British soccer star David Beckham, whose personal style was unconstrained by EuroAmerican conventions of masculine identity. (Figure 13.28.) He frequently changed his hairstyles, sometimes buzz cut short, other times shoulder length; he also polished his fingernails, wore an abundance of jewelry and accessories, donned sarongs and the briefest of swimwear, and scrupulously dressed in color-coordinated clothing that fitted well. In a 2009–10 ad campaign for Armani underwear, he modeled various styles from trunk boxers to sheer bikinis.

At the beginning of the 2000s, the ultraslim, fitted look of the 1960s was revived by men's suit designers, and the silhouette became the suit look of the new millennium. (Figure 13.29.) Tailoring of the new suit styles, reported *WWD*, was "in the vein of softness, unstructured with a natural, rounded shoulder." In addition, details such as lapels and pocket flaps were scaled down to emphasize the new, trim proportions. Some designers also shortened the jacket skirt to emphasize the lanky look of the narrow sleeves and trouser legs. A favorite jacket style of young men was the one-button closure, which emphasized their long, lean torso and youthful, trim waistline. Likewise, trousers were cut with a low-rise waistband and plain, unpleated front. To be even more slimly fitted, some trousers were darted in front. Suit trouser cuffs, which had largely disappeared at the start of the decade, returned at the end. The cuff was deep—about an inch and a half—and cropped short, just at the ankles so as not to break the center crease over the shoe, causing the cuff to gap.

One of the most prominent names in the shrunken suit look of the decade was New York designer Thom Browne, whose custom suits were priced in the $5000 range. With the delivery of each Thom Browne suit also came a sheet of style rules:

- Rule #1: Only the middle button on the jacket should be buttoned when you are wearing it closed.
- Rule #2: The pocket square in the breast pocket should be just peeking out (no more than 1/8 of an inch).
- Rule #3: The last button on the cuff of the jacket should be left unbuttoned.
- Rule #4: The button-down collar of the white oxford shirt should remain unbuttoned.
- Rule #5: Please do not iron the oxford shirts after washing.
- Rule #6: The trousers should be worn high-waisted so that the cuff of the trouser falls above the ankle.
- Rule #7: The neckties have been pretied, but please remember to keep the knot very tight when tying the necktie.
- Rule #8: The necktie should be worn long, with the tip of the tie tucked into the waist of the trousers.

FIGURE 13.28. British athlete David Beckham epitomized the new millennium's metrosexual with a personal style that defied the conventions of EuroAmerican masculine dress. Photo of Beckham dressed in Manchester emblazoned jacket carrying a mailpouch shoulder bag, 2003.

FIGURE 13.29. Men's suits of the new century were ultraslim with natural shoulders, narrow sleeves, and scaled down details such as lapels and pocket flaps. Often called skinny or shrunken suits by the fashion press, some new styles included shortened jacket skirts and ankle-high trouser cuffs. Summer sharkskin suit from C.P. Company, 2009.

- Rule #9: The tie bar should be clipped so that it falls halfway between the collar of your shirt and the waistband of the trousers.
- Rule #10: The shoes should be worn without socks.

The trim, soft casing of the skinny suit was further enhanced by improved fabric technologies. Textile mills developed new methods of producing "**high twist**" **wool** yarns by tightly coiling two strands of the finest, softest fibers. The result was a more elastic and yet stronger fabric that could more readily bounce back to shape, staying relatively wrinkle-free compared to previous wool fabrics. The various grades of these nanoperformance cloths are referred to as Super 100s numbered in tens up to Super 200s. The best tailored suits usually used Super 130s since the higher the grade, the more delicate and high-maintenance the fabric.

In 2008, the era of the Man in the Gray Flannel Suit was revived with the critically acclaimed TV series *Mad Men,* which takes place in the early 1960s when the trim, snug-fitting cut of the Continental look became universal. The influence of the TV drama also inspired a renewed interest in the classic looks of President Kennedy, whose photos of his two-button suits and casual sportswear were frequently reproduced in menswear editorials. *GQ* referred to the revival of the iconic Continental look as "Eisenhower chic," a formulaic corporate "uniform," just as it had been fifty years earlier: "dark, trim suit; crisp, white dress shirt; narrow, diagonally striped repp tie; and a pair of wingtips," accented with a white pocket square, slide belt, and tie bar. Replication of the fifties masculine dress formula was a stylish way for men without the requisite slender collegiate build needed for a skinny suit to look current and be comfortable.

With the acceptance of business casual dress in most workplaces, though, sport coats became a preferred substitute for suits. For winter months, trimmed down tweed styles were commonly recommended in fall preview magazine articles. However, even unconstructed cotton styles became a year-round option since the colors, textures, and textile patterns were so varied. (Figure 13.30.) In 2008, Italy's Cantarelli produced a true reversible sport coat with a solid navy side with brass buttons that reversed to a navy pin striped side with navy buttons. Other incarnations of the navy blazer, in single- or double-breasted styles, were touted in the fashion press as a must-have wardrobe staple for all men. Unlike the nineteenth-century original, which was viewed as active sports attire worn only for boating or tennis, the millennial blazer served as a versatile anchor to a wide variety of looks ranging from a casual layer over a screenprinted T-shirt and chinos or jeans to the traditional spectator dress of the polished resort habitué.

For most men, twenty-first-century formalwear was the tuxedo. Style guides usually directed the uncertain male to the traditional black tux with a notch collar, a look that has varied little since the suit style made its debut at the New York Tuxedo Park Club in the 1880s. "Opting for a classic doesn't make you a square; it makes you a gentleman," cajoled one editor. For a man wishing to make more of a personal style statement, he might choose a peak or shawl collar, or perhaps opt for midnight blue instead of black. Whichever collar type or dark fabric a man might select, there were still pitfalls of formal dress that separated the knowledgeable sophisticate from the uniformed "prom date." Foremost was the fit. All up-and-coming young men were advised to buy a tux rather than rent to ensure a proper fit "like a suit of armor." Hand-tied bowties were a requirement although, to dress down a tux for a less formal daytime event, a narrow long tie in solid black was sometimes acceptable. Cummerbunds were passé.

Despite the conformist demands of traditionalists, though, some millennial designers experimented with ways to break the 130-year-old rules of the tux while preserving the es-

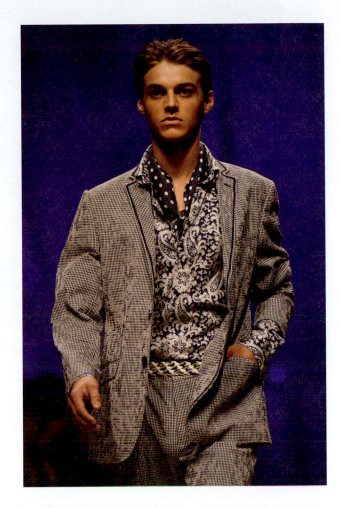

FIGURE 13.30. Sport coats were constructed with the same slim, narrow proportions and natural shoulders as skinny suit jackets. For millennial men, the sport coat served as a suit substitute for the workplace and as a versatile casual look when dressed down. Left, bold pattern mixing from Etro, 2009; right, deconstructed blazer from Jil Sander, 2008.

sence of the style. Designs by Dolce and Gabbana included suits in royal blue satin with white piping and white side stripes on the trousers; basic black tuxedo jackets were enlivened with sumptuous allover jet beadwork except for the satin shawl collar. (Figure 13.31.) Variations of millennial tuxedos by other designers included bottle green or burgundy velvet jackets with black bowties and black trousers.

With the dominance of the skinny, shrunken look in suits and sport coats, young men needed trim fitting dress shirts to fit comfortably beneath the jackets. "Most guys don't know it, but they're walking around with way too much shirt—baggy arms, sagging sides, balloon

FIGURE 13.31. Although menswear style guides adhered to a strict protocol for the tuxedo, some avant-garde designers experimented with variations that offered millennial men options for greater self-expression. Jet beaded tuxedo jacket and black satin trousers from Dolce and Gabbana, 2010.

FIGURE 13.32. With the decade-long wars in Afghanistan and Iraq dominating news headlines, military looks became a prevalent influence in men's fashion. Army shirt by John Varvatos, 2011.

backs," admonished *GQ*. "Just because a shirt's neck and sleeves are the right size doesn't mean the rest of the shirt will fit you." Ready-to-wear makers responded with skinny shirts cut with narrow sleeves, tapered side seams, and darted backs—revival constructions from the 1960s and 1970s. In 2009, Brooks Brothers added a line of "extra slim fit" broadcloths and oxfords in a variety of patterns and colors. A regular size 15 1/2 × 34 shirt was reduced from 51 1/2 inches across the chest to 43 1/2 inches. The following year, Calvin Klein Body shirts were introduced with an ad campaign stating simply, "Slim. Contoured. Defined."

One of the innovative dress shirt designs of the decade was the Prada French cuff, introduced in 2007. Instead of the traditional turn-back style, which many men viewed as too much fabric and too pretentious, the Prada French cuff was a regular sleeve cuff with cuff-link holes instead of buttons. The shirts came with pearl button links as an alternative to jewelry cuff links.

FIGURE 13.33. The variety of casual sportswear tops provided young men with a broad range of looks from the menacing concealment of hoodies to the whimsy of screenprinted manga and similar graphic images. Left, hoodie jacket, from Jerzees, 2008; right, manga T-shirt by Lucien Pellat-Finet, 2009.

Similarly, by the end of the decade, collars of skinny dress shirts were pared down by almost a third of standard styles. The rounded corner club collar, suggested *Details,* could "impart freshness, making a point collar seem, well square."

Among the most popular trends in men's shirts and casual jackets of the decade was the military look. As the first decade of the new century came to a close, the U.S. war in Afghanistan had been ongoing nine years, and the war in Iraq seven years, both continually dominating global news headlines. Military styled shirts and jackets, usually in a shade of olive green, included epaulets, multiple pockets with flaps, assorted buckles, exposed zippers, metal buttons, appliqued rank patches, and stenciled or embroidered insignia. (Figure 13.32.) Military uniform detailing such as epaulets and pocket flaps "make you look tough," suggested a *GQ* editor, possibly as compensation for the frail appearance of the prevailing super skinny silhouettes. But not all military inspired looks were in shades of army green. Roberto Cavalli's military jacket was in yellow edged with sienna piping. Dolce and Gabbana embellished their military officers' dress jackets with sumptuous frogging, braid, and embroidery. Burberry's military coat was turquoise with a rappelling cams belt.

Another prevalent sportswear look of young millennial men was the **hoodie**—any variety of hooded knit shirt, fleece top, or vest. (Figure 13.33.) Although the hoodie was far from new, previously hooded garments—commonly emblazoned with sports logos—were largely worn for utility in cold weather. Instead, the twenty-first-century hoodie became imbued with the cachet of the menacing, inner-city hoodlum who wore a hoodie with the hood up year round as a

Yoke front white jeans by Ermanno Scervino, 2010.

Low rider jeans by Dsquared2, 2008.

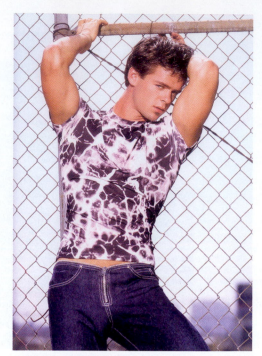

Zip-around waistband jeans by Pedro Diaz for Pistol Pete Jeans, 2004.

FIGURE 13.34. Retro styles of men's jeans included new interpretations of sixties hiphuggers and revamped traditional looks such as well-worn "dirty denim" and pristine white varieties. Skintight skinny jeans emphasized trim, youthful physiques, and were often worn with ankle-high cuffs or rolled hems to expose sockless feet.

sort of disguise or concealment. For warmer weather, light weight jerseys and even sleeveless hoodies were widely available, many with huge, multicolored screenprints over the front and back. Teens and collegiates especially liked skull and tattoo graphics or oversized logos from Ecko, Billabong, and Enjoi.

Denim shirts, and their cousins, chambray work shirts, were another favorite casual look in the second half of the decade. The simplicity of the work shirt, though, was transformed into high style looks with embellishments ranging from lavish embroidery to metal studs. Where Ralph Lauren's RRL branded denim shirts were accented with small, studded snowflakes on the shoulders of the Western-cut yokes, Trussardi completely covered the entire surface of theirs with whorls of studs.

Although style guides continually cautioned that only shirts with short, finished tails should be worn untucked, many men preferred the comfort and look of untucked shirt tails irrespective of the shirt cut. As with young women's styles, many young men arranged the casual, thrown-together look with shirt tails extending from beneath buttoned cardigans or pullovers, fleece tops, sport coats, and outerwear jackets. Some collegiates were spotted on campus with the anti-prep look of button down oxfords worn with the back and only one side of the front tail tucked, the other half of the front tail hanging loose over the front of the jeans or khakis.

Logos continued to be significant to certain segments of male consumers. Not only was the logo a style comfort zone for many men—predictable in quality, fit, and looks—but for others, the brand marketing provided a particular masculine identity some men embraced: athletic, or nautical, or country club. Some logoists were content with a quiet statement such as Louis Vuitton's polo shirt with an unobtrusive "LV" logo on the chest priced at $300. For other men, size mattered. In addition to replacing the thumbnail-scale polo rider logo with the embroidered Big Pony, Ralph Lauren also introduced a hand-sized heraldic lion embroidered in golden thread on some polo shirts in 2006. Lacoste, too, upsized its croc logo five times the original size on polo shirts.

For men of all ages, the comfortable, uncomplicated T-shirt was the favorite, most universal top. It draped easily, hanging loosely from the shoulders without binding seams or cumbersome closures, and was expected to be worn untucked. At the beginning of the 2010s, young men opted for T-shirts with deep, plunging V-necks that bared the chest. Screen-printed T-shirts allowed millennial men to express their pluralistic personalities, sports loyalties, hobby interests, social convictions, and political affiliations. For teens, **manga T-shirts**, imprinted with the big-eyed Japanese cartoon characters of manga comics and anime films like the one shown in Figure 13.33, reflected the globalization of pop culture. A resurgence in protest message T-shirts recalled the activist looks of the late 1960s and early 1970s. In the United States, both sides of the abortion issue asserted their views across their chests during marches. Participants in annual Gay Pride parades displayed their unity against discrimination with rainbow-embellished T-shirts. One of the best-selling T-shirt messages against the war in Iraq read "We will not be silent" written in both English and Arabic as a protest against the Bush administration's remarks that critics of the war were unpatriotic.

Men's jeans, as with women's styles, became even more widely varied in design in the 2000s. One of the most prevalent looks was a revival of the tight fitting hiphugger styles of the late sixties, now commonly called low riders. (Figure 13.34.) As in the 1960s, the style particularly appealed to slim young men although some baby boomers whose fitness routines kept them trim also opted for the nostalgia of the new hiphuggers. Other varieties of jeans ranged from basic "dirty denim" produced by assorted designer labels to painter's styles with cargo pockets and hammer loops at the side seams. Distressed jeans with threadbare holes and frayed edges were called "Destroyed Jeans" by I●N●C International Concepts. Designer labels and distinctive topstitching or embroidery on the back pockets held as much appeal for Gen Y men as for their Gen X predecessors. In 2008, Ralph Lauren's kelly green jeans included multiple polo players embroidered on the hip coin pocket. Ed Hardy jeans were embroidered over substantial portions of the thighs or backside with his exuberant tattoo designs and massive logo. Pedro Diaz redefined the everyday jeans with an exposed zipper that extended up from the fly and around the waistband. Prices for designer label jeans were commonly in the $150–$300 range, with 2010 styles from Balmain at $1300 a pair.

To wear jeans belted or unbelted was a constant topic of editorials and consumer questions-to-the-editor columns. As one editor noted, "A belt tends to improve the looks of any pants with belt loops. If you have the sort of waistband overhang often referred to as love handles . . . that's all the more reason to wear a belt, as it will help prevent the waistband of the pants from rolling over from the pressure of flab spillage." Many men opted for belts

FIGURE 13.35. At the end of the decade, tailored shorts were influenced by the ultraslim look of skinny jeans and pants. Leg lengths of shorts were cropped to mid-thigh and the fit was trim. Left, white cotton shorts and silk shirts from Etro, 2010; right, cotton shorts, crewneck sweater, and cardigan by Salvatore Ferragamo, 2009.

because the variety was so inviting. White belts drew attention to slender waists and narrow hips, metal studded belts added a touch of masculine toughness, colorful tattoo belts expressed a wearer's whimsy, and bottle cap belts with car seatbelt buckles projected an avant-garde confidence.

More important than belted or beltless, though, was the length of the jeans legs. Where once "highwater" pant hems were viewed as the look of rock stars like Michael Jackson or, on the other end of the spectrum, the styleless dress of pocket-protector-wearing nerds of the eighties, now the ankle-baring length was deliberate and trendy. Cropped leg hemlines reinforced the skinny, shrunken fit. If the jeans were too long, then rolling the cuffs high was an easy solution.

Not all trousers were thigh- and calf-hugging remakes of the 1960s Levi's "13s" (cut so narrow that the circumference at the leg opening hem measured 13 inches). Indeed, as a 2010 Docker's ad noted, skinny jeans were regarded as one of the "strange and humiliating rites of passage" young men had to endure. Instead, roomy cargo pants with multiple pockets continued to be common into the 2010s. Likewise virtually every boy, teen, and man had at least one pair of full-cut khakis whether in off-white "stone" (also called "putty" in some catalogs) or in the pale ochre to olive palettes. And as noted with suit trousers and jeans, the new khakis, too, were recommended in style editorials to be hemmed "so they barely touch the top of your shoes." However, even with fuller cut styles of pants, fit was still important. As *GQ* cautioned Gen X and Gen Y young men, "Walking around with a sagging waistline and what looks like a fistful of rocks in your oversize cargo pockets is not cool."

Although most American men steadfastly clung to their baggy, shin-length shorts, European men began to opt for shorter, trim tailored shorts at the end of the decade. (Figure 13.35.) The skinny look of jeans and pants emphasized the muscular contours of men's legs, which sportswear designers took to the next level with a return of eighties' styled short shorts. Like jeans and pants, tailored shorts were usually pleatless and cut narrow for an ultraslim fit. Cargo styles of short shorts, with abbreviated patch pockets, were mass produced as "hiking shorts." In her 2010 spring collection, Miuccia Prada went one step further with as-

FIGURE 13.36. Throughout the first decade of the new century, a diversity of skirts for men appeared on the runways and in collections of menswear designers. Left, men's skirt and shoulder bag by Vivienne Westwood, 2006; right, men's skirts from Comme des Garcon Homme, 2008.

sorted thigh-high "raw-hemmed" suit shorts, or basically cut-offs with finely fringed, unraveling edges.

As with designers of women's fashions, menswear designers used runway shows to present drama and fantasy styles for the new-age male. One of the most talked about looks of the new millennium was the wide array of skirts for men. (Figure 13.36.) Gaultier, Westwood, Galliano, and McQueen were among many designers offering varieties of men's skirts and other gender-bending clothes. As a modern concept, though, skirts for men were not unique to the 2000s but had a legacy dating back to the 1960s when male hippies donned wrap skirts, kaftans, and long tunics as a way to express their anti-establishment view of gender rules and stereotypical identities.

Men's Sports Attire and Outerwear 2000–Present

The most prevalent active sports attire for most men of the new century varied little from the previous decade. Long baggy nylon or polyblend shorts prevailed. (Figure 13.37.) They were

FIGURE 13.37. Although the snug, skinny look for suits, jeans, and pants prevailed in the new century, men still preferred the long, baggy fit of athletic shorts. New nanotechnologies were applied to fiber and fabric production, making performance sports clothing more durable and comfortable and providing the freedom to move from hot to cold environments and still feel dry. Left, muscle shirt and running shorts from Tek Gear, 2009; right, Adidas logo T-shirt and tennis shorts, 2010.

comfortable, cool, and functional for almost any sports and fitness regimen. Any oversized cotton T-shirt—often including the basic white undershirt—served as a sports top. Long shorts and T-shirts were cheap and available in large assortments of colors and fabrics from every mass merchandiser.

The more serious athlete, though, studied the recommendations and consumer reports in health and fitness magazines on advances in new fabrics and constructions of performance clothing. Twenty-first-century nanotechnology transformed fibers on the molecular level to produce fabrics and clothing that provided the freedom to move from hot to cold environments and still feel dry. The advanced moisture wicking of textiles kept athletes cool and neutralizer fabrics eliminated odors. For winter sports, nanotechnology produced fleece that repelled water and resisted static.

However, despite the benefits of compression support constructions of some active sportswear, a new generation of young American men adopted the fear of exhibitionism and usually avoided any type of spandex active sportswear. Even though idolized champions such as seven-time Tour de France winner Lance Armstrong were repeatedly in TV news reports and featured in sports magazines dressed in second-skin spandex, the American male was wary. This persistent fear of peer pressure over common sense was a topic of countless men's studies books and magazine articles. "As for the spandex fear, get over it," chastised *GQ* in a 2007 review of cycling clothing. "You don't want to be one of these jokers trying to gut it out in army shorts; bike seats aren't beanbag chairs. If nothing else, your junk will thank you."

Through much of the decade, coats and outerwear jackets reflected the shrunken, skinny look of suits. Sleeves were narrow, bodies were slim, and details were minimal. Hemlines were

Kneebreaker trench coat by Junya Watanabe, 2006.

Duffle coat by Frank Leder, 2009.

Greatcoat by Dior Homme, 2010.

FIGURE 13.38. Much of men's outerwear followed the trim, shrunken trend of suits and sportswear. At the end of the decade, designers revived the eighties big look, producing voluminous greatcoats with oversized details.

cropped short on topcoats. "A topcoat should be trim," advised a style guide in 2007. "It should reach to just above your knee, and it should be the same size as the suit you wear not a size larger." Traditional peacoats, duffles, and leather jackets in scaled down versions were favorites of young men. (Figure 13.38.) Trench coats, the preferred all-weather style for men of all ages, were also reduced in proportions and details.

At the beginning of the 2010s, though, some men's topcoats once again became massive and long, reminiscent of the big look of the eighties. "Narrow? No more," proclaimed *WWD's* 2010 report on men's collections. "The grand coat made a dramatic entrance of voluminous proportions." Many styles were mid-calf in length and others swept the ankles. Sleeves were capacious and details like pockets, belts, and buttons were oversized. Shoulders were broad and squared to support huge Napoleonic collars and hand-span lapels.

Men's Underwear and Swimwear 2000–Present

After somewhat of a hiatus during the 1990s, men's fashion underwear resurged in the new century with more varieties of cuts, colors, patterns and prints, and fabrications since the

Bikini by John Galliano, 2010.

Sport boxerbriefs with contoured pouch from Mundo Unico, 2008.

FIGURE 13.39. The notion of underwear as fashion resurged in the new century with greater varieties of cuts, colors, prints, and fabrics since the 1970s. New constructions included reengineered front pouches for more comfortable support and new microfiber fabrics with a luxurious feel.

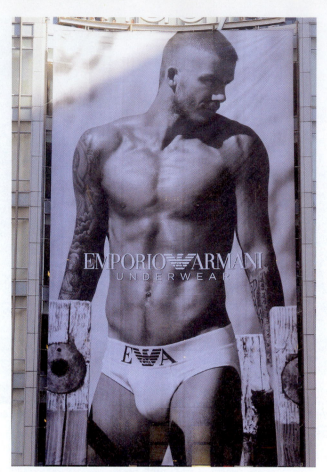

Armani briefs (five-story billboard), 2010.

1970s. New makers such as 2(X)ist, N2N, and C-IN2, among others, entered the lucrative underwear market with aggressive magazine ad campaigns that targeted a new generation of young, fit males. Big name designers like Armani, Dolce and Gabbana, and Sean John branded the waistbands of sexy, luxury styles with bold logos. (Figure 13.39.) "Trade in your baggy boxers for a pair of the season's best formfitting briefs," exclaimed *GQ* in 2008. Among the more popular cuts of formfitting underwear for men under forty were boxerbriefs. In the early 2000s, square-cut versions called **trunks** were made with a lowered waistband to better fit beneath low rider jeans. The look was made popular in mass media, movies, and on TV programs whenever a young male character had to be undressed: in 2005, for instance, the promotional print and broadcast images for the TV reality program *Manhunt* depicted the male model contestants all wearing white trunk-cut boxerbriefs.

For men who were more comfortable with traditional woven boxers, styles narrowed to reduce bunching beneath skinny pants and jeans. "If boxers are too bulky, you're wearing the wrong kind," advised *GQ*. "You're thinking of the old Ivy League boxer, which is almost literally having proportions similar to Everlast [boxing] trunks; modern boxer shorts are trim and close to the body, similar to the shorts worn by the 1973 world-champion New York Knickerbockers."

New support constructions included reengineered front pouches that lifted and projected the genitals for more comfortable support and sexualized display beneath skintight jeans. In

Board shorts, 2008.

FIGURE 13.40. For the majority of American men, the long, baggy board shorts that first reappeared in the late eighties remained the preferred swim attire of the new century. Revivals of formfitting square-cut trunks and briefs followed trends of fashion underwear. In the competitive arena, new technologies of construction and nanofabrics were applied to body-covering swimwear designed to maximize performance.

Retro sixties low-rise square-cut trunks from Simons, 2009.

2007, Calvin Klein introduced the Steel collection of briefs, boxerbriefs, and trunks in two new fabrications, an enhanced fine cotton and a new, "ultra-luxe microfiber," each with a tagless, metallic logo waistband. Undershirts from makers such as Spanx were made of high-quality, ring-spun cotton with flat-lock side seams that promised to firm the chest, flatten the stomach, improve posture, and support the lower back.

Fashion underwear color palettes and prints became as vibrant as their seventies pre-decessors. Camouflage prints complemented the popular military look of sportswear. Vividly detailed tattoo prints by Ed Hardy were a favorite with collegiates. One of the best selling styles of 2009 reported by Baskit was a pink mesh jockstrap. "Guys want to be sexy too," concluded a *New York Times* editorial on the men's underwear industry in 2007.

For swimwear, long, baggy **board shorts** remained the most common look pool- and beach-side for men of all ages. (Figure 13.40.) Most men did not consider much beyond the color or print when selecting their board shorts despite the numerous suggestions about body types and fit in catalogs and magazines. A six-paged "GQ Primer" on "how to buy a swimsuit" in 2009 reminded men that "if you don't pay attention, you'll end up with board shorts droop-ing past your knees or elastic-waist dad trunks cinching your love handles." Even as swimwear makers and style editorials emphasized that new swimsuits were "short but not tight," beaches abounded with the long, baggy look that resembled a "hand-me-down cheerleading skirt."

Speedo LZR Racer swimsuit, 2008.

FIGURE 13.41. Since the late eighties, traditional styles of ties have remained fairly standardized at 3 1/2 to 4 inches wide at the end of the blade. In the new century, skinny ties were reintroduced to Gen Y young men as a complement to the ultraslim styles of suits and sportswear. Anna Sui logo necktie, jacket, and trousers, 2003.

In 2000, a new type of neck-to-ankle bodysuit swimwear made of a high-tech fabric called **Fastskin** was introduced at the Olympics. The material was developed with the aid of computers to simulate the smooth, V-shaped ridges of sharkskin, which reduced the drag of friction even better than the swimmer's shaved bare skin. In 2008, the high-tech Speedo LZR (pronounced "laser") Racer, which covered the swimmer from neck to ankles, was credited with establishing over thirty world records in swimming during the Beijing Olympics.

Men's Accessories 2000–Present

To complement the dominant skinny look in much of young men's wear, skinny ties reappeared. (Figure 13.41.) At 1 1/2 to 2 inches in width, though, skinny ties were distinct from "slim" ties, which were about 2 1/2 to 2 7/8 inches in width. Slim ties in school stripes and pin point dots from Brooks Brothers and other more conservative menswear makers were the recommended finishing touch for the new skinny suits of young execs.

For men who still preferred the subdued wider power tie, at 3 1/2 inches at the end of the blade, knots were a way of subtle self expression. The versatile **Shelby knot** (popularized by news anchorman Don Shelby) was wider than a four-in-hand but not as thick as a half-Windsor. New emphasis was also placed on the arrangement of a tie's dimple. The "**sorchetta**" was a double-dimple knot initiated by style makers in Italy.

Beginning in the late 1990s, and especially in the first decade of the new millennium, jewelry for men underwent a resurgence of popularity not seen since the iconoclastic excesses of the 1960s peacock male. Gold and titanium chain necklaces from the disco era reappeared beneath open collars, some with retro pendants such as blunted razor blades (once used by partiers for cutting cocaine), dog tags to complement military looks, skulls, and tribal symbols. Large black steel finger rings were studded with oversized red jasper or other colorful natural stones. David Yurman's rings were inlaid with dinosaur bone or capped with sculpted scarabs, wasps, or Mycenaean shields. At the end of the decade, multiple bracelets became a revival seventies trend, especially combinations of silver-studded leather and silver chains of varying widths. "The more wrist pieces you wear, the better each looks," suggested *GQ* in 2007. Rubber bracelets such as the yellow Livestrong band from the Lance Armstrong Cancer Foundation promoted causes. Less subtle but equally symbolic was **bling-bling** (more commonly shortened to just "bling"), a term coined by a rapper group in the late nineties meaning flashy jewelry, particularly oversized diamond-studded pieces, or a showy style of dress that represented disposable wealth and the confidence to display it. (Figure 13.42.)

The body piercings that once had hallmarked the shock values of the urban punk style in the 1970s were now ubiquitous among young men worldwide. Varieties of pierced earrings for men expanded from the simplicity of the punk safety pin, silver stud, or tiny gold hoop to ornate Celtic crosses, dangling chains, and sociopolitical symbols. Some men now wore pairs rather than solo earrings, or even multiples in each ear. In addition, tongues, lips, noses, eyebrows, navels, nipples, and genitals were pierced and plugged with studs and hoops of varying sizes and metals.

Men's shoes became almost as varied, and sometimes extreme, as women's styles. Lug soled shoes that had emerged in the late nineties developed even thicker rubber cleats and

FIGURE 13.42. At the end of the twentieth century and into the new millennium, men's jewelry reflected the pluralism of masculine style. Men expressed their personalities, social status, and emotional sentiments with a wide variety of jewelry ranging from subtle and simple to opulent and ostentatious. Left, rubber Livestrong wristband for the Lance Armstrong Cancer Foundation; right, rapper Curtis "50 Cent" Jackson displaying his bling-bling, 2003.

higher heels in the '00s. (Figure 13.43.) By middecade, men's styles began to adopt the wide, squared toes that had developed in women's shoes a couple of years earlier. Also following the trends of women's styles, versions of men's poulaines with long, sharply pointed toes were a trend with younger men in the second half of the decade. With the shorter pants hemlines, new attention was focused on eyecatching footwear. One of the more popular revivals for dressing down a suit and dressing up chinos or jeans was the **bit loafer** named for the horse harness bit hardware attached to a strap or metal bar across the vamp. The *Mad Men* influence and renewed interest in the looks of the Kennedy years inspired a resurgent popularity of boat shoes, which, as one 2008 editorial noted, "made the leap from being the footwear of choice for Nantucketers and Key West stoners to required gear for downtown rock kids and style boys." For logoists, Louis Vuitton embedded the heels of slip-ons with an "LV" and debossed the logo signature on the side of wingtips in 2007.

Studded, square-toe slip-on by Mark Nason, 2007.

Fifties revival of the bush boot by Kenneth Cole, 2005.

Rubber cleated Sketchers, 2004.

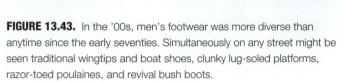

"The Funeral" boots from Illex Kinni, 2009.

FIGURE 13.43. In the '00s, men's footwear was more diverse than anytime since the early seventies. Simultaneously on any street might be seen traditional wingtips and boat shoes, clunky lug-soled platforms, razor-toed poulaines, and revival bush boots.

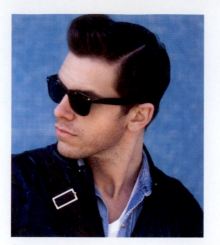

Glued pompadour, 2009.

Dreadlocks and circle beard, 2009.

Bed head hair glues, 2008.

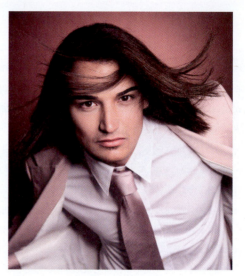

Long hair, 2010.

FIGURE 13.44. Hairstyles of millennial men remained broadly diverse with cuts ranging from buzz-cut short to waist-length long. Hundreds of haircare products for men such as fixative sprays, gels, and nonpermanent colors provided even more options for distinctive looks ranging from revivals of fifties-style pompadours to the studied casualness of the bed head.

As pant leg hems climbed to the ankles, socks became an important accessory. The prevailing sartorial guideline of the eighties and nineties had been to wear the color of socks that preserved the visual line of the trousers to the shoes, which usually meant mostly dark solid colors. Millennial men, though, opted for striking colors that popped against gray or navy worsted suit trousers or casual khakis and jeans: red, turquoise, yellow. In warm weather, many men bared ankles and went sockless, even with suits (a recommendation by premier men's suit maker Thom Browne). However, to avoid blisters and damp discomfort when trudging along hot city pavements in leather oxfords, and yet still flash the trendy bare skin at cropped hemlines, footie **loafer socks**, also called **no-show socks**, were a solution.

The principal head gear for men of all ages in the 2000s remained the baseball cap. Trucker hats, a variation of the visor-front baseball cap with a mesh back and industrial logo patch or screen print on the front, became a pop culture fad when Ashton Kutcher and other young celebrities donned them. At the end of the decade, trim fedoras and narrow brim trilbies were revived as part of the urban exec *Mad Men* influence. Justin Timberlake and Johnny Depp were often photographed in assorted trilbies and pinch-front fedoras, and similarly, in 2009, Matthew Bomer adopted a pared down fedora to complement his slim suits in the TV series *White Collar,* furthering the popularity of the urban look for many young men. Fashion editors revisited men's style archives to explain how fur felt hats were blocked and to clarify the distinctions between a fedora, trilby, porkpie, and derby.

Pocket squares were repeatedly emphasized in fashion editorials as a key accessory for self-expression, both in casual and business dress. Colorful print handkerchiefs added personality to a blazer with jeans. A sharp-edged, squared white pocket square reinforced the polished look of a well-tailored suit. A fresh idea was the **shibori**, or twisted textured pocket square made with manipulated fabrics that created a three-dimensional floral effect. Dimension was also added to cotton pocket squares with frayed edges, forming a delicate fringe.

Men's Grooming and Hairstyles 2000–Present

The vast variety of men's hairstyles in the new century reflected the pluralism of a globally connected society. The fifties style pompadours that had been revived at the end of the 1990s reached even greater heights with fresh interpretations in the '00s. (Figure 13.44.) As *GQ* noted of the new big hair looks, "If you've got great hair, flaunt it (while you still have it.)" A variation of big hair called a bed head was a mussed, spiky look that appeared as though the wearer had just rolled out of the sheets, when in fact men actually spent considerable time applying gels and "glues," to preserve the studied arrangement of locks. In 2007, L'Oréal introduced the StudioLine Weather or Not "extreme spiking glue" advertised as "rain proof, sweat proof, life proof." For added personality, some glues were tinted with bright colors and shimmering metallics. In the early 2010s, adolescent boys (and girls) adopted a fringy bowl cut with full bangs swept forward to the eyebrows popularized by the Canadian pop star Justin Bieber.

Facial hair also became a way for men to express their personalities and distinguish themselves from the herd. Favorite looks for young men included the **soul patch**, a tuft of beard just beneath the lower lip but not extending onto the chin; **chinstrap beards**, long sideburns that connected under the chin along the jawline; and **circle beards**, also called goatees, consisting of a mustache and narrow beard that encircled the mouth.

The hairless torso aesthetic that emerged in the late eighties persisted into the new century. In 2005, the movie *Forty-Year-Old Virgin* emphasized the extremes some men went to, such as the excruciating pain of hair removal by body waxing. "**Manscaping**" extended beyond simply shaving "sweater" torsos and waxing "bearskin" backs to include careful trimming of nose and ear hair, plucking eyebrows, and even shaping pubic hair. Makers of grooming products such as Gillette promoted the hairless, youthful look with online videos of shaving methods. The smooth, hairless torso is "something the ladies really appreciate," assured the narrator of one shaving video in 2010.

Besides manscaping, the most prevalent body enhancement of the new century for Gen Y men was tattoos. (Figure 13.45.) "Tats" were still somewhat regarded as a rebellious statement because of their permanence and their legacy with tough guy sailors, convicts, and inner city gang members. At the end of the decade, though, tattoos had become so common that one editor complained, "Want to rebel? Keep it all-natural."

FIGURE 13.45. Many millennial men found self-expression, personal identity, and social rebellion with tattoos.

FIGURE 13.46. Established designers capitalized on the indulgence of Gen X parents and affluent baby boomer grandparents by offering high style fashions for children from cradle through high school. Infant's playsuit by Stella McCartney for Baby Gap, 2011.

Children's Clothing 2000–Present

Probably more than in any previous era, children of the new century were keenly style and brand conscious. The Internet allowed computer savvy children and teens access to volumes of pop culture information, including real-time reports, videos, and photos of what their favorite TV, movie, and music idols were wearing. Through social networking sites, children exchanged ideas of fads and style trends with peers on a national and even global scale. The fashion industry reached out to this ever-expanding market with ads on teen-targeted sites. In 2003, *Teen Vogue* was launched, quickly followed by their Web site, which provided teen membership blogs and fashion giveaways. Designers offered children high style, logo branded fashions just like those favored by their older siblings and classmates. Gen X parents and baby boomer

FIGURE 13.47. Girls of the new millennium were more fashion savvy and style conscious than any generation before, due in part from Internet blogs, online retailers, and social networking Web sites. Designers catered to this expanding market with high style, diminutive adaptations of women's fashions. Left, girls' boho looks, 2009; right, jacket, jeans, and ruffled skirt from Pinko, 2011.

FIGURE 13.48. Comfortable, baggy hip-hop looks of oversized screenprinted T-shirts and jeans dominated boys' looks through most of the '00s. In the second half of the decade, teen boys adopted the styles of their favorite pop culture idols, including skinny jeans and military inspired shirts and jackets. Left, jeans and hoodie from Liv Jo Junior, 2008; right, boys' Calvin Klein logo sportswear, 2009.

grandparents were indulgent, spending billions of dollars online and at specialty stores like Gap Kids and Benetton or designer boutiques in upscale department stores. (Figure 13.46.)

For most girls, denim skirts, jumpers, and jeans remained the preferred wardrobe choices for school and play. But to emulate big sister, school girls also opted for miniskirts, swing tops over leggings, and layered looks that mixed vivid colors and textile patterns just like those worn by characters on TV series like the *Gilmore Girls* and *7th Heaven*. (Figure 13.47.) High school girls followed the style leads of young celebrities like Britney Spears and Miley Cyrus in experimenting with clothes that projected a nubile sensuality: painted-on-tight low rider jeans, sometimes worn with a thong panty that showed above the waistband; contouring shrunken sweaters; and cropped tops that exposed midriffs. As with collegiate young women, teen girls also donned assorted boyfriend styles, from rolled khakis and cardigans to military jackets and unconstructed blazers.

For many boys, the baggy, oversized hip-hop look persisted well into the new century. Boys' hoodies were screenprinted with tattoo graphics for teens and comic book supervillians and heroes or Harry Potter and *Avatar* creatures for schoolboys. Designers' logos were embroidered, appliquéd, and screenprinted on T-shirts, sweatshirts, sweaters, jackets, and jeans. (Figure 13.48.) Distressed jeans and cargo pants and shorts were topped by long, oversized T-shirts or untucked oxford button downs. By the beginning of the 2010s, many teen boys abandoned baggy looks for skinny jeans and shrunken military jackets.

Review

Fashion pluralism in the new millennium became much more youth-driven and global with the expanded growth of the Internet. Style blogs, e-tailers, and social networking Web sites provided instantaneous information on new trends and a constant flow of cross-cultural exchanges from around the world. An eco- and ethical-consciousness influenced designers and consumers alike. Clothing makers responded to the new global paradigm with a focus on niche marketing that targeted specific customers in the pluralistic consumer arena.

Women's fashions reflected the balkanized market with a continued interest in revivals from designers, now called "heritage" looks, particularly from the sixties and seventies. Boho (bohemian) and "tribal" looks represented a blending of retro hippie styles with global cross-cultural influences. New romantique styles, renamed "romance novel" looks, included a renewed popularity of the Empire waist, puff sleeves, and an abundance of lace, ruffles, bows, and rosettes. The youth oriented skinny look included skintight low rider jeans, shrunken cardigans and T-shirts, and little cropped tops. Boyfriend styles, called the "borrowed" look in editorials, ranged from plain front khakis, tennis sweaters, and blazers to men's style underwear and swim trunks. Even military styles permeated women's fashions.

Men's fashions of the twenty-first century were also guided by the Gen Y youth market, with an eye on retro Continental looks of the *Mad Men* sixties. Ultraslim suits with fitted silhouettes, natural shoulders, narrow sleeves, and even shortened jackets and ankle-high trouser cuffs were the prevailing trend. Although baggy hip-hop looks lingered for many men—oversized jeans, cargo pants, board shorts, and drooping T-shirts—by the second half of the decade, skinny jeans, unpleated khakis, tapered dress shirts, fitted sport coats, and shrunken T-shirts indicated a return of the sexualized male. Tailored shorts were shortened to mid thigh. Formfitting fashion underwear and briefer swimwear reflected the new masculinity.

review questions

1. How has the Internet furthered the pluralist balkanization of women's and men's fashions in the 2000s?

2. What were some of the key niche looks of women's fashions in the 2000s?

3. In the twenty-first century, what were some sources of fantasy that inspired experiment and innovation among designers? Identify three designers discussed in the chapter and how they expressed their runway inventiveness.

4. What is nanotechnology and how has it been applied to clothing production?

5. How did men's suit styles of the new millennium change from those of the 1990s? Which heritage era was a source of inspiration for twenty-first-century suit designers?

6. What global events of the 2000s inspired the military looks in menswear? What design elements characterized the military look?

7. What changes in men's fashions indicated a return to the sexualized peacock male?

research and portfolio projects

Research

1. Write a research paper on today's five top couture houses. Who are their chief designers and what is innovative about their collections? Which business practices, such as licensing, eco- or ethical manufacturing, or brand marketing, have added to the profitability of each?

Portfolio

1. Find ten women's revival styles, each of a different historical era, in current magazines. Mount enlarged photocopies or digital scans of each image on an 11×14 board. Beneath each image write a description of the revival and the original period inspiration for the look. Explain how the revival has been adapted to modern tastes. Include details about each designer or maker, fabrics, colors, and date.

dress terms

absurdists: a Parisian group of avant-garde fashion designers

admiral jacket: double-breasted sport coat with metal buttons and grosgrain trim

bed head: the arranged mussed hair look for both men and women achieved with fixative gels or glues

bit loafer: men's slip-on shoes named for the horse harness bit hardware attached to a strap or metal bar across the vamp

bling-bling: flashy jewelry, especially diamonds and an abundance of gold, or a showy style of dress

board shorts: men's long, baggy swim trunks modeled after the surfer jams of the eighties

boho (bohemian) style: a blending of retro hippie-gypsy looks with cross-cultural tribal influences

borrowed look: the adaptation of men's clothing styles to women's fashion; also called boyfriend styles

boyfriend style: menswear influences on women's ready-to-wear; also called the borrowed look in some fashion editorials

boyshorts: women's square-cut underwear modeled after men's boxerbriefs

chinstrap beard: long sideburns that connected under the chin along the jawline

circle beard (also called a goatee): a mustache and narrow beard that encircled the mouth to the chin

electronic clothes: garments constructed with electrically conductive textiles interwoven with microscopic wires used to enable electronic devices such as cell phones and GPS tracking

Fastskin: a branded synthetic fabric that simulated sharkskin applied to swimsuits

green fashions: clothing and accessories made of sustainable (organic, natural) fibers and materials

high twist wool: yarns made by tightly coiling two strands of the finest, softest wool fibers

hoodie: any variety of hooded shirt, fleece top, jacket, or vest

L.E.D.s: acronym for light-emitting diodes, an electronic semiconductor device that produces light from an electric current

loafer socks: a form of footie socks worn by both men and women; also called no-show socks

low riders: a new form of women's and men's hiphugger pants cut extremely shallow at the inseam

manga T-shirts: T-shirts screenprinted with the big-eyed Japanese cartoon characters of manga comics and anime films

manscaping: the process of trimming or removing body hair

metrosexual: a heterosexual male with high standards of style and taste, a quality usually attributed to gay men

nanotechnology: the science of reconfiguring the size and properties of molecules; see smart fabrics

no-show socks: see loafer socks

peep toes: new term for open-toed shoes

poulaines: shoes of the Middle Ages with long, pointed toes

Shelby knot: a tie knot wider than a four-in-hand but not as thick as a half-Windsor popularized by news anchorman Don Shelby

shibori: twisted textured fabric used in fashion and accessories such as men's pocket squares

shrug sweater: see shrunken cardigan

shrunken cardigan: women's tight-fitting cardigan with a high, cropped waistband and sometimes short or half sleeves

shrunken look: tops with cropped hems, shortened sleeves, and a tight fit that appeared to pull button closures and strain the fabric

skyscraper pump: women's platform shoes with spike heels at five inches or more

smart fabrics: textiles produced with nanotechnology finishes that can wick perspiration away from the body, repel insects, block the sun's UV rays, and resist stains

sorchetta: a double dimple necktie knot that originated in Italy

soul patch: a tuft of beard just beneath the lower lip but not extending onto the chin

sustainable fabrics: textiles made from organically grown natural fibers from plants and animals

tankini: women's swimsuit comprised of a tanktop and bikini bottom

tantoo: the silhouette of a shape or initial resulting from the application of an adhesive-backed decal to skin prior to sunbathing

tats: the abbreviated term for tattoos

trash fashion (also "trashion")**:** garments and accessories sewn, woven, or crocheted from recycled plastic bottles, food packaging, inner tubes, soda can pop top chainmail, and plastic grocery bags

tribal looks: fashions with a pre-industrial or cross-cultural aboriginal design, including historical and global national costume styles

trilby: a narrow brimmed fedora often accented with a leather band or buckle

trunks: men's square-cut underwear made with a lowered waistband modeled after sixties style swimwear

tubini: a two-piece swimsuit with a bandeau "tube" top, some of which extended to the hips in a short skirt; bottoms varied from bikini to square cuts

whalefin: the V-shaped back of a bikini thong

14 The Fashion Makers

The Preeminence of the Designer

Over the 30,000-year history of human dress, the significance of the individual designer as the acknowledged arbiter of style has been relevant only since the mid-nineteenth century. Numerous names of clothing and accessory designers, along with the evidence of their contributions to the history of fashion and style, populate the preceding pages of this survey. Some designers—and the looks they created—have come to be inextricably associated with a specific period, such as Christian Dior and the 1950s, while others, like Yves St. Laurent, have dominated several decades. Many other once prominent designers have been relegated to footnotes in specialized studies on fashion. Countless others have been lost, decade by decade, to anonymity in history. We get a glimpse of the magnitude of this loss in the 1928 study of the fashion industry by economist Paul Nystrom, who reported that there were 80,000 dressmaking shops in Paris alone, from which "not less than 25,000 . . . *new designs* in women's apparel" were created each year. And this is but a sliver of time and place in the global arena of fashion history.

It should be noted, too, that, although the words couturier and designer are often use interchangeably, there is a pronounced distinction. In the 1972 book, *Couture,* contributing writer and former Balmain Directrice Ginette Spanier emphasized the difference. A true couturier was a master of the craft of cut and fit who always strove for perfection. "I have seen the lining of a dress started over five times because the dart at the bust was not at the perfect angle even though the lining did not show through the dress," noted Spanier. "Of such stuff is the haute couture made."

On a less lofty pedestal were those designers who possessed a more fundamental working knowledge of their craft and primarily focused on style innovation and pioneering inventiveness. One is reminded of the simplicity of Mary Quant's designs or the nontraditional approaches of Paco Rabanne and Kansai Yamamoto. This is not to negate the significance or influence of these designers in the realm of fashion history, though.

Fashion show at the House of Dior, 1956.

The third tier in the rarified dominion of fashion design is that of the fashion product stylist. This sometimes pejorative label has been applied, for example, to commodity ready-to-wear makers whose efforts most often focused on choosing new colors or fabrics for standardized garments such as men's dress shirts, and basic clothing like polo shirts, sweatshirts, turtlenecks, T-tops, and the like. For a number of branded stylists, successful marketing and product merchandising rather than fashion innovation have provided them with the cachet of a designer. Ralph Lauren, who himself often denies the label of fashion designer, is one of the premier thematic stylists of today.

The importance of the designer from a historical perspective also may be determined by the era in which he or she worked. As fashion historian Linda Watson noted, in the century and a half since Worth became the first couturier, the designer "was considered a dictator, then a director, and a suggestor." Through the 1950s, the fashionistas, retail buyers, ready-to-wear manufacturers, and journalists eagerly awaited the semiannual shows in Paris to learn what the dictators of fashion had prescribed that the modern, stylish woman, man, and child *must* be wearing in the coming season. In the 1960s, though, when the youth cult of the era inspired individualism, the designer as director emerged. "Do your own thing" was a common phrase, to which designers responded with a broad spectrum of looks that blended space-age innovations with historic costume and street styles. This idea of the customer's quest for personal style continued to gain momentum through the seventies and eighties. Since the end of the 1980s, the designer has largely provided suggestions for a fragmented, niche market filled with consumers who choose and mix looks that define a style of their own.

Dressmakers and Artistes

As the end of the twentieth century drew to a close, the duality of fashion as an art form as well as an industry became more sharply evident than during any previous period. From the perspective of many in the world of fashion, particularly designers, the business half has become the dominant of the two. It is the financiers, corporate conglomerates, and marketers who have taken over, preferring, it seems, to work with dressmakers rather than artistes. In 1999, the fashion corporate raider, Bernard Arnault, who had acquired Dior, Givenchy, and Louis Vuitton, among others, succinctly stated, "The reason to be a designer is to sell. Fashion is not pure art. It is creativity with the goal of having as many customers as possible wearing the product." Those designers who understood this shift in the fashion paradigm continued to thrive, finding their niche and defining the parameters in which their creativity could be expressed.

Garment labels, 1937.

For those designers who were unable or unwilling to understand the nature of the beast in its fin de siècle form, few continued to succeed on their own terms. The consequences more often than not were dire. In recent memory is the example of Isaac Mizrahi, a case study which still echoes down New York's Seventh Avenue. Mizrahi was the most prolific American designer of the 1990s, offering one innovation after another under his own label and winning a number of "best designer" awards. Despite the adoration of the fashion press, though, sales were disappointing. "Look, it is all I can do to make fabulous clothes," the designer later explained; "I can't imagine how it will translate at retail." The reality of retail, though, eventually forced the closing of the House of Mizrahi in 1998. (He later learned retail fashion marketing during his five-year alliance with Target Stores and, in 2008, headed ready-to-wear label Liz Claiborne.) The era of the designer as dictator, or even as director, had passed.

Yet, the reality signs were clearly evident everywhere for the business-savvy designer to recognize (or at least for the silent business partner to read). In 1994, for instance, a Paris-based market research firm asked European women, "Who or what do you emulate when you try to be fashionable?" Seventy percent of the respondents answered, "No one; I just want to maximize me." Designers as the creative force of fashion had to adapt to this new global pluralism. No longer did the design talents, in league with the trend setters of high society and style journalists, determine what everyone would wear season after season. The successful designer of the twenty-first century is an amalgam of artiste, dressmaker, and retailer. The artiste provides glamour, fantasy, and innovation—fashion as drama and high art; the designer as dressmaker provides the market with fashion as real, wearable styles that allow each customer to "maximize me"; the designer as retailer understands commodity marketing, public relations, and the industry's business cycles.

In the following biographical index are 100 of the most famous and important names in fashion design of the past 150 years. The designers featured here have been selected by the author for their innovation in fashion design, for their imaginative leadership in the fashion industry, and especially for their enduring legacy in the realm of fashion history.

Adolfo

(b. 1933)

Born in Havana, Cuba, Adolfo Sardina came from an affluent family of lawyers. As a boy he visited Paris with his sophisticated aunt, who introduced him to couture fashion. He later became a milliner at the House of Balenciaga, where he learned the importance of cut, fit, and line. In 1948, he moved to New York to design hats for Bergdorf Goodman. During the 1950s, as chief designer for the millinery wholesaler, Emme, he established the distinct techniques of shaping hats by cut and stitching rather than wires and padding. In 1962, he began his own design firm, expanding into clothing as well as hats. Adolfo won the Coty Award twice for millinery (1955 and 1969). Throughout the sixties, he utilized theatrical design elements for styles such as a melton officer's greatcoat with epaulets and large brass buttons, Gibson Girl blouses, organdy jumpsuits, and patchwork evening skirts. During the 1970s and 1980s, his collections featured tailored designs with clean, straight lines. His fashions were a favorite of Washington, D.C., socialites, particularly Nancy Reagan. He retired in 1993.

Adri

(1934–2006)

Adri was the label name for the Missouri-born Adrienne Steckling. She studied at the Parson's School of Design where Claire McCardell lectured. In the fifties, Adrienne designed for the ready-to-wear maker B.H. Wragge, followed in the sixties by a design position with Anne Fogarty, Inc. In 1972, she established her own line of clothing with an emphasis on easy, comfortable separates. She won a Coty American Fashion Critics "Winnie" in 1982.

Adrian, Gilbert

(1903–1959)

Adrian was born into a fashion family; his parents owned a successful millinery shop in Connecticut. His first work as a designer was in the theatre, which led to a career as a studio costumer in Hollywood during the 1920s and 1930s. His slouch hat for Greta Garbo in *A Woman of Affairs* (1929) set a style trend for the next ten years. Similarly he popularized the snood during World War II, which he created for Heddy Lamarr in *I Take This Woman* (1939). His "Letty Lynton" dress with its wide shoulders and ruffled sleeves was designed for Joan Crawford in the movie of the same name (1932), and was widely copied by ready-to-wear makers who sold thousands of the style. Among his most famous Hollywood creations was the white satin gown cut on the bias to accentuate the voluptuous figure of Jean Harlow in *Dinner* at *Eight* (1933). Adrian left the studios in 1942 to open his own atelier in Beverly Hills. Although never taken seriously by the fashion press due to his theatre pedigree, he won a Coty American Fashion Critics "Winnie" in 1945. He became famous for exquisitely tailored suits designed with complex cuts and precision stitching.

Alaia, Azzedine

(b. 1940)

Tunisian art student Azzedine Alaia went to Paris in the late fifties where, over the next two decades, he worked in a succession of jobs in the fashion industry. By the 1970s, he had secured a following of clients, including Tina Turner and Paloma Picasso, who encouraged him to launch his own label. His first show was held in New York in 1982. The body-conscious designs of Alaia were perfect for the eighties: little black dresses and acetate knit halter gowns that accentuated the slender, curvaceous figure. In the 1990s, his use of hardware such as rivets and industrial zippers combined with formfitting technotextiles showed the influence of Mugler and Montana.

Albini, Walter

(1941–1983)

Originally a fashion illustrator in Paris, Walter Albini returned home to Italy in 1960 where he worked as a ready-to-wear designer for Krizia and Basile. In 1965, he opened his own salon, designing glamorous clothes inspired by the costumes featured in movies of the 1930s and 1940s, particularly the styles of Katherine Hepburn and Marlene Dietrich. Throughout the 1970s, Albini integrated elements of global ethnic costumes and hippie-styled layering of mixed looks into his sophisticated, cleverly cut sportswear creations.

Amies, Hardy

(1909–2003)

Hardy Amies was one of Britain's most prolific and famous fashion designers. In the 1930s, he trained at the couture house of Lachasse where he became managing director as well as chief designer. During World War II, Amies developed collections of beautifully tailored suits within the rationing restrictions of the government's Utility Scheme. In 1945, he opened his own couture salon, making dresses for most of London society, including Princess Elizabeth. He is best known for his superbly tailored tweed suits and sumptuous ball gowns. In 1955, he was awarded the royal warrant by the Queen. In 1961, he expanded his venture to include menswear.

Armani, Giorgio

(b. 1934)

The one word most frequently associated with Giorgio Armani is perfectionist; a secondary label is deconstructionist. Armani began his fashion career as a department store menswear buyer where he first developed a keen eye for garment cut and construction as well as an understanding of the fashion retail business. In the 1960s, he became a designer with suit manufacturer Nino Cerruti and later with Emanuel Ungaro. After Armani established his own firm in 1975, he began to deconstruct men's suits by rethinking the fit and removing the padding, interlining, and stiffness. He combined luxurious fluid fabrics with perfect cuts and superb tailoring to design a new form of men's suit. The result was an understated elegance, comfort, and a sensuous masculinity. In 1980, he was catapulted to international prominence when he designed the wardrobe for Richard Gere in

American Gigolo. Throughout the eighties, the Armani label was the quintessential symbol of the successful yuppie, male or female. Armani also applied his principles of cut, fit, and quality fabric to designing women's fashions—an unusual reverse transition in the industry. His designs are always well represented at highly publicized events such as the Oscars.

Ashley, Laura
(1925–1985)

The manufacturing empire of Laura Ashley, Ltd., began in 1953 as a cottage industry in rural England when she and her husband, Bernard, began hand-printing textiles for use in table linens and head scarves. In 1968, Ashley opened a shop selling cotton short-sleeve smock tops and voluminous dresses with capacious patch pockets. As the business grew during the 1970s, she created ankle-length dress styles based on Victorian and Edwardian models—a look sometimes called "milkmaidism." The high collars, billowing sleeves, and petit-print textiles recalled an era of innocence before the First World War. During the 1980s, her frilly blouses and floral print dresses were popular with women who preferred the Romantique look to that of the powersuit wardrobe. Since 1990, the company has expanded its lines to include more international styles made with blended fabrics and jersey knits. Her love of prints, patterns, and textiles were additionally applied to a coordinating total look approach to home furnishings including upholstery, wallpaper, paints, furniture, fixtures, china, and decorative accessories.

Balenciaga, Cristobal
(1895–1972)

When Balenciaga retired in 1968, many fashion aficionados declared that true haute couture had ended for all time. In more than fifty years, Balenciaga was the benchmark by which most other couturiers were measured. Each collection he designed made a clear, pertinent fashion statement that evolved logically from previous collections. Balenciaga began as a tailor in Spain and, in 1916, opened a dressmaking shop. He escaped Franco's repressive regime in 1937 and went to Paris to reopen his atelier. Unlike Worth, Poiret, and Dior, whose innovations altered the course of fashion, Balenciaga created styles of enduring perfection—the classicist's view of scale, proportion, and balance achieved by the perfect cut. His guiding principle of design was the elimination of detail. His colors were of Spain: brilliant reds and yellows, Mediterranean turquoises, and warm earthtones. In many instances, his designs were also ahead of their time. He forecasted the New Look in 1939 with designs featuring cinched waists and rounded shoulders and hips. In 1956, his loose chemise dress, called the sack, anticipated the fuller looks of the sixties. His name is still associated with a stand-away collar design and the use of oversized buttons.

Balmain, Pierre
(1914–1982)

Although the Balmain family owned a wholesale drapery business, young Pierre was initially interested in architecture, which he began studying in Paris. Instead of completing his studies, though, he became an illustrator for Robert Piquet in the early 1930s. He then spent five years with Edward Molyneux, after which he joined the house of Lucien Lelong. At Lelong, he collaborated with Dior and they considered opening an atelier together, but Balmain instead opened his own salon in 1945. From the start, his glamorous but nonfussy designs appealed to society's elite. He dressed royalty, statesmen's wives, and Hollywood stars. Among his famous clients were the Duchess of Windsor, the Queen of Siam, and Sophia Loren.

Giorgio Armani, 1992.

Balenciaga, 1927.

In the fifties, he popularized the sheath dress worn with loose, full jackets. He set trends with cossack capes and full coats with half belts. In 1951, he expanded into ready-to-wear with designs that successfully translated French fashion into clothing for the taller American woman.

Bates, John

(b. 1935)

Most famous for his 1960s costume designs for Diana Riggs in *The Avengers*, John Bates was one of the most innovative British designers of the Swinging London era. He trained at the Chelsea couture house of Herbert Sidon in the 1950s and became the chief designer of the ready-to-wear maker Jean Varon in the 1960s. He introduced tube dresses with matching tights in 1964 and popularized cutaway looks, including dresses with a bare midriff. In 1972, he launched his own label with superbly crafted maxi coats and sophisticated evening wear. After his business went bankrupt in 1980, he moved to Wales and continued designing for select clients.

Beene, Geoffrey

(1927–2004)

Throughout his life, Geoffrey Beene retained the soft Southern accent he acquired as a boy in his native Louisiana. He changed his plans to pursue a medical degree and, according to lore, became interested in fashion upon seeing Adrian's designs for Joan Crawford in *Humoresque* (1946). He studied in New York at the Traphagen School of Fashion Design followed by the Académie Julian and the Molyneux tailoring studio in Paris. During the fifties, Beene worked for a number of U.S. ready-to-wear makers, including Teal Traina. In 1963, he set up his own company. He was noted for his use of bold colors and for the unusual mixing of materials such as rhinestones and flannel or jersey and taffeta. Many of his designs presented unexpected touches of fantasy like football jersey evening gowns replete with player numbers on the back. He described his boutique line, named Beene Bag in 1971, as "romanticized sportswear." A feud with the trade paper *Women's Wear Daily* began in 1967 when he refused to provide advance details of the wedding dress he designed for President Johnson's daughter. Despite the clash with *WWD* that lasted for decades, Beene's firm thrived, and the designer won eight Coty awards.

Blass, Bill

(1922–2002)

Before the Second World War, Bill Blass worked as a fashion artist for ready-to-wear manufacturers. Following a stint in the military, he joined the Anna Miller company as a designer through the 1950s. When the firm merged with another ready-to-wear maker, Maurice Rentner, Blass became a vice president until he bought the company in 1967. Three years later he renamed the company Bill Blass. He is best known for his American luxury sportswear characterized by simple, soft lines and a fluid fit. This same simplicity of line was combined with sumptuous fabrics and rich details for elegant, urbane evening wear throughout the sixties and seventies. In the 1980s, he created cocktail dresses with exaggerated ruffles and opulent trimmings that well suited the exhibitionism of the nouveau riche of the era. His keen business acumen led to more than thirty licensing agreements, including accessories and bed linens. In addition, he launched a high-style, moderately priced sportswear line called Blassport in 1972. He won numerous fashion awards and held three honorary doctorates.

Bohan, Marc

(b. 1926)

As a boy, Marc Bohan had been encouraged to design clothing by his milliner mother. After receiving his diploma in art from the Lycée Lakanal in 1946, he spent the next ten years designing for three of the most prestigious houses in Paris: Piquet, Molyneux, and Patou. He joined the house of Dior in 1958 and was sent to London to design the ready-to-wear collections. When Yves St. Laurent left Dior in 1960, Bohan became creative director and returned to Paris. Over the following three decades, he produced traditionalist couture. His designs were understated and elegant. Among his most notable looks were the fur-trimmed collection of 1965 based on the costumes of the movie *Dr. Zhivago* (1965), and his evening gowns with large, bustle-like bows. In 1990, he returned to London to take over at Hartnell, where he ended his career when the financially ailing firm finally closed.

Capucci, Roberto

(b. 1929)

Trained at the Accademia delle Belle Arti in Rome, and apprenticed under Emilio Schumberth, the precocious Roberto Capucci opened his own salon at the age of twenty-one. A decade later he was persuaded to relocate to Paris, but returned to Rome after six years. Capucci was one of the first post–World War II Italian couturiers to enjoy international fame. His design style is often compared to that of Balenciaga—crisp, architectural, and meticulously cut and draped. His critics frequently accused him of viewing his fashion designs as more important than the wearer. He constantly experimented, extending the perimeters of design with daring new cuts and striking use of fabrics. His 1985 ball gowns of pleated rainbow taffeta appeared to be engineered as a series of gigantic shoulder-to-floor bows—an ideal look for the exhibitionism of the decade.

Cardin, Pierre

(b. 1922)

As a teenager during World War II, Pierre Cardin was apprenticed to a tailor in Vichy, making suits for women. After the war, he went to Paris and worked for Paquin and Schiaparelli. He joined Dior in 1947 just as the New Look was launched. Three years later, Cardin established his own firm. During his early career, he also designed costumes for theatre and movies, which had a significant impact on his fashion designs. In the fifties, Cardin's bubble skirts were the precursor of the 1980s pouf dresses, and his loose chemises were the prototype for the revivals of the 1990s. In the sixties, he applied similar design solutions to both genders, for which he is often credited with the creation of unisex fashions. He pushed the

Bill Blass, 1986.

Marc Bohan, 1965.

boundaries of cut and inventiveness, including knit tube dresses, tabard tops over bodystockings, and bias cut spiral dresses that featured Op Art cutouts and plastic geometric appliques. The Cardin name became known worldwide through his aggressive licensing program that appeared on products ranging from furniture and luggage to wigs and cookware.

Carnegie, Hattie

(1889–1956)

When Hattie Carnegie's family immigrated to the United States, they changed their Viennese name from Kanengeiser to that of the richest man in America—Carnegie. As a teenager, Carnegie worked in the millinery department of Macy's where she learned the basics of design and retail. In 1909, she opened a hat shop with a partner who made dresses. Although Carnegie could not sew or draw, she had a keen fashion eye and understood the stylistic needs of the American woman. She imported Paris couture and produced adaptations with an American feel under the label Hattie Carnegie Originals. She also employed some of America's leading designers, including Claire McCardell and Norman Norell. Carnegie expanded her business interests beyond retail to include her own ready-to-wear factories and distribution.

Cashin, Bonnie

(1915–2000)

Inspired to clothing design by her mother, who was a dressmaker, and by her study of art and dance, Bonnie Cashin became a costume designer for the theatre in the 1930s while still a teenager. She expanded her repertoire by also designing ready-to-wear sportswear in the thirties, but then went to Hollywood as a costume designer for 20th Century Fox in the 1940s. In 1949, she opened her own business in New York, where she created clean, uncomplicated designs despite the prevalence of the cinched and tight-fitting New Look. She was one of the first American designers to develop layered looks with easy, functional garments that could be added or discarded as the climate or weather demanded. She is most often associated with popularizing the poncho. Many of her sportswear designs, based on squares, rectangles, and triangles, have a timeless quality and are still relevant today.

Cassini, Oleg

(1913–2006)

As a boy, Oleg Cassini helped his mother run an exclusive dress shop in Florence. In the 1930s, he trained at Patou in Paris before going to New York, where he worked for various ready-to-wear makers. In 1940, Cassini went to Hollywood as a costumer for the movie industry, working for a while under Edith Head. He was engaged to Grace Kelly but eventually married Gene Tierney. He opened his couture salon in 1950 and was best known for glamorous sheath dresses and opulent evening wear. In 1961, he became the official designer for Jacqueline Kennedy. The Empire waist gowns and tailored suits he designed for the First Lady were widely copied around the world, as were his little pillbox hats.

Castelbajac, Jean-Charles de

(b. 1950)

At age eighteen, Castelbajac began designing clothing for his mother's ready-to-wear company in France. In 1975, he opened his own business. His modernist, high-tech designs revealed the influence of Pierre Cardin and Paco Rabanne. Though his clothing was a skillful mixture of fantasy and futurism, the attitude was most always functional and natural. In the 1980s, he became famous for "wearable art" featuring handpainted fabrics and revivals of Pop Art imagery. He also designed for the theatre, cinema, and concert arena, including costumes for the Rolling Stones and Talking Heads.

Cavanagh, John

(1914–2003)

In 1932, John Cavanagh became an assistant to Molyneux in Paris. After serving in the British army during World War II, he returned to Paris and worked for Pierre Balmain. In 1952, Cavanagh opened his own couture shop in London, designing elegant, understated styles with long, lean lines that appealed to English high society. Among his notable clients were Princess Alexandra, Princess Marina, and the Duchess of Kent. His salon closed in 1974.

Cerruti, Nino

(b. 1930)

At age twenty, Nino Cerruti became head of the Italian textile firm his family had established in 1881. In his early years, he produced avant-garde menswear with clean, superb tailoring—in particular his "Hitman" collection of 1957 and a knitwear line in 1963. Armani worked for him a number of years, learning the importance of the perfect cut and line. In 1967, Cerruti opened a boutique in Paris and launched his luxury ready-to-wear label. A women's line followed in 1977. He also designed costumes for over sixty movies, including eighties aspirational looks for *Wall Street* and *Baby Boom*. He retired in 2001.

Chanel, Gabrielle (Coco)

(1883–1971)

The details of Chanel's childhood and teenage years were purposely kept obscure by the designer throughout her lifetime. As a young woman, she was mistress to a number of wealthy and powerful men, one of whom backed her first shop in 1914. Over the next few years, Chanel introduced revolutionary designs that were based on her own preference for comfortable and practical clothes. She created simple chemise dresses to be worn without corsets, reducing the stiff linings for a lighter, less rigid fit. Her early suits were made of jersey, a fabric typically used for casual tops and underwear. Chanel particularly liked to adapt menswear to women's fashions, including the pea jacket and oversized cardigans. In the 1920s,

Oleg Cassini, 1961.

John Cavanagh, 1950.

Coco Chanel, 1960.

she expanded on the practical trouser styles first worn by working women during World War I and designed bell-bottom "yachting pants" and wide-legged day pajamas. By the 1930s, the Chanel look was already classic—the little black dress, the collarless suit jacket and slim skirt, and an abundance of colorful costume jewelry. She closed her salon at the start of World War II in 1939, but remained in Paris where she became the mistress of a German officer. After the war, she barely escaped having her head shaved as a collaborator, and fled to Switzerland. In 1954, she was persuaded to return to Paris and reopen her salon, in part to boost sales of her fragrances. She resumed producing the classic Chanel suit in soft tweeds or jersey—a timeless style that changed little, even a decade after her death. The house of Chanel was revitalized when Karl Lagerfeld became designer for the firm in 1983.

Claiborne, Liz

(1929–2007)

A Belgian by birth, Liz Claiborne studied fine arts before winning a *Harper's Bazaar* fashion design contest in 1949. She worked for various New York ready-to-wear makers, including Tina Leser and Omar Kiam. During the sixties she was instrumental in designing collections of mix-and-match separates that crossed the typical categories of special occasion clothing. In 1976, she formed her own company based on divisions that produced primarily youthful, well-made sportswear particularly suited to the American market. She retired in 1989.

Clarke, Ossie

(1942–1996)

While still an art student at the London Royal College of Art, Ossie Clarke began designing clothing for the boutique Quorum in the early sixties. He had an instinctive feel for the female anatomy, producing body-conscious dresses with plunging necklines, open backs, and ethereal wrap-around silhouettes. He married textile designer Celia Birtwell and used many of her fabrics in his collections.

Courréges, Andre

(1923–2012)

Although trained to be a civil engineer, Courréges changed careers and returned to school to study textiles and fashion design. In 1949, he joined Balenciaga and, over the next decade, learned from the Spanish master to be a serious perfectionist in cut and design. In 1961, he opened his own atelier. Along with Pierre Cardin and Paco Rabanne, Courréges led the visionary thrust of minimalist fashion design in the sixties. Because his styles were geometric, sharp-edged, and uncluttered, with a disciplined reduction of excess material and superfluous decoration, he came to be known as the "space age" designer. His futuristic collections featured stark, trapeze-style dresses and coats and tube-shaped pants cut on the bias. His stiff, square miniskirts were declared by *Vogue* in 1965 to be the shortest. He also popularized calf-high white go-go boots. In the seventies, his designs lost the edginess of his earlier work, but retained the well-tailored, delineated line of the master couturier.

Crahay, Jules Francois

(1917–1988)

During his teenage years, Crahay worked in his mother's dressmaking shop in Liège, and later for the house of Jane Regny in Paris. In 1952, he became the chief designer for Nina Ricci, creating superbly tailored suits and sumptuous evening wear. In 1963, he moved to Lanvin where he directed the collections for twenty years. He is best known for his trendy peasant and gypsy styles of the late sixties.

De La Renta, Oscar

(b. 1932)

While studying fine art in Madrid, some of Oscar De La Renta's fashion sketches were shown to the wife of the U.S. Ambassador who subsequently commissioned him to design her daughter's debut gown. The dress was featured on the cover of *Life* magazine and De La Renta's career in fashion was set. He worked at the Madrid couture house of Balenciaga until 1961 when he went to Paris as an assistant to Antonio del Castillo at Lanvin. In 1963, he joined Castillo at Elizabeth Arden in New York, and in 1965, established his own firm. De La Renta is best known for sophisticated suits and especially opulent evening wear, often elaborately trimmed with embroidery, ruffles, and other lavish ornamentation. Among his clients were Jackie (Kennedy) Onassis, Liza Minelli, Nancy Reagan, Faye Dunaway, and Joan Collins.

Demeulemeester, Ann

(b. 1954)

Experimental and deconstructive, Ann Demeulemeester is one of today's most imaginative fashion designers. Trained at the Royal Academy of Fine Arts in Antwerp, she freelanced until launching her own line in 1985. In 1992, she opened her showroom in Paris, and four years later, presented her first menswear collection. Her style is a blending of punk and gothic with a decided influence from the Japanese Big Look of the 1980s. Madonna and Courtney Love have donned designs by Demeulemeester.

Andre Courrèges, 1970.

Oscar de la Renta, 1990.

Christian Dior, 1956.

Dior, Christian

(1905–1957)

The pivotal point in twentieth-century fashion was created by a shy, middle-aged Frenchman whose 1947 New Look shook the world of style. As a teenager, parental pressure had forced Dior to study political science in preparation for a diplomatic career. He instead wanted to be an architect, but ended up managing an art gallery. When the Great Depression interrupted that venture he occasionally found work as a freelance fashion illustrator for magazines and couture houses. In 1938, his impoverished years as a gypsy ended when he became a design assistant to Robert Piquet. During World War II, he worked for Lucien Lelong in Paris, where he met the millionaire fabric manufacturer, Marcel Boussac. In 1946, Boussac offered to finance Dior as an independent couturier, and the forty-one-year-old designer opened his own atelier. The following February, he presented his first collection, which he named the Corolle line. The New Look, as it was dubbed by *Harper's Bazaar,* was an instant sensation and spectacularly successful. Dior had launched a counterrevolution that was actually more anachronistic than new: cinched waists, padded hips, tight bodices, and huge skirts that harkened back to the Edwardian era. But his timing was impeccable. After years of austerity and privations during the Depression and Second World War, women enthusiastically bought the New Look. Dior's colleagues likewise responded to this reassuring fashion statement with design adaptations of their own. Not only did Paris couture flourish again, but Dior led its evolution from the more sedate, formal process of prewar years to the choreographed drama and theatre it is today. His fashion shows were spectacle and high art with their ballets of models swirling full skirts and yards of fabric provocatively past the audience as the name of each style was announced. Dior was also a consummate marketer, keeping demand high for his creations with new collections every six months that built on the previous looks but offered something fresh and significant. In the tradition of Balenciaga, the cut and the line were all important to Dior—color was almost incidental. In addition, lucrative licenses for jewelry, scarves, hosiery, furs, perfume, gloves, and even men's ties helped to expand the House of Dior into a multimillion dollar empire. When Dior died suddenly of a heart attack in 1957, he was succeeded briefly by his assistant, Yves St. Laurent. In 1960, Marc Bohan assumed leadership of the house until 1989, when Gianfranco Ferré replaced him. The baton then passed to the brilliant maverick, John Galliano, in 1996, followed by Raf Simons in 2012.

Dolce & Gabbana

Domenico Dolce (b. 1958) and **Stefano Gabbana** (b. 1962)

The widely publicized fantasy designs of Dolce & Gabbana are scintillating visions of mixed metaphors and Italian stereotypes. Sexy corsets and cleavage are accessorized with rosary beads and sequined icons; bold Mafioso pinstripe suits are offset by the simplicity of little black dresses and headscarves of Sicilian widows. Dolce & Gabbana achieved worldwide fame when they created the costumes for Madonna's *Girlie Show* tour in 1993. Though they have been noted for the sensuality and glamour of vintage Hollywood since they launched their label in 1985, Stefano insists the duo principally designs "clothes women can wear to work." The D&G logo is also licensed for a variety of accessories, as well as $30–$600 signature jeans.

Ellis, Perry

(1940–1986)

With a master's degree in fashion merchandising, Perry Ellis began his career as a sportswear buyer for a department store in the 1960s. He went to John Meyer as design director in 1968, and six years later to the Vera Company. The success of his Portfolio sportswear collections earned him his own label in 1978, and a Coty the following year. The clean lines and natural, textured fabrics of his clothes are in the Anne Klein tradition. Although he experimented with exaggeration—particularly unusual proportions—his designs never slipped into fantasy. His menswear looks were ideal for the career woman of the 1980s.

Fath, Jacques

(1912–1954)

Fath tentatively emerged on the Paris fashion scene in 1937 with a small collection of twenty designs. He had an innate understanding of the movement and sensuality of feminine form and a forward-looking genius that even anticipated the fitted New Look styles of a decade later. He often draped fabric directly onto a live model rather than working from sketches. His clothes were sexy and young without being vulgar. In 1948, he was invited by the U.S. ready-to-wear maker, Joseph Halpert, to translate that European feel into designs for the American market. Nearly half the revenue of the Fath firm came from boutique sales. He died of leukemia at age forty-two in 1954.

Fendi, Adele Casagrande

(1897–1978)

The Italian leather and fur design house founded by Adele Casagrande Fendi in 1918 is today one of the world's most important fashion empires. Her five daughters gradually assumed leadership of the firm beginning in 1954, and the third generation has already been elected to the board of directors. In 1962, the company engaged Karl Lagerfeld to add his high fashion aesthetic to Fendi's fur collections. Since then, Lagerfeld has helped redirect the Fendi label from anonymity to a high-profile brand. The Fendi logo with its tete-beche F's is famous globally and has become an aspirational symbol for the fashion conscious. The firm's chic accessories have sold extremely well and continue to be in demand around the world.

Jacques Fath, 1950.

Gianfranco Ferre, 1990.

Ferré, Gianfranco

(1945–2007)

In the late sixties, Ferré studied to be an architect and initially worked in the design studio of a Milan furniture company. By the early 1970s, he had applied his architect's sense of form, outline, and study of detail to designing fashion accessories and jewelry. In 1972, he began designing ready-to-wear freelance, and established his own house in 1978. His intellectual approach to fashion design produced clothing with all the power and beauty of modern sculpture. He was artistic director for Dior from 1989 to 1996, and afterward continued his own label collections, including Ferre Sport and Ferre Studio.

Fogarty, Anne

(1918–1981)

While studying drama and working as a fashion model, Anne Fogarty began designing freelance for various New York ready-to-wear makers. In 1948, she joined the Youth Guild and won a Coty for her 1951 "Paper Doll" dresses. She then spent five years designing for Saks Fifth Avenue before establishing her own company in 1962. Her clothes were soft and feminine in subtle color palettes.

Fortuny, Mariano

(1871–1949)

As a young man, Fortuny was a painter and an inventor. He designed set decorations for the theatre and became fascinated with the effects of light. In the 1890s, he began to experiment with textiles and dyes, developing new methods of printing and stencilling silk, cotton, and particularly rich, lustrous velvets. He registered a pleating process of running horizontal folds of fabric between copper plates and ceramic tubes to create permanent irregular accordion pleats resembling those of ancient Greek textiles. He viewed his clothing concepts more as inventions than fashion. His dress designs were far removed from the precision cutting and corseted fit of haute couture. His famous Delphos gown was a loose-fitting, cylindrically shaped garment made of pleated silk that fluidly draped over the body and tied into place with cords like the ancient Ionic chiton. It was often worn with a pleated overblouse or kimono style jacket. The timeless simplicity of Fortuny's clothing designs and the superlative hand-made textiles used to construct them are as stunning and captivating today as when first created. Museums and collectors still vie to acquire them whenever possible.

Galanos, James

(b. 1924)

After completing his studies at the New York Traphagen School, James Galanos succeeded in selling design sketches to several ready-to-wear makers, including Hattie Carnegie. He briefly worked with Robert Piquet in Paris and at Columbia Pictures in Hollywood. In 1951, he opened his own design firm in California. His luxurious ready-to-wear clothes were expensive because he used the finest materials combined with the flawless cutting of the couturier. His evening wear designs were a favorite at the White House court of the Reagans. Galanos was elected to the Coty Hall of Fame in 1959. He retired in 1998.

Galliano, John

(b. 1960)

Often described as incurably romantic, John Galliano is one of the most talented and inventive designers of the twenty-first century. His rise to preeminence was slow and difficult despite *Vogue's* acclaim of his college graduate collection in 1984. He was twice named British Designer of the Year. In 1994, he moved to Paris, and two years later was appointed design director at Dior. A couturier at heart in the tradition of Balenciaga and Vionnet, Galliano has become the unequalled modern master of the bias cut. He has resurrected many of the special cut and construction techniques of the great couturiers to create fashions that are a remarkable blend of innovation, history, and superb craftsmanship. In 2011, he was fired from Dior, following a scandal where he made antisemitic remarks in public, for which he was found guilty in court.

Gaultier, Jean Paul

(b. 1952)

From the beginning of his career, Gaultier's witty and eclectic style has challenged the French fashion establishment. His first job was with Cardin in 1970, followed by a series of ready-to-wear makers before launching his own label in 1978. Since then, he has successfully produced both couture and ready-to-wear that have run the gamut in menswear from tailored suits to kilts and in womenswear from corset dresses to luxurious evening gowns. His inspiration is often from the London street scene, especially punk looks, as well as global ethnic costume. Gaultier's more unorthodox designs are for the very young and self-assured, such as Madonna, who wore his mix of satin corsetry and black bondage costumes during her 1990 *Blonde Ambition* tour.

Gernreich, Rudi

(1922–1985)

Born in Austria, Gernreich's family fled their Nazi occupied homeland and moved to California in 1938. Through much of the forties, he was a dancer and costume designer for his troupe, during which he developed a fascination with fabrics and body-based clothing. In the 1950s, he freelanced, designing youthful sportswear for boutiques such as Jax in Los Angeles. In 1964, he established his own firm. Gernreich is often considered

John Galliano, 2006.

Hubert de Givenchy, 1985.

America's answer to Courrèges, Quant, and Cardin. His fashion ideas were revolutionary. During the youthquake of the sixties, his futuristic designs included dresses with plastic inserts, transparent blouses, bodystockings, and the nylon "No-Bra" bra. He is best remembered for his designs of swimwear in the mid-1960s that scandalized the fashion world, such as the topless monokini and the first unisex thong.

Givenchy, Hubert de

(b. 1927)

Trained at Fath, Piquet, Lelong, and Schiaparelli in the 1940s, Givenchy opened his own atelier in Paris at age twenty-five. Inspired by his mentor, Balenciaga, Givenchy strove for perfection of cut and line in his haute couture designs rather than avant-garde innovation. His luxurious, high style evening dresses were a favorite look for many of the world's most elegant women, including Jacqueline Kennedy, the Duchess of Windsor, and especially Audrey Hepburn, for whom he designed costumes for *Funny Face* (1957) and *Breakfast* at *Tiffany's* (1961). In 1988, Givenchy sold his label to LVMH, retiring in 1995.

Grès, Alix

(1903–1993)

As a young woman, Alix Grès studied to become a sculptor. During those early years, she earned money by selling toiles of her clothing designs to various Paris fashion houses. In 1934, she opened her own salon as Alix, but changed the label brand to her husband's name, Grès, following World War II. She preferred to work in silk and wool jersey, which she fluidly draped and molded to the feminine form with deceptively precise construction. Decade after decade, her classically simple dress designs transformed women into elegant, living statues.

Gucci, Guccio

(1881–1953)

Rather than work in his family's failing straw hat factory, Gucci ran away to London, where he got a job as a maitre d' at the Savoy. When he returned home to Florence in 1922, he opened a saddlery and leather shop producing small accessories with equestrian motifs and harness or stirrup hardware. In the 1930s, he designed the logo of the interlocking G's for his alliterative name (although some sources credit his son Aldo with that icon). The Gucci style and superior product quality sustained the business over the decades. During the aspirational 1980s, the Gucci brand enjoyed a surge in popularity among status-conscious yuppies. In 1989, Dawn Mello, the former president of Bergdorf Goodman, became creative director for the firm and revitalized the label with new best-selling reinterpretations of Gucci classics, including the bamboo bag and small leathers with the hand-shaped clasp. From 1994 till 2004, Tom Ford's fashion designs for the Gucci label were a must-have for trend setting celebrities and fashionistas worldwide.

Halston

(1932–1990)

A true son of the American Midwest. Roy Halston Frowick was born in Iowa and attended school in Indiana and Illinois. During the 1950s, he operated his own millinery salon in Chicago designing for celebrities such as Deborah Kerr and Gloria Swanson. In 1957, he moved to New York to work for Lilly Dache, and the following year joined Bergdorf Goodman as milliner. In 1966, he began designing ready-to-wear for the store with great success. Two years later, he opened his own salon. Halston recognized in the late sixties that women were beginning to tire of the gypsy and European fancy-dress styles of the era. Instead, he offered clean-line, classic designs based on minimalist art: jersey halter dresses, ultrasuede shirtwaists, boxy jackets, day-into-night cashmere chemises, and denim pantsuits. Among his jet-set clients were Liza Minelli, Ali McGraw, Bianca Jagger, and Diana Vreeland. In 1974, he was elected to the Coty Hall of Fame.

Jacobs, Marc

(b. 1964)

Following his graduation from Parson's School of Design in 1984, Marc Jacobs designed on his own for two years before going to Perry Ellis as a sportswear designer. He has repeatedly received rave reviews for his collections of simple, American-style clothes, frequently made of luxurious materials. In 1997, Jacobs took the post of creative director at Louis Vuitton, where he has designed fashions that, in his words, are "deluxe but that you can throw in a bag and escape town with."

James, Charles

(1906–1978)

By many accounts, Charles James was the greatest couturier of the twentieth century. Balenciaga, Dior, and Mainbocher were among the preeminent masters who have paid homage to him, and in later years, Halston sought him out to design for his salon. At age nineteen, James began his career as a milliner in Chicago. Between 1928 and 1947, he ranged between the United States and Europe, designing for private clients, department stores, and the salons of Hardie Amies and Elizabeth Arden. He was a genius and knew it. His contrary, eccentric personality usually led to disastrous business and personal relationships. Bankruptcy and litigation followed him wherever he settled. For him, nothing superseded his design work. His approach to fashion design was a rare blend of intellect and artistry. Over the years, he developed about 200 design modules engineered

Halston, 1968.

Donna Karan, 2004.

with interchangeable parts from which he could create thousands of variations. His sumptuous ball gowns were masterpieces of mathematical precision and sculpted elegance. His petal gowns of the early 1950s are the quintessential James design with their foliate bodices and flowing, monumental skirts. Although he retired in 1958, he continued to teach at the Pratt Institute and the Rhode Island School of Design. The last years of his life were spent meticulously documenting his work.

Johnson, Betsey

(b. 1942)

During her studies at Syracuse University, Betsey Johnson designed sweaters and knitwear for herself and friends. Upon graduation in 1964, she began her career as a journalist with *Mademoiselle,* but continued to design clothes freelance. In 1969, she began her own boutique, "Betsey, Bunk and Nini" and, in 1978, established her sportswear label, Betsey Johnson. Among her quirky, clever, and fun creations were cowhide wrap miniskirts, a clear vinyl dress kit that came with paste-on stars, silver motorcycle suits, and jersey "noise" dresses trimmed with jangling grommets or shower curtain rings.

Kamali, Norma

(b. 1945)

After graduation from New York's Fashion Institute of Technology in 1964, Norma Kamali worked as an airline stewardess for a few years. Her trips to Europe inspired her to open a boutique with her husband in 1968. After her divorce a decade later, she established her label OMO (On My Own). Her inventive designs in utilitarian materials such as fleeced cotton ran counter to the structured, formal styles of the 1980s, and presaged the chic comfort looks of the nineties. Among her most influential styles were sleeping bag coats padded with eiderdown, short rah-rah skirts, parachute fabric pantsuits, and disposable all-white holiday ensembles made of nylon paper.

Karan, Donna

(b. 1948)

While attending classes at Parson's School of Design in New York, Donna Karan went to work as a sketcher for Anne Klein, which eventually led to a permanent design position there. She left briefly to work for the ready-to-wear maker, Addenda, returning to Anne Klein in 1968. Following Klein's death in 1974, Karan co-designed with Louis Dell' Olio until 1984, when she set out on her own. Her collections of practical, wearable clothes were designed with the young urban career woman in mind. Her sportier range of styles bear the label DKNY.

Kawakubo, Rei

(b. 1942)

In 1966, Rei Kawakubo left her job in advertising to pursue freelance fashion design. Three years later, she founded Tokyo's Comme des Garçons but did not open her first shop until 1974. When she first showed in Paris in 1981, her iconoclastic approach to design shocked the French fashion establishment. For Kawakubo, fashion was a fine art expressed with a new conceptual aesthetic. Although her work is founded in Japanese rather than European clothing traditions, her designs do not exhibit the restrained formality of the tea ritual and Noh theatre, but rather evoke the violent drama of the samurai warrior and the Kabuki performance. Her slashed, crumpled, and knotted designs with random ruching, irregular seams, and unfinished edges look accidental but are actually precisely planned and cut. Kawakubo has consistently strived to unravel preconceived ideas of fashion, fit, and gender. Her collection of 1996 included removable padded humps—dubbed the Quasimodo look by the press—that recontoured the natural body into a fresh perspective of physical beauty.

Kenzo

(b. 1939)

Kenzo Tadaka studied at the Bunka College of Fashion in Tokyo before going to Paris in 1965 to design freelance. In 1970, he opened a boutique, which he named Jungle Jap because it was decorated with jungle prints. Young trendsetters were immediately drawn to Kenzo's wearable smocks, tunics, wide-legged pants, and similar clothing based on traditional Japanese styles. His most significant impact was made with his vibrant, contemporary knitwear, especially vividly colored sweaters. Unlike his fellow Japanese designers, Kenzo avoids conceptual fashion design with its deconstructionist cuts and radical silhouettes, and instead focuses on easy-to-wear clothing for both men and women.

Khanh, Emmanuelle

(b. 1937)

During the late 1950s, Emmanuelle Khanh began her fashion career as a model for Balenciaga and Givenchy. She started to design clothes in 1959, working for Dorothee Sis and Cacharel through the 1960s. In 1970, she established her own label. Khahn rejected the structured stiffness of haute couture in favor of interpretations of the soft, fluid looks of the 1930s. Her "Droop" collections featured slim, clinging dresses and long, gentle jackets. She is often credited with introducing the sixties' youthquake to France through her sexy, body-conscious clothes.

Christian Lacroix, 1985.

Karl Lagerfeld, 1990.

Klein, Anne

(1923–1974)

From age fifteen into her mid-twenties, Anne Klein worked for various ready-to-wear makers on New York's Seventh Avenue. In 1948, she and her husband, Ben Klein, founded Junior Sophisticates. Twenty years later she launched Anne Klein & Co. Klein's clothing epitomized the ease and comfort of American sportswear. She championed soft, comfortable materials—even jersey for evening wear—and clean, simple lines in her designs. Her mix-and-match separates were sensible wardrobe solutions for the modern American woman, a concept that her successor, Donna Karan, continues to build upon.

Klein, Calvin

(b. 1942)

A graduate of New York's Fashion Institute of Technology in 1962, Calvin Klein worked as a coat designer until he started his own firm six years later. Key to Klein's success was his keen understanding of the times in which he designed: the disco era of the seventies, the status-conscious eighties, and the simplified nineties. His classic sportswear collections in natural fabrics have had a timeless appeal to both women and men; his color sense introduced an international flavor to American clothing. In 1993, his versatile talents were acknowledged by the fashion world when he was voted both Womenswear and Menswear Designer of the Year. Klein's marketing acumen is unsurpassed, and his sexually charged advertising campaigns have made his label a world-famous brand. In addition to his ready-to-wear, the Klein signature is affixed to shoes, handbags, furs, fragrances, and bed linens.

Lacroix, Christian

(b. 1951)

In college, Christian Lacroix studied art history to become a curator, and fell in love with the fancifulness, splendor, and opulence of the Rococo era. His wife, Françoise, encouraged him to direct his interests and talents toward fashion rather than museum work. He got a job as a sketcher at Hermès and later became a design assistant to Guy Paulin. In 1981, Lacroix joined Patou as chief designer, where, with wit and daring, he created fashions that blended modern street influences with the sumptuousness and grandeur of the eighteenth century. Although highly skilled in couture cut and construction, Lacroix was less concerned with wearability than fun and theatricality. His pouf dresses, usually in alarming color combinations, were ideal for the exhibitionism of the 1980s. In 1987, he established his own salon in Paris with the backing of LVMH. His love of color and decoration was applied with enthusiasm to his ready-to-wear collections launched in 1988 and to his sportswear line begun in 1994.

Lagerfeld, Karl

(b. 1938)

At age seventeen, Karl Lagerfeld won a fashion design competition, which landed him a job working for Balmain. Three years later, he went to Patou, and then freelanced for various ready-to-wear makers, including Krizia. In 1963, he started working for Chloé, where he remained for twenty years. He also continued to freelance throughout the 1960s and 1970s, including designing furs for Fendi, shoes for Valentino, and menswear for Club Roman. In 1983, he went to Chanel as design director, revitalizing the label with endless variations of the little Chanel suit. Young American women especially responded to the fresh ideas Lagerfeld created for the House of Chanel as well as the deluxe ready-to-wear for his own KL label. Decidedly confident and astonishingly prolific, Lagerfeld is one of the most influential designers of today.

Lanvin, Jeanne

(1867–1946)

As a young girl of thirteen, Jeanne Lanvin was apprenticed to a dressmaker. In 1890, she opened a millinery shop in Paris. When her customers took notice of the dresses she designed for her younger sister and her daughter, Lanvin produced copies to sell in the store. She introduced a line of matching mother-daughter dresses and, in 1926, menswear. The House of Lanvin was the only couture salon that dressed all ages of the family. Her "robes de style" collections of the 1910s were based on eighteenth-century looks, and remained popular into the 1920s. Although Lanvin favored designing picturesque frocks and romantic clothing based on the full-skirted styles of earlier eras, she also produced lavishly embroidered deco opera capes, sleek dinner pajamas, and exotic evening wear with Asian influences.

Laroche, Guy

(1923–1989)

While still in his mid-teens, Guy Laroche went to Paris to apprentice with a milliner. After World War II, he designed hats in New York, but returned to France in 1949 to design ready-to-wear for Jean Desses. By the time Laroche opened his own house in 1957, he had mastered an architectural style of couture cutting and precision tailoring that was often compared to that of Balenciaga. In 1960, he added a line of ready-to-wear, and over the next two decades created lively collections that particularly appealed to young women—delicate Empire dresses in the sixties and superbly tailored pantsuits in the seventies. The Laroche empire of couture, women's ready-to-wear, and licensed products expanded in 1966 when he began designing menswear.

Lauren, Ralph

(b. 1939)

Born Ralph Lipschitz in the Bronx, New York, Lauren began his fashion career in retail. He had no design training and often negates the label of designer. "I never learned fashion; I was never a fashion person," Lauren told *Vogue* in 1992. Yet he is a skilled fashion product designer and a superb marketer who went from selling men's neckwear to head of a multimillion dollar fashion empire. In 1967, he established the "Polo by Ralph

Jeanne Lanvin, 1936.

Ralph Lauren, 1987.

Lucien Lelong, 1938.

Lauren" label for men's ties, which he expanded to include men's ready-to-wear the following year. In 1971, he launched his women's sportswear line. Rather than cut and silhouette, Lauren focuses on themes and narratives with his fashion product styling, especially the looks of the American West and of the gentrified Ivy League East. His sophisticated advertising campaigns, featuring tableaus of waspish beautiful people in old-money settings particularly appealed to the nouveaux riches of the aspirational eighties. He, as the ultimate customer of the Lauren label, often appears in his own ads.

Lelong, Lucien

(1889–1958)

Lucien Lelong went to work as a designer in his family's textile and dressmaking business in 1907. Following his release from military duty after World War I, he opened his own house. During the hard times of the Great Depression, Lelong developed a line of ready-to-wear, one of the earliest Paris designers to do so. While serving as President of the Chambre Syndicale de la Couture during the Second World War, he courageously persuaded the occupying Germans not to relocate the Paris couture industry to Berlin. As a designer, Lelong was better known for his superior workmanship of luxurious fabrics rather than for innovative styles. Dior, Balmain, and Givenchy were among the fashion luminaries who trained at the House of Lelong.

Mainbocher

(1890–1976)

Main Rousseau Bocher studied art and music in Chicago, New York, and Europe. After serving with an American hospital unit during the First World War, he went to Paris to pursue a singing career. In 1922, he abandoned his musical ambitions and became an illustrator for *Harper's Bazaar*. A year later, he went to French *Vogue* as a fashion editor. Abruptly in 1929, he decided to open a couture atelier, holing up in his studio for months practicing cutting and draping techniques. As the only American to open a couture salon up to that time, he merged his first and last names into one for a more French sound. His connections through fashion journalism ensured success when he opened in 1930; his collections of elegant and refined designs sustained that success. He achieved worldwide notoriety in 1937 when he designed the wedding dress and trousseau for Wallis

Simpson, the Duchess of Windsor. He closed his Paris salon in 1940 just ahead of the German occupation and reopened it in New York where he remained until his retirement in 1971. The designs of Mainbocher were elegantly simple with crisp, clean lines, often cut on the bias in the tradition of Vionnet. His sumptuous evening suits were usually made with a long, dark skirt and a contrasting jacket, often luxuriously trimmed with fur.

McCardell, Claire

(1905–1958)

Purposeful is the one word that best seems to describe Claire McCardell's clothing. Her approach to design was to allow the body to determine what a garment should look like with none of the artificial pretensions of shoulder pads, boned linings, or superficial decoration. She studied at Parson's School of Design, and began her career in 1929 as a sketcher for a ready-to-wear maker. During the 1930s, she evolved as a designer of simple clothing in basic fabrics that included her popular "monastic"—a bias-cut tent dress that could be worn loose or belted. In 1940, she began designing under her own label, creating what is often referred to as the foundation of the American look in clothing—sporty styles that were relaxed, comfortable, and most especially, practical.

McFadden, Mary

(b. 1938)

Having studied fashion at the Traphagen School of Design and sociology at Columbia, Mary McFadden began her career with Dior as public relations director in 1962. In 1970, she became a special projects editor for *Vogue.* Three years later she created a collection of tunics from rare African and Chinese silks that were featured in the magazine. She continued to design and founded her own business in 1976. Her classic silhouettes were austerely cut but enlivened with exotic, cross-cultural prints and kinetic pleating. Her trademark looks are slim dresses and quilted jackets, often of sumptuous hand-printed textiles.

McQueen, Alexander

(1969–2010)

Self-styled as a "fashion schizophrenic," Alexander McQueen produced both exhibitionistic styles—such as the bloody, tattered lace dresses for his 1996 "Highland Rape" collection—as well as wearable. luxury clothing like his superbly tailored suits for Givenchy. Even before he graduated from London's St. Martin's School of Art and Design, he had considerable experience and technical skill with his craft. He had apprenticed at a Savile Row tailor, had done pattern cutting at Kohji Tatsumo in Tokyo, and had worked at Romeo Gigli in Milan. When he presented his graduate collection in 1992, his designs caught the attention of a *Vogue* editor who included pieces in a magazine shoot that fall. In 1996. McQueen again made fashion headlines with his low-cut "bumster" pants that displayed the "plumber's crack" frequently parodied in skits twenty-years earlier on *Saturday Night Live.* That year he also was voted British Designer of the Year and received the invitation to design for the House of Givenchy. Despite his irreverence for the house founder, referring to the shadow of Hubert de Givenchy as "irrelevant," McQueen's fashions for the label nevertheless continued to follow the master couturier's tenets of the perfect cut and wearability. McQueen died at age 40 by suicide.

Missoni

Missoni, Rosita (b. 1931) and Ottavio (b. 1921)

The Italian knitwear company, Missoni, was founded in 1953 by the husband-and-wife team, Tai (Ottavio) and Rosita. After World War II, he had begun manufacturing knit athletic wear, and she had come from a family of bedding textile makers. Tai created the bold, geometric textile patterns and Rosita developed the garment shapes by draping directly on live models. The knitwear they produced was sold under other labels until 1966

Claire McCardell, 1954.

Alexander McQueen, 2006.

when they presented their first collection under their own name. Their vibrantly colored sweaters, jackets, suits. coats, and dresses were produced in limited runs, making them popular international status symbols. In 1997, the reins of the firm were handed to the duo's daughter, Angela.

Miyake, Issey

(b. 1935)

A graphics design graduate of Tama University, Issey Miyake went to Paris in 1964 to study at the Chambre Syndicale de la Couture. He then worked for Guy Laroche and Givenchy in Paris and for Geoffrey Beene in New York until 1971 when he launched his own label. Along with his compatriots, Rei Kawakubo and Yohji Yamamoto, Miyake revolutionized traditional perspectives of bodies and clothing. He once noted that, in the West, the body determines the cut of a garment, but in Japan, it is the fabric. He is often compared to Fortuny in his exploration of the properties and aesthetics of textiles. For him, technology was an art form, and he was constantly researching new fibers and fabrics. "Taking the spirit of the kimono" in all his work, his clothing designs de-emphasized the body and focused on freedom of movement. His Issey Sport collections were loose, comfortable, and wearable garments, designed to be mixed and matched and layered.

Mizrahi, Isaac

(b. 1961)

Described as a "shooting star" by the press with his debut in 1989, Isaac Mizrahi was a casualty of the cut-throat fashion business barely a decade later. He graduated from Parson's School of Design in New York in 1982 and worked for Perry Ellis and Calvin Klein before setting up his own shop in 1992. His witty creativity mixed unusual fabrics and vibrant colors for sportswear designs that were fresh and fun in the nineties. Despite the success of his collections, his ready-to-wear operations were not financially successful, and he was forced to close his firm in 1998. In the new millennium, Mizrahi found his niche as a style host on cable TV programming. In 2004, he began designing moderately priced ready-to-wear for Target Stores and, in 2008, joined Liz Claiborne.

Molyneux, Edward

(1891–1974)

Edward Molyneux was working as an illustrator when one of his sketches won a design contest sponsored by the House of Lucile in 1911. He traveled with Lucile (Lady Duff Gordon) to her salon branches in Paris, New York, and Chicago, learning all aspects of the couture business. After a distinguished career as captain during World War I, in which he was wounded three times and lost an eye in battle, he opened his own salon in Paris in 1919. From the mid-1930s through World War II, he was based in London where he dressed the English elite. He opened salons in the playgrounds of his clientele: Monte Carlo, Cannes, and Biarritz. He achieved worldwide notoriety when he designed the wedding gown and trousseau for Princess Marina of Greece in 1934. The simple classicism of his petit-print silk dresses and softly tailored suits was achieved by the perfect cut and proportion. His elegant style was an understatement of the British upper classes. As the vision of his remaining eye began to fail, he retired in 1950.

Montana, Claude

(b. 1949)

In the late sixties, Claude Montana began designing papiermaché jewelry decorated with rhinestones that he sold in London street markets. In 1972, he returned home to Paris and joined the MacDouglas leather firm for five years before starting his own label in 1977. Throughout the 1970s, he produced leather and knit fashions with strong, masculine shapes. Since much of his early work was in black leather, he was often accused of producing fascistic or fetishistic costumes, so he began to introduce potent color palettes of plums, reds, and in the eighties, jeweltones. In the 1980s, Montana's aggressive outlines of the broadest shoulders, cinched waists, and narrow hips complemented the power-dressing of the era. Between 1989 and 1992, his couture creations for Lanvin brought him new respect as a craftsman in the tradition of his idol, Balenciaga.

Mori, Hanae

(b. 1926)

Encouraged by her husband, whose family operated a textile business, Hanae Mori returned to college to study fashion design after the births of her two sons. In the early fifties, her family connections provided opportunities for costume design work in Japanese cinema. By the mid-1950s, she had opened a boutique in Tokyo selling ready-to-wear. She opened a couture salon in New York in 1973, followed four years later by one in Paris. Despite the Western styling of Mori's fashions, she had drawn much from her cultural background, especially evening wear based on the obi-belted kimono. She used her own fabrics, dyed and printed to her specifications in Kyoto. Hanae Mori retired in 1999, and her daughter-in-law, Penelope Mori, became creative director of the house.

Mugler, Thierry

(b. 1948)

Thierry Mugler began making his own clothes at age fourteen. In the sixties, he danced with a ballet company and later worked as a window decorator for a department store. He continued designing clothes and presented his first collection for Cafe de Paris in 1971. Two years later, he began designing under his own label. Mugler's styles reshaped the body into an ideal female and male silhouette. Women are made to look like goddesses and men as superheros—both with an electric, aggressive sexuality. Like Jean Paul Gaultier and Azzedine Alaia, who have been influenced by Mugler, he designs for individuals with aplomb and unique personal style.

Edward Molyneux, 1929.

Thierry Mugler, 1993.

Muir, Jean

(1933–1995)

Fashion was not an art to Jean Muir; it was a craft—a trade—requiring technical expertise and skilled workmanship. She started out as a salesclerk in Liberty's London store in 1950. She trained in the made-to-measure department there, eventually working her way up to sketcher. In 1956, she went to Jaeger as a designer for seven years, followed by four years designing for the Jane & Jane label with the Susan Small organization. In 1966, she began designing under her own name. Muir's classic designs could be deceptive in their simplicity, requiring as many as eighteen pattern pieces to construct a basic coat. For her dresses, she preferred soft fabrics such as jersey and suede for a fluid, flattering fit.

Norell, Norman

(1900–1972)

Born Norman Levinson, Norell left his Indianapolis home in 1919 to go to New York to study fashion. He graduated from the Pratt Institute and began his career as a costume designer for the New York studio of Paramount Pictures. During the mid-1920s, he also designed for a theatre costume company and a ready-to-wear maker. In 1928, he went upscale when he joined Hattie Carnegie. Thirteen years later, the clothing manufacturer Anthony Traina persuaded him to form Traina-Norell. In 1960, Norell established his own company. His legacy is simple, precisely tailored silhouettes. He was a trendsetter who introduced long evening skirts topped with sweaters, fur-lined trench coats, after-six culottes, and harem pants. His elegant, sophisticated clothes, made of luxurious fabrics, were equal to the fashions of Paris at the time. His leadership in American high style influenced the next two generations, including Halston, Galanos, and Mizrahi.

Paquin, Jeanne

(1869–1936)

Soon after Isador and Jeanne Paquin were married in 1891, they established a couture house in Paris. Madame Paquin, as she came to be known, had learned her craft at the Maison Rouff. Her collections helped popularize the hobble skirt and the Directoire revivals of the 1910s. She made a fortune selling design models for reproduction and exporting to department stores around the world. By most accounts, she is often regarded as the first major female couturier. Although she retired in 1920, the Paquin house remained open into the 1950s.

Patou, Jean
(1887–1936)

Jean Patou began his fashion career as a boy working in his father's tannery and his uncle's fur business. His first salon had just been opened when the First World War erupted in 1914. After the Armistice, he reopened his salon with modern sporty fashions that appealed to the active, emancipated woman of the era. A prolific designer, his large collections had to be shown in two parts—the morning for sportswear and casual-wear, and the afternoon for suits and formal styles. In 1929, Patou altered the fashion silhouette of the boyish flapper by shifting waistlines back to their natural position and lengthening hemlines—a presage of the look of the thirties. He also understood the importance of publicity. In 1925, he made headlines when he imported six tall American beauties as showroom models. Patou's simple, comfortable, and wearable designs were a permanent influence on fashion, comparable to that of Chanel. Both Chanel and he despised each other and were jealous of the other's success and innovation. The debate persists today which of the two had the most profound influence on modern women's fashion.

Poiret, Paul
(1879–1944)

As a teenager, Paul Poiret began his career selling design sketches to Paris couture houses, including that of Madeleine Cheruit. In 1896, he went to work as a designer for Doucet from whom he learned the business of couture as well as personal refinement and elegance. In 1900, Poiret went to the House of Worth, but felt stifled and went out on his own four years later. His lifelong love of exoticism and orientalism was first piqued during the Russo-Japanese War (1905) when Eastern artwork, prints, and textiles became widely popular in Paris. Later in the decade when he saw the lavish, ornamental costumes by Bakst for the Ballets Russes, he developed a complete collection of oriental-inspired styles, including harem pants and feathered skirts. In 1908, he recut the flared, bell-shaped skirts of the Edwardian era into a radically new form that tapered tightly to the ankles, creating the hobble skirt. The new look made him both notorious and famous worldwide. Capitalizing on this fame, he toured Europe and the United States with his collections in the years before the First World War. During the war he converted his salon into a uniform factory and then joined the French army. When he reopened in 1919, the fashion world had changed significantly. Patou and Chanel had redefined clothing for the modern woman but he attempted to dress them in the richly ornamental styles of prewar years. He could not understand the demand for what he called Chanel's "poverty de luxe." His firm was bankrupt by the end of the twenties and he died in poverty.

Potter, Clare
(1903–1999)

In the 1920s, Clare Potter studied fashion design at the Pratt Institute of Design and, immediately afterwards, began her career in fashion, working in ready-to-wear on Seventh Avenue. In 1936, she gained national recognition through the Lord & Taylor "American Look" campaign, winning the store's first design award two years later. In 1946, she won a Coty Award for her casual sportswear, and in 1948, launched her own ready-to-wear label Timbertop, named after her farm in West Nyack, NY. During the 1940s and 1950s, she was a leading force in women's sportswear, helping to popularize a colorful casual look worldwide.

Paul Poiret, 1922.

Emilio Pucci, 1960.

Prada, Miuccia

(b. 1949)

Miuccia Prada is the granddaughter of the founder of the Italian luxury leather goods maker bearing the family name. She joined the firm in 1978 where she immediately revolutionized the staid look of Prada products with her innovative use of unusual combinations of materials. In 1985, she made fashion headlines with the introduction of a line of black nylon handbags and backpacks, which became the logo insider's badge of membership. Four years later, she launched her first ready-to-wear collection. In 1992, she developed a less expensive line of women's apparel with the Miu Miu label, her nickname. The following year, she was honored with the prestigious Council of Fashion Designers of America International Award. In 1995, she expanded the brand with a successful line of menswear. Her husband, Patrizio Bertelli, led the company's commercial and retail strategies. Under his leadership as CEO, the design house grew into an international conglomerate adding labels such as Fendi, Jill Sander, Azzedine Alaia, and Helmut Lang to its portfolio of brands. When the company went public in 2011, it had over 250 stores in 65 countries and was valued at $13 billion.

Pucci, Emilio

(1914–1992)

The fashion career of the aristocratic Marchese Emilio Pucci de Barsento began in 1947 when *Harper's Bazaar* photographed him wearing ski pants he had designed. The magazine invited him to design some women's winter wear, which was subsequently sold in New York stores like Lord & Taylor's. In 1950, he opened a couture salon in the Palazzo Pucci in Florence, producing smart and easy sportswear in boldly colored prints and abstract patterns. His palazzo pyjamas became a favorite resort ensemble of the jet-set and were worn by Elizabeth Taylor, Grace Kelly, and Lauren Bacall. Pucci fashions and accessories quickly became the chic label to own and, today, vintage pieces are highly sought after collector's items.

Quant, Mary

(b. 1934)

The youthquake that would rock the fashion world of the 1960s had its roots in British and American urban street scenes of the late fifties. When Mary Quant opened her boutique in 1955, which she named Bazaar, she was young and energetic, creative, and totally attuned to the social changes emerging at the time. Initially her shop sold ready-to-wear, but Quant became frustrated with trying to find clothing that young people wanted, so she began to design her own. She was inspired by what dancers wore to rehearsals, especially easy tops, short skirts, and colorful tights and leggings. Although she never claimed to have created the miniskirt, her designs nevertheless popularized the look in "swinging London" with hemlines rising above the knees by 1960 and to mid-thigh by 1963. Her simple designs sold so well that she began exporting to the United States under the Ginger Group label. After 1970, she became increasingly involved with her cosmetics lines and licensed products, including accessories and home textiles, and her creative fashion leadership waned.

Rabanne, Paco

(b. 1934)

Paco Rabanne began his fashion career by applying his training as an architect to designing hardline fashion goods such as handbags, shoes, jewelry, and even buttons. In 1965, he began exploring the use of modern materials for clothing. The following year he presented his first collection of dresses made from a chain mail of plastic disks, which were more sculpture than clothing. Subsequent designs included molded Plexiglas garments and dresses made of crinkled paper, aluminum plates, or leather tiles riveted together. Although the press declared his designs unwearable, his futuristic ideas were revolutionary in the 1960s. He was in constant demand as a costume designer for movie studios and the ballet. The influence of his sculptural and architectonic creations is evident in the experimental work of the next generation, particularly Miyake's molded corsets and Versace's chain mail designs. He retired in 1999.

Rhodes, Zandra

(b. 1942)

Trained as a textiles designer in the early 1960s, Zandra Rhodes began to make dresses that she felt best interpreted her fabric designs. In 1968, she bought an interest in the Fulham Road Clothes Shop and launched her own label. Far ahead of the fashion curve, her conceptual chic collections of the 1970s incorporated street styles and punk looks, including dresses with embroidered rips and safety pin jewelry. In the eighties, her effervescent crinoline and bubble dresses were of tulles, silks, and chiffons in vibrant colors and exotic handprinted abstract patterns. Over the years, Rhode's fantastic and inventive designs have been added to the collections of museums and collectors around the world who, like Rhodes herself, view her creations as works of art.

Ricci, Nina

(1883–1970)

At age thirteen, Nina Ricci went from making clever clothes designs for her dolls to an apprenticeship with a dressmaker. As she honed her skills in cutting and draping, she worked her way up to become a premier couturier. With the encouragement of her husband, Louis Ricci, a jeweler, and assisted by her son, Robert Ricci, she opened her own Paris salon in 1932. Her designs were not at the vanguard of fashion, a role she yielded to contemporaries like Elsa Schiaparelli. Instead, she established a reputation for providing superbly made chic styles to wealthy mature women. During the 1950s, she collaborated with Jules Francois Crahay and, after 1963, Gérard Pipard became her chief designer.

Mary Quant, 1968.

Paco Rabanne, 1989.

Zandra Rhodes, 1985.

Rochas, Marcel

(1902–1955)

Marcel Rochas was one of the most innovative and influential designers of the thirties and forties. With the encouragement of his friend Paul Poiret, he opened his Paris salon in 1924. He is thought to have created the broad-shouldered military look ahead of Schiaparelli, who made the silhouette her trademark. He also anticipated Dior's New Look with his long, full skirts of 1941 and his long-line corset, or guepiere, of 1946. Many of his ensembles featured three-quarter length coats, well before the style became widely popular, and he is one of the first couturiers to construct skirts with pockets.

Rykiel, Sonia

(b. 1930)

Christened the "Queen of Knitwear" by the American press, Sonia Rykiel began her lifelong work with knits by making her own warm and easy maternity clothes in the early sixties. She then designed figure-hugging sweaters for her husband's boutique, Laura, until 1968, when she opened her own shop. Her fluid, softly feminine knit skirts, jumpers, jackets, capes, scarves, and pants were comfortable but never baggy. In the 1970s, she added menswear, childrenswear, and home textiles to her label. Although untrained in couture, she became vice-president of the Chambre Syndicale du Pret-à-Porter des Couturiers, a post she held for twenty years.

St. Laurent, Yves

(1936–2008)

At age seventeen, Yves St. Laurent won a fashion design contest in 1954, which, the following year, led to a job as Christian Dior's assistant. The skinny, emotionally fragile St. Laurent immersed himself in his work, absorbing all he could from the master of the house. When Dior died suddenly in 1957, St. Laurent was appointed head designer by the board of directors. His first collection, based on the little girl silhouette of the trapeze line, was a huge success. Subsequent collections were less well received, and his 1960 Left Bank collection inspired by the street looks of beatniks, shocked Dior patrons. When he was drafted for military service during the Algerian War, he was replaced at Dior by the more conservative Marc Bohan. After a few weeks of vicious harassment in the army, St. Laurent had a nervous breakdown and was released. With his business-savvy companion, Pierre Berge, at his side, he opened his own house in 1962. Four years later, he launched his ready-to-wear line, Rive Gauche, a menswear line in 1974, and childrenswear in 1978. His YSL signature became world famous and the initials signed almost everything to do with fashion, including accessories, swimwear, fragrance, and bed linens. St. Laurent is universally regarded as a genius and the greatest designer of the last forty years. Where Dior owed an allegiance to the past, St. Laurent preferred to break new ground, to surge ahead with visionary experiment and inventiveness like Schiaparelli before him, whom he often cited as a significant influence. Among his most noteworthy creations were his Mondrian dresses of 1965 and the Rich Fantasy Peasant collection of 1976. He introduced a masculine flavor to many women's styles that have since become fashion staples: safari jackets, pantsuits, and particularly, tuxedo jackets. However, many of his more avant-garde looks were not a complete success, such as his transparent blouses of the sixties and their periodic revival in the eighties and early nineties. As a result, his career has been a roller coaster of rhapsodic acclaim and scathing criticism from the fashion press, which often pushed the high-strung St. Laurent into periods of depression and substance abuse. In 1983, the New York Metropolitan Museum of Art presented a retrospective exhibit of his work, the first living designer to be so honored. On his thirtieth anniversary in 1992, he passed design direction of his ready-to-wear line to Alber Elbaz, so he could concentrate his efforts on couture. He retired in 2004.

Sant' Angelo, Giorgio

(1936–1989)

Brought up in Argentina and educated in Italy and France, Giorgio Sant' Angelo initially worked as a textile designer in the early sixties. In 1966, he began to design ready-to-wear under his own label, winning a Coty only two years later. He was an influential designer during the youthquake of the 1960s, creating popular interpretations of patchwork hippie styles and peasant looks. During the seventies, he was in and out of favor, but rebounded in the 1980s with his body-conscious designs of Lycra and richly ornamented, hand-beaded sweaters.

Scaasi, Arnold

(b. 1931)

Born Arnold Isaacs, he reversed the letters of his last name for added flair. He studied fashion at the Montreal Design School and at the Chambre Syndicale in Paris. He trained at Paquin before going to New York as assistant to Charles James. In 1957, he began his own ready-to-wear line, followed by his haute couture salon in 1964. His specialty was superbly made evening wear in luxurious fabrics. Among the famous women he dressed were Elizabeth Taylor, Ivana Trump, and First Lady Barbara Bush.

Schiaparelli, Elsa

(1890–1973)

Elsa Schiaparelli arrived in Paris from New York in 1922 following a divorce from a husband who had abandoned her and their daughter. With no money or training for a job, fate intervened when a department store buyer saw her wearing a black sweater with a white trompe l'oeil bow collar she had designed. The store ordered forty of the sweaters and Schiaparelli was in the fashion business. In 1927, she opened her own shop and produced easy, comfortable sportswear in the American mode as well as wildly eccentric, witty designs that sensationalized the fashion world throughout the thirties. She had collaborated with some of the most prominent avant-garde artists of the era, most notably Salvadore Dali, to merge art and fashion. Her inventiveness was boundless. She made sumptuous gowns elaborately embroidered with amusing, graphical images by Jean Cocteau. Her hats were shaped like lamb cutlets, ice cream cones, or upside down high heel shoes. Buttons were padlocks, drawer pulls,

Yves St. Laurent, 1962.

Elsa Schiaparelli, 1938.

Pauline Trigère, 1962.

butterflies, or miniature sculptures of acrobats and circus ponies. She popularized the broad, padded shoulder silhouette that remained a major fashion look through the Second World War. In 1940, Schiaparelli fled the war and returned to the United States for the duration. She reopened her Paris salon in 1945, but fashion had changed and Dior's New Look soon dominated. She retired after her last collection in 1952, living comfortably from the sale of her perfumes.

Simpson, Adele

(1903–1995)

While studying fashion design at the Pratt Institute in the mid-twenties, Adele Simpson also worked for a ready-to-wear maker, gaining valuable practical experience. After designing for various firms during the thirties and forties, she founded her own company in 1949 by buying out Mary Lee, Inc. Simpson's conservative designs were chic and current without being ahead of their time. In the 1950s, she produced a widely popular chemise dress with attached belts that could be fastened in the front or back. Her practical and versatile coordinates were a particular favorite of politician's wives, ranging from Mamie Eisenhower to Rosalyn Carter.

Trigère, Pauline

(1912–2002)

By the age of ten, Pauline Trigère already possessed sufficient sewing skills to assist her parents with their tailoring business. Later, when she was apprenticed to a couture house in Paris, she only stayed briefly because there was nothing more they could teach her. In 1937, she came to the United States and worked at Hattie Carnegie. In 1942, she opened her own business. She was a master of cutting and draping, preferring to work directly with the fabric on a mannequin. The intricate construction of her ready-to-wear was nearer couture than to mass production. Her urban chic clothes blended French high style with American simplicity and ease. She introduced coats and dresses with detachable collars and scarves, and dresses with attached jewelry. Her outerwear made her famous, particularly reversible coats and capes with vibrant colors on the inside.

Ungaro, Emanuel

(b. 1933)

As a young boy, Emanuel Ungaro was trained to sew by his tailor father and worked in the family business until 1955. He then went to Paris and apprenticed with Balenciaga for six years, followed by a brief period with Courrèges. In 1964, Ungaro opened his own company. At the peak of the youth-oriented sixties, his architectural A line dresses and futuristic coats and suits were inspired by Courrèges but made with the skillful discipline of Balenciaga. When he began to collaborate with fabric designer Sonia Knapp, his clothes became softly flowing and fluid. He became a brilliant colorist, mixing prints and layers for more grown-up looks than his earlier work.

Valentino

(b. 1932)

The Italian Valentino Clemente Ludovico Garavani studied at the Accademia Dell'Arte in Milan and the Chambre Syndicate in Paris. At age nineteen, he won a fashion contest and was offered a job by Jean Desses. Five years later he went to Guy Laroche and, in 1959, returned to Italy to open a couture house in Rome. Instead of succumbing to the youth cult of the sixties, Valentino made a name for himself with collections of elegant, glamorous designs. His 1968 White collection became world-famous when Jacqueline Kennedy selected a dress from the group for her marriage to Aristotle Onassis. In 1969, Valentino launched his women's ready-to-wear line, followed in 1972 by menswear. His gracefully cut gowns with dramatic touches like big bows and lavish beadwork or embroidery recall the feminine elegance of the thirties and fifties. Over the years Valentino's design empire expanded to include licenses for jewelry, sunglasses, leather goods, perfume, home products, and even an Alfa Romeo edition. He retired in 2008 after his final couture show.

Versace, Gianni

(1946–1997)

Gianni Versace began his fashion career assisting his dressmaker mother in Calabria, Italy. In the 1970s, he designed for various Milan firms before opening his own business in 1978. He quickly became known as an originator, especially in the development and use of new fabrics and trimmings. His leather accented knitwear for both men and women was widely copied. He worked directly on the model, creating bias-cut styles that sensuously wrapped the body. Versace's sexy, richly colored designs were a favorite of the high-profile social elite, including Elton John, Sting, Prince, George Michael, Madonna, and Princess Diana. When he was murdered at his Miami, Florida, home by a deranged fan in 1997, his sister, Donatello, assumed the mantle of head designer for the Versace label.

Vionnet, Madeleine

(1876–1975)

Apprenticed at age eleven to a Paris seamstress, Madeleine Vionnet became highly skilled at dressmaking by the time she was sixteen. She worked for various houses in London and Paris, including Doucet, before opening her own business in 1912. After being closed during the First World War, Vionnet resumed her design work in 1922. Hers was the creative vision of a sculptor who dressed the body in fabric with a minimalist perfection. Although she did not invent the bias cut, as is often stated, she mastered the technique and sewed ingenious seams that fluidly followed the body and its movement. She ordered fabric produced two yards wider than usual to accommodate her masterful cuts. To Vionnet, the pinnacle of her craft was a dress made with a single seam that achieved the perfect fit. She was not a colorist, preferring shades of white, and used decorative

Emanuel Ungaro, 2002.

Gianni Versace, 1992.

Vivienne Westwood, 1988.

embellishments sparingly. After she retired at the outbreak of World War II, she was virtually forgotten outside of the fashion industry. Yet she is idolized even today by contemporary designers who recognize that her unequalled, almost mysterious techniques had once transformed simple geometric shapes of fabric into liquid sculptures.

Westwood, Vivienne

(b. 1941)

Undisputedly one of the most courageous and influential designers of the last thirty years, Vivienne Westwood unleashed her quirky, eccentric creativity on the world of fashion in 1970 when she opened a boutique in London's King's Road. Through her association with Malcolm McClaren and his anarchic pop group the Sex Pistols, Westwood provided her customers with the attitudinal looks that reflected the urban youth culture of the time. Her confrontational styles were based on leather and rubber fetishism, raw sexuality, and especially punk. At the beginning of the 1980s, she began a long-running interest with historic silhouettes—exploiting and reinventing the aesthetics of the past. Her thematic collections have included Pirates, Buffalo Girls, Anglomania, Mini-Crini, and Witches. Among her fashion shockwaves have been underwear worn on the outside, constricting corset dresses, the cage crinoline, S&M platform shoes, and a men's sweater twinset with pearls. She was voted British Designer of the Year in 1991 and received the Order of the British Empire the following year.

Worth, Charles Frederick

(1825–1895)

Universally acclaimed as the Father of French couture, Worth was an Englishman who inauspiciously arrived alone in Paris in 1845 with little money and no connections. Since he had apprenticed in London at a draper's shop and later with a tailor, he found work as a sales clerk at the House of Gagelin. He met his wife there and began to dress her in his own designs. When so many customers expressed interest in Mme. Worth's gowns, he was permitted to open a shop in the store. In 1858, he opened his own salon, becoming a favorite of Empress Eugenie, then the world's arbiter of fashion. In the early 1860s, he reshaped the crinolined gown into an oval with a flattened front and an enormous train. By 1868, he had discarded the crinoline and began the radical transition to the bustle. Worth changed the role and status of the clothing designer from that of dressmaker, who primarily executed the ideas of the customer, to that of the style creator who guided the fashionable elite with his ideas of what was current and suitable for them. After his death in 1895, the House of Worth continued under the directorship of his sons and grandsons until 1954 when it was taken over by Paquin.

Yamamoto, Kansai

(b. 1944)

Trained as a civil engineer, Kansai Yamamoto instead turned to fashion design while studying at Nippon University. He worked for Hisashi Hosono Studio before establishing his own label in 1971. Four years later he presented his first Paris show. His work was a dynamic blend of ancient Japanese forms with Western sportswear styles such as sumptuous satin pyjamas emblazoned with giant embroidered cartoon graphics. He designed David Bowie's spectacular wardrobe for Ziggy Stardust. His shows were extravaganzas, one of which attracted more than 40,000 people to a stadium in New Delhi in 1998.

Yamamoto, Yohji

(b. 1943)

Yohji Yamamoto began his career assisting his war widow mother with her dressmaking business. He got his degree from the Bunka College of Fashion in Tokyo and worked as a freelance designer until starting his own firm in 1972. In 1981, he opened a shop in Paris and began showing his collection as part of fashion week. His intellectual, nontraditional designs, with their tears and slashing, illogical pocket flaps, and asymmetrical closures, created a sensation with the press. He was constantly exploring the relationship of fabric and body. Yamamoto's clothing was draped, wrapped, and knotted to disavow gender, sexual exhibitionism, and the conventional view of fashion glamour.

dress terms

A Line: one of Dior's 1955 collections that featured dresses, suits, and coats that were narrow and fitted at the top and widened from the bust or waist in a straight line to the hem

absurdists: a Parisian group of avant-garde fashion designers

admiral jacket: double-breasted sport coat with metal buttons and grosgrain trim

afro: full, bushy hair worn by African-American men and women

á la disposition printing: a technique of fabric roller printing in which patterns were designed specifically for the edges of skirt flounces

aniline dyes: synthetic dyestuffs first developed in the 1850s

Apache scarf: American adaptations of the ascot worn by men in the late 1960s

art deco (also known as moderne): a decorative art style featuring geometric shapes and a pure linearity

ascot: a wide, scarf-like cravat that filled the open neckline of the vest

Atome: the name given to the 1946 bikini swimsuit design by Jacques Heim

Australian bush boots: men's short ankle shoes with side elastic panels

B-Boys: inner city street looks of the 1980s that included Kangol hats, big gold chains, sneakers without laces, and oversized quilted jackets

baby doll gown: women's smock-like shortie nightgown with short, ruffled bloomers

baby doll pajamas: women's pajama sets with hip-length tops and bloomer bottoms

back-strap shoes: women's shoes with a tab of material stitched across the heel that buckled

baggies: men's and women's high-waisted trousers with wide legs

Bakelite and Catalin: brand names of phenolic plastics used for costume jewelry, buttons, and ornaments

bal collar: banded type of turned-down collar derived from the Scottish balmacaan topcoat

ballet slippers: women's wide, flat slip-on shoes

balloon shoes: men's broad, square-toed shoes of the 1920s

balmacaan: raglan sleeve overcoat with narrow, turned-down collar

basques: short, skirt-like tabs attached at the waist of women's bodices and jackets

battle jacket: civilian version of the military jacket with big pockets, buttoned waistband, and fly front

batwing sleeve: a deep, softly draped, dolman sleeve style, wide at the shoulder tapering to a close fit at the wrist

bavolet bonnet: a close fitting hat style with a ruffle at the back of the neck

bed head: the arranged mussed hair look for both men and women achieved with fixative gels or glues

beehive hairstyle: high, cylindrical arrangement of long hair popular in the mid-1960s

beetle crushers: men's thick, crepe-soled shoes

bell bottoms: pants with flared cuffs

bermuda shorts: tailored, knee length shorts for both women and men

bertha: a wide, deep collar usually attached to the edge of the low, open neckline

bikini: women's two piece swimsuit of the late 1940s with a bandeau or bra-cut top and low waisted bottom

bishop's sleeve: women's sleeve with a fullness between the elbow and wrist

bit loafer: men's slip-on shoes named for the horse harness bit hardware attached to a strap or metal bar across the vamp

blade cut suit: see drape cut suit

blanket cloth: thick, flannel fabrics in bold plaids and patterns used for men's bathrobes

blazer: a variant of the men's sack coat made with patch pockets and worn as casual attire, particularly for sports events

bling-bling: flashy jewelry, especially diamonds and an abundance of gold, or a showy style of dress

Bloomer dress: women's long, baggy trousers worn with a short skirt named for Amelia Bloomer who wore them while on tour as an advocate for women's rights

boa: a decorative scarf made of feathers or materials cut or knit in a feathery treatment

board shorts: men's long, baggy swim trunks modeled after the surfer jams of the eighties

boater: shallow, cylindrical straw hats worn by both men and women

bobbysoxers: teenage girls who wore turned down white cotton socks with saddle oxfords or penny loafers

body stocking: long sleeve, one-piece knit suit; also called a catsuit

bogolanfini cloth: African inspired textiles made of cotton cloth painted or handstamped with patterns of geometric symbols in a mixture of black, mineral-rich mud, sometimes intensified with vegetable dyes

boho (bohemian) style: a blending of retro hippie-gypsy looks with cross-cultural tribal influences

bold look: the term applied to menswear of the late 1940s in which accessories were vividly colored and patterned

bolero jacket: a woman's short, cropped jacket or vest, often with a rounded cutaway front

bolla: a string tie affixed with decorative holder

bomber's jacket: men's short leather or fabric jacket with high pockets and banded bottom

borrowed look: the adaptation of men's clothing styles to women's fashion; also called boyfriend styles

bosom front shirt (also shield front or breastplate front): the front panel of men's shirts often made of fine linen and embellished with tucks or pleats; the slit closure usually fastened with two or three buttons

bowler: see derby

boxerbriefs: men's underwear that combined the snug fit of knit briefs with the square cut and longer legs of traditional boxers

boyfriend style: menswear influences on women's ready-to-wear; also called the borrowed look in some fashion editorials

boyshorts: women's square-cut underwear modeled after men's boxerbriefs

brassiere: various forms of bust support garments

breastplate front: see bosom front shirt

bretelles: a pair of decorative braces for women's bodices that attached at each shoulder and tied together at the waist

broomsticks: men's tight fitting pants cut with leg hems between thirteen and seventeen inches in circumference

bulb-toe shoe: men's shoes with a wide bulbous-shaped toe

Burberry: any of a type of men's or women's outerwear or rainwear made of a weather resistant gabardine

bust bodice: an early form of brassiere

bust improver: padding for the decollete bodice

cabochon: large rounded clasps or pins used as ornaments on women's hats

caesar cut: men's hairstyle of the mid-nineties cropped very short at the sides with a short fringe of bangs combed forward in a point over the forehead

cage crinoline: a petticoat reinforced with hoops of whalebone or watch spring steel

camiknickers (also chemiknickers): a type of short slip with a button or loop at the hem that could be fastened to form a divided underskirt

camisole: a form of short sleeved or sleeveless underbodice

canadienne: men's goatskin jacket with fleece lining

canezou: various decorative tops ranging in style from short muslin jackets to elaborate neckline fillers

capote: a bonnet style made with a soft fabric crown and rigid brim

capri pants: women's and men's casual pants cropped just above the ankles

car coat: any variety of men's or women's coat cropped between the upper thighs and hips to allow greater freedom of motion for driving

Carnaby Street looks: young men's mod styles that included vividly colored shirts, tight hiphugger pants, and brightly hued ascots, scarves, and neckties; named for the shopping district in London's Soho section

carrick: a men's or women's overcoat with layers of three to five capes sewn to the collar

cashmere: a soft textile made from the silken hair of goats from the Kashmir region of Central Asia

cavalier collar: a woman's collar designed as a high band that flared into a shallow roll similar to styles of the 1590s

celluloid: a nineteenth-century type of plastic produced from cotton and cellulose

cellulose acetate: a cellulose-based fiber used in the production of rayon

Chelsea boots: men's short ankle boots with pointed toes, elastic side gussets, and Cuban heels

chemisette: a type of underbodice made with a decorative front panel to fill open necklines

chesterfield topcoat: a men's or women's topcoat with a velvet collar and a fly front that concealed the buttons

chinos: khaki-colored cotton twill trousers

chinstrap beard: long sideburns that connected under the chin along the jawline

cigarette silhouette: the slim, tubular cut of women's outerwear during World War II

circle beard (also called a goatee): a mustache and narrow beard that encircled the mouth to the chin

circle skirt: fully round skirts usually worn with crinolines by girls and teenagers

cloche: women's close-fitting, high-crowned hat with shallow brim

cloverleaf lapels: the rounded points on notched lapels

clutch coat: a wrap style of coat popular with the flapper

coachman's coat: a men's heavy overcoat featuring a fitted bodice, full skirt in the back, and large flap pockets

coat front shirt: men's shirts of the 1890s designed with a button front closure from the collar to the hem

cocoons: slim wrap coats worn by young women in the early postwar years

collar grips: a metal clasp affixed to the tips of the collar behind the knot of the necktie to hold the collar smooth on men's dress shirts

collarettes: wide capelets with a dog collar neckline used as an attachment to Edwardian women's outerwear

combinations: women's underwear made with the camisole and drawers sewn together

constructed swimsuit: women's swimwear with various engineered devices to sculpt, control, and idealize the female body

Continental suit: a variety of Italian inspired looks, including shortened jackets with natural shoulders, shaped waistlines, narrow lapels, and rounded fronts

corselette: an all-in-one corset style of the 1920s that encompassed the bust and hips

corset amazone: a corset style made from elasticized fabric

corset waist: a form of corset that fully covered the upper torso and included breast support with shoulder straps

cossack pajamas: men's sleepwear suit with tunic top cut with an off-center closure and a stand-up round collar

covert coat: a women's loose-fitting, three-quarter length overcoat made of twill (covert) wool

cravat: men's neckwear variously tied or knotted at the front of the throat

crepeset: permanently textured or crimped monofilament nylon fabric

crinolette: a flat front petticoat with steel half hoops of widening sizes top to bottom

crinoline: a dense fabric woven of horsehair and linen

crinoline petticoat: a petticoat made with wide, thick bands of crinoline applied around the hem

crusher: low, round-top hat with turned-up, saucer-like brims; named for its light, three-ounce weight

cuirass bodice: a sheath-like bodice that fit tightly over the hips, producing a long-line dress silhouette

culottes: short styles of the split skirt

cummerbund: a men's vividly colored sash worn with formal wear in place of a vest

cyberstyle: a futuristic look of the late 1990s that combined technotextiles with street looks and elements of historic dress

dressing sacque: a woman's loose dressing robe

dressing-gown coat: women's wrap coats of the 1970s

duffle coat: men's hooded, square-shoulder coat with patch pockets and rope frogging that hooked over wooden pegs

dungarees: jeans

duster: long, waterproofed coats for men and women initially used for motoring in open cars; also, a women's knee-length housecoat

duvet coat: women's oversized quilted jacket or coat of the late seventies

 Earth Shoes: "negative heel" styles of low shoes made with molded soles shaped with lowered heels and elevated toes

egg-point toes: women's flat shoes with wide, rounded toes

elasticized fabrics: textiles produced in the early nineteenth century from yarns made with rubber

electronic clothes: garments constructed with electrically conductive textiles interwoven with microscopic wires used to enable electronic devices such as cell phones and GPS tracking

elephant bells: women's and men's pants of the early 1970s that fitted snugly about the hips and thighs but flared into enormous bell shapes over the feet

Empire waist: a high waistline positioned just under the bosom

Eton suit: boy's short jacket, trousers, and white shirt with a turned-down collar named for the London boys' school where the ensemble was a required uniform

 dashiki: long, T-cut tunics made of kente cloth or fabrics evocative of African heritage

deconstruction: the rejection of conventional rules of clothing cuts, form, or fit

deerstalker cap: a men's sports cap with turned-up earflaps

denim: a heavy cotton twill named for the French serge de Nimes

derby: a men's round crown hat with a narrow brim

dishrag shirt: men's short sleeve knit shirt with mesh bodice

ditto suit: a men's three-piece combination of lounge jacket, vest, and trousers all made of the same fabric

dog-collar neckline: high, stiff collars of Edwardian women's fashions

drape cut suit: men's jacket style of the 1930s featuring broad, unpadded shoulders, a smooth fit across the shoulder blades, roomy armholes, a tapered waistline, and rolled lapels; also called London cut and blade cut

dress coat: men's formal suit jacket with a cut-in front cropped above the waistline and tails in the back variously shaped as a "coffin" or "swallow's tail"

 fall front bodice: two pieces of lining material that fastened across the inside front of an Empire waist bodice to lift the bust

fall front closure: the drop-front flap of men's trousers through the 1830s

Fashion Avenue: the name generally applied to the New York City apparel market located on Seventh Avenue

Fastskin: a branded synthetic fabric that simulated sharkskin applied to swimsuits

Fauntleroy suit: a boy's velvet or satin suit that included knee breeches, short jacket, and a wide falling-band collar

fedora: a men's hat with a high, conical crown with a deep crease front to back

ferrule: the metal tips of laces and bolla strings used to prevent unraveling

fichu: cape-like or scarf covering for open necklines

flamenco pants: women's pants of the mid-1960s with a low-rise waistline and flared legs below the knees; a precursor to bell bottom hiphuggers

flare coat: a capacious coat that flared from the shoulders to the hem without a marked waistline

fly front: the vertical slit in the front of men's trousers or drawers

folklorica: women's fashions and accessories of the late 1970s that featured peasant or folk art motifs and decorative embellishments

French blue: a pale shade of blue popular for men's suit jackets and dress shirts of the early 1950s

French wrists: turned-back cuffs that fastened with cuff links

gabardine: a closely woven twill fabric

gaiter boot: a style of men's and women's shoe made with leather vamps over the instep and toes and a fabric upper around the ankles

Gatsby suit: men's suit styles of the mid-1970s with jackets that were padded and shaped in the style of the English drape cut of the 1930s

gauchos: midi-length versions of culottes

gigot: a form of leg-of-mutton sleeve padded with feather pillows in the Romantic Age

glam or **glitter rock styles:** androgynous looks of the early 1970s that included sequined or rhinestone-studded tops and pants, platform shoes, and feathery haircuts for both women and men

go-go boots: any of a variety of boots, but usually the short white styles with flat heels and wide uppers; named for the wild go-go dancing of the period

goring: triangular or tapered pieces of cloth used to shape garments

granny dress: ankle-length calico dress often made with Victorian details such as high collars, puffed sleeves, and ruffled hemlines

Grecian bend profile: women's silhouette of the bustle era in which the torso appeared to tilt forward as a balance to the skirt volume in the back

green fashions: clothing and accessories made of sustainable (organic, natural) fibers and materials

grippers: men's boxer style underwear with a snap-closure fly

grunge: a youth pop culture look of the early 1990s that emphasized a disheveled casualness and ensembles of distressed and mismatched clothing

guards coat: an adaptation of the dark blue, double breasted greatcoat of the British Grenadiers with center back pleat and half belt

guimpe: a bust-to-hips corset; see also waspie

H Line: one of Dior's 1954 collections that featured dresses with a dropped waistline

handkerchief skirt: skirt style draped with uneven, pointed hemlines resembling handkerchiefs

Hawaiian print shirt: casual, short sleeve sport shirts in vividly colored, tropical motif prints

headwrap: a cloth headcovering worn by black women as an expression of their African heritage

Hessian boot: a men's high boot with a heart-shaped top and a tassel at the dip in the center

high twist wool: yarns made by tightly coiling two strands of the finest, softest wool fibers

hiphuggers: men's and women's pants cut with a low waistline that fitted tightly about the hips

hipster: a women's high-waist swimsuit bottom of the 1990s that was a revival of a style from the forties

hobble skirt: a slim, tube skirt that tapered to a narrow opening at the hemline, some with a strip of material at the ankles called a hobble garter

homburg: a shorter version of the fedora; named for a style adopted by the Prince of Wales after his visit to a hat factory in Homburg, Germany

hoodie: any variety of hooded shirt, fleece top, jacket, or vest

hot pants: city short shorts of the early 1970s often made of upscale materials

house coat: men's dressing gown worn over regular clothes during late night or early morning hours

huaraches: an adaptation of Mexican peasant sandals with woven leather toes and a strap at the heel

intarsia: Italian word meaning inlaid applied to complex knitwear patterns that appear to have inset panels

Inverness cape coat: a men's heavy travel coat that included a circular cape that covered the shoulders and arms to the elbows

Ivy League style: conservative men's suits with columnar, straight hanging jackets and unpleated, narrow trousers

jabot blouse: women's blouses of the 1920s with frilly neck treatments and a wide cut that could form a deep blouson over the skirt waistband

Jack Tar suit: a boy's or girl's sailor suit featuring a middy top and nautical trousers or skirt

jacquard: a fabric with an intricately woven design of raised patterns

Janeiro jacket: the 1950s adaptation of the mess jacket

jeans: denim work pants named after the "genes" or Genoese sailors who brought boatloads of the material from France

jockey boot: a men's tall boot worn with the snug top turned down

Jockey briefs: men's formfitting knit underwear cut with high leg openings, an elasticized waistband, and a Y-front closure; introduced in 1934

jupe-culottes (also called Turkish trousers): women's wide-legged pantaloons of the early 1910s

Kevlar: aramid fiber used in protective clothing as "soft body armor"

kilties: shoes with a turned-down fringed tongue

kimono trousers: women's baggy, Japanese inspired trousers resembling harem pants

knee-breaker coat: men's outerwear of the 1960s and early 1970s cropped at or slightly above the knees

knickerbockers: knee breeches worn by both men and women for sports activities, especially bicycling and golf

L-85 regulations: restrictions and guidelines for making clothes instituted by the U.S. War Production Board in 1942

L.E.D.s: acronym for light-emitting diodes, an electronic semiconductor device that produces light from an electric current

last: industry term applied to the shape of a shoe; also, shoe-shaped forms, usually of wood, inserted into shoes for storage to preserve the shape

leggins: high, buttoned spats worn by men and women over their shoes for sports activities

leghorns: wide-brimmed straw hats named for the type of bleached wheat straw used in their construction

leisure suit: casual menswear of the early 1970s that featured shirt-like jackets with wide collars and matching trousers, usually of polyester double knits or stretch denim

Lido shoes: any variety of women's thick, cork soled shoes of the 1930s

lingerie look: the excessive use of laces and ribbons as decoration for Edwardian women's fashions

loafer socks: a form of footie socks worn by both men and women; also called no-show socks

loafers: a moccasin style of slip-on casual shoe introduced from Norway in the 1930s

London cut suit: see drape cut suit

Louis heel: women's shoe style with high curved heel similar to that popularized by Louis XV

lounge suit: see ditto suit

loungers: men's moccasin style slip-on shoes

low riders: a new form of women's and men's hiphugger pants cut extremely shallow at the inseam

mackintosh: a raincoat made from layers of sheet rubber cemented to fabric; named for the inventor of the material, Charles MacIntosh

manga T-shirts: T-shirts screenprinted with the big-eyed Japanese cartoon characters of manga comics and anime films

manscaping: the process of trimming or removing body hair

Mao collar: the French term for the rounded stand-up collar on men's jackets and shirts of the late 1960s; named for Chinese Communist leader Mao Tse-tung

marcel: a hair curling device used in salons of the 1920s and 1930s for "permanent" waves

Marie Stuart collar: a high standing collar that curled out into five points

martingale coat: a variety of women's wide or fitted coats with half belts in the back

maxi: a skirt or coat with a hemline near or to the ankles

Mercedes toque: a woman's hat with a circular crown and a brim turned straight up the same height as the crown

Merino wool: soft, supple wool from specially bred sheep in England and Spain

mess jacket: men's dinner jacket cropped at the waist and resembling a naval officer's dinner dress

metrosexual: a heterosexual male with high standards of style and taste, a quality usually attributed to gay men

Miami Vice look: a men's sporty suit look of the 1980s that included unconstructed jackets worn with the sleeves pushed up, colored T-shirts, relaxed fit trousers, and shoes with no socks

middy: a square-collar sailor's shirt named after midshipmen worn by Victorian women and children; also, a dress silhouette of the mid-1950s with a dropped waistline and fitted torso

midi: a skirt or coat with a hemline at mid-calf

milkmaidism: the English term applied to women's Victoriana revivals

minaret tunic (also called a lampshade tunic): short, panniered tunics that flared into a funnel shape from the waist

miniskirt: dress or skirt with a hemline above the knees

mod look: short for "modern" or "modernist" fashions for women and men of the mid-1960s

monk: men's shoe style with a single strap and buckle over the instep rather than laces

morning coat: men's semi-formal day jacket cropped at the waist in the front with a knee-length skirt that was cut away in a tapering contour of the tails at the back

mushroom puff sleeve: a tight, cylindrical sleeve capped at the shoulder by a shallow, flattened puff

mutton chops: men's long, bushy side whiskers

 **nainsook:** a woven striped cotton from India whose name means "delight the eye" in Hindi

nanotechnology: the science of reconfiguring the size and properties of molecules; see smart fabrics

Neapolitan: a smooth, horsehair fabric used for women's winter bonnets

negligee shirt: men's casual shirt with attached turn-down collar; also called a "soft shirt"

negligee: a woman's loose nightgown or dressing robe

Nehru suit: menswear style of the late 1960s that featured a tunic-style jacket with a rounded stand-up collar; named for Indian prime minister Jawaharlal Nehru

New Look: the term applied by the fashion press in 1947 to describe Christian Dior's debut collection; the look featured rounded shoulders, full busts, cinched waists, and spreading skirts

no-show socks: see loafer socks

norfolk jacket: a men's loose-fitting jacket with an attached belt and double box pleats from shoulder to hem

notched collar: the V-cut gap formed at the intersection of the lapel and collar piece

Nureyev cap: Russian worker's cap with short visor and wide headband; named for ballet dancer Rudolf Nureyev

nylon: an amide synthetic used to produce resilient yarns used in textiles

 organdy: a stiff, transparent fabric of silk or cotton

outing sack suit: men's suits made with a sack jacket with patch pockets and bold patterned textiles

oxford: a stout, low shoe for men and women, often designed with contrasting tones of material

Oxford bags: trousers with wide legs worn by young men of the 1920s

 pagoda sleeve: a Victorian style of sleeve cut with a narrow fit at the upper arm and an abrupt flare from the elbow to the wrist; also, in the 1930s, an exaggerated sleeve with a high, peaked shoulderline

paisley: gourd or pod-shaped motifs richly decorated with intricate patterns

pajamas (pyjamas in Britain): men's trouser sleepwear suit

palazzo pajamas: women's wide-legged evening pants

paletot: a women's three-quarter length cape with two or more layers and slits for the arms

Palm Beach suit: men's lounge style suit made of lightweight tropical fabrics; named for the Florida resort in the 1930s

panama hat: a high crowned straw hat that became popular during the construction of the Panama Canal

pannier bustle: a thin, padded form of bustle worn with the narrow skirts of the early 1880s

pantalettes: women's long drawers of mid-calf or ankle length

pantyhose: seamless, one-piece knit hose, combining stockings and panty, introduced in the mid-1960s

peacock revolution: the hedonistic changes in menswear in which men adopted colorful clothes and styles that broke with conventional masculine dress

peaked lapel: the wide, pointed style of lapel first popular on suit jackets of the 1920s

pedal pushers: casual pants cropped just below the knees for women and men

peep toes: new term for open-toed shoes

pegged trousers: men's trousers cut full around the hips and thighs and tapering to a close fit at the ankles

pelisse: a long, capacious overcoat, usually lined with fur

peplum: a short skirt attached at the waist of bodices or jackets

permanent press: treated fabrics that resist wrinkling, introduced in 1964

Peter Pan collar: low, rounded neckline with a petal-shaped collar used on women's and children's clothing

phenolic plastic: a resinous plastic made from benzene used in the manufacture of jewelry, accessories, and trimmings

pinched-crown hat: men's brimmed hat with a pair of dents in the front of the crown

plastron: a woman's frilly lace neckpiece often embellished with ribbon bows

plus fours: loose, baggy knickerbocker trousers worn by both men and women in the 1920s and 1930s for sports activities, and by men as casual country attire

polo shirt: short-sleeve knit shirt with placket button closure and knit Eton collar

pompadour: women's hairstyles arranged up on the head in a high bouffant shape with various knots at the back

poodle cloth: a nubby, deep pile wool fabric resembling the texture of poodle fur

pouf dress (also called bubble dress): a bouffant cocktail dress of the 1980s constructed with a voluminous, rounded skirt

poulaines: shoes of the Middle Ages with long, pointed toes

powersuit: men's and women's business suits of the 1980s usually designed with an inverted triangle silhouette formed by broad padded shoulders and tapered, narrow hips

prêt-à-porter: French high-style, high quality ready-to-wear tailored to the U.S. market

Prince Albert coat: the name given to men's dressy frock coats of the last quarter of the 1800s

princess bodice: a style of dress made of one long piece (or long gored pieces) from the shoulder to the hem with no waist seam

pullman robe: men's tailored dressing robes

punk look: the self-styled look of disaffected youths of the mid-seventies, such as clothes and accessories slashed and pinned together or embellished with images and found objects that could create shock value

 qi pao dress: an Asian sheath usually with a mandarin collar and slit skirt

Qiana: Du Pont synthetic silk introduced in 1968

 raccoon skin coat: long, voluminous fur coat with large collar worn by collegiate men and flappers of the 1920s

racer: a sleek, one-piece tank-style swimsuit initially worn by men in competition sports of the 1910s and 1920s; also, a women's one-piece swimsuit with an open back and wide shoulder straps modeled on Olympic swimsuits of the 1940s

rain topcoats: outerwear made of moisture-resistant nylon or polyester fabrics

rainy-daisies: skirts with shortened hemlines worn for walking on rainy days or for sports activities

rayon: a synthetic fabric commonly known as artificial silk

reticule (also redicule): a women's small purse of assorted types

rio: women's string bikini introduced on the beaches of South America in the early 1970s

rockabilly: a youth look that incorporated vintage casualwear of the fifties with modern retro-styles

Romantique: women's fashions that featured frilly, feminine elements of nineteenth-century styles

rubberized thread: spun yarns reinforced with an application of vulcanized rubber used to create elasticized fabrics

S

S-bend corset: corset designed with a straight-line busk and long hipline that thrust the chest forward and shifted the hips back into a kangaroo stance

sack coat: a men's short coat cut to hang straight from the shoulder with no seam or tapered line at the waist

seersucker: a puckered textile that derived its name from the Persian "shirushakar"

serge de Nimes: a heavy cotton twill from which the word "denim" was derived

Sergeant Pepper suits: menswear of the mid-1960s that blended a form of Edwardian dandyism with psychedelic patterned fabrics and color combinations; named for the costumes of the mythical band in the Beatles' *Yellow Submarine*

Shelby knot: a tie knot wider than a four-in-hand but not as thick as a half-Windsor popularized by news anchorman Don Shelby

shell toes: sneakers worn without the laces

shibori: twisted textured fabric used in fashion and accessories such as men's pocket squares

shield front: see bosom front shirt

shirtwaist: women's blouses of various styles and fabrics

shirtwaister: the 1950s version of the shirtwaist dress with a fitted bodice and full skirt

shrug sweaters: see shrunken cardigan

shrunken cardigan: women's tight-fitting cardigan with a high, cropped waistband and sometimes short or half sleeves

shrunken look: tops with cropped hems, shortened sleeves, and a tight fit that appeared to pull button closures and strain the fabric

silk shantung: a nubby silk weave

singlette: lightweight step-in underwear favored by young women of the 1920s

skanties: women's brief style panties of the 1930s

skimp: a girl's long sweater extending to mid-thigh worn with tights or form-fitting knit pants

skinheads: a counterculture group of disaffected young men who shaved their heads and dressed in working class garb

skinny ties: men's thin neckties

skyscraper pump: women's platform shoes with spike heels at five inches or more

slacks: the generic term applied to women's or men's tailored casual trousers

slim jims: men's string neckties

slip: the generic term usually applied to petticoats and chemises since the 1920s

slop shops: early retail tailor shops specializing in ready-made clothing for men

slope: men's hairstyle of the late 1990s with a short fringe of bangs gelled to rise vertically from the forehead

slope-crown hat: men's styles of hats in the 1940s that featured a crown blocked higher in the front than the back

smart fabrics: textiles produced with nanotechnology finishes that can wick perspiration away from the body, repel insects, block the sun's UV rays, and resist stains

snap-brim fedora: men's hat with a pliable, wide brim and high, tapered crown

snood: chenille or silk cord hair net

sorchetta: a double dimple necktie knot that originated in Italy

soul patch: a tuft of beard just beneath the lower lip but not extending onto the chin

space age style: sleek, minimalist women's and men's fashions of the mid-1960s with clean, smooth lines and simple shapes

speedsuit: men's one-piece swimwear with short trunks and a tanktop

spencer: a women's Empire jacket cropped to fit just below the bosom

split raglan coat: men's outerwear with sleeves that featured a set-in effect in the front but diagonal raglan seams in the back

spool heels: women's shoes with thick, rounded heels resembling a spool of thread

spool torso: a fitted dress bodice of the early post World War II years

stilettos: women's shoes with thin, high spiked heels

stirrups: strips of fabric sewn to the cuff of men's trousers that fit under the instep of a shoe

suburban: another name for car coat

surfer jams: revivals of young men's long, shorts-style swim trunks in retro colors and prints from the 1960s

sustainable fabrics: textiles made from organically grown natural fibers from plants and animals

swank suit: a less extreme variation of the zoot suit, featuring a jacket with broad, padded shoulders, trim waist, and wide lapels

swim-walker: men's knit, bermuda-length swim trunks

T

tail coat: see dress coat

tankini: women's swimsuit comprised of a tanktop and bikini bottom

tantoo: the silhouette of a shape or initial resulting from the application of an adhesive-backed decal to skin prior to sunbathing

tats: the abbreviated term for tattoos

technotextiles: synthetic materials produced in the 1990s that were applied to apparel and accessories

Teddy boys: British working class teenagers of the early 1950s who dressed in a mock Edwardian style with long, boxy suit jackets, string ties, and cuffless trousers cropped at the ankles

tennis shoe: sport shoe with rubber sole and canvas upper originally worn on tennis courts

toggle coat: another name for duffle coat

toppers: women's loose fitting coats usually cropped at the waist or high on the hips

toppers: women's loose-fitting coats usually cropped at the waist or high on the hips

toque: a woman's tall, brimless hat usually tapering to the top

toreador: a narrow four-in-hand necktie knot

torpedo bra: bra with spiral cup stitching and padded linings that enlarged and separated the breasts into a stylization of the bosom

tournure: a bustle frame of steel, duck, tapes, and laces worn in the mid-1880s

toy hat: miniaturized versions of women's hat styles popular in the late 1930s

trapeze line: a dress or coat cut featuring a full, tent shape with a high bust and back that fell from the shoulders

trash fashion (also "trashion'): garments and accessories sewn, woven, or crocheted from recycled plastic bottles, food packaging, inner tubes, soda can pop top chainmail, and plastic grocery bags

tribal looks: fashions with a pre-industrial or cross-cultural aboriginal design, including historical and global national costume styles

trilby: a narrow brimmed fedora often accented with a leather band or buckle

trouser drawers: men's ankle length underwear commonly made of knit fabrics

trunks: men's square-cut underwear made with a lowered waistband modeled after sixties style swimwear

tubini: a two-piece swimsuit with a bandeau "tube" top, some of which extended to the hips in a short skirt; bottoms varied from bikini to square cuts

tunic suit: a boy's skirted top worn over pantaloons or trousers

Turkish trouser: a form of women's trousers from the mid-1800s featuring voluminous legs fastened at the ankles

turtlesuit: men's one-piece fitted body shirt and underwear with a snap closure crotch

tuxedo: a version of the men's sack coat that incorporated elements of the dress coat such as satin lapels; named for New York's Tuxedo Park Club

twosome swimsuit: men's one-piece swimwear with short trunks and a tank of a contrasting color or pattern

Tyrolean: men's hat of the 1930s with a wide brim, tapered crown, and feather in a corded hatband

U

ulster: a capacious, mid-calf length topcoat with varying details

umbrella-back coats: women's outerwear with triangular gores set into the back collar that flared into deep organ pipe folds

Union Jack jacket: mod sport coat constructed with red, white, and blue panels stitched together to resemble the British flag

union suits: one-piece underwear for both men and women; so named for the union of the top and drawers

utility look: the simplified, utilitarian styles of World War II fashions

V

vandyking: a form of trim cut in points resembling the sharply pointed beard of the artist Anthony Van Dyck

vanity case: handbag cosmetic containers with small, touch-up amounts of makeup and a mirror

velcro: nylon strips of material with a filament nap of hooks that held fast when pressed together

vest suit: a women's or men's long, sleeveless top with matching trousers or skirt popular in the early 1970s

Victoriana: clothing and accessories that featured revivalisms from the age of Queen Victoria (1837–1901)

viscose rayon: fabric made from synthetic yarns produced with viscous cellulose

waists: another name for shirtwaists

wash-and-wear: clothing made from synthetic or chemically treated fabrics that were shrink- and wrinkle-resistant

waspie: a constricting corselette popular in the early years of the New Look

Wellington boot: a men's high boot with a curving top in the front and a dipped curve in the back; named for the British general who defeated Napoleon at Waterloo

weskit: a men's jacket with a short, vest-cut hemline

whalefin: the V-shaped back of a bikini thong

wrapper: a woman's loose dressing robe

 Y Line: one of Dior's 1955 collections that featured dresses with balloon sleeves and other shoulder emphasis over slim skirts

zazous: young Frenchmen of World War II who dressed in long jackets with baggy, pegged trousers

zipper: a slide closure of interlocking teeth affixed to fabric or other material

zoot suit: an urban American men's suit of the early 1940s with an oversized, padded jacket and baggy, pegged trousers

bibliography

Adams, James. *Dandies and Desert Saints: Styles of Victorian Manhood*. Ithaca, NY: Cornell, 1995.

Agins, Teri. *The End of Fashion: The Mass Marketing of the Clothing Business*. New York: William Morrow, 1999.

Angeloglou, Maggie. *A History of Make-up*. London: Macmillan, 1965.

Armstrong, Nancy. *Victorian Jewelry*. New York: Macmillan, 1976.

Arnold, Janet. *Patterns of Fashion: English Women's Dresses and Their Construction 1660–1860*. London: Wace, 1964.

Ashdown, Emily. *British Costume During XIX Centuries*. London: T. C. and E. C. Jack, 1910.

Ashelford, Jane. *The Art of Dress: Clothes and Society 1500–1914*. London, National Trust, 1996.

Baclawski, Karen. *The Guide to Historic Costume*. New York: Drama, 1995.

Bailey, Adrian. *The Passion for Fashion: Three Centuries of Changing Styles*. Limpsfield, UK: Dragon's World, 1988.

Bailey, Perkins, ed. *Men's Wear: History of the Men's Wear Industry 1890–1950*. New York: Fairchild, 1950.

Baines, Barbara. *Fashion Revivals from the Elizabethan Age to the Present Day*. London: B. T. Batsford, 1981.

Baker, Patricia. *Fashions of a Decade: The 1940s*. New York: Facts on File, 1992.

_____. *Fashions of a Decade: The 1950s*. New York: Facts on File, 1991.

Ball, Joanne. *The Art of Fashion Accessories: A Twentieth Century Retrospective*. Atglen, PA: Schiffer, 1993.

Barber, Elizabeth. *Women's Work: The First Fifty Years*. New York: W. W. Norton, 1994.

Barfoot, Audrey. *Discovering Costume*. London: University of London, 1959.

Barnard, Malcolm. *Fashion as Communication*. London: Routledge, 1996.

Barnes, Ruth, and Joanne B. Eicher, eds. *Dress and Gender: Making and Meaning*. New York: Berg, 1992.

Bassett, Lynne Zacek. *Modesty Died When Clothes Were Born*. Hartford, CT: Mark Twain House and Museum, 2004.

Batterberry, Michael, and Ariane Batterberry. *Mirror, Mirror, A Social History of Fashion*. New York: Holt, Rinehart and Winston, 1977.

Battersby, Martin. *Art Deco Fashion: French Designers 1908–1925*. New York: St. Martin's, 1974.

Baudot, Francois. *The Allure of Men*. New York: Assouline, 2000.

_____. *Elsa Schiaparelli*. New York: Universe, 1997.

_____. *Fashion: the Twentieth Century*. New York: Universe, 1999.

Beaton, Cecil. *The Glass of Fashion*. London: Weidenfeld and Nicolson, 1954.

Bell, Quentin. *On Human Finery*. New York: Schocken, 1976.

Benson, Elaine, and John Esten. *Unmentionables: A Brief History of Underwear*. New York: Simon and Schuster, 1996.

Berendt, John. *Esquire Fashions for Men*. Rev. ed. New York: Harper and Row, 1966.

Biddle, Julian. *What Was Hot: A Rollercoaster Ride Through Six Decades of Pop Culture in America*. New York: MJF, 2001.

Bigelow, Marybelle. *Fashion in History: Western Dress, Prehistoric to Present*. Minneapolis, MN: Burgess, 1979.

Binder, Pearl. *The Peacock's Tail*. London: Harrap, 1958.

Black, J. Anderson, and Madge Garland. *A History of Fashion*. New York: William Morrow, 1981.

Blanc, Charles. *Art in Ornament and Dress*. Detroit: Tower, 1971.

Blanchard, Tamsin. *Antonio Berardi: Sex and Sensibility*. New York: Watson-Guptill, 1999.

Bond, David. *Glamour in Fashion*. London: Guinness, 1992.

Bonner, Paul, ed. *The World in Vogue*. New York: Viking, 1963.

Bordo, Susan. *The Male Body: A New Look at Men in Public and in Private*. New York: Farrar, Straus and Giroux, 1999.

Bosker, Gideon, and Lena Lencek. *Making Waves: Swimsuits and the Undressing of America*. San Francisco: Chronicle, 1988.

Boston, Lloyd. *Men of Color: Fashion, History, Fundamentals*. New York: Artisan, 1998.

Boucher, Francois. *A History of Costume in the West*. London: Thames and Hudson, 1967.

Bowman, Sara, and Michel Molinare. *A Fashion for Extravagance: Art Deco Fabrics and Fashions*. New York: E. P. Dutton, 1985.

Bradfield, Nancy. *Costume in Detail 1730–1930*. Boston: Plays, 1968.

Bradley, Carolyn G. *Western World Costume*. New York: Dover, 2001.

Bradshaw, Angela. *World Costumes*. New York: MacMillan, 1969.

Braun-Ronsdorf, Margarete. *Mirror of Fashion: A History of European Costume 1789–1929*. New York: McGraw-Hill, 1964.

Breward, Christopher. *The Culture of Fashion*. Manchester, UK: Manchester University, 1995.

_____. *The Hidden Consumer: Masculinities, Fashion, and City Life 1860–1914*. Manchester: Manchester University, 1999.

Brooke, Iris. *English Costume 1900–1950*. London: Methuen, 1951.

_____. *A Short History of European and American Shoes*. London: Pitmans, 1972.

Brown, Marcia. *Unsigned Beauties of Costume Jewelry*. Paducah, KY: Collector, 2000.

Brown, William. *American Men's Shirts 1750–1900*. Gettysburg, PA: Thomas, 1999.

Bruzzi, Stella, and Pamela Church Gibson, ed. *Fashion Cultures: Theories, Explorations, and Analysis*. London: Routledge, 2001.

Bryk, Nancy, ed. *American Dress Pattern Catalogs 1873–1909*. New York: Dover, 1988.

Buck, Anne. *Victorian Costume and Costume Accessories*. New York: Thomas Nelson, 1961.

Burrow, Ed J., ed. *A History of Feminine Fashion*. London: Ed J. Burrow, 1928.

Buttolph, Angela, et al. *The Fashion Book*. London: Phaidon, 1998.

Buxbaum, Gerda. *Icons of Fashion of the Twentieth Century*. Munich: Prestel Verlag, 1999.

Buzzaccarini, Vittoria de. *Elegance and Style: Two Hundred Years of Men's Fashions*. Milan: Lupetti, 1992.

Byrde, Penelope. *Nineteenth Century Fashion*. London: B. T. Batsford, 1992.

Calasibetta, Charlotte. *Essential Terms of Fashion*. New York: Fairchild, 1986.

Calthrop, Dion C. *English Costume from William I to George IV 1066–1830*. London: Adam and Charles Black, 1937.

_____. *English Dress from Victoria to George V*. London: Chapman and Hall, 1934.

Campbell, Emily, et al. *Inside Out: Underwear and Style in the UK*. London: Black Dog, 2000.

Carnegy, Vicky. *Fashions of a Decade: The 1980s*. New York: Facts on File, 1990.

Carter, Ernestine. *The Changing World of Fashion*. New York: G. P. Putnam's Sons, 1977.

_____. *With Tongue in Chic*. London: Michael Joseph, 1977.

Cashen, Marilynn. *A Moment in Time: Images of Victorian Fashions from the Mid-1800s*. South Plainfield, NJ: MAC, 1992.

Cassin-Scott, Jack. *Costume and Fashion in Color 1760–1920*. New York: MacMillan, 1971.

_____. *The Illustrated Encyclopedia of Costume and Fashion from 1066 to the Present*. London: Studio Vista, 1998.

Cassini, Oleg. *In My Own Fashion, an Autobiography*. New York: Simon and Schuster, 1987.

Castelbajac, Kate de. *The Face of the Century: One Hundred Years of Makeup and Style*. New York: Rizzoli, 1995.

Cawthorne, Nigel. *The New Look: The Dior Revolution*. Edison, NJ: Wellfleet, 1996.

Celant, Germano. *Giorgio Armani*. New York: Harry N. Abrams, 2000.

Chadwick, Luie. *Fashion Drawing and Design*. London: Batsford, 1926.

Chenoune, Farid. *A History of Men's Fashion*. Paris: Flammarion, 1993.

Chic Simple Partners. *Men's Wardrobe*. New York: Alfred A. Knopf, 1993.

Clark, Fiona. *Hats*. New York: Drama, 1982.

Cobrin, Harry. *The Men's Clothing Industry: Colonial Times Through Modern Times*. New York: Fairchild, 1970.

Cole, Shaun. *The Story of Men's Underwear*. New York: Parkstone, 2010.

Coleman, Elizabeth. *Changing Fashions 1800–1970*. Brooklyn, NY: Brooklyn Museum, 1972.

_____. *Of Men Only: A Review of Men's and Boy's Fashions 1750–1975*. Brooklyn, NY: Brooklyn Museum, 1975.

_____. *The Opulent Era: Fashions of Worth, Doucet, and Pingat*. New York: Thames and Hudson, 1990.

Coleridge, Nicholas. *The Fashion Conspiracy*. London: Heinemann, 1989.

Connickie, Yvonne. *Fashions of a Decade: The 1960s*. New York: Facts on File, 1991.

Connolly, Joseph. *All Shook Up: A Flash of the Fifties*. London: Cassell, 2000.

Contini, Mila. *Fashion from Ancient Egypt to the Present Day*. New York: Odyssey, 1965.

Cooper, Wendy. *Hair: Sex, Society, Symbolism*. New York: Stein and Day, 1971.

Cosgrave, Bronwyn. *The Complete History of Costume and Fashion from Ancient Egypt to the Present Day*. New York: Checkmark, 2000.

Costantino, Maria. *Fashions of a Decade: The 1930s*. New York: Facts on File, 1992.

_____. *Men's Fashion in the Twentieth Century: From Frock Coats to Intelligent Fibres*. London: B. T. Batsford, 1997.

Cox, Caroline. *Lingerie: A Lexicon of Style*. New York: St. Martin's, 2000.

Craik, Jennifer, ed. *The Face of Fashion: Cultural Studies in Fashion*. London: Routledge, 1994.

Crawford, M. D. C. *One World of Fashion*. New York: Fairchild, 1947.

Cremers-Van de Does, Eline. *The Agony of Fashion*. Trans. Leo Van Witsen. Poole, UK: Blandford, 1980.

Cumming, Valerie. *Understanding Fashion History*. New York: Costume and Fashion Press, 2004.

Cunningham, Patricia, ed. *Dress in American Culture*. Bowling Green, OH: Bowling Green State University, 1990.

Cunnington, C. Willett. *English Women's Clothing in the Nineteenth Century*. New York: Dover, 1990.

Cunnington, C. Willett, and Phillis Cunnington. *A Dictionary of English Costume 900–1900*. Philadelphia: Dufour, 1960.

_____. *The History of Underclothes*. London: Michael Joseph, 1951.

Cunnington, Phillis. *Children's Costume in England from the Fourteenth to the End of the Nineteenth Century*. London: Adam and Charles Black, 1965.

_____. *Costume in Pictures*. London: Herbert, 1981.

_____. *Handbook of English Costume in the Nineteenth Century*. London: Faber and Faber, 1970.

_____. *A Picture History of English Costume*. New York: MacMillan, 1960.

Dalrymple, Priscilla. *American Victorian Costume in Early Photographs*. New York: Dover, 1991.

D'Assailly, Gisele. *Ages of Elegance, Five Thousand Years of Fashion and Frivolity*. London: MacDonald, 1968.

Davenport, Millia. *The Book of Costume*. New York: Crown, 1948.

Daves, Jessica. *Ready-Made Miracle*. New York: G. P. Putnam's Sons, 1967.

de la Haye, Amy, and Cathie Dingwall. *Surfers, Soulies, Skinheads and Skaters*. New York: Overlook, 1996.

de la Haye, Amy, and Elizabeth Wilson, ed. *Defining Dress: Dress as Object, Meaning and Identity*. Manchester, UK: Manchester University, 1999.

de la Haye, Amy, and Shelley Tobin. *Chanel, the Couturier at Work*. New York: Overlook, 1995.

de la Haye, Amy, ed. *The Cutting Edge: Fifty Years of British Fashion, 1947–1997*. Woodstock, NY: Overlook, 1997.

_____. *Fashion Source Book: A Visual Reference to Twentieth Century Fashion*. Secaucus, NJ: Wellfleet, 1988.

Deloffre, Claude, ed. *Thierry Mugler: Fashion, Fetish, Fantasy*. Los Angeles: General, 1998.

de Marly, Diana. *Christian Dior*. New York: Holmes and Meier, 1990.

_____. *Fashion for Men: An Illustrated History*. New York: Holmes and Meier, 1989.

_____. *The History of Haute Couture 1850–1950*. New York: Holmes and Meier, 1980.

_____. *Worth: Father of Haute Couture*. New York: Holmes and Meier, 1991.

de Montebello, Philippe, et al. *The Imperial Style: Fashions of the Hapsburg Era*. New York: Metropolitan Museum of Art, 1980.

Diamonstein, Barbaralee. *Fashion: The Inside Story*. New York: Rizzoli, 1988.

Di Grappa, Carol. *Fashion: Theory*. New York: Lustrum, 1980.

Dior, Christian. *Christian Dior's Little Dictionary of Fashion*. London: Cassell, 1954.

Doran, John. *Habits and Men with Remnants of Record Touching the Makers of Both*. New York: Widdleton, 1865.

Dorner, Jane. *Fashion in the Forties and Fifties*. New Rochelle, NY: Arlington House, 1975.

_____. *Fashion: the Changing Shape of Fashion Through the Years*. London: Octopus, 1974.

Downey, Lynn, et al. *This is a Pair of Levi's Jeans: The Official History of the Levi's Brand*. San Francisco: Levi Strauss, 1995.

Drake, Nicholas. *The Fifties in Vogue*. New York: Henry Holt, 1987.

_____. *The Sixties: A Decade in Vogue*. New York: Prentice Hall, 1988.

Earnshaw, Pat. *Lace in Fashion from the Sixteenth to the Twentieth Centuries*. New York: Drama, 1985.

Edwards, Tim. *Men in the Mirror: Men's Masculinity and Consumer Fashion*. London: Cassell Academic, 1997.

Emmet, Boris. *Montgomery Ward Catalogue and Buyer's Guide*. New York: Dover, 1969.

English, Bonnie. *A Cultural History of Fashion in the Twentieth Century*. New York: Berg, 2007.

Epstein, Diana. *Buttons*. New York: Walker, 1968.

Evans, Caroline. *Fashion at the Edge: Spectacle, Modernity, and Deathliness*. New Haven: Yale University, 2003.

Evans, Mary. *Story of Textiles*. Boston: Little, Brown, 1942.

Evans, Mike, ed. *Key Moments in Fashion*. New York: Hamlyn, 1998.

Ewing, Elizabeth. *Dress and Undress*. New York: Drama, 1978.

_____. *Everyday Dress 1650–1900*. London: B. T. Batsford, 1984.

_____. *History of Children's Costume*. Charles Scribner's Sons, 1977.

_____. *History of Twentieth Century Fashion*. Lanham, MD: Barnes and Noble, 1992.

Farrell-Beck, Jane, and Colleen Gau. *Uplift: The Bra in America*. Philadelphia: University of Pennsylvania, 2002.

Feldman, Egal. *Fit for Men: A Study of New York's Clothing Trade*. New York: Public Affairs, 1960.

Feldman, Elane. *Fashions of a Decade: The 1990s*. New York: Facts on File, 1992.

Finlayson, Iain. *Denim: An American Legend*. New York: Fireside, 1990.

Fischer-Mirkin, Toby. *Dress Code: Understanding the Hidden Meanings of Women's Clothes*. New York: Clarkson N. Potter, 1995.

Flocker, Michael. *The Metrosexual Guide to Style: A Handbook for the Modern Man*. Cambridge, MA: Da Capo, 2003.

Flugel, J. C. *The Psychology of Clothes*. London: Hogarth, 1950.

Flusser, Alan. *Clothes and the Man*. New York: Villard, 1985.

_____. *Dressing the Man: Mastering the Art of Permanent Fashion*. New York: HarperCollins, 2002.

Foster, Vanda. *A Visual History of Costume in the Nineteenth Century*. London: B. T. Batsford, 1982.

Frankel, Susannah. *Visionaries: Interviews with Fashion Designers*. New York: Harry N. Abrams, 2001.

Fraser, Kennedy. *The Fashionable Mind*. New York: Alfred A. Knopf, 1981.

Fukai, Akiko, et al. *Fashion: A History from the Eighteenth to the Twentieth Century*. Los Angeles: Taschen America, 2005.

Gaines, Jane, and Charlotte Herzog, ed. *Fabrications: Costume and the Female Body*. New York: Routledge, 1990.

Gale, Bill. *Esquire's Fashions for Today*. New York: Harper and Row, 1973.

Garland, Madge, et al. *Fashion 1900–1939*. London: Idea, 1975.

_____. *Fashion: A Picture Guide to Its Creators and Creations*. Harmondsworth, UK: Penguin, 1962.

Geijer, Agnes. *A History of Textile Art*. London: Phillip Wilson, 1982.

Gere, Charlotte. *European and American Jewellery 1830–1914*. London: Heinemann, 1975.

Gernsheim, Alison. *Fashion and Reality*. London: Faber and Faber, 1963.

_____. *Victorian and Edwardian Fashion*. New York: Dover, 1981.

Gillow, John. *World Textiles: A Visual Guide to Traditional Techniques*. Boston: Bulfinch, 1999.

Ginsburg, Madeleine. *The Hat: Trends and Traditions*. Hauppage, NY: Barron's Educational, 1990.

Glynn, Prudence, and Madeleine Ginsburg. *In Fashion: Dress in the Twentieth Century*. London: George Allen and Unwin, 1978.

Glynn, Prudence. *Skin to Skin: Exoticism in Dress*. New York: Oxford University, 1982.

Gold, Annalee. *One World of Fashion*. New York: Fairchild, 1987.

Goldthorpe, Caroline. *From Queen to Empress: Victorian Dress 1837–1877*. New York: Metropolitan Museum of Art, 1988.

Gorsline, Douglas. *What People Wore*. New York: Viking, 1952.

Graham, Nicolas. *A Brief History of Shorts: The Ultimate Guide to Understanding Your Underwear*. San Francisco: Chronicle, 1995.

Grass, Milton. *History of Hosiery: From the Piloi of Ancient Greece to the Nylons of Modern America*. New York: Fairchild, 1955.

Graveline, Noel. *Jeans: Levis Story*. Paris: Minerva, 1990.

Greeley, Horace, et al. *Great Industries of the United States*. Hartford, CT: Burr and Hyde, 1872.

Greenwood, Kathryn, and Mary Murphy. *Fashion Innovation and Marketing*. New York: MacMillan, 1978.

Griffin, Gary. *The History of Men's Underwear from Union Suits to Bikini Briefs*. Los Angeles: Added Dimensions, 1991.

Gross, Elaine, and Fred Rottman. *Halston: An American Original*. New York: HarperCollins, 1999.

Gross, Kim. *Chic, Simple Men's Wardrobe*. New York: Alfred A. Knopf, 1998.

Gutner, Howard. *Gowns by Adrian: The MGM Years 1928–1941*. New York: Harry N. Abrams, 2001.

Hall, Carolyn. *The Forties in Vogue*. New York: Harmony, 1985.

_____. *The Thirties in Vogue*. New York: Harmony, 1985.

_____. *The Twenties in Vogue*. New York: Harmony, 1983.

Hall, Lee. *Common Threads: A Parade of American Clothing*. Boston: Bulfinch, 1992.

Hannah, Barry, et al. *Men Without Ties*. New York: Abbeville, 1994.

Hansen, Joseph, et al. *Cosmetics, Fashions, and the Exploitation of Women*. New York: Pathfinder, 1986.

Harris, Alice. *The White T*. New York: Harper Style, 1996.

Harris, Jennifer, ed. *Textiles: Five Thousand Years*. New York: Harry N. Abrams, 1993.

Harris, Kristina. *The Child in Fashion 1750–1920*. Atglen, PA: Schiffer, 1999.

_____. *Victorian and Edwardian Fashions for Women 1840–1919*. Atglen, PA: Schiffer, 1995.

Harrison, Martin. *Beauty Photography in Vogue*. New York: Stewart, Tabori and Chang, 1987.

Harvey, John. *Men in Black*. Chicago: University of Chicago, 1995.

Heard, Gerald. *Narcissus: An Anatomy of Clothes*. New York: E. P. Dutton, 1924.

Hecht, Ann. *The Art of the Loom: Weaving, Spinning, and Dyeing Across the World*. New York: Rizzoli, 1990.

Herald, Jacqueline. *Fashions of a Decade: The 1920s*. New York: Facts on File, 1991.

_____. *Fashions of a Decade: The 1970s*. New York: Facts on File, 1991.

Hill, Daniel Delis. *Advertising to the American Woman 1900–1999*. Columbus: Ohio State University, 2002.

_____. *American Menswear from the Civil War to the Twenty-First Century*. Lubbock: Texas Tech University, 2011.

_____. *As Seen in Vogue: A Century of American Fashion in Advertising*. Lubbock: Texas Tech University, 2004.

_____. *History of Men's Underwear and Swimwear*. San Antonio: Daniel Delis Hill, 2011.

_____. *History of World Costume and Fashion*. Columbus, OH: Prentice Hall, 2010.

Hill, Margot, and Peter Bucknell. *The Evolution of Fashion: Pattern and Cut from 1066–1930*. London: B. T. Batsford, 1967.

Hix, Charles. *Looking Good: A Guide for Men*. New York: Hawthorn, 1977.

_____. *Man Alive: Dressing the Free Way*. New York: Simon and Schuster, 1984.

Holland, Vyvyan. *Hand Coloured Fashion Plates 1770–1899*. London: B. T. Batsford, 1955.

Hollander, Anne. *Seeing Through Clothes*. New York: Avon, 1978.

Holmes, Martin. *Stage Costumes and Accessories in the London Museum*. London: Her Majesty's Stationery Office, 1968.

Hoobler, Dorothy, and Thomas Hoobler. *Vanity Rules: A History of American Fashion and Beauty*. Brookfield, CT: Twenty-First Century, 2000.

Howell. Georgina. *In Vogue: Seventy-Five Years of Style*. London: Conde Nast, 1991.

Hunt, Marsha. *The Way We Wore: Styles of the 1930s and '40s*. Fallbrook, CA: Fallbrook, 1993.

Hurlock, Elizabeth. *The Psychology of Dress: An Analysis of Fashion and Its Motives*. Manchester, NH: Ayer, 1980.

Jobling, Paul. *Man Appeal: Advertising, Modernism, and Menswear*. Oxford, UK: Berg, 2005.

Joselit, Jenna Weissman. *A Perfect Fit: Clothes, Character, and the Promise of America*. New York: Metropolitan, 2001.

Jouve, Marie-Andree. *Balenciaga*. New York: Universe, 1997.

Kaiser, Susan. *The Social Psychology of Clothing*. New York: Macmillan, 1990.

Karpinski, Kenneth. *Red Socks Don't Work: Messages from the Real World About Men's Clothing*. Manassas Park, VA: Impact, 1994.

Keenan, Brigid. *Dior in Vogue*. New York: Harmony, 1981.

Kemper, Rachel. *Costume*. New York: Newsweek, 1977.

Kennedy, Sarah. *The Swimsuit*. London: Carlton, 2007.

Kerr, Rose. *One Hundred Years of Costumes in America*. Worcester, MA: Davis, 1981.

Keyes, Jean. *A History of Women's Hairstyles 1500–1965*. London: Methuen, 1967.

Klein, Kelly. *Underworld*. New York: Alfred A. Knopf, 1995.

Koda, Harold. *Extreme Beauty: The Body Transformed*. New York: Metropolitan Museum of Art, 2001.

Kunzle, David. *Fashion and Fetishism*. Totowa, NJ: Rowman and Littlefield, 1992.

Kurella, Elizabeth. *The Complete Guide to Vintage Textiles*. Iola, WI: Krause, 1999.

Kutchta, David. *The Three-Piece Suit and Modern Masculinity: England 1550–1850*. Berkeley: University of California, 2002.

Kybalova, Ludmila. *The Pictorial Encyclopedia of Fashion*. Trans. Claudia Rosoux. London: Hamlyn, 1968.

Laver, James. *Children's Fashions in the Nineteenth Century*. London: B. T. Batsford, 1951.

_____. *A Concise History of Costume and Fashion*. London: Thames and Hudson, 1979.

_____. *Costume and Fashion*. London: Thames and Hudson, 1995.

_____. *Dress: How and Why Fashions in Men's and Women's Clothes Have Changed During the Past Two Hundred Years*. London: John Murray, 1950.

_____. *Edwardian Promenade*. Boston: Houghton Mifflin, 1958.

_____. *Modesty in Dress*. London: Heinemann, 1969.

_____. *Victoriana*. New York: Hawthorne, 1967.

Lee, Sarah, ed. *American Fashion*. New York: Fashion Institute, 1975.

Lee-Potter, Charlie. *Sportswear in Vogue Since 1910*. New York: Abbeville, 1984.

Lees, Elizabeth. *Costume Design in the Movies*. London: BCW, 1976.

Lehnert, Gertrud. *A History of Fashion in the Twentieth Century*. Cologne: Konemann, 2000.

_____. *Fashion: A Concise History*. London: Laurence King, 1998.

Lester, Katherine, and Rose Kerr. *Historic Costume*. Peoria, IL: Charles A. Bennett, 1977.

Levin, Phyllis. *The Wheels of Fashion*. Garden City, NY: Doubleday, 1965.

Levitt, Sarah. *Victorians Unbuttoned*. Boston: Allen and Unwin, 1986.

Ley, Sandra. *Fashion for Everyone, the Story of Ready-to-Wear 1870s–1970s*. New York: Charles Scribner's Sons, 1975.

Liberman, Alexander, ed. *On the Edge: Images from One Hundred Years of Vogue*. New York: Random House, 1992.

Lipovetsky, Gilles. *The Empire of Fashion*. Trans. Catherine Porter. Princeton, NJ: Princeton University, 1994.

Lobenthal, Joel. *Radical Rags: Fashions of the Sixties*. New York: Abbeville, 1990.

Loring, John. *Tiffany in Fashion*. New York: Harry N. Abrams, 2003.

Lurie, Alison. *The Language of Clothes*. New York: Henry Holt, 2000.

Lussier, Suzanne. *Art Deco Fashion*. New York: Bulfinch, 2003.

Lynam, Ruth, ed. *Couture*. Garden City, NY: Doubleday, 1972.

Mackrell, Alice. *An Illustrated History of Fashion: Five Hundred Years of Fashion Illustration.* New York: Drama, 1997.

_____. *Art and Fashion: The Impact of Art on Fashion and Fashion on Art.* London: B. T. Batsford, 2005.

_____. *Paul Poiret.* New York: Holmes and Meier, 1990.

MacPhail, Anna. *The Well-Dressed Child: Children's Clothing 1820–1940.* Atglen, PA: Schiffer, 1999.

Maeder, Edward. *Hollywood and History: Costume Design in Film.* London: Thames and Hudson, 1987.

_____. *Salvatore Ferragamo: Art of the Shoe 1896–1960.* New York: Rizzoli, 1992.

Malossi, Giannino, ed. *Material Man: Masculinity, Sexuality, Style.* New York: Harry N. Abrams, 2000.

Mansour, David. *From Abba to Zoom: A Pop Culture Encyclopedia of the Late 20th Century.* Kansas City, MO: Andrews McMeel, 2005.

Marcus, Stanley. *Minding the Store.* New York: Little Brown, 1974.

Marks, Susan. *In the Mood for Munsingwear.* St. Paul, MN: Minnesota Historical Society, 2011.

Martin, Richard, and Harold Koda. *Cubism and Fashion.* New Haven: Yale University, 1999.

_____. *Giorgio Armani: Images of Man.* New York: Rizzoli, 1990.

_____. *Jocks and Nerds: Men's Style in the Twentieth Century.* New York: Rizzoli, 1989.

_____. *Splash! A History of Swimwear.* New York: Rizzoli, 1990.

Martin, Richard. *American Ingenuity: Sportswear 1930s–1970s.* New York: Metropolitan Museum of Art, 1998.

_____. *Charles James.* New York: Universe, 1999.

_____. *Fashion and Surrealism.* New York: Rizzoli, 1996.

_____. *Versace.* New York: Universe, 1997.

McClellan, Elisabeth. *History of American Costume 1607–1870.* New York: Tudor, 1969.

McDowell, Colin. *Fashion Today.* New York: Phaidon, 2000.

_____. *Hats: Status, Style, and Glamour.* New York: Rizzoli, 1992.

_____. *A Hundred Years of Royal Style.* London: Muller, Blond, and White, 1985.

_____. *McDowell's Directory of Twentieth Century Fashion.* Englewood Cliffs, NJ: Prentice Hall, 1985.

_____. *Shoes: Fashion and Fantasy.* London: Thames and Hudson, 1992.

_____. *The Man of Fashion.* London: Thames and Hudson, 1997.

McNabb, Nan. *Body Bizarre, Body Beautiful.* New York: Fireside, 1999.

McNeill, Peter, and Vicki Karaminas, eds. *The Men's Fashion Reader.* London: Berg, 2009.

McRobbie, Angela. *British Fashion Design: Rag Trade or Image Industry?* London: Routledge, 1998.

_____. *In Culture Society: Art, Fashion, and Popular Music.* London: Routledge, 1999.

Mears, Patricia. *American Beauty: Aesthetics and Innovation in Fashion.* New York: Fashion Institute of Technology, 2009.

Meller, Susan, and Joost Elffers. *Textile Designs: Two Hundred Years of European and American Patterns.* New York: Harry N. Abrams, 1991.

Mendes, Valerie, and Amy de la Haye. *Twentieth-Century Fashion.* London: Thames and Hudson, 1999.

Mendes, Valerie. *John French: Fashion Photographer.* London: Victoria and Albert Museum, 1984.

Metzner, Sheila. *Form and Fashion.* Santa Fe, NM: Arena, 2001.

Milbank, Caroline. *New York Fashion.* New York: Harry N. Abrams, 1996.

Mo, Charles. *Evening Elegance: One Hundred Fifty Years of Formal Fashions.* Charlotte, NC: Mint Museum of Art, 1998.

Moffitt, Phillip, et al. *The American Man 1946–1986.* New York: Esquire, 1986.

Montgomery, Florence. *Textiles in America 1650–1870.* New York: W. W. Norton, 1983.

Moore, Doris. *Fashion Through Fashion Plates 1771–1970.* New York: Clarkson Potter, 1971.

Morris, Bernadine. *The Fashion Makers.* New York: Random House, 1978.

_____. *Valentino.* New York: Universe, 1996.

Morris, Bob, and Ben Widdicombe. *The Blue Jean.* New York: Powerhouse, 2002.

Muir, Robin. *Clifford Coffin: Photographs from Vogue 1945 to 1955.* New York: Stewart, Tabori, and Chang, 1997.

Mulvagh, Jane. *Costume Jewelry in Vogue.* London: Thames and Hudson, 1988.

_____. *Vogue: History of Twentieth Century Fashion.* London: Viking, 1988.

Mulvaney, Jay. *Jackie: The Clothes of Camelot.* New York: St. Martin's, 2001.

Mulvey, Kate, and Melissa Richards. *Decades of Beauty: the Changing Image of Women 1890s–1990s.* New York: Reed Consumer, 1998.

Newman, Cathy. *Fashion.* Washington, DC: National Geographic Society, 2001.

Nixon, Sean. *Hard Looks: Masculinities, Spectatorship and Contemporary Consumption.* New York: St. Martin's, 1996.

Norris, Herbert. *Nineteenth-Century Costume and Fashion.* Mineola, NY: Dover, 1999.

Nunn, Joan. *Fashion in Costume 1200–1980.* New York: Schocken, 1984.

Nystrom, Paul. *Economics of Fashion.* New York: Ronald, 1928.

O'Hara, Georgina. *The Encyclopaedia of Fashion.* New York: Harry N. Abrams, 1986.

O'Keefe, Linda. *Shoes: A Celebration of Pumps, Sandals, Slippers, and More.* New York: Workman, 1996.

Olian, Joanne. *Authentic French Fashions of the Twenties.* New York: Dover, 1990.

_____. *Children's Fashions 1860–1912.* New York: Dover, 1993.

Omelianuk, Scott, and Ted Allen. *Esquire's Things a Man Should Know About Style.* New York: Riverhead, 1999.

Packer, William. *The Art of Vogue Covers 1909–1940.* New York: Bonanza, 1980.

_____. *Fashion Drawing in Vogue.* New York: Thames and Hudson, 1983.

Parsons, Frank. *The Psychology of Dress.* Garden City, NY: Doubleday, Page, 1921.

Pavia, Fabienne. *The World of Perfume.* New York: Knickerbocker, 1996.

Peacock, John. *The Chronicle of Western Fashion from Ancient Times to the Present Day.* New York: Harry N. Abrams, 1991.

_____. *Fashion Accessories: The Complete Twentieth-Century Sourcebook.* New York: Thames and Hudson, 2000.

_____. *Fashion Source: The 1920s.* New York: Thames and Hudson, 1997.

_____. *Fashion Source: The 1930s.* New York: Thames and Hudson, 1997.

_____. *Fashion Source: The 1940s.* New York: Thames and Hudson, 1998.

_____. *Fashion Source: The 1950s.* New York: Thames and Hudson, 1997.

_____. *Fashion Source: The 1960s.* New York: Thames and Hudson, 1998.

_____. *Fashion Source: The 1970s.* New York: Thames and Hudson, 1997.

_____. *Fashion Source: The 1980s.* New York: Thames and Hudson, 1998.

_____. *Men's Fashion: The Complete Sourcebook.* London: Thames and Hudson, 1996.

Perrot, Philippe. *Fashioning the Bourgeoisie: A History of Clothing in the Nineteenth Century.* Trans. Richard Bienvenu. Princeton, NJ: Princeton University, 1987.

Poiret, Paul. *My First Fifty Years.* Trans. Stephen Guest. London: Victor Gollancz, 1931.

Polhemus, Ted. *Street Style: From Sidewalk to Catwalk.* London: Thames and Hudson, 1994.

_____. *Style Surfing: What to Wear in the Third Millennium.* New York: Thames and Hudson, 1996.

Probert, Christina. *Hats in Vogue since 1910.* New York: Abbeville, 1981.

_____. *Lingerie in Vogue since 1910.* New York: Abbeville, 1981.

_____. *Shoes in Vogue since 1910.* New York: Abbeville, 1981.

_____. *Swimwear in Vogue since 1910.* New York: Abbeville, 1981.

Raymond, Walter, ed. *Menswear: Seventy-Five Years of Fashion.* New York: Fairchild, 1965.

Ribeiro, Aileen. *Dress and Morality.* New York: Holmes and Meier, 1986.

_____. *Ingres in Fashion.* New Haven: Yale University, 1999.

_____. *The Visual History of Costume.* New York: Drama, 1997.

Ribeiro, Aileen, and Valerie Cumming. *The Visual History of Costume.* London: B. T. Batsford, 1989.

Robinson, Julian. *Body Packaging: A Guide to Human Sexual Display.* Los Angeles: Elysium Growth, 1988.

_____. *The Fine Art of Fashion: An Illustrated History.* New York: Bartley and Jensen, 1989.

Roetzel, Berhard. *Gentlemen: A Timeless Fashion.* Cologne: Konemann Verlagsgesellschaft, 1999.

Rosenblum, Robert. *Jean-Auguste-Dominique Ingres.* New York: Harry N. Abrams, 1990.

Ross, Geoffrey Aquilina. *The Day of the Peacock: Style for Men 1963–1973.* London: V&A, 2011.

Ross, Josephine. *Beaton in Vogue.* New York: Clarkson N. Potter, 1986.

Ruby, Jennifer. *Costume in Context: The 1920s and 1930s.* London: B. T. Batsford, 1988.

_____. *Costume in Context 1930–1945.* London: B. T. Batsford, 1995.

_____. *Costume in Context: The 1960s and 1970s.* London: B. T. Batsford, 1989.

_____. *Costume in Context: The Edwardians and the First World War.* London: B. T. Batsford, 1988.

_____. *Costume in Context: Underwear.* London: B. T. Batsford, 1996.

_____. *Costume in Context: The Victorians.* London: B. T. Batsford, 1994.

_____. *People in Costume: The 1970s and 1980s.* London: Chrysalis, 1988.

Rudofsky, Bernard. *Are Clothes Modern?* Chicago: Paul Theobald, 1947.

Russell, Douglas. *Costume History and Style.* Englewood Cliffs, NJ: Prentice Hall, 1983.

Ruttenber, Edward. *The American Male: His Fashions and Foibles.* New York: Fairchild, 1948.

Sato, Pater. *Fashion Illustration in New York.* Tokyo: Graphic-Sha, 1985.

Schnurnberger, Lynn. *Let There Be Clothes: 40,000 Years of Fashion.* New York: Workman, 1991.

Schoeffler, O. E., and William Gale. *Esquire's Encyclopedia of Twentieth Century Men's Fashions.* New York: McGraw-Hill, 1973.

Seeling, Charlotte. *Fashion: The Century of the Designer 1900–1999.* Cologne: Konemann Verlagsgesellschaft, 1999.

Selbie, Robert. *The Anatomy of Costume.* New York: Crescent, 1977.

Shaw, William. *American Men's Wear 1861–1982.* Baton Rouge: Oracle, 1982.

Sherwood, James. *Bespoke: The Men's Style of Savile Row.* New York: Rizzoli, 2010.

Shover, Edna. *Art in Costume Design.* Springfield, MA: Milton Bradley, 1920.

Sichel, Marion. *Costume Reference: 1918–1939.* Vol. 8. Boston: Plays, 1978.

_____. *Costume Reference 1939–1950.* Vol. 9. London: B. T. Batsford, 1987.

_____. *Costume Reference: Edwardians.* Vol. 7. New York: Chelsea House, 1978.

_____. *Costume Reference: Regency.* Vol. 5. New York: Chelsea House, 1978.

_____. *Costume Reference: Victorians.* Vol. 6. New York: Chelsea House, 1986.

_____. *History of Children's Costume.* London: Batsford Academic and Educational, 1984.

_____. *History of Men's Costume, Roman to 1930s.* London: B. T. Batsford, 1984.

_____. *History of Women's Costume.* London: Batsford Academic and Educational, 1984.

Simonds, Cherri. *Costume Jewelry.* Paducah, KY: Collector, 1997.

Smith, Desire. *Fashion Footwear 1800–1970.* Atglen, PA: Schiffer, 2000.

Spignesi, Stephen. *American Firsts: Innovations, Discoveries, and Gadgets Born in the USA.* New York: Barnes and Noble, 2004.

Squire, Geoffrey. *Dress and Society 1560–1970.* New York: Viking, 1974.

_____. *Dress, Art and Society.* London: Studio Vista, 1974.

Steele, Valerie. *The Corset: A Cultural History.* New Haven: Yale University, 2001.

_____. *Fashion and Eroticism: Ideals of Feminine Beauty from the Victorian Era to the Jazz Age.* New York: Oxford University, 1985.

_____. *Fifty Years of Fashion: New Look to Now.* New Haven: Yale University, 1997.

_____. *Handbags: A Lexicon of Style.* New York: Rizzoli, 2000.

_____. *Men and Women, Dressing the Part.* Washington, DC: Smithsonian Institution, 1989.

_____. *Paris Fashion: A Cultural History.* New York: Oxford University, 1988.

_____. *Red Dress.* New York: Rizzoli, 2001.

_____. *Shoes: A Lexicon of Style.* New York: Rizzoli, 1999.

Strong, Roy. *Gianni Versace: Do Not Disturb.* New York: Abbeville, 1996.

Stuart, Dorothy. *Boy Through the Ages.* London: George Harrap, 1947.

Summers, Leigh. *Bound to Please: A History of the Victorian Corset.* New York: Oxford University, 2001.

Swan, June. *Shoes.* London: B. T. Batsford, 1982.

Swenson, Marge, and Gerri Pinckney. *New Image for Men: Color and Wardrobe.* Costa Mesa, CA: Fashion Academy, 1983.

Taylor. Lou. *The Study of Dress History.* Manchester, UK: Manchester University, 2002.

Thieme, Otto Charles. *Simply Stunning: Two Hundred Years of Fashion from the Cincinnati Art Museum.* Cincinnati: Cincinnati Art Museum, 1988.

Thieme, Otto, et al. *With Grace and Favor: Victorian and Edwardian Fashion in America.* Cincinnati: Cincinnati Art Museum, 1993.

Tilberis, Elizabeth, ed. *Vogue: Seventy-Five Years.* London: Conde Nast, 1991.

Tilke, Max. *Costume Patterns and Designs.* New York: Frederick A. Praeger, 1957.

Torrens, Deborah. *Fashion Illustrated: A Review of Women's Dress 1920–1950.* New York: Hawthorne, 1975.

Tortora, Phyllis, and Keith Eubank. *Survey of Historic Costume.* Fifth ed. New York: Fairchild, 2010.

Tozer, Jane, and Sarah Levitt. *Fabric of Society: A Century of People and Their Clothes 1770–1870.* Manchester, UK: Laura Ashley, 1983.

Tucker, Andrew. *London Fashion Book.* London: Thames and Hudson, 1998.

Turnudich, Daniela, ed. *1940s Hairstyles.* Longbeach, CA: Streamline, 2001.

Uzanne, Octave. *Fashion in Paris: The Various Phases of Feminine Taste and Aesthetics from 1797 to 1897.* London: William Heinemann, 1898.

Versace, Gianni. *Rock and Royalty.* New York: Abbeville, 1996.

_____. *Signatures.* New York: Abbeville, 1992.

Vreeland, Diana. *Allure.* Boston: Bulfinch, 2002.

Walkley, Christina. *Dressed to Impress 1840–1914.* London: B. T. Batsford, 1989.

Warwick, Edward, et al. *Early American Dress.* New York: Benjamin Blom, 1965.

Watson, Linda. Vogue: *Twentieth Century Fashion.* London: Carelton, 1999.

_____. *Vogue Fashion: Over 100 years of Style by Decade and Designer.* Ontario: Firefly, 2010.

Waugh, Norah. *Corsets and Crinolines.* London: B. T. Batsford, 1954.

_____. *The Cut of Women's Clothes 1600–1930.* New York: Theatre Arts, 1968.

Webb, Wilfred. *The Heritage of Dress.* London: Times Book Club, 1912.

Wheeler, R. E. M. *Costume 1558–1933.* London: Lancaster House, 1934.

White, Palmer. *Elsa Schiaparelli: Empress of Paris Fashion.* London: Aurum, 1986.

_____. *Poiret.* New York: Clarkson Potter, 1973.

Wilcox, Claire. *Radical Fashion.* London: Victoria and Albert Museum, 2001.

Wilcox, Claire, and Valerie Mendes. *Modern Fashion in Detail.* Woodstock, NY: Overlook, 1991.

Wilcox, Turner. *Dictionary of Costume.* New York: Charles Scribner's Sons, 1969.

_____. *Five Centuries of American Costume.* New York: Charles Scribner's Sons, 1963.

_____. *The Mode in Costume.* New York: Charles Scribner's Sons, 1958.

_____. *The Mode in Footwear.* New York: Charles Scribner's Sons, 1958.

_____. *The Mode in Furs.* New York: Charles Scribner's Sons, 1951.

_____. *The Mode in Hats and Dresses.* New York: Charles Scribner's Sons, 1945.

Wilson, Carrie. *Fashions Since Their Debut.* Scranton, PA: International Text, 1945.

Winters, Peggy, et al. *What Works in Fashion Advertising.* New York: Retail Reporting, 1996.

Worrell, Estelle. *American Costume 1840–1920.* Harrisburg, PA: Stackpole, 1979.

Wykes-Joyce, Max. *Cosmetics and Adornment.* New York: Philosophical Library, 1961.

Yarwood, Doreen. *The Encyclopedia of World Costume.* New York: Bonanza, 1978.

_____. *Fashion in the Western World 1500–1990.* New York: Drama, 1992.

Zahm, Volker. *The Art of Creating Fashion.* Pocking, Germany: Mondi, 1991.

Advertising Periodicals

Advertising Age (1930 to present)
Adweek (1960 to present)
Journal of Advertising (1960 to present)
Printers' Ink (1888–1967)

Fashion, Costume, and Popular Culture Periodicals

Allure (1991 to present)
American Magazine (1876–1956)
Apparel Arts (1931–1957)
Arthur's Home Magazine (1852–1898)
Bride's (1934 to present)
CIBA Review (1937–1975)
Collier's (1888–1957)
Cosmopolitan (1886 to present)
Country Gentleman (1853–1955)
Delineator (1873–1937)
Details (1982 to present)
Dress (1975 to present)
Ebony (1945 to present)
Elle (1985 to present)

Esquire (1933 to present)
Essence (1970 to present)
Fashion Theory (1997 to present)
Flair (1950–1951)
Fortune (1930–present)
Glamour (1939 to present)
Genre (1991 to 2009)
Gentlemen's Quarterly (GQ) (1957 to present)
Godey's Lady's Book (1830–1898)
Good Housekeeping (1885 to present)
Graham's (1839–1858)
Harper's Bazaar (1867 to present)
Ladys' Book (1830–1839)
Ladies' Companion (1834–1844)
Ladies' Home Journal (1883 to present)
Ladies' Repository (1841–1876)

Ladies' World (1880–1918)
Life (1936–1972)
Look (1937–1971)
M (1983–1992)
Mademoiselle (1935–2001)
McCall's (1876 to present)
McClure's (1893–1929)
Men's Guide to Fashion (MGF) (1984–1991)
Men's Vogue (2006–2009)
Men's Wear (1890–1983)
Mirabella (1989–2000)
Modern Bride (1949 to present)
Munsey's (1889–1979)
National Geographic (1888 to present)
Peterson's Magazine (1837–1898)

Redbook (1903 to present)
Rolling Stone (1967 to present)
Sassy (1988 to present)
Saturday Evening Post (1821–1969)
Seventeen (1944 to present)
Sew News (1984 to present)
Threads (1985–1991)
Town & Country (1846 to present)
Vanity Fair (1913–1936, 1983 to present)
Vogue (1892 to present)
Vogue Pattern Book (1925 to present)
W (1971 to present)
Woman's Day (1937 to present)
Woman's Magazine (1896–1920)
Women's Wear Daily (1910 to present)

photo credits

Chapter 1

F. 1-2: Francois Henri Mulard (1769–1850) "Portrait of a lady wearing a white dress with a paisley shawl and holding a glove." Ca. 1810, Oil on canvas, 39.4 × 31.7 in./100 × 80.6 cm. Photo by H. Churchyard. **F. 1-4:** Madame de Senonnes, 1814–16 (oil on canvas) by Jean Auguste Dominique Ingres (1780–1867). Musee des Beaux-Arts, Nantes, France/Giraudon/The Bridgeman Art Library. **F. 1-5 (left):** Ingres, Jean Auguste Dominique (1780–1867). Mme. Riviere. Oil on canvas, 116 × 90 cm. Louvre, Paris, France. Reunion des Musees Nationaux/Gerard Blot/Art Resource, NY. **F. 1-5 (right):** The Design Library, New York, USA/The Bridgeman Art Library International. **F. 1-16:** Bibliotheque Nationale de France. **F. 1-20:** Bibliotheque des Arts Decoratifs, Paris, France/Archives Charmet/The Bridgeman Art Library International. **F. 1-22:** Sir William Beechey "Portrait of a Young Girl (Little Mary)". Philadelphia Museum of Art: Gift of Mrs. John S. Williams, 1946. 1946-88-1.

Chapter 2

F. 2-3: Winterhalter, Franz Xaver (1805–1873). Empress Eugenie surrounded by the ladies of her court, 1855. Oil on canvas, 300 × 420 cm. Chateau, Compiegne, France. Reunion des Musees Nationaux/Art Resource, NY. **F. 2-5 (bottom right); F. 2-13; F. 2-17; F. 2-27 (center); F. 2-27 (right):** www.antique-fashion.com/Karen Augusta.

Chapter 4

F. 4-8 (left): National Archives and Records Administration; **(right):** © CORBIS All Rights Reserved.

Chapter 5

F. 5-1 (1st row, 4th image): Used with permission of General Electric; **(2nd row, 3rd image):** Courtesy Bell & Howell, Inc.; **(2nd row, 4th image):** Used with permission from RCA Trademark Management S.A. **F. 5-2 (left):** Courtesy, Goodrich Corporation; **(right):** Courtesy, Talon. **F. 5-11:** Photo used courtesy of Macy's Archives. **F. 5-17 (left):** Courtesy of Ferguson Archives. **F. 5-20 (top):** CORBIS-NY. **F. 5-22 (bottom, 3rd image):** Courtesy The John B. Stetson Company; **(bottom, 4th image):** By permission of In Mocean Group, LLC.

Chapter 6

F. 6-1 (left): Russell Lee/Library of Congress; **(right):** CORBIS-NY. **F. 6-3:** Crown Zippers. **F. 6-4 (left):** Courtesy Spiegel Brands Inc. **F. 6-6 (bottom left, bottom center):** Photo used courtesy of Macy's Archives. **F. 6-9:** Courtesy of Ferguson Archives. **F. 6-13 (bottom right):** Courtesy of Ferguson Archives. **F. 6-14 (right):** Courtesy Cartier Archives © Cartier. **F. 6-15 (left):** Courtesy, Revlon. **F. 6-16 (3rd row, 2nd image):** Photo used courtesy of Macy's Archives. **F. 6-17 (top left, top right):** Courtesy of Whiting & Davis, A Sperian Company. **F. 6-22 (right):** We would like to acknowledge and thank Phillips-Van Heusen Corporation, the owner of the VAN HEUSEN, IZOD, and ARROW trademarks. **F. 6-28 (left):** Used with permission from Jockey International, Inc. **F. 6-29 (left):** By permission of In Mocean Group, LLC. **F. 6-32 (left):** Courtesy Swank, Inc.

Chapter 7

F. 7-1 (left): Image copyrighted by Chevron Corporation and/or its subsidiaries and used with permission; **(center):** Courtesy 3M Corporation; **(right):** Courtesy Navistar, Inc. **F. 7-2 (top):** ENKA®, Used by permission; **(bottom right):** Photo used courtesy of Macy's Archives. **F. 7-5 (left):** AP Wide World Photos. **F. 7-6 (left):** Courtesy of Ferguson Archives; **(right):** We would like to acknowledge and thank Phillips-Van Heusen Corporation, the owner of the VAN HEUSEN, IZOD, and ARROW trademarks. **F. 7-12:** Courtesy of Ferguson Archives. **F. 7-14 (center, right):** Courtesy Spiegel Brands Inc. **F. 7-20 (top row):** Courtesy Spiegel Brands Inc.; **(2nd row, 3rd image; 2nd row, 4th image; bottom left):** Courtesy The John B. Stetson Company; **(bottom right):** Revlon. **F. 7-21 (top left):** Courtesy Georg Jensen; **(bottom left):** Courtesy Spiegel Brands Inc. **F. 7-23:** © Bettmann/CORBIS. **F. 7-26 (bottom right); F. 7-28; F. 7-30; F. 7-36 (center):** Courtesy Spiegel Brands Inc. **F. 7-35 (left):** Courtesy Unilever.

Chapter 8

F. 8-1 (center): Courtesy of AT&T Archives and History Center; **(right):** Courtesy Chrysler LLC. **F. 8-2:** Used with permission from RCA Trademark Management S.A. **F. 8-3:** Courtesy of Ferguson Archives. **F. 8-8 (top left):** ENKA®, Used by permission; **(bottom right):** Celanese. **F. 8-12 (top right; bottom left):** Courtesy of Warnaco. **F. 8-14:** By permission of In Mocean Group, LLC. **F. 8-15 (top left):** Photo used courtesy of Macy's Archives; **(bottom):** Courtesy Brown Shoe Company, Inc. **F. 8-17 (top right):** Coty, Inc. Used by permission. **F. 8-18 (1st row, 1st image):** ENKA®, Used by permission; **(1st row, 2nd image):** Revlon; **(4th row, 1st image):** Photo used courtesy of Macy's Archives; **(4th row, 2nd image):** Courtesy The John B. Stetson Company. **F. 8-19 (1st row, 1st image):** Courtesy Spiegel Brands Inc. **F. 8-22 (center):** By permission of In Mocean Group, LLC. **F. 8-23:** We would like to acknowledge and thank Phillips-Van Heusen Corporation, the owner of the VAN HEUSEN, IZOD, and ARROW trademarks. **F. 8-24 (left):** John Kobal Foundation/Hulton Archive/Getty Image. **F. 8-24 (right):** We would like to acknowledge and thank Phillips-Van Heusen Corporation, the owner of the VAN HEUSEN, IZOD, and ARROW trademarks. **F. 8-27 (right):** Used with permission from Jockey International, Inc. **F. 8-28 (right):** Courtesy Perform Group LLC. **F. 8-29 (top left; bottom left; bottom right):** Courtesy The John B. Stetson Company. **F. 8-30 (top left):** Courtesy Spiegel Brands Inc.; **(top center):** Courtesy Wolverine World Wide, Inc. **F. 8-35 (left):** Photo used courtesy of Macy's Archives. **F. 8-36 (top left; right):** Courtesy Spiegel Brands Inc.; **(bottom left):** Dickies®, Williamson-Dickie Manufacturing Company.

Chapter 9

F. 9-1 (left): Ad used with the permission of Polaroid Corporation; **(center):** TRADEMARKS, CAMPBELL SOUP COMPANY. ALL RIGHTS RESERVED; **(right):** Courtesy Chrysler LLL. **F. 9-4 (bottom):** Bill Ray/Life Magazine/Getty Images Inc. **F. 9-5 (left):** Image courtesy Knoll, Inc. **F. 9-6 (top right):** Collection of Phoenix Art Museum, Gift of Mort and Marilyn Bloom 2005.106 and 2005.99; **(bottom right):** Campbell's Soup's "Souper Dress", 1966, silkscreen printed paper, cellulose and cotton. Collection of Phoenix Art Museum, Gift of Stephen and Gail Rineberg. Photo by Ken Howie. **F. 9-7:** Larry_Ellis/Getty Images Inc.—Hulton Archive Photos. **F. 9-8:** Courtesy of Ferguson Archives. **F. 9-10 (left):** Ron_Case/Getty Images Inc.—Hulton Archive Photos; **(right):** John Dominis/Getty Images/Time Life Pictures. **F. 9-11 (top left):** Courtesy of Revlon; **(top center; top right):** University of Rhode Island Library; **(bottom left):** Getty Images Inc.—Hulton Archive Photos; **(bottom right):** Photo Courtesy of the National Cotton Council of America. **F. 9-12 (top left):** Getty Images Inc.—Hulton Archive Photos; **(top center):** Courtesy of Ferguson Archives; **(bottom):**

Ian Showell/Getty Images Inc.—Hulton Archive Photos. **F. 9-14 (top left):** Courtesy Kayser-Roth Corporation—Makers of HUE and No Nonsense. **F. 9-15:** Celanese. **F. 9-16 (right):** By permission of In Mocean Group, LLC. **F. 9-17 (right):** Courtesy Spiegel Brands Inc.; **(bottom left):** Courtesy Mason Companies, Inc. **F. 9-19 (left):** Getty Images Inc.—Hulton Archive Photos; **(center):** Jack Robinson/Getty Images Inc.—Hulton Archive Photos; **(right):** Bob Grant/Fotos International/Getty Images Inc. **F. 9-21 (1st row, 4th image; 2nd row, 2nd image):** Commercial Pattern Archive, University of Rhode Island Library, Special Collections; **(2nd row, 1st image):** Courtesy of Ferguson Archives; **(2nd row, 3rd image):** Photo courtesy of the National Cotton Council of America; **(bottom):** Copyright Trevira. **F. 9-22 (top left):** Courtesy of Ferguson Archives; **(top right):** Courtesy Hanes Brands Inc. **F. 9-23:** Getty Images. **F. 9-24 (left):** Getty Images Inc.—Hulton Archive Photos; **(right):** Hulton Archive/Getty Images. **F. 9-25:** Getty Images Inc.—Hulton Archive Photos. **F. 9-27 (right):** We would like to acknowledge and thank Phillips-Van Heusen Corporation, the owner of the VAN HEUSEN, IZOD, and ARROW trademarks. **F. 9-31 (right):** Courtesy of Ferguson Archives. **F. 9-32:** Evening Standard/Getty Images. **F. 9-33 (left):** Courtesy of Ferguson Archives. **F. 9-35:** Steve_Wood/Getty Images Inc.—Hulton Archive Photos. **F. 9-36 (top left):** Courtesy Spiegel Brands Inc.; **(top right; bottom right):** Courtesy of Ferguson Archives. **F. 9-37 (2nd image):** Courtesy of Ferguson Archives; **(3rd and 4th image):** Courtesy Spiegel Brands Inc.

Chapter 10

F. 10-1 (left; top right): Courtesy of Ferguson Archives. **F. 10-3 (top left):** Courtesy Sears® Brands, LLC.; **(bottom left):** Courtesy Spiegel Brands Inc.; **(bottom center):** Courtesy Bobbie Brooks, Incorporated; **(bottom right):** University of Rhode Island Library. **F. 10-7 (top):** Courtesy of Ferguson Archives; **(bottom center; bottom right):** Photo used courtesy of Macy's Archives; **P. 355:** Courtesy of Ferguson Archives. **F. 10-9 (left; right):** Photo used courtesy of Macy's Archives. **F. 10-11:** University of Rhode Island Library. **F. 10-12:** Maidenform. **F. 10-13:** Courtesy Jones Apparel Group. **F. 10-14 (left):** Courtesy of Ferguson Archives; **(right):** By permission of In Mocean Group, LLC. **F. 10-16 (bottom):** Courtesy of Ferguson Archives. **F. 10-17 (left):** University of Rhode Island Library. **F. 10-18 (1st row, 2nd image):** Michael Ochs Archive; Getty Images Inc.; **(2nd row, 1st image):** Photo used courtesy of Macy's Archives. **F. 10-19 (right):** Courtesy of Ferguson Archives. **F. 10-23:** Courtesy of Ferguson Archives. **F. 10-26:** Dickies®, Williamson-Dickie Manufacturing Company. **F. 10-28:** Archive photo provided by Gant. Used by permission. **F. 10-29 (right):** Courtesy of Ferguson Archives. **F. 10-32:** Keystone/Hulton Archive/Getty Images. **F. 10-33:** Commercial Pattern Archive, University of Rhode Island Library, Special Collections. **F. 10-34 (left):** Courtesy Earth, Inc., Waltham, MA-www.EARTH.US; **(right):** © Dorling Kindersley. **F. 10-36 (right):** Robin Platzer/Getty Images/Time Life Pictures. **F. 10-37:** Courtesy of Ferguson Archives. **F. 10-38 (top center):** Courtesy of Ferguson Archives; **(top right):** Courtesy of Ferguson Archives. **F. 10-39 (bottom left):** Courtesy Spiegel Brands Inc.

Chapter 11

F. 11-2: Bustier, 1980–81 (fibreglass resin & felt) by Miyake, Issey (b.1938). National Gallery of Victoria, Melbourne, Australia. The Bridgeman Art Library. **F. 11-3 (right):** Photo used courtesy of Macy's Archives. **F. 11-8:** The Museum at FIT. **F. 11-9:** Courtesy Vivienne Poy, 1985. **F. 11-10:** Paul Chesley/Getty Images Inc.—Stone Allstock. **F. 11-11:** Courtesy DINA BAR-EL. **F. 11-15 (right):** Photo used courtesy of Macy's Archives. **F. 11-16:** Maidenform. **F. 11-17 (top left):** Faberge; **(top right):** Courtesy of Pepsi-Cola North America. **F. 11-18 (left):** George Rose/Getty Images Inc.; **(center):** By permission of In Mocean Group, LLC. **F. 11-19 (left):** Courtesy of Warren Edwards Shoes; **(right):** Courtesy Grendha Shoes Corp. **F. 11-20 (top left):** Necklace, Courtesy Franklin Mint, 1988; **(top center):** Courtesy, Dinny Hall, www.dinnyhall.com; **(bottom center):** Courtesy, Black, Starr and Frost. **F. 11-22 (left):** Tim Graham/Getty Images. **F. 11-23 (left):** Courtesy of Ferguson Archives. **F. 11-25 (bottom right):** Reprinted with permission from Brawn, LLC. All rights reserved. **F. 11-28:** Courtesy Visage as an English design company. **F. 11-30 (right):** Photo used courtesy of Macy's Archives. **F. 11-35:** Giorgio Brutini is a registered trademark of Harbor Footwear Group, Ltd. Used by permission. **F. 11-37 (left):** Courtesy

Eminence; **(right):** Photo used courtesy of Macy's Archives. **F. 11-39 (left; right):** Courtesy of Ferguson Archives. **F. 11-40 (right):** Photo used courtesy of Macy's Archives. **F. 11-41 (right):** Courtesy of Ferguson Archives

Chapter 12

F. 12-1 (left): Courtesy of Ferguson Archives; **(center):** Jean-Pierre Muller/Agence France Presse/Getty Images; **(right):** Pierre Verdy/Getty Images Inc. **F. 12-3:** The Museum at FIT. **F. 12-5 (left):** Pierre Verdy/Getty Images Inc.; **(right):** Richard Drew/AP Wide World Photos. **F. 12-6:** Courtesy of Ferguson Archives. **F. 12-7 (bottom):** Courtesy of Ferguson Archives. **F. 12-8 (right):** Lionel Chironneau/AP Wide World Photos. **F. 12-9 (left):** Andrea Bucci/Getty Images/Time Life Pictures; **(right):** Courtesy of Ferguson Archives. **F. 12-12 (left):** Courtesy of Ferguson Archives; **(right):** DMI/Getty Images/Time Life Pictures. **F. 12-16:** Brand X Pictures/Getty Images. **F. 12-17 (bottom):** Mark Mainz; Getty Images Inc. **F. 12-18 (top left):** Urbano Delvalle/Getty Images Inc. **F. 12-20 (bottom right):** Henning Christoph/DAS FOTOARCHIV/Getty/Photolibrary/Peter Arnold, Inc. **F. 12-21 (left):** Getty Images. **F. 12-22 (left):** Salvatore Ferragamo SPA; **(center):** Courtesy of Ferguson Archives. **F. 12-27:** Getty Images Inc.—Hulton Archive Photos. **F. 12-28 (left):** Getty Images. **F. 12-29:** AP/Wide World Photos. **F. 12-33 (bottom):** Courtesy of Ferguson Archives. **F. 12-35 (right):** Courtesy of Ferguson Archives.

Chapter 13

F. 13-2 (left): Getty Images. **F. 13-3 (right):** Image courtesy of WeSC – WeAretheSuperlativeConspiracy. **F. 13-4:** Getty Images. **F. 13-5 (top):** Vlisco, Frozen Dreams 2009, photography Fritz Kok; **(bottom):** Image courtesy of Cris Barros. **F. 13-6:** Kevin Mazur/WireImage for Rounder Records/Getty Images. **F. 13-7 (left):** Andrew H. Walker/Getty Images for IMG; **(right):** Mike Marsland/WireImage/Getty Images Inc. **F. 13-8 (left):** Neilson Barnard/Getty Images For IMG; **(right):** Winslow/St. Clair/Splash News/Newscom. **F. 13-9:** FILIPPO MONTEFORTE/AFP/Getty Images. **F. 13-10 (left):** Image courtesy of Paul Empson for Lucien Pellat-Finet, 2009; **(right):** Venturelli/WireImage/Getty Images. **F. 13-11:** Jeff Fusco/Getty Images. **F. 13-12 (1st row):** Eric Ryan/Getty Images Inc.; **(2nd row, 1st image):** Jean-Pierre Muller/Agence France Presse/Getty Images; **(2nd row, 3rd image):** Kiyoshi Ota/Getty Images Inc.; **(3rd row, 1st image):** Francois Guillot/Agence France Presse/Getty Images; **(3rd row, 2nd image):** Karl Prouse/Catwalking/Getty Images Inc.; **(3rd row, 3rd image):** Dave M. Benett/Getty Images Inc. **F. 13-13 (left):** Noel Quidu/ZUMA Press – Gamma; **(right):** Radu Sigheti/CORBIS-NY. **F. 13-14:** Sam Ogden/Photo Researchers, Inc. **F. 13-15 (left):** Garments by Úna Burke, Photography: Rebecca Parkes, Creative Direction: Úna Burke, Hair and Make-up: Faye Hayward; **(center):** REUTERS/Jacky Naegelen; **(right):** REUTERS/Benoit Tessier. **F. 13-16:** Dimitrios Kambouris/WireImage/Getty Images Inc. **F. 13-18 (center):** Image courtesy of Stylesight; **(right):** zumawirewestphotosthree288458. **F. 13-19 (left):** Getty Images; **(center):** © Ipatov | Dreamstime.com; **(top right):** © Thoth11 | Dreamstime.com; **(bottom right):** By Permission of Cynthia Moore. **F. 13-20 (left):** Ocean/Corbis RF; **(right):** © Corbis. **F. 13-21 (left):** © Luke MacGregor/Reuters/CORBIS All Rights Reserved; **(right):** Pete Saloutos/Jupiter Images. **F. 13-22 (left):** © Stefano Rellandini/Reuters/Corbis Rights Reserved; **(center):** Lluis Gene/Agence France Presse/Getty Images; **(right):** © age fotostock/SuperStock. **F. 13-23 (1st row, 1st image):** Image courtesy of Stylesight; **(1st row, 2nd image):** By Permission of Cynthia Moore; **(1st row, 3rd image):** Image courtesy of Stylesight; **(2nd row, 1st image):** Image courtesy of Andreia Chaves; **(2nd row, 2nd image):** Image courtesy of Stylesight; **(2nd row, 3rd image):** Heavy Machine Designs; **(3rd row, 1st image):** By Permission of Cynthia Moore; **(3rd row, 2nd image):** By Permission of Cynthia Moore. **F. 13-24 (top center; bottom):** Getty Images. **F. 13-25 (top):** © Robert Freeman/Corbis. All Rights Reserved. **(bottom):** Getty Images. **F. 13-26 (left):** Jason Kempin/WireImage/Getty Images Inc.; **(center):** © Monsoon/Photolibrary/Corbis. All Rights Reserved. **(right):** © Radius Images/Corbis. **F. 13-27 (top left):** Design Pics/Corbis RF; **(top center):** Karl Prouse/Catwalking/Getty Images; **(top right):** Fernada Calfat/Getty Images for IMG. **F. 13-28:** Phil Noble/Pool/Reuters Media News, Inc./CORBIS-NY. **F. 13-29:** © WWD/Condé Nast/Corbis. All Rights Reserved.

F. 13-30 (left): OLIVIER MORIN/AFP/Getty Images; **(right):** © Giulio Di Mauro/epa/Corbis. All Rights Reserved. **F. 13-31:** Venturelli/WireImage/Getty Images. **F. 13-32:** Victor VIRGILE/Gamma-Rapho via Getty Images. **F. 13-33 (left):** © Jason Todd/Rubberball/Corbis/Corbis RF; **(right):** Image courtesy of Paul Empson for Lucien Pellat-Finet, 2009. **F. 13-34 (left):** © Matteo Bazzi/epa/Corbis. All Rights Reserved; **(center):** Karl Prouse/Catwalking/Getty Images Inc. **F. 13-35 (left):** ALBERTO PIZZOLI/AFP/Getty Images; **(right):** GIUSEPPE CACACE/AFP/Getty Images. **F. 13-36 (left):** Bryan Bedder/Getty Images Inc.; **(right):** Chris Moore/Catwalking/Getty Images Inc. **F. 13-37 (left):** Diane Collins and Jordan Hollender/Jupiter Images; **(right):** © JUSTIN LANE/epa/Corbis. All Rights Reserved. **F. 13-38 (left):** Chris Moore/Catwalking/Getty Images Inc.; **(center):** Image courtesy of Gregor Hohenberg for Frank Leder, 2009; **(right):** Image courtesy of Stylesight. **F. 13-39 (left):** Image courtesy of Stylesight; **(center):** © Shift Foto/Corbis. All Rights Reserved; **(right):** C Flanigan/Getty Images. **F. 13-40 (top left):** ZUMA Press/Newscom; **(top right):** © Ben Welsh/Corbis. All Rights Reserved; **(bottom right):** Getty Images for Speedo. **F. 13-41:** Mark Mainz/Getty Images Inc. **F. 13-42 (right):** AP Wide World Photos. **F. 13-43 (right):** Ryan Heywood/Nouvelle Vague. **F. 13-44 (top center):** © Jonathan Downey/iStockphoto.com; **(top right):** SGranitz/WireImage for ESPN; **(bottom right):** © Radius Images/Alamy. **F. 13-45:** Cultura/AGE Fotostock America, Inc—Royalty-free. **F. 13-46:** Dave M. Benett/Getty Images. **F. 13-47 (left):** © Fotosearch/AGE Fotostock; **(right):** TORSTEN SILZ/AFP/Getty Images/Newscom. **F. 13-48 (left):**

TORSTEN SILZ/AFP/Getty Images; **(right):** ALBERTO PIZZOLI/AFP/Getty Images.

Chapter 14

F. 14-1: General Motors Corporation. Used with permission, GM Media Archives. **F. 14-3:** Andrea Blanch/Getty Images. **F. 14-4:** Lipnitzki/Getty—Roger Viollet Collection. **F. 14-5:** Ron Galella/Getty Images—WireImage.com. **F. 14-6:** Getty Images Inc.—Hulton Archive Photos. **F. 14-7:** © Oleg Cassini. Used by permission. **F. 14-8:** Getty Images Inc.—Hulton Archive Photos. **F. 14-9:** Photo: Roger Schall (C) Collection Schall. **F. 14-10:** Reg_Lancaster/Getty Images Inc.—Hulton Archive Photos. **F. 14-11:** CORBIS-NY. **F. 14-12:** Getty Images. **F. 14-13:** Getty Images Inc.—Hulton Archive Photos. **F. 14-14:** Christian Dior. **F. 14-15:** Eric Ryan/Getty Images Inc. **F. 14-16:** Cary Wolinsky/Aurora Photos, Inc. **F. 14-17:** Bernard Gotfryd/Getty Images. **F. 14-18:** The Donna Karan Company LLC. **F. 14-19:** Abbas/Magnum/Magnum Photos, Inc. **F. 14-20:** Mike Segar/Reuters America LLC, A Thomson Reuters Company. **F. 14-21; F. 14-25:** Dave M. Benett/Getty Images Inc. **F. 14-27:** Steve Eichner/Getty Images—WireImage.com. **F. 14-28:** Lipnitzki/Roger Viollet/Getty—Roger Viollet Collection. **F. 14-29; F. 14-31; F. 14-32; F. 14-33:** Getty Images Inc.—Hulton Archive Photos. **F. 14-36:** Carlos Alvarez/Getty Images Inc. **F. 14-37:** Dave Cheskin/AP Wide World Photos. **F. 14-38:** Getty Images Inc.—Hulton Archive Photos.

index

Page numbers in *italics* indicate an image appears on that page.